Second Edition

The

companion

Neil Bradley

Addison-Wesley

An imprint of PEARSON EDUCATION

Harlow, England · London · New York · Reading, Massachusetts · San Francisco · Toronto · Dan Mills, Ontario · Sydney
Tokyo · Singapore · Hong Kong · Seoul · Taipei · Cape Town · Madrid · Mexico City · Amsterdam · Munich · Paris · Milan

PEARSON EDUCATION LIMITED

Head Office:
Edinburgh Gate
Harlow CM20 2JE
Tel: +44 (0)1279 623623
Fax: +44 (0)1279 431059

London Office:
128 Long Acre, London WC2E 9AN
Tel: +44 (0)20 7447 2000
Fax: +44 (0)20 7240 5771
Website: www.awl.com/cseng

First published in Great Britain in 2000

© Pearson Education Limited 2000

The right of Neil Bradley to be identified as the Author of this Work has been asserted by him in
accordance with the Copyright, Designs and Patents Act 1988.

ISBN 0 201 67486 6

British Library Cataloguing in Publication Data
A CIP record for this book can be obtained from the British Library

Library of Congress Cataloging in Publication Data
Applied for.

10 9 8 7 6 5 4 3 2

Typeset by the Author
Printed and bound in the United States of America

The Publishers' policy is to use paper manufactured from sustainable forests.

Preface

The **Extensible Markup Language** is a powerful publishing and document interchange format. Developed by the *World Wide Web Consortium*, it was released, to widespread acclaim, in 1998. **XML** has a superficial resemblance to HTML, the established language of the Web, but information held in this format is self-describing – it can be extracted, manipulated and formatted to the requirements of any target audience or publishing medium.

XML should be of interest to HTML designers who need more flexibility to manage and customize their documents, to SGML users seeking advanced yet modestly priced applications, and to software developers requiring a flexible storage or interchange format that has powerful supporting tools.

The XML Companion serves the **programmer**, **analyst** or **consultant** involved in the management, processing, transfer or publication of XML documents. Detailed study of XML is supported by the inclusion of cross-referenced 'road maps' of the building blocks that comprise the standard, and an extensive glossary. Related standards for cataloguing, linking and styling XML files are also covered in detail.

This edition

The first edition of this book was completed within weeks of the release of the XML standard. Since that time, no significant pressure to modify or enhance the core standard has emerged. Justification for a new edition of this book therefore rests upon the high degree of activity surrounding XML. Complementary standards for processing, presenting and merging XML data have since been released, and this edition provides detailed coverage of **DOM 1.0**, **SAX 1.0**, **CSS 2** and **Namespaces 1.0**. Other standards have progressed, but are still being refined, so this edition simply describes later, more stable drafts of XSL (now divided into **XSL** and **XSLT**) and XLL (now divided into **XLink** and **XPointer**). Other proposed standards have only very recently emerged. The next version of HTML (**XHTML**) will be an application of XML (instead of SGML), and the **XML Catalog** proposal defines a standard scheme for managing the mapping of entity identifiers to local system files. A new scheme for navigating around XML documents, called **XPath**, will be utilised by the linking and styling standards.

This opportunity has been taken to rectify a number of minor syntactic and grammatical mistakes, as well as a few factual errors, and thanks are due to readers of the first edition for highlighting many of these issues.

Very little material from the first edition has been omitted, so the new book is a little larger than before. Despite this, it is hoped that the book can still serve as a 'companion' for those who are constantly on the move.

Acknowledgements

A repeated thanks to all those mentioned in the first edition of this book, as their contributions remain relevant. In addition, a number of readers of the first edition have contributed suggestions and observations that have helped improve the quality of this work, and their efforts are appreciated. Finally, thanks once again to Adobe for *FrameMaker+SGML* (which was used both in the preparation and publication of this book).

Feedback

Comments and suggestions for a possible future edition are welcome. They should be sent to the author, who can be found at *neil@bradley.co.uk*. Updates, additions and corrections can be obtained from the author's Web page, located at '*http://www.bradley.co.uk*', which also contains links to various XML and SGML related sites.

Neil Bradley
August 1999

Contents

Related standards

Reference

1. Using this book

Book structure

The chapters in the first part of this book, *The XML Specification*, cover the features of the core language. They should be read in the order provided, as they each build on concepts described in previous chapters. The second part, *Working with XML*, provides supporting material, such as techniques for designing, processing and managing XML documents. The *Adjunct Standards* section covers standards for linking, styling and processing XML data. The *Related Standards* section covers existing standards that have influenced the design of XML, or can be used in conjunction with XML in many working environments. Finally, the *References* section includes condensed information on a number of topics, including a Road Map of the XML standard and a glossary.

Although XML is heavily influenced by SGML and HTML, familiarity with these languages is not assumed. The text describes XML in isolation, starting from first principles. However, it is recognized that many readers will be familiar with one or both of these languages, and some of the features and limitations of XML could surprise or confuse readers with prior expectations. Notes targeted at these audiences appear at relevant points in the text (see below). These notes should be ignored by readers unfamiliar with the language concerned.

HTML Note: Although XML is similar in appearance to HTML, there are many fundamental, and some counter-intuitive differences in approach. These notes highlight and explain any differences, as they are encountered.

SGML Note: Although XML is similar in concept to SGML, there are many limitations and a few differences of approach. These notes draw attention to details that may otherwise be missed.

Style conventions

Names or terms that appear in **bold style** have specific meaning within XML or related technologies, and appear in bold typeface on their first occurrence, and thereafter whenever their roles are further defined. They are described in the *Glossary*, and each occurrence is referenced in the *Index*.

Text appearing `in a mono-spaced font` represents example data, usually an XML fragment. Larger examples are separated from the text:

```
This is a sample line of text.
```

XML has a superficial resemblance to SGML and HTML. To avoid confusion, whenever example fragments of these languages appear they are preceded by one of the following comments:

```
<!-- SGML -->
<!-- HTML -->
```

In addition, when the discussion includes XML examples in close proximity to HTML or SGML examples, each XML fragment will be preceded by the following comment:

```
<!-- XML -->
```

Though bold typeface may be used to emphasize part of an example, such as '`look at `**`this`**` word`', it does not have the significance described above.

Examples of presented material (printed or displayed output) appear as follows:

This is a presented material.

Words displayed in *italic style* are either quotations or simple 'attention grabbers'.

For the sake of clarity, element and attribute names are capitalized in the text, such as 'the Name element contains a name', but are fully lower case in XML fragment examples, as in '`<name>Smith</name>`', despite the fact that names are case-sensitive in the XML standard.

A name that is followed by a superscript number, such as Letter[84], is an XML construct that is described by a numbered chart in Chapter 21 (see the introduction to that chapter for a full explanation).

Note that UK spelling conventions are used in the text, but some terms and keywords appear with US spelling when consistency with a standard described in this book is important. For example, 'centre' is used in the text but 'center' is a parameter value in the HTML table formatting model.

2. Overview

This chapter provides a brief tour of the XML data format, and associated standards. Note that the initial *Concepts* section in each of the following chapters describes specific features introduced here in more detail.

What is XML?

Although computers are now able to handle electronic documents that contain images, music and video, many documents are still bound within a text framework. For text and other media to be combined, exchanged and published, it must be organized within some kind of infrastructure. The **XML** standard provides such a platform. The name 'XML' is an acronym for **'Extensible Markup Language'** (with 'X' replacing 'E' for aesthetic impact). This language is not owned or dominated by any single commercial interest. It was developed by the W^3C (the *World Wide Web Consortium*), and has been shaped by experience of previous markup languages.

XML is an ideal data format for storing structured and semi-structured text intended for dissemination and ultimate publication on a variety of media. Indeed, XML has its roots in this domain. An XML document contains special instructions, called **tags**, which enclose identifiable parts of the document. The fragment below is taken from a technical manual, and illustrates just one application of XML:

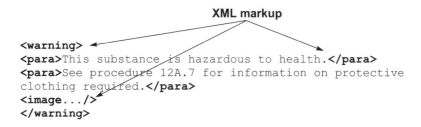

Beyond the world of publishing, information passed between programs and computer systems is becoming richer and more complex as new network-based applications are devised. Such information needs to be **self-describing**, so that the client software can interpret and perform user-driven actions on the data without needing to reconnect to the server. Despite its historical roots in publishing, XML is also suited to the task of unambiguously identifying complex data structures that may never be viewed or printed:

```
<transaction>
<time date="19980509"/>
<amount>123</amount>
<currency type="pounds"/>
<from id="X98765">J. Smith</from>
<to id="X56565">M. Jones</to>
</transaction>
```

An example of a standard that utilizes XML in this way is **SMIL** (the *Synchronized Multimedia Integration Language*), which employs XML markup to identify and manage the presentation of files containing text, images, sound and video fragments to create a multi-media presentation.

An XML document has both a logical and a physical structure. The logical structure allows a document to be divided into named units and sub-units, called **elements**. The physical structure allows components of the document, called **entities**, to be named and stored separately, sometimes in other data files so that information can be reused and non-XML data (such as image data) can be included by reference. For example, each chapter in a book may be represented by an element, containing further elements that describe each paragraph, table and image, but image data and paragraphs that are reused (perhaps in other documents) are stored in separate entity files.

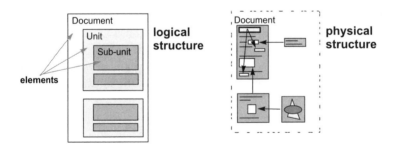

The logical structure involves a number of constraints that must be obeyed in all valid XML documents. A document can be checked for conformance using a **parser**, which reports any errors it finds. Documents composed of a number of entities must first be assembled, using an **entity manager**. The standard describes software that can perform both these functions as an **XML processor**, though the term 'parser' is commonly promoted to mean the same thing.

XML is actually a **meta-language**, meaning that it is a language that describes other languages. There is no pre-defined list of elements. XML provides complete freedom to employ elements with names that are meaningful to the application. However, it is possible to prevent tag-naming anarchy with an optional mechanism for pre-defining the elements allowed in a specific class of documents. A **DTD** (*Document Type Definition*) defines the elements allowed, and a **validating parser** compares the DTD rules against a given document to determine the validity of the document. This feature allows software translation filters to be developed with confidence that the markup used during document preparation conformed to a known specification, and was applied consistently. A number of industry standards for data exchange and publication may be defined in terms of a suitable DTD (there is a DTD for the SMIL format mentioned above). In the example below, tags called Warning, Para, Image, Emph and Keyword are all defined, for use in appropriate locations in all relevant documents:

```
<!ELEMENT warning  (para*, image?)>
<!ELEMENT para     (#PCDATA | emph | keyword)*>
<!ELEMENT image    EMPTY>
<!ELEMENT emph     (#PCDATA)*>
<!ELEMENT keyword  (#PCDATA)*>
```

XML documents can be created and edited using existing text editors and word processors, but specialist XML-sensitive editors also exist. These editors use the DTD to guide authors, preventing both XML syntax errors and logical document structure errors from occurring. Typically, the tags are replaced by icons selected from a menu of suitable options within the current context. In the first example below, a selected word can be enclosed by those elements appearing in the menu (Emph and Keyword). In the second example, the change of cursor location dictates a different range of insertion possibilities.

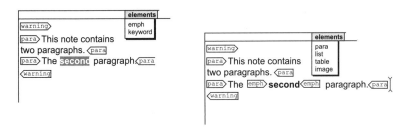

XML encourages the use of elements with names that describe the nature of an object, as opposed to describing how it should be displayed or printed, and this **generalized markup** approach has one fundamental advantage over traditional style-based instructions. The information is self-describing, so can be located, extracted and manipulated as desired. However, this move away from style-specific formatting means that an appropriate presentation of the document cannot be produced automatically. It is not obvious (at least to a computer program) how the content of an element called Paragraph or Emphasis should be presented, let alone one named Company or Pricecode. A **style sheet** is therefore needed to specify an output format for each element. The great advantage of this approach is that alternative style sheets can be applied at any time, changing the format to suit the intended audience, or the capabilities of the publishing medium. An advanced style sheet language should be able to generate standard text, such as a prefix, and also rearrange components of the document, as well as perform the more basic task of selecting appropriate fonts and styles:

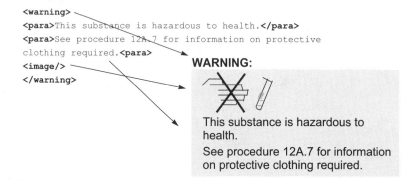

One of the great benefits of electronic publishing in general is that software can help the reader navigate to referenced text using **hypertext** links. An adjunct standard to the XML specification defines an advanced hypertext linking scheme, which may be employed by browser software to provide powerful document navigation options, including cross-document, multiple and bi-directional links. The linking scheme also includes implied links such as 'find the second occurrence of the name "Napoleon" in the third chapter'.

```
/book/chapter[3]/string::2,"Napoleon"
```

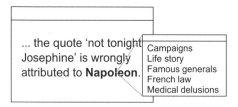

Data exchange applications

Wherever complex data must be exchanged between two programs, XML has the potential to be a suitable format. XML has certain application in a number of already identified domains, such as **push technology**, **EDI** (*Electronic Data Interchange*) and general meta-data applications (**MCF**, **XML-Data** and **RDF**).

XML may be used as an exchange format for **relational database** systems. In this scenario, the XML tags are being used as a convenient data wrapper during transfer of records, fields and relationships between systems. When the data is derived from multiple tables, connected by **one-to-many** relationships, the structured yet repeatable nature of XML elements is ideal for storing any number of related data fields.

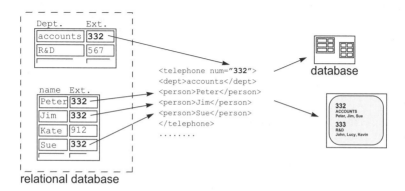

Standards for the exchange of meta-data have been suggested by various parties, including Microsoft (XML-Data), Netscape (MCF), and more recently the W^3C (RDF). All these variants attempt to define common approaches to making data self-describing by assigning an additional layer of significance to specific XML markup.

Although **EDI** has been a reality for some years, this technology has been based on proprietory (and often expensive) solutions. There is now a lot of activity in this field based around the use of XML and the Internet, aiming not only to reduce the price of electronic commerce solutions through the use of standard tools (such as Web browsers), but also to bring much needed standardization to this domain.

Traditional Web technology has been described as 'pull technology', because the Web browser 'pulls' the HTML encoded documents from the Web server, which simply waits for requests for a Web page or other data file. The Web client is active, and the server is passive. The concept behind push technology is that the Web server pushes, or sends, data to each client, without waiting for a request. The client browser is updated dynamically, as the base information changes. One obvious application for this is a news update service. The Microsoft **CDF** push technology format is an XML application.

Increasing interest in client-sided scripting technology is a reaction to the realization that complex services, requiring a high degree of processing power, are best provided by the client computer. The server can then concentrate on its prime purpose, which is to deliver the software and data to each client. For example, a Java program can read and make sense of XML data, and can respond sensibly to operations requested by the applet. Optional data may be hidden or revealed, a table of contents may be created, expanded or retracted, or information may be rearranged or styled in different ways, without further interaction with the Web server.

Software modules and applications have been developed to interpret XML data, and provide access to it via the **SAX** and **DOM** interface standards. Note that the tools developed primarily for publishing applications (described below) may be utilized here. For example, document browsers can be used to produce elegantly styled data printouts.

Document publishing applications

XML can be used to mark up semi-structured documents, such as reference works, training guides, technical manuals, catalogues, academic journals and reports. Among many other niche applications, XML can also be used to mark up patents, examination papers, financial statements and research papers. New and more specialized uses include support for the presentation of data in the next generation of mobile telephone.

All the features of a typical document can be represented by XML tags. Taking the example of a reference book, objects such as chapters, titles, notes, paragraphs, lists and tables can all be explicitly identified by name:

```
<chapter>
<title>An example XML fragment</title>
<note>
<para>This note contains two paragraphs.</para>
<para>The second paragraph.</para>
</note>
</chapter>
```

XML also facilitates the generation and management of **meta-data**, which is information *about* information (just as a meta-language is a language that describes languages). Taking the reference book example, typical meta-data would include the table of contents, the index and the date the book was commissioned from the author. None of these items are part of the text of the book, but simply background information or an aid to searching or classification. XML is able to directly store meta-data, such as the commissioning date, yet keep it separate from the document text so that it will never appear in the published document. But it is also possible for software to generate meta-data, when it is required, from the body of the text. For example, the table of contents and index can be produced automatically, because each title and each indexed term is explicitly identified. In the following example, the chapter titles are 'real' content when they appear at the top of each chapter, but are considered to be meta-data when reused to build the contents page:

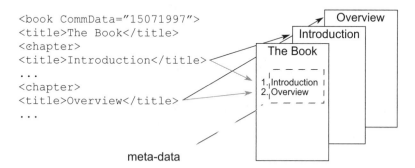

```
<book CommData="15071997">
<title>The Book</title>
<chapter>
<title>Introduction</title>
...
<chapter>
<title>Overview</title>
...
```

meta-data

The move to XML can result in a long-term cost benefit, due to the high level of automation achievable once the core data is held in a controlled and structured format – in some cases allowing fully automated publication, in appropriate formats, to paper, CD-ROM and the Internet.

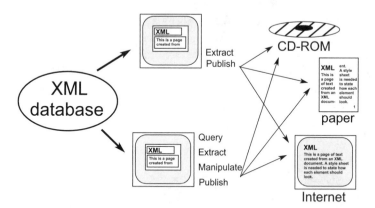

But XML does not stand in isolation. Beyond the core syntax specification, XML includes optional standards for enabling hypertext links (**XLink** and **XPointer**) and output formatting (**XSL** and **XSLT**). The linking and formatting schemes exploit and conform to a new standard, called **XPath**, which defines an expression language for interrogating XML data structures. There are draft and *de facto* standards for the coding of mathematical formulae, chemical formulae, and tabular material. In addition, established and developing standards further complement and enhance the scope of XML.

Together, the standards described below offer an independent and powerful approach to disseminating and publishing information.

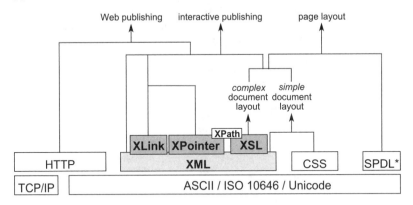

* or PostScript

ASCII is a long-established standard for electronic storage and transfer of text. **Unicode** and **ISO/IEC 10646** are more extensive versions of ASCII. **HTTP** is the Internet protocol that underpins the Web. **CSS** (*Cascading Style Sheets*) is a simple style sheet language, aimed primarily at on-screen formatting, first developed for HTML (and currently supported by the popular Web browsers), but usable with XML without modification. It may be utilized by applications that do not require the power of the XSL style sheet mechanism. **SPDL** (*Standard Page Description Language*) describes exactly how information is to be placed on a page (and is therefore a vendor-neutral equivalent of **PostScript**). Composition software takes the formatting-tagged document, along with font information and page or column area details, to create a description of the content of each page in SPDL format.

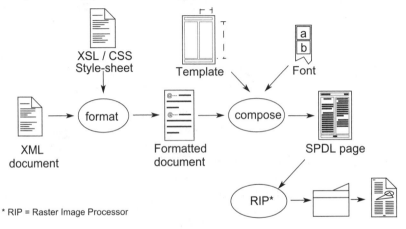

* RIP = Raster Image Processor

Historical context

XML builds on the principles and conventions of two existing languages, **HTML** and **SGML**, to create a simple yet powerful mechanism for information storage, processing and delivery. XML is based primarily on SGML, but inherits some characteristics from HTML, and contains additional features that are aimed at its use on the Internet.

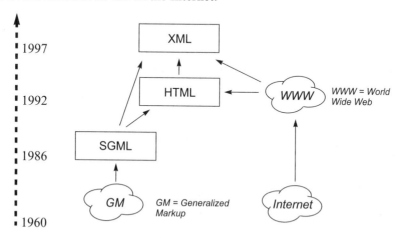

The generalized markup concept emerged in the early 1960s, but did not become well established until the introduction of SGML, which was ratified by the **ISO** in 1986, and remained essentially unchanged in its first ten years of use. It is a measure of how robust SGML was from the beginning that a decade passed before even minor revisions were considered necessary. Indeed, the specification for SGML was perhaps too advanced, with several of its features to this day under-utilized. Yet it is the very power of SGML that has been its major handicap. Development of software to support even a typical subset of the language is a huge programming task. SGML-aware applications have therefore tended to be slow in arriving, incomplete or error-prone, yet at the same time expensive in comparison with proprietary solutions. A large number of experts in the field considered that a simplified version of SGML was needed to make the generalized markup approach attractive to a wider audience.

The Internet has recently become an established medium for information retrieval and exchange. This medium was a natural platform for a hypertext service, linking documents around the world into a **World Wide Web** of information. But a tagging language was needed to provide the linking mechanism, and to apply some basic text formatting to the document containing these links. The **HTML** language was developed to meet this need. Although the syntax of SGML was largely adopted by HTML, its principles were not. Only in later incarnations was HTML made fully compatible, and could then be described as an application of SGML (and defined by a suitable DTD). Although a standards committee is responsible for the development of HTML, vendors of the most popular Web browsers have also added incompatible tags for commercial advantage, causing considerable confusion. Yet HTML provides no mechanism for allowing document authors to extend the language by adding their own tags.

The pressure to simplify SGML coincided neatly with the pressure to enhance HTML, and the W^3C saw the need for a new language to fill the gap. In 1996 the process began with the definition of ten design goals that the new language should satisfy (see Chapter 20). XML version 1.0 was formally released on 10 February 1998.

The future

The most influential software vendors have backed this standard, and have released numerous products to support it, and XML is at the heart of a number of initiatives (available from http://www.oasis-open.org/cover/xml.html). The future of XML is almost certainly secure. But there remains the question about its continued relationship with SGML and HTML, and whether there is room for all three languages.

HTML should survive. It has some unique features that XML does not aim to replicate, and is particularly suited to form-based interaction with the user. Also, there are times when customized tags are unnecessary, and even counter-productive. Such examples as displaying information extracted from a database, and creating marketing-oriented Web sites, illustrate the point. In the first case, a DTD has no useful role to play, and, in the second case, the constraints of structured markup would stifle creativity in design. Finally, Web browsers are simply more efficient when dealing with formatting markup they natively understand, particularly when a style sheet is not needed. HTML should remain a popular standard, and one that will gradually improve. It should, however, soon become an application of XML (instead of SGML), to be called **XHTML**.

XML is also unlikely to replace SGML in the near future. There are a number of additional features in SGML that still have their uses in serious document management and publishing applications. But once XML is fully established, there will no doubt be pressure to extend its capabilities. It may eventually match, or even surpass SGML in capability, though it is also possible that these languages will grow together, and eventually be harmonized into a single language.

For the time being, there is plenty of room for all three languages. Each has its own strengths and weaknesses, yet they have enough commonality in syntax to assist users who need to work with more than one of them.

Syntax overview

The following illustration includes examples of almost all the important features of the XML format, and is therefore more complex than would typically be the case. Many of the mechanisms shown are optional. Those readers with experience of HTML or SGML will be familiar with at least some of the markup appearing in this illustration. The next three chapters explain this markup in detail:

Note.XML

```
<?XML version="1.0" encoding="UTF-8" standalone="no" ?>
<!DOCTYPE Note SYSTEM "Note.DTD" [
<!ENTITY XML "eXtensible Markup Language">
<!ENTITY history  SYSTEM "History.XML">
<!ENTITY XMLimage  SYSTEM "/ents/XML.TIF" NDATA TIFF >
<!ENTITY  % images "INCLUDE"> ]>
<note>
<p>The  &XML; format is a very important move
to bringing the benefits of structured markup
to the masses.</p>
&history;
<p>The following image shows a fragment of XML:</p>
<image filename="XMLimage" />
<p>The tags  <![CDATA[<note>, <p> and <image../> are
used in this document]]>.</p>
</note>
```

XML.TIF

History.XML

```
<?XML encoding="UTF-8" ?>
<p>Its roots can be seen in HTML, in that the tags
have the same delimiters,  &#60; and &#62;, but its
real ancestry is SGML.</p>
<p xml:space="preserve" xml:lang="en-GB">
  --- XML ---
  |       |   |
SGML    HTML</p>
```

Note.DTD

```
<!-- The Note DTD version 1.3 -->
<!NOTATION TIFF SYSTEM "TIFFVIEW.EXE" >
<!ENTITY % images "IGNORE" >
<![%images[<!ENTITY % noteContent "p | image">]]>
<!ENTITY % noteContent "p">
<!element note (%noteContent;)*>
<!element p (#PCDATA)>
<!element image EMPTY>
<!attlist image filename ENTITY #REQUIRED>
```

Note: For quick reference, the same fragments appear in Chapter 20, with labels to identify the features and references to the page numbers of relevant chapters or sections (see page 405).

3. Document markup

This chapter introduces the concept of electronic document markup in general, and describes XML document markup convention s in detail.

Concepts

XML is concerned with describing the content of documents that are stored in electronic format, in a form that is accessible to both people and computer software. An XML format data file contains a mixture of document text and XML markup, which organizes and identifies the components of a document.

Traditional markup

The simplest form of electronic document is a basic **text file**. The file is considered to contain a **data stream**: a linear sequence of characters that are read and processed by software in strict order.

```
                Text File Format.
    This document explains how text data can
  be formatted with varying degrees of com-
  plexity to improve readability.
```

In traditional **typesetting** systems, **markup** instructions are used to facilitate more flexible formatting by **composition** software. The software accepts and outputs normal characters according to the current style setting, but detects markup characters and interprets them as instructions. Such an instruction, or **tag**, may for example dictate a switch to another **font**, or signify a line break, but will not itself appear in the presented text.

```
Are you going to *ITA Scarborough *ROM fair?
```

Are you going to *Scarborough* fair?

When composing for paper output, the physical limitations of the page area require the document to be split into page-sized blocks, in a further step called **pagination** (making pages). Advanced pagination engines have a complex task to perform, including balancing the text on each page and inserting headers and footers.

Modern word processors and DTP systems hide markup codes from the author by employing a **WYSIWYG** (*What You See Is What You Get*) interface. The markup still exists, in one form or another, though it may take the form of a less intelligible (to humans), more efficient machine-readable scheme.

Most **typesetting languages** comprise an allowed list of tags, each one having a pre-defined purpose. Of particular interest, in comparing this approach with XML, is that these systems tend to focus on the appearance of the information, and the language comprises a set of instructions for specifying the appearance and location of the text on the page.

Some typesetting languages allow a commonly used sequence of formatting instructions to be grouped and stored, for reference by a single tag whenever they are needed. The **macro** concept involves the use of named groups of instructions, called **macro definitions**, and references (**macro calls**) to these groups.

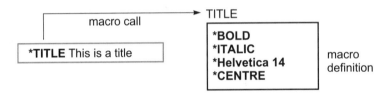

This technique introduces the concept of **generic** coding, because the macro name is likely to reflect its intended use, not the style of the following text. A macro called '*TITLE' has an obvious meaning. It is only necessary to identify a title in the document, and apply this macro to it, not to remember and apply a series of style tags. The document author need not be concerned with either specifying or understanding the formatting codes held in the macro definition. In addition, the author need not be concerned with the final appearance of the title. Most modern word processors and DTP packages have 'style sheet' definition facilities, which can be considered an equivalent concept.

Elements

XML markup builds on the concept of macro-based typesetting languages. Usually, the tags do not specify a required presentation style, but identify the nature of each component of the text. XML tags usually surround an identified object in the data stream. A **start-tag** and an **end-tag**, together with the data enclosed by them, comprise an **element**. In this way, an XML document identifies discrete objects.

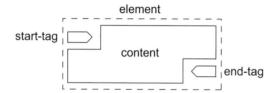

As with more traditional markup, the start-tag and end-tag are embedded in the data stream:

```
Are you going to <name>Scarborough</name> fair?
```

The data is typically prepared for publishing by mapping element tags to conventional typesetting tags (perhaps using a style sheet). This approach allows the choice of output style to be changed at any time:

XML elements may contain further, embedded elements, and the entire document must be enclosed by a single **document element**. The document structure **hierarchy** may be visualized as boxes within boxes (or Russian dolls), or as branches of a **tree** (for convenience often shown on its side, as in the example below). In a typical example, a Book element may contain a number of Chapter elements, and each Chapter element may in turn contain a number of Section elements.

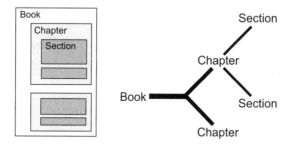

Each element must be completely enclosed by another element. For example, a section may not straddle two chapters.

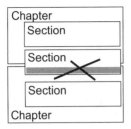

When describing the relationship between element structures, the terminology of the family tree is often adopted (an analogy that clearly fits a tree-like view of structures). From the perspective of a specific Chapter element, adjacent Chapter elements are **siblings**, like brothers or sisters, the Book element is its **parent**, and any contained sections are its **children**.

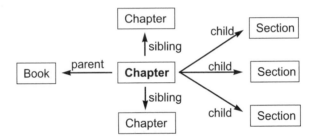

The Book element is the **ancestor** to all other elements, including the Section elements and all their children. All elements directly or indirectly enclosed by a Chapter element are **descendants** of that element.

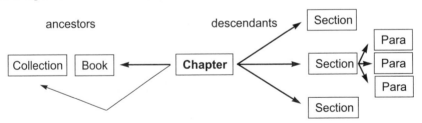

It can be deduced that every element has a single parent, and any number of siblings, except for the document element which has no parent and no siblings. Elements that have no children are termed **leaf** elements.

The degree to which an element's content is organized into child elements is often termed its **granularity**. When there are many descendants this is described as a 'fine granularity', and when there are few descendants this is termed a 'coarse granularity', though in practice this term may be used simply to describe a document in which some potentially recognizable objects have not been explicitly identified and tagged.

Some hierarchical structures may be **recursive**. An element may directly or indirectly contain instances of itself, in which case it may be termed a **nested element**. In a typical example, a list consists of a number of items, and each item may contain a further complete list. The List and Item elements may therefore be nested:

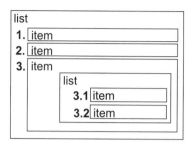

The presence of hierarchical and recursive structures allows formatting to be applied on a context-sensitive basis. The content of a Title element may be formatted differently, for example depending on whether it occurs directly within a book, chapter or section, and the indentation of a list can be increased if it resides within another list. Although different elements could be defined for each context, that approach could require many more elements, increasing the complexity of the document.

It is possible to pre-define which elements are allowed within other elements. An optional **DTD (*Document Type Definition*)** contains rules for each element allowed within a specific class of documents. See Chapter 5 for details. A DTD for the book example would declare the existence of elements called Book, Chapter and Section, and state that the Chapter element can only contain Section elements. When a DTD is *not* in use, the document may still be deemed valid, providing that the tags are not corrupted, and also providing that elements are properly contained as described above.

HTML Note: A DTD is not directly relevant to HTML because the tags allowed and rules dictating their use are already hard-wired into **HTML-aware** editors and Web browsers. However, DTDs for each version of HTML *do* exist, primarily to codify the standard, but also for the benefit of SGML users (who may employ SGML tools to create, modify, store or validate HTML documents).

SGML Note: The DTD is an *optional* feature of XML. The SGML standard is being amended so that it also allows this.

Attributes

It is possible for an element to hold additional information about its content beyond just its name. For example, the target audience for the content of a particular Paragraph element may be governed by a security level value, and each paragraph may be associated with a particular author. This 'information about information' is termed **meta-data**, and is stored in an **attribute**. As a single element may contain more than one attribute, it is necessary for each attribute to have a name, such as Security or Author.

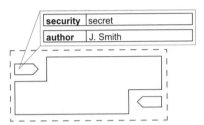

When a DTD is not in use, the attribute value is simply considered to be a unit of text. No distinction is made between numeric values such as '123', keywords such as 'secret', and names such as 'J. Smith'. But when a DTD is in use, more control can be exerted over the range of values allowed for each attribute. An attribute is associated with a particular element by the DTD, and is assigned an **attribute type**. A **character data** attribute may have a value that consists of general characters (this is equivalent to the informal value allowed when no DTD is used). A **name token** attribute, however, may contain only a single word, so does not allow embedded spaces. A name token may be further restricted to one word from a group of words in an **enumerated** attribute (the word enumerate means 'count', 'reckon up one by one', or more appropriately 'go through a list of...'). The DTD may also specify a default value. This is the assumed value to be applied when no attribute value is given by the document author. In other cases, the DTD assigns special roles to an attribute, such as whether it forms part of a hypertext link.

Some attributes are reserved by the XML standard, or will be reserved by future adjunct standards. In all cases, the attribute names begin 'xml:'. For example, the standard reserves the name 'xml:lang' for an attribute that holds information on the human language used in the content of the element, and is recognized as such by all XML-aware applications (a user may wish to see only the content of elements conforming to a specific language, or a spell-checking application may switch dictionaries as the language changes).

Special instructions

An XML document may contain instructions to the XML processor. These instructions are contained within **markup declarations**.

Many documents are likely to contain just one markup declaration, the optional **document type declaration**, which identifies the document element and may contain document structure building rules (see Chapter 5):

```
<!DOCTYPE MyBook SYSTEM "MyBook.DTD">
```

It is possible to add a **comment** to an XML document. The comment is never considered part of the document text, so would not appear in published output. A comment may be inserted by a document author or editor to mark text that needs further treatment. But comments are more typically employed in a DTD, where they help to organize and document the rules that it contains.

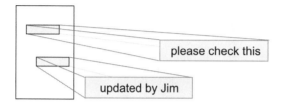

It is also possible to identify a block of text as **character data**, which will not contain markup, so any markup characters appearing in the text can be safely treated as normal text characters.

The intention of XML is to be independent of specific composing or pagination requirements. However, such dependencies cannot always be avoided. An XML document may contain instructions to a specific application using a **processing instruction**.

At the top of an XML document (before the document type declaration) there should be a processing instruction that identifies the version of XML in use, specifies the character set used, and possibly indicates whether a DTD is required for accurate processing. This is called the **XML Declaration** (even though it is actually a processing instruction):

```
<?XML version="1.0" encoding="UTF-8" standalone="YES" ?>
```

Traditional markup

Without any kind of formatting markup in a text file, the content can be viewed as a single, very long line of data, including text and simple formatting codes (such as the carriage return (**CR**) character and line feed (**LF**) character):

```
Text File Format.[CR]This document explains how...
```

However, a browser or word processor would normally interpret and obey the formatting codes and also insert **soft line-breaks** to break the line into screen or column width units to improve legibility:

```
Text File Format.[CR]
This document explains how text data can be formatted
with varying degrees of complexity to improve
readability.
```

Note that MS-DOS systems use CR and LF in sequence, whereas the Apple Macintosh uses only CR, and UNIX uses only LF (the issue of line-ending codes is relevant to XML, and their interpretation in an XML document is discussed in Chapter 7).

Further crude formatting of text files can be achieved using multiple spaces or tab characters:

```
          Text File Format.[CR]
   This document explains how text data can be form-
atted with varying degrees of complexity to improve
readability.
```

However, simple text files do not include stylistic information such as bold, underline or italic formatting. In order for the data file to specify stylistic information (and improved formatting options) an implied significance can be given to certain character sequences. Many typesetting systems and word processors take this approach. In the example below there are two markup tags, '*ITA' and '*ROM'. In this fictional markup language, the first instruction switches on an **italic** font, and the second instruction switches on a **roman** (normal) font. In this example, the place name *Scarborough* appears in italic typeface when the data is printed:

```
Are you going to *ITA Scarborough *ROM fair?
```

Are you going to *Scarborough* fair?

An issue that arises in text-based data formats is that some characters must be given special significance in order to distinguish markup tags from data. A **markup delimiter** character (or characters) identifies the start, and perhaps also the end of an instruction embedded in the text. In the markup language described above, the '*' and the following space serve as markup delimiters, so that '*ITA' is identified as a tag to be obeyed, not text to be printed. The problem is that a document author may wish to use the same characters in the text, and this could easily confuse software designed to detect the markup. One common solution is to introduce the concept of an **escape code**: a markup tag that is used to represent characters that would otherwise be difficult or impossible to include. The escape code itself has a markup delimiter, so that it can be recognized as such, so the first and most obvious use of the escape code is to represent the data character used as its own delimiter. For the example above, the code '**' may represent a single asterisk (C and Java programmers will be familiar with the use of '\\' to represent a single '\' character).

Among the limitations of the markup approach described above is the problem of preserving formats defined previously. Taking the example above, if the entire phrase were embedded in a bold paragraph, the '*ROM' instruction would inadvertantly disable the bold style, in addition to the italic style:

```
*BOL Are you going to *ITA Scarborough *ROM fair?
```

Are you going to *Scarborough* fair?

In order to avoid this problem, some markup languages apply styles to a range of text. Each style is switched on using one tag, and switched off by a complementary tag. This is known as 'toggling'. HTML takes this approach, and includes tags such as '<i>' and '</i>' to enable and disable italic styling. An HTML-aware browser would render the example below correctly:

```
<b>Are you going to <i>Scarborough</i> fair?</b>
```

Are you going to *Scarborough* fair?

Note that it was initially acceptable practice in HTML to overlap these structures. In the following example, the word 'fair' will appear in italic, but not in bold. It may seem like reasonable behaviour, but this practice is now discouraged (and is not legal in XML documents):

```
<b>Are you going to <i>Scarborough</b> fair?</i>
```

Are you going to *Scarborough* fair?

Elements

XML tags usually surround an identified object in the data stream. A **start-tag** (**STag**[40]) and an **end-tag** (**ETag**[42]), together with the data enclosed by them, represent an **element**[39]. The start-tag is delimited using the '<' and '>' characters. The end-tag is delimited by '</' and '>':

```
Are you going to <name>Scarborough</name> fair?
```

Element names are case-sensitive, so 'name', 'NAME' and 'Name' refer to different elements. The name appearing in the end-tag must also exactly match the name that appears in the start-tag. Although case-sensitivity allows different elements with the same name to be defined and used, this is not advisable when it would be confusing for document authors.

Each element must be completely enclosed by another element, except for the ancestor of all other elements (the 'root' or **document element**). Some hierarchical structures may be recursive. An element may directly or indirectly contain instances of itself. Nested structures may cause difficulties for programmers or to composing software, as there is no theoretical limit to the level of nesting, yet each level requires consideration of output style:

```
<list>
    <item>
        <list>
            <item>
                <p>Nested Item</p>
```

As the '<' and '>' characters take the role of markup delimiters, they should never also appear as data characters because of the ambiguity and confusion this would cause. A document author should use a form of escape code instead. '<' represents '<' and '>' represents '>' (though an XML-aware editor may perform this substitution on the author's behalf, behind the scenes, while still presenting the true characters on-screen). See Chapter 4 for more details.

```
<p>The &lt;p&gt; tag is used to start a paragraph.</p>
```

The **p** tag is used to start a paragraph.

Content types

Some elements are able to contain data, possibly including both child elements and text. These are known as **container elements**.

An element that does not directly contain text, but contains other elements, is said to have **element content** (see **children**[47]). A Book element has element content if it can contain only Chapter elements. Similarly, a Section element may perhaps contain only Paragraph and List elements:

```
<section>
    <p>...</p>
    <p>...</p>
    <list>...</list>
</section>
```

If a DTD is not in use, it is impossible to know for certain that an element has only element content. In the example above, a human reader will deduce from the names of the tags that the Section element does not directly contain text, but software cannot decide so easily. Just because there is no actual text between the child elements in the example, this does not mean that there cannot ever be. Whether this matters or not depends on a number of factors, mainly concerned with how an application might interpret line-end codes, and also has implications for advanced hypertext linking schemes.

Spaces and line-end codes in element content are not usually considered part of the document, so the meaning of the document is not affected by the following rearrangement:

```
<section><p>...</p><p>...</p>
<list>...</list>

</section>
```

However, at some point in the hierarchy the actual document content must appear. At this point, an element may contain text, or a mixture of text and child elements. An element that contains a mixture of elements and text is said to have **mixed content (Mixed[51])**. For example, a Paragraph element may, perhaps, be allowed to contain both text and Emphasis elements. An element that happens to contain only text is informally said to have **data content**, though this is still officially classified as mixed content.

```
<p>This paragraph contains an <em>emphasized
phrase</em> in the middle.</p>
```

Line-ending codes are significant in text content. The example above shows the ideal, or safe way to format the content of a mixed content element. The line-end code after the word 'emphasized' should be considered equivalent to a space character by an application that is formatting the text for display or print. There is much more information on line-ending and space significance in Chapter 7.

Finally, an element may have *no* content. Any instance of an element that may contain text could just happen to contain no text:

```
<name><init></init><lastname>Smith</lastname></name>
```

There is another form of markup that may be used to represent an element with no content. The end-tag is not used, and the start-tag has a slightly different syntax, ending with '/>' instead of '>':

```
<name><init/><lastname>Smith</lastname></name>
```

Some elements may not be *allowed* to contain data. A typical example is a placeholder for an image. Such an element is formally termed an **empty element (EmptyElemTag[44])**. Both forms of markup described above may be applied, but the abbreviated version is strongly advised, for brevity and for compatibility with SGML systems.

Spanning structures

Empty elements may be used to describe a block of text that spans proper structures. In the example below, the Revision empty element indicates the start of some revised text, and the Revision End empty element indicates the end of the block. The revised text begins in one paragraph, and ends in another. However, **composition** software designed for XML structures may not be able to switch on or switch off a specific style from the location of an empty element, and a **parser** is certainly not able to validate these blocks for missing block-start or block-end tags. This mechanism can be used for extracting block-spanning material, but only for non-XML processing, as the embedded structures will be invalid when taken out of context:

```
<p>In this paragraph there is
some <rev/>revised text.</p>
<p>This text is also changed,
but <revend/>this text is not.</p>
```

In this paragraph there is
some **revised text.**

This text is also changed,
but this text is not

Attributes

An **Attribute**[41] provides additional information about an element. Attributes are embedded in the element start-tag. An attribute consists of an **attribute name** and an **attribute value** (**AttValue**[10]). The attribute name precedes its value, and they are separated by an equals sign.

The attribute value is also enclosed by quotes, because it may contain spaces and it would otherwise be impossible to detect the end of a value when it is followed by more attributes. In the example below, there are two attributes on the Topic element. The Keywords attribute currently has a value of 'XML SGML', and the Id attribute currently has a value of 'x123'. If the quotes were not present, it would be assumed that the Keywords attribute had a value of 'XML SGML id=x123', and if the space character was interpreted as a value terminator, the Keywords attribute would be assumed to have a value of just 'XML':

```
<topic keywords="XML SGML" id="x123">
<title>Generalized Markup</title>
...
</header>
```

Both the name and the value are case-sensitive, so great care must be taken to ensure consistency. There must be at least one space between the element name and the first attribute, and spaces may also optionally appear around the equals sign:

```
<topic keywords = "XML SGML" id   =   "x123"  >
```

Although double quotes are usually used, it is possible to use single quotes instead. One reason for using single quotes would be to enclose a value that contained a double quote+ as part of the text:

```
<bolt diameter='2"'>
```

If both types of quote are used in the value, it is necessary to 'escape' one of them by using an escape code ('"' for the double quote or ''' for the single quote (apostrophe)).

SGML Note: The surrounding quotes are required, and the attribute name must always appear.

Any tab, carriage return or line feed is considered to be equivalent to a space character, and will be translated into a space (further manipulation of white space is performed for some attribute types when a DTD is in use). The combination CR then LF is translated into a single space. The following examples are therefore equivalent:

```
name='John Smith'
name='John
Smith'
```

HTML Note: Most HTML users will be familiar with the short-hand form '`<hr noshade>`' or '`<ol compact>`'. The attribute name is not present, and the attribute has only one allowed value, such as 'compact'. When the value is not present, the element has an implied value, such as 'shaded' or 'not compact', so its presence acts as a simple switch-on instruction. As XML requires the presence of the attribute name, the equals symbol and the surrounding quotes, this technique is not available.

Reserved attributes

There are some universal characteristics that elements in many different applications may share. These may include the human language of the text they contain, and the importance or otherwise of non-visible spaces and formatting characters surrounding the text. To avoid conflict with user-defined attribute names, the prefix 'xml:' is reserved by the standard for these and other purposes. There are only two **reserved attributes** in the XML core standard.

Languages

There are any number of reasons why it may be useful to identify the language used for the text contained in a particular element. The '**xml:lang**' attribute name is reserved for storage of both language and sometimes also country details (as the same language may differ slightly between countries). The value of this attribute is a single token, or code, which conforms to one of three possible schemes, as outlined below, and defined in **RFC 1766**.

The content may comprise a simple two-character language code, conforming to **ISO 639** (Codes for the representation of names of languages). For example, 'en' represents English. A list of these codes is shown in Chapter 20 (see page 438).

```
<para xml:lang="en">This is English text.</para>
```

Alternatively, the content may be a user-defined code, in which case it must begin with 'x-' (or 'X-'). For example, 'x-cardassian'. Finally, the code may be one that is registered with **IANA** (the *Internet Assigned Numbers Authority*), in which case it begins with 'i' (or 'I-'). For example, 'i-yi' (Yiddish).

It is possible for sub-codes to exist, separated from each other and from the main code by a hyphen, '-'. If the first sub-code is two letters (and is not part of a user-defined code) then it must be a country code, as defined in **ISO 3166**, such as 'GB' for Great Britain (see page 440 for a list of country codes).

```
<instruction xml:lang="en-GB>
Take the lift to floor 3.</instruction>
<instruction xml:lang="en-US>
Take the elevator to floor 3.</instruction>
```

Note that although attribute values are case-sensitive, interpretation of these codes is not case-sensitive, so any combination of upper- and lower-case letters may be entered, though convention dictates that lower-case be used for language codes and upper-case for country codes, giving 'en-GB'.

Significant spaces

Some space characters, line-end codes and tabs may be inserted into an XML document to make the markup more presentable, but without affecting the actual content of the document. The following two examples should normally be considered equivalent, in that published output should be identical:

```
<book><chapter><section><p>The first paragraph.</p>...

<book>
  <chapter>
    <section>
      <p>The first paragraph.</p>
```

Some XML-aware software is able (in certain circumstances) to distinguish space characters in elements that contain other elements (as in the Book, Chapter and Section elements above) from spaces in elements that contain text (as in the Paragraph element above), which is termed **significant white space**. It is normally assumed that spaces in elements of the first type are not part of the document, so can be considered to be **insignificant white space**. Yet in some circumstances the document author may wish this space to be considered significant, in which case the **xml:space** attribute may be used to override the default handling. The 'xml:space' attribute has two possible values, 'default' (the assumed value when this attribute is not present) and 'preserve'. All white space in an element can be explicitly made significant, even though it may only contain child elements.

Most publishing applications are liable to reduce multiple spaces back to a single space, and replace line-end codes with spaces. The 'preserve' value may also be interpreted as an override to these actions, but this is not made explicit in the standard. Chapter 7 covers this topic in more detail.

Declarations

An XML document may contain instructions to the XML processor. These instructions are contained within **markup declarations**. Legal instructions include definitions of entities (described in Chapter 4), comments and character data sections (described below), as well as core DTD building constructs (described in Chapter 5).

A markup declaration is delimited by the characters '<!' and '>'.

```
<! ... >
```

Markup declarations are sometimes used to group a number of other declarations. The embedded declarations are held in a subset structure, identified using the square bracket characters '[' and ']':

```
<! ... [
   <! ..... >
   <! ..... >
]>
```

There are various kinds of markup declaration. A specific declaration type is indicated using a keyword, which must appear at the start of the declaration, without any intervening spaces. The declaration types described below have the following keywords:

```
<!DOCTYPE ..... >
<!-- ..... -->
<![CDATA[ ..... ]]>
```

The remainder, which are described in later chapters, have the following key-words:

```
<!ENTITY ..... >
<!NOTATION ..... >
<!ELEMENT ..... >
<!ATTLIST ..... >
<![IGNORE[ ..... ]]>
<![INCLUDE[ ..... ]]>
```

Document type declaration

One declaration that, if used at all, must appear before the document element, is called the **document type declaration (doctypedecl**[28]**)**. The keyword 'DOC-TYPE' is used to indicate a document type declaration:

```
<!DOCTYPE MyBook>
```

The example above shows a document type declaration in its simplest form. It merely identifies the name of the document element, which it precedes. More complex variants are used to hold entity definitions (see Chapter 4) and contain the DTD (see Chapter 5). These more complex variants use the square bracket groups:

```
<!DOCTYPE MyBook [
......
]>
```

Comments

It is possible to add a comment to an XML document, using a **comment (Comment**[15]**)** declaration. The comment is never considered part of the document text, so would not appear in published output. The keyword '--' identifies a comment declaration. For backward compatibility with SGML, the declaration must also end with the same two characters, and two adjacent hyphens must not appear within the comment text:

```
<!-- This is a comment -->
<!-- This is an -- ILLEGAL -- comment -->
```

SGML Note: A markup declaration can contain only one comment, and nothing but that comment. It is not possible to embed comments in element and attribute list declarations.

Comments may be inserted by a document author or editor to mark text that needs further treatment. But they should probably not be used if they need to be preserved when the document is processed. Some tools (such as those reading the document using the SAX API discussed in Chapter 14) will 'lose' the comments. It is often a better idea to use an element, possibly called Comment, instead (style sheet languages are able to prevent such elements from being included in published output). Comments are more typically employed in DTDs, where they help to organize and document the rules that they contain.

Character data sections

When a document author wishes to use characters that could be confused with markup delimiters, such as '<' and '&', it is normal practice to employ an **entity reference**, such as '<' and '&'. But this is hardly intuitive, and such text is difficult to read. If one portion of a document contains many characters of this type, the use of entity references could be considered unacceptable. Consider the following example:

```
Press the &lt;&lt;&lt;ENTER&gt;&gt;&gt; button.
```

Press the <<<ENTER>>> button.

It is therefore possible to identify a block of text as **character data**, which will not contain markup. As markup characters are not expected in character data, there is no possibility of confusion when using markup-related characters in the text. A **Character Data Section (CDSect[18])** declaration identifies a character data document segment. The keyword '[CDATA[' begins the declaration, and ']]>' ends it:

```
<![CDATA[Press the <<<ENTER>>> button.]]>
```

Press the **<<<ENTER>>>** button.

Entity references are also ignored:

```
<![CDATA[In XML the &lt; reference is built-in.]]>
```

In XML the **<** reference is built-in.

SGML Note: The other marked section types, 'IGNORE', 'INCLUDE', 'TEMP' and 'RCDATA' are not available in an XML document instance, though the first two of these are available in the external subset of a DTD.

Processing instructions

Unlike comments and character data sections, a **processing instruction (PI[16])** contains information required by a specific application expected to process the XML data. It is not therefore specified by a markup declaration, the contents of which must be obeyed by all applications. Instead, it is bounded by the characters '<?' and '?>':

```
<? ..... ?>
```

The content begins with a keyword (a **PITarget**[17]), significant to the application that will understand the instruction, followed by a space, then the instruction itself, which may include any valid XML characters. The syntax used for the content is assumed to be significant only to the target application. In the example below, a Paragraph contains two processing instructions, each forcing a new page in the required syntax of differing pagination applications (which happen not to be able to interpret an otherwise more suitable Pagebreak element).

```
<p>It would be nice to end the page
<?ACME-WP   (NEW PAGE)?>
<?BigDTPSystem   DO:page-break?>
<pagebreak/>
here.</p>
```

Processing instructions are used to provide information about an XML document (see the next section), and to identify a style sheet that is to be used to format the document (see Chapter 13).

XML declaration

A special tag should appear at the start of an XML document to impart some important information about that document. This tag is called the **XML Declaration** (**XMLDecl**[23]). It may contain three pieces of information: the version of XML in use, the character set in use, and the importance or otherwise of externally defined markup declaration to accurate interpretation of the document content.

```
<?xml version="1.0" encoding="UTF-8" standalone="yes" ?>
```

Note that, despite its official name, this information is not contained within a markup declaration, but within a processing instruction. Also, the target name is 'xml'; upper-case letters cannot be used.

The **version** parameter tells the XML processor which version of XML the document conforms to. At present there is only one version, identified as '1.0'.

The optional **encoding** parameter reveals the character encoding scheme used in the document. If this information is not present, then 'UTF-8' encoding is assumed. See Chapter 16.

The optional **standalone** parameter indicates whether or not an externally defined set of declarations contain information that affects interpretation of the content of the document. See Chapter 5.

If the XML declaration is not present, the version of XML in use is assumed to be '1.0'. It is probable that the XML declaration will not be optional in later versions of the language, as it would otherwise not be possible to detect which version is in use. Other defaults adopted are the same as listed above for missing parameters (the character set encoding is assumed to be UTF-8, except where other sets can be inferred from the first characters read, and the processing of externally defined entity declarations is assumed to be required).

4. Physical structure (entities)

A single XML document may be distributed among a number of separate data files, facilitating component reuse within that document and throughout other documents, and allowing non-XML data to be included. This chapter describes the mechanism used to support this feature.

Concepts

The XML specification includes a facility for physically isolating and separately storing any part of a document. For example, each chapter in a book may be stored separately, or a picture may be required at a certain point in the text. Each unit of information is called an **entity**, and each entity is assigned a name so that it can be identified.

The only entity which is not assigned an entity name is the **document entity**. This is the data file that is considered to represent the entire document, and is selected by the user or given to the **parser**, generally by reference to the name of the file containing it.

In simple cases the document entity may be the only entity (in which case the techniques described in this chapter are irrelevant). In other cases the document entity may contain the majority of the document content, with other entities used to fill some gaps. At the other extreme, it may be nothing more than a framework, used primarily to position the content of other entities.

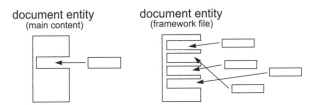

document entity
(main content)

document entity
(framework file)

An entity is defined using a special markup tag, called an **entity declaration**, which appears at the top of the document entity. It declares the existence of an entity, gives it a name for future reference, then either directly holds the content of the entity, or points to a file that holds it.

Entities are employed by inserting references to them within the text. An **entity reference** identifies the entity required, and its location in the text indicates where the content should appear. There may be any number of references to the same entity, and the content replaces each reference.

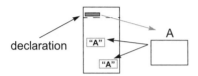

A hierarchy of entities may be built, beginning with the document entity. However, it is not permitted for an entity to directly or indirectly contain a reference to itself (a cyclical relationship would confuse XML processing software).

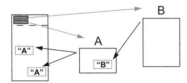

Use of an entity would normally be considered in one of the following circumstances:

- the same information is used in several places, and duplication would be both error-prone and time-consuming
- the information may be represented differently by incompatible systems
- the information is part of a large document that for practical reasons must be split into manageable units
- the information conforms to a data format other than XML.

To meet these disparate needs, two basic concepts combine in different ways to provide a number of different types of entity. First, a distinction is made between XML data and data that conforms to another format. Second, the entity content may be stored within the main document, when it is known as an **internal entity**, or in a separate file, when it is known as an **external entity**. The combinations allowed are 'internal text entity', 'external text entity' and (external) 'binary entity'.

The simplest form of entity is an **internal text entity**. This type of entity allows a document author to pre-define any phrases or other text fragments that will be used repeatedly in the document. For example, in a book on XML the name 'Extensible Markup Language' may appear often. To avoid keying the whole name, and also to prevent the misspellings that may result from this tedious task, an internal text entity, perhaps named 'XML', may be created to hold the text.

An entity may be too large to be conveniently stored in the declaration. It may, for example, consist of several paragraphs of text. Alternatively, the entity content may need to be accessed from a number of documents, and it would be both time-consuming and error-prone to redefine it in each one. Both problems can be solved by storing the text in a separate data file. Using an **external text entity**, the size of the information unit is not limited, the content is easy to edit in isolation, and the entity can be referenced from declarations in each document.

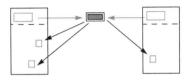

Another use of external text entities is to group several internal entities. For example, letters and symbols not covered by ASCII, such as accented European letters, Greek letters and mathematical symbols, have standard ISO entity declarations, and are grouped into entity files. The most commonly required are:

- **ISOnum** (symbols, including '<', '>' and '&')
- **ISOlat1** (accented Western European letters)
- **ISOgrk1** (Greek letters)
- **ISOpub** (publishing characters)
- **ISOtech** (technical symbols)

Whether it is stored internally or externally, an entity that contains XML data is known as a **parsed entity**, because it can be validated by an XML parser. A parsed entity contains **replacement text**, meaning that the content of the entity replaces the reference to it in the data stream.

Many documents include information that cannot be represented by a simple text format. Even the simplest documents typically contain drawings or photographs. Other media types, such as sound and video, are now being incorporated into documents as well. XML is able to reference an external entity that contains binary data. This is termed a **binary entity**. A binary entity *must* be defined externally, because it may contain characters that would confuse an XML processor. For the same reason, binary entities cannot be merged into the document by the XML processor. Instead, they must be handled by the application itself. The XML processor provides the name and location of the file, along with the notation it uses. The application is expected to use this information to either process the data directly, or launch another application that can deal with it. For example, a browser could either merge in a binary entity directly, so that the user is not even aware of this mechanism, or it may insert an icon which prompts the user that an entity is present, and can be viewed by selecting it.

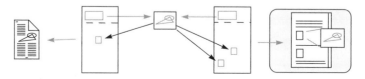

The author of a document may use entities to aid construction of that document. The author of a DTD may also use entities to aid construction of the DTD. It follows that it is possible for both parties to inadvertently define the same entity, as the document author cannot be expected to read a DTD file to see if a particular entity name is already in use. For example, if the DTD author defines an entity called 'Styles' to group the names of elements that affect the style of a range of text, this should not prevent a document author from also defining an entity called 'Styles' to hold a paragraph describing the aesthetic options available on a new motor car. This potential conflict is avoided through the use of two kinds of entity. A **general entity** is an entity that may be referred to within the document instance, and is therefore available to document authors. A **parameter entity** is an entity that may only be referenced within markup declarations, and is therefore generally the province of DTD designers. These types of entity are distinguished from each other by a minor variance in syntax. A general entity called 'Styles' cannot be confused with a parameter entity of the same name.

There are two circumstances under which an entity declaration is not required. First, there are a small number of characters ('<' (less than), '>' (greater than), '&' (ampersand), ' ' ' (apostrophe) and ' " ' (closing quote)) that could be confused with markup delimiters, making it difficult for software to distinguish 'real' characters from markup delimiters. The use of references for these characters is so important that declarations are not required, as they are already built-in to the XML processor. Second, although the XML character sets include many characters, most of these characters cannot be generated directly from the keyboard. Using a special form of reference, called a **character reference**, any character can be represented simply by specifying the value of that character in the ASCII/Unicode character set. This scheme also provides another mechanism for specifying characters that would normally be interpreted as markup. Note that an XML-aware editor may hide these complications from authors, allowing delimiters and extended characters to be inserted using keyboard short-cuts, and displaying them normally, yet creating character references when saving the data to disk.

Defining an entity

A declaration is required to announce the existence of an entity. The general purpose and format of declarations is covered in Chapter 3. Entities must be defined before the first reference to them in the data stream, and are declared in the **document type declaration** (**doctypedecl**{28}). The '**ENTITY**' keyword identifies an **entity declaration** (**GEDecl**{71} or **PEDecl**{72}):

```
<!DOCTYPE MyBook [
<!ENTITY .......>
]>
```

The name can be any length, but the characters allowed in the name are restricted to those defined in the **Name**{05} rule. The name must therefore begin with a letter, '-' or ':', and optionally consist of further letters, digits and the symbols '.', '-', '_' and ':'. Legal names include ':MyEnt' and 'my.ent'. An entity name is case-sensitive, so an entity named 'MyEntity' is *not* the same as an entity named 'myentity', or another named 'MYENTITY':

```
<!ENTITY MyEntity .......>
```

It is possible to define the same entity more than once, but only the first declaration is acknowledged. This rule is important because it allows a document author to specify which optional and alternative portions of a DTD are to be used in that document. See Chapter 5 for details.

```
<!ENTITY myentity "content of 'myentity'">
<!ENTITY myentity "THIS CONTENT IS IGNORED">
```

For each entity, there may be any number of **entity references** (including none). Each reference effectively 'points to' a specific entity by referring to its name. The content of that entity then replaces the reference.

SGML Note: There is no option to define a default entity.

Internal text entities

The replacement text of an **internal text entity** is contained within quote delimiters that follow the entity name:

```
<!ENTITY XML "eXtensible Markup Language">
```

Either single or double quotes may be used. When double quotes are used, it is not possible to also include a double quote in the text, as this would inadvertently signify the end of the entity. However, it would be possible to include a single quote without ambiguity. One reason for choosing single quotes as delimiters would be to allow double quotes to appear in the text:

```
<!ENTITY DemoEntity 'The rule is 6" long.'>
```

A reference to a general text entity appears at the point in the text where the entity content is required. The ampersand character, '&', acts as the start delimiter, and the semi-colon character, ';', completes the reference. The name of the entity appears between these characters:

```
The &XML; format includes entities.
```

An XML processor removes the entity reference, and inserts the replacement text in its place. The receiving application may not be aware of this activity, and therefore be ignorant of the existence of the original entity:

```
The eXtensible Markup Language format includes entities.
```

SGML Note: The semi-colon is always required, even when followed by a space. Entities are either XML data or binary types; there are no other types, such as 'CDATA' or 'SUBDOC'.

Built-in entities

Every XML processor has a small number of entity declarations built in. Document authors must use the references listed below instead of the actual characters:

- < for '<'
- > for '>'
- & for '&'
- ' for ' ′ ' (in attribute values delimited by the same character)
- " for ' ″ ' (in attribute values delimited by the same character)

The angle bracket entities must be used in place of the actual character within text, so as to avoid confusing the XML processor, which assumes that every occurrence of these characters represents markup delimiters.

```
<p>The &lt;p&gt; tag is used to represent a paragraph.</p>
```

The <p> tag is used to represent a paragraph.

The ampersand entity is used within text to avoid confusing an XML processor, which assumes that the '&' character represents the start delimiter of a general entity reference.

```
<title>&XML; &amp; &CSS;<title>
```
eXtensible Markup Language **&** Cascading Style Sheets

The quote entities are used within internally defined entity replacement text. They are needed when both types of quote appear in that text, and a conflict with the delimiter character would otherwise be unavoidable.

```
<!ENTITY sample "Use &quot; and 'as delimiters.">
```
Use " and ' as delimiters.

Character entities

A character entity reference has the same format as a text entity reference, except that the hash symbol, '#', is inserted after the ampersand. A decimal or hexadecimal value is used to identify the character required.

A decimal value in the range '0' to '255' represents a character from the extended ASCII set, ISO 8859/1, as used under Windows, Sun UNIX and as the Web default (see Chapter 20 for a chart of this set). The reference '<' refers to the less-than symbol, '<' (and is equivalent to '<'). A decimal value in the range '256' to '65535' represents an additional character from the larger Unicode/ISO10646 set (see Chapter 16).

A hexadecimal value is preceded by an additional 'x' character. The reference '<' refers to the '<' character, because the hexadecimal value 3C is equivalent to the decimal value 60. Just as the decimal notation, which is also known as base ten, has symbols for nine unitary values, so the hexadecimal notation, also known as base 16, has symbols for 15 unitary values, including all the usual digits plus an additional six ('A' = 10, 'B' = 11, 'C' = 12, 'D' = 13, 'E' = 14 and 'F' = 15). So '3C' represents three multiplied by 16, plus 12, giving 60.

Larger values may be used to refer to any Unicode character, such as '￸'.

Parameter entities

A **parameter entity** declaration (used in DTD construction) is defined by including a percent sign, '%', after the 'ENTITY' keyword. A general entity of the same name may be declared by omitting the '%' symbol:

```
<!ENTITY % AnEntity "(para | list)" >
<!ENTITY   AnEntity "This is an entity" >
```

In order to distinguish a parameter entity reference from a general entity reference with the same name, the parameter type has a different start delimiter character. The '%' symbol is used in place of the '&' symbol:

```
%AnEntity;
```

When the entity reference appears in markup, a space character is added to the start and end of the content as it replaces the reference. This is to ensure that the entity contains complete tokens. The example below actually creates three tokens, 'emph', 'supersc' and 'ript' (not 'superscript').

```
<!ENTITY % PartModel "emph | supersc" >
<!ELEMENT para  (%PartModel;ript)*>
```

See Chapter 5 for details on the use of parameter entities, and for an explanation of this markup.

External text entities

The location of an **external text entity** is provided by a **system identifier**, which is indicated using the 'SYSTEM' keyword, followed by a quoted string that locates the file. The system identifier must conform to the URL standard. See Chapter 11 for details.

```
<!ENTITY myent SYSTEM "/ENTS/MYENT.XML" >
```

An additional mechanism for locating an external entity can be provided, using a **public identifier**. This method of identifying remote information is more flexible, as it offers more information on the content of the data file, and at the same time does not directly specify the location and name of the file. The keyword 'PUBLIC' is used to indicate a public identifier:

```
<!ENTITY myent PUBLIC
       "-//MyCorp//ENTITIES Superscript Chars//EN" .....>
```

See Chapter 10 for details on a standard that describes a recommended format for such identifiers.

Using both a public and system identifier has the advantage of allowing local resources to be used when they are available, and is particularly suited to Web usage. The application should first test the public identifier against a **catalog** of locally stored entities. If the entity already exists on the local system, it does not have to be fetched from a remote Web server. Should the public identifier not resolve to any locally held entities, the system identifier is then used to fetch the entity from the server.

When a public identifier is used, the system identifier must still be present, but as it must follow the public identifier, there is no requirement to include the 'SYSTEM' keyword, and in fact this keyword must *not* be entered:

```
<!ENTITY myent PUBLIC "...." "/ents/myent.ent">
```

SGML Note: The system identifier is *always* required.

Binary entities

A binary entity is very similar to an external text entity. The public and system identifiers are used in the same way to locate the data file containing the entity. But there is an additional requirement to identify the format of the data, so that it can be associated with an application that understands this format. After the system declaration, there is a notation declaration, consisting of the 'NDATA' keyword, followed by a format name. In the example below, the file 'JSphoto.tif' is identified as a 'TIFF' file. Although, in this case, it may be thought possible to identify the format from the filename extent of '.tif', that mechanism cannot be relied upon:

```
<!ENTITY JSphoto SYSTEM "/ENTS/JSphoto.tif" NDATA TIFF>
```

References of the kind discussed previously cannot be used to refer to binary entities. Instead, an empty element is used, with an attribute specified to be of type 'ENTITY' (see Chapter 5):

```
Here is a photograph <pic name="JSphoto"/> of J. Smith.
```

Character defining entities

When a large number of declarations are needed, it can be inconvenient to place them within the document type declaration. Instead, they can be placed in a separate file, which is itself referenced using a parameter entity. This is common practice for including lists of entities representing non-ASCII characters.

The document author includes an entity declaration and a reference to it such as:

```
<!ENTITY % ISOnum PUBLIC "ISO 8879:1986//ENTITIES
                  Numeric and Special graphics//EN"
                  "/ents/isonum.ent">
%ISOnum;
```

The file called 'isonum.ent' contains further declarations, such as:

```
<!ENTITY excl "!">
<!ENTITY reg "*REG*">
```

These sets may be customized to contain application-specific codes, such as '*REG*', to generate the required character. They were first defined for SGML, which has traditionally relied upon the very limited ASCII character set. In theory, they are not required in XML, which utilizes the more extensive Unicode character set. However, operating systems and applications that do not work with Unicode could use this mechanism instead.

Usage limitations

There are many places that an entity reference could be placed, including in the text content of an element, in an attribute, in other entity values, and also within DTD-building declarations. However, there are differing restrictions that apply, depending on the type of entity concerned.

Note: As much of the following discussion refers to DTD markup, readers unfamiliar with SGML would be advised to return to this section after reading the following chapter.

General text entity references

General text entity references may be used in the content of an element.

```
<para>TimeCorp Int. is located at &TimeCorpAddress;</para>
```

They may also appear in internal entity content, but they are not replaced by their content in this location. This is because it is more powerful for such references to be replaced in the context of the documents that the enclosing entity finally appears in. In the following example, the content of Division only replaces its reference when the content of TimeCorp replaces references in each document instance. This allows for Division to have different values in different documents.

```
<!ENTITY TimeCorp "TimeCorp Int. (&Division;)">

<!ENTITY Division "Watches">
...
<title>Accounts for &TimeCorp;</title>
```

Accounts for TimeCorp Int. (**Watches**)

```
<!ENTITY Division "Clocks">
...
<title>Accounts for &TimeCorp;</title>
```

Accounts for TimeCorp Int. (**Clocks**)

Apart from this (and within an attribute default value), they may not appear in the DTD, in either the internal or external subsets. The following example contains two general entities that are incorrectly used:

```
                              <!-- ERROR -->
<!ELEMENT para (#PCDATA | emph | &MoreTokens;)>
<!-- ERROR -->
&MoreDeclarations;
<!ELEMENT emph (#PCDATA)>
```

An attribute value cannot represent the name of a general entity. The following example will *not* identify the entity declared above:

```
<!ATTLIST book owner ENTITY>
...
            <!-- ERROR -->
<book owner="TimeCorp">
```

However, an attribute value may contain a normal reference to an internal entity, though not to an external entity:

```
<!ENTITY TimeCorp "MyCorp International">
<!ENTITY TimeCorpAddress SYSTEM "address.xml">

                          <!-- ERROR -->
<book owner="&TimeCorp; at &TimeCorpAddress;">
```

Binary (unparsed) entity references

When the entity content is not XML data, textual references are not allowed at all. The following example therefore contains a number of errors:

```
<!ENTITY MyPic SYSTEM "../pics/pic.tif" NDATA TIFF>
<!-- ERROR -->
&MyPic;                         <!-- ERROR -->
<!ELEMENT chapter  (para | list | &MyPic;)*>
                <!-- ERROR -->
<book ="&MyCorp; (&MyPic;)">
                        <!-- ERROR -->
<title>Financial Report (&MyPic;)</title>
```

The only place that the name of such an entity can appear is as an attribute value, when that attribute is of type ENTITY or ENTITIES:

```
<!ENTITY MyPic SYSTEM "../pics/pic.tif" NDATA TIFF>
<!ATTLIST pic  name ENTITY #REQUIRED>

<title>Financial Report (<pic name="MyPic">)</title>
```

Parameter entity references

Parameter entity references cannot be used in the document instance. The following example contains two errors; they are not detected as errors, but are simply treated as text:

```
                <!-- ERROR -->
<book owner="%AnEntity;">
                    <!-- ERROR -->
<title>All About %AnotherEntity;</title>
```

   All About %AnotherEntity;

They are only used in the DTD, and specifically between declarations, within element and attribute declarations, and within internal entity values.

5. Logical structure (the DTD)

A significant feature of XML is its ability to create a template for document markup, so that the placement of elements and their attributes can be controlled and validated. This chapter explains the purpose, scope and syntax of these templates.

Note: See Chapter 6 for a discussion on practical issues surrounding the development of document structure templates. The template for this book is included as an example in Chapter 20.

Concepts

The most significant feature that XML inherits from SGML is the concept of a **DTD** (a *Document Type Definition*). The DTD is an optional, but powerful feature of XML that provides a formal set of rules to define a document structure. It is a similar, but more powerful equivalent to style templates typically found in word processors and DTP packages. DTDs are typically defined to describe such document types as journals, training guides, technical manuals and reference books, amongst many others, as well as to help define other standards that utilize XML syntax.

The DTD establishes formal **document structure** rules. It defines the elements that may be used, and dictates where they may be applied in relation to each other. It therefore specifies the document **hierarchy** and **granularity**.

A DTD comprises a set of declarations that define a document structure tree. This tree is related to, but not identical to, the tree structure of any document that conforms to the DTD. Unlike a document tree, the DTD tree contains a node for each option, but does not contain any repetition. In the example below, the DTD tree describes a book as containing a number of Chapter elements, with each chapter containing either a number of Paragraph elements or a single Sections element. A particular document tree has a node for each actual chapter and paragraph element present, and may omit some of the optional elements, such as the Sections element.

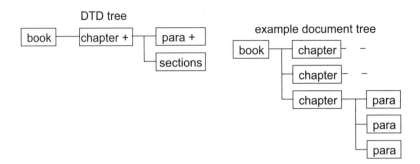

Each specified element must either be a **container element**, or be empty (a place-holder). Container elements may contain text, child elements, or a mixture of both, and the use of child elements can be controlled in a number of ways.

A child element may be required. For example, every book must have a title, so the Book element must have a Title child element.

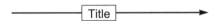

A child element may be optional. Tables sometimes have a title, but not always, so a Table element could have an optional Title child element.

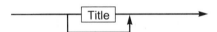

A child element may be repeatable. For example, a list has a number of items so a List element would have repeatable Item child elements.

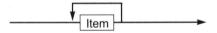

A child element may be both optional *and* repeatable. For example, a chapter may have preliminary paragraphs, but (as in this book) may not always do so.

The DTD also specifies the names of **attributes**, and dictates which elements they may appear in. For each attribute it specifies whether it is optional or required, and what kind of value it may hold. An attribute can hold a simple text phrase, a token, list of tokens, hypertext link anchor, or a reference to an entity or notation. An attribute may also have a default value, to be applied only if no value is supplied by the document author. For example, a DTD may define Version and Date attributes for the Book element, and a Section Number attribute for the Section element. The Version attribute value may default to '1.0'.

Some **XML processors** are able to read the DTD, and use it to build the document model in memory. The template is then compared with the content of a document instance to search for errors. Such processors are said to include a **validation** feature, and to include a **validating parser** module. A **batch validation** process involves comparing the DTD against a complete document instance, and producing a report containing any errors or warnings. For example, if the DTD states that a title must appear in every chapter, but the Title element is missing from one chapter, this is flagged as an error. The recipient of a document instance from another source may perform batch validation to ensure the document is correct, before loading it into a database, or attempting to edit it. Software developers should consider batch validation to be analogous to program compilation, with similar errors detected. **Interactive validation** involves constant comparison of the DTD against a document as it is being created. The application simply prevents an illegal operation. For example, if the DTD states that a Paragraph element can contain only Emphasis and Keyword elements, the editor may only make these elements available for insertion when the cursor is located within a Paragraph element:

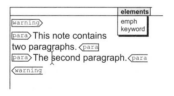

HTML Note: There are SGML DTDs that describe HTML 2.0, HTML 3.2 and now HTML 4.0. These DTDs are not compatible with XML, primarily because they use some of the additional features of SGML.

Creation of a DTD is no trivial exercise, but there are several important benefits to having one. Programmers can write extraction and manipulation filters without fear of their software ever processing unexpected input. Style sheets can be written with the same degree of confidence, and a style rule can be defined for each element in the DTD. Using an XML-aware word processor, authors and editors can be guided and constrained to produce conforming documents (though XML itself allows user-defined elements to be added, editors designed to be used in a controlled environment may be configured to disallow this).

Caution: Parsing a document does not replace careful visual checking of the document content. For example, a parser cannot detect a missing chapter, or the inadvertent use of a bulleted list instead of a numbered list. Likewise, if the title of a book appears in the Author element, and vice versa, this cannot be detected.

Some documents will not require the creation of a DTD. Where raw information is automatically tagged by software for reading by a specific client program, the tagging can be relied upon to be accurately generated. Although
strict rules will apply, these will probably be defined only by a written specification. In fact, much more specific checks may be made by the receiving software than could be implemented in the DTD. For example, the content of a
Date attribute may be checked for valid values in the format 'ddmmyyyy'.
Also, where documents are created on an ad hoc basis for one-off projects, the
effort of producing a DTD may be too great for the reward.

The declarations that comprise the DTD may be stored at the top of each document
that must conform to these rules. Alternatively, and more usually, they may be
stored in a separate data file, referred to by a special instruction at the top of each
document. Finally, there may be good reason to split the declarations between these
two locations. Some declarations are stored within the document, where they are
described as the **internal subset** of the DTD. The remaining declarations, stored in
a separate data file, are described as the **external subset** of the DTD.

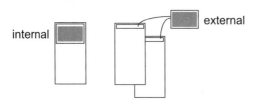

When an external subset applies to many documents, which is almost always
the case, each document is known as a **document instance**, as it is just one
instance in the set of related documents. The external subset is considered to
be the second part of the DTD. Though this often does not matter, there are
cases where it is important because it gives the document author some control
over how the external subset is used in a particular document.

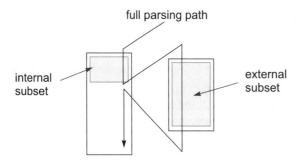

One way in which the document author can be given access to optional con-
figurations is by allowing the author to include instructions that enable or dis-

able declarations in pre-defined segments of the external subset. A **conditional section** encloses a number of other declarations, and contains a keyword that renders the content 'visible' or 'invisible' to XML processing software.

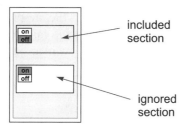

included
section

ignored
section

DTD structure

A DTD is composed of a number of declarations. Each declaration conforms to the markup declaration format, '<!......>', and is classified using one of the following keywords:

- ELEMENT (tag definition)
- ATTLIST (attribute definitions)
- ENTITY (entity definition)
- NOTATION (data type notation definition)

Declarations are grouped together, and held within a **document type declaration (doctypedecl[28])**:

```
<!DOCTYPE MYBOOK [
<!-- The MYBOOK DTD appears here -->
<!....>
<!.......>
]>
```

This mechanism effectively makes the DTD part of the document it describes. The problem with this approach is that a DTD is only worth defining if it is going to apply to a set of documents, and this technique would require the same declarations to appear in every document. This is not only inefficient, but also difficult to manage, as changes to the DTD must then be repeated in each document. To resolve this problem, some or all of the declarations can be stored in an **external subset (extSubset[30])** file. This file can then be referenced from all relevant documents:

```
<!DOCTYPE MYBOOK SYSTEM "../DTDS/MYBOOK.DTD"[
<!-- Some of MYBOOK DTD appears here -->
<!....>
]>
```

Typically, only a few document-specific declarations are left in the **internal subset**. They may define special characters, commonly used phrases or embedded images that are not used elsewhere. In such cases, all the important document structure describing declarations are contained in the external subset file, which is why many people describe this file as *the* DTD file, despite the technical inaccuracy of this statement. Although it is possible to put element declarations in the internal subset, and thereby create document-specific structure models, caution is advised. DTD-specific processing software and style sheets cannot be developed with confidence when some documents arbitrarily redefine the rules.

An entity declaration in the internal subset can be used to override the value of an entity in the external subset. To understand how this is done, two important points must be recalled. The first point is that when an entity is defined more than once, only the first declaration is used. The second point is that the internal subset is processed before the external subset. Therefore, if an entity is declared in the internal subset that has the same name as one in the external subset, it will be processed first, and take precedence. In the example below, a local entity declaration is used to define the content of an element that is defined in the external subset:

```
<!DOCTYPE MYBOOK SYSTEM "C:\DTDS\MYBOOK.DTD" [
<!ENTITY % paraModel "#PCDATA | SUB | SUP">
]>
```

This technique can also be used to exert some control over the use of optional or alternative segments of the DTD, but involves the use of conditional sections, which are described later.

Attribute list declarations work in a similar way. An attribute specified in a declaration within the internal subset overrides a definition in a declaration in the external subset.

SGML Note: The SGML specification has recently been updated so that it also allows this.

Element declarations

An **element declaration** (**elementdecl**[45]) is used to define a new element and specify its allowed content. The keyword '**ELEMENT**' introduces an element declaration. The name of the element being declared follows, separated by at least one space character:

```
<!ELEMENT title ..... >
```

An element name must begin with a letter, an underscrore character, '_', or a colon, ':' (though there are restrictions on the usage of the colon), and may additionally contain digits and some other punctuation characters ('.' and '-'). The element name can be of any length. Valid names include 'P', 'X:123' and 'aVeryLongElementName'. Beyond these restrictions, there are no rules or official recommendations for assigning names to elements.

A statement of the legal content of the element is the final required part of the declaration. An element may have no content at all, may have content of only child elements, of only text, or of a mixture of elements and text. If the element can hold no child elements, and also no text, then it is known as an **empty element**. The keyword 'EMPTY' is used to denote this. In the example below, the Image element is declared to be an empty element, as it is used only to indicate the position of the image. When child elements are allowed, the declaration may contain either the keyword 'ANY', or a **model group**. An element declared to have a content of 'ANY' may contain all of the other elements declared in the DTD (in practice, however, this approach is rarely used because it allows too much freedom, and therefore undermines the benefits that derive from defining document structures).

```
<!ELEMENT p ANY>
<!ELEMENT image EMPTY>

<book><p>There is an image at this point<image.../> in the
text.</p></book>
```

Note that an element that is allowed to hold child elements, text, or both, may just happen to have no content at all. In this case it is legal to employ both a start-tag and end-tag, or to use an empty element tag (**EmptyElemTag[44]**).

```
<title></title>

<title/>
```

Likewise, an element declared to be empty may be represented by a start-tag, immediately followed by an end-tag, though there must be no elements or text between these tags.

A model group is used to describe enclosed elements and text. The structure of a model group can be complex, and is explained fully in the next section.

```
<!ELEMENT book (para*, chapter+)>
```

SGML Notes: The optional minimization codes, '- -' and their variants, never appear in an XML DTD because minimization is not supported (though a DTD can be compliant with both SGML and XML by replacing these characters with a parameter entity, which in the XML version must have an empty replacement value). It is not possible to embed comments within other declarations. Also, an element cannot be declared to have CDATA or RCDATA content.

Model groups

A **model group** is used to define an element that has mixed content or element content. An element defined to have **element content (children[47])** may contain only **child** elements. An element defined to have **mixed content (Mixed[51])** may contain a mixture of child elements and free text. When applied, however, this element may equally contain only text, or only child elements, and it is not possible to specify the order in which text and elements may intermix.

A model group is bounded by brackets, and contains at least one **token** that may be the name of an included element. In this way document hierarchies are built. For example, a model group used in the declaration for a Book element may refer to embedded Front Matter and Body elements, '(fmatter, body)'. The declarations for these elements may in turn specify the inclusion of further elements, such as Title and Chapter.

Sequence control

When a model group contains more than one content token, the child elements can be organized in different ways. The organization of elements is controlled using two logical connector operators: ',' **(sequence connector)** and '|' **(choice connector)**.

SGML Note: The 'and' connector, '&', is not available. The reason for not including this connector type is related to the added complexity it introduces to document structure models, which complicates development of parser software. At the loss of some flexibility for document authors, it can simply be replaced by the sequence connector. See Chapter 19 for details.

The **sequence (seq[50])** rule '(a, b, c)' indicates that element A is followed by element B, which in turn is followed by element C.

Note that other markup, such as comments and processing instructions, may be legally inserted between these elements. Such markup is invisible to the document structure. In an article, for example, it may be important for the title to appear first, followed by the author's name, then a summary.

```
<article>
  <!-- this is an article -->
  <title>Article Title</title>
  <?PAGE-BREAK?>
  <author>J. Smith</author>
  <summary>This is an article about XML.</summary>
  ...
</article>
```

The **choice (choice[49])** rule '(a | b | c)' indicates a choice between the elements A, B and C (only one can be selected).

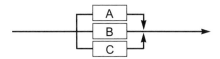

It is not legal to mix these operators because this would introduce ambiguity in the model. The rule '(a, b, c | d)' is invalid, for example, because it may indicate that 'D' is an alternative to *all* the other elements, or that 'D' is an alternative only to element C (A and B still being required).

The solution to this problem is to use enclosed model groups. Further brackets are placed according to the meaning required – '((a, b, c) | d)' indicates the first meaning, whereas '(a, b, (c | d))' indicates the latter. In this way, operators are not actually mixed in the same group. In the last example, the outer model group makes use of the choice connector and the inner model group makes use of the sequence connector.

Quantity control

The DTD author can also dictate how often an element can appear at each location. Occurrence rules are governed using **quantity indicators**.

If the element is required and may not repeat, no further information is required. All of the previous examples indicated a required presence (except where the '|' connector specified a choice of elements).

In an article, the Title element may be required, but the Author element may be absent. If an element is optional, and cannot repeat, it is followed by a question mark, '?'. For example, '(a, b?)' indicates that element B is optional.

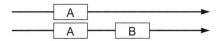

A Book element may require the presence of at least one embedded Chapter element. If an element is required and may repeat, the element name is followed by a plus, '+'. For example, '(a, b+)' indicates that element B must appear, but may also repeat.

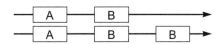

An Article element may contain any number of Author elements, including none. If an element is optional, and also repeatable, the element name is followed by an asterisk, '*'. The '*' may be seen as equivalent to the (illegal) combination '?+'. For example, '(a, b*)' indicates that element B may occur any number of times, and may also be absent.

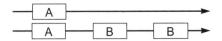

The DTD author can ensure that an element appears at least twice. For example, a list that contains a single item should not be a list at all. A List element may therefore be obliged to hold more than one Item element. This can be achieved using the model '(item, item+)', though care must be taken to place the '+' occurrence symbol after the second Item, as the alternative would be ambiguous, for reasons described below.

A model group may itself have an occurrence indicator. The entire group may be optional, required or repeatable. The example '(a, b)?' indicates that the elements A and B must either occur in sequence, or both be absent. Similarly, the example '(a, b)*' indicates that the sequence A then B may be absent, but if present may also repeat any number of times. The example '(a, b)+' indicates that elements A and B must exist, but may also then repeat.

Note: When creating a DTD, there may be several ways to achieve a required effect. The briefest representation possible should always be used for the sake of clarity. For example, the rule '(a+)?' is more simply defined as '(a*)', though '(a+, b+)' should not be confused with '(a, b)+', which is a very different model.

Text

The locations where document text is allowed are indicated by the keyword '**PCDATA**' (*Parsable Character Data*), which must be preceded by a **reserved name indicator**, '#', to avoid confusion with an element that has the same name (as unlikely as this seems). This keyword represents zero or more characters. An element that may contain only text would be defined as follows:

```
<!ELEMENT emph (#PCDATA)>

<emph>This element contains text.</emph>
```

There are strict rules which must be applied when an element is allowed to contain both text and child elements. The PCDATA keyword must be the first token in the group, and the group must be a choice group. Finally, the group must be optional and repeatable. This is known as a **mixed content** (**Mixed**[51]) model:

```
<!ELEMENT emph   (#PCDATA | sub | super)*>
<!ELEMENT sub    (#PCDATA)>
<!ELEMENT super  (#PCDATA)>

<emph>H<sub>2</sub>O is water.</emph>
```

SGML Note: These strict rules are to avoid the ambiguities that alternative arrangements have caused in SGML DTDs. Most SGML DTD authors have adopted these restrictions as an informal rule.

Model group ambiguities

Some care should be taken when creating model groups as it is possible to confuse the parser. There are several ways to inadvertently create an ambiguous content model.

Ambiguities arise when the element encountered in the data stream matches more than one token in the model. The example below illustrates such a case. On encountering an Item element, the parser cannot tell whether it corresponds to the first token in the group (the optional item) or to the second (the required item). If the parser assumes the first case then discovers no more Item elements in the data, an error will result (because the second item is required). If the parser assumes the second case, then encounters another item, an error will also result (because no more Item elements were allowed). The parser is not expected to look ahead to see which situation is relevant, because some examples of this problem would require the parser to search a long way (possibly to the end of the document), complicating the process and hindering efficiency. The example below could be made valid simply by switching the '?' to the second token:

```
(item?, item)
```

If alternative model groups contain the same initial element, the parser cannot determine which model group is being followed:

```
((surname, employee) | (surname, customer ))
```

On encountering a Surname element, the parser is unsure which model group is active and, as before, will not look ahead to determine which is in use. Such problems can be resolved by redefining the model groups as follows:

```
(surname, (employee | customer ))
```

One severe cause of ambiguity in mixed content models has been avoided by only allowing the choice connector in such models. This decision was made in response to the problems that using other connector types in SGML has raised in the past.

Attribute declarations

Attributes are declared separately from the element, in an **attribute list declaration** (**AttlistDecl**[52]). All the attributes associated with a particular element are usually declared together, in a single attribute list declaration. An attribute declaration is identified by the keyword '**ATTLIST**'. The name of the element that will contain the declared attributes appears first:

```
<!ATTLIST  chapter ... .....
                   ... .....>
```

When there is more than one declaration for a particular element, the individual attribute definitions are combined. However, the first declaration takes precedence when the same attribute is redefined in declarations that are encountered later. The first definition is retained. Note that this allows an attribute declaration in the internal subset to override external definitions, though this is not usually advisable as it alters the document model for individual documents.

The rest of the declaration consists of at least one **attribute definition** (**AttDef**[53]). An attribute definition specifies the name of an attribute, dictates an **attribute type** (**AttType**[54]), and sometimes provides a **default value**.

Attribute name and value type

The first parameter in the declaration is the attribute name, which is of type **Name**[05], and therefore follows the same restrictions on character usage as element names. In the example below, three attributes are defined for use in the Sequence List element:

```
<!ATTLIST  seqlist first .....
                   offset .....
                   type ..... >
```

The second parameter describes the type of the attribute, which can restrict the range of possible values it may hold:

- CDATA
- NMTOKEN
- NMTOKENS
- ENTITY
- ENTITIES
- ID
- IDREF
- IDREFS
- notation
- name group

For example:

```
<!ATTLIST  seqlist first  CDATA
                   offset NMTOKEN
                   type   ( alpha | number )>
```

SGML Note: This is a subset of the types allowed in SGML. The missing types are 'NUMBER', 'NUMBERS', 'NAME', 'NAMES', 'NUTOKEN' and 'NUTOKENS'.

Three of these types are divided into singular and plural forms, for example 'NMTOKEN' and 'NMTOKENS'. The plural form simply indicates a series of values that conform to the same restrictions as the singular form. As a NMTOKEN attribute may contain '123abc', a NMTOKENS attribute may therefore contain '123abc 987xyz thirdToken'.

All attribute types are considered case-sensitive. This means that any difference in letter case is important. For example, 'MyToken' is not considered the same as 'mytoken' and 'MYTOKEN'.

The **CDATA** type indicates a simple string of characters, providing exactly the same flexibility as would be allowed if a DTD was not in use.

```
<book author="J. Smith">
```

The **NMTOKEN** type indicates a word, or token, with the same limits on character usage as previously described for the attribute name, except that there are no special restrictions on the first character, so a token can begin with a digit. White space is used to separate tokens when a value is allowed to contain multiple token values.

```
<doc size="A4">

<picture boundary="5 12 35 55">
```

The **ENTITY** type is a special case, indicating that the attribute value is actually an entity reference. For example, an element may be used as a placeholder for images:

```
<!ENTITY ACMElogo ..... >
<!ELEMENT picture  EMPTY>
<!ATTLIST picture  file ENTITY ...>

<picture file="ACMElogo">
```

The **ID** and **IDREF** types are also special cases, used to provide a platform for hypertext linking. They are covered in detail in Chapter 12.

It is possible to embed non-XML data within an element. However, the embedded data must conform to an identified format. The name is used to link various references to the data type, found in notation declarations (see below), entity declarations and attribute declarations. In an attribute declaration, the **NOTATION** option specifies which data types may be embedded within the element. The **notation type** (**NotationType**[58]) declaration begins with the keyword 'NOTATION', and concludes with a list of previously defined notation names, such as 'TeX'. Because the embedded data does not conform to XML syntax, the XML processor must assume that the element has ended when it encounters the end-tag start delimiters, '</' (so this combination must not appear in the embedded data). In the example below, the Format attribute to the Image element has been defined to be a notation attribute:

```
<!ATTLIST image format    NOTATION (TeX | TIFF) >

<image format="TeX">
-$${ \Gamma (J^psi ......
</image>
```

The **name token group** option restricts values to one of a finite set. For example, the definition '(left | right | centre)' specifies that the value must be one of these tokens:

```
<title align="centre">
```

In some cases, it is practical for a group to contain a single option:

```
<!ATTLIST list  type  (indented)  .....>
```

In this example, the List element has an attribute called Type, which can take only one value, 'indented'. An application should assume that a missing value indicates the alternative form:

```
<list> <!-- normal list -->

<list type="indented"> <!-- indented list -->
```

HTML & SGML Note: Recall that the attribute name, equals sign and quotes are all required in XML, so '<list indented>' is not allowed.

Attribute values are 'normalized' before they are passed to an application. In all cases, any line-end codes are replaced by spaces to create a simple string of text. Then all entity references are replaced by the entity content. Finally, for attribute types other than CDATA, multiple spaces are reduced to a single space and surrounding spaces are removed. The attribute values below are normalized to 'X123', 'John Peter Smith' and '15mm 35mm':

```
<!ENTITY MiddleName "Peter">
<!ATTLIST pic     id    ID          #REQUIRED
                  owner CDATA       #REQUIRED
                  size  NMTOKENS    #REQUIRED >

<book id=" X123" owner="John     &MiddleName;
         Smith " size="15mm     35mm " >
```

Note that CDATA attributes are allowed to contain general entity references.

Default attribute values

The final parameter is the **default value (DefaultDecl[60])**, which specifies a default value to be applied when the document author does not enter a value. Alternatively, this parameter can be used simply to state that the document author must enter a value, or that the value is optional. It is even possible for a default value to be made compulsory (the only value allowed for this attribute).

The DTD can specify that a particular attribute must be present each time the element it belongs to is used. This is termed a **required attribute**. If a value is not given, an error is reported. The '**#REQUIRED**' keyword is used for this purpose. In the example below, the DTD dictates that the Separator Character attribute to the Sequence List element is a required token. This token must be provided every time a Sequence List element is used:

```
<!ATTLIST seqlist sepchar   NMTOKEN  #REQUIRED>
```

Alternatively, the DTD may specify that the attribute can be absent. This is an **implied attribute**. When a value is not explicitly provided, the application just assumes some default behaviour. The '**#IMPLIED**' keyword is used for this purpose. In the example below, the DTD dictates that the Offset attribute to the Sequence List element is an implied token (which, if used, specifies an indentation width for the list items):

```
<!ATTLIST seqlist sepchar   NMTOKEN  #REQUIRED
                  offset    NMTOKEN  #IMPLIED >

<seqlist sepchar="*">...</seqlist>

<seqlist sepchar="*" offset="5mm">...</seqlist>
```

An attribute may be required, yet also given a **default value**. When an explicit value is not provided in the document, this default value is used. The benefits of this approach are that each time the default value is applicable, the size of the data file or stream is reduced, and a document author has less work to do. In the example below, the Type attribute is a choice group, with possible values of 'alpha' and 'num' (indicating an alphabetical list or a numeric list). When a value is not specified, the default is 'num' (numerical list), perhaps because this is deemed to be the most frequent requirement:

```
<!ATTLIST seqlist sepchar    NMTOKEN  #REQUIRED
                  offset     NMTOKEN  #IMPLIED
                  type       (alpha|num) "num" >

<seqlist sepchar="*">              <!-- numeric -->

<seqlist sepchar="*" type="num">   <!-- numeric -->

<seqlist sepchar="*" type="alpha"> <!-- alpha    -->
```

Note that a default value can *not* be added to required or implied attributes. It is an alternative to these types of attribute. It can, however, be considered as a special kind of required attribute, as the XML processor is guaranteed to be given a value, by the DTD author if not by the document author.

If a default value is preceded by the keyword '**#FIXED**', then the provided value is the only value the attribute can take. This may seem odd, but using this feature the DTD author can place permanent markers that attach application-specific roles to DTD-specific elements or attributes. Xlink and HyTime utilize this concept to identify elements and attributes with linking roles, and it also has a possible role in the Namespaces standard to identify the namespaces allowed.

Reserved attributes

Attribute names beginning 'xml:' are reserved for use in the standard, and the attributes **xml:lang** and **xml:space** are already assigned meanings. Previous examples have shown these attributes embedded in element start-tags. But when a particular element always has the same value for one of these attributes, it is more economical to store this information in the attribute declaration. For example, when elements called English and German are defined to hold text in each of these languages, it would be sensible to define suitable values in the DTD. The document author then only has to insert the relevant element.

```
<!ATTLIST english  xml:lang NMTOKEN "en">
<!ATTLIST german   xml:lang NMTOKEN "de">
```

Note that this example illustrates another possible use for the #FIXED feature. It would not be wise to allow a document author the option to override the values attached to each of these elements.

Multiple declarations

More than one attribute list declaration can be assigned to the same element. The attribute definitions they contain are combined. When the same attribute name appears, the first declaration has precedence.

```
<!ATTLIST book  id  ID #REQUIRED
                type (novel | fact) #REQUIRED>
<!ATTLIST book  type (thick | thin) "thin"
                author CDATA #IMPLIED>
```

```
<book id="X123" type="fact" author="J. Smith">
```

For reasons of backward compatibility with SGML, which does not allow this, using multiple declarations is not advised. In any case, there seems to be little advantage in doing this. For reasons already stated, it is certainly not a good idea to include overriding declarations in a document's internal subset.

Parameter entities

Just as a document author may use a general entity to avoid unnecessary repetition, so a DTD author may use a **parameter entity** (**PEReference**[69]) in a similar fashion to aid construction of the DTD. The use of entities can reduce the workload, make authoring errors less likely and clarify the DTD structure (although they can also, if used too frequently, render the DTD unintelligible). For example, a model group that is in common use may be stored in an entity:

```
<!ENTITY % common   "(para | list | table)">
```

Within element declarations a reference is made to the parameter entity:

```
<!ELEMENT chapter - -  ((%common;)*, section*) >
<!ELEMENT section - -  (%common;)*>
```

Note that an entity reference must not be qualified by an occurrence indicator. In the example above, a model group is used to hold the '%common;' reference. It would not be legal to use '%common;*' instead. The double pair of brackets this introduces into the model has no effect, though to avoid such redundancy, models defined in entity declarations tend not to include the brackets. But omitting brackets in the entity declaration can also cause problems if the DTD author forgets, and also omits them in the element declaration. In the end, this is just a matter of personal preference.

A space character is added to the start and end of the content as it replaces the reference. This is to ensure that the entity contains complete tokens. The following example would break the Superscript element into two tokens, 'supersc' and 'ript', and this would be illegal anyway because there would be no vertical bar between them.

```
<!ENTITY % PartModel "emph | supersc" >
<!ELEMENT para  (%PartModel;ript)* > <!-- ERROR -->
```

Using this feature, portions of a DTD may be stored in separate files, for reuse in other DTDs. Parameter entities are also useful when used in conjunction with conditional sections, as described in the next section.

Conditional sections

Portions of a DTD may be identified as optional segments, which can be easily included or excluded from processing to build alternative document models. This facility is provided using **conditional sections (conditionalSect[61])**. Once a segment of the document is marked, the content is made visible or invisible to XML processing by changing a single keyword.

Marking the DTD segment for possible exclusion is achieved by surrounding the appropriate declarations with an **included section (includeSect[62])** declaration. An included section declaration is an example of a markup declaration that includes a subset. It is therefore indicated by the declaration start characters, '<!', and an open square bracket, '['. This is followed by the keyword 'INCLUDE'. However, unlike the CDATA construct described previously, spaces *are* allowed around the keyword. The contents are enclosed by embedded square brackets, and the declaration is closed with the combination ']]>'.

```
<![INCLUDE[
      ......
]]>
<![   INCLUDE   [
      ......
]]>
```

Just surrounding some declarations with an included section has no effect on the processing of the DTD. The included section declaration is effectively invisible. The only reason for its presence is that it allows the segment to be 'switched out' easily. Simply changing the word 'INCLUDE' to 'IGNORE' converts the included section declaration into an **ignored section (ignoreSect[63])** declaration. The content of an ignored section is not processed by an XML processor. The embedded declarations are effectively omitted from the DTD:

```
<![IGNORE[
    <!-- THIS COMMENT IS NOT PROCESSED -->
]]>
```

Entities may be used to facilitate the use of conditional sections. If marked sections are used to define optional parts of the DTD, or to create two variants of the same DTD within one file, then the active group of marked sections at any one time can be defined using an entity. In the example below, all the conditional sections containing parameter entity reference 'MyStandard' are to be included (along with all their embedded element and attribute list declarations), and the other marked sections are to be ignored. The effect is to include the first Text entity declaration, which includes the Temp element:

```
<!ENTITY % MyStandard "INCLUDE">
<!ENTITY % MyVariant  "IGNORE">
```

```
<![%MyStandard;[
        <!ENTITY % Text "#PCDATA | sup | sup | temp">
]]>
<![%MyVariant;[
        <!ENTITY % Text "#PCDATA | sup | sup">
]]>
```

By redefining such entities in the internal subset, a document author can choose to omit or include pre-defined (tightly controlled) segments of the DTD, though software that pre-**compiles** the DTD into some more accessible binary format may not permit this kind of flexibility.

SGML Note: The included and ignored section markup cannot be used in a document instance. In XML, this is purely a DTD feature.

When two conditional sections are used to select alternative entity definitions, as in the example above, there is a simple technique that can be employed to dispense with one of them. This technique depends once again on remembering that duplicate entity definitions are ignored. There is therefore no need to surround the second entity declaration, or declarations, with included section markup. In the following example, the second Text entity declaration is ignored if the first is included by setting the MyStandard entity value to 'INCLUDE':

```
<!ENTITY % MyStandard "INCLUDE">
...
<![ %MyStandard; [
        <!ENTITY % Text "#PCDATA | sup | sup | temp">
]]>
<!ENTITY % Text "#PCDATA | sup | sup">
```

Finally, it should be noted that these declarations can only be used in the external subset. It is not possible to use them in a document's internal subset, or in any external entity referred to from this place.

Notation declarations

An element or entity may contain non-XML format data. An element declaration must specify which formats may be embedded, and an entity declaration must specify which format *is* embedded. In both cases, this is done by referring to a notation name, which is defined in a **notation declaration** (**NotationDecl**[82]).

As with other declaration types, a notation declaration begins with the '<!' delimiter and ends with '>'. The keyword '**NOTATION**' identifies a notation declaration, and is followed by the notation name, which is at the discretion of the DTD author but should be an obvious name for the format:

```
<!NOTATION TeX ..... >
```

Note: $\mathrm{T_{E}X}$ is a typesetting language.

The notation name is followed by an external notation identifier, possibly involving both a public and a system identifier. If no information on the format is available, and no application is identifiable that can process the data, the declaration must be present in its minimum form, which includes a system identifier with no value (the keyword 'SYSTEM' followed by two quotes):

```
<!NOTATION PIXI SYSTEM "">
```

When an application is available that can process the data, the system identifier should specify the location and name of that application (though this approach may not work well across the Internet, where the location and name of the user's application will not be known in advance):

```
<!NOTATION TIFF SYSTEM "C:\APPS\SHOW_TIF.EXE">
```

Information about the data format should be provided, if present, in the public identifier:

```
<!NOTATION TeX PUBLIC "-//MyCorp//NOTATION TeX
  Help File//EN" "C:\APPS\SHOW_TEX.EXE">
```

The declared notation may be referred to in entity declarations, following the '**NDATA**' (notational data) keyword. Note that the parser can make no use of this information, but passes it to the application (which, it is hoped, can).

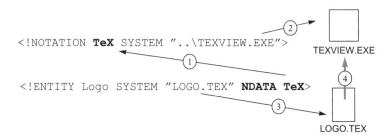

The declared notation may also be referred to in attribute declarations, for elements that contain formats other than XML (but conforming to legal XML character usage).

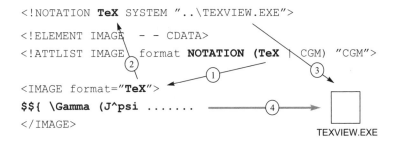

DTD processing issues

When a document contains neither an internal nor external DTD subset, there are some restrictions on the use of markup:

- Attributes cannot have a default value, so must always be specified in full.
- Attributes cannot be entity references, identifiers or identifier references, nor a token or series of tokens. All attributes are assumed to be simple strings (CDATA).
- Attributes cannot be made compulsory. All attributes are optional, and implied if not present.
- Entities cannot be defined, and the only entity references that can (and should) be used are the hard-wired references: '<', '>', '&', ''' and '"'.

Also, because no document structure rules are available, it is not possible to determine which elements have element content, as opposed to mixed content. Therefore, all spaces and line-end codes may be considered part of the document:

```
<p>Here is a list:</p>
<list>
<item>
<p>First item</p></item>
<item><p>Second item</p></item>
<item>
<p>Third item</p></item></list>
```

Here is a list:

First item
Second item

Third item

These restrictions are relatively trivial in the cases where software is both generating and processing the document. The document rules need not be passed
from application to application if they are already built into both applications. The writer program can easily ensure that required attributes are always
produced, and repeated generation of 'default' values takes no effort. Unnecessary spaces and line-end codes can also be consistently avoided. It is also
assumed that the client application can perform its own check for required
attributes, and determine for itself which of the attributes hold either references to entities or hypertext link codes.

Internal DTD processing

When present, an internal DTD subset must be processed. Typically, this subset contains document-specific declarations, such as local entity definitions.
The following example shows an internal subset that contains a single entity
declaration. This declaration must be read so that the reference in the paragraph can be expanded when the document is presented:

```
<!DOCTYPE Note [
<!ENTITY XML "Extensible Markup Language">
]>
<note>
<p>The &XML; format includes entities.</p>
</note>
```

Though much less common, the internal subset may also contain document structure building declarations. Even a non-validating parser needs to read these declarations, as they may contain default or fixed attribute values, or attributes that
provide the name of a binary entity (indicating that the element should be
replaced by the content of that entity). For example, the DTD may state that a
Security attribute is required in every paragraph, and that it has a default value of
'secret' (as in a typical government department). Without reading the attribute list
declaration, it would not otherwise be possible to tell that the second paragraph
in the example below should not be presented to all readers:

```
<!ATTLIST para   security  (secret|normal) "secret">
...
<para security="normal">A normal paragraph.</para>
<para>A secret paragraph.</para>
```

For this reason, an XML processor that is not capable of reading and interpreting element and attribute declarations should abort processing the document if they are present.

External DTD processing

Typically, an external subset contains document structure rules. Although some
applications may not be very interested in the external subset, especially when they

have no intention of validating the content for correct structure, they still need to know if entities or attribute values of the kinds described above are stored there. The **standalone** parameter of the **XML declaration** includes the keyword 'yes' or 'no', to inform a non-validating XML processor whether or not the external subset of the DTD must be read for the document to be processed accurately.

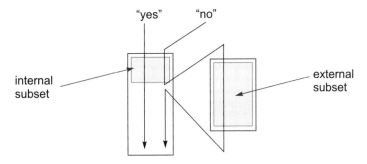

When no information is provided, the value 'no' is assumed as a default, so external processing is assumed to be necessary (unless, of course, there *is* no external subset). It follows that the parameter need only be included when an external subset exists, but is not needed to interpret the document content:

```
<?XML ..... standalone="yes" >
```

6. Document modelling (DTD design)

This chapter explores issues relating to the development of a document model or template, including document analysis, future-use analysis and general DTD design. It focuses on the more complex needs of professional document publishing.

Analysis

DTDs are important documents. They are used to guide authors and ensure that relevant documents conform to agreed standards. If a DTD is in some way inadequate, or simply defines inappropriate rules, the implications can be enormous. Correcting a problem with the DTD later may also necessitate appropriate modifications to thousands of documents. Changes to software filters and style sheets may also need to be made. Great care should therefore be taken to ensure that the DTD is correct first time.

The creation of a document model requires a number of skills that in most cases cannot be found in any single person. Specifically, it is necessary to consider the features and limitations of the XML syntax (and possibly some of the adjunct standards), the level of complexity and its impact on any bespoke software development, the existing document model (which may not be fully apparent from simply studying previously published material and style guides) and likely future electronic publishing or information dissemination needs. The following roles are likely to be spread across a small number of individuals:

- document author or editor
- editorial system administrator
- software developer or integrator
- XML consultant
- database designer

Document analysis

It is typically the case that a new XML-based system replaces a system that adopted procedural markup principles, whether an old-fashioned typesetting system or a more modern DTP package. Existing books or documents to some degree conform to in-house style guides (whether formally defined, loosely described in notes, or existing simply in the heads of senior editorial staff), and naturally form the foundation of document analysis. The better the style guide, and the more rigorously it was previously applied, the easier it is to define a suitable DTD.

Studying existing documents reveals much about the required structure. However, nothing can replace having an author or editor with widespread experience of the content of these documents involved in the process. When the document collection is vast, only a small proportion of the material can be assessed, and it is very important that the selected material be representative of the whole collection.

Another important principle to adopt is to be realistic about the technology and its capabilities. DTP operators have become accustomed to a degree of artistic freedom that cannot be sustained in an XML environment. XML is usually implemented because it can improve the efficiency of publishing and republishing to different target audiences on a variety of media. Software is used to provide the necessary automation, but programs require predictable input. Utilities that locate, extract, manipulate and present information from XML documents must be given manageable tasks to perform. In particular, regard must be given to the limitations of style sheets and structure-oriented publishing products. Creating complex coding structures to deal with structures that appear infrequently may not be practical. One common example of such a problem is a small, vertically aligned fragment, as shown below. Compromise may be in order. Perhaps these structures can be formatted slightly differently, more simply, without any loss of legibility.

```
        300
         25.6
  and    1.3
```

For every feature identified in existing documents, the following set of questions may be asked:

- can it be given a name?
- does it always appear?
- may there be more than one?
- must it always appear before (or after) some other feature?
- does it deconstruct into smaller objects (to which these same questions apply)?
- is some of the textual content always the same (if so, it could be generated automatically)?

The answers to these questions form the basis of a document specification. Every object in the document is given a descriptive name, and is assigned rules governing where and how often it may appear, and what it may contain.

Database schema analysis

All or part of an XML document may consist of data extracted from a relational database. If the database schema has been created professionally, there should be documentation that describes the design. Database analysis frequently involves the production of entity relationship diagrams (or E-R diagrams), which may be of use in helping determine the XML data model. The reverse is also true; an existing XML document model may be used to help design the database schema, including the E-R diagrams describing it. In either case, it is interesting to compare DTD definitions with entity relationship diagrams. An 'entity' in this case may be equivalent to an XML element.

In a **one-to-one** relationship, one entity is related to one other entity. For example, a chapter may contain one title, and that title belongs only to that chapter (note that the Chapter element is not mandatory to the Title element if the Title element may also be used elsewhere):

If the Title element is not mandatory, the black circle is replaced with an empty circle:

In a **one-to-many** relationship, a single entity is related to many instances of another entity. For example, a Chapter element may (or perhaps must) contain at least one Paragraph element:

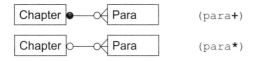

Alternative relationships can also be described in XML, and in the **SSADM** (*Structured Systems Analysis and Design Method*) version of an E-R diagram. For example, a Chapter element may contain either a set of Paragraph elements or a single Sections element (note that the Title element may be part of a chapter or a section):

```
(Title?, (Para+ | Sections))
```

These diagrams say nothing about the order of appearance because relational databases have no concept of internal order (though output may be sorted alphabetically).

Future-use analysis

Analysis should not end at describing current practice, unless it is certain that the data will never be put to new purposes. A major reason for adopting XML is the possibilities it offers for information reuse. The advent of electronic publishing has been a major factor in popularizing the generalized markup approach. In addition, the benefit of using databases to locate information is now well appreciated, and it is relatively simple to extract such information from XML documents. Analysis must therefore include looking ahead to the features offered by these new publishing media, and to possibilities for niche publications derived from subsets of the data.

One benefit of electronic publishing over traditional paper publishing is the capability of software to provide hypertext links. The original document may contain obvious linking text, such as 'see section 9 for details', but there may also be other, more subtle links 'hidden' in the document structure. In both cases, it is necessary to determine a linking strategy, including a scheme for producing unique link values for each target object.

The issue of granularity is often raised at this point, because future-use analysis tends to identify structures that need to be identified, but which have no distinctive visual appearance in existing paper products. For example, while a person's name may be highlighted in the document, it is unlikely that the last name will be styled differently to the first name, yet an online publication or associated database may be envisaged that includes a list of names, sorted by last name. To achieve this automatically, each part of the name should be tagged.

The name *John Smith* is very popular.

```
The name <name><f>John</f><s>Smith</s></name> is
very popular.
```

DTD design

Ultimately, the results of document and future-use analysis combine to form a plan from which a suitable DTD can be constructed. But a single plan can be implemented in many different ways. There are choices to make, such as whether or not to adapt an existing DTD, whether to describe a feature of the document with an element or an attribute, and what names to assign to each element and attribute. Even the layout of the DTD deserves consideration, such as the arrangement of declarations, the use of comments, and the division of the DTD into reusable entities.

Naming options

There are few restrictions on the naming of elements, but some guidelines are worth considering.

A coherent policy on the use of upper-case and lower-case letters is essential, as element names are case-sensitive. The most obvious options are all lower-case ('myelement') and all upper-case ('MYELEMENT'), though mixed-case ('MyElement') has the benefit of clearly distinguishing each part of a name derived from multiple words. Consistency is particularly important, so if an underscore character is used to separate words within one element name, this character should be used for the same purpose in all compound element names. Lower-case letters are generally considered to be easier on the eye (on the few occasions when raw XML data should need to be directly viewed), and make documents compressed for transfer smaller (because the exact same words are more likely to appear in the document text).

The other factor to consider is the length of the name. Unfortunately, there are two conflicting aims to keep in mind. The desire to create unambiguous, self-describing structures would tend to suggest the need for longer names. Clearly, the name 'PriceCode' is more meaningful than 'PC', or even 'PriCd'. But in contradiction to this is the need to minimize document size, so as to increase the speed of transfer over networks. One solution is to use short names for commonly used elements, and long names for infrequently used elements. This approach addresses both problems, as document authors will use the shorter named elements so frequently that memorizing their meaning is hardly an issue, and, at the same time, document size is not greatly affected by the increased length of a few, rarely used elements. The naming of attributes should follow the same considerations, with a reasonable balance between clarity and brevity, perhaps also taking into account the likely number of occurrences of the element, and of the attribute itself. Note that HTML tends to follow these rules, with 'p' standing for 'paragraph', a commonly used element, and 'frameset' representing an entire document containing frames.

Element or attribute

Analysis of the content of an element may result in identification of information that at first sight could be represented either by a child element or by an attribute, and even expert DTD designers may make different choices. Even so, there are some guidelines that may assist in making this decision.

If the embedded information may itself contain sub-structures, then an element should be used, because attributes are not capable of holding structured markup. For example, if the title of a book may contain superscript and subscript characters, or emphasized words, it should be held in a Title element, not a Title attribute to a Book element.

If the information is a small unit of text that cannot itself contain markup, it can reasonably be represented by an attribute. It is a particularly strong candidate if it is purely administrative information that may not even appear on the published document, such as a draft version number.

If the information is a simple choice from a given number of options, then an attribute should almost certainly be used, as it is possible to restrict the value to one of a pre-defined set of values, and the full set of options can (with a typical XML-aware editor) be presented for document authors to choose from.

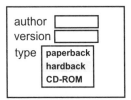

When in doubt, and a small number of attributes are involved, an element should probably be used. In a typical XML-aware editor, it is often inconvenient to switch between element inserting mode and attribute editing mode. Similarly, it is easier to provide visual feedback of the current value with an element. Some products and style sheet languages have limited or non-existent capabilities for presenting attribute values.

To summarize, an attribute is usually easier to manage. It can be constrained and validated by a parser, whereas text in an element cannot. However, style sheets tend to have limited capabilities for extracting, styling and positioning an attribute on-screen or on the page.

Industry standard DTDs

Some government organizations and industry-wide standardization committees have produced standard DTDs. There are powerful reasons for considering the adoption of such a DTD. Consider the case of two organizations who wish to both produce and exchange documentation. By adopting a standard DTD, both organizations avoid the costs associated with document analysis and DTD design. In addition, information can be exchanged between these organizations with a minimum of fuss. The recipient is at a particular advantage, as this organization will have a data repository that understands the document structures, and style sheets already configured to present it. The DTD itself is already available, so does not have to be exchanged along with the data.

But there are also some drawbacks to using an industry standard DTD. The needs of one organization will rarely match the needs of another. Each party will tend to make different decisions concerning the content of their documentation, even in tightly regulated industries, perhaps for reasons of commercial advantage, or because their products differ in some detail. First, the DTD may not identify every feature of the documents produced by the implementor, in which case important information will either not be tagged at all, or be tagged inappropriately, and such information will then be difficult to identify when it is required for indexing, styling or extraction. Second, the DTD may contain elements that will never be used by the implementor, and the presence of these elements on selection menus will both confuse authors and add unnecessary work for software developers (who may be unaware that they are not used). Third, in order to attempt to satisfy the varying needs of many organizations in the industry, the DTD rules may be too flexible. For example, the DTD may allow an author name to appear before or after a publication title, and also allow it to be absent (if there is no author), despite there being an in-house style rule that states an author's name must always appear, and that it must precede the title. Every unnecessary degree of freedom will also add to the work of software filter and style sheet developers. Worse still, there may be more than one mechanism included to model a particular data structure, due to compromises made by various contributors to the design during development of the DTD, and it would be unfortunate if document authors were able to choose a model at random. Note that a subtle variant or combination of the first two factors may be encountered. For example, if a standard DTD contains several elements to describe paragraph levels, such as P0, P1 and P2, but the implementor only requires a single level of paragraph, then there are both unnecessary elements which are to be ignored (P1 and P2), and an inappropriately named element for a simple paragraph, P0 (which would be better named Para, or just P).

Assuming that, for the reasons described above, the standard DTD is not a perfect fit, it would be natural to consider that DTD worthless, and to start again. But in most cases it is appropriate to adopt a pragmatic approach, by taking account of an appropriate standard DTD, but modifying it to fulfil the real need. Although this approach undoubtedly hinders the transfer of documents between organizations that have modified the DTD, in subtly different ways, there will be at least some commonality remaining to reduce confusion. For example, if the DTD contains an element called PriceCode, the modified DTDs are likely to retain this name.

The DTD designer should therefore compare the results of analysis against a suitable standard. Redundant elements should be removed, additional ones added, and loose occurrence rules tightened. This process is not as destructive as it first looks when considering how to transfer data to an organization using the standard (or their own variant of it). Tightening of context and occurrence rules has no effect on the validity of the documents when parsed against the original DTD (the recipient's parser does not know or care that the documents were created using a stricter data model). Also, removal of redundant elements usually has no implication beyond making them unavailable to document authors, providing they were originally optional elements. Only the addition of new elements guarantees problems, which can simply be resolved by either removing or renaming these elements before the data is transferred.

Tables

Industry standards have an important role in defining models for constructs that are difficult to render, and the most common example of this is tabular matter. Tables provide a special problem for designers of viewing and editing applications. Structures like paragraphs, lists and warnings form a simple linear sequence, but table cells are arranged into a two-dimensional grid. An application must recognize which elements represent column or row boundaries. The presence of border lines, cells that straddle over adjoining rows and columns, and the various ways in which text can be aligned within each cell, all complicate the issue still further. These features may be described using additional elements or attributes, but if every document model designer adopts a different approach, an application that is required to present the information in a tabular format has little chance of being able to interpret the markup.

In the SGML community, recognition of this problem quickly led to the establishment of a *de facto* standard. From a few competing models, widespread use of applications that support the DTDs developed for the US Department of Defense meant that the **CALS table** model was the inevitable winner. This table model requires the use of specific elements, including Table, Thead, Tbody, Tfoot, Row and Entry. This model also influenced, to some extent, the approach taken to add table support to HTML. Introduced in HTML 2.0, this scheme has been extended in later versions, and is now quite similar to the CALS model (see Chapter 18 for details). Due to the fact that XML is aimed primarily at the Web, it seems likely that the HTML model will become the *de facto* standard.

Although there is nothing to prevent the creation of XML elements that reflect the names of HTML elements, such as Table, Tr (table row), Th (table header) and Td (table data), freedom to use names that are more meaningful to the content of the cells is an important XML principle. For example, when the table contains a list of product codes and prices, the following structure may be deemed more appropriate:

```
<prices>
  <prod><code>XYZ-15</code><price>987</price></prod>
  <prod><code>XYZ-22</code><price>765</price></prod>
</prices>
```

In this example, the information is sufficiently well identified for product details to be automatically located and extracted, and a specialized search engine can locate the price of a specific product. The content can also be presented in a number of different ways. Nevertheless, the most obvious presentation format is a tabular structure. Close study of the elements reveals that the Prices element is analogous to the HTML Table element, the Prod element encloses a single row of data, and the Code and Price elements both represent individual cells.

But an application must be informed of the specific significance of each of these elements. This can be achieved using a style sheet. Fortunately, the CSS specification now includes property values that map an element name to a table part role (see Chapter 17 for full details). The values 'table', 'table-row' and 'table-cell' may be used in the display property:

```
prices { display:table }
prod   { display:table-row }
code   { display:table-cell }
price  { display:table-cell }
```

XYZ-15	987
XYZ-22	765

Care should be taken when defining the data structure to adopt a row-oriented approach, as shown in the example above, so that the elements can be mapped easily to the HTML model. It is not possible to map elements in a structure that takes a column-oriented approach, as in the example below:

```
<table>
  <products>
    <code>XYZ-15</code>
    <code>XYZ-22</code>
  </products>
  <prices>
    <price>987</price>
    <price>765</price>
  </prices>
</table>
```

Another strategy that could be used is to adopt the HTML table model, using namespaces to make the rendering engine aware of the significance of the HTML elements.

Architectural forms

When an application is tuned to a specific DTD, it can assign significant roles to specific elements. For example, an HTML-aware Web browser recognizes and responds in different ways to each occurrence of the Image, Table and Form elements encountered in a document. But when a specialized application must perform specific tasks on data that conforms to a variety of different DTDs, standardized element and attribute names cannot be expected. Although the ideal solution would be to harmonize the DTDs, it may be impractical to enforce this, particularly when the DTDs were produced by different authorities, or were developed primarily for other purposes. For example, an indexing application may need to identify the author and title of each document in a collection that is composed of documents from many different sources.

An **architectural form** is a mechanism that enables standard templates to be added, as an extra layer of meaning, to documents that conform to diverse markup models. Taking the example above, in documents conforming to one DTD, the title may be tagged with an element called Title, and the author name with an element called Author, but in another DTD these elements may be named Tel and Auto Foreign language DTDs may further increase the range of possibilities, including 'Titel' and 'Verfasser' (the German equivalents of 'title' and 'author').

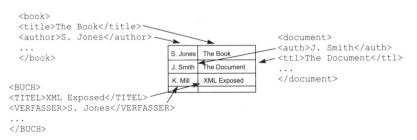

It would certainly be useful if all applications that perform identical functions could understand documents conforming to various DTDs, without any further preparation by the user of a particular application. If all applications adopt the architectural form mechanism, and an independent group devises an appropriate architectural form, this laudable goal can be achieved. One obvious candidate is hypertext linking. Each browser must be made aware of the linking elements and attributes in order to provide active linking. The **HyTime** standard (ISO/IEC 10744) takes this approach, as does the XLink scheme (described in Chapter 12).

Typically, an architectural form involves the use of significant, or 'reserved' attribute names. When a DTD is analyzed, and some elements are found to contain these attributes, the application can match its capabilities to documents conforming to this DTD. For example, the application may have the capability to create a simple database table of names and works, as shown above, and assign significance to elements that contain attributes named IndexTitle and IndexName. But to keep the number of reserved attributes to a minimum, the fixed attribute type may be used to distinguish roles. For example, a single attribute called WorkIndex could be defined, with possible values of 'TITLE' and 'NAME', but having a different fixed value in each element:

```
<!ATTLIST title      WorkIndex CDATA #FIXED "TITLE">
<!ATTLIST author     WorkIndex CDATA #FIXED "NAME">
```

The reason for using fixed attributes is to prevent document authors from changing the values. In fact, document authors can completely ignore these attributes, as they are in effect required attributes with default values.

Of course, it is possible for a reserved attribute, such as 'WorkIndex', to conflict accidently with an attribute of the same name already residing in the DTD. In some cases, it is hoped, this is avoided by assigning very specific names, such as 'xml-link' (XML Linking scheme), 'HyTime' and 'SDARULE' (see below). A more secure workaround is to define a single required reserved attribute, which is used to override the default names for other reserved attributes. The XML Linking scheme uses this approach, and has an attribute called 'xml-attributes', which is used to specify a substitute name for each reserved attribute named.

There is a standard for the use of architectural forms, released by the ISO under the designation ISO 10744, though this is aimed at their use in SGML documents. Applications that are expected to process documents containing unknown architectural form markup need some indication that one or more forms are present, and which ones are present. A processing instruction of the following form is likely to be accepted for use with XML:

```
<?IS10744:arch name=MyForm ?>

<!ATTLIST book MyForm NMTOKEN #FIXED "MyForm-Document">
```

Case study (the ICADD initiative)

Some practical issues regarding the use of architectural forms can be covered through analysis of a 'real world' application, an attempt to help print-impaired readers by making documents accessible in large print, braille or voice synthesis forms. The **ICADD** (*International Committee for Accessible Document Design*) organization produced a suitable SGML DTD for use with software that can re-publish information in these forms. Although developed for use with SGML, there is no reason why it cannot be applied to XML documents.

The software developed by ICADD to process documents relies upon a bespoke DTD, so that both generic and formatting tags can be unambiguously translated (in the same way that Web browsers have relied upon conformance to the HTML element set in order to present material). The ICADD DTD is relatively simple, and contains the following basic elements:

Anchor	(mark spot on page)	Lhead	(list heading)
Au	(author)	List	
B	(bold)	Litem	(list item)
Book	(document element)	Note	
Box	(sidebar information)	Other	(emphasize)
Fig	(figure title)	Para	
Fn	(footnote)	Pp	(print page number)
H1–H6	(header levels)	Term	(or keyword)
Ipp	(Ink print page)	Ti	(title of book)
It	(italic)	Xref	(cross reference)
Lang	(language)		

In order to make a wide variety of information available via this means, it would normally be necessary to either impose the ICADD DTD on all contributors, or translate information between DTDs. Clearly both options have drawbacks. The first may be impossible. The second is very costly because such translations can rarely be performed without human guidance. For these reasons, the **SDA** (*SGML Document Access*) architectural form was developed. When SDA rules are embedded in a DTD, a special converter application knows how to map document instances into the ICADD DTD format, without manual intervention.

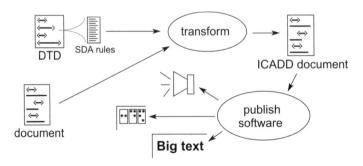

A number of special attributes are defined. They are **SdaRule**, **SdaForm**, **SdaBdy**, **SdaPart**, **SdaPref** and **SdaSuff**. Each dictates a different action to be taken by the transformation software. For example, the **SdaForm** attribute is used to map an element to an ICADD DTD element. In the following example, the Title element is mapped to the Ti element:

```
<!ATTLIST  title  SDAFORM CDATA #FIXED "ti">

<title>The Title</title>

<ti>The Title</ti>
```

The **SdaPref** attribute is used to specify a prefix to be generated. In the following example, the original meaning of the Abstract element is kept intact by specifying that the paragraph is to be preceded by an appropriate header:

```
<!ATTLIST  abstract
              SDAFORM CDATA #FIXED "para"
              SDAPREF CDATA #FIXED "<h1>Abstract</h1>">
<abstract>The Abstract</abstract>

<h1>Abstract</h1>
<para>The Abstract</para>
```

Writing the DTD

A DTD can be written using a standard text editor, providing that the DTD author understands the declarations that comprise it, as described in the previous chapter. However, some thought should be given to the location and layout of the declarations. An illegible DTD is difficult to analyze and maintain.

The DTD should contain a header that describes its purpose and scope, and identifies the current version and the author (including contact details):

```
<!-- XML BOOK DTD
        DTD for The XML Companion
        AUTHOR: N.Bradley (neil@bradley.co.uk)
        VERSION: 1.3 (13/9/97) -->
```

In some respects, the rules of the XML language dictate the layout. Notation declarations should appear first, and entity declarations should follow. Most DTD authors then place element declarations in order of their approximate location in the structure hierarchy, starting with the document element and ending with in-line elements. Attribute declarations tend to be placed immediately after the elements to which they apply. When short element or attribute names are used, comments should be employed to supply the full name:

```
<!-- Company President -->
<!ELEMENT compres .....>
<!ATTLIST compres ........>
```

When more than one attribute is being defined, each attribute should be specified on a separate line:

```
<!ATTLIST book    version    CDATA            #REQUIRED
                  date       CDATA            #REQUIRED
                  author     CDATA            #IMPLIED
                  type       (fiction|none)   "none"
                  pages      NUMBER           #IMPLIED>
```

Although aligning parts of the definition in columns, as shown above, is the most common approach used, there is no universal consensus that this is the best technique. The reader is left to consider whether the following is more, or less, legible than the example above:

```
<!ATTLIST book    version CDATA #REQUIRED
                  date CDATA #REQUIRED
                  author CDATA #IMPLIED
                  type (fiction|none) "none"
                  pages NUMBER #IMPLIED >
```

The XML tags used to construct a DTD have a complex syntax, and do nothing to help the author see the document structure they create. It is therefore far too easy to make a syntactic mistake when generating the necessary markup, or to create an incorrect document model that allows elements to appear where they should not (or not appear where they should). There are products that can overcome both these problems, by hiding the markup behind a visual interface which includes icons for each element, and lines that illustrate how they form hierarchical structures. The author receives visual feedback on the document model as it is built, and the software generates the necessary markup when the authoring process is complete. Such tools are also useful for interpreting DTDs developed elsewhere, and for training editorial staff. On the negative side, the generated DTD file may not be formatted or organized exactly as desired.

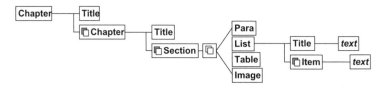

Note that an alternative approach may be considered. There is no reason why a DTD cannot be developed for the construction of other DTDs (see the final case study below). An XML-aware document editor could then be used to construct the DTD, eliminating syntax errors and ensuring required items are included, though not providing the visual feedback described above. In addition, software must be developed to map the resulting document instance into DTD building declarations.

Debugging the DTD

When a DTD has been developed using a standard text editor, it may contain errors, such as content models that refer to elements which do not exist. Some XML parsers are able to detect such errors, and they should be used after completing the DTD.

The time needed for testing the document model defined by the DTD is often underestimated. Even relatively simple DTDs usually contain a surprising number of possible document structures. Testing should involve the production of one (or if necessary two) conforming documents that contain all possible combinations of elements. This process should reveal any gaps or redundancies in the structure, and the resulting document becomes a useful product for the purposes of training future authors and editors. If realistic data is placed in this document, it may also be used to test translation software and style sheets.

Even if a DTD design tool is not used to construct the DTD, these tools can be useful for revealing content models in a tree form that is easy to analyze.

Case study (this book)

For the first case study, it is imagined that this book is part of a collection of 'companion' books, which conform to a standard style and layout. The editors of existing books and authors of new books are to use XML-aware word processors in order to ensure consistency of structure and style. All new issues will then be paginated automatically. Initial analysis will focus on one book in the range, *The XML Companion*.

This book obviously follows general structure conventions, including division into three main segments: front-matter, body and back-matter.

```
<!ELEMENT book   (front, body, back)>
```

Front-matter

The front-matter segment contains, amongst other items, the title, author's name, publisher, date of publication, copyright information, contents, dedication and preface:

```
<!ELEMENT front     (title, edition, author,
                     publisher)>
<!ELEMENT title     (#PCDATA)>
<!ELEMENT edition   (#PCDATA)>
<!ELEMENT author    (first, second, e-mail?)>
```

```
<!ELEMENT first      (#PCDATA)>
<!ELEMENT second     (#PCDATA)>
<!ELEMENT e-mail     (#PCDATA)>
<!ELEMENT publisher (pub-name, address)

<front>
<title>The XML Companion</title>
<edition>First Edition</edition>
<author>
<first>Neil</first>
<second>Bradley</second>
<e-mail>neil@bradley.co.uk</e-mail>
</author>
<publisher>
<pub-name>Addison Wesley Longman Ltd</pub-name>
<address>Edinburgh Gate, Harlow, Essex, CM20 2JE,
United Kingdom</address>
</publisher>
</front>
```

Body

At first sight, the body of the book appears to be a simple sequence of chapters. However, close study of the contents list reveals a higher level of structure. Although not named, this can be thought of as book divisions. It may be decided that this layer is not mandatory in the series of books:

```
<!ELEMENT body     ((chapter*, division+) | chapter+)>
<!ELEMENT division (title, chapter+)>

<body>
<division>
<title>The XML Standard</title>
...
</division>
<division>
<title>Working with XML</title>
...
</division>
...
...
</body>
```

Note that the Part element contains a Title element, which has already been defined and used to title the book. The purpose of a particular Title instance is dependent on its context, so it is easy to distinguish a book title, which appears in one style in the first pages, from a part title that appears in the contents. The Title element is also used in other contexts:

```
<!ELEMENT chapter (title, (...))>
```

Most chapters contain headings, some larger than others. In fact, there are two levels of heading, and it may be tempting to define elements called Header-one and Header-two, which surround only the heading text. However, another way to look at this is to recognize that the headings are identifying a block of text, just as the heading to this section is identifying a DTD-building case study. In this case, the whole block of text should be isolated, perhaps by an element named Section, and the heading text itself is then identified by an embedded Title element. The smaller headings are identifying sub-sections. The advantage of this approach is that it becomes possible to extract the sections and sub-sections for possible reuse in other publications. In addition, a hypertext link to a section may return the entire section to the browser.

```
<!ELEMENT chapter       (title, ..., section*)>
<!ELEMENT section       (title, (..., sub-section*))>
<!ELEMENT sub-section   (title, (...))>
```

At the next level down in the book structure, there are miscellaneous 'block'-level structures. They are called blocks because they do not share horizontal space on the page with other elements. The most obvious block-level element is the Paragraph element. In addition, there are List, Table, Graphic and Markup Paragraph elements. As all these block structures may be used in various places, it is appropriate to create an entity to hold the content model that groups them:

```
<!ENTITY % Blocks       "(para | list | markup-para |
                        graphic | table)*" >
```

Blocks can be used as introductory material in a chapter and section, and form the content of sub-sections:

```
<!ELEMENT chapter       (title, %Blocks;, section*)>
<!ELEMENT section       (title, (%Blocks;, sub-section*))>
<!ELEMENT sub-section (title, (%Blocks;))>
```

The Markup Paragraph is used to hold multi-line fragments of XML example data. The content appears in a different, mono-spaced font, and is indented (as in the fragment above this paragraph). So that the author can control line-break positioning in the example data, each line is enclosed by a Markup Line element:

```
<!ELEMENT markup-para   (markup-line*)>
<!ELEMENT markup-line   (#PCDATA | ... )*>

<markup-para>
<markup-line>Line one of markup</markup-line>
<markup-line>Line two of markup</markup-line>
</markup-para>
```

The List element contains further block-type elements, called Item, which contain the text of each item in the list.

```
<!ELEMENT list          (item+)>
<!ELEMENT item          (...)>

<list>
<item>Item One</item>
<item>Item Two</item>
<item>Item Three</item>
</list>
```

The List element contains a Type attribute to specify whether it is a numbered or random (bulleted) list. It defaults to random, as this is the most common type:

```
<!ATTLIST item        type   (number|random)  "random">
```

For tables, the popular CALS model is used. This is to take advantage of the capabilities of some SGML-aware typesetting and DTP software. In future, this model may be replaced by the HTML table model.

The Graphic element is empty because it is a placeholder for an image. It contains an Identifier attribute, which holds an entity name. An entity declaration is required for each picture in the book.

```
<!ELEMENT graphic      EMPTY>
<!ATTLIST graphic      id     ID        #IMPLIED
                       ident  ENTITY    #REQUIRED>
```

There are various classes of in-line element, which may be used in varying combinations within the block-level elements. To help describe these classifications, three entities are defined:

```
<!ENTITY % SuperSub "sup | sub" >
<!ENTITY % Hilite   "markup | emph-strong | emph-weak" >
<!ENTITY % Inline   "(#PCDATA | %Hilite; |
                    %SuperSub; | x-ref)*" >
```

The Superscript/Subscript entity refers to superscript and subscript text, such as 'H_2O' and 'element[39]'. The Hilite entity refers to the Markup, Emphasis Strong and Emphasis Weak elements, which are used to enclose example fragments within a paragraph. Typically, different fonts would be used to identify them in the text. In this book, the Markup element content is presented in a mono-spaced font, as in 'this is markup', the Emphasis Weak element content is presented in italic typeface, for '*important terms*', and the Emphasis Strong element content is presented in bold typeface, for '**key terms**'. The Inline entity includes the previous entities and adds the #PCDATA token and Cross Reference element (X-ref). Each element definition is carefully designed to avoid including itself:

```
<!ELEMENT markup         (#PCDATA | %SuperSub; |
                         emph-strong | emph-weak)*>
<!ELEMENT emph-strong    (#PCDATA | markup | emph-weak |
                         %SuperSub; | x-ref)*>
<!ELEMENT emph-weak      (#PCDATA | markup |
                         emph-strong | %SuperSub; |
                         x-ref)*>
<!ELEMENT sup            (#PCDATA)>
<!ELEMENT sub            (#PCDATA)>
<!ELEMENT x-ref          (#PCDATA)>
```

The Markup Line element can, in addition, contain a Presented element. This is used to show the published output, using a sans-serif font:

```
<!ELEMENT markup-para  (markup-line*)>
<!ELEMENT markup-line  (#PCDATA | ... | presented )*>

<markup-para>
<markup-line>XML fragment</markup-line>
<markup-line>
<presented>XML fragment</presented>
</markup-line>
</markup-para>

XML fragment
```

XML fragment

Some markup fragments may be quite large, in which case it is likely that a page-break would naturally appear somewhere within it. The Splitable attribute is used to specify whether or not the block can be split across pages. The default value of 'loose' means that a page-break may appear within the block. The alternative value of 'together' means that the lines must be kept together (even at the expense of leaving white space at the bottom of the page).

```
<!ATTLIST markup-para  splitable
                       (loose | together) "loose">
```

Back-matter

The back-matter consists of only the Glossary element. The Glossary element is a simplified version of a Chapter. There is no Title element, because the title 'Glossary' can be assumed, and can therefore be generated automatically:

```
<!ELEMENT back      (glossary)>
<!ELEMENT glossary  (para*, section*)>
```

The index is generated automatically, so no data or tags are required.

Case study (a DTD for DTDs)

A DTD can be considered to be a structured document in its own right, and can therefore be described using another DTD. This makes for an interesting case study, not least because modelling DTD constructs serves to reinforce the concepts covered in Chapter 5.

Why a DTD for DTDs?

Two concepts combine in this example to create a powerful new approach to working with DTDs. First, there are a number of advantages to using XML document syntax for codifying document structure rules, in place of the DTD-building constructs described in an earlier chapter. The DTD can take advantage of

XML document processing tools, such as parsers that can check that the DTD is well-formed, and browsers that can format and present the DTD, using style sheet languages such as CSS or XSL. The second advantage is that a DTD can then be written to describe this model, so the DTD creation can be performed using a standard XML editor, which can use the 'DTD for DTDs' to guide the author. Note that this DTD is also an XML document, so can also be easily validated and presented. The obvious disadvantage to this approach is that XML syntax is more verbose than the existing syntax for DTD construction, and is therefore less appropriate for transfer of data over networks.

Of course, these documents are not 'true' DTDs, in the sense presently under-stood by XML-sensitive software. However, it should be a simple matter to automatically convert document structures into the current DTD syntax:

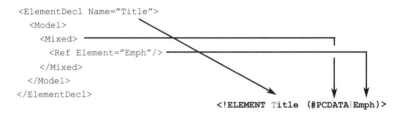

```
<ElementDecl Name="Title">
  <Model>
    <Mixed>
      <Ref Element="Emph"/>
    </Mixed>
  </Model>
</ElementDecl>
```

`<!ELEMENT Title (#PCDATA|Emph)>`

Note that in this case study, future-use analysis is not appropriate (nobody can say what version 2 of XML will include), and document analysis is not necessary because there is a clearly defined specification for the structure of a DTD, as described in Chapter 21 (markupdecl[29]), though some attempts to improve upon current DTD technology are included.

The DDML Proposal

Considering the benefits described above, it is not surprising that a number of proposals have been presented to redefine DTDs using XML syntax. This effort has been coupled with attempts to extend the capabilities of the DTD. The latest proposal released at the time of writing was **DDML** (*Document Definition Markup Language*). DDML was developed from contributors to the XML-Dev mailing list. The W^3C are considering submissions, including this latest one, as the starting point for development of a schema language for XML. It is not possible to say at this time whether the final standard will be the same, or even similar to, the scheme described below.

For reasons of space, only a core subset of the proposal is presented here. Many attributes, and some elements, have been omitted. The full proposal is available from http://www.w3.org/TR/NOTE-ddml.

DTD Outline

The document element is named DocumentDef. This element directly contains elements representing each type of declaration allowed in the external subset: ElementDecl, AttGroup, Notation and UnparsedEntity:

```
<!ELEMENT DocumentDef (Doc?, More?,
                        (ElementDecl | AttGroup |
                         Notation | UnparsedEntity )*
                      )>
```

Note that comments declarations are not included. In order to bind comments more tightly to individual constructs, an optional Doc element is allowed in a number of circumstances, included at the top of the DTD itself. In addition, extensions to the DTD schema are given a placeholder in the form of the More element:

```
<DocumentDef>
  <Doc>This is a DTD</Doc>
  <More><MyExtension>...</MyExtension></More>
</DocumentDef>
```

Element declarations

The element declaration contains the same prefix options, for documenting and possibly extending the scheme, then a Model element that contains the element model, and finally an optional AttGroup element for attaching attributes to the element:

```
<!ELEMENT ElementDecl (Doc?, More?, Model, AttGroup? )>

<ElementDecl>
  <Doc>This is an ELEMENT</Doc>
  <More><MyExtension>...</MyExtension></More>
  <Model>...</Model>
  <AttGroup>...</AttGroup>
</ElementDecl>
```

The reason why the AttGroup element is also allowed directly within the DocumentDef element is to enable construction of global definitions that can be reused in a number of elements. This is clearly an extension of what is possible now in a DTD, though the proposal does not describe how these global definitions are actually to be linked to elements that need to use them.

The Model element must cater for sequential and optional content models, empty elements, elements that can have any content, PCDATA models and mixed models. In the simpler cases, this element just contains an appropriate empty element called Any, Empty or PCData. A model that contains a single element includes a Ref element (see below) to name the element:

```
<!ELEMENT Model (Doc?, More?,
                (Ref | Choice | Seq | Empty | Any |
                 PCData | Mixed )))>

<Model><Ref Element="SingleElement"/></Model>

<Model><Any/></Model>    <!-- ANY -->

<Model><Empty/></Model>  <!-- EMPTY -->

<Model><PCData/></Model> <!-- (#PCDATA) -->
```

More complex models refer to a number of other elements. This is done using a Ref element, with a required NMTOKEN attribute called Element. An attribute is used to ensure that the name is present, and that it is a single token (does not contain spaces):

```
<!ELEMENT Ref  EMPTY>
<!ATTLIST Ref  Element NMTOKEN #REQUIRED>

<!-- A element -->
<ref Element="A"/>
```

An element may occur optionally, or be able to repeat. A Frequency attribute is used to hold this information. This is an enumerated attribute that allows for the values 'Required', 'Optional' (?), 'ZeroOrMore' (*) and 'OneOrMore' (+). The default value is 'Required':

```
<!ATTLIST Ref Frequency ( Required | Optional |
                          ZeroOrMore | OneOrMore )
                          'Required'>
<!-- A+ -->
<ref Element="A" Frequency="OneOrMore"/>
```

The Mixed element represents a mixed model, which simply states which elements may be included with the text content:

```
<!ELEMENT Mixed (Ref+)>
```

This element does not need to include the PCData element shown previously as both its presence and its location (it must be the first token) can be inferred:

```
<!-- ( #PCDATA | A )* -->
<Mixed><Ref Element="A"/></Mixed>
```

The Choice and Seq elements can contain direct references to elements in the choice or sequence group, but can also contain groups of the opposite type. As both models are irrelevant unless they contain at least two tokens, the following models ensure that at least two tokens are included:

```
<!ELEMENT Seq (( Choice | Ref | Model ),
               ( Choice | Ref | Model )))>

 <!-- ( A, B ) -->
<Seq><Ref Element="A"/><Ref Element="B"/></Seq>
```

```
<!ELEMENT Choice (( Seq | Ref | Model ),
                  ( Seq | Ref | Model ))>

<!-- ( A | B ) -->
<Choice><Ref Element="A"/><Ref Element="B"/></Choice>
```

They can also contain more Model elements. This allows the following model to be represented:

```
<!-- (A, B, (C, D)+, E ) -->
<Seq>
  <Ref Element="A"/>
  <Ref Element="B"/>
  <Model>
    <Seq Frequency="OneOrMore">
      <Ref Element="C"/>
      <Ref Element="D"/>
    </Seq>
  </Model>
  <Seq Element="E"/>
</Seq>
```

Attributes

Attribute definitions can be stand-alone, for reuse in various elements (an advance on the current DTD capability), or can be assigned to a specific element by storing the definition in the ElementDecl element, following the Model element. An AttGroup element is used in both cases, acting as a wrapper for a number of individual attribute definitions, which are represented by AttDef elements:

```
<!ELEMENT AttGroup (Doc?, More?,(AttDef+|AttGroup)*)>
<!ELEMENT AttDef   (Doc?, More?, Enumeration? )>
<!ATTLIST AttDef    Name      NMTOKEN        #REQUIRED
                    Type ( CData | ID | IDRef | IDRefs |
                           Entity | Entities | NmToken |
                           NmTokens | Notation |
                           Enumerated )         'CData'
                    Required ( Yes | No )    'Yes'
                    AttValue #CDATA          #IMPLIED>

<!-- <!ATTLIST A B ID #REQUIRED
                C (X|Y) "Y"> -->
<AttGroup>
  <Doc>Documentation for Attributes</Doc>
  <AttDef Name="B" Type="ID" Required="Yes">
  </AttDef>
  <AttDef Name="C" Type="Enumerated"
          Required="No" AttValue="Y">
    <Enumeration>
      <EnumerationValue Value="X"/>
      <EnumerationValue Value="Y"/>
    </Enumeration>
  </AttDef>
</AttGroup>
```

One obvious weakness in this scheme is that it allows an ID to have a default value, which the standard does not permit.

As it may be useful to include comments in enumerated lists and in each entry in the list, the empty elements shown above are just a short-hand form to be used only when such comments are not present:

```
<!ELEMENT Enumeration (Doc?, More?,
                                EnumerationValue+ )>
<!ELEMENT EnumerationValue (Doc?, More?)>
<!ATTLIST EnumerationValue Value CDATA #REQUIRED>

<Enumeration>
  <Doc>This is the X and Y list</Doc>
  <EnumerationValue Value="X">
    <Doc>This is the X value, short for 'Xtreme'</Doc>
  </EnumerationValue>
  <EnumerationValue Value="Y">
    <Doc>This is the Y value, short for 'YES'</Doc>
  </EnumerationValue>
</Enumeration>
```

No mechanism is supplied in the proposal for linking global attribute definitions to individual elements, though the full DTD does include Id attributes which uniquely identify each definition, so could be used in some kind of linking scheme.

Notations

Notation declarations are created with the Notation element, which contains Name, PubidLiteral and SystemLiteral attributes to hold the notation name, the public identifier (if any) and the system identifier (if any):

```
<!ELEMENT Notation (Doc?, More?)>
<!ATTLIST Notation  Name           NMTOKEN  #REQUIRED
                    PubidLiteral   CDATA    #IMPLIED
                    SystemLiteral  CDATA    #IMPLIED>

<!-- <!NOTATION A PUBLIC "B" "C"> -->
<Notation Name="A"
          PubidLiteral="B"
          SystemLiteral="C"/>
```

Unparsed entities

Only entities that cannot be parsed can be declared, using the UnparsedEntity element. A required Notation attribute is included to ensure that only unparsable entities are defined using this element:

```
<!ELEMENT UnparsedEntity (Doc?, More?)>
<!ATTLIST UnparsedEntity  Name           NMTOKEN  #REQUIRED
                          Notation       NMTOKEN  #REQUIRED
                          PubidLiteral   CDATA    #IMPLIED
                          SystemLiteral  CDATA    #IMPLIED>
```

```
<!-- <!ENTITY A PUBLIC "B" "C" NDATA "X"> -->
<UnparsedEntity Name="A" Notation="X"
                PubidLiteral="B" SystemLiteral="C">
  <Doc>This is Entity A</Doc>
</UnparsedEntity>
```

The assumption is that general entity management is outside the scope of a schema language. However, it is hard to see where such definitions should be defined, when globally available to all documents, if this scheme is used in preference to existing DTDs. Perhaps other entity declaration elements will appear in a later version of the proposal.

Miscellaneous features

Most elements have Id attributes, which could be used in some advanced linking scheme (possibly XLink), and perhaps also to attach free-floating attribute definitions to multiple elements, and to include definitions in other DTDs.

Many elements have an Ns attribute which is used to hold a namespace name (not a prefix, but the full URL), which can be referenced from elsewhere. The intent is to overcome the present limitation, where prefixes have be 'hardcoded' into ELEMENT declarations, thus limiting the freedom of document authors to choose non-conflicting prefixes as required.

7. White space issues

This chapter explains how spaces and line-end codes used to format the data file are easily confused with document formatting characters, how SGML-based and HTML-based systems cope with this issue, describes an XML mechanism for preserving all space, and concludes with suggestions for default handling of ambiguous spaces in XML documents.

White space

The term '**white space**' is used to describe a number of miscellaneous characters that have no visual appearance, but in some way affect the formatting of a document. The space character is usually used to separate words, and the tab character is usually used to help horizontally align columns of text, though either may also be used in markup to separate attributes and other parameters. The **carriage return** and **line feed** characters are used by most systems, either alone or in combination, to indicate the start of a new line in the text.

The $S^{\{03\}}$ rule in the XML standard represents any combination of these characters, and is used in various scenarios.

At certain locations in the body of the document, the significance of space characters and line-end codes can be set by the document author. In other circumstances, their significance is determined by the processing application. White space becomes an issue for XML processing when it is not certain that it is intended to be present in the published document. Ambiguities may arise when a document author introduces line-end codes just to make it easier to read the text using a standard text viewing utility, or to edit the text in a standard text editor.

Line-end normalization

The ASCII standard includes two special characters that may be interpreted as a signal to end a line of text. These are the **CR** (Carriage Return) and **LF** (Line Feed) characters. The names of these characters are taken from the actions of a typewriter. When starting a new line, the lever on the typewriter carriage forces the roller to move the paper up by one line (the line feed), then the user pushes the carriage to the right so that the next letter will appear at the left edge of the paper (the carriage return). The line feed character has an ASCII value of 10, and the carriage return character has an ASCII value of 13. On IBM mainframe systems, these characters are used to surround one record of text, so are given the names 'record start' and 'record end', but MS-DOS/Windows systems use the pair together as a line-end code sequence. The Macintosh and UNIX platforms use just one of these characters to signify a line-end.

An XML processor uses the line feed character to terminate lines. This is compliant with UNIX. When a carriage return is encountered in the data stream, the XML processor converts this to a line feed (so dealing with Macintosh input). When both characters are found together, in the sequence CR followed by LF, the carriage return is removed (so dealing with MS-DOS/Windows input). A sequence of identical line-end codes, such as three carriage returns in a row, *are* treated separately.

```
A Macintosh[CR]
data file.[CR]

A Unix[LF]
data file.[LF]

An MS-DOS[CR][LF]
data file.[CR][LF]
```

White space in markup

Within markup, all white space is equivalent to a single space character, and may be used to separate attributes and other parameters. The two examples below are deemed to be equivalent:

```
<book issue="3" date="15/3/97" >

<book
issue   = "3"
date    = "15/3/97"   >
```

Element content space

Document authors may choose to insert white space, particularly line-end codes, around elements that contain other elements, in order to improve the presentation. For example, the second document fragment below is easier to read than the first:

```
<!-- element content -->
<!ELEMENT sec     (auth,e-mail,...)>
<!ELEMENT auth    (first, second)>
<!-- mixed content -->
<!ELEMENT first   (#PCDATA)>
<!ELEMENT second  (#PCDATA)>
<!ELEMENT e-mail  (#PCDATA)>

<sec><auth><first>Neil</first><second>Bradley</second></
auth><e-mail>neil@bradley.co.uk</e-mail>...

<sec>
<auth>
  <first>Neil</first><second>Bradley</second>
</auth>
<e-mail>neil@bradley.co.uk</e-mail>...
```

In this example, the Section element directly contains a line feed character, and the Author element directly contains two line feeds and two spaces. It is clear that these white space characters are not part of the document text. The fact that it occurs in elements that are only allowed to contain other elements is a clue to this fact. A validating parser has access to the DTD, so is able to determine which elements can only contain other elements. Such parsers are obliged to inform the application of white space characters in element content (termed **ignorable white space**). With this information, a publishing application may choose to omit these characters from the presented document.

There is one obvious limitation to this technique. A non-validating parser cannot tell which elements have element content by design (as opposed to by accident in a specific instance), so cannot distinguish white space so easily. In fact, one reason for including a **standalone** value of 'no' in a document is to warn such parsers that they cannot process the document without misinterpreting some of the white space.

Some may consider this technique to be inadequate even when a validating parser is in use. For example, the Paragraph and Emphasis elements below both have mixed content, so are not distinguished by this mechanism, yet many would argue that the leading and trailing spaces in the Paragraph element should be removed, but that spaces in the same positions in the Emphasis element should not:

```
<para> A paragraph with<emph> space </emph>. </para>
```

Ambiguous space issues are discussed later, and the suggested solution completely ignores this XML feature.

Preserved space

A distinction is made between the act of leaving all white space characters intact, and **normalizing** white space back to a single character. When left intact, the white space is said to be **preserved**. When normalized, it is said to have **collapsed**, and this is usually what is desired.

The document author has some control over normalization of white space in the text, using a reserved attribute named 'xml:space'. If this attribute is applied to a specific element, and given a value of 'preserve', then all white space in that element is deemed to be significant:

```
<para xml:space="preserve">Mrs White
13 Acacia Avenue
Newtown
England</para>
```

Mrs White
13 Acacia Avenue
Newtown
England

More advanced formatting is possible using multiple spaces to align text. However, care must be taken over which font is used to present the content. Each character has a different width in most fonts. Unless the same font is used to present the material as was used to create it, the output will be distorted. The safest approach is to use a **mono-spaced** (fixed-pitch) font.

```
<preform xml:space="preserve">

      O
   --I--
     I
    / \
</preform>
```

A fixed pitch font must also be used to display the content, but it does not have to be the same font, as the space character is the same width as other characters in all fixed-pitch fonts.

```
      O
   --I--
     I
    / \
```

If a variable-pitch font is used to present the material, the content is distorted because the space character is no longer the same width as other characters.

```
    O
  --|--
    |
   /\
```

If an element embedded within a preserved element has content which must not be preserved, the same attribute may be used to explicitly collapse its content, 'xml:space="collapse"', though this is an unlikely scenario.

When an element is created specifically to hold pre-formatted text, its content status can be set in the DTD:

```
<!ELEMENT preform (#PCDATA)>
<!ATTLIST preform xml:space #FIXED "preserve">

<preform>
     O
   --I--
     I
   / \
</preform>
```

Ambiguous space

Earlier, it was suggested that ambiguities may arise as to whether some white space is intended to be part of the document, or is just present to make the data file more readable. Consider the following example:

```
Is this line of text:[CR]
to be kept separate from this one?
```

Is this line of text:
to be kept separate from this one?

Is this line of text: to be kept separate from this one?

Markup introduces further problems. The following example could be treated in two different ways. The problem is deciding whether or not the line-end code after the Paragraph start-tag is significant, and part of the text of the document. Perhaps the line-end code should be interpreted as a space, though most people would argue that it should not. Similarly, the line-end code at the end of the text may be omitted or retained. Although retaining it would usually have no visual impact, there is no guarantee of this (the '^' symbol is used below to represent spaces that are otherwise impossible to see).

```
<para>[CR]
This paragraph is bounded by element tags.[CR]
</para>
```

^This paragraph is bounded by element tags.^

This paragraph is bounded by element tags.

Note that these issues are quite separate from style sheet considerations. For example, though there is no space in '`<name><f>Dick</f><s>Whittington</s></name>`', this is a reasonable construct because a style sheet would be used to add a space between the first and second names. In these cases, additional formatting rules are applied to specific elements.

According to the standard, there are no issues relating to ambiguities in the use of white space, as it is assumed that different rules or conventions may be applied in different applications. Some consider this decision 'to ignore the issue' as naive, if only because the same XML processors, document handling software libraries, editors and browsers should be universally applicable. However, it is true to say that some applications of XML will vary widely from others, and the same rules may not always be suitable.

The following text therefore concentrates on information that is to be published. In this arena, it is possible to look to SGML and HTML solutions for some guidance. Existing product vendors are certain to play an important role in determining *de facto* rules for white space handling. HTML-based editors and browsers, and SGML-based document management systems and pagination engines, are being adapted for use with XML. Unfortunately, there is no agreement between SGML and HTML regarding white space handling. It is therefore necessary to look at both in isolation, before attempting to define a position for XML.

Note that in the following discussion, the term 'ignored' will be used to describe a white space character that appears in the data file, but is not considered to be part of the document it contains, so will not appear when the document is presented. An XML-aware application should remove these characters if it is preparing the content for display.

HTML

Rules for white space handling in HTML have arisen in a haphazard fashion, though the two most popular browsers are now almost compatible.

It is useful to first define two classes of element. An **in-line element** does not generate a break in the flow of the text, whereas a **block element** contains text that is separated from preceding and following text. The Emphasis element is an in-line element, whereas the Paragraph element is a block element:

```
<p>This block element contains an <em>in-line</em>
element, which does not break the flow of the
text.</p>
<p>This paragraph block is separated from the
previous block.</p>
```

This block element contains an **in-line** element which does not
break the flow of the text.

This paragraph block is separated from the previous block.

Note that the CSS style sheet language allows the default settings for each element in the HTML format to be changed. For example, the Paragraph element could be changed into an in-line element.

Except for text contained in the Preformatted element, a Web browser removes any white space not considered to be part of the actual document. All white space between block elements is ignored. All white space preceding the first 'genuine' character in a block element, and all but one trailing white space character is also ignored. A fixed amount of vertical space is reinserted between block elements as they are presented:

```
<p>The first paragraph.</p>[CR]
[CR]
[CR]
<p>^^^The second paragraph.^^^</p><p>[CR]
^^^[CR]
^^^The third paragraph.[CR]
^^^</p>
```

The first paragraph.

The second paragraph.^

The third paragraph.^

Within a block element, all line-end codes are replaced by a space, and multiple spaces are reduced to a single space. The browser reinserts its own line-end codes when presenting the material, at points dependent on the width of the screen or frame:

```
<p>This paragraph is split over[CR]
lines.^^^The browser may reinsert some^^^[CR]
line-end codes as it 'composes' the[CR]
paragraph.
```

This paragraph is split over lines. The browser may reinsert some line-end codes as it 'composes' the paragraph.

The only disagreement between Netscape Navigator and Microsoft Internet Explorer is in regard to comments. Explorer simply ignores them, but Navigator also ignores an immediately following line-end code. This may be considered dangerous, as demonstrated in the following example, where two words are inadvertently joined together. Comments should therefore not be placed on the same line as any text.

```
<p>The following words are joined<!-- COMMENT -->[CR]
together in Netscape.</p>
```

The following words are **joinedtogether** in Netscape.

SGML

The advantage that HTML-aware applications have over SGML-aware applications is that they already 'know' the meaning and purpose of each element in the language they are processing. On the surface, an SGML application can only deduce a few characteristics of the document structure from its DTD construction. In particular, a distinction is made between an element that has element content, as opposed to one that has mixed content. A typical Chapter element has element content, such as lists, paragraphs and tables, and an element called Emphasis may have mixed (or only text) content.

This concept seems to be analogous to the block and in-line distinction made in HTML. But both the Emphasis element and the Paragraph element have mixed content, despite one of these elements being a block element, and the other an in-line element.

In SGML, the focus is on the line-end codes rather than on white space in general. Specifically, two characters are defined in the SGML standard that take the roles of record delimiters. The **RS (Record Start)** character identifies the start of a record (or line) and the **RE (Record End)** character identifies the end of a record (or line). By default they are mapped to the ASCII characters LF and CR respectively. It is, therefore, strictly speaking incorrect to think of the CR plus LF combination as indicating the end of a line on MS-DOS/Windows systems, when the second character is really indicating the start of the next line.

In element content, both these characters are simply ignored.

The record start character is ignored everywhere (except in markup), but the record end character may be interpreted as a space (or retained as a line-end code) within text.

```
[RS]<chapter>[RE]
[RS]^^^[RE]
[RS]<p>A normal[RE]
[RS]paragraph.</p>[RE]
```

A normal paragraph.

If a line of text contains only markup declarations (including comments) and/or processing instructions, the record end code is also ignored. Note the similarity of this behaviour to comment handling in Netscape Navigator.

Finally, the record end character is also ignored if it immediately follows a start-tag, or immediately precedes an end-tag. Again, this is similar behaviour to the HTML browsers, except that only the one character is affected:

```
<para>[RE]
This paragraph is bounded by element tags.[RE]
</para>
```

This paragraph is bounded by element tags.

Note that multiple white space within a line is not normalized down to a single space in SGML.

```
<para>This is a ^^^ paragraph.</para>
```

This is a ^^^ paragraph.

Hyphenation

Many documents are converted into SGML or XML format directly from previously typed or published material (possibly using OCR/ICR technology). This material often contains hyphens at the end of lines, where the author or publishing software has chosen to split a word so as to better balance the text over lines.

This paragraph is too long to comfortably fit on one line of text.

In this case, an application may be intelligent enough to simply remove the line-end code (not replace it with a space), and also remove the hyphen, though it must be careful not to remove the hyphen from a double-barrelled word, such as 'line-end'. Fortunately, the extended character sets described in this book have a special 'soft hyphen' character (character 176, '°'), which looks the same as a normal hyphen, but is interpreted as one that *can* be safely removed. The normal hyphen is assumed to be a 'hard' hyphen, which must be retained.

Recommendations

It seems desirable to provide rules that allow some latitude to the author, while producing common sense 'standardized' output. If the standardization authorities are unwilling to tackle this subject, the best we can hope for is consensus amongst application developers. There has been much discussion on this topic in the XML news groups, and many people have contributed thoughts based on experience with SGML and HTML. The following is the author's own stab at a set of rules, but the reader should be prepared to discover the 'real' rules as they emerge.

If Web browsers become the first major applications that process XML for presentation (as, at the time of writing, seems most likely), then HTML conventions should be of most relevance to XML. A style sheet is needed to identify block elements and in-line elements, but CSS and XSL both have this capability. This would probably be appropriate, because the block/in-line definitions are more informative in this regard than the element/mixed model details that a DTD can supply, and a DTD may not even be available.

When a space mode is not made explicit for a particular element, the application should imply a default setting, which it should additionally interpret as implying 'collapsed' mode. If the DTD or document author requires preserved content for a specific element, the XML-Space attribute should be used.

A string of white space characters should be reduced to a single character, except when 'preserve' mode is in operation:

```
<para>A ^^^ normal
^^^paragraph.</para>
```

A normal paragraph.

When a line of text consists of nothing but comments and/or processing instructions, the entire line should be removed, including the line-end code.

```
<para>A normal
<!--Comment-->
paragraph.</para>
```

A normal paragraph.

The line-end code after 'normal' becomes the space between this word and 'paragraph'. The middle line is effectively non-existent. Actually, this rule is implied from previous rules. The comment is removed anyway, leaving two consecutive line-end codes. The normalization process then converts the first one to a space and removes the second.

To summarize the rules, in the order they should be applied:

- block and in-line elements must be identified (using a configuration file or style sheet)
- white space surrounding a block element should be removed
- a line containing nothing but declarations and/or comments should be entirely removed
- leading and trailing white space inside a block element should be removed (except when content is explicitly preserved)
- a line-end code within a block element should be converted into a space (recall that alternative line-end codes are already normalized to a line-end code)
- a sequence of white space characters (including converted line-end codes) should be reduced to a single space character

8. Namespaces

This chapter describes a standard for building documents that include components from different domains, defined within disparate DTDs.

Compound documents

It is possible for a single XML document to contain fragments that are defined in different DTDs. This ability resolves a number of issues. To facilitate rendering of complex structures in a browser, it may be necessary to embed HTML elements within a document that does not otherwise conform to this standard. For example, HTML tables are powerful, and well supported by the popular Web browsers, so it would be useful to be able to simply use HTML elements when a table is needed. This is actually just one case of the general need to match data to the expectations of widely used tools that have a specific purpose, beyond the individual domains that DTDs are associated with. Another example would be a Web crawler searching documents for specific forms of meta-data to improve the classification of sites for a search engine (but see Architectural forms in Chapter 6 for another approach).

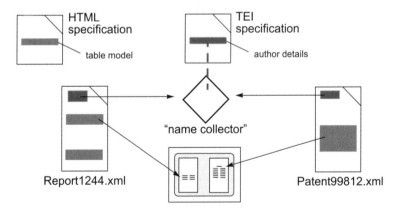

The XSLT standard, described later, also requires this concept to allow the mixing of formatting instructions with target document element tags.

The well-formed nature of all XML structures makes it relatively simply to embed 'foreign' structures in documents. However, there are still two issues which must be addressed. The first problem is to identify which schema a particular element belongs to. The meaning of the element must not be ambiguous. The second, related problem is how to avoid duplication of element and attribute names, as there is nothing to prevent different schemas defining objects with the same names.

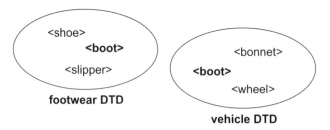

There is a third issue, concerning the validation of documents containing fragments from different DTDs, but this problem can only be properly addressed after the Namespaces scheme has been described.

The standard

The Namespaces standard, or 'Namespaces in XML' to give it its full title, is a scheme for building documents from fragments defined in different domains, by addressing the problems outlined in the previous section. It was produced by the W^3C, and gained recommended status in January, 1999. The standard can be found at http://www.w3.org/TR/1998/REC-xml-names.

A single schema (or DTD) is considered to own a '**namespace**', an environment in which all element names are unique, and all attribute names (within the context of a particular element) are also unique. Any reference to an element name is therefore unambiguous. Any reference to an attribute within a particular element is also unambiguous. The term **multiple namespaces** is used to describe the concept of a single document that contains information defined in a number of namespace domains.

This standard focuses on solving the two issues raised above. First, it provides a mechanism for identifying the namespaces used in the document. Second, it identifies which namespace a particular element or attribute belongs to.

Namespace identification

Most standards can now be identified with a specific location on the Web. For example, HTML 4 is defined at http://www.w3.org/TR/REC-html40. As these Web addresses must by definition be unique, this string of characters can be deemed to be a suitable namespace identifier. Using a URL as an identifier has two major benefits over any alternatives. First, it is already known to any-one interested in the DTD or standard in question, and second, it is genuinely informative to any readers of the document who were not aware of its exist-ence, as they can use the identifier to find and read the standard itself.

The Namespaces standard uses URLs to identify each namespace, but it must be understood that Namespace-aware applications do not have to be con-nected to the Internet. In this context, a URL is purely a useful and well-known text string. An application is only expected to compare the URL against a list of standards it can meaningfully process.

Elements and attributes from different namespaces are distinguished from each other by adding a prefix to the name. The prefix is separated from the name using a colon. The resulting object is known as a **qualified name**.

```
prefix:name
```

Having noted that URLs are a good way to uniquely identify a namespace, it also has to be said that they are not suitable for use as element and attribute prefixes. First, they tend to be quite long, as in the HTML example above, but, more importantly, they often contain characters that are not allowed in element and attribute names. To solve this problem, the standard includes a mechanism for defining short, legal prefixes, and for mapping them to the full URL identifier.

It cannot be left to the standard's bodies to define the prefix, because the collision problem could easily re-emerge. The DTD or document author has full control over prefix names, and can avoid conflicts simply by ensuring that each prefix is unique within the confines of the document, or class of documents concerned.

Using namespaces

Namespaces are defined using attributes. The attribute name 'xmlns' is used to declare a namespace, and at the same time declare the prefix that will stand in for the full URL in element and attribute names. The remainder of the attribute name itself is used for this purpose. The prefix name is separated from the 'xmlns' part of the name using a colon. This can be confusing at first, because the namespace prefix is defined by the attribute name suffix. The value of the attribute is the URL. In the following example, the HTML 4.0 namespace is referenced, and given the local prefix 'X':

```
<X:html xmlns:X="http://www.w3.org/TR/REC-html40">
  ...<X:p>An HTML paragraph.</X:p>...
</X:html>
```

Although namespaces may typically be defined within the root element, as in the example above, they can actually be specified in any element. In the following example, an HTML table has been included in an XML document:

```
<Q:para>A normal paragraph</Q:para>
<X:table xmlns:X="http://www.w3.org/TR/REC-html40">
  ...<X:td>An HTML table cell.</X:td>...
</X:table>
<Q:para>A normal paragraph</Q:para>
```

An element may declare more than one namespace:

```
<Q:book xmlns:Q="file:/DTDs/book.dtd"
        xmlns:X="http://www.w3.org/TR/REC-html40">
  ...<Q:para>A normal paragraph.</Q:para>...
  ...<X:td>An HTML table cell.</X:td>...
</Q:book>
```

Note that this example is perfectly legal XML. It does not contain duplicate attribute names, as might first appear. The suffixes serve the purpose of making these attributes unique.

Attributes from one namespace can be used in elements from another. The attribute names contain the same prefixes as the elements to distinguish them. The following example of a House element contains two Style attributes. The first one is from the house namespace, and explains what kind of property the House element describes. The second one is an HTML attribute that is used to format the content of the element (in this case colouring the text red):

```
<Q:house Q:style="Georgian" X:style="color:red">
```

Simplification techniques

When every element and attribute has a prefix, the document can become difficult to read, and the extra characters certainly add to its size. Fortunately, the standard includes the concept of a **default namespace**.

Attributes automatically default to the namespace of the element they are in. Taking the example above, the first Style attribute can be simplified immediately:

```
<Q:house style="Georgian" X:style="color:red"
```

Elements can also belong to a default namespace, but this is done by declaring the namespace using an attribute named 'xmlns', with no suffix:

```
<book xmlns="file:/DTDs/book.dtd"
      xmlns:X="http://www.w3.org/TR/REC-html40">
  ...<para>A normal paragraph.</para>...
  ...<X:td>An HTML table cell.</X:td>...
</book>
```

The default namespace can be changed at any point in the document hierarchy. This should be done when a sufficiently large XML fragment is embedded.

```
<book xmlns="file:/DTDs/book.dtd"
      xmlns:X="http://www.w3.org/TR/REC-html40">
  ...<para>A normal paragraph.</para>...
  ...<X:td>An HTML table cell.</X:td>...
  ...<para>A normal paragraph.</para>...
  ...<html xmlns="http://www.w3.org/TR/REC-html40">
    ...<td>An HTML table cell.</td>...
  ...</html>
  ...<para>A normal paragraph.</para>...
</book>
```

DTD issues

In order to parse documents against a DTD, it is necessary to include the prefixes in the element definitions:

```
<!ELEMENT document (shoe|boot|slipper|
                    veh:bonnet|veh:boot|veh:wheel)*>
```

This means that prefix selection is performed by the DTD author instead of the document, but this should not be a problem as the DTD author should be aware of which namespaces are allowed in all documents that conform to the DTD.

The namespace definition can also be included in the DTD, and shows one good use of the FIXED attribute type:

```
<!ATTLIST document xmlns:veh #FIXED "file:///c:/veh.dtd">
```

The DTD must also include references to all allowed children in the element content models, regardless of the namespace they may belong to. This requirement complicates DTD construction hugely.

However, Namespace-aware XML parsers may in future be able to validate documents against the original collection of DTDs referenced, so avoiding the need to add prefixes to the declarations, and the need to anticipate where fragments from one namespace may be inserted into elements from another. However, this approach comes at the cost of being unable to specify constraints on where fragments from one namespace can appear within documents from another.

9. Processing XML data

Issues involved in developing software to read and write XML documents are covered in this chapter, as well as the circumstances that determine when it is necessary to process a DTD in order to accurately interpret the markup in a document.

Concepts

As an electronic data format, it is very important that software applications be able to read and write XML documents easily.

Developing software to generate XML output is a trivial matter. Most programming languages have the capability to output strings of text to a file, and it is only necessary to include XML tags in these strings:

```
PRINT #FileNum "<para>This is a paragraph.</para>"
```

However, reading an XML document can be complicated by a number of issues and features of the language. The various ways in which white space can be used to format the data file may cause problems of interpretation. It may be necessary for entities to replace all references to them, and for attribute values to be processed. Finally, the DTD may need to be processed, either to add default information, or to compare against the document instance in order to validate it.

Developers of applications that take XML as input should not have to write the code that interprets and parses the markup. Most programming languages have the capability to incorporate software libraries, and a number of XML libraries already exist. Programmers wishing to read XML data files need an XML-aware processing module, termed an **XML processor**. The XML processor is responsible for making the content of the document available to the application, and will also detect problems such as file formats that the application cannot process, or URLs that do not point to valid resources.

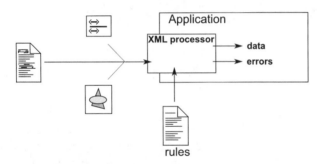

Two fundamentally different approaches to reading the content of an XML document are known as the '**event-driven**' and '**tree-manipulation**' techniques. In an event-driven approach, the document is processed in strict sequence. Each element in the data stream is considered an event trigger, which may precipitate some special action on the part of the application. The tree approach provides access to the entire document, allowing its contents to be interrogated and manipulated in any order. Event-driven processing is akin to a motorist finding a destination by following road signs (as they are encountered). The tree-manipulation approach is more like studying a map before commencing the journey (the driver can choose the best route in advance).

Application developers should be able to incorporate pre-packaged software libraries that perform event-driven or tree-manipulation processing. There are already a number of such packages. The application must communicate with one of these libraries through an API (an *Application Programmers Interface*), but the developer may find it difficult to adopt newer and better products from different vendors if the API differs each time. Standards have therefore been developed for both the event-driven and tree-driven approaches, called **SAX** and **DOM** respectively.

Writing XML

To produce XML data, it is only necessary to include XML tags in the output strings:

```
PRINT #FileNum "<para>This is a paragraph.</para>"

fprintf(stdout, "<para>This is a paragraph.</para>\n");
```

However, one decision that has to be made is whether to output line-end codes, as in the examples above, or whether to omit them. In many respects it is simpler and safer to omit line-end codes. But if the XML document is likely to be viewed or edited using tools that are not XML-aware, this approach makes the document very difficult to read. Some text editors will only display as much text as will fit on one line in the window:

```
<book><front><title>The Book Title</title><author>J...
```

Although some editors are able to display more text by creating 'soft' line breaks at the right margin, the content is still not very legible.

```
<book><front><title>The Book Title</title><author>J.
Smith</author><date>October 1997</date></front><body>
<chapter><title>First Chapter</title><para>This is the
first chapter in the book.</para><para>This is the ...
....
```

It would seem to be more convenient to break the document into separate lines at obvious points in the text, as in the example below. However, there may be a problem for the recipient application in determining which line-end codes are there purely to make the XML data file more legible, and which form a crucial part of the enclosed document. This issue is covered in detail in Chapter 7.

```
<book>
<front>
<title>The Book Title</title>
<author>J. Smith</author>
<date>October 1997</date>
</front>
<body>
<chapter>
<title>First Chapter</title>
<para>This is the first chapter in the book.</para>
<para>This is the ...
```

Reading XML

Due to the complications that can arise when reading an XML data file, in many cases it is advisable for the application to utilize an existing XML processor module or library. The XML processor hides many complications from the application.

The XML processor has at least one sub-unit, termed the **entity manager**, which is responsible for locating fragments of the document held in entity declarations or in other data files, and handling replacement of all references to them.

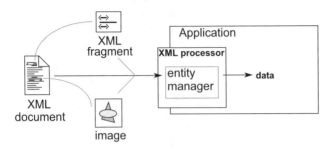

Most XML processors also include an integrity checker, or **parser**. The parser compares the data file content against the pre-defined document structure rules. See Chapter 5 for details.

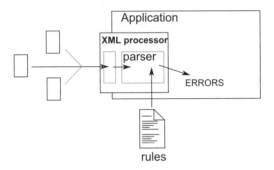

The XML processor ultimately delivers data to the application, but there are two distinct ways in which this can be done. The first, and simplest, is to pass the data directly to the application as a stream. The application accepts the data stream and reacts to the markup as it is encountered. This is termed **event-driven** processing because the application can only react to events. The alternative approach involves the XML processor holding onto the data on the application's behalf, and allowing the application to ask questions about the data and request portions of it. Data can be processed out of sequence, in a 'random access' manner. This is termed tree processing, though more commonly known as the **tree-walking** approached. A tree, or group of trees can be stored in a data structure called a **grove**. These concepts are described in more detail later.

Event processing

The simplest method of processing an XML document is to read the content as a stream of data, and to interpret markup as it is encountered. The software therefore responds to 'events' in the data stream. This simply means that the application reacts to information contained in XML markup as it is encountered in the data stream. A general-purpose programming language, such as 'C', may be used, with functions to deal with markup as it is encountered. If contextual processing is required, the current location in the document structure may be tracked using variables to indicate which elements are currently open.

The following example shows a 'C' function that is called each time a start-tag is encountered while reading the XML data stream. The first test detects paragraph elements, then sets a global flag to indicate to later events that a paragraph is currently being processed. Similar flags are tested to determine if the paragraph is within a chapter or appendix, and if not, further activity is undertaken:

```
void ProcessOpenTag( char tagname[] )
{
  if ( ! strcmp( tagname, "para" ) )
  {
    inPara = TRUE;
    if (( inChapter == FALSE ) && ( inAppendix == FALSE))
    {
      /* must be in Introduction - copy content to
         new summary book */
      ...
    }
  }
}
```

If out-of-sequence processing is required, such as needing to collect all the titles in a document for insertion at the start of the document as a table of contents, then a 'two-pass' process is needed. In the first pass, the titles are collected. In the second pass, they are inserted where they are required.

Those readers familiar with the CALS or HTML 4.0 table models may have wondered why the element representing the footer section appears before the body section element. This design avoids the necessity for two-pass processing; the footer text is read first, so it can be printed at the bottom of each page that contains a reference to it, or permanently displayed beneath a scrollable pane that contains the body rows.

Simple API for XML (SAX 1.0)

To reduce the workload of the application developer, and make it easy to replace one parser with another, a common event-driven interface has been proposed for object-oriented languages such as Java. The **SAX** standard (standing for *Simple API for XML*) has not been developed by an official standards body, but has nevertheless emerged as a *de facto* standard, and is free for commercial use. It is described in detail in a later chapter.

Tree manipulation

More advanced processing options are available when the entire XML document is made available to the software, in what may be termed a 'random-access' method. Software that holds the entire document in memory needs to organize the content so that it can be easily searched and manipulated. There is no need for multi-pass parsing when any part of the document can be accessed instantly. Applications that benefit from this approach include XML-aware editors, pagination engines and hypertext-enabled browsers.

Although each program may adopt its own techniques for physically handling the data, a standard for describing the requirements of such programs is useful. The abstract description of the model for SGML documents is called a **grove**, and the grove scheme is equally applicable to XML. The name 'grove' is appropriate because it mainly describes a series of trees. For example, a single grove may contain the DTD tree and the document instance tree, as well as smaller trees for some attribute values, such as a list of name tokens. However, the name has been made into an acronym, standing for 'Graph Representation Of property ValuEs'. A grove is a 'directed graph of nodes'. Each **node** is an object of a specified type: a package of information that conforms to a pre-defined template. A node that represents a person may contain information on the name, date of birth and current address of that person. Each of these items is known as a **property**. A property has a name and a value, so can be compared to an attribute. A node that describes a person may have a property called 'age' which holds the value representing the age of an individual. A node must have a type property, and name property, so that it can be identified, or referred to.

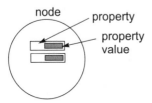

For example, there is a pre-defined type called 'element', which has a property called 'gi' to hold the name of the element. This node type also has properties that describe the content of the element and any attributes it contains.

A node may also contain properties that refer to other nodes, and the connection is known as an **arc**. A single property may refer to a single other node, or contain a list of references to other nodes. For example, an element node may refer to several attribute nodes. The arc is labelled according to the name of the property, and may be one of three possible relationship types: 'subnode' (child node), 'irefnode' (internal reference node) or 'urefnode' (unrestricted/ external reference node).

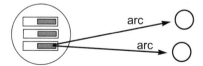

In the simplest case, nodes may be organized into a tree structure, using the subnode type in a designated 'content' property, which is suitable for describing the content of an XML document. Even following just the content property nodes, a program can build an accurate picture of the document content. It is possible to process all the children of a specified element.

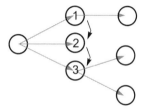

It is also still possible to extract the content of an element (or the entire document, when starting at the root element), in sequential order, though the technique is more complex than for simple event-driven processing. It is necessary to use recursive iteration techniques to traverse nodes that represent all the descendants:

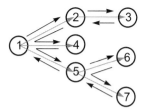

The real power of this approach is that it becomes possible to target a specific node for analysis or extraction. It also becomes possible to delete document fragments (branches), or move or copy them to other locations:

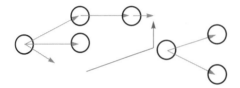

The arcs between nodes do not have to follow a tree-like structure. It is possible for a node to refer to any other node, regardless of its position in the grove, providing that it is an irefnode type. As groves may be multi-directional, even cyclic, they can also represent a DTD structure that includes nested element models. For example, a node that represents a List element declaration points to other nodes describing the elements the list may contain. Assuming this is only an Item element, there will be an arc from the List node to the Item node. But assuming that the Item element may also be able to contain a complete list, the Item node will also contain an arc back to the List node (as well as to other elements):

```
<!ELEMENT list (item+)>
<!ELEMENT item (list|para)*>
```

As node list properties are distinguished by their type, it is possible to ignore parts of the grove that are of no interest. For a particular application, a **grove plan** is determined. For example, the **HyTime** hypertext scheme includes elements, pseudo elements and data entities, but ignores comments and processing instructions. The **DSSSL** stylesheet mechanism also uses a grove plan to model the document, allowing parts of a document to be moved or duplicated, as required, to produce a published document.

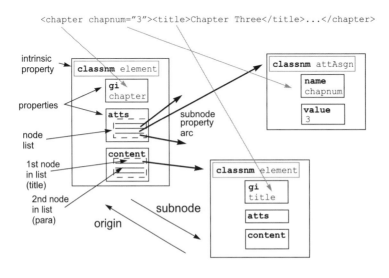

XML-aware applications that adopt the grove scheme must create a physical representation of the abstract concepts the grove describes. Techniques may differ according to programmer preference and the strengths and weaknesses of the chosen programming language.

Document Object Model (DOM 1.0)

To reduce the workload of the application developer, and make it easy to replace one parser with another, a common tree-walking API has been proposed for object-oriented languages such as Java. The **DOM** standard (standing for *Document Object Model*) has been developed for this purpose, and is free for commercial use. It is described in detail in a later chapter.

Events or trees?

Having chosen a parser that supports both event-driven and tree-walking approaches, and perhaps even the SAX and DOM standards, an application developer may wonder which approach to choose. A number of factors can influence this decision.

Event-driven benefits

With the event-driven approach, the parser does not have to hold much information about the document in memory. Each piece is extracted from the document and passed immediately to the application, after which it can be discarded. There is no danger of the parser needing large amounts of memory, or of running out of memory while parsing large documents.

The document structure does not have to be managed in memory, either by the parser or, depending on what it needs to do, by the application. This can make parsing very fast.

Following on from the last point, the fact that the application receives pieces of the document in the order in which they were encountered means that it does not have to do anything special in order to process the document in a simple linear fashion, from start to end.

Tree-walking benefits

Some data preparation tasks require access to information that is further along the document. For example, to build a table of contents section at the beginning of a book, it is necessary to extract all the titles. With the entire document held in memory, the document structure can be analyzed several times over, quickly and easily.

When an application needs to reorder components in a document that has been parsed, or needs to build a new document but in a non-linear fashion, the data structure management module may be profitably utilized by the application to manage the document components on its behalf.

With this approach, the entire document can be validated as well-formed, and possibly also conformant to a particular DTD, before passing any of it to the application. A document that contains errors can be rejected before the application begins to process its contents, thereby eliminating the need for messy roll-back routines.

Other considerations

The memory usage advantage of the event-driven approach may be only theoretical. Some parsers provide access to the document via a SAX API, but only after parsing the whole document and building the tree model in memory. While this can still be useful, the memory usage and speed advantages are lost.

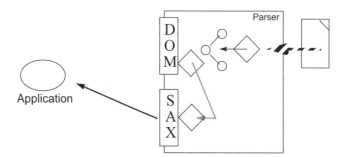

More effective parsers do the opposite of this. If the application uses an event-driven API, the parser need not build a document tree, but if the application uses a tree-walking API, it can itself use the event-driven API to build its tree model.

The linear processing issue in the tree-walker approach can be largely overcome if the parser has a convenient sequential tree-walking class (as most now have). An example of this is demonstrated in Chapter 15 (*The Sun tree-walker*).

Transformation tools

When the intent is simply to change an XML document structure into a new structure, there are often simpler ways to do this than to develop an application that reads in the source data, performs the transformation, then writes out the new structure. Providing that the transformations required are not too ambitious, there are existing tools on the market that can perform the transformation process. They are configured using scripting languages of various kinds.

The following example uses a popular scripting language to convert Para elements into either P or H2 elements, depending on what the parent element is (creating HTML output from the source XML document):

```
element para
 do when parent is description
  output "<P>%c</P>"
 else when parent is intro
  output "<H2>%c</H2>"
 done

<intro>
  <para>Introduction</para>
</intro>
<description>
  <para>Description.</para>
</description>
```

These tools can usually do much more advanced things, such as changing the order of elements, sorting them, and generating new content automatically.

Although initially designed to assist XSL in the processing of data for formatting and presenting, the XSLT language can also be used purely to transform one XML document into another XML document, or (due to its similarity to XML) into an HTML document. The following example performs the same operation as the script above:

```
<xsl:template name="intro/para">
 <H2></xsl:apply-templates></H2>
</xsl:template>
<xsl:template name="description/para">
 <P></xsl:apply-templates></P>
</xsl:template>
```

See Chapter 13 for details on XSLT.

10. Managing XML documents

Many XML documents have a long or repeating life cycle between creation and obsolescence. Apart from general issues of document management that apply to all types of electronic document, the XML language has features which may be utilized by software designed to simplify the creation and long-term management of documents. This chapter describes the options available, from the simplest 'stuff the files in a directory' solution, to the most advanced document management systems.

Concepts

When XML is used to describe the content of large, complex, structured or semi-structured documents, created over a long period of time, perhaps authored by a large team, for ultimate publication and possible republication in a number of forms, or on a variety of media, then management becomes an important issue. Information stored in electronic form must be managed if it is too important to be misplaced, corrupted or stolen.

The simplest way to manage XML documents is to store them in a fixed location within the file system. In the example below, the main documents are stored in the 'docs' directory, common text entities are stored in the 'entity' directory and image entities are stored in the 'images' directory. Necessary configuration files, such as the DTD and character entity lists, are stored in the 'config' directory:

```
\work\xml\docs\X123456.xml
              X123457.xml
              X123458.xml
        \entity\disclaim.xml
               rights.xml
        \images\0001.tif
               0002.tif
               0003.tif
        \config\article.dtd
               isolat1.ent
               isogrk1.ent
```

The operating system is designed to be a suitable storage medium for documents, and standard features of the operating system may be utilized to prevent unauthorized access to some or all the directories. The URL-based linking scheme embodied in XML is also ready-made for file-to-file linking. A standard XML browser would allow users to follow links between documents. All desktop applications expect to work directly with files, so do not need customizing. And best of all, this approach is free.

There are, however, a number of weaknesses with this approach. It is difficult (and in some cases impossible) to control access to specific documents. It is certainly impossible to control access to parts of a document. Documents tend to have short, and therefore cryptic file names (essential in older operating systems, and still desirable), so may not be easy to identify. Two operators may simultaneously access the same document without realizing, and only changes made by the operator who saves the work last are retained. The status and history of a particular document are not stored, and there is no means to identify and notify an operator when the document is ready for a specific process. Retained versions of the same document are also difficult to manage.

Another issue to be addressed with this technique is management of entities. A URL provides a fixed location for each entity, and must be edited if the entity is moved to a new location. A **public identifier** overcomes this limitation by assigning a unique name to the entity, which is indirectly matched to a location address via a catalogue file, which may conform to a standard such as the **XML Catalog** standard.

Some of these issues can be partly solved by adding a simple **database** to the system. The database can hold **meta-data** on the document pool, including **fields** to hold such items as the full document name, its current status, and any keywords or other details that would aid other ways of identifying the document, as well as a pointer to the file containing the document.

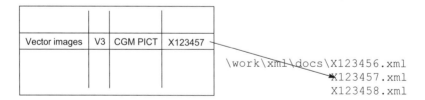

Such a database is of particular benefit if it is accessed by a front-end program that is also able to launch another application, using the content of the locator field to generate a complete file path, which it passes to the application. The user may enter a keyword, for example, receive a list of possible document titles, select one of the titles, then receive the complete document, which may be automatically passed to a suitable editor for amending or viewing.

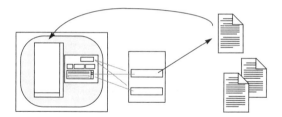

A simple system would utilize a **flat-file database**, where all the meta-data is held in a single database table, but **relational database** technology is now widely available and no longer expensive. These systems allow information to be linked across database tables, and therefore facilitate removal of repeated information. For example, where each document may be created by a single author, but each author may have written several documents, it is wasteful and problematic to store the author's details with each document. Relational databases also tend to have more powerful **query** capabilities, and many use the **query language** called **SQL** (*Structured Query Language*).

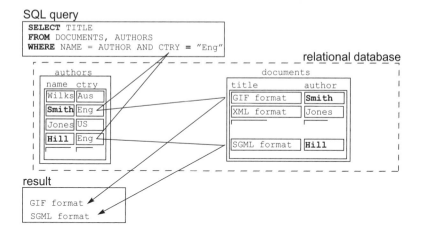

This approach is taken by more advanced **document management** systems, which also use the database to provide version tracking and project grouping facilities. A document is 'checked-out' when requested, so other users cannot access it and inadvertently overwrite any amendments.

Some document management systems also incorporate, or link into, an existing professional **workflow** tracking system. When such a document management system also includes other features aimed at 'factory' production of documents, it is also termed an **editorial system**. Many publishers, for example, use an editorial system for production of books, journals and magazines. Additional features may include tracking of operator time spent on each document.

The solutions discussed to this point are generic to all data formats. An editorial system, for example, would typically manage text files, images and page layout files. None of these solutions take advantage of the structured nature of XML documents. An author or editor wishing to amend one paragraph in a book should not need to check-out and open the entire book, or even one chapter of it. It should be possible to identify and access a single paragraph, check-out the paragraph and edit it in isolation, allowing others access to neighbouring text blocks at the same time. A document **component management** system (also sometimes termed a 'compound document management system') can 'pull apart' an XML document, storing each element separately. A query can locate a specific element, such as a paragraph, and this single unit can be checked-out for editing. This allows documents to share standard blocks of text, or documents to be assembled from standard components (a particular requirement of maintenance manuals for equipment, such as engines, which are available in almost limitless variations).

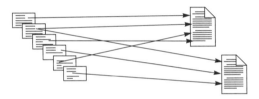

With this approach, the actual document is stored inside the database tables. The major advantage of this is that the data is protected by the system to the same degree as the meta-data. It is included in incremental backups, and hidden from unauthorized users. The major disadvantage is that relational databases are not particularly suited to storage of hierarchical data structures. However, **object databases** are more suitable (these concepts are explored in more depth later).

A search engine may have a number of techniques for locating documents that contain specified words or phrases. The most basic technique employs an **inverted word index**, which is a simple list of all the words used in a collection, sorted alphabetically, with links back to the documents containing these words. Typically, the search engine records the exact location of the terms in the original document. XML-aware versions of such a product could also record the start and end location of each element embedded in the file, and by comparing offset values determine which elements contain the terms. This allows for targeted searching. For example, it would be possible to locate all documents containing the word 'Wellington' within an element called Name, and by this means avoid all documents about footwear and military aircraft.

```
FIND "Wellington" IN Name AND "Waterloo" IN Title
```

External entity management

When documents are connected via system identifiers, problems arise if some of the documents are moved. If many documents in a local collection all reference a file, or files, in another location, and those files are subsequently moved, it may be necessary to edit all the local files to reflect the new locations. Avoiding this scenario requires the use of **entity management** techniques.

Using public identifiers

An **entity manager** uses **public identifiers** to locate external entities. Entries in catalogue files simplify the management of entities (though they complicate transfer of data over the Internet). The various means by which the entity manager can provide access to an external entity can be illustrated using the example of an external DTD, as specified in the document type declaration. However, the following explanations apply equally to all external entity declarations.

A public identifier always assumes use of a catalogue file, but descriptive text replaces the file name in the document type declaration:

```
<!DOCTYPE mybook
          PUBLIC "-//MyCorp//DTD My Book//EN"  ""  >
```

The keyword 'PUBLIC' identifies this example as a public identifier. The catalogue file simply matches the delimited text to a specific data file on the local system.

```
PUBLIC "-//MyCorp//DTD My Book//EN" C:\XML\MYBOOK.DTD
```

Although the use of catalogue files simplifies the maintaining of XML document storage, each XML-aware software application may use its own syntax for the catalogue filing system, in which case the information must be repeated for each application. In an attempt to avoid this unnecessary duplication, the **SGML Open** group has produced a standard format for SGML documents, and more recently a proposal has emerged for XML documents, called **XML Catalog**.

Formal public identifiers

A formal, but not compulsory, definition for the format of public identifiers exists (originally defined for use with SGML). A **formal public identifier** has a rigid structure composed of several parts – the **identifier type**, the **owner identifier**, the **public text class**, the **public text description** and the **public text language**. A public identifier should either conform strictly to the rules described below, or ignore this standard completely. Adopting the look, but not the rigid rules of a formal public identifier would be confusing to people attempting to interpret it.

The **identifier type** describes the status of the URL. For a public identifier to be guaranteed unique, it must be **registered**. The **ISO** standard **ISO 9070** covers the generating of a unique public identifier. A **registered owner identifier** has the symbol '+' for the identifier type. An **unregistered owner identifier** has the symbol '-' (hyphen). An **ISO owner identifier** contains the text 'ISO 8879:1986'. The identifier type is separated from the rest of the name by a double solidus, '//':

```
<!ENTITY ..... PUBLIC "+//.....">
<!ENTITY ..... PUBLIC "-//.....">
<!ENTITY ..... PUBLIC "ISO 8879:1986//..">
```

Note: There has been a change of character separating the ISO numbers from the dates. Originally a hyphen, '-', it has changed to a colon, ':'. For example, 'ISO 8879-1986' has become 'ISO 8879:1986'.

The owner identifier is the name of the person or organization that owns the entity content (or perhaps of just the identifier itself). The owner identifier is not applicable in the case of ISO entities, as the identifier type has already established that ISO is the owner. Another double solidus separates the owner identifier from following details:

```
"+//MyCorp//.....""
"-//MyCorp//.....""
"ISO 8879:1986//.....""
```

The **public text class** comprises a keyword that specifies the type of information contained by the entity. The classes of possible relevance to XML are listed here (there are several others used in SGML). The 'DTD' class indicates that the remote data file contains a **Document Type Definition**, possibly including declarations for elements, entities and short references. The 'ENTITIES' class indicates that the remote data file contains an **entity set**, containing declarations only for entities (commonly for character sets, such as the ISO sets). The 'NOTATION' class indicates that the remote data file contains **character data** that documents the format of a notation. The 'TEXT' class indicates that the remote data file contains a **text entity**:

```
"-//MyCorp//TEXT .....""
```

The **public text description** is free text that provides additional information about the content of the external data:

```
"-//MyCorp//ENTITIES Superscript Chars .....""
```

The final component is the **language**, which is a keyword from the list provided in **ISO 639** (see Chapter 20). It is separated from the public text description by a double solidus '//'. The keyword for the English language, for example, is 'EN' (note that letter-case is not really significant, but despite the conventions used in this and other examples, lower-case letters are now recommended):

```
"-//MyCorp//ENTITIES Superscript Chars//EN"
```

XML Catalog format

The scope and syntax of the proposed **XML Catalog** format (see http://
www.ccil.org/~cowan/XML/XCatalog.html) is derived in part from an earlier
attempt to define a standard for SGML documents. The version described
below is the draft version 0.4.

SGML Open origins

Two problems were identified by the SGML Open committee relating to the
locating of entities on a system. First, when each application that accesses SGML
entities uses its own catalogue format, entity location details must be duplicated.
Second, the recipient of an SGML document consisting of several files (not
merged using **SDIF**) needs a simple method to identify the base document and all
of its components. Both problems are solved by defining a common catalogue format. The 'SGML Open Technical Resolution 9401:1995 (Amendment 1 to
TR9401)' paper on entity management defines such a format. This simple format
comprises a number of identifier mappings consisting of a keyword, followed by
a public identifier or entity name and an equivalent system identifier. In the example below, the file 'MYBOOK.XML' is identified as the base document (the starting-point). The DTD is located in the system file 'BOOK.DTD', and the first
chapter of the document is referred to by an entity called 'chap1', which is associated with a file named 'CHAPTER1.XML':

```
DOCUMENT   "MYBOOK.XML"
PUBLIC     "-//myCorp//DTD My DTD//EN"    BOOK.DTD
ENTITY     "chap1"                        CHAPTER1.XML
```

Introducing XML Catalog

The XML Catalog proposed standard is a private initiative, but is already
widely accepted and incorporated into several parsers. This standard defines
a simple mechanism for mapping public identifiers to local system identifiers,
and is derived in part from the more extensive SGML Open standard.

Note that the name 'XCatalog' was formerly used for this standard. The name
was changed due to a conflict with the name of a commercial product.

The XML Catalog standard allows public identifiers to be mapped to system
identifiers (URLs), existing system identifiers to be mapped to other (locally
relevant) system identifiers, a base location to be defined from which relative

URLs can be given a context, a mechanism for incorporating one catalogue within another (much like the external entity mechanism), and another for delegating some mappings to other catalogues.

Catalog syntax

There is a choice of syntax for encoding mappings and other features in a catalogue file, each aiming to satisfy a different need. First, a format that is backward compatible with SGML Open catalogues is defined for the purposes of incorporating older SGML tools into an XML system. Second, an XML-based format is defined to take advantage of XML tools. For example, it is possible to create or edit a catalogue file using an XML editor, which can use the DTD shown below to guide the author. It seems likely that the second format will become dominant over time, with the former disappearing as reliance on SGML tools decreases, or as these tools are upgraded to work with the new format. However, the same features are enabled in both formats, so converting between formats is a task that can be automated. The following examples are directly equivalent:

```
BASE   "file:/xml/"
PUBLIC "-//ACME//DTD MyBook//EN" "DTDs/MyBook.DTD"

<XMLCatalog>
  <Base href="file:/xml/" />
  <Map PublicId="-//ACME//DTD MyBook//EN"
       HRef="DTDs/MyBook.DTD" />
</XMLCatalog>
```

Mapping public identifiers

The most fundamental reason for the existence of this standard is to provide a product-independent mechanism for dealing with external entities that are referenced using a public identifier. The **Map** element provides a system identifier equivalent that software can use to actually locate the entity. In the following examples, an entity called '-//ACME//DTD MyBook//EN' is given a location 'DTDs', and a filename of 'MyBook.DTD':

```
PUBLIC "-//ACME//DTD MyBook//EN" "DTDs/MyBook.DTD"

<Map PublicId="-//ACME//DTD MyBook//EN"
     HRef="DTDs/MyBook.DTD" />
```

Mapping system identifiers

The heavy emphasis on using system identifiers rather than public identifiers in XML, due to its perceived use as primarily a language of the Web, where catalogues do not (yet) exist, means that public identifiers will often not be present in an entity declaration. Only a system identifier will exist. However, the issue of mapping identifiers to locally relevant URLs often remains. This standard therefore allows a global system identifier to be mapped, or more accurately remapped to a local identifier, using the **Remap** element (the older format uses the keyword 'SYS-TEM'). In the following examples, the file 'MyBook.DTD' has no location context in the system identifier, but is mapped to the 'DTDs' directory locally:

```
SYSTEM "MyBook.DTD" "DTDs/MyBook.DTD"

<Remap SystemId="MyBook.DTD"
       HRef="DTDs/MyBook.DTD" />
```

Base locations

The example above includes a relative URL as the system identifier. This is commonly done to make it easy to move collections of documents and entities to a new system location without needing to edit all the paths. When a relative URL is included in a document, the path is considered to be relative to the source document. In this case, however, there is no source document.

In this situation, the location of the catalogue file itself is used as the default base location:

```
        HRef="DTDs/MyBook.DTD"

/XML/catalog.xml     -----------
        ...                        \
        DTDs/MyBook.DTD   <--------
```

However, it is possible to override this default by including an instruction that names a specific base location, using the **Base** element:

```
BASE "-//ACME//DTD MyBook//EN" "DTDs/MyBook.DTD"

<Map PublicId="-//ACME//DTD MyBook//EN"
     HRef="DTDs/MyBook.DTD" />
```

Extending and delegating

In large-scale systems, a single catalogue file may be too large to be either processed or maintained comfortably. It is therefore possible for a number of separate catalogue files to contain references to each other. Common sets of mappings can be grouped together, and included in various 'main' catalogue files using the **Extend** element (the keyword 'CATALOG' is used in the older syntax). In the following example, a number of mappings for entities related to the ACME company are held in a catalogue file called 'ACME.CAT':

```
CATALOG "ACME.CAT"

<Extend HRef="ACME.CAT" />
```

A more sophisticated mechanism is provided for delegating related groups of entities, with similar public identifiers, to specialist catalogue files. For example, a number of entities may all begin with the prefix '-//ACME'. The **Delegate** element is used to identify the prefix, as well as the catalogue file to delegate the mappings to:

```
DELEGATE "-//ACME" "ACME.CAT"

<Delegate PublicId="-//ACME" HRef="ACME.CAT" />
```

When an entity such as '-//ACME//DTD MyBook//EN' is encountered, the 'ACME.CAT' file is opened, and a matching public identifier is searched for in that file.

The DTD

The DTD for catalogue documents that comply with the XML variant of the draft is shown below:

```
<!ELEMENT Map        EMPTY>
<!ATTLIST Map        PublicId  CDATA   #REQUIRED
                     HRef      CDATA   #REQUIRED>

<!ELEMENT Remap      EMPTY>
<!ATTLIST Remap      SystemId  CDATA   #REQUIRED
                     HRef      CDATA   #REQUIRED>

<!ELEMENT Delegate EMPTY>
<!ATTLIST Delegate PublicId  CDATA   #REQUIRED
                     HRef      CDATA   #REQUIRED>

<!ELEMENT Extend     EMPTY>
<!ATTLIST Extend     HRef      CDATA   #REQUIRED>

<!ELEMENT Base       EMPTY>
<!ATTLIST Base       HRef      CDATA   #REQUIRED>
```

Note that the enclosing root element is not part of this DTD fragment, as it is envisaged that these mapping declarations may appear as part of larger configuration file structures. If it were included, it would probably have something like the following definition:

```
<!ELEMENT XMLCatalog    ( Base?,
                          (Map | Remap | Delegate)+,
                          Extend* ) >
```

The name '**XMLCatalog**' should certainly be used to ensure maximum portability of catalogue documents between systems.

Database storage

An XML document can be broken into its hierarchical components and stored in a relational database. Consider the following document fragment:

```
<para>An example
<em>paragraph<xref> idref="#para"></em>
that demonstrates
<em>disassembly</em>
into hierarchical structures.</para>
```

Breaking this fragment into its components reveals three levels of structure. The Paragraph element has a total of five children, including two elements and three pseudo-elements (text strings). The first Emphasis element has two children; first a pseudo-element, then an empty element. The second Emphasis element has one child, the pseudo-element string 'disassembly'.

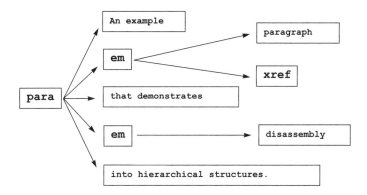

A simple method of storing this information in a relational table assigns a record with a unique identifier to each element and pseudo-element.

element	id	parent	childNum	string
para	100	???	?	
	101	100	1	An example
em	102	100	2	
	103	100	3	that demonstrates
em	104	100	4	
	105	100	5	into hierarchical structures

Other fields in the record contain a reference to its parent element, and a child number that records its position in relation to its siblings. The five rows shown above demonstrate how the five siblings of the Paragraph element are numbered, '1' to '5', and refer to their parent, '100'.

The first Emphasis element contains two children:

	106	102	1	paragraph
xref	107	102	2	

The second Emphasis element contains one child pseudo-element:

	108	104	1	disassembly

Using this simple scheme, it would be possible to reconstruct the original paragraph using queries that refer to the identifiers. For example, to find the children of the Paragraph element, the following query would retrieve them:

```
SELECT element, id WHERE parent = ParaId
```

More efficient designs would utilize multiple tables, particularly to separate elements hierarchies from textual content, and to store attribute values.

This approach allows a user to access and edit part of a document in isolation, and to choose how large a unit to edit. It also allows two users to work on different parts of the same document at the same time, but does not allow one user to edit part of a document that is already in use by another. In the above example, two users could be editing the content of the two Emphasis elements without affecting each other, but one user could not edit the entire paragraph while the other amends one of the Emphasis elements, as this would lead to conflicts.

Relational databases have their limitations. Specifically, it is not a simple matter to represent information that does not fall into a simple tabular model. XML elements have many relationships, none of them tabular. Each element has a parent, and may have children, creating a hierarchical relationship. Each element may have siblings, and must know its position in the sequence. Although it is possible to define fields to hold sequential and hierarchical relationships between elements, as demonstrated in the example application above, such a model requires a considerable amount of software support to cope with amendments to the document. An alternative **object database** technology has emerged. Instead of tables built from rows containing fields, a much looser structure is built using uniquely identifiable units of information, or objects, containing 'attributes' that hold either simple data or pointers to other objects. Just as in XML, each attribute has a name and a value. In the example below, object 'A' contains two attributes, one called 'colour' that contains the value 'red', and another called 'ptr' that contains a list of pointers (to objects 'B' and 'C'):

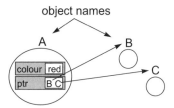

Object database technology has primarily been developed for permanent storage of data objects created by object-oriented software applications. But this technology is also suited to the storage of XML documents, as it can more easily describe sequential and hierarchical relationships. An XML document can be decomposed into its constituent parts, as described previously, using attributes to hold the name of the element, and an array of pointers to identify child elements, in the order that they appear in the document.

However, the additional power of this approach comes at the cost of performance, and this technology is still considered by many to be inadequate for industrial strength applications. Despite this, the relational database vendors have replied to the threat with the **object-relational database**, which is essentially an object layer that sits on top of an existing relational database product, offering a compromise on both performance and object awareness. Most SGML/XML document management systems utilize object or object-relational database systems.

11. Navigation (URL and XPath)

This chapter describes the URL scheme for locating documents on local and remote computer systems, and an XML-specific scheme, called XPath, for identifying document sub-structures. XPath will be incorporated into several XML-related standards, including XPointer, XQL and XSLT. Readers intending to cover one or more of these topics are advised to read this chapter first. Variations and standard-specific extensions are explained in later chapters, as appropriate.

Locating documents (URLs)

The need to locate documents on the Internet led to the development of the **URL** (*Uniform Resource Locator*) scheme. This scheme can also be used to identify resources on a local intranet, or even on the local machine. They are used in Web browsers, to find the home page of a Web site, then to navigate around the site from this page. In XML, URLs are used to locate entities (see Chapter 4) and, as in HTML, to allow hypertext links between documents (see Chapter 12). Even the Namespaces specification refers to URLs, though only to provide a universally known identifier for each domain.

Strictly speaking, the URL scheme is going to be just part of a wider scheme, known as the **URI** standard. This part of the URI standard is used to create references to files, using a file specification that includes at least a file name, but may also include a path to the file, and the protocol to be used to access it.

UNIX syntax conventions are used, including the use of '/' (step separator) and '..' (parent directory). The full path to the file may be supplied, starting at the root directory, '/' (see below for extra requirements to identify files on local disk drives). The protocol appears first, and is separated from the rest of the URL by two forward slashes, '//'. The host then appears, followed by the location and the name of the resource:

```
protocol://host/location/resource
```

A number of server-based applications may be listening simultaneously for requests over the Internet, and to avoid confusion each one listens on a different port number. By default, an application that can deal with requests using the HTTP protocol listens on port 80, but it is possible to have multiple applications listening on other port numbers, such as 1234. To connect to an application not using the default port, it is necessary to quote the number in the URL. It follows the host name, and is preceded by a colon:

```
protocol://host:1234/location/resource
```

Some of these components may not be needed. Relative URLs (see below) do not require the protocol and host information, and in the simplest case of all, only the resource name is required.

Characters allowed in a URL are restricted to upper-case and lower-case letters, digits, and the symbols '$', '+', '.', '-' and '_'. All other characters are represented by a special code, comprising a percent symbol, '%', followed by a hexadecimal two-digit ASCII character value ('%00' to '%FF'). For example, '%20' represents a space, and the percent symbol itself must be represented by the code '%25':

```
... xml%20files/myfile.xml
```

Local resources

When the file is stored on a local storage device that is 'visible' to the operating system as part of its file system, then strictly speaking there is no protocol involved, but the name '**file:**' should appear. Note the three forward slashes in the following example of an entity declaration; the third one represents the system root directory:

```
<!ENTITY ent9 SYSTEM "file:///c:/ents/e9.xml">
```

In fact, there remains some confusion about using the '//' symbols after 'file:'. Possibly because this is not a true access protocol, unlike the others described below, some applications expect these symbols to be omitted. It may be necessary to formulate the URL as shown in the following example, where the single '/' after 'file:' is the root directory identifier. Fortunately, most software can cope with both forms:

```
<!ENTITY ent9 SYSTEM "file:/c:/ents/e9.xml">
```

Note that on Windows systems, the drive letter is then required, followed by a colon, as shown above. On Macintosh systems, the drive name must appear, as in the following example:

```
<!ENTITY ent9 SYSTEM "file://Macintosh%20HD/ents/e9.xml">
```

Remote resources

The real power of URLs is their ability to identify resources on file systems that are not visible to the local system. In particular, any file on any system connected to the Internet can be accessed using a URL.

The most common protocol used for file downloading is **HTTP** (the *Hyper-Text Transfer Protocol*), specified using the protocol name '**http:**':

```
<!ENTITY ent9
      SYSTEM "http://www.XMLserve.com/entities/e9.xml">
```

When the file to be downloaded is not part of the hypertext system, but simply a binary data file that is to be accessed and viewed, or stored locally, then the **FTP** (*File Transfer Protocol*) mechanism is also popular, as it is optimized to provide safe, fast downloading. The protocol name is '**ftp:**':

```
<!ENTITY ent9
      SYSTEM "ftp://www.XMLserve.com/software/upgrade.zip">
```

Relative URLs

Once a file has been located using a URL, there may then be a need to locate other files on the same system. The simplest way to do this is to use a **relative URL**. These URLs are shorter and simpler, as they simply identify a resource by its location relative to the source file. The protocol and host name need not be repeated. In fact, when the resource is in the same directory as the source, it is only necessary to provide its name:

```
entity9.xml
```

When the resource is in a sub-directory, the URL begins with the name of the directory:

```
<!ENTITY ent9 SYSTEM "entities/entity9.xml">
```

```
/xml/document.xml
      /entities/entity9.xml
```

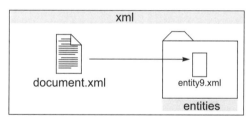

When the resource is elsewhere on the system, it is necessary to 'back out' of the current directory. This is done using the '..' symbols, which make the parent directory the new current directory. A relative link to a file in a directory which shares the same parent directory as the source document may appear as follows:

```
<!ENTITY ent9 SYSTEM "../entities/entity9.xml">
```

```
/xml/docs/document.xml
       /entities/entity9.xml
```

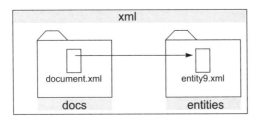

Relative URLs make maintenance of related files much easier. A collection of documents and directories can be moved to another system, without needing to edit the URLs, providing that the documents retain their locations relative to each other.

Queries and fragments

The required resource may not be an existing, static file, residing on a disk. It may be data that needs to be generated from information provided in the URL. The classic example is a URL that requests information that resides in a database, and requests to the popular Web search engines take the following form, with a question mark character, '?', preceding the query:

```
<!ENTITY jamesAddress SYSTEM "ftp://www.XMLserve.com/cgi/
go-get-it?find=Address&name=James">
```

Alternatively, a URL may lead on to further information that specifies just part of the identified resource, using the '#' symbol. This is known as a **fragment identifier** (and is not strictly part of the URL scheme). In HTML, the fragment identifier usually refers to the value of the Href attribute in the Anchor element:

```
<link href="../myfiles/detail.xml#part3">
See details, part 3
</link>
```

The same kind of link can be made in an XML document, when using the XPointer standard:

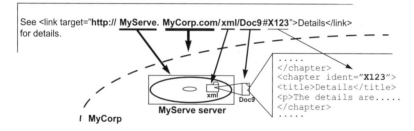

However, the XML scheme goes beyond simply referring to an identifier value. Using familiar expression, it allows fragments of a document to be located by context (in the following example, a link is made to the introduction title):

```
<link href=".../docs/abc.xml#xptr(book/intro/title)">
See the introduction.</link>
```

Inside XML documents (XPaths)

The meaning of an element can depend on its context. For example, a Title element that is embedded within a Book element will have very different content to a Title element that is embedded within a Name element. The format will certainly differ, and a query that is used to extract a list of book titles should not include entries such as 'Mr', 'Dr' and 'Ms'.

The hierarchical document structure can be exploited to pinpoint a particular element of interest. To obtain the last name of the author of a book, it should be possible to identify each element in the hierarchy in order to ensure that the correct Name element is selected. The list of elements could be 'Book', 'Front' (front-matter information), 'Author', 'Name', and finally 'Last'. In the following example, this would select the name 'Smith', but not the name 'Jones':

```
<book>
  <front>
    <author>
      <name>
        <first>John</first>
        <last>Smith</last>
  </name></author></front>
  ...
  <chapter>
    ...
    <name><init>F</init><last>Jones</last></name>
```

A number of XML-related standards discussed in later chapters involve 'tunnelling in' to XML documents in order to target specific elements, attributes, other markup constructs, or even text fragments. The proposed XQL standard may be used to locate and extract information of interest, and needs a mechanism for specifying the queries to do this. The proposed XPointer standard will be used to create hypertext links to objects that do not have unique identifiers, and requires a mechanism for identifying each target object by its location. The proposed XSLT standard needs to match formatting templates to appropriate elements in the source document in order to transform or style the content.

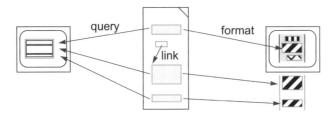

It can be seen that these needs are similar. The developers of the XPointer and XSLT working groups agreed that it would be appropriate to adopt a common approach, and the XQL proposal also follows this lead. Skills developed learning one of these standards should be of great benefit when learning one of the others. Learning all three becomes easier than it would otherwise be. The same expression could even be used across standards. For example, an expression created for XSLT, to identify and style each occurrence of some significant document object, could be copied to XQL in order to query and extract the same objects for analysis.

The proposed **XPath** scheme described here naturally exploits the sequential and hierarchical context of elements in an XML document. For example, it is possible to select the first paragraph in each chapter of a book, in order to give it a different style to all other paragraphs (using XSLT), to create a hypertext link to the paragraph that is separated from the current paragraph by five intermediate objects (using XPointer), and to retrieve a list of all author names that appear in the bibliography section of a textbook (using XQL). The draft standard can be obtained from www.w3.org/TR/XPath.

Expressions

XPath uses a text string that contains meaningful symbols. This is called an '**expression**'. The exact syntax of this scheme has been crafted to avoid problems when including navigation instructions in URLs, and also utilizes widespread knowledge of techniques used in command-line operating systems such as UNIX and MS-DOS. Symbols such as '/' ('\' on MS-DOS and ':' on the Macintosh), '..', '.' and '*' have existing and appropriate meanings to these audiences. It is also no coincidence that the first two of these have the same purpose as they have in URLs.

The following simple example identifies a Title element that is the direct child of a Book element:

```
book/title
```

Limitation of IDs

It could be argued that navigation techniques are not needed when elements contain unique identifiers. Indeed, when a specific element needs to be extracted using a query, or linked to from a source element, or styled in a different way to others of its kind, then the presence of a unique identifier is invaluable. Referring to the unique identifier is the most direct, and often the only way to locate such an element.

However, there are limitations to this technique. First, assigning unique identifiers to every element in a document can be an arduous task. Second, identifiers cannot be used to isolate individual comments, processing instructions, or ranges of text. Third, the identifier of a required element may not be known. Fourth, it would not be convenient to identify a lot of similar objects by listing all their identifiers.

A large XML document may contain thousands of elements. It would be very difficult to invent meaningful identifiers for them all. The difficulty can be illustrated by considering the paragraphs in this section. It is not obvious what meaningful identifiers they could be given. The obvious solution would be to give them simple identifiers, such as 'P1', 'P2' and 'P3'. There may be good reasons to do this, but not to return a list representing the first paragraph of each chapter. Of course, such identifiers are very useful when a specific paragraph is the target of a hypertext link, and the link must be retained even if the paragraph is moved (this topic is covered further in Chapter 6).

A hypertext link may wish to target only a short range of text in a large paragraph. XML includes no mechanism for assigning an identifier to such a range.

When a list of all document authors needs to be retrieved from a document just received from another party, it would be necessary to open the document and note the identifiers in order to use them to extract the values.

All the paragraphs in this section are styled in the same way. It should not be necessary to list all their identifiers in order to apply the same style to them all (using XSL).

Expressions

An expression is a string of text that consists of instructions for selecting an element, attribute, other markup structure, or a range of text. As stated above, an expression is a simple string. Some symbols have special meaning in an expression, including '/', '*', '.' and '..'. There are no line feeds permitted, and allowed characters are constrained by the various environments in which they may be used. The most limiting of these is the constraints of the URL standard.

How expressions are used depends on the technology in question, and on the application of that technology. Typically, however, an expression may appear in an attribute, in a URL, or in a variable that is passed to a database.

```
http://MyCorp.org/getQuery?/book/front/title

<xsl:pattern match="chapter/title">...</xsl:pattern>
```

Perhaps the simplest expression is one that identifies an element type of interest. In the following example, the expression matches Para elements:

```
para
```

Expressions may also be used to select attributes, comments, processing instructions, or ranges of text between elements. The term **node** is used to represent every item of significance in an XML document, including elements. The expression '**node()**' represents any such item. The expressions '**text()**', '**processing-instruction()**' (processing instruction) and '**comment()**' represent any object of these types.

Expressions are used in different ways for different purposes. Some expressions are location paths, used to identify and extract, link to or reuse targeted information in the document. Some location paths can take the role of a pattern, and be used, in XSLT, to match style sheet rules to a currently selected element.

Location paths

Expressions identify items by their location in the hierarchical document structure. A 'path' is a series of steps to a target location. A **location path** may burrow-down into the structure, skip over siblings, or work back up the structure, and there are two distinct types of path to consider, termed 'relative' and 'absolute'.

Relative paths

A **relative path** is one that starts from an existing location in the document structure.

The simplest form of relative path has already been shown:

```
para
```

In this case, the reference is to paragraphs that happen to be child elements of a currently selected element. In fact, this is an abbreviation of '**child::**...', a more verbose pattern, which makes the meaning more explicit. This pattern selects all child elements that have the given name:

```
child::para
```

To re-emphasize the point, this expression is not selecting children of a paragraph, but children of the *current* element that have the name 'para'. The current element may, perhaps, be a Chapter element:

```
<chapter>
  <title>A TITLE</title>
  <para>First paragraph</para>
  <para>Second paragraph</para>
</chapter>
```

In some standards, such as XQL, there is no concept of a current element. Each time a pattern is used, it is a query that searches the entire document. On these occasions, a relative path may not be appropriate at all.

However, some applications may process a document from start to finish, selecting each element in turn, so that all elements become the current element. In this scenario, the pattern shown above would eventually apply to all paragraphs in the document, as they will all be children of an element that is selected at one point or another. Indeed, in XQL this pattern would select all paragraphs in the document. XSLT also uses a similar concept to match style templates to elements in a document to be formatted (but in that case asks the question in reverse – having encountered an element, it asks if the name (and possibly the location) of the element matches the pattern).

An objection may be raised to the suggestion made above that all elements are the children of other elements. The root element has no parent, so a book should not be selected by the pattern 'book'. However, even the root element has a parent node. This node represents the entire document, including any markup, such as comments and processing instructions, that may surround the root element.

Multiple steps

When a pattern includes a number of steps, they are separated from each other using the '/' symbol. The steps in the pattern are read from left to right. Each step in the path creates a new context for remaining parts of the path. The following example includes two steps. First, the Book element is selected and made the current context, then each Title element in the book is selected:

```
book/title
```

Both steps in this pattern refer to child elements. However, it is important to emphasize that the '/' symbol itself is not denoting a parent/child relationship, but merely serves to separate the steps. It is used in many other circumstances. This is made more clear when the verbose form is used:

```
child::book/child::title
```

Wildcards

Sometimes, the names of elements between the context element and the required descendant may not be known, but this does not need to be an obstacle. The '*' symbol is used as a 'wildcard', standing in for any element name.

This technique can also be used to select elements in a number of different contexts simultaneously. For example, it may be necessary to select all chapter titles, and also the title of an introduction. While it would be possible to use two separate patterns, the third example below meets both requirements:

```
book/intro/title
book/chapter/title

book/*/title
```

This approach can be dangerous, however. The example above may inadvertently also select titles in other structures, such as an Appendix element that follows the Chapter elements. Used with care, though, it is a powerful technique.

The unabbreviated version simply adds the asterisk symbol to the 'child::' expression:

```
child::*
```

Although multiple asterisks can be used to indicate unknown elements at several levels in the pattern, using this technique it is still necessary to know exactly how many levels deep the required elements are. When the elements to be selected lie at different levels of the document structure, this tool is not suitable. A more powerful facility is provided by selecting all descendants. In the abbreviated syntax, a double-slash is used, '*//*'. In the following example, paragraphs that occur anywhere within a chapter are selected:

```
chapter//para

<chapter>
  <para>...</para>
  <note>
    <para>...</para>
  </note>
</note>
```

The more verbose version of this uses the '**descendant-or-self::**' expression. This expression is used to select all descendant nodes, but including the original context node itself (in this case, the Chapter element). Finally, the children of each of these nodes is tested to see if any are Para elements:

```
child::chapter/descendant-or-self::node()/child::para
```

Note the 'node()' in the second step above. Normally, the parameter is used to filter out unwanted element types, but in this case there must be no restrictions on the elements that may appear at intermediate levels.

It is also possible to use this approach to select all occurrences of a given element at any level *directly* within the current context. However, for reasons that will become clear later, using '*//*' at the beginning of the expression would not produce the desired effect. Instead, it is first necessary to explicitly declare that the starting-point is the current element. This is done using a full-point, '.'. The following example selects all paragraphs within the current element:

```
.//para
```

The more verbose equivalent of the '.' operator is the expression '**self::**'. As the current object may be an element, or the node representing the entire document, the parameter should again be 'node()'.

The verbose equivalent of this is in fact *very* verbose. First, the 'self::' expression is used to identify the current element as the start-point. Second, the 'descendant-or-self::' expression is used to indicate that all descendants, and the current node itself, are to be selected. Third, the 'child::' expression is used to indicate which children of these objects are to be selected:

```
self::node()/descendant-or-self::node()/child::para
```

Parents and grandparents

The parent of the context element is denoted using '..'. This mechanism can be used to select siblings of the current element. The following example selects a Title element that shares the same parent as the context element:

```
../title
```

The equivalent verbose syntax is '**parent::**':

```
parent::node()/child::title
```

The reason for needing 'node()' here, instead of just '*', is to cater for the parent of the root element, which is not an element, but a node that represents the entire document. The '*' symbol only represents elements (or, in one special circumstance, attributes), whereas a 'node()' test matches any node, including the node that represents the entire document.

To move up to the grandparent element, the '..' notation is simply repeated, as another step. The following patterns select the title of a chapter, when the current element is embedded within a section of the chapter:

```
../../title
```

```
parent::node()/parent::node()/child::title
```

This technique for accessing ancestors of the context element can be clumsy when many intermediate levels exist, and does not work at all when the number of levels is unknown. A more advanced technique for accessing ancestors is described later.

Absolute paths

In some circumstances, a relative path is not suitable. For example, it may be necessary to select the title of the book, regardless of the current context. The location relative to the document as a whole may be known, whereas the offset from the current location (if there *is* a current location) may not. In this case, an **absolute path** is used.

Essentially, an absolute path is the same as a relative path, except for the first step. It may begin with a '/' symbol, indicating the root of the document:

```
/book/title
```

Using the '//' expression, it is possible to select all occurrences of a specific element type. Unlike simply stating the element name, this technique ensures that all matching elements are selected, whatever the context:

```
//para
```

Another kind of absolute path is one that begins from a specific 'anchor point' in the document. An element that has a unique identifier can be targeted using the '**id()**' function:

```
id("para33")...
```

Other paths

Selection does not have to be from amongst the children of the context node. It has already been shown that parents and further ancestors of the current element can be selected. Many other options are available, and each can be thought of as a direction, or an '**axis**'.

Parents, children and siblings can be selected using the 'parent::', 'child::', '**preceding-sibling::**' and '**following-sibling::**' axis expressions:

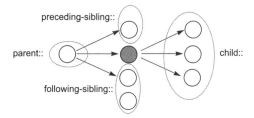

Note that sibling elements are neatly divided into those that appear before the context element, and those that appear after:

Previous siblings are counted backwards from the context element (in reverse order). The counting order is important. In the following example, the paragraph immediately preceding the current paragraph is selected:

```
preceding-sibling::para[1]

<para>Target paragraph.</para>   <----
<note>A note</note>                  |
<para>Source paragraph.</para>   -----
```

Following siblings are counted up from the context element:

following (younger) siblings

In the following example, the next Para element is selected:

```
following-sibling::para[1]

<para>Source paragraph.</para>   -----
<note>A note</note>                  |
<para>Target paragraph.</para>   <----
```

Ancestors and descendants can be searched for matching criteria using the '**ancestor::**' and '**descendant::**' functions:

Notice that descendants include children, not just lower levels in the hierarchy. Elements are counted in 'breadth' order, meaning that all sub-elements of one element are counted before going on to the next, at each level.

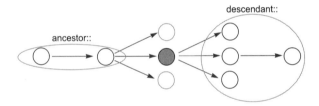

Ancestors are counted backwards up the hierarchy. Siblings of each ancestor element are ignored:

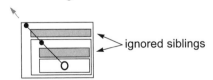ignored siblings

There is no abbreviated format for this. To select the title of the chapter containing the current element, the following verbose instruction is necessary:

```
ancestor::chapter/title
```

The current context node can be included in ancestor and descendant searching. The '**ancestor-or-self::**' and 'descendant-or-self::' functions are employed for this purpose. The search works as described above, except that in both these cases the context element itself is the first node in each list:

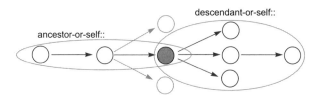

The current context node itself can be selected using 'self::'. The attributes of the context node can be selected using '**attribute::**'. All elements preceding the context element in the document can be selected using '**preceding::**'. This includes all descendants of elements that precede the context element, or are ancestors of the current element. Similarly, '**following::**' selects from all elements that follow the current element:

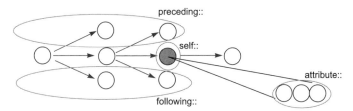

Essentially, the preceding function takes a flattened view of the document, and provides access to all elements that occur (and are completed) before the context element is encountered.

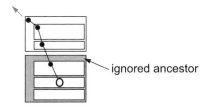

The following function provides the same service for the remainder of the document:

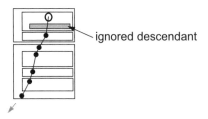

ignored descendant

Patterns

A **pattern** is a form of expression that is used, not to find objects, but to establish if a specific object matches some given criteria. Location paths may be used in patterns to decide if a currently selected element is in a significant contextual location. For example, paragraphs tend to be styled in different ways in a book, depending on where they appear. A paragraph in the introduction may be styled differently to one in a chapter, and a paragraph anywhere within a warning section may need to be highlighted. Location paths are suitable for use as patterns, and the circumstances described above can be coded as '/book/intro/para', 'chapter/para' and 'warning//para'. In the XSLT standard, templates are matched to elements in a source document using such patterns.

Because there is no concept of a source location in patterns, the symbols '.' and '..' are meaningless, as are many of the path step types, such as 'ancestor-or-self::'.

In fact, only the abbreviated format is allowed for patterns. The '/' and '//' instructions are permitted, including an initial '/' or 'id(x)'. When both these are absent, the ancestry of the current element is simply compared against the pattern. For example, 'warning//para' matches when the current element is a paragraph, and this paragraph is within a Warning element.

The '|' symbol may be used to specify multiple patterns. For example, 'note|warning|caution|/book/intro' matches all Note, Warning and Caution elements, as well as an Intro element that is a child of the Book element.

Predicate filters

Location paths are quite indiscriminate. At most, it is possible to specify a particular element type to select, within a given context. Often, a long list of matches is made. For example, the path 'book/chapter/para' selects all the paragraphs in all the chapters, when it may be necessary to select or process only the first paragraph in each chapter. A **predicate filter** is used to remove unwanted items from the list to create a new list. Square brackets, '[' and ']', are used to hold the predicate.

```
para [....]
```

The results of the test or tests is a single boolean value, true or false, and the selection only succeeds when the value is true.

Position tests

The '**position()**' function returns the sequential location of the element being tested. This value can be compared to a required location. The following example selects only the first paragraph:

```
para[position()=1]
```

This form of query can be abbreviated to just a number. The following test is equivalent to the one above:

```
para[1]
```

This number does not refer to the position of the element amongst all sibling elements, but only amongst those elements already selected by the pattern. In this case, as only Para elements are selected, the position refers to the first Para element in the list. To select a Para element only when it is the first *child* of its parent, a more complex expression is required. The following example illustrates this, and shows that it is necessary to first select all the sibling elements, using '*', then check both the position and the name of each element. In this case, the element is only selected if it is the first in the list, and is also a Para element (see below for the purpose of the 'and' expression):

```
*[position() = 1 and self::para]
```

Note that a similar technique can be used to select all occurrences of elements of more than one type. In the following case, all paragraphs and notes are selected (see below for the purpose of the 'or' expression):

```
*[self::note or self::para]
```

Locating the last sibling, when the number of elements in the list is unknown, can be achieved using the '**last()**' function. The following pattern applies to the last paragraph (*not* to the last sibling, if it happens to be a paragraph):

```
para[last()]
```

The '**count()**' function has the same purpose, but requires a parameter to specify the node list to count. It is not clear as to why there need to be two functions instead of one, apart from the fact that 'last()' counts the current list of nodes (selected by the location path), whereas other functions that can omit a parameter default to the current node, which in this case would always mean a return value of '1'. Using this function, it is possible to discover how many occurrences of a particular element there are in a document. The following example selects notes that contain a single paragraph:

```
child::note[count(child::para) = 1]
```

An element may have an identifier, and this unique value can be used to select the element. The '**id()**' function is used for this purpose:

```
chapter[id("summary")]
```

This function can be used at the start of a location path:

```
[id("chapter_9")/title]
```

Contained element tests

The name of an element can appear, in this location representing an element that must be present as a child for the test to succeed. In the following example, a Note element is only selected if it directly contains a Title element:

```
child::note[title]
```

The value of an element can be tested:

```
child::note[title="first note"]

<note>
  <title>first note</title>
  ...
</note>
```

Attribute tests

Attributes can be selected (usually for reuse elsewhere, in XSLT) and elements can be selected depending upon the presence or value of a specific attribute. The '**@**' symbol is used to represent an attribute, and precedes the name of the attribute. The following example selects the Author attribute of the Book element:

```
book/@author
```

The following example selects every paragraph with a Type attribute value of 'secret':

```
para[@type='secret']
```

The verbose equivalent of '@' is '**attribute::**':

```
para[attribute::type='secret']
```

Boolean tests

Many expressions, including those described above, are either valid or invalid in a given circumstance. A boolean test is performed, with a result of 'true' or 'false'. The tests shown above are only successful if the expression returns a 'true' value. The '**not()**' function can be used to reverse the result, and so greatly extends the number of tests that can be made. For example, all notes except for the third one, a note that does not contain a Title element, and all chapters except for one with a specified identifier, can all be selected:

```
note[not(position() = 3)]

note[not(title)]

chapter[not(id("summary"))]
```

The '**boolean()**' function evaluates an embedded expression and returns a boolean value. All numbers except zero are considered to be true, and a node list that contains at least one entry is also true. A text string is true if it contains at least one character. All the following tests return 'true' (assuming, in the last case, that there is at least one Title element):

```
boolean(3)

boolean("some text")

boolean(title)
```

It follows that the following expression returns false:

```
not(boolean(3))
```

Comparisons also return a boolean result. The most obvious comparison is for equality, using the equals symbol, '='. An example of such a comparison appeared above.

```
note[position() = 3]
```

This example compares two numbers. It is also possible to compare boolean expressions and strings:

```
note[title = "first note"]
```

Testing for non-equality is possible using '!='. For example, to select all but the last note:

```
note[position() != last()]
```

Other comparisons can be made that require the expressions to be interpreted as numbers. These are tests for the first expression being greater than the second, using '>', and the other way around, using '<'. By combining symbols, it is also possible to test whether the first expression is greater than or equal to the second one ('>='), or less than or equal to ('<='). The two examples below are equivalent, as they both filter out the first two Note elements:

```
note[position() > 2]

note[position() >= 3]
```

Note that the '<' and '>' symbols are significant in XML. When inserting expressions into an attribute, while not using an XML-aware editor, it is necessary to remember to use '<' and '>' to represent these characters.

An expression can be divided into separate sub-expressions, and the whole expression can be considered to be true only if all the sub-expressions individually evaluate to true, using an '**and**' expression. In the following example, a Note element is selected only if it is preceded by at least two others, and followed by at least one more:

```
note[position() > 2 and position() < last()]
```

Alternatively, the whole expression may succeed when at least one of the sub-expressions is true, using an '**or**' expression. In the following example, both the second and fourth Note elements are selected:

```
note[position() = 2 or position() = 4]
```

The value of the XML attribute 'xml:lang' can be tested against a specific language code using the '**lang()**' function. The parameter of this function is the language code to test the current node against. If the attribute is not present, or the language it specifies is different, a value of false is returned. Otherwise, a value of true is returned:

```
note[lang("en")]

<note xml:lang="en-uk">...</note>
```

Finally, the '**true()**' and '**false()**' functions simply return a value of true or false respectively.

Strings

String objects can be analyzed to discover if they contain specific characters or sub-strings. The '**contains()**' function returns 'true' if the string contains the given text. The first parameter is the string to test. The second parameter is the string to find in the first string. In the following example, each Note element is tested to see if it contains the word 'hello':

```
note[contains(text(), "hello")]

<note>This note says 'hello'</note>
```

Note that, in this example, the string to test is the child node of the Note element, which of course needs to be a text node, as represented by 'text()' for the first parameter. But only the first node is tested. The test will fail if the word is actually in a sub-element, or following a sub-element. The safer way to use this function is to refer to the Note element itself, using '.' (the current node). Although the Note element node does not contain the string, its children may do, and these are analyzed too:

```
note[contains(., "hello")]

<note>This note says <emph>hello</emph></note>
```

If the specified text needs to appear at the start of the string, the function '**starts-with()**' should be used instead:

```
note[starts-with(., "Hello")]

<note>Hello there</note>
```

The '**string()**' function converts an embedded expression into a string. For example, the following test selects Note elements that contain the character '2':

```
note[starts-with(., string(2))]

<note>This is note number 2</note>
```

When converting a number into a string, an invalid number is converted to the string 'NaN', and an infinite value is converted to the string 'Infinity' (negative infinity becomes '-Infinity' and negative zero becomes '0').

The '**translate()**' function converts characters according to a mapping scheme. The first parameter is the string to convert. The second parameter lists the characters to modify in the source text, and the third parameter lists the replacement values. One use for this function is to allow case-insensitive text comparisons, as in the following example, which matches both of the Note elements below:

```
note[starts-with(
        translate(normalize(.),
          "abcdefghijklmnopqrstuvwxyz",
          "ABCDEFGHIJKLMNOPQRSTUVWXYZ"),
            "HELLO THERE")]
```

```
<note>  Hello There</note>
```

```
<note>HELLO there</note>
```

Additional characters in the second parameter represent those characters that are to be removed from the source string. To convert semi-colons to commas, while also removing all existing plus symbols from a string, the following would be used:

```
translate(.,  ";+",  ",")
```

A leading or trailing fragment of a string can be extracted, providing that the fragment ends or begins with a given character or character sequence. The 'substring-before()' function takes two parameters, first the string to extract text from, then the character or characters that terminate the prefix to be extracted. The 'substring-after()' function works in the same way, but extracts text from the end of the string. For example, to retrieve just the year from a date:

```
substring-after(  .,  "/"  )
```

```
<date>12/08/1999</date>
```

To extract any fragment of a string, the 'substring()' function takes three parameters. First, the source string, then the character offset position, and finally the number of characters to extract. This can be used like the 'contains()' function, with the added constraint that the required string must occur at a specified location:

```
note[substring(., 9, 5) = "XPath"]
```

```
<note>This is XPath</note>
<note>This XPath is not a match</note>
```

When using namespaces, element names are separated into two parts: a local part, such as 'h1', and a namespace part, such as 'html', giving a complete name of 'html:h1'. The 'namespace()' function returns the namespace part of the first node in the list that forms its parameter. The 'local-part()' function returns the local part of the name.

```
*[namespace(.)  = "html"]
```

```
<html:h1>An HTML Header One</html:h1>
<html:p>An HTML paragraph.</html:p>
```

```
*[local-part(.)  = "h1"]
```

```
<html:h1>An HTML Header One</html:h1>
```

The '**normalize()**' function removes leading and trailing spaces, and reduces a sequence of white space down to a single space character. This is very useful when used with the example above, to ensure that the match is still made, even when there are spaces in and around the string:

```
note[starts-with(normalize(.), "Hello there")]

<note>   Hello    there</note>
```

A number of strings can be concatenated into a single string, using the '**concat()**' function, which takes one or more string parameters:

```
concat(., "append this", " and this")
```

Finally, the number of characters in a string can be determined using the '**string-length()**' function:

```
note[string-length(.) = 15]

<note>fifteen letters</note>
<note>123456789012345</note>
```

Numbers

Objects can be converted to numbers, using the '**number()**' function. Boolean expressions are interpreted as '1' for 'true' and '0' for 'false'. Strings that cannot be interpreted as a valid number are translated to a special default value called 'not-a-number' (or 'NaN' for short).

Real numbers can be converted to integers. Using the '**round()**' function, the real number is rounded, up or down, to the nearest integer equivalent. Using the '**floor()**' function, the number is rounded down to the nearest integer, so '3.1' becomes '3', and using the '**ceiling()**' function, the number is rounded up, so '3.1' becomes '4'.

The '+' and '-' operators may be used, and the following two examples are equivalent:

```
note[ 3 ]                    note[ 1 + 2 ]
```

The '**mod**' operator supplies the remainder of a truncated division. For example, '9 mod 4' returns '1' (there is a remainder of one after dividing nine by four). This feature is good for selecting alternate items, such as even numbered paragraphs:

```
para[ position() mod 2 = 0 ]
```

Multiple filters

Multiple predicate filters are used when both an abbreviated position and another type of test need to be combined, because they must not appear

together. The following example first selects company names, then extracts
the third name in this list:

```
child::name[company][3]

<names>
  <name><person>...</person></name>
  <name><company>...</company></name>
  <name><company>...</company></name>
  <name><person>...</person></name>
  <name><company>...</company></name>
  <name><person>...</person></name>
</names>
```

The order in which these two tests are made is very important. Only elements that
successfully pass the first test are subjected to the second. Reversing the order of
the tests in the example axbove therefore produces a very different result. This
time, the third name is selected, providing that it is also a company name:

```
child::name[3][company]

<names>
  <name><person>...</person></name>
  <name><company>...</company></name>
  <name><company>...</company></name>
  <name><person>...</person></name>
</names>

<names>
  <name><person>...</person></name>
  <name><company>...</company></name>
  <name><person>...</person></name> <!-- NOT SELECTED -->
</names>
```

Multiple predicate filters are also useful in other circumstances, although in
many cases a single filter can be used that includes the 'and' token. The second
example above can be reformulated as follows:

```
child::*[position() = 3 and self::company]
```

12. Hypertext links (XLink and XPointer)

This chapter covers the inherent hypertext linking features of the XML language, plus the more extensive capabilities provided by the proposed XLink and XPointer adjunct standards.

Warning: Most of the material in this chapter is derived from two draft proposals. Later drafts, or the release versions of the XLink and XPointer standards, may differ from this description.

Concepts

Publishers of printed material typically provide a number of features to assist with locating required information. This may include a table of contents, numbered pages, sections and chapters, and an index. Some of these navigation techniques may become irrelevant when the document is published electronically. Document browsers have a number of new features for locating required material, including full-text and keyword searching, and most include a **hypertext linking** capability. In the simplest case, when the reader encounters such text as 'see *More Information* for details', a software link provides instant access to the specified section.

The simplest kind of link can be visualized as a length of string, attached to the document at both ends with a pin. One pin represents the '**source**' (or start-point) of the link. This would typically be a phrase that directs the reader's attention to other information. From here, the string leads to the '**target**' (end-point) pin, which is located at the start of the required text. This is termed a '**basic link**'.

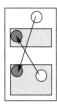

The document browser emphasizes source text, providing a visual clue to the user that it is possible to instantly access the material referenced.

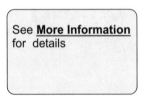

Formally, the target object is called a **resource**, and the source is a **linking element**. The act of moving from the linking element to the resource is termed a **traversal**.

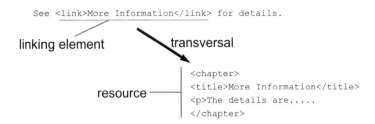

The XML Syntax specification described in previous chapters includes reserved attribute types which enable a simple linking scheme to operate. In this scheme, source and target attributes hold a matching **locator** value. This facility is backward compatible with SGML, so will work with SGML-aware browsers.

```
                                   locator
See <link target="X123">More Information</link> for details.


    <chapter ident="X123">
    <title>More Information</title>
    <p>The details are.....
    </chapter>
```

XML places no restriction on the names of elements and attributes that have significance in this linking scheme. For example, a linking element could be called 'A' (Anchor), 'Xref' or 'Link', and the attribute that contains the locator of the resource may be called 'Href', 'At' or 'Target'. The attribute that holds the locator value in the linking element is identified in the DTD, using a special attribute type.

A parser uses the special attribute types to identify the attributes that hold locator codes, and from this identifies source and target elements. Using this information, it can detect target elements that claim the same identifying code, and references that do not refer to any target present in the document, and are therefore considered to hold 'hanging pointers' (or 'broken' links).

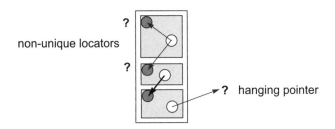

non-unique locators

? hanging pointer

From this description of how XML links work and are validated, a fundamental weakness becomes apparent. The source and destination points must reside in the same document. Links between documents are not supported. While limiting, this restriction can be surmounted. A collection of XML documents may be merged together for publication. This technique is quite common when preparing material for publication on CD-ROM.

Single-direction links to target objects in the same document are a primitive form of hypertext linking. Proposals for more advanced forms of linking appeared decades ago. Readers who are familiar with HTML and the World Wide Web will already be aware of a scheme that allows links to be made to other documents. Indeed, this scheme is incorporated into the new **XLink** standard. But this standard goes well beyond the capabilities of HTML too.

SGML Note: Although HyTime has already been developed for use with SGML, it has not been widely implemented. If software support for the linking schemes described in this chapter is more forthcoming, there is no reason why they cannot also be applied to SGML documents.

The XLink specification provides a similar feature to the primitive one-directional linking scheme described above, but makes it possible to traverse links between documents (as HTML users are already able to do). This is termed a **simple link**.

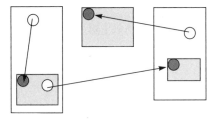

Documents are identified using the **URL** mechanism (see Chapter 11), which is already familiar to users of Web browsers, and objects in the documents that have a unique identifier can be targeted explicitly. However, there may be times when it is necessary to provide a link to an object that has no unique identifier, or does not comprise the entire content of the target element. Those responsible for preparing the text may not have been able to identify the elements that will be linked to, and the cost of adding unique values to all elements may not have been justifiable. The proposed **XPointer** standard therefore allows a resource to be identified by its contextual location. This information is simply added to the URL, in place of a document fragment name, to be interpreted by the browser after the document has been received, or in the form of a query that the server processes in order to return the required item:

```
http://.../xml/doc9#xptr(/intro/title)
```

```
http://.../xml/doc9?xptr(/intro/title)
```

The navigation techniques provided by the **XPath** standard (described in Chapter 11) are exploited by the XPointer standard. This is a very flexible technique, as a selection of examples can demonstrate. A resource can be identified as:

- the third chapter
- the second child element in the third chapter
- the fifth paragraph in the fourth chapter
- the second occurrence of the phrase 'A little learning is a dangerous thing' in the fifth chapter
- the second paragraph in the section with an identifier of 'Sec12'.
- the last-but-one item in the first list of the third chapter
- the second list with a Type attribute value of 'indented'
- the first paragraph with a Level attribute value of 'top-secret', in the first section with a Level attribute value of 'secret'

In addition, XPointer includes a technique for addressing uniquely identified objects that, by use of a minimization technique, retains full compatibility with the HTML mechanism for linking to objects within Web pages. In fact, this feature of XPointer can be informally considered to be part of the XLink standard, as it is the one feature of XPointer that is needed to provide even simple links within documents:

```
http://.../xml/doc9#sect2.1
```

```
<section id="sec2.1">...</section>
```

Xpointer also offers a very simple scheme for identifying an element by its location in the document tree, by counting elements at each level. This is called a **'tumbler'** mechanism, or **'stepwise addressing'** scheme:

```
http://.../xml/doc9#/3/2
```

```
<book>
  <title>Book Title</title>
3 <chapter>...</chapter>
  <!-- third child of this book -->
  <chapter>
    <title>Chapter Title</title>
2 <!-- second child of this chapter -->
    <section id="sec2.1">...</section>
```

Xpointers also allow the target of a hypertext link to be a range of elements, rather than a single element. For example, the target of a link could be a block of text consisting of three consecutive paragraphs.

An XPointer also allows a range of text within an element to be identified as the link resource, even if the string contains or spans across elements:

```
string::1,"here to here."

<line>Select the text from <emph>here</emph></line>
<line> to <emph>here</emph>. But not this.</line>
```

Select the text from *here*
to here. But not this.

The means by which a link can be activated, and the presentation technique required once it has been activated, can be influenced by attributes in the linking element. A link could be activated by the person reading the document (a '**user**' link), or directly by the application (an '**auto**' link). Once activated, by whichever means, the application may 'jump' to the specified resource ('**replace**' the original text), display the resource in another window (create a '**new**' window), or even insert the resource into the original text, replacing the linking element ('**embed**' it). These concepts can be combined in different ways to produce a variety of effects. The default combination would typically be 'user' and 'replace', which duplicates the linking action of HTML-based Web browsers. The user must select the link to activate it, and the new text simply replaces the original in the main window:

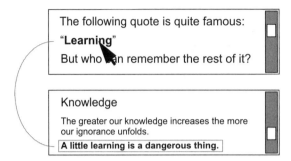

However, if embedding is required, the resource is displayed between the paragraphs, as it might appear in a printed version of the document.

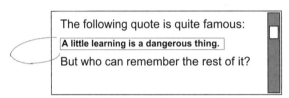

Finally, the browser can open a new window to display the resource, leaving the original window on-screen.

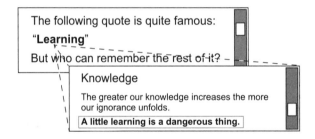

When a link is activated automatically, it is followed as soon as the linking element appears on-screen. A typical reason for selecting this option is to immediately present the resource on-screen, in conjunction with the 'embed' option. The user need not be aware that a link even exists. Note that this particular combination replicates the functionality of the XML entity feature, though without needing the equivalent of an entity declaration. Another typical use (again when used in conjunction with the 'embed' option) is to refer to the title of another section of the document. The actual title is keyed only once, at the top of the section concerned. It is automatically repeated wherever the section is referenced. The advantage of this approach is that a change to the section title need only be made in one place, and all references are updated the next time they are displayed.

The links described above are very limited. The linking element is embedded in the text, so cannot be used in a read-only document, and is also one-directional. Although a browser may be able to return from the resource using a 'back' button, this is not equivalent to being able to start from the other end of the link. To do that, it would be necessary to include another simple link at the other end. It is sometimes desirable to have two-directional, or even multi-directional links. For example, a number of online works may contain some material on a famous person, such as Napoleon. A book on warfare may include a chapter on his campaigns; a book on famous French people may include a chapter on his life; and a book on psychiatry may include a case study of someone who thought they were this historical character. Using an **extended link**, all these resources can be cross-related. An extended link contains a number of **locator** elements, each one pointing to a resource. The extended link may still be an in-line element, located at one of the resources:

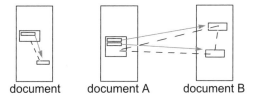

document   document A   document B

Note that the concept of 'source' and 'target' are no longer relevant here. The ends of the link have equal status, even if one is a single word reference and the other is an entire book.

It is generally neater to separate the extended link from all the resources it identifies. An **out-of-line** link provides this facility. Strangely, perhaps, an out-of-line link may physically appear in-line, in the sense that it is placed in the flow of text. But this only makes the linking mechanism difficult to find. A more obvious place to put out-of-line links is at the top of the document:

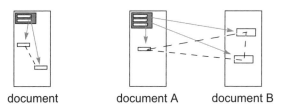

document   document A   document B

It is important to note that a document may not contain any information on the links it contains, as in 'document B' in the example above, because its linked resources are identified in another document. The possible absence of linking markup in a participating document has interesting repercussions. A document that cannot be edited, perhaps because it resides on a remote system and is not owned by the link creator, can nevertheless be remotely provided with links, both to other parts of the same document, and to other documents.

However, there is also a disadvantage to this approach. A processor given 'document B' would be unaware of the existence of the first document, and therefore of any links between them. A mechanism called an **extended link group** is used to overcome this problem. A number of **extended document** pointers are used to identify all the interlinked documents. They are contained in an **extended group** element. By this means, all the documents concerned hold pointers to each other.

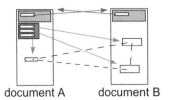

document A   document B

Using this technique, a browser reading 'document B' is told to read also the documents it points to, including 'document A', which contains the extended links. But the obvious new problem this approach raises is illustrated below. A significant problem is that when many documents are linked, every document contains pointers to every other document. While creating all these links is one issue, maintaining them can be a far more severe issue. If a document is added to or removed from the collection, or the entire collection is moved to a different location, a great deal of editing is required.

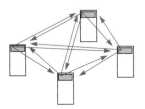

The solution is to use a special 'link group' file. This is a file that contains nothing but links to all the files in a collection. It can be thought of as the hub of a wheel, with spokes leading out to all the documents. This file may also contain all the extended links, making them more accessible, and all link maintenance is then performed in a single file. Each document contains a single reference (to the hub file). Note, however, that linking cannot start from a read-only document, as it would not contain the link to the link group file, unless the browser is also given the link group file at the same time.

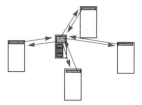

There are still two problems that a browser attempting to collect together all the documents may encounter. The first is that following every document link into and back out of the link group inevitably means following the same path repeatedly, and going around in circles. The second is that a document may contain links to other groups, leading to potentially unlimited links, and giving the browser the impossible task of trying to incorporate them all.

To avoid both these problems, it is possible to state in an attribute how many **link steps** may be taken from the original document. Typically, only two steps are needed. Step one takes the browser to the hub file. Step two takes it to every document indicated in this file.

When the user selects an extended link, the browser cannot know which other resource the user may wish to link to. It is therefore necessary to label each resource, so the browser can give the user a choice. A resource is given a **resource title**, which contains a brief description. This description may be presented in a selection window.

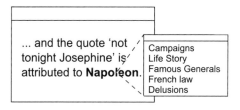

There is also a way to identify categories of link. A **link role** can be assigned to each locator, which is used by the system to apply a different style to the linking element content, or to affect linking behaviour in some way. For example, if all links are classified as 'internal' (referring to objects in the same document) or 'external', then these links can be given distinctive colours so that users will be aware of the distinction. Actions may also vary. Perhaps internal links would be made by scrolling to the new location, while external links would be made by opening a new window for the other document.

XML syntax basic links

The XML standard includes a primitive linking scheme, inherited from the SGML standard. This single-direction, in-line link works only when both the source and target are contained within the same document and relies upon the two special attribute types, 'ID' and 'IDREF'. Using this technique, the target object must be enclosed by an element that has an attribute defined to be of type **ID**. A unique value must be placed in this attribute.

```
<!ELEMENT section (...) >
<!ATTLIST section target ID #REQUIRED>

<section target="S6">
<title>This is Section 6</title>
...
...
...
</section>
```

Every reference to that object must be contained within an element that has an attribute defined to be of type **IDREF**. For example, a referencing element called 'XRef' may use an attribute called 'Link' to point to the required object:

```
<!ELEMENT xref (...) >
<!ATTLIST xref link IDREF #REQUIRED>

<para>Please refer to
<xref link="S6">Section 6</xref>
for more details</para>
```

An XML parser uses the ID and IDREF attribute type designators to identify and validate these values. Every ID value must be unique, to avoid ambiguity, and every IDREF value must match the value of an attribute of type ID in order to avoid hanging pointers.

The following fragment is invalid because two sections have the same identifier value:

```
<section target="S6">
<title>This is Section 6</title>
...
</section>
<section target="S6"> <! -- ERROR -->
<title>This is Section 7</title>
```

The following fragment is invalid because no element with an identifier matches the reference value:

```
<book>
<section target="S1">
<title>This is Section 1</title>
<para>Refer to <xref link="S0"> <!-- ERROR -->
Section 7</xref> for more details.</para>
</section>
<section target="S2">
<title>This is Section 2</title>
...
```

The link code is limited to alphabetic or numeric characters, and the symbols '-' and '.', but must start with an alphabetic character. Valid examples include 'X-123', 'peter' and 'ABC.DEF'. Names are case-sensitive, so a target value of 'mytag' will not be matched with a source value of 'MyTag'.

It is possible that some XML-aware browsers may only implement this facility, rather than the more complex XLink scheme described below. As this technique is backward compatible with SGML, an SGML parser and SGML-aware browser will understand the use of these attributes, and treat the XML document as an SGML document containing active links.

The inability of this scheme to operate between documents is not always an issue. When publishing to paper or CD-ROM, it is often convenient for the entire publication to be contained in a single data file, and it is common practice to merge a large number of small documents into one large document for these purposes. When this is the case, linking can be supported providing that two DTDs are used. The DTD used during creation of the individual documents assigns the attribute type CDATA to the source attributes, so that no checking takes place on their values. The publishing DTD assigns the IDREF type instead, but is otherwise probably identical. Checking and activation of links then only takes place after construction of the entire publication. Note that there is no problem with using ID types in both DTDs, as this type simply ensures that the values are unique.

XML linking specification

The proposed XML linking specification (**XLink**) describes a number of schemes for representing links that are able to span across documents, locate multiple sources, and point from and into read-only documents.

Identifying links

The advanced linking features described here are not based on reserved attribute types, and an XML parser is therefore unable to recognize and validate the links. It is assumed that there is another layer of software, an 'XML link processor', which interrogates the parsed document instance, and possibly also the DTD, in order to detect and activate linking features.

When a DTD is in use, the **architectural form** approach is used, using significant attribute names to identify linking elements. For example, the attribute name 'xml:link' is deemed significant to such a software module. There is a built-in mechanism for changing the names of these reserved attributes in order to avoid conflicts with other attributes. The reserved attributes may also be stored directly within the document, and it is necessary to do this if no DTD is in use. In the example below, a specific instance of the Link element is identified as a (simple) linking element:

```
<link xml:link="simple" href="..." >the link</link>
```

```
<!ATTLIST link    xml:link    CDATA  #FIXED  "simple"
                  href        CDATA  #REQUIRED>
<link href="..." >the link</link>
```

Types of link

Different types of link are specified using the **xml:link** attribute, which can take the value '**simple**', '**extended**', '**locator**', '**group**' or '**document**'. Simple links are one-directional. Extended links are multi-directional. Many concepts are relevant to both simple and extended links, including the use of URLs to locate the resource and the ability to define the behaviour of the link.

Simple links

As a simple link contains only one resource locator, this locator is stored in the linking element itself, using the **Href** attribute:

```
See <simple href="...">book 9</simple> for details.
```

HTML Note: This feature is identical in nature to the use of the Anchor element, and it is also no coincidence that the default locator attribute name is 'Href'. In fact, as the element name 'Simple' is only a suggestion in the standard, it is possible to emulate HTML completely by naming the linking element 'A' (anchor) instead.

Although there are a number of features that can be explicitly defined using attributes, almost all are optional (Role, Title, Content Role, Content Title and Behaviour), or have default values (Inline defaults to 'true'). Only the Href and xml:link attributes are required, and when a DTD is in use the xml:link attribute should be defined there (to avoid unnecessary duplication, and to make things simpler for document authors):

```
<!ATTLIST simple      xml:link CDATA #FIXED "simple" >
```

Note that this example illustrates a suitable use of the #FIXED feature, as document authors should never need to change the value, and in fact must be prevented from doing so. In reality, a document author would not even need to be aware of its existence.

When a DTD is not in use, the xml:link attribute must be present in the start-tag:

```
<simple href="http://ProcMan.xml#Sec9" xml:link="simple">
See Section 9 of the Procedures Manual.
</simple>
```

The simplest form of locator is a code that identifies an object in the same document. These 'local' references must be preceded by a hash symbol, '#', as described in Chapter 11. The resource is identified by an element that contains an identical value (but without the hash symbol) in its **Id** attribute. It is assumed that this attribute is actually defined in a DTD to be of type ID, and it is not clear how this attribute would be identified when no DTD is in use. In fact, a very small part of the XPointer standard is used here, and the example below is an abbreviation for the XPointer expression '`#xptr(id("X123"))`':

```
<chapter id="X123">



<simple href="#X123">
```

Title and Role

It is useful for simple links to be labelled, so that the user can decide whether it would be profitable to follow the link. For example, if the name 'Scarborough' is highlighted in the title of the song 'Are you going to Scarborough fair?', it is not immediately obvious where the link leads to, and why. A label, containing the word 'location', that perhaps appears when the cursor is placed over the name, makes it obvious that the resource says something about the location of the town. The **Title** attribute is used to hold this label. It will be shown later how this label is even more useful, indeed vital, when multiple links are involved.

```
<!ATTLIST link ...
                    title CDATA #IMPLIED>
```

```
... are you going to
<link href="#X123" title="Location">Scarborough</link>
fair?
```

When many links are in use, it is possible that they can be divided into meaningful groups. For example, it may be possible to divide links into 'local' and
'remote' categories, or into 'describe' and 'next topic' categories. The **Role**
attribute is used to create categories of link that can be accessed by specialized
browsers. A general browser may simply use the Role attribute value to apply
different styles to the linking text (both CSS and XSLT are able to apply different styles to an element, depending on the value of one of its attributes). A
more specialized browser may perform role-specific actions as well, or instead.

```
<!ATTLIST link ...
                    role CDATA #IMPLIED>
```

```
... are you going to
<link href="#X123" role="describe">Scarborough</link>
fair?
```

Extended links

Extended links refer to a number of resources by including embedded resource
locators. Each locator is stored in a **locator** element, and all related locator elements are grouped within an **extended** element. The 'xml:link' attribute is used
to identify elements that take these roles. The DTD author must ensure that
the extended element can contain the locator element, as well as any DTD-
specific elements appropriate at this point:

```
<!ELEMENT para        (#PCDATA | extend | emph ) >
<!ELEMENT extend      (#PCDATA | locate | emph) >
<!ATTLIST extend      xml:link="extended" ... >
<!ELEMENT locate      (#PCDATA) >
<!ATTLIST locate      xml:link="locator" ... >
```

```
<para>Here are
<extend>some <emph>extended</emph>
links:
<locate href="...">Locator 1</locate>,
<locate href="...">Locator 2</locate>.
</extend>
</para>
```

Here are <u>some</u> *extended* links: **Locator 1**, **Locator 2**.

A browser should recognize that the embedded Locate elements form a related group and deduce that it would be useful to dynamically produce links between them all (in this case, between the fragment shown above, the fragment identified as 'Locator 1', and the fragment identified as 'Locator 2').

Content Role and Content Title

In the example above, each resource to be linked was referred to in the text, and these references were treated as labels by enclosing them in Locate elements. But this may not always be the case, and the problem then arises as to how the user can know that there is more than one resource, and how the user can select one of these resources. The **Title** attribute can be used to overcome these problems.

```
<locate title="location" role="explain" href="..."/>

<locate title="history" role="explain" href="..."/>
```

But the extended link itself, if it is an in-line link, should also have a title and role, so that other resources can provide meaningful pointers to it. The attributes **Content Role** and **Content Title** serve this purpose.

```
<!ATTLIST extend ...
                 content-role  CDATA  #IMPLIED
                 content-title CDATA  #IMPLIED>

<song>
<title>Are you going to
<extend content-title="song" content-role="reference">
Scarborough
<locate title="location" role="explain" href="..."/>
<locate title="history" role="explain" href="..."/>
</extend>
fair?</title>
...
</song>
```

The content title is presented to users browsing other documents who may wish to link to this one, in this case depending on whether or not the user wishes to learn the lyrics to a song about Scarborough.

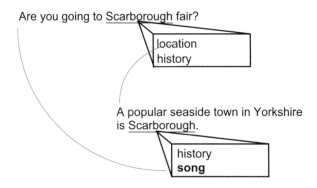

Out-of-line links

A distinction needs to be made between **in-line links** and **out-of-line links**. Previous examples have all been in-line, though there are two slightly different interpretations of what 'in-line' actually means. Within the XLink specification, this term denotes 'a link that serves as one of its own resources'. Elsewhere, however, it has been defined as a link source that is embedded within the text, forming an **anchor** that will move with the reference text if preceding text is edited.

HTML Note: Most HTML users will be familiar with the action of the Anchor element (A). This element sometimes encloses one resource, using the Name attribute, while at the same time also pointing to another resource, using the Href attribute.

An out-of-line link, according to the XLink specification, is a link that 'does *not* serve as one of its own resources'. Although it is possible for the linking element to be physically 'in-line', for practical reasons it is generally kept away from the text of the document, and points to both the source and destination (using an **extended link**). However, the terms 'source' and 'destination' are interchangeable when discussing out-of-line links. The concept of bi-directional linking is not only possible, but is actually difficult to avoid. Typically, such links reside in a separate 'linking file':

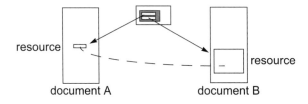

Note that it is also possible for a simple link to be out-of-line, but it would not then enclose (identify) the source text of the link, so the concept is practical in only very special cases. The standard suggests a role for them in adding properties to the target object.

The **Inline** attribute must be set to 'false' to specify an out-of-line link (indicating that the content is not itself considered to be a resource):

```
<extend inline="false">
  <locate href="..."/>
  <locate href="..."/>
</extend>
```

Out-of-line links should be considered when:

- a read-only document is involved
- different links are required for different groups of people, where seeing others' links is confusing
- link management is an issue

Extended link groups

When bi-directional, out-of-line links are stored in another file (perhaps a linking file), the browser cannot tell from simply reading the current document that it contains resources that are linked to other resources. It would be useful if the browser could be informed which documents contain links to each other, so that it can locate the linking elements and highlight all linked resources in the current document. Other documents in a group of interlinked documents can be identified using the **Group** element, containing a **Document** element for each document in the group. The 'xml:link' attribute identifies elements that take these roles. Each Document element locates a document using an **Href** attribute.

However, simply following link groups to accumulate all the links can be dangerous. If document A contains a link group that refers to document B, and document B contains a link group to document A, the accumulating process will take forever. Either the application must be clever enough to avoid revisiting documents already included, or it can take note of the **Steps** attribute, which contains a value stating how many steps to take. When each document simply points to a hub document, they should have a Step value of '2', indicating that the hub document itself (step 1), and all documents referred to there (step 2), including itself, should be read:

```
<group steps="2">
  <document href="DocumentHub"/>
</group>
```

Of course, the collection of documents may not conform to the same DTD, and some may not contain elements with unique identifiers. Fortunately, this facility can make use of 'extended pointers' to identify a resource by its contextual location.

If some of these documents are read-only, then link groups cannot be added to them. It must be assumed either that the user is not starting from a read-only document, so that the links can be established first, or that the browser has also been given the hub file to read.

Extending URLs

XLink and XPointer rely upon the **URL** scheme, described in Chapter 11, to link to remote documents. Locating documents is identical to locating entities. The following example creates a link to a fragment of another document:

```
<link href="../myfiles/detail.xml#part3">
See details, part 3
</link>
```

Note that the '#' symbol and the text that follows it are not part of the URL standard, and this text can be interpreted in different ways, depending on the application. In this case, there is a useful, deliberate, yet superficial resemblance to HTML usage, where the text following the '#' symbol refers to a unique element identifier (in HTML, this would refer to the value of a Name attribute in an Anchor element). In this context, however, the text is interpreted as an XPointer, and it just so happens that the abbreviation for the XPointer function 'xptr(id("x"))' (described below) is just 'x', so emulating the HTML meaning. But the Xpointer standard is much more powerful, and there are many keywords and symbols that are used to allow selection of an element that has no unique identifier, but does have a unique contextual location. See Chapter 11 for details.

When the XPointer is to be processed by a Web server, so that it can return only the required document fragment that matches the query, a query operator is used, as represented by the question mark character, '?':

```
../myfiles/detail.xml?...
```

XPointers

XPointer expressions are simply added to the end of a URL, when linking to objects in other documents.

The XPointer standard is heavily dependent on the proposed XPath standard, which supplies the general mechanism for identifying objects in a document by their context, rather than by a unique identifier. After the fragment identifier, '#', an XPointer expression is identified by a schema specifier, 'xptr', with the expression itself enclosed by brackets:

```
../thedoc.xml#xptr(...)
```

For example, to link to the title of a book introduction, the following abbreviated or full XPath expressions can be used:

```
../thedoc.xml#xptr(/intro/title)
../thedoc.xml#xptr(/child::intro/child::title)
```

Relative links

It is difficult to understand why the following should be true, but all XPath expressions are considered to be absolute addresses. If the expression does not begin with '/' then its presence is implied. This means that the following two examples are deemed to be equivalent:

```
../thedoc.xml#xptr(intro/title)
../thedoc.xml#xptr(/intro/title)
```

Relative linking is possible, but only by using a 'here()' function at the beginning of the expression. The following example links to the next paragraph:

```
<para>See the next
<link target="#xptr(here()/../following-sib-
ling::para[1]))">paragraph.</xlink>
</para>
<para>This is the target paragraph.</para>
```

A similar mechanism is provided for relative links that are defined out-of-line, using the 'origin()' function at the beginning of the expression. This function represents the node that the user is traversing from. This feature only seems to make sense when an extended link contains references to two resources, with the second one defining a location relative to the first, as in the following example, which links two adjacent paragraphs. However, if this is the intention, it serves only as a form of shorthand, as it would always be possible to include the full path to the second resource:

```
<extend inline="false">
  <locate href="#xptr(id("chap1")/para[5])"/>
  <locate href="#xptr(origin()/following-sib-
ling::para[1])"/>
</extend>
```

Unique end-points

The '**unique()**' function can be used in predicates to determine whether or not the expression locates a single object in the document. Often, a hypertext link should have a single end-point, so that a user following the link will 'arrive' at a precise location. This function returns true if the current node list contains a single node. In the following example, the link will not be created if the chapter contains more than one title:

```
.../chapter[3]/title[unique()]
```

This is of course equivalent to the slightly more verbose example below:

```
.../chapter[3]/title[count()=1]
```

In some circumstances, it may be better to ensure that the link succeeds by adding more constraints. From the example above, it could be more appropriate to select the first title of the chapter. This is guaranteed to be unique:

```
.../chapter[3]/title[1]
```

Ranges

The '**range::**' axis is used to specify a target that consists of a number of objects that occur in sequence. The start-point and end-point of the range are given as two separate location paths, separated by a comma:

```
range::path1,path2
```

The following example selects the first three paragraphs of a specific chapter:

```
range::/book/chapter[3]/para[1],/book/chapter[3]/para[3]
```

However, the first path creates a context location from which the second path can be specified. The following example is less verbose, but equivalent to the one above:

```
range::/book/chapter[3]/para[1],following::para[2]
```

Note the value '2' in the last part of the expression above. This is the second paragraph after the currently selected paragraph, making it the third paragraph in the chapter.

Strings

Designating a string of text as a link resource is accomplished using the '**string::**' axis. The first parameter is the occurrence to locate, and the second is the string to find. The following example selects the third occurrence of the string 'find me' within the second chapter of the book:

```
/book/chapter[2]/string::3,"find me"
```

Two further parameters can be added to select just part of the given string. In the following example, only the word 'me' is selected, providing that it occurs within the string 'find me here':

```
/book/chapter[2]/string::3,"find me here",6,2
```

The first of these parameters is the position number, which must not be zero. The value '6' indicates a position just before the sixth character (character six is to be included in the selection). The next parameter value is the number of characters to select from this position.

A negative number can be used for the position value, indicating a count backwards from the end of the string. A value of '-1' indicates a position immediately preceding the last character in the string. The following example has the same result as the one above:

```
/book/chapter[2]/string::3,"find me here",-7,2
```

A length of zero is permitted, and indicates a point between characters (an insertion point, if editing were allowed). The reserved word 'end' may be used as a position value, indicating a position beyond the final character:

```
/book/chapter[2]/string::3,"find me here",end,0
```

find me here●

The string can be omitted, though the quotes must still appear. This indicates that any string will match. For example, it would be possible to select the first ten characters:

```
/book/chapter[2]/string::1,"",1,10
```

Any old text string.   Some other text string.

Predicate tests can be made. The standard suggests their use to isolate a particular occurrence of the string, despite the fact that the first parameter already fulfils this function. The example below is perhaps more realistic, though the same effect could be achieved by placing the predicate elsewhere in the expression:

```
string::3,"note or para text",1,2,[parent::para or
                                   parent::note]
```

Multiple white space characters are normalized to a single space when matching strings, and embedded markup is ignored. The string can even start in one element and end in another.

```
..."match this text"...

<para> match    <emph>this</emph>        text</para>
```

Link behaviour

The means by which a link can be activated, and its behaviour once it has been activated, can be influenced by attributes in the linking element. The **Actuate** and **Show** attributes suggest which action to take, though they may be ignored by the application.

The **Actuate** attribute has a value of '**auto**' or '**user**'. The default value is defined in the DTD, but would typically be 'user', which indicates that the link is only traversed when explicitly selected by the user. When this attribute is set to 'auto', the link is activated automatically, as soon as the linking element is presented to the user. A typical reason for selecting 'auto' is to immediately present the resource on-screen (in conjunction with the 'embed' Show option), such as to refer to the title of another section of the document.

The **Show** attribute specifies how the new material is to be presented, and has a value of '**replace**', '**embed**' or '**new**'.

The '**replace**' value dictates behaviour familiar to users of HTML browsers when following a hypertext link. The browser replaces the source text with the resource required (it 'jumps' to the new location). This method is ideal when the user is simply skipping to a more interesting portion of the document (perhaps never to return). When used in conjunction with the 'auto' actuate option, transfer takes place automatically, which is useful when the document has been moved to another location, leaving behind only a redirection document.

```
<xlink show="replace" actuate="auto">This page has
moved.</xlink>
```

When the Show attribute has a value of '**embed**', the resource is brought to and embedded in the source text, at the point from which it was referenced (this is formally termed a **transclusion**). In the following example, both the chapter number and title replace the reference text. The text 'Section 7' is missing from the source document. When used in conjunction with the 'auto' option, reference replacement may even be transparent to the user (if it happens quickly enough). The title and number of the chapter are inserted into the reference text as it is displayed, which means it can be altered at any time, with all references automatically updated. But the disadvantage is that the XML document is harder to understand and work with when using editing and viewing tools that are not link-aware.

```
As stated in Chapter
<xref source="|MSnum" show="embed"/>
(<xref source="|MStitle" show="embed"/>), ...

<chapter>
<num link="MSnum">7</num>
<title link="MStitle">Market Research</title>
```

As stated in Chapter 7 (Market Research), . . .

As shown above, it is advisable to use the '|' in place of the '#' symbol when referring to the target text, as it would not be a good idea to insert the *whole* document into the source text.

Note: This is reminiscent of an entity reference being replaced by the entity content. However, the link approach has the advantage that there are no declarations to create, and the resource can also be accessed elsewhere using more conventional linking techniques.

If the Show attribute has a value of '**new**', the browser should open a new window to display the resource, leaving the original window on-screen. This approach could be used to display elements that contain entity references to graphics, so the image appears in its own window, or to display comments or annotations. It may also be used to create a help system. The disadvantage is that the user must explicitly close the window to avoid clutter, and perhaps even to reveal the original window.

```
A <xref show="new" source="#chap6">picture</xref>
of Scarborough.
```

The Show and Actuate attributes also appear in the extended link element, where they provide default values for all embedded links. In the following example, the first and last locators have inherited Show values of 'new'. The other locator overrides the default.

```
<extend show="new">
<locate href="..." />
<locate href="..." show="embed"/>
<locate href="..." />
</extend>
```

Another attribute, called **Behavior**, is provided, to hold more detailed information on how to process the link, though the standard does not specify the syntax or scope of its usage.

Attribute name conflicts

Attribute names are important to the more complex linking schemes described in this chapter. A 'link-aware' application identifies relevant elements and attributes from these names.

- xml:link
- role
- href
- title
- inline
- content-role
- content-title
- show
- actuate
- behavior
- steps

However, it is possible that one or more of these names are already in use in the DTD to which these features are to be added. It could be imagined that a linking element already contains an attribute called Show, which is used for some DTD-specific purpose. If it is not possible to rename the original attribute, the only way to avoid a clash is to rename the linking attribute. Fortunately, there is a mechanism by which this can be done, while still allowing an application to identify it.

The purpose of the **xml-attributes** attribute is to change the names of the other attributes, when this is needed (though it obviously cannot be used to rename itself). This attribute contains pairs of values, separated by spaces. The first value in each pair is the name of one of the reserved attributes. The second value in each pair is the replacement name. The following example renames the Show attribute to Xshow:

```
<!ATTLIST link
      xml-attributes CDATA #FIXED   "show xshow"
      xshow  (embed|replace|new)    "replace">
      show   (normal|secret)        "normal">
```

To additionally rename the Title attribute to Xtitle, further parameters are added:

```
<!ATTLIST link
   xml-attributes CDATA #FIXED "show xshow title xtitle"
   xshow (embed|replace|new)   "replace"
   xtitle         CDATA        #IMPLIED>
```

It may be more common for the Href attribute to be mapped to another name, one that is more intuitive for document authors unfamiliar with HTML conventions:

```
<!ATTLIST link
        xml-attributes   CDATA   #FIXED      "href target"
        target           CDATA   #REQUIRED>

<link target="X123">...</link>
```

When considering new names to be given to reserved attributes, it could be tempting to give them names such as 'xml-title' and 'xml-show', but names beginning 'xml', 'XML', 'Xml', and other combinations, are reserved for special purposes within the XML language.

Link value strategies

Apart from the usual constraints on the characters allowed in a name, a link-aware application will not be concerned with the characteristics of a unique identifier. It will only care that the name is valid and unique. However, document authors are usually required to generate identifiers for new objects, or refer to existing identifiers when creating a reference. The scheme chosen for assigning identifiers must be convenient to use.

One approach is to simply assign the next available sequential value. If the last object defined had an identifier of 'X-77776', then the next object will have an identifier of 'X-77777'. These identifier numbers may be assigned automatically by authoring or database software, but authors must look up target values from a list or perform a search when inserting references, and this can be a time-consuming, costly process.

A simpler technique that many HTML users will be familiar with is assigning the title, or an abbreviation of the title, to a locator:

```
<xref idref="#Summary">...</xref>
```

This approach is suitable for small documents (such as most Web pages), especially when distinctive titles are used in the document, though standards for abbreviating longer titles must obviously be established, or there will still be a need to check each reference against the target locator. For example, one scheme would dictate that the identifier should be built from the first five (legal) characters of the first word, a dash, then the first letter of each subsequent word, and all letters are folded to lower-case, so 'Contents List' becomes 'conte-l'. Duplicate names are still a danger using such a scheme. For example, 'Contemporary Life' would be coded in the same way as the example above.

For long, numbered documents, an abbreviated reference scheme may be considered. This scheme makes use of the navigation methods devised for printed output, such as 'see Chapter 7, Paragraph 12', but codifies this information, giving something like 'ch7pa12'. This approach allows for automatic genera-tion of resource identifier values, and document authors can deduce the target value from the reference text.

```
see <xref idref="#ch7pa12">Chapter 7, Paragraph 12</xref>
```

Naturally, the problem with this approach is that when new material is inserted into the document, the numbering of material beyond this point will often change. However, updating affecting identifiers and references is a task that can be automated.

13. Document formatting (XSL and XSLT)

This chapter describes XSL, a proposed style sheet standard, and XSLT, a proposed standard for transformation of XML structures, which together complement XML by describing how the content of an XML document should be arranged and formatted for presentation.

Warning: These are draft proposals that have not been ratified by the W^{3}C. Some details may have changed since the publication of this book, though recent drafts have become increasingly stable.

Concepts

XML documents are intended to be easily read by both people and software, but it is not expected that people interested in the material these documents contain will wish to see the tags. To publish information held in XML format, it is necessary to replace the tags with appropriate text styles. **XSL** (the *XML Stylesheet Language*) is being developed to meet this requirement, with the assistance of **XSLT** (the *XSL Transformation* standard).

An unofficial but widely recognized forum for discussing the implementation, use and future direction of XSL can be accessed by registering with major-domo@mulberrytech.com, including 'subscribe xsl-list' in the body of the message. An archive of past correspondence can be accessed from http://www.mulberrytech.com/xsl/xsl-list.

Style sheets

To present an XML document on paper or screen, the use of style sheets is almost essential. The content of an XML element, such as a Paragraph element, has no explicit style. A text editor will certainly present the text in a default font, but this setting is not retained when the document is passed to another application, such as a browser. Even were this not the case, a single style for all text is hardly acceptable in published material, where readers demand variety and helpful visual clues as to the structure of the information. To illustrate this point, consider the following example XML fragment:

```
<title>An example of style</title>
<intro><para>This example shows how important style is
to material intended to be read.</para></intro>
<para>This is a <em>normal</em> paragraph.</para>
<warning><para>Styles are important!</para></warning>
```

Apart from removal of the XML tags, the presented version below is not styled or formatted in any way:

An example of style This example shows how important style is to material intended to be read. This is a normal paragraph. Styles are important!

Using a style sheet, this XML fragment could be presented in the following format:

An example of style

This example shows how important
style is to material intended to be read.

This is a **normal** paragraph.

WARNING: Styles are important!

Web browsers that work with HTML do not need a style sheet to present a document, because the elements allowed in an HTML document are pre-defined, and their roles are well known. The browsers apply a default style to the content of each type of element. Nevertheless, a style sheet standard has been developed for use with HTML. The **CSS** language was developed in 1996 to give document authors more control over screen presentation (see Chapter 17 for details). Fortunately, this standard contains features that allow styles to be applied to elements beyond the HTML set, so it may also be used to style XML documents. Recent releases of the most popular Web browsers are able to use this language to format XML. However, CSS is a relatively weak language, despite some recent innovations. At the other extreme, **DSSSL** (the *Document Style Semantics and Specification Language*) has been developed over many years for use with SGML. It was finally released as an ISO standard in 1996, but due to its complexity there is still little software support. The XSL format was designed to fill a void between the simple CSS and complex DSSSL standards, and has features that are derived from both.

As explained above, the use of style sheets with XML documents is not an option, as it is with HTML. This could be seen as a weakness of the language, but there are several good reasons for using style sheets, regardless of this fact.

A single style sheet may be shared by a number of documents, so reducing the amount of effort needed to create large numbers of documents that need to be formatted in the same way. As the rules in a style sheet are targeted at specific elements, the style sheet is therefore closely associated with a DTD. Indeed, the DTD acts as a specification document for style sheet authors as it details every element that will be encountered, and every possible contextual arrangement of these elements.

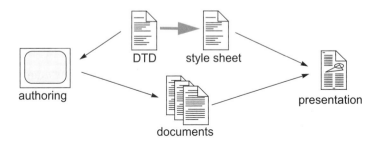

An XML document can be associated with more than one style sheet. In this way, without needing to edit the document itself, its contents can be styled in many different ways, customized to the needs of various target audiences and the characteristics of different media types. For example, an emphasized phrase may be printed using an italic style on paper, but, due to the current limitations of computer displays, may be styled in bold or in red on-screen. As another example, visually impaired people may wish to have the document presented in larger type, or in braille.

```
<title>This is a title</title>
<p>This paragraph contains
a <em>highlighted</em> term.</p>
```

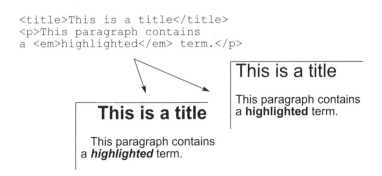

Styling with XSL

The XSL standard is really just a set of formatting objects, such as blocks, in-line objects and table cells, each having numerous properties that can be utilized to format the content in a professional way. In this first version of XSL, all the allowed formatting objects are rectangular. Text is said to 'flow' into these rectangular regions. For example, a Title element could be assigned to be a 'block' object, a Price element could be assigned to be a 'table cell' type, and an Emphasis element could be defined as an 'inline-sequence' type. Each flow object type has its own set of characteristics. For example, a 'block' object includes a characteristic to determine the size of the gap between the current block and the one above.

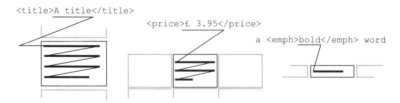

Being an abstract standard, XSL formatting instructions can take any number of concrete forms, but the most obvious form they can take is XML markup, with elements representing object types and attributes representing their characteristics. Indeed, a DTD has been specified in the standard for just this purpose. For obvious reasons, this is called the **Formatting Objects DTD**, or **FO DTD** for short. It includes elements such as 'block', and attributes such as 'text-align'. In a conforming document, these elements contain the text to be rendered in the given format.

```
<block text-align="centered">This is a normal,
centred paragraph.</block>
```

Transforming with XSLT

Most XSL processing engines should be able to accept an XML document that complies with the FO DTD, then interpret the instructions and format the content. However, it is not expected that documents will ever be authored to this DTD. Such an approach would obviously negate the entire philosophy of XML. Used in this way, XML would become just another typesetting language. XML documents should be self-describing, not self-formatting. Instead, source documents need to be converted into this form, using a transformation engine, which is where the companion XSLT standard plays its very important role. The new document should be considered to be a temporary file, to be deleted as soon as it has served its purpose in the process of publishing the document.

The XSLT standard describes a mechanism for manipulating source XML data into a form suitable for publishing. XSLT is able to:

- add prefix or suffix text to the content
- remove, create, reorder and sort elements
- reuse elements elsewhere in the document
- transform data from one XML format to another XML format, or to HTML
- specify the XSL formatting objects to be applied to each element class

An XSLT processor takes an existing XML document as input, and generates a new XML document as output. The output document can conform to a different DTD to the input, and this transformation is specified using a style sheet that conforms to the XSLT standard.

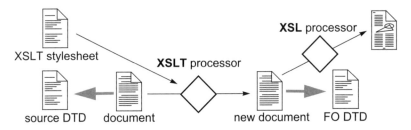

Transformations are performed in accordance with **template** rules embedded in the style sheet. Templates are matched to elements in the source document using Path expressions, as described in Chapter 11. The original element tags are removed in the process, and typically replaced with new 'output' tags.

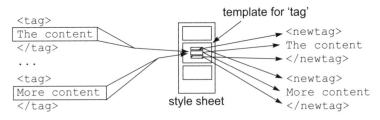

The following example shows a single rule, specifying that emphasized text should be presented in-line, styled in bold, according to the XSL standard, as described by the FO DTD:

```
                              An <emph>emphasized</emph> word.

<template match="emph">
   <fo:inline-sequence font-weight="bold">
      <apply-templates/>
   </fo:inline-sequence>
</template>                   An emphasized word.
```

Note the use of namespaces to distinguish XSLT transformation instructions from XSL formatting instructions, in this example using 'fo:' prefixes for the FO DTD elements. Namespaces are covered in detail in Chapter 8.

When documents are encoded in XML, it may be possible to omit information that never varies, which can be described as 'template' text. For example, if every paragraph that would normally begin with the word 'CAUTION' is tagged using a Caution element, there is no need actually to include this word each time a warning is tagged. Instead, it can be generated automatically when the content of the Caution element is presented. This approach reduces the size of the document and the effort involved in the data entry task, but also provides more options for presenting the material. For example, in one publication the word 'CAUTION' may be deemed redundant, as the text is to be presented in red, bold lettering. But when the prefix is needed, XSLT allows it to be added to the content automatically.

```
<caution>This is a caution</caution>
```

CAUTION: This is a caution ***

The order in which material is created may not always be the same order as it should be presented. The needs of authors and editors can be very different from those of the ultimate readers. In addition, information in documents aimed at different audiences may need to be omitted in some cases, or moved to a more (or less) prominent position in others. XSLT is able to omit material, and move information units to new locations in the document. It is also able to sort a list into alphabetical order, and even create new elements. In the following example, the summary is moved to the top, and the secret paragraph is omitted from presentation:

```
<para>This is the FIRST paragraph.</para>
<secret>Not everyone can read this.</secret>
<summary>This summary may appear first
in some cases.</summary>
```

This summary may appear first in some cases.
This is the FIRST paragraph.

Finally, when the XML philosophy has been applied rigorously, redundancy is avoided by omitting material that already appears elsewhere. For example, if a book review contains a number of keywords, marked-up within the review text, then it would be wasteful to repeat these keywords in another place, even if this would be useful for searching purposes, or to present to readers as a list. XSLT is able to locate and reuse information elsewhere in the document:

```
<book>
<review>This book covers <kw>XML</kw> and <kw>XSL</kw>,
as well as the <kw>CSS</kw> styling language.</review>
</book>
```

KEYWORDS: XML, XSL, CSS

This book covers **XML** and **XSL**, as well as the **CSS** styling language.

The ability to reuse and sort information can be very useful for building table-of-contents lists.

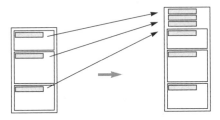

The same element may need to be presented differently, depending on its location in the document. For example, the content of a Paragraph element may be presented in larger text than normal if that instance of the element appears within an introduction section, or bolder if it occurs inside a Warning element. This concept leads to a potential problem concerning specificity. When a paragraph is detected in the document, more than one rule may be thought to apply to it. Perhaps there is a rule for paragraphs in general, and another rule for paragraphs within Warning elements. Some rules can also be given a higher priority than others. Much of the effort and skill needed to develop style sheets involves ensuring that the correct rule is used in each circumstance.

XSLT was previously just one part of the draft XSL standard, but has now been extracted into a separate standard of its own. The reason for this follows from a widespread belief that XSL was attempting to do two very different things, and that the first of these things – the manipulation of XML structures – while useful for reordering information, adding template text and building content lists, is also very useful for many non-publishing applications. Confusingly, the other half of the specification, which deals with identifying the format to apply to the text, retains the name XSL. Useful applications can now be developed that implement just the XSLT standard, with the expectation that the complementary formatting application, when needed at all, will be developed elsewhere. Of course, some publishing and browsing applications will implement both.

One implication of the separation of XSLT from XSL is that an XSLT document can still sometimes be considered to be a style sheet, even when it does not produce output that conforms to the FO DTD. Apart from XSL FO elements, the most obvious output format is HTML. Indeed, at least one of the popular Web browsers that claims to support XSL actually implements only the XSLT standard, and requires that the style sheet transform source documents into HTML format, as in the following example (which translates Para elements into HTML-conformant P elements):

```
<template match="para">
  <html:p><apply-templates/></html:p>
</template>
```

Selecting a style sheet

Choosing which style sheet file to use when presenting an XML document is a task that can be performed in any number of ways. A browser could simply allow the user to select from a list of all known style sheets, and a typesetting system may allow a style sheet to be specified prior to processing a number of similar documents. But one of the most obvious techniques is to include an appropriate instruction in the XML document itself. Alternatively, because there is an obvious relationship between a DTD and a style sheet (one defines the document structure rules that the other must apply appropriate styles for), the instruction could appear in the DTD instead. A standard format for such an instruction has been produced by the W³C. Version 1.0 of the '*Associating Style Sheets with XML documents*' standard was released in June, 1999, and can be found at http://www.w3.org/TR/xml-stylesheet.

An XML processing instruction is used for this purpose, and the target name for the style sheet processing instruction is '**xml-stylesheet**'. All rendering software should recognize and interpret a processing instruction with this target name:

```
<?xml-stylesheet ... ?>
```

This processing instruction must occur before the root element.

A number of parameters can be included in the processing instruction, and each one takes the same form as an attribute appearing in a start-tag. The 'attribute' names, and the values each may take, are the same as those defined in the HTML standard for attributes of the Link element. The Href and Type attributes locate and identify the style sheet, and specify the kind of style sheet by its MIME type, which in this case would be 'text/xsl':

```
<?xml-stylesheet href="mystyles.xsl" type="text/xsl" ?>
```

When a choice of style sheets is available, the processing instruction may be repeated. Each one should be given a suitable title so that a user could select the one they wish to apply from a menu. The default style sheet can be identified, as all the others would include an Alternative pseudo-attribute with a value of 'yes':

```
<?xml-stylesheet  href="mystyles.xsl"
                  type="text/xsl"
                  title="default" ?>
<?xml-stylesheet  href="myBIGstyles.xsl"
                  type="text/xsl"
                  title="bigger font"
                  alternative="yes" ?>
```

Another reason for including multiple references would be to associate style sheets conforming to other style sheet languages, such as CSS, so that a rendering engine can choose the one that it understands, or one that it provides the most support for:

```
<?xml-stylesheet  href="mystyles.xsl"
                  type="text/xsl"
                  title="default" ?>
<?xml-stylesheet  href="mystyles.css"
                  type="text/css"
                  title="default" ?>
```

XSLT

An XSLT style sheet is identified by the namespace http://www.w3.org/XSL/ Transform/1.0. This format is defined by a DTD in an appendix to the standard, which describes the 34 elements, and their attributes, which may be used to construct style sheets. Most of these elements are used only to support complex requirements, and it is often possible to build a useful style sheet using just three of them. The elements and attributes defined in the DTD are shown in the table below, sorted into alphabetical order:

Element	Attributes
apply-imports	*(none)*
apply-templates	select, mode
attribute	name, namespace, xml:space
attribute-set	name, use-attribute-sets
call-template	name
choose	xml:space
comment	xml:space
copy	xml:space, use-attribute-sets
copy-of	select
element	name, namespace, xml:space, use-attribute-sets
fallback	xml:space
for-each	select, xml:space
if	test, xml:space
import	href
include	href
key	name, match, use
locale	name, decimal-separator, grouping-separator, infinity, minus-sign, NaN, percent, per-mille, zero-digit, digit, pattern-separator

message	xml:space
number	level, count, from, format, lang, letter-value, grouping-separator, grouping-size, sequence-src
otherwise	xml:space
param	name, select
processing-instruction	name, xml:space
preserve-space	elements
sort	select, lang, data-type, order, case-order
strip-space	elements
stylesheet	result-ns, default-space, indent-result, id, xmlns:xsl*, xml:space, result-version, result-encoding, extension-element-prefixes
template	match, name, priority, mode, xml:space
text	*(none)*
transform	(*see* stylesheet)
value-of	select
variable	name, select
when	test, xml:space
with-param	name, select

* Note that the DTD defines the attribute 'xmlns:xsl' for use in declaring the namespace for XSLT elements. It may be necessary to add at least one more attribute, to declare the namespace for the output document, such as 'xmlns:fo' or 'xmlns:html'.

General structure

The root element is named **Stylesheet**. All embedded elements that form part of the XSLT standard must conform to this namespace.

```
<stylesheet xmlns="http://www.w3.org/XSL/Transform/1.0">
   ...
</stylesheet>
```

The element name **Transform** may be used as an alternative to Stylesheet:

```
<transform xmlns="http://www.w3.org/XSL/Transform/1.0">
   ...
</transform>
```

Note that, for the sake of clarity, examples in this book use the default namespace, so no prefixes appear on the XSLT elements. In the standard itself, the prefix 'xsl:' is used in the examples, but this is simply a matter of preference.

An XSLT style sheet may also contain elements that are not part of this standard, but are to be output to create the new document. These elements must conform to another namespace:

```
<stylesheet xmlns="http://www.w3.org/XSL/Transform/1.0"
            xmlns:X=".......">
   ...
   ... <X:my-element>...</X:my-element>...
</stylesheet>
```

The default action of any XSLT processor is to simply transform a document, in most cases producing an XML output file. However, in special cases, the processor may be capable of performing extra services. Specifically, it may be part of a larger application that is able to interpret the resulting document and format its contents for presentation. The **Result Namespace** attribute is used to identify the prefix that represents the namespace concerned:

```
<stylesheet  xmlns="http://www.w3.org/XSL/Transform/1.0"
             xmlns:X="......."
             result-ns="X">
```

When this prefix maps to the namespace http://www.w3.org/XSL/Format/1.0, then the processor is requested to interpret the output elements that conform to the XSL specification, and format the data accordingly. No output file is actually created.

The Stylesheet element may be embedded within a larger XML document. This can be appropriate when the style sheet only applies to the document containing it. The processing instruction used in the document to identify a style sheet simply refers to the embedded sheet, using an XPointer. The Stylesheet element must have an **Id** attribute for this to work:

```
<?xml-stylesheet type="text/xsl" href="#MyStyles" ?>
<X:book>
  <stylesheet id="MyStyles" ...>
     ...
  </stylesheet>
  ...
</X:book>
```

Anticipating that there will in future be more than one version of XML, the **Result Version** attribute can be used to specify which version of XML should be used for the output file. Similarly, the **Result Encoding** attribute can be used to specify a character set encoding scheme other than the input format:

```
<stylesheet ... result-version="2.0"
                result-encoding="ISO-8859-1" >
```

White space

When processing the source document, an XSLT processor creates a tree of nodes, including nodes for each text string in and between the markup tags. If the source document contains only white space characters between two markup constructs, a text node may be created. Alternatively, this white space may be discarded. In the following example, text nodes will (or will not) be created around the Para element. By default, all white space is preserved, but it is possible to remove the white space by setting the **Default Space** attribute on the Stylesheet element to 'strip'.

```
<book>  <para>A paragraph.</para>

</book>
```

From this starting-point, individual elements can be added to the (initially empty) list of white space preserving elements, using the **Preserve Space** element, and removed from the list using the **Strip Space** element. In both cases, the **Elements** attribute contains a list of space separated element names. In the following example, only the Pre and Poetry elements preserve white space:

```
<stylesheet ... default-space="strip">
  <preserve-space elements="pre poetry"/>
  ...
</stylesheet>
```

The **Indent Result** attribute can be used on the Stylesheet element to ensure that the output data file contains indents to reveal the hierarchical structure of the document

```
<stylesheet ... indent-result="yes">

<!-- OUTPUT -->
<book>
  <title>The Title</title>
  <chapter>
    <title>The Chapter Title</title>
    <para>The only paragraph.</para>
  </chapter>
</book>
```

The default value is 'no':

```
<stylesheet ... indent-result="no">

<!-- OUTPUT -->
<book>
<title>The Title</title>
<chapter>
<title>The Chapter Title</title>
<para>The only paragraph.</para>
</chapter>
</book>
```

When the XSLT processor reads the style sheet, ignorable white space is stripped from all elements, except from within the **Text** element. This element is used to ensure that white space is not removed, as in the following example, where a single space must be preserved between the presentation of an attribute value, and the presentation of the content of the element (the other elements are explained later):

```
<value-of select="@security"/>
  <text> </text>
  <apply-templates/>
```

Templates

The body of the style sheet consists of at least one transformation rule, as represented by the **Template** element:

```
<template ... >
  ...
</template>
```

In practice, a style sheet would normally contain a great many rules, each one defining the transformation to be applied to a specific element in the source document, using the **Match** attribute. The following example demonstrates two rules: one for all Para elements, and one for Emphasis elements:

```
<template match="para">
  ...
</template>
<template match="emph">
  ...
</template>
```

Those familiar with CSS rules will recognize that this is equivalent to 'para {...}' and 'emph {...}'.

Sometimes, the content of an element may need to be formatted differently, depending on its context. More specific rules can be defined using the XPath scheme described in Chapter 11. For example, to specify a format for paragraphs that are directly contained within a Warning element, the following would apply:

```
<template match="warning/para">
  ...
</template>
```

Those familiar with CSS2 rules will recognize that this construct is equivalent to 'warning > para {...}'.

Imports and inclusions

Multiple style sheets may share some definitions. To avoid unnecessary repetition, common sets of rules may be placed in a separate style sheet, and referenced from other style sheet files:

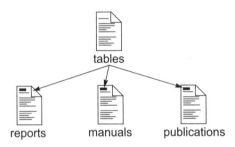

Sets of rules can be imported using the **Import** element. This element may be used repeatedly, to import a number of other resources. They must all occur before the style rules. This element has an **Href** attribute that identifies a file to import by its URL:

```
<stylesheet ...>
  <import href="tables.xsl">
  <import href="colours.xsl">
  <template ...>...</template>
```

Imported rules are not considered to be as important as other rules, which can affect selection of a rule when conflicts occur. See below for more details on this issue.

Rules in other files can also be inserted. This is a similar concept to importing, except that the **Include** element can be used anywhere (after the Import elements), and included rules are not considered to be less important than other rules. It also uses an **Href** attribute to locate the file to be included:

```
<include href="...">...</include>
```

Priorities

When an XSLT processor attempts to find a matching rule for an element in the source document, it may find more than one that matches. For example, a paragraph in a Warning element would match both of the rules shown above ('para' and 'warning/para'). In fact, the more specific rule is chosen, as it is assumed that this is more appropriate.

Each rule is actually given a priority value. Rules that simply name an element have a priority value of '0'. Rules that are more specific than this have a priority value of '0.5'. Less specific rules have a value of '-0.5'. This includes the wildcard, '*', and such general functions as 'text()' or 'processing-instruction()'.

When more than one complex rule still matches the current element, it is necessary to explicitly give one rule a higher priority than the others, using the **Priority** attribute. For example, it may be appropriate to specify that a paragraph in a Warning element is more specific than one in a Chapter element, if all warning paragraphs (whether within a chapter or not) are to be formatted in the same way:

```
<template match="chapter//para"> <!-- priority = 1 -->
  ...
</template>
<template match="warning//para" priority="2">
  ...
</template>
```

If the Priority attribute is not used, or not used correctly, an XSLT processor may still detect multiple complex rules for a given element. In this case, it should report an error, but may choose to simply select the last rule it detects (the rule nearest the end of the file).

This mechanism is not needed to cater for conflicts between rules in the main style sheet, and other rules in an imported file. Imported rules are considered to be less important. In addition, rules in one imported file are considered to be less important than rules in another that is imported later.

Recursive processing

Typically, it is necessary to process all elements in a document, starting with the root element, then working through its children, but processing the descendants of each child before proceeding to the next (in the same manner as shown for linear processing of a DOM tree, as discussed in Chapter 15). In XSLT, this does not happen automatically. It is necessary to do two things. First, the **Apply Templates** element must be used to indicate that children of the current element are to be processed. In the example below, the Emphasis element rule is only triggered if the Paragraph rule contains this instruction, and the text within the Emphasis element is only processed (presented) if the same instruction is included:

```
<para>An <emph>emphasized</emph> word.</para>
<template match="para">
  <apply-templates/>
</template>
<template match="emph">
  <apply-templates/>
</template>
```

However, this is not sufficient on its own. The problem that remains occurs when some elements do not require specific formatting, so no rule is supplied for them. If such objects contain other elements that do require formatting, these embedded objects will not be processed. For example, if an Animal element existed within the paragraph, and there was no rule for this element, but it could contain the Emphasis element, then the emphasized text would not be formatted:

```
<para>A <animal><emph>Giraffe</emph></animal> is
an animal.</para>
```

To eliminate this problem, a rule is needed to act as a catch-all, representing the elements not covered by explicit formatting rules. All XSLT processors should include an implied rule that acts as if the following rule were present. Following the XPath standard conventions, this rule uses the wildcard operator, '*', to represent any element, and '/' to represent the root of the document.

```
<template match="/|*">
  <apply-templates/>
</template>
```

Although this is an implied rule, it can also be included explicitly, so that its default action can be modified. For example, the Apply Templates element could be removed, in which case the content of elements that do not have an associated rule will not be processed.

Similarly, a built-in rule is needed to present the text content of every element. This rule uses the 'text()' function to achieve this (the content of this template is explained later):

```
<template match="text()">
  <value-of select="."/>
</template>
```

Note that comments and processing instructions are, by default, not processed. Explicit rules similar to the one above, but using the 'processing-instruction()' or 'comment()' functions, must be included to process these items.

Selective processing

The Apply Templates element can take a **Select** attribute, which overrides the default action of processing all children. Using XPath patterns, it is possible to select specific children, and ignore the rest. In the following example, the rule targets only Name elements with a Type attribute value of 'company':

```
<template match="names">
  <apply-templates select="name[@type='company']"/>
</template>
```

It is also possible to select elements that are located elsewhere in the document. The '..' operator is used to select the parent, and the '/' operation at the beginning of an expression selects the whole document, from where it is possible to zero in on the required information. The following example inserts chapter titles into the introduction of a book:

```
<template match="intro">
  <apply-templates select="//chapter/title"/>
</template>
```

When the Select attribute is not present, it is implied, having the value of 'node()' to represent all children of the current element.

The Apply Templates element can be used more than once in a template. In the following example, chapter titles are inserted into the introduction, but after the content of the Introduction element itself:

```
<template match="intro">
  <apply-templates/>
  <apply-templates select="//chapter/title"/>
</template>
```

Output formats

In the examples above, the content of each element in the source document is identified and processed, but no actual formatting is applied. Furthermore, the element tags from the source document are discarded in this process. Yet an XSLT transformation tool is expected to write out a new XML document, possibly using the FO elements described later, or possibly using HTML elements to format the content for Web browser display. One way to do this is simply to insert the appropriate elements into the templates. For example, to enclose the content of a Paragraph element in HTML P elements, the following would apply:

```
<template match="para">
  <html:p><apply-templates/></html:p>
</template>
```

This is an interesting approach that has both strengths and weaknesses. One of the major weaknesses concerns the building of an XSLT DTD for guided authoring and validation, and is discussed later. The other major problem is that the style sheet must, of course, be a properly well-formed XML document, so it is not possible to alter the hierarchical structure from that in the source document. For example, if the source document contained a list of Firstname and Secondname elements, not directly enclosed by an element that represents each whole name, but in the output document an enclosing element *was* needed, it would not be possible to do the following:

```
<!-- ERROR (overlapping structures) -->
<template match="firstname">
  <html:p><apply-templates/>
</template>
<template match="lastname">
  <apply-templates/></html:p>
</template>
```

However, this approach ensures that the output document will be well-formed, as a side effect of the whole style sheet needing to be well-formed.

Comments and processing instructions can be inserted into the output document using the **Comment** and **Processing Instruction** elements. The Comment element simply contains the text to be output in an XML comment tag. The Processing Instruction element also has a **Name** attribute, which is used to hold the target application name for the processing instruction:

```
<template match="book">
  <processing-instruction name="ACME">
   INSERT_TOC
  </processing-instruction>
  <comment>This is the HTML version</comment>
   <html:body><apply-templates/></html:body>
</template>
```

```
    <?ACME INSERT_TOC?>
    <!--This is the HTML version-->
    <body>...</body>
```

Prefix and suffix text

A template is also able to contain text that needs to be added to the content of the given element. If this text appears before the Apply Templates element, it becomes a prefix to the content. If this text appears after the Apply Templates element, it becomes a suffix. The following example inserts the prefix 'NOTE:' and suffix ']' around the content of a Note element:

```
<template match="para">
  <html:p>NOTE: <apply-templates/> ]</html:p>
</template>
```

Sorting elements

When the source document contains a list of items that are not arranged in alphabetic order, it is possible to ensure that these items are sorted in the output document. The **Sort** element is used within the Apply Templates element to sort the elements it selects:

```
<list>
  <item>ZZZ</item>
  <item>MMM</item>
  <item>AAA</item>
</list>

<template match="list">
  <apply-templates><sort/></apply-templates>
</template>
```

Note that, contrary to the impression given by earlier examples, the Apply Templates element is not really an empty element, and further scenarios covered later also require this element to be present as a container element.

In the simple default form shown above, the sort key is simply the content of the child elements. The item 'AAA' will appear first in the output document. By adding a **Select** attribute to the Sort element, it is possibly to be more explicit. For example, the Item elements may contain an attribute which is to serve as the sort key:

```
<list>
  <item sortcode="Z">...</item>
  <item sortcode="M">...</item>
  <item sortcode="A">...</item>
</list>

<sort select="@sortcode"/>
```

It is even possible to add more sort keys by using more Sort elements. The second occurrence of the Sort element indicates a sub-key. For example, a list of names may need to be sorted first by surname, then, within each surname group, by first name as well:

```
<template...>
  <sort select="second-name"/>
  <sort select="first-name"/>
</template>
```

Sorting order is also affected by the optional **Order** attribute, which takes a value of '**ascending**' (the default) or '**descending**', and possibly also by the **Lang** attribute, which identifies the language of the text. In addition, the **Data Type** attribute, which has a default value of 'text', can be given a value of 'number', which specifies that the items should be sorted by numeric value. For example, in text '12' would appear before '7', because the first digit has a lower ASCII value, but in number mode '7' is obviously a smaller value than '12', so appears first. Finally, the **Case Order** attribute specifies whether 'a' appears before 'A' ('**lower-first**') or the other way around ('**upper-first**').

Automatic numbering

In many XML documents, list items are not physically numbered in the text, making it easy to insert, move or delete items without having to edit all the other items. In such circumstances, the style sheet must add the required numbering. In the simplest case, a list of item numbers is added by inserting the **Number** element at the appropriate position relative to the content:

```
<template match="item">
  <number/><apply-templates/>
</template>
```

In this simple case, each Item element is assigned a number based on its sequential position amongst other elements of the same name. Elements of different types are ignored, and numbering restarts within each parent element (in this case, within each list). This default action is equivalent to using the **Level** attribute, with a value of '**single**' (this is single level numbering). Explicitly changing this value to '**any**' dictates that numbering does not reset, so the items in each list simply continue one large sequence, throughout the entire document.

More complex numbering is made possible by allowing a value of '**multiple**' in the Level attribute. This option indicates that the number will consist of several parts, possibly separated by punctuation. The **Format** attribute is used to indicate the type of numbering to use at each level, and the punctuation that appears between levels. For example, '1. A.' indicates numbering of the larger items using digits, and the second level items using letters, with full-point characters after each part. The token 'A' represents alphabetic ordering, with 'AA', 'AB', 'AC' following 'Z'. The token 'a' represents the lower-case equivalent. Leading zeros in a numeric token add the given amount of padding to each value. For example, '001' indicates a sequence of '001' ... '002' ... '099' ... '100' ... '101'. Upper- and lower-case roman numerals are represented by the tokens 'I' and 'i' respectively.

The **Count** attribute is used to list the elements that are to be included in the multi-part count, with vertical bars separating the element names (and the current element does not have to be one of them, as demonstrated in the example below).

Putting all this together, it is possible to number the title of a section (using a letter) in such a way that it also includes the number of the chapter (using a digit) that it is in:

```
<chapter>
  <section>
  <title>First section of Chapter One</title>
```

```
<template match="section/title">
  <number level="multi"
          count="chapter|section"
          format="1.A"/>
  <apply-templates/>
</template>
```

1.A First section of Chapter One

2.C Third section of Chapter Two

The **From** attribute is used to specify an element from which numbering must start, and is particularly useful with Level values of 'any'. In the following example, all Table elements are numbered sequentially within each chapter, regardless of how many other structures surround any particular table:

```
<template match="table">
  <number level="any" from="chapter"/> <apply-templates/>
</template>
```

In large numbers, groups of digits are often separated using a comma or full point character. The **Grouping Separator** attribute specifies which symbol to insert between groups, such as ',', and the **Grouping Size** attribute indicates how many digits to place in each group (and is typically set to '3').

```
<number ... grouping-separator=","
            grouping-size="3"
            format="1"/>
```

999,999 Large item
1,000,000 Even larger item

In some languages, there is more than one means to create a sequence that does not use digits. In English, this applies with the alphabetic sequence 'a, b, c, d' and roman numerals 'i, ii, iii, iv'. In English, it is easy to distinguish between these sequences as they start with a different letter, 'a' and 'i' (or 'A' and 'I'), but in some languages this may not be the case. To assist with this distinction, the **Letter Value** attribute can be used. It takes a value of 'alphabetic' ('a, b, c' in English) or 'other' ('i, ii, iii, iv') in English. The following example selects a Greek character sequence, but ensures that the sequence uses 'classical' Greek characters:

```
<number format="&#x03B1"
        letter-sequence="other" />
```

When numbering elements that are also sorted, the numbering is applied first, so, using the techniques described above, the numbers will not be in sequence in the final document. In some cases, this may be the desired result, but in other cases it will be necessary to sequentially number the elements in their final order. This can be achieved using the **Value** attribute, which calculates the number from the expression it holds. The most obvious use of this attribute is to hold the 'position()' function, which returns the sequential position of the element:

```
<number value="position()" format="1)" />
```

Modes

An earlier example showed how to copy chapter titles for reuse in a table of contents. However, the same templates would be activated, so the style of the title text would be the same in both locations. If they are to be presented in 18pt Arial at the top of each chapter, they will appear in the same style in the table of contents. This may be the desired result, but typically information that is copied and reused elsewhere must also be styled in a different way (the chapter titles in this book are not as large in the table of contents as they are at the top of each chapter). This can be achieved using modes to define templates for use in different circumstances.

The **Mode** attribute is added to the Template element. In the Apply Templates element, it is also used, but this time to select a template only from those that have a matching mode name. Taking the title example, there should be two rules for styling the Title element. This implies the need for two modes. All the examples above used the default mode, which does not require specific identification, but a second mode requires a unique name to identify it. In this case, chapter titles are normally translated into HTML H1 elements (large headings), but when reused in the Introduction element, are rendered in H3 elements (smaller headings):

```
<template match="intro">
  <apply-templates
          select="//chapter/title" mode="TOC" />
</template>

<template match="chapter/title">
  <html:h1><apply-templates/></html:h1>
</template>

<template match="chapter/title" mode="TOC">
  <html:h3><apply-templates/></html:h3>
</template>
```

Variables and templates

A style sheet often contains a number of templates that produce output that is identical, or very similar, and XSLT includes some mechanisms for avoiding such redundancy.

Variables may be declared and used in the style sheet, using the **Variable** element. The name of the variable is given in the **Name** attribute, and the value of the variable is the content of the element. The following example creates a variable called 'Colour', and gives it the value 'red':

```
<variable name="Colour">red</variable>
```

Alternatively, the value can be generated from an expression in the **Select** attribute.

The variable is used by inserting a variable reference into an attribute. A variable reference is identified by a leading '$' symbol.

In order to insert the value into output text, the variable must be placed in the **Select** attribute of the **Value Of** element:

```
<html:h1>The colour is
        <xsl:value-of select="$Colour"/>.</html:h1>
```

The colour is **red**.

A variable can also be used in output elements. In the following example, a variable is used to specify the border width. However, note that in this case it is necessary to enclose the variable in curly brackets, '{' and '}', which signify a text expression. Without the brackets, the variable will not be recognized:

```
<variable name="Border">3pt</variable>
...
...<fo:block border-width="{$Border}">...
```

The brackets shown above actually indicate a string expression. In order to use curly brackets as normal in an attribute value, they must be escaped by repeating the character. '{{' represents '{' and '}}' represents '}'. As shown above, string expressions may include variable references, but in addition they may contain literal text, enclosed by quotes, and XPath expressions.

When the same formatting is required in a number of places, it is possible to simply reuse the same template. Instead of a Match attribute, a **Name** attribute is used to give the template a unique identifier. Elsewhere, within other templates, the **Call Template** element is used to activate the named template, also using a **Name** attribute to identify the template required:

```
<template name="CreateHeader">
  <html:hr />
  <html:h2>***** <apply-templates/> *****</html:h2>
  <html:hr />
</template>

<template match="title">
  <call-template name="CreateHeader" />
</template>

<template match="head">
  <call-template name="CreateHeader" />
</template>
```

Such a mechanism is even more useful when the action performed by the named template can be modified, by passing parameters to it that override default values. To assist with this, a special type of variable can be used. The **Parameter** element defines a variable, using the **Name** attribute to assign it a name, but differs from other variables in that the element content is only the default value:

```
<param name="Prefix">%%%</param>
```

The default value can be overridden by a parameter value. Parameters can be passed to a named template by use of the **With Parameter** element, which names the parameter in its **Name** attribute, and gives the parameter a value in its content (or its Select attribute expression):

```
<with-param name="SecurityLvl">3</with-param>
```

The With Parameter element is placed within the **Call Template** element in order to pass the parameter name and value to the template that is being called:

```
<call-template name="CreateHeader">
  <with-param name="Prefix">%%%</with-param>
  <with-param name="SecurityLvl">3</with-param>
</call-template>
```

The following example shows that the named template holds the default values for these parameters, how these parameters are used, and what is presented if the parameters shown above are passed to the template:

```
<template name="CreateHeader">
  <param name="Prefix">*****</param>
  <param name="SecurityLvl">0</param>
  <html:hr />
  <html:h2>
    <value-of select="$Prefix"/>
    Security = <value-of select="$SecurityLvl" />-
    <apply-templates/>
    *****</html:h2>
  <html:hr />
</template>
```

> %%%Security = 3-The Header To Present *****

Displaying and reusing attribute values

Attribute values in the source document may be copied to appropriate attributes in the output document, and may also be inserted into element content for display, using the **Value Of** element introduced above. Attributes are identified by the '@' prefix.

To simply copy the value into an output attribute, a string expression is used. The following example shows how to copy a name from the Fullname element, containing a First and Second attribute, into a Person element that just contains a single Name attribute:

```
        <full-name first="John" second="Smith"/>

<template match="full-name">
  <X:person name="{@first} {@second}"/>
</template>

        <person name="John Smith"/>
```

To copy the value into element content text, the Value Of element is needed:

```
        <full-name first="John" second="Smith"/>

<template match="full-name">
  <X:person>
    <value-of select="@first"/>
    <value-of select="@second"/> -
    <apply-templates/>
  </X:person>
</template>

        <person>John Smith - ... </person>
```

Creating and copying elements

An element can be created in the output document using the **Element** element, with the element name specified using the **Name** attribute, and an optional namespace specified using the **Namespace** attribute. At first, there appears to be little point to this, as the following two examples are equivalent, and the first is easier to create and understand:

```
<template match="third-header-level">
  <html:h3>
    <apply-templates/>
  </html:h3>
</template>

<template match="third-header-level">
  <element namespace="html" name="h3">
    <apply-templates/>
  </element>
</template>
```

However, the key to using this construct is the Name attribute, which can take an expression instead of just a pre-defined name. In this way, the name of the element can be modified by use of a variable. For example, a parameter passed to a named template may specify the header level to output in an HTML document. The named template below by default creates an H3 element, but a parameter passed to it may change this, perhaps to an H5 element:

```
<template name="CreateHeader">
  <param-variable name="HeaderLvl">3</param-variable>
  <element namespace="html" name="h{$HeaderLvl}">
    <apply-templates/>
  </element>
</template>
```

```
<h3>the default header</h3>
```

Elements can also be created that are copies of the source element, using the
Copy element. This element is simply replaced by the original element that
triggered this template. For example, to add a prefix to all HTML header elements, the following template would suffice:

```
<template match="h1|h2|h3|h4|h5|h6|h7">
  <copy>
    Header: <apply-templates/>
  </copy>
</template>
```

Note that original attributes are not preserved when the Copy element is used,
but a solution to this problem is outlined below.

In order to attach attributes to elements created (perhaps using the Element
or Copy element), the **Attribute** element can be used. This element takes a
Name attribute to hold the name of the attribute to be created, and optionally
a **Namespace** attribute to hold the namespace prefix. The content of this element is the attribute value. In the following example, a Style attribute is added
to the headers:

```
<template match="h1|h2|h3|h4|h5|h6|h7">
  <copy>
    <attribute name="style">color: red</attribute>
    Header: <apply-templates/>
  </copy>
</template>
```

As noted above, the Copy Of element does not preserve original attributes. It
is possible to resurrect source attributes using the Attribute element along
with the Value Of element, which is used to select and insert the original value
of the attribute:

```
<attribute name="style">
  <value-of select="@style"/>
</attribute>
```

Sets of attributes can be defined within the **Attribute Set** element, which is
given a name using the **Name** attribute. These sets can be used in various
places, using the **Use Attribute Set** attribute:

```
<attribute-set name="class-and-colour">
    <attribute name="style">color:red</attribute>
    <attribute name="class">standard</attribute>
</attribute-set>

<template match="h1|h2|h3|h4|h5|h6|h7">
  <copy use-attribute-sets name="class-and-color" />
    Header: <apply-templates/>
  </copy>
</template>
```

Note that this attribute can also be used on the Element element, and on the Attribute Set element itself (to merge sets).

Source document elements can also be selected and copied out to the destination document using the **Copy Of** element, which uses a **Select** attribute to identify the document fragment or set of elements to be reproduced at the current position. The elements that match the selection criteria are not processed against the templates. All descendant elements and attributes are retained, unlike using the Copy element described above. For example, if the source document contains numerous H1 and H2 header elements, it would be possible to reproduce them at the start of an HTML output document as follows:

```
<template match="body">
  <body>
    <copy-of select="//h1 | //h2" />
    <apply-templates/>
  </body>
</template>

      <body>
        <h1 id="intro">Introduction</h1>
        <h2>Secondary header</h2>
        <h1>Main Text</h1>
        ...
      </body>
```

This technique can also be used to copy the current element to the output, while retaining its attributes and contents. An earlier example demonstrated adding a prefix to a header. This example can be reformulated, replacing the Copy and Apply Templates elements with the Copy Of element. All attributes are taken care of, but elements embedded within the headers will not be styled:

```
<template match="h1|h2|h3|h4|h5|h6|h7">
  <html:p>Header:</html:p>
  <copy-of select="."/>
</template>
```

Repeating structures

When creating tabular output from source elements, or some other very regular structure, a technique is available that reduces the number of templates needed significantly, and in so doing improves the clarity of the style sheet. For example, consider the need to transform the following structure into a tabular format:

```
<countries>
  <country>
    <name>United Kingdom</name>
    <capital>london</capital>
  </country>
  <country>
    <name>United States</name>
    <capital>Washington</capital>
```

```
    <borders>Canada</borders>
    <borders>Mexico</borders>
  </country>
</countries>
```

To create an HTML table for this data, with one row for each country, the following four templates would normally be needed:

```
<template match="countries">
  <html:table><apply-templates/></html:table>
</template>
<template match="country">
  <html:tr><apply-templates/></html:tr>
</template>
<template match="name">
  <html:th><apply-templates/></html:th>
</template>
<template match="capital | borders">
  <html:td><apply-templates/></html:td>
</template>
```

This would require some study to deduce the exact nature of the conversion to be applied. To clarify this example, the output would be as follows:

```
<!-- OUTPUT -->
<table>
  <tr><th>United Kingdom</th>
      <td>London</td>
  </tr>
  <tr><th>United States</th>
      <td>Washington</td>
      <td>Canada</td>
      <td>Mexico</td>
  </tr>
</table>
```

Using the **For Each** element, a single template can be used instead. The **Select** attribute applies the enclosed template to each occurrence of the matching element. This mechanism is particularly useful when there are multiple levels of structures, as in the variable number of bordering countries in this example:

```
<template match="countries">
  <html:table>
  <for-each select="country">
    <html:tr>
    <html:th><apply-templates select="name"/></html:th>
    <html:td><apply-templates select="capital"/>
    </html:td>
    <for-each select="borders">
      <html:td><apply-templates/></html:td>
    </for-each>
    </html:tr>
  </for-each>
  </html:table>
</template>
```

Conditions

When a template transforms a source document element into formatted output, it is possible to vary the output depending on certain conditions. In the simplest case, some part of the formatting can be optional, and only instantiated when a specific condition is true. The **If** element encloses the optional formatting instructions, and uses a **Test** attribute to check the condition. This feature can be used to reduce the number of templates needed. For example, if alternating paragraphs are to be coloured differently, the first template below produces the same effect as the following two. Note that, to keep the example well-formed, it is necessary to specify the HTML open tag once, then use the Attribute element to add an appropriate attribute value to this element (the attribute is not added to the If element, but to the nearest output element, which in this case is the P element):

```
<template match="para">
  <html:p>
    <if test="position() mod 2 = 0">
      <attribute name="style">color: red</attribute>
    </if>
    <if test="not(position() mod 2 = 0)">
      <attribute name="style">color: blue</attribute>
    </if>
    <apply-templates/>
  </html:p>
</template>

<!-- VERBOSE ALTERNATIVE -->
<template match="para[position() mod 2 = 0]">
  <html:p style="color: red">
    <apply-templates/>
  </html:p>
</template>
<template match="para[not(position() mod 2 = 0)]">
  <html:p style="color: blue">
    <apply-templates/>
  </html:p>
</template>
```

The saving can be more significant in some cases, as in the following example, where an attribute can take a number of different values, each one producing a different format:

```
<p type="normal">A normal paragraph</p>
<p type="secret">A secret paragraph</p>
<p type="optional">An optional paragraph</p>
```

```
<template match="para">
  <html:p>
  <if test="@type='normal'">
    <attribute name="style">color: black</attribute>
  </if>
  <if test="@type='secret'">
    <attribute name="style">color: red</attribute>
  </if>
  <if test="@type='optional'">
    <attribute name="style">color: green</attribute>
  </if>
  ...
  <apply-templates/></html:p>
</template>
```

```
<!-- OUTPUT -->
<p style="color: black">A normal paragraph</p>
<p style="color: red">A secret paragraph</p>
<p style="color: green">An optional paragraph</p>
```

However, this technique can still be quite clumsy. It does not prevent two or more tests from succeeding, and does not provide a catch-all condition in case all others fail. The **Choose** element solves both these problems. It contains **When** elements for each case, and an **Otherwise** element that is activated when none of the explicit cases apply. The When element has a **Test** attribute, which works as described for the If element:

```
<template match="para">
  <html:p>
  <choose>
    <when test="@type='normal'">
      <attribute name="style">color:black</attribute>
    </when>
    <when test="@type='secret'">
      <attribute name="style">color:red</attribute>
    </when>
    <when test="@type='optional'">
      <attribute name="style">color:green</attribute>
    </when>
    <otherwise>
      <attribute name="style">color:yellow</attribute>
    </otherwise>
    ...
  </choose>
  <apply-templates/>
  </html:p>
</template>
```

Local number formats

The 'format-number()' function takes three parameters. The first is the number to format. The second is a string that specifies how to format this number. The third is a string that gives location specific formatting details. The formatting specification (the second parameter) is interpreted in different ways, depending on the language and country conventions, as given by the third parameter 'locale', but in general specifies how to format a number according to a template pattern. For example, a pattern of '00.00' specifies two digits before and after the decimal point. The specification for this pattern has been borrowed from Java. For full documentation, see http://www.sun.com/products/jdk/1.1/docs/java.text.DecimalFormat-Symbols.html.

A locale can be defined in an XSLT style sheet using the **Locale** element. The **Name** attribute gives the locale a name, for reference from the 'format-number()' function. The **Decimal Separator** attribute defines the character to use as the separator in decimal numbers, and the **Grouping Separator** attribute defines the character to use between groups of digits:

```
<locale  name="UK" decimal-separator="."
                   grouping-separator="," />
    99,999.123
```

A number of other attributes are used to specify how characters are interpreted in a number format expression.

Keys

The XML linking system, using the ID and IDREF special attribute types, is quite limited. First, without a DTD it is not possible to identify these attributes. Second, there is only one set of identifiers, which means that every identifier in the document must be unique. Third, the name of the identifier must conform to the constraints of XML names, and in particular spaces are not allowed in the identifier. Fourth, an element can have only one identifier. Fifth, the identifier must take the form of an attribute value. An alternative scheme can avoid all these limitations.

XSLT allows keys to be defined and associated with particular elements. Every key has a name, a value, and a node to which it is associated. A set of keys are defined using the **Key** element:

```
<key ... />
```

The **Name** attribute provides a name for a set of identifiers. When only one set is needed, a name such as 'global' may be considered. The **Match** attribute specifies the elements to be included in this set of identifiers, using an XPath pattern. For a global set, this would be '*' (representing all elements). Finally, the **Use** attribute is an XPath expression that identifies the location of the identifier values. If the identifier is in an attribute called 'id', then the expression would be '@id':

```
<key name="global" match="*" use="@id" />

<book id="book">
  <chapter id="chap1">...</chapter>
  <chapter id="chap2">...</chapter>
</book>
```

The following example creates a set of keys specifically for Name elements, where the unique key values are taken from the content of the embedded Employee Number elements. Note that the values in this example would not be valid XML ID names, as they begin with digits and have spaces in them:

```
<key name="nameKeys"
     match="name"
     use="employnum/text()" />

<name>
  <first>John</first><second>Smith</second>
  <employnum>12345 X12</employnum>
</name>
<name>
  <first>Peter</first><second>Jones</second>
  <employnum>18887 X12</employnum>
</name>
```

A new function called 'key()' has been added to those provided by XPath. It works in similar fashion to the 'id()' function, but this function takes two parameters; the first parameter identifies a key set to use, such as 'global' or 'names', and the second may be the value to locate:

```
key("global", "chap2")/para[3]

key("names", "18887 X12")/first
```

Of course, it is possible to create equivalent expressions that do not rely upon this feature, as the following examples demonstrate. However, it is expected that processing will be much more efficient when keys are used, as the processor can create a list of key values in advance of template processing:

```
chapter[id="chap2"]/para[3]

name[employnum="18887 X12"]/first
```

Messages

The style sheet may pass a message to the XSLT processor, which should provide some means to further pass this message on to the user, perhaps in a pop-up window, or as output to the command line. The **Message** element contains the XML fragment to be displayed. The standard does not say what restrictions should apply to this fragment in order to guarantee that the processor can interpret it. The safest option is to enter only text. This element cannot be used at the top level of the style sheet, but only within templates and other structures. Its most obvious purpose is to assist with debugging:

```
<template match="weird-element">
  <message>The WEIRD element has occurred</message>
  <html:p><apply-templates/></html:p>
</template>
```

Style sheet DTD issues

In theory, one of the most obvious benefits of using the XML data format for XSLT style sheets is that an XML editor can be used to assist in the construction of a style sheet. Such editors can prevent errors from occurring in the markup, ensure that the style sheet conforms to the constraints of the XSLT standard, and help the author by indicating which elements and attributes are available in any context. However, these editors need a DTD to do these things, and this requirement raises one or two issues.

As a starting-point, the XSLT standard includes a DTD that defines the XSLT elements and attributes. But this DTD alone may not be sufficient. The fact that XSLT markup can be mixed with output markup means that a DTD may need to be defined that includes both sets of elements.

For example, a style sheet that specifies FO output would be different to one, even for the same data source, that specifies HTML output, and the DTDs should differ accordingly. For this reason, the XSLT DTD includes a parameter entity, called **Result-Elements**, which must be defined as required. The following examples illustrate different definitions for this entity:

```
<!ENTITY % result-elements "fo:block |
                            fo:inline-sequence | ... ">
<!ENTITY % result-elements "html:p | html:emph | ... ">
```

The DTD must, of course, also contain the definitions for the elements concerned. While the draft XSL specification includes a DTD for FO elements, unfortunately it does not accurately describe the attributes allowed on each element (instead, it includes only attributes that represent properties that apply to the object, not those that can be used to set inherited properties).

For example, the Inline Sequence element only contains an Id attribute, yet in reality is used to specify a number of inherited properties, so needs to be able to include such attributes as FontWeight. Hopefully, the final standard will include a DTD that can be merged with the XSLT DTD to provide a single DTD for creation of FO-based style sheets.

However, this problem can be avoided entirely, by using the Element and Attribute elements throughout the style sheet. In this scenario, the XSLT DTD is sufficient for all needs. However, the style sheets will be harder to read. The second example below is not as easy to interepret as the first:

```
<template match="book">
  <html:html>
    <html:head>
      <html:title>The Document</html:title>
    </html:head>
    <html:body style="color:blue">
      <apply-templates/>
    </html:body>
  </html:html>
</template>


<template match="book">
  <element name="html" ns="html">
    <element name="head" ns="html">
      <element name="title" ns="html">
       The Document
      </element>
    </element>
    <element name="body" ns="html">
      <attribute name="style">color:blue</attribute>
      <apply-templates/>
    </element>
  </element>
</template>
```

XSL

The XSL standard defines a number of formatting objects, such as 'block', 'table-cell' and 'display-graphic', and a number of formatting properties, such as 'border-color', 'table-width' and 'font-size'. Note that Chapter 20 includes two tables, one listing all the formatting objects, and one listing all the properties.

Representation format

The objects and properties described below have an abstract existence, and need to take some concrete form in order to be used. XML is, of course, an ideal data format for holding both the text content of the document, and formatting to be applied to this text. Each formatting object can be represented by an element from the FO (Formatting Objects) DTD, which is defined in an annex to the standard. Formatting properties are defined using attributes to these elements. The text content of the element is the text to be rendered according to the object type and formatting properties defined in the enclosing elements.

Of course, this use of XML goes against the spirit of the standard, in that the elements describe the appearance, not the meaning of their content. Normally, however, this XML document would be generated directly from another, more descriptive document, and will not have any life span beyond its immediate use to control the XSL formatter engine. An XSL processor is expected to receive input from the XSLT processor, though in some cases an implementation may be able to receive an XML document that conforms to the FO DTD instead, created by other means. For example, there are many general-purpose XML processing tools on the market that could easily output an FO-compliant document.

General presentation model

XSL creates formatting objects to hold the content to be presented. Formatting objects create rectangular areas. Although there will often be a single rectangle for a given object, more may be created. For example, a paragraph object may span two pages. These rectangular areas are placed adjacent to each other to create the flow of material onto the screen or page.

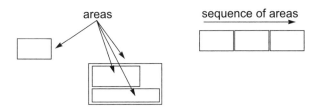

Areas are divided into four categories: area-containers, block-areas, line-areas and inline-areas (including individual character glyph-areas). In descending scale, these areas represent such objects as page zones, such as the heading and body columns, paragraphs and title, lines of text, embedded inline elements, and individual characters.

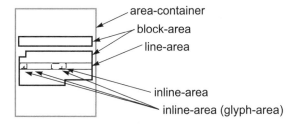

An area-container has a coordinate system, by which embedded objects can be placed, defining the 'top', 'bottom', 'left' and 'right' directions, and is able to contain other area-containers. For example, an area that represents a page may contain other areas that represent columns within the page:

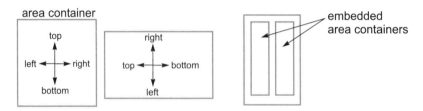

Area-containers may also contain block-areas. The placement of block-areas within area-containers depends on the 'writing mode'. It is not assumed that inline-areas flow from left to right, or that block-areas flow from top to bottom. The writing mode determines the inline-progression direction within a block, and block-progression direction within an area-container. For English documents, this would be progression from left to right and from top to bottom respectively.

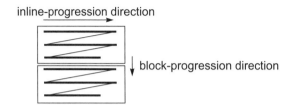

Property names like 'left', 'right', 'top' and 'bottom' are supported, but are often inappropriate in XSL, due to the fact that the writing mode may dictate flow of material in different directions. The terms 'start', 'end', 'before' and 'after' are preferred. The term 'start' refers to a position before the content in the flow direction. In an English document, the writing mode is 'lr-tb' (left-to-right lines in top-to-bottom blocks). In this case, the 'before' position is above the block concerned. In another language, a 'tb-rl' direction may be specified, in which case the before position is to the right:

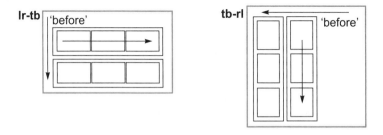

In an English document, block-areas are stacked from top to bottom within an area-container. In this writing mode, the 'space-before' property on a block element refers to space above the block.

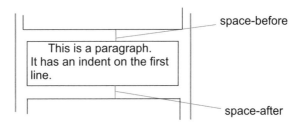

When a block-area is too long to fit in the area-container, another block-area may be created in the next area-container. For example, a paragraph that spans pages requires two block-areas to be created for it.

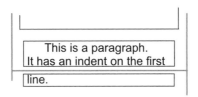

A block-area may contain more block-areas. For example, a list can be considered to be a block that contains further blocks, one for each item in the list. Again, these contained blocks are placed adjacent to each other, in the same direction (as dictated by the writing mode). They may be separated from each other using a 'display-space'.

Embedded blocks may be narrower than the enclosing block, in the non-writing-mode direction, using indent properties. Note that the 'start-indent' and 'end-indent' property values always refer to the edge of the area-container (not to the edge of an enclosing block).

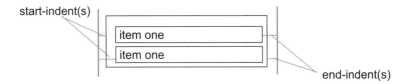

Blocks may instead contain line-areas, which are adjacent to each other in the line-progression direction. By default, they are simply stacked on top of each other (in English documents), but properties are available to create space between them. Note that a line-area has no correspondence with any element in a source document, but is created by the XSL formatter as needed.

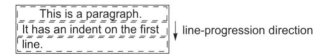

line-progression direction

However, line-areas can contain inline-areas, which correspond with XML inline elements. Inline-areas are stacked within a line-area in the inline-progression direction. For English documents, this is left to right. When a formatted inline element spans lines, additional inline-areas are created.

inline-progression direction

...<emph>first line</emph>...

Inline-areas are drawn from an initial position-point, and it is possible to adjust this point upward ('ascender-height') or downward ('descender-depth') in relation to neighbouring inline-areas. When the inline-area is placed in the line-area, an escapement-point is also established, at the end, and becomes the default location for the next position-point.

position point   escapement point   placement path

Inline-areas may be stacked within other inline-areas, and ultimately every character glyph creates an inline-area (which is then known as a glyph-area).

Kerning can be achieved by adjusting the position of the escapement point. In the second example below, the escapement point for the letter 'V' has been moved to the left, because it is followed by an 'A' character (which may overlap without the lines touching):

CSS-compatible formatting objects

Many of the XSL formatting object types correspond with established CSS display property types:

XSL	CSS
block	display:block
inline-sequence	display:inline
list-item	display:list-item
table	display:table
table-caption	display:table-caption
table-header	display:table-header-group
table-footer	display:table-footer-group
table-row	display:table-row
table-cell	display:table-cell
table-column	display:table-column

The first two of these types are the most important, as they are used to represent general text blocks, such as titles and paragraphs, and significant ranges of text within these blocks, such as emphasized words.

```
<fo:block ...>...</fo:block>
<fo:block ...>...</fo:block>
<fo:block ...>...</fo:block>

...<fo:inline-sequence ...>...</fo:inline-sequence>...
```

XSL includes a large number of additional formatting objects for handling pages, page regions and footnotes, graphics, lines, characters and hypertext links. These are discussed later.

CSS-compatible formatting properties

Many of the formatting options available in XSL are derived from properties provided in CSS. To avoid unnecessary duplication, explanations given in Chapter 17 are not repeated here (and the decision to explain these concepts in the later chapter is due to the fact that CSS is a well-established standard, while XSL is still in draft form). Out of a total 207 XSL properties, 82 have the same name and purpose as a CSS property, and in most cases they inherit exactly the same value options. For example, XSL incorporates the CSS 'font-weight' property, and all the CSS defined value options ('bold', 'normal', 'bolder', 'lighter', '100', '200', '300', etc.). For these properties, it is a trivial matter to map CSS to XSL. The property name becomes the attribute name, and the value becomes the attribute value:

```
emph { font-weight: bold } /* CSS style */

<!-- XSL style -->
<fo:inline-sequence font-weight="bold">
```

However, in some cases the property/attribute values allowed differ. The 'text-align' property adopts the 'centered' and 'justified' values from CSS, while omitting 'left' and 'right', and adding 'start', 'end', 'page-inside' and 'page-outside'. In fact, this example highlights a general difference in approach. Where CSS refers to left and right positions, XSL allows for languages that are written from right to left. The terms 'start' and 'end' are more appropriate in this circumstance. See below for more details.

Most font information is identical to CSS. The 'font', 'font-family', 'font-size', 'font-size-adjust', 'font-stretch', 'font-style', 'font-variant' and 'font-weight' properties are identical. See *Font styles* and *Fonts and styles* (CSS2) in Chapter 17.

```
Some <fo:inline-sequence font-family="Helvetica"
                  font-size="12pt"
                  font-size-adjust="none"
                  font-style="italic"
                  font-variant="small-caps"
                  font-weight="bold" >Very Special
formatting</fo:inline-sequence>
```

Some *VERY SPECIAL* formatting

Text styles are largely the same. The 'text-decoration', 'vertical-align', 'text-align' (but added 'page-outside' value), 'text-indent', 'letter-spacing', 'word-spacing', 'text-transform', 'text-shadow' and 'line-height' are used in the same way. See *Text Styles* in Chapter 17.

```
Some <fo:inline-sequence text-decoration="underline"
                  vertical-align="super"
                  letter-spacing="1pt"
                  word-spacing="2pt"
                  text-transform="lowercase"
                  text-shadow="normal">Very
Special</fo:inline-sequence> formatting
```

some <u>very special</u> formatting

```
<fo:block text-align="right"
        text-indent="3em"
        line-height="16pt" >...</fo:block>
```

Note that the 'text-decoration' property can be affected by the XSL 'score-spaces' property, which defaults to 'false', and indicates whether or not a line runs above, through or below spaces in the range of text to be highlighted:

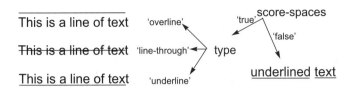

Background colours and pictures are the same, including 'background', 'background-attachment', 'background-color', 'background-image', 'background-repeat' and 'background-position'. In addition, the 'color' (foreground) property is the same. See *Colours and backgrounds* in Chapter 17.

```
<fo:block background-color="red"
...</fo:block>

<fo:block background-image="boat.gif"
          background-attachment="fixed"
          background-repeat="repeat-x">
          background-position="top">...</fo:block>
```

Defining the characteristics, size and position of an area box is the same, using the 'visibility', 'clip', 'clear', 'float', 'height', 'width', 'min-height', 'min-width', 'max-height' and 'max-width' properties. Positioning boxes using the 'position' property, perhaps over other boxes, using 'z-index', also works in the same way. See *Boxes* and *Display options* in Chapter 17.

Border details are the same. This includes 'border', 'border-left', 'border-right', 'border-top' and 'border-bottom. Also 'border-style', 'border-left-style', 'border-right-style', 'border-top-style' and 'border-bottom-style'. Also 'border-width', 'border-left-width', 'border-right-width', 'border-top-width' and 'border-bottom-width'. Also 'border-color', 'border-left-color', 'border-right-color', 'border-top-color' and 'border-bottom-color' (though the 'transparent' option has been added and only hexadecimal values are otherwise allowed). See *Boxes* (CSS1) and *Boxes* (CSS2) in Chapter 17.

```
<fo:block border="1pt dashed red">...</fo:block>

<fo:block border-width="1pt 2pt 1pt 2pt"
          border-style="dashed"
          border-color="#FF0080" >...</fo:block>
```

Similarly, margin and padding details are the same, including 'margin', 'margin-left', 'margin-right', 'margin-top' and 'margin-bottom'. Also 'padding', 'padding-left', 'padding-right', 'padding-top' and 'padding-bottom' (although percentage values are not allowed). See *Boxes* in Chapter 17.

```
<fo:block margin="1pt"
          padding="2pt">...</fo:block>
```

Many table properties are the same. This includes the 'table-layout', 'caption-side' (though some options have been added), 'empty-cells', 'speak-header' (see *Aural Styles* (CSS2) in Chapter 17), 'border-collapse' and 'border-spacing' properties. See *Tables* in Chapter 17.

Aural style sheets have been adopted wholesale from CSS. This includes the 'volume', 'speak', 'pause', 'pause-after', 'pause-before', 'cue', 'cue-after', 'cue-before', 'play-during', 'azimuth', 'elevation', 'speech-rate', 'voice-family', 'pitch', 'pitch-range', 'stress', 'richness', 'speak-punctuation' and 'speak-numerals' properties. See *Aural styles* (CSS2) in Chapter 17 for an in-depth discussion on this topic.

CSS also has some page-oriented properties, which have been adopted. Page size is controlled by the 'size' property. Control of objects affected by page boundaries uses the CSS 'widows', 'orphans' and 'page-break-inside' properties. See *Printed output* (CSS2) in Chapter 17.

Start and end additions

A number of properties have been added to those provided by CSS, simply to give direction-neutral equivalent instructions. The 'start', 'end', 'before' and 'after' locations are directly equivalent to existing positions, such as 'left', 'right', 'top' and 'bottom', but map to different ones depending on the language concerned, and the type of formatting object concerned. In all cases, they take the same possible values as those already discussed.

For borders, the 'border-before-width', 'border-before-style', 'border-before-color', 'border-after-width', 'border-after-style', 'border-after-color', 'border-start-width', 'border-start-style, 'border-start-color', 'border-end-width, 'border-end-style' and 'border-end-color' properties have been added.

For margins, the 'padding-before', 'padding-after', 'padding-start' and 'padding-end' properties have been added.

Finally, as already mentioned, the 'text-align' property also accepts 'start' and 'end' values.

Block-level objects

The Block element has already been demonstrated, and is used to enclose any simple block of text, such as a paragraph or title. Text styles can be defined, margin, border and padding attributes may be added, text may be aligned in different ways, hyphenation can be controlled, and the whole block can be removed from the flow and positioned explicitly:

```
<fo:block>A block of text.</fo:block>
<fo:block>Another block of text.</fo:block>
```

A block of text.

Another block of text.

The 'text-indent' property is used to indent the first line of text in a block, and the 'last-line-end-indent' property similarly indents the last line of text, though a negative value is typically used here to create an 'outdent' for such items as page numbers in content lists:

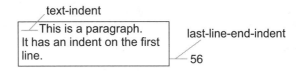

The 'text-align' property takes the values 'left', 'right', 'center' or 'justify':

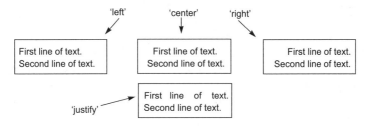

Graphics between text blocks are represented by Display Graphic elements, with an Href attribute to locate the graphic file, and optional Height and Width attributes to define a fixed area into which the graphic must be placed, or Minimum Width, Minimum Height, Maximum Width, Maximum Height, and the Scale attribute to provide more flexibility to render the graphic:

```
<fo:display-graphic href="boat.gif" width="5cm"
                    height="7cm" />
```

When a set of blocks are written in a different writing mode to the main text, this set can be enclosed in a Display Included Container element, which over-rides the current writing mode.

A rule can be drawn horizontally or vertically between text blocks, using the Display Rule element, which has Length, Rule Orientation, Rule Style and Rule Thickness attributes:

```
<fo:display-rule length="8cm"
                 rule-orientation="horizontal"
                 rule-style="solid"
                 rule-thickness="2pt" />
```

When a number of consecutive text blocks have some properties in common, these properties can be specified on a containing Display Sequence element to eliminate unnecessary duplication:

```
<fo:display-sequence border="3mm" >
  <fo:block>...</fo:block> <!-- inherited border -->
  <fo:block>...</fo:block> <!-- inherited border -->
</fo:display-sequence >
```

Inline objects

Individual characters can be represented by the Character element. The Character attribute provides the Unicode value for the character, and the Vertical Align attribute can be used to move the character up or down relative to surrounding characters:

```
H<fo:character character="2" vertical-align="sub"/>O is
water.
```

This object type can also be used to individually style characters, and to enclose individual characters in borders.

The first object inside a Block element may be a First Line Marker element, which specifies the properties to apply to the first line of text, once the pagination engine has determined from the font size and the width of the area the actual range of characters this applies to. It is an initial empty element:

```
<fo:block font-size="12pt"><fo:first-line-marker font-
size="14pt"/>The first line of text in this paragraph is in
a larger font than the rest</fo:block>
```

A graphic can be presented within a line of text, using the Inline Graphic element. Again, the Href attribute is used to identify the graphic file, and the Height, Width, Scale and other attributes described for block graphics can be used to control the size of the image produced:

```
<fo:block>Here is a picture of a boat: <fo:inline-graphic
href="boat.gif"/>.</fo:block>
```

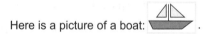

Here is a picture of a boat: .

Rule lines can be drawn inline, as well as between blocks. The Inline Rule element takes the same attributes, but creates an inline area.

```
<fo:block>Chapter 9:
<fo:inline-rule length="3cm" width="1pt/> Summary
</fo:block>
```

Chapter 9: ———— Summary

The Inline Sequence element has already been demonstrated. It has the same purpose as the Display Sequence element, but for inline objects instead of block objects:

```
<fo:block>A <fo:inline-sequence font-weight="bold">bold</
fo:inline-sequence> word.</fo:block>
```

A **bold** word.

The current page number can be inserted into the text using the Page Number element:

```
This text is on page
<fo:page-number font-weight="bold"/>.
```

This text is on page **123**.

Similarly, it is possible to insert the page number of another object, using the Page Number Citation element. The Reference Identifier attribute provides the unique identifier of the object in question. Note that most objects can have Id attributes to facilitate the use of this feature.

```
Please refer to the summary on page
<fo:page-number-citation ref-id="chap9"
                          font-weight="bold" />.

<fo:block id="chap9">To summarize, ...</fo:block>
```

Please refer to the summary on page **987**.

Lists

Lists can take two forms. In both cases, the List Block element is used to enclose a number of items. In the simplest case, the items are a sequence of List Item elements. Alternatively, the block may directly contain a sequence of labels followed by contents, using the List Item Label and List Item Body elements.

```
<fo:list-block>
  <fo:list-item>...</fo:list-item>
  <fo:list-item>...</fo:list-item>
</fo:list-block>
```

```
<fo:list-block>
  <fo:list-item-label>...</fo:list-item-label>
  <fo:list-item-body>...</fo:list-item-body>
  <fo:list-item-label>...</fo:list-item-label>
  <fo:list-item-body>...</fo:list-item-body>
</fo:list-block>
```

In fact, these elements are also used in the List Item element, so the real difference is only the optional element surrounding each label/content pair. The more verbose format is required to specify borders around items:

```
<fo:list-item padding="2mm" border="1mm">
  <fo:list-item-label>...</fo:list-item-label>
  <fo:list-item-body>...</fo:list-item-body>
</fo:list-item>
```

Both the label and content parts of each item contain block-level elements, such as the Block element.

```
<fo:list-item-label>
  <fo:block>LABEL</fo:block>
</fo:list-item-label>
<fo:list-item-body>
  <fo:block>FIRST BLOCK IN CONTENT</fo:block>
  <fo:block>SECOND BLOCK</fo:block>
</fo:list-item-body>
```

The label part is placed next to the content. Two attributes are used as shown below to determine the width of the label and content parts. When the labels and bodies are not grouped in List Item elements, the space between each pair is given in the Space Between List Rows attribute:

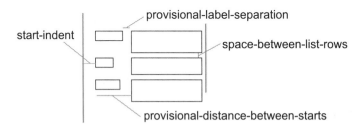

Tables

When a table has a caption, the main element is called Table And Caption. This element contains a Table Caption element and a Table element. When no caption is present, the main element is the Table element:

```
<fo:table>...</fo:table>

<fo:table-and-caption ... >
  <fo:table-caption>...</fo:table-caption>
  <fo:table>...</fo:table>
</fo:table-and-caption>
```

The Table And Caption element contains a Caption Side attribute to specify which side of the table the caption should appear ('before' for above the table in English), as well as the usual border and margin properties:

```
<fo:table-and-caption caption-side="after">
```

The caption itself contains block-level elements:

```
<fo:table-caption >
  <fo:block>Example Table</fo:block>
</fo:table-caption>
```

The Table element contains the actual table grid. The model follows the HTML approach (see Chapter 18), and has at least one major improvement over the capabilities of CSS (see Chapter 17) to render XML structures in a grid format. Specifically, the Number Columns Spanned and Number Rows Spanned attributes allow cells to span into further columns and/or rows. Note that material covering table structures in Chapters 17 and 18 is not repeated here, and it is recommended that the appropriate sections in these chapters be read before studying the examples below.

The grid is composed of cells within rows within body, header and footer blocks, using the Table Header, Table Body, Table Footer, Table Row and Table Cell elements:

```
<fo:table>
  <fo:table-header>...</fo:table-header>
  <fo:table-footer>...</fo:table-footer>
  <fo:table-body>...</fo:table-body>
</fo:table>

<fo:table-body>
  <fo:table-row>...</fo:table-row>
  <fo:table-row>...</fo:table-row>
</fo:table-body>

<fo:table-row>
  <fo:table-cell>...</fo:table-cell>
  <fo:table-cell>...</fo:table-cell>
  <fo:table-cell>...</fo:table-cell>
</fo:table-row>
```

The Table element has Table Width and Table Height attributes, the Table Row element includes a Row Height attribute, and the means to control page breaks before and after the row (using the May Break Before Row and May Break After Row attributes, which default to "no"):

```
<fo:table>
  <fo:table-header>
    <fo:table-row row-height="24pt">
      <fo:table-cell n-columns-spanned="2">
        <fo:block>Headings</fo:block>
      </fo:table-cell>
    </fo:table-row>
    <fo:table-row row-height="24pt">
      <fo:table-cell>
        <fo:block>Head 1</fo:block>
      </fo:table-cell>
      <fo:table-cell>
        <fo:block>Head 2</fo:block>
      </fo:table-cell>
    </fo:table-row>
  </fo:table-header>
  <fo:table-body>
    <fo:table-row row-height="16pt"
                  may-break-before="yes">
      <fo:table-cell>
        <fo:block>cell 1</fo:block>
      </fo:table-cell>
      <fo:table-cell n-rows-spanned="2">
        <fo:block>span down</fo:block>
      </fo:table-cell>
    </fo:table-row>
    <fo:table-row row-height="16pt">
      <fo:table-cell>
        <fo:block>cell 2</fo:block>
      </fo:table-cell>
    </fo:table-row>
  </fo:table-body>
</fo:table>
```

Headings	
Head 1	Head 2
cell 1	span
cell 2	down

The Table Row element is optional. When cells are not embedded in row elements, some of the Table Cell elements need to use Starts Row and Ends Row attributes:

```
<fo:table-body>
  <fo:table-cell starts-row="yes">
    <fo:block>1,1</fo:block>
  </fo:table-cell>
  <fo:table-cell ends-row="yes">
    <fo:block>1,2</fo:block>
  </fo:table-cell>
  <fo:table-cell starts-row="yes">
    <fo:block>2,1</fo:block>
  </fo:table-cell>
  <fo:table-cell ends-row="yes">
    <fo:block>2,2</fo:block>
  </fo:table-cell>
</fo:table-body>
```

Borders and padding can be applied at all levels in this structure.

Hypertext links

A range of text can be enclosed in a Simple Link element, which is used to provide a mechanism for hypertext linking to another object. It has an Internal Destination attribute that is used to refer to the Id of another object in the same document, or an External Destination attribute that contains a URL to an external resource:

```
See <fo:simple-link internal-destination="chap9">Chapter
9</fo:simple-link> for details.

See <fo:simple-link external-destination="file:///
book3.xml">Book 3</fo:simple-link> for details.
```

The Show Destination attribute is used to control how the link is traversed. It takes the value of 'replace' (scroll to the location), the default value, or 'new' (create a new window for the resource).

The Indicate Destination attribute is used to specify that the destination text is to be highlighted in some way, when set to 'true' (the default value is 'false').

Alternative document fragments

When publishing electronically, it is possible to hide and reveal portions of the document depending on user actions. For example, allowing the opening and collapsing of portions of a contents list can be supported using this feature. The Multi Switch element contains a number of Multi Case elements, each one holding an alternative document fragment.

```
<fo:multi-switch>
  <fo:multi-case>...</fo:multi-case>
  <fo:multi-case>...</fo:multi-case>
  <fo:multi-case>...</fo:multi-case>
</fo:multi-switch>
```

The content of the first Multi Case element with an Initial value of 'true' is presented. The others remain hidden, initially, but can be revealed later. They are all identified using a Name attribute, for later selection:

```
<fo:multi-case name="first">...</fo:multi-case>
<fo:multi-case name="second" initial="true">
  <fo:block>THIS PORTION IS SHOWN FIRST</fo:block>
</fo:multi-case>
```

Within each document fragment, there may be any number of Multi Toggle elements, which are used to switch the view to one of the other fragments. The Switch To attribute refers to the name of the fragment to swap in:

```
<fo:multi-case name="closed" initial="true">
  <fo:block>Heading
    <fo:multi-toggle switch-to="opened" >
    [+]
    </fo:multi-toggle>
  </fo:block>
</fo:multi-case>

<fo:multi-case name="opened">
  <fo:block>Heading
    <fo:multi-toggle switch-to="closed" >
    [back]
    </fo:multi-toggle>
  </fo:block>
  <fo:block>- Item 1</fo:block>
  <fo:block>- Item 2</fo:block>
</fo:multi-case>
```

An entire case block may be hidden, because it is embedded within a single case of a larger block. It may then be revealed again. By default, when this happens the case with the Initial attribute value of 'true' is presented, regardless of which case was selected when the entire block was previously hidden. This behaviour can be changed to reveal the previously selected case by changing the Auto Restore attribute value to 'false':

```
<fo:multi-switch auto-restore="false" >...
```

Alternative properties

The style of a range of blocks, or range of text, may need to depend on the state of the environment. An example given in the standard refers to the way that the colour of a hypertext link source may vary, depending on whether the link has been visited recently, or is currently selected. The Multi Properties element contains a number of initial, empty Multi Property Set elements, each one providing the style to apply under a given circumstance, identified using the State attribute. These elements are followed by the document fragment to be styled:

```
<fo:multi-properties>
<fo:multi-property-set state="visited"
                       color="#FF0000" />
<fo:multi-property-set state="active"
                       color="#00FF00" />
<fo:multi-property-set state="inactive"
                       color="#0000FF" />
This text to be coloured depending on the state.
</fo:multi-properties>
```

Floating objects and footnotes

In paged output, it may be inconvenient to place an object, particularly a large object, at the location implied by its physical position in the document source. For example, large tables and figures are often moved to a location where they create the least possible disruption to the flow of text, and the page balance, such as to the top of the next page or column. The Float element is used to contain such items, indicating to the pagination engine that it may move the content as appropriate. Only block-level elements can be used in the Float element:

```
<fo:float><fo:table>...</fo:table></fo:float>
```

Similarly, a footnote is usually placed at the bottom of the first page that contains a reference to it, and it is of course not possible to determine in advance where a page-break may occur. The Footnote element contains the footnote text, which will float to the base of the page, and may also contain a reference to the footnote:

```
Here is a reference<fo:footnote>
<fo:footnote-citation>*</fo:footnote-citation>
<fo:block>* The footnote</fo:block>
</fo:footnote> to a footnote.
```

Both the Float and Footnote elements can only be applied within block-level elements, such as the Block element.

Building pages (the text flow)

The Flow element contains all the block-level objects that constitute the main text flow content of the document. For example, a simple flow may just contain a title and a paragraph, separated by a line:

```
<fo:flow flow-name="xsl-body" >
   <fo:block>This is a Title</fo:block>
   <fo:display-rule.../>
   <fo:block>This is a paragraph.</fo:block>
</fo:flow>
```

The Flow Name attribute identifies the page region into which the content should flow. In the first version of XSL, the possible regions are represented by specific elements, such as Region Body (the other regions are Region Before (the header), Region After (the footer), Region Start (left border) and Region End (right border)).

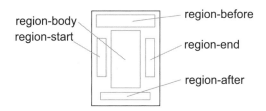

To flow text into the body region, the Flow Name attribute needs to take the value 'xsl-body'. Likewise, 'xsl-before' for the 'region-before' area, 'xsl-after' for 'region-after', 'xsl-start' for 'region-start' and 'xsl-end' for 'region-end'. Regions are described in detail later.

A large flow naturally occupies more than one page. As extra pages are added, a sequence of pages is created. To reflect this fact, the Page Sequence element contains the Flow element. The Page Sequence element may also contain any number of objects that are to be repeated in the same place on each page in the sequence, which is termed static content. The Static Content element contains block-level elements, and once again it targets an area on the page within which these objects are to be presented, using the 'flow-name' attribute. The most obvious use for this feature is to place headers and rule lines on each page:

```
<fo:page-sequence>
  <fo:static-content flow-name="xsl-before" >
    <fo:block>The XML Companion</fo:block>
    <fo:display-rule.../>
  </fo:static-content>

  <fo:static-content flow-name="xsl-after" >
    <fo:display-rule.../>
  </fo:static-content>

  <fo:flow>...</fo:flow>
</fo:page-sequence>
```

A page sequence must also include information on how different page master templates are to be used in the sequence. For example, it is common for the first page to have a different template to all following pages, and in some cases the template for odd-numbered pages will be different to the one for even-numbered pages, even if only to vary the margins for the purposes of book binding on left and right pages.

```
<fo:page-sequence>
  <fo:sequence-specification>
    ...
  </fo:sequence-specification>
  <fo:static-content>...</fo:static-content>
  <fo:static-content>...</fo:static-content>
  <fo:flow>...</fo:flow>
</fo:page-sequence>
```

The Sequence Specification element specifies this information in embedded elements that represent single pages, repeatable pages and alternating pages. The order in which these elements appear within the Sequence Specification element is significant.

The empty Sequence Specifier Single element represents a single page in the output, and simply refers to a page master that defines the layout of this page, using the Page Master Name attribute:

```
<fo:sequence-specifier-single
          page-master-name="FirstMaster" />
```

Note that an 'overflow' value of 'scroll' can be applied to ensure that only a single, scrollable page is generated, which is suitable for online browser viewing of the text.

The Sequence Specifier Repeating element represents one or more pages in the output, but allows for a separate page master for the first page, by including two attributes called Page Master First and Page Master Repeating:

```
<fo:sequence-specifier-repeating
          page-master-first="FirstMaster"
          page-master-repeating="OthersMaster" />
```

The Sequence Specifier Alternating element is much more sophisticated. Apart from once again allowing a first page template to be specified, using the Page Master First attribute, different master templates can be specified for odd and even pages (representing right and left sides of a physical page), using the Page Master Odd and Page Master Even attributes. One reason to do this would be to set different widths for the inner margins and outer margins, taking account of the area hidden by page binding (although, in this book, the margins are the same width (leading to the impression that the outer margins are wider), left and right templates are still used in order to alternate the heading content between the book title and the chapter title). Different master pages can be defined for the last page, depending on whether this page is odd or even, using the Page Master Last Odd and Page Master Last Even attributes. In addition, another template can be defined to cater for the possibility that the text will end on an odd-numbered page, using the Page Master Blank Even attribute (in this book, a completely blank side is presented at the end of each chapter that concludes on a right-hand side):

```
<fo:sequence-specifier-alternating
          page-master-first="FirstMaster"
          page-master-odd="OddMaster"
          page-master-even="EvenMaster"
          page-master-blank-even="BlankMaster" />
```

The enclosing Page Sequence element also specifies the initial page number (using the Initial Page Number attribute). It is probable that this will default to '1' for the first page sequence (there may be more than one), and one higher than the last number for subsequent sequences. The Format, Grouping Separator, Letter Value and Grouping Size attributes described for XSLT (see *Automatic numbering* above) may be used to describe how the page number is to be presented. In the following example, pages are numbered from '5', using roman numerals (as in the preface pages of this book):

```
<fo:page-sequence initial-page-number="3"
                  format="i">...
```

A number of page sequences may occur, so that, for example, a preface can be numbered separately from the body of the text, and chapters can all start on right-hand pages. These elements are all children of the Root element, which, unsurprisingly, is the root element of the entire style sheet:

```
<fo:root>
  ...
  <fo:page-sequence initial-page-number="3" format="i">
    ...
    <fo:flow >
      <fo:block>Prelims</fo:block>...
    </fo:flow>
  </fo:page-sequence>

  <fo:page-sequence initial-page-number="1" format="1">
    ...
    <fo:flow>
      <fo:block>Chapter One</fo:block>...
    </fo:flow>
  </fo:page-sequence>

  <fo:page-sequence>
    ...
    <fo:flow>
      <fo:block>Chapter Two</fo:block>...
    </fo:flow>
  </fo:page-sequence>
  ...
</fo:root>
```

As discussed above, page sequences flow text into pages that conform to a pre-defined template, properly termed a page master. Page masters are defined before the page sequences that use them, within the Layout Master Set element.

```
<fo:root>
  <fo:layout-master-set>...</fo:layout-master-set>
  <fo:page-sequence...>...</fo:page-sequence>
  <fo:page-sequence...>...</fo:page-sequence>
</root>
```

This element in turn contains at least one Simple Page Master element, each one defining a single template, such as an initial page, a left-side page, or a right-side page. Each template also has a name, held in the Page Master Name attribute, which is referred to from the sequence specifier elements.

```
<fo:root>
  <fo:layout-master-set>
    <fo:simple-page-master
        page-master-name="FirstMaster"...>
      ...
    </fo:simple-page-master>
    <fo:simple-page-master
        pagemaster-name="LeftMaster" ...>
      ...
    </fo:simple-page-master>
  </fo:layout-master-set>
  <!-- page sequences -->
  ...
</fo:root>
```

Each page master has a writing direction, specified using the Writing Mode attribute (for English, its value would be 'lr-tb' (left to right, top to bottom)), a height and width, specified using the Size attribute, or by the Page Height and Page Width attributes, and a margin (which should define the non-print area of the page). Also, the Reference Orientation attribute is used to change the printing direction from top to bottom, as represented by the value '0' degrees, to landscape, using a value of '90' degrees or '270' degrees.

```
<fo:simple-page-master page-master-name="MasterX"
                       margin="1cm" size="12cm 8cm"
                       writing-mode="lr-tb"
                       reference-orientation="0">...
```

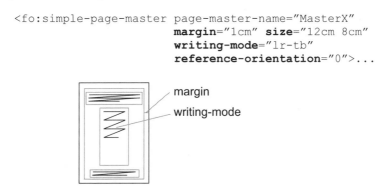

margin

writing-mode

Each template is defined by specifying the active regions on each page, using the 'region-...' elements mentioned earlier. The only required region is represented by the Region Body element. The others are all optional, but if present must appear in the order shown below:

```
<fo:simple-page-master ...>
  <region-body .../>    <!-- main flow -->
  <region-before .../>  <!-- header -->
  <region-after .../>   <!-- footer -->
  <region-start .../>   <!-- left margin -->
  <region-end .../>     <!-- right margin -->
</fo:simple-page-master>
```

These areas can be given their own reference orientation (text in the margins could be made vertical) and writing mode, and have borders and padding. In addition, the body region has attributes that define the number of columns in the area (the Column Count attribute), the width of the gap between these columns (the Column Gap attribute), the background colour, and the width of any border around the area:

```
<fo:simple-page-master ...>
  <fo:region-body column-count="2"
                  column-gap="1em"
                  background-color="#000000"
                  border-width="1pt"
                  margin="4pt"/>
  ...
</fo:simple-page-master>
```

Note that a number of objects, including the Block and Table elements, have a Span attribute, which defaults to a value of 'none', but can be set to 'all', meaning that the content of this element is allowed to span all columns.

The size of the body region is determined by deducting the margins and padding from the size of the whole page area (minus its own margins). The other areas are placed in the margins around the body area, and their height (in the case of the before and after areas) or width (in the case of the start and end areas) is specified using the Extent attribute:

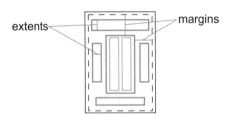

Hyphenation

More care is usually taken in splitting words across lines on paper than on the screen, and hyphenation is a common way to balance the need to put as many words on each line as possible, while not reducing the space between words to such a degree that it is not possible to read the text. The 'hyphenate' property defaults to 'false', but can be set to 'true', so enabling the hyphenation of words.

The character to be inserted by the formatter at the end of the line when hyphenating a word can be specified using the Hyphenation Character attribute. Normally, the hyphen character, '-', is specified.

Many typesetting systems and DTP packages have access to a hyphenation dictionary, showing acceptable break-points in each word. When such a dictionary is not available, the system needs to follow some simple rules instead, and one criterion that could be used involves counting the characters at each side of the break. The Hyphenation Push Character Count property specifies the minimum number of characters that need to be pushed onto the next line, and the Hyphenation Character Count attribute specifies the minimum number of characters to be retained on the original line. Typically, these values would both be set to '2':

```
<fo:block hyphenate="true"
          hyphenation-char="-"
          hyphenation-push-char-count="2"
          hyphenation-remain-char-count="2">...
```

14. SAX 1.0

SAX (the *Simple API for XML*) is a standard API for event-driven processing of XML data, allowing parsers to deliver information to applications in digestible chunks. This chapter describes the SAX standard in detail, and illustrates its use within a popular Java parser.

Background

Many XML parsers can work in a stand-alone manner. They accept a reference to an XML document, read the XML data and simply report whether they conform to the rules of the standard, and possibly also the rules of a given DTD. While useful for validating XML data, this does nothing to assist an application that needs to access the content. Fortunately, many parsers are also able to pass information extracted from XML constructs to an application, but to do this they must include an API that the application can access.

Each parser vendor develops APIs that match the capabilities of their parser, often solving the same problems in subtly different ways. Of course, this leads to incompatibilities. The XML community quickly recognized that there would be a great degree of overlap in functionality between parsers, as they would all be basically doing the same thing, and that it would be useful to have a standard API for processing XML documents. This would mean that, providing an application only used these common functions, it would be a trivial task to replace one parser with another, and programmers would be able to transfer their skills to new products that used different parsers.

SAX was developed, by members of the XML-DEV mailing list, to meet this aim. Version 1.0 was released in May 1998, and is free for both private and commercial use. The standard is available from www.microstar.com/SAX/roadmap.html.

A large number of SAX-compliant parsers have been developed, in a wide variety of computer languages, and most are freely available for download over the Web. For reasons explored elsewhere, most of these parsers are Java applications, and this language has been chosen for the examples that follow.

Call-backs and interfaces

The application instantiates a parser object, supplied by the parser developer (in this case IBM), and instructs it to parse a specified XML document or data stream. As the parser processes the XML data, it detects significant items, such as an element start-tag, or a comment. It also detects any well-formed, and possibly also any DTD, errors. But the parser also needs to send all this information back to the main application. The SAX API is mainly concerned with the means by which the parser is able to return this information, using a 'call-back' mechanism.

Depending on the need, the application creates one or more objects that contain methods that the parser must call when appropriate events occur. The application may only wish to be informed of document markup: the element start-tags, end-tags and text content (as well as any white space), the comments and processing instructions, and the document start and end. But it may also wish to be informed of calls to external unparsed entities, and declarations of notations. Or it may wish to be informed of errors. When errors occur, it may need to be able to determine the location of these errors. Finally, it may wish to be informed of all calls to external entities, and be given the opportunity to intercept and redirect these calls. The application passes references to these objects to the parser, so that it can call the methods.

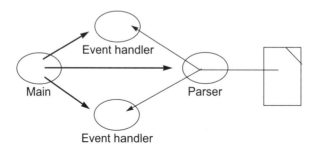

So that the parser will accept the objects, they must belong to a class that defines one or more of the SAX interfaces (located at '**org.xml.sax.***'). The parser can then be certain that the necessary methods are present, and call them when appropriate events occur.

The SAX interfaces are:

- Parser (implemented by the parser itself)

- DocumentHandler

- AttributeList

- ErrorHandler

- EntityResolver

- Locator

- DTDHandler

These interfaces are discussed in detail below.

Java implementation

There are some important activities involved in parsing, navigating and processing documents that the SAX standard does not cover. For example, writing out a structure into XML format is outside the scope of the standard. These features, if implemented at all, will differ in operation between parsers. For the sake of providing working examples, a specific parser has been chosen. In this case, the IBM Java parser is used throughout.

To use the IBM parser, the following import statements are required:

```
import org.xml.sax.*;
import com.ibm.xml.parsers.*;
```

IBM provide a number of classes for parsing an XML file or data stream, including one called ValidatingSAXParser. This class (as well as a non-validating equivalent) implements the first interface discussed below:

```
ValidatingSAXParser myParser;
...
try {
  myParser.parse("file:/doc.xml");
}
catch( SAXException err ) {...}
```

NOTE: This example shows the simpler variant of the parse method, which takes a URL string locating a data file. When the data is not stored in a file, a more complex variant is used. This variant is described later.

The parser

The parser developer creates a class that actually parses the XML document or data stream. This parser class implements the **Parser** interface, which defines the following methods:

```
void  parse(InputSource src)
                  throws SAXException, IOException;
void  parse(String src)
                  throws SAXException, IOException;

void  setDocumentHandler(DocumentHandler doch);
void  setErrorHandler(ErrorHandler errh);
void  setDTDHandler(DTDHandler dtdh);
void  setEntityResolver(EntityResolver entres);
void  setLocale(Locale loc) throws SAXException;
```

These methods fall into two groups. The larger group of 'set...' methods is used by the application to register with the parser classes that conform to other interfaces. Most of these methods are described later, as the interfaces they register are discussed. The only one worth discussing now is the '**setLocale**' method, which is used to tell the parser what language to use for error messages and warnings (which the parser may ignore).

After registering one or more of these objects with the parser, the application will call one or other of the '**parse**' methods, as demonstrated above.

The parser begins to read the XML source data, but as soon as it encounters a meaningful object, such as the start-tag of an element, it stops reading, sends the information to the main application by calling an appropriate method in one of the objects registered with the parser, and waits for this method to return before continuing.

Document handlers

In order for the application to receive basic markup events from the parser, the application developer must create a class that implements the **DocumentHandler** interface. This interface defines methods that handle different kinds of event:

```
void  startDocument() throws SAXException;
void  endDocument() throws SAXException;
void  startElement(String name, AttributeList atts)
                                throws SAXException;
void  endElement(String name) throws SAXException;
void  characters(char ch[], int start, int length)
                                throws SAXException;
```

```
void  ignorableWhitespace(char ch[], int start,
                          int length)
                              throws SAXException;
void  processingInstruction(String target, String data)
                              throws SAXException;
void  setDocumentLocator(Locator myLoc);
```

Some of these methods are included in the diagram below, which shows the application creating an object belonging to a class that implements the DocumentHandler interface (containing the methods listed above), then creating the parser object (which implements the Parser interface, so contains the parse method), which is then told to begin reading the XML data file, and in turn triggers appropriate methods in the first object as notable items are encountered.

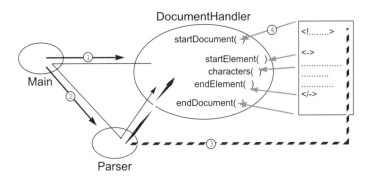

In order for this to work the parser object needs to be given a reference to the DocumentHandler object. The main application passes such a reference to the parser by calling its 'setDocumentHandler' method.

```
ValidatingSAXParser myParser =
                    new ValidatingSAXParser();

myDocHandlerClass myDoc = new myDocHandlerClass();

MyParser.setDocumentHandler(myDoc);

// now begin parsing...
```

Note that it is common practice for a single object to be developed that handles all the events that the parser will activate, and also activates the parser itself. In this case, each 'set...' method is simply passed the word 'this' (a reference back to the current object).

```
class MyClass implements DocumentHandler {
...
MyParser.setDocumentHandler(this);
```

The first method called is always the 'startDocument' method, and the last called is always the 'endDocument' method. These methods are useful for general housekeeping, such as initializing variables and opening and closing files.

```
public void startDocument ()
{
  InChapter = false;
  InChapterTitle = false;
  NextTitle = 1;
}
```

The '**startElement**' method is called when a start-tag is encountered in the data stream. It is passed the name of the element and its attributes (using another class that is described below). The '**endElement**' method is called when an end-tag is encountered, and is also passed the name of the element (as all element end-tags must be present in XML, this information is potentially redundant, unless it is intended as a mechanism to isolate empty elements). The examples below set flags that are used to identify a title inside a chapter. A later example shows how this information is used to extract all the chapter titles:

```
public void startElement (String name,
                          AttributeList atts)
{
  if ( name.equals ("chapter") ) InChapter = true;
  if ( name.equals ("title") && InChapter == true )
                               InChapterTitle = true;
}
public void endElement (String name)
{
  if ( name.equals ("chapter") ) InChapter = false;
}
```

The '**characters**' method is called when a string of text is encountered. It is passed a character array, but it is not assumed that the string completely fills this array, nor that it starts at the beginning of the array, so start and length values are also passed. The example below shows how to convert this information into a simple string:

```
public void characters (char ch[], int start, int length)
{
  String chars = new String( ch, start, length );

  if ( InChapterTitle == true )
               ChapterTitle [NextTitle++] = chars;
}
```

The '**ignorableWhitespace**' method is called when a string of ignorable white space characters is encountered. This is white space that appears in elements that are only allowed to contain elements. When a DTD is not in use, this method is unlikely to be called at all, because it is not then possible for the parser to distinguish between elements that can contain text, and elements that can only contain other elements. The parameters are the same as for the characters method.

The '**processingInstruction**' method is called when a processing instruction is encountered, and is passed both the target application name and the actual instruction:

```
public void processingInstruction(String target,
                                  String data)
{
  if ( target.equals("ACME") )
  {
    // target is ACME processor
    if ( data.equals("new_page") )
    {
      // page break here
    }
  }
}
```

Attribute lists

When the parser informs the application that an element start-tag has been encountered, it calls the startElement method, as described above. However, a start-tag may contain one or more attributes. It would not be possible to pass details of each attribute as individual parameters, because it is unknown in advance how many there could be. There is no practical limit to the number of attributes an element can contain.

The solution is to create a 'wrapper' object for all attribute details. This object must implement the **AttributeList** interface, which defines the following methods:

```
int     getLength();
String  getName(int i);
String  getType(int i);
String  getType(String name);
String  getValue(int i);
String  getValue(String name);
```

An attribute value may not be physically present in the start-tag, but be supplied as a default value from the DTD. There is no way to distinguish between attributes defined explicitly, and those that are supplied by the DTD. Note that it does not hold any information on attributes defined in the DTD that are both implied, and happen not to appear in the start-tag. It is therefore not possible, using the SAX API, to reconstruct a DTD from analysis of documents that conform to it.

To ascertain how many attributes are present in this object, the '**getLength**' method is called. This method returns an integer value representing the number of attributes, and a value of zero indicates that no attributes are present. Each attribute is identified by a simple index value. The first attribute has an index value of zero. It follows that the last attribute has an index value one less than the value returned by the getLength method. To discover the name of one of the attributes, the 'getName' method is called, along with its index value. This example retrieves the name of the last attribute:

```
String lastAttribute = null;
int totalAtts = atts.getLength();
if ( totalAtts > 0 )
        lastAttribute = atts.getName(totalAtts - 1);
```

Similarly, to get the value of an attribute, the 'getValue' method is called. Unsurprisingly, the attribute value with a given index number matches the attribute name with the same index number:

```
lastAttValue = atts.getValue(totalAtts - 1);
```

When a DTD is in use, each attribute is assigned a data type, such as CDATA, ID or NMTOKEN. The 'getType' method returns this information. If the parser is unable to get this information from the DTD, perhaps because it is not a validating parser, then it substitutes the default catch-all type, 'CDATA'. The following example partially reconstructs the original attribute list declaration (but makes a few unjustifiable assumptions about default values and requirement status):

```
public void startElement(String name,
                        AttributeList atts)
{
  System.out.print( "<!ATTLIST " + name + " " );
  for( int i = 0; i < atts.getLength(); i++ )
  {
    System.out.print( atts.getName(i) + " " +
                      atts.getType(i) + " " +
                      "#IMPLIED \"" +
                      atts.getValue(i) + "\" \n");
  }
  System.out.print( "> \n" );
}
```

When the application is only interested in a specific attribute, a simpler mechanism is provided for ascertaining its value. Instead of stepping through the attributes in sequence, looking for the one with the correct name, it is possible to simply request the value of a named attribute. If the attribute is not present, a null value is returned. The following example extracts the value of the Id attribute, regardless of which element is being processed:

```
public void startElement(String name,
                        AttributeList atts)
{
  String ID = atts.getValue("Id");
}
```

The type of a named attribute can be discovered in the same way, though this seems to be a much less valuable feature. If the application already knows the name of the attribute it wants, it probably already knows what data type its values conform to as well.

Error handlers

If the application needs to be informed of warnings and errors, then it can implement the **ErrorHandler** interface. This interface includes the following methods for intercepting warnings and errors:

```
void  warning(SAXParseException err)
                             throws SAXException;
void  error(SAXParseException err)
                             throws SAXException;
void  fatalError(SAXParseException err)
                             throws SAXException;
```

These methods all work in the same way, and just react to different levels of problem.

Typically, the same object that handles normal document events will also handle error events. These methods then just become additional event handlers in the main event-handling object. To inform the parser where to send error events, the object must be registered in the same way that the document handler is, but using the 'setErrorHandler' method instead:

```
class MyClass implements DocumentHandler,
                        ErrorHandler {
  ...
myParser.setDocumentHandler( this );
myParser.setErrorHandler( this );
```

The following example simply displays a message each time a warning is triggered by the parser:

```
public void  warning(SAXParseException err)
{
  System.out.println( "WARNING: " + err );
}
```

Locators

An error message is not particularly helpful when no indication is given as to where the error occurred. To a greater or lesser extent, depending on the type or error concerned, all errors could be traced to an exact point in the data, and this information is vital for correcting such errors.

Most parsers count line feed characters as the document is parsed, so can report which line of text the error occurred on (note that this ability alone supplies a very good reason for including line feeds in the text). Some parsers may even keep track of the number of characters they have read from the current line, so can provide even more precise information.

To complicate matters, a single XML data stream may be derived from a number of data sources (that reference each other using external entities), and the line number alone is not sufficient in these cases. It is also necessary to know which source file or stream the parser was working through at the time.

The parser can tell the application the entity, line number and character number of the warning or error, by instantiating an object that belongs to a class that implements the **Locator** interface, then giving the application a reference to this object. The Locator interface defines the following methods:

```
int      getLineNumber();
int      getColumnNumber();
String   getSystemId();
String   getPublicId();
```

Most of these are self-explanatory, given the discussion above. The '**getLineNumber**' method returns the line number of the error ('-1' if this information is not available). The '**getSystemId**' and '**getPublicId**' methods return their respective source location information types. The '**getColumnNumber**' method returns the number of the column where the error occurred (again, '-1' if not available). The column is actually just the character position within the line.

The parser will continue to update this object each time it finds an error. But the main application needs access to it. It should be recalled that the DocumentHandler interface includes a method called '**setDocumentLocator**'. This method is used by the application to obtain a reference to the object:

```
Locator myLocator;
...
public void setDocumentLocator(Locator aLocator)
{
  myLocator = aLocator;
}
```

The following example shows the locator being used to provide a more informative error message:

```
Locator myLocator;
...
public void error(SAXParseException err)
{
    int ln = myLocator.getLineNumber();
    int ch = myLocator.getColumnNumber();
    String ent = myLocator.getSystemIID();
    System.out.println( "ERROR (" + err + ")" +
                        " at " + ln + ":" + ch +
                        " in file " + ent );
}
```

DTD handlers

External entity data that does not conform to the XML syntax cannot be processed by the parser, so is not passed on to the application. The application would therefore not know of its existence. To overcome this limitation, a mechanism is provided for the parser to tell the application about any binary entity declarations it encounters, as well as any notation declarations. Using this information, the application can locate the binary entities, and perhaps call other applications that can handle them.

The **DTDHandler** interface must be implemented by a class in the main application. Then an object instantiated from this class needs to be passed to the parser, in the now familiar way, this time using the **setDTDHandler** method. Once again, an application would typically implement this interface in the same class as the event-handler methods:

```
class MyClass implements DTDHandler {
...
myParser.setDTDHandler(this);
```

The class that implements this interface must include the following methods:

```
void notationDecl(String name, String publicId,
                  String systemId )
                               throws SAXException;

void unparsedEntityDecl(String name, String publicID,
                        String systemID,
                        String notationName)
                               throws SAXException;
```

The final parameter of the '**unparsedEntityDecl**' method provides the name of a notation. The details of this notation should have already been passed to the '**notationDecl**' method.

Input sources

While it is possible to parse documents by passing the **parse** method a string representing a file or other data source identified by a URL, it is also possible to specify a byte stream or a character stream instead. This is very useful when the application is reading data directly from another application, perhaps over a network.

The **InputSource** class contains methods that specify the exact nature of the data source. An InputSource object can be passed to the parser when parsing is set to commence (instead of the string that gives the parser a URL), and has further uses that are described later. This class includes the following methods:

```
InputSource();
InputSource( String SystemID );
InputSource( InputStream byteStream );
InputSource( Reader characterStream );

void   setPublicId( String publicId );
void   setSystemId( String systemId );
void   setByteStream( InputStream byteStream );
void   setCharacterStream( Reader characterStream );
void   setEncoding( String encoding );

String       getPublicId();
String       getSystemId();
InputStream  getByteStream();
Reader       getCharacterStream();
String       getEncoding();
```

There are a large number of methods in this interface. However, most of the 'set...' methods are just alternative means to using the constructor to define the input source, and the last five methods are only normally only used by the parser, to extract the information supplied by the application.

The following example demonstrates using this object to pass a string containing XML markup to the parser.

```
String text = "<note>This is a note</note>";
StringReader myReader = new StringReader( text );
myInputSource = new InputSource();
myInputSource.setCharacterStream( myReader );
...
myParser.parse( myInputSource );
```

Entity resolvers

Using the interfaces and classes discussed so far, the application is not aware of the physical structure of the XML data. The parser contains an entity manager that hides this complexity from the application, which sees the data as a single data stream.

However, it has already been shown that it can be useful to know more about each entity, if only to be able to provide useful error reports when problems are encountered within them. It would also be useful to be able to intercept an entity reference, and redirect the parser to another resource, or simply to a local copy of the named resource. An application could implement a catalogue feature using this scheme (assuming that the parser does not already have such a facility). For example, it could resolve public identifiers into local system identifiers.

It is possible to intercept references to entities using the **EntityResolver** interface. The application needs to create a class that implements this interface, which defines the following single method:

```
InputSource resolveEntity( String publicId,
                           String systemId );
```

Each time the parser encounters an entity reference that resolves to an external entity (but not to a binary entity), it stops and passes the system and/or public identifier to the main application, using the '**resolveEntity**' method. It waits for the method to return, either with a null value, which signifies that the parser should just continue as normal, or alternatively with a replacement data file, or data stream to process.

This method returns an **InputSource** object. The following example shows how to return a locally valid system identifier, to a file called 'disc.xml' in the 'xml' directory, whenever an entity is encountered that has a system identifier of 'Disclaimer', or a public identifier of '-//MyCorp//TEXT Disclaimer//EN':

```
public InputSource resolveEntity( String publicID,
                                  String systemID)
{
  if ( systemID.equals("Disclaimer") ||
    publicID.equals("-//MyCorp//TEXT Disclaimer//EN") )
      return ( new InputSource( "file://xml/disc.xml") );
}
```

Handler bases

When the application only needs to do something very simple with the XML source data, implementing all the interfaces described above may seem like too much effort. It would be useful if there were a ready-made class that implemented all the interfaces, providing some sensible default behaviour for each event, which could be subclassed to add application-specific functionality. The SAX API includes a class called **HandlerBase** that does this.

The following example demonstrates a very simply application that just reads processing instructions and presents their contents:

```
import org.xml.sax.HandlerBase;
...
public class myHandler extends HandlerBase( ) {
{
  public void myHandler(){}

  public void processingInstruction(String target,
                                    String content) {
    System.out.println( target + "\t" + content );
}
```

It is still necessary to locate and activate the parser, passing this class to the parser as the handler of the various interfaces.

15. DOM 1.0

Most XML parsers are able to build a tree model of an XML document as it is parsed, then allow the main application access to this model via an API. The arguments for and against using a standard API are the same as for the SAX approach discussed in the previous chapter, but in addition the major Web browser developers agreed that there was a need to provide a similar capability for accessing HTML elements from scripts in a Web page.

DOM (the *Document Object Model*) was developed by the W^{3}C, primarily to specify how future Web browsers and embedded scripts should access HTML and XML documents. There is a core standard that applies to both HTML and XML (available from http://www.w3.org/TR/REC-DOM-Level-1/), and is concerned with defining an interface to document instance constructs common to both (elements, attributes, comments, processing instructions and text content). There are extensions for more specific HTML processing, but they are not described in this chapter.

See Chapter 20 for a list of all DOM methods.

Java implementation

The DOM has an object design that assumes the use of object-oriented programming and scripting languages, such as C++, Java and JavaScript. The following examples are all Java code fragments, but the principles are the same for other languages.

The DOM standard is composed of a number of interfaces. In Java, these interfaces are defined in the package org.w3c.dom. Typically, a parser developer will implement these interfaces, and replace them with classes that have the same names. The application developer then only needs to import this package and use these classes. The following examples assume this scenario.

There are some important activities involved in parsing, navigating and processing documents that the DOM standard does not cover. Tree-walking a DOM structure, and writing out a structure into XML format, are both outside the scope of the standard. These features, if implemented at all, will differ in operation between parsers. For the sake of providing working examples, a specific parser has been chosen. In this case, the SUN Java parser has been used throughout.

To use the SUN parser, the following import statements are required:

```
import org.w3c.dom.*;
import com.sun.xml.tree.*;
import org.xml.sax.*;
```

Note that the SAX package is needed. This may appear strange, but some SAX objects are used in this implementation.

SUN provide a class for parsing XML, called XmlDocument. The createXmlDocument method in this class is used to parse the XML file or data stream, build the document tree, and return a reference to a node that represents the entire document:

```
try {
  Document myDoc =
     XmlDocument.createXmlDocument("file:/doc.xml", true);
  ...
}
catch( IOException err ) {...}
catch( SAXException err ) {...}
catch( DOMException err ) {...}
```

Again, note that this implementation requires trapping of SAX errors, as well as DOM errors.

The example above demonstrates parsing of the file 'doc.xml', with the 'true' value indicating that the parser should validate the document against its DTD. None of this is part of the DOM standard. However, the method returns a reference to a DOM object of type Document. This class is described in detail later. For now it is necessary only to know that it contains methods for extracting information about the parsed document, including a reference to the root element, which is represented by a Node object.

Nodes

Essentially, the DOM standard defines interfaces that are used to manage nodes. Nodes describe elements, text, comments, processing instructions, CDATA sections, entity references and declarations, notation declarations, and even entire documents. Nodes are also used to represent attributes of an element, though these nodes are not strictly part of the document tree.

There are some additional node types defined for ease of managing groups of nodes, including two that hold lists of nodes, and one that is useful for transferring nodes to another part of the document tree.

The **Node** interface is at the heart of the DOM scheme. In fact, this is practically the only interface that is needed, though several others subclass it to provide additional, more specific functionality, depending on the type of the object the given node represents. All of the interfaces shown in this diagram are discussed in detail later:

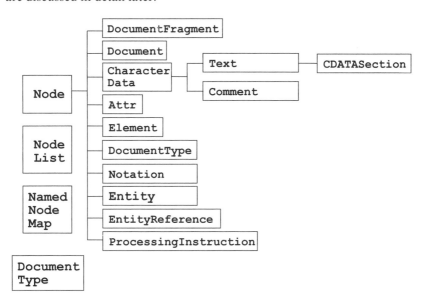

The Node interface itself defines a number of methods, and they can be divided into three broad categories. First, each node has characteristics, such as its type, name and value. Each node also has a contextual location in the document tree, and provides access to its relatives (its parent, siblings and children). Finally, each node has the capability to modify its contents – the nodes that represent its children.

Node characteristics

Each node carries some important information about itself, including its type and its name, but possibly also its value, attributes and contextual location. The following methods are supplied to provide access to this information:

```
short         getNodeType();
String        getNodeName();
String        getNodeValue() throws DOMException;
void          setNodeValue(String nodeValue)
                                throws DOMException;
boolean       hasChildNodes();
NamedNodeMap  getAttributes();
Document      getOwnerDocument();
```

Note that attribute handling is discussed later.

As a node can be any XML object, it is often necessary to determine what it represents before performing other operations on it. The **getNodeType** method is used to determine its type. A short integer value is returned, its value matching one of the following constants:

```
ELEMENT_NODE = 1
ATTRIBUTE_NODE = 2
TEXT_NODE = 3
CDATA_SECTION_NODE = 4
ENTITY_REFERENCE_NODE = 5
ENTITY_NODE = 6
PROCESSING_INSTRUCTION_NODE = 7
COMMENT_NODE = 8
DOCUMENT_NODE = 9
DOCUMENT_TYPE_NODE = 10
DOCUMENT_FRAGMENT_NODE = 11
NOTATION_NODE = 12
```

The following example shows how to use this information to detect that a node represents an element:

```
if ( MyNode.getNodeType() == Node.ELEMENT_NODE )
{
  // process element
}
```

Every node also has a name. In the case of nodes that represent elements, this is the element name, such as 'Para'. In other cases, a fixed name is used, such as '#comment' for all comment nodes. It should be clear from this that the node name is not a unique node identifier. An individual node can be uniquely identified only by its location in the document tree.

The **getNodeName** method returns the name of the node, and the **getNode-Value** method returns the value of the node. The following table shows, for each node type, the values returned by these methods:

Type	Interface name	Name	Value
ATTRIBUTE_NODE	Attr	*attribute name*	*attribute value*
DOCUMENT_NODE	Document	#document	*NULL*

Type	Interface name	Name	Value
DOCUMENT_FRAGMENT_-NODE	DocumentFrag-ment	#document-fragment	*NULL*
DOCUMENT_TYPE_NODE	DocumentType	*DOCTYPE name (root element name)*	*NULL*
CDATA_SECTION_NODE	CDATASection	#cdata-section	*CDATA content*
COMMENT_NODE	Comment	*entity-name*	*content string*
ELEMENT_NODE	Element	*tag name*	*NULL*
ENTITY_NODE	Entity	*entity name*	*NULL*
ENTITY_REFERENCE_NODE	EntityReference	*entity name*	*NULL*
NOTATION_NODE	Notation	*notation name*	*NULL*
PROCESSING_INSTRUCTION_NODE	ProcessingInstruct-ion	*target string*	*content string*
TEXT_NODE	Text	#text	*text string*

The value of a node can be replaced using the **setNodeValue** method. A string is passed to this method. In this way, the content of a text string, attribute, comment, processing instruction (instruction part only) and CDATA section can be modified.

Most types of node cannot have children. For example, a child of a comment makes no sense. The only nodes that can have children are Element, Document and DocumentFragment node types. There is a simple method to determine whether a node has children or not. The **hasChildNodes** method returns a boolean value of true if it has:

```
if ( MyNode.hasChildNodes() )
{
    // process children of MyNode
}
```

When a node has attributes, they can be accessed using the **getAttributes** method, which returns an object of type **NamedNodeMap** (described later). In practice, only Element nodes can have attributes, and the Element interface includes some alternative ways to process attached attributes in a simpler way.

```
NamedNodeMap myNodeMap = MyNode.getAttributes();
```

Node navigation

Every node has a specific location in the document hierarchy. When processing a document via the DOM interface, it is usual to use nodes as stepping-stones. Each node therefore has methods that return references to surrounding nodes:

```
Node      getFirstChild();
Node      getLastChild();
Node      getNextSibling();
Node      getPreviousSibling();
Node      getParentNode();
NodeList getChildNodes();
```

Using only two of these methods (**getFirstChild** and **getNextSibling**) it is possible to traverse the entire tree. The other four methods offer convenient ways to go back to the first sibling (**getFirstChild**), travel back up the tree structure (**getParentNode**), go backward through the list of siblings (**getPreviousSibling**), and to iterate through all children (**getChildNodes**).

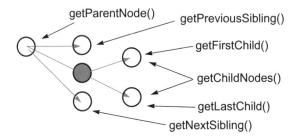

In the following example, after testing that a given node has children, references to the first and second child are obtained. The second reference will be null if the given node has only one child:

```
if ( myNode.hasChildNodes() )
{
  Node firstChild = MyNode.getFirstChild();
  Node secondChild = firstChild.getNextSibling();
}
```

Node manipulation

Structures in a DOM tree can be edited. Each node has methods that allow its children to be modified. Child nodes can be removed, added, replaced and copied.

```
Node   removeChild(Node oldChild) throws DOMException;
Node   insertBefore(Node newChild, Node refChild)
                             throws DOMException;
Node   appendChild(Node newChild) throws DOMException;
Node   replaceChild(Node newChild, Node oldChild)
                             throws DOMException;
Node   cloneNode(boolean deep);
```

A child node can be detached from its location in the tree by use of the **removeChild** method. The removed node still exists, and a reference to it is returned, but it no longer has a location in the tree. Other methods described below may be used to reattach it to another part of the document.

New nodes can be appended to the child list of a given node. These new nodes may be existing nodes already detached from another part of the tree, as described above, or may be manufactured using methods in the Document interface. The **appendChild** method is used to pass a reference to the new node. Another reference to the new node is returned by this method. The reason for doing this is to allow for the case where no reference exists until after the node has been added, as in the following example (which uses a 'factory' method of the Document interface, as discussed later). This example then goes on to remove the new node immediately:

```
Node addedNode =
     theParent.appendChild(doc.createElement("para"));
theParent.removeChild( addedNode );
```

Alternatively, a new node may need to be inserted between existing nodes in the child list. In this case, it is necessary to identify the location, and this is done by referring to the node that the new node must precede. The **insertBefore** method therefore takes two parameters. First, the reference to the new child node, and second, a reference to the existing node in the list.

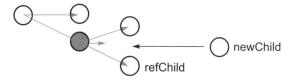

In the following example, a paragraph node is appended to the list, then a note is inserted before the paragraph:

```
Node paraNode =
     theParent.appendChild(doc.createElement("para"));
theParent.insertBefore( doc.createElement("note"),
                        paraNode );
```

Using the methods described above, it is of course possible to replace one node with another. The original can be removed, then the replacement can be inserted before its next sibling (or appended, in the case that the original was the final node in the list). But this process can be simplified using the **replaceChild** method.

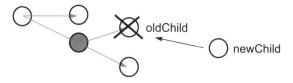

This method takes two parameters, the first being a reference to the new node, the second being a reference to the node to be removed. The method returns a reference to the replaced node.

When editing a document, it may be a common requirement to create copies of existing nodes, or whole branches of the tree, for use elsewhere. The **cloneNode** method creates a new node that has the same type, name and value as the given node. This method takes a boolean value which, when set to 'true', indicates that copies should also be made of all the children of the node, and all descendants of those children. In this way, entire branches of the tree can be copied. When set to 'false', only the selected node is copied, and the new copy therefore has no children. These two modes are known as 'deep' and 'shallow' cloning:

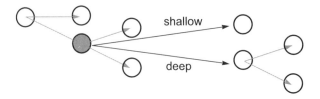

The Sun tree-walker

Although the main benefit of using the DOM (over the SAX approach) is that it provides a way to process an XML document in a random order, the ability to process the tree in sequential order often remains relevant. In practice, this means traversing the nodes in a very specific manner that is often termed 'tree-walking'.

Using the navigation methods described previously, tree-walking is a difficult process. A recursive technique is required to process all the children of each node before continuing on to the next sibling of that node. The rules that need to be followed are:

- if there are children, move to the first child, otherwise...

- if there further siblings, move to next sibling, otherwise...

- move to the nearest ancestor that has further siblings, and on to its next sibling, otherwise...

- if there are no ancestors with following siblings then stop

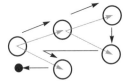

Achieving this requires careful management of references to various nodes. While the DOM does nothing to help with this activity, many parsers include software that performs the tree-walking process. A method may be included that simply returns a reference to the next node in the tree, effectively hiding the complexities described above. In the case of the Sun parser, a class called TreeWalker contains the following methods:

```
void TreeWalker( Node startPoint );
Node getCurrent();
Node getNext();
Node getNextElement( String tagName );
```

The TreeNode constructor method is given a reference to the node to start walking from. To read an entire document, this would be a reference to the root element:

```
Element currentElement = rootElement;
TreeWalker myWalker = new TreeWalker( currentElement );
```

Thereafter, each call to the getNext method returns a reference to the next node in the sequence. A return value of null indicates completion of the process. The following example reads an entire document and reports all occurrences of the 'para' element:

```
while ( currentElement != null )
{
  if ( currentElement.getName().equals("para") )
      System.out.println( currentElement.getName() );
  currentElement = myWalker.getNext();
}
```

Searching for all occurrences of a particular element is a very common requirement, so Sun have included another method that simplifies this task even further. The getNextElement method is given the name of the element, and only returns references to nodes with this name. Using this method, the example above can be simplified:

```
currentElement = myWalker.getNextElement("para");
while ( currentElement != null )
{
  .....
  currentElement = myWalker.getNextElement("para");
}
```

However, there is a standard DOM technique that achieves the same effect, using a method called getElementsByTagName (described later).

Documents

An entire XML document is represented by a special type of node. The **Document** interface extends the Node interface, adding a number of methods for extracting information about the document, and for creating objects that can be used to build a new document.

The following methods are included for obtaining information about the document:

```
DocumentType       getDoctype();
DOMImplementation getImplementation();
Element            getDocumentElement();
NodeList  getElementsByTagName(String tagName);
```

The **getDoctype** method provides access to information about the document, such as the DOCTYPE name (the name of the root element), and lists of entity declarations and notation declarations, via a DocumentType interface object (explained later).

The **getImplementation** method provides access to information concerning the capabilities of the DOM-compliant package. It returns a reference to an object that can be queried for information on whether or not a specific feature is supported. For example, it can be asked whether or not HTML extensions are available. The DOMImplementation interface is discussed in detail later.

The **getDocumentElement** method is perhaps the most important one in this list. It returns a reference to the node that represents the root element. It should be noted at this point that the node that represents the entire document has child nodes, including one that represents the root element. Other nodes are present if the root element is surrounded by markup, such as comments and processing instructions. It is therefore possible to gain a reference to the root element by searching through the document's children for the first (and only) node that represents an element, though this method is not as efficient as simply asking for the root element using the getDocumentElement method. This method returns an object of type Element (described later).

Often, a document needs to be searched for all occurrences of a specific element. For example, an application may need to extract the content of all title elements in order to construct a contents list for the document. The **getElementsByTagName** method returns a reference to an object that holds a list of matching element nodes. The NodeList interface used to hold the list is discussed later.

Factory methods

When reading an XML document into a DOM structure, all the nodes are created by the parser from the XML source. However, the DOM can be used to create new documents, or the application may need to add new structures to a document that has been read from file. It must therefore be possible for the application to create new nodes as they are needed, before attaching them to the tree (using the append or insert methods described previously). The Document interface contains a number of so-called 'factory' methods for this purpose:

```
Element             createElement(String tagName)
                                    throws DOMException;
DocumentFragment createDocumentFragment();
Text                createTextNode(String data);
Comment             createComment(String data);
CDATASection        createCDATASection(String data)
                                    throws DOMException;
ProcessingInstruction
        createProcessingInstruction(String target,
                                    String data)
                                    throws DOMException;
Attr                createAttribute(String name)
                                    throws DOMException;
EntityReference   createEntityReference(String name)
                                    throws DOMException;
```

These methods return references to nodes of various types that are discussed in detail later. The following example shows creation of a Para element:

```
Element MyElem = MyDoc.createElement("para");
```

Document types

Information about a document beyond the actual content hierarchies and text is encapsulated in an object of type **DocumentType**, which is returned by the **getDoctype** method described above.

This interface contains the following methods:

```
String          getName();
NamedNodeList getEntities();
NamedNodeList getNotations();
```

The **getName** method returns the name of the document, which is the word appearing after the DOCTYPE keyword, and is also the name of the root element.

The **getEntities** and **getNotations** methods return an object that contains a list of nodes that represent entities or notations declared in the document and DTD.

Elements

Nodes that represent elements are often the most common type of node to be found in a document tree structure. The DOM standard includes an **Element** interface that extends the Node interface to add element-specific functionality. These methods fall into two groups: general element methods and attribute management methods.

General element processing

The additional general-purpose methods in the Element interface are:

```
String    getTagName();
NodeList  getElementsByTagName( String name );
void      normalize();
```

The **getTagName** method returns a string that holds the element name. This method is identical in function to the underlying getNodeName method. It is simply more descriptive, within this context.

The **getElementsByTagName** method returns a list of all descendant elements that have the given name. This is the same method as the one in the Document interface, but lists only elements found within the source element node, rather than across the entire document.

When editing text, an application may split, delete, rearrange and create new Text nodes. At the end of editing, there may be adjacent Text nodes. While this is not illegal, and would not be noticed if the next task was simply to write out the text to an XML file, there are reasons why it is sometimes useful to be able to tidy up the structure. The **normalize** method cleans up the fragment of the tree within the element. In practice, this means that adjacent Text nodes are simply merged together.

Perhaps the most important reason for normalizing the text is to avoid confusing an advanced hypertext linking system that identifies ranges of text by their absolute location in the tree, or by counting nodes (see the XPointer standard).

Attribute management

Elements may contain attributes. The getAttributes method in the Node interface, briefly shown earlier, can be used to gain access to all the attributes of an element, and provides all the functionality necessary. But it is an unwieldy device when only simple operations are needed, and it is for this reason that additional methods have been defined in the Element interface to do simple things with attributes:

```
String getAttribute( String name );
void   setAttribute( String name, String value )
                                throws DOMException;
void   removeAttribute( String name )
                                throws DOMException;

Attr   getAttributeNode( String name );
void   setAttributeNode( Attr newAttr )
                                throws DOMException;
void   removeAttributeNode( Attr OldAttr )
                                throws DOMException;
```

The value of a given attribute can be retrieved as a string value using the **getAttribute** method. If the named attribute is not present in the element (and also not defined with a default value in the DTD), then an empty string is returned.

The value of a specific attribute can be changed by naming the attribute and supplying the replacement value. The **setAttribute** method therefore takes two string parameters. The named attribute is created if not already present.

An attribute can be removed using the **removeAttribute** method.

The second set of methods have identical functions and very similar names, but work with Attr objects instead of strings. The Attr interface provides a wrapper for an attribute with methods that provide more information about the attribute. It is discussed later.

These simple methods cannot supply all the information that might be necessary. They are inadequate when the name of the required attribute is not known, or when it is necessary to distinguish between values explicitly added to the element by a document author, and values that have been supplied by a default in the DTD. They also cannot determine the type of an attribute. To do these, and other complex things, it is necessary to use the underlying getAttributes method and work with NamedNodeMap and Attr objects, which are described below.

Attributes

Some of the methods in the Element interface return objects of type **Attr**. This interface is used to hold information on individual attributes.

Attribute characteristics

The following methods are available (beyond the underlying Node methods):

```
String  getName();
String  getValue();
void    setValue( String value );
boolean getSpecified();
```

The **getName** and **getValue** methods are exactly the same as the underlying getNodeName and getNodeValue methods.

The value of an attribute can be changed using the **setValue** method. The string passed to this method replaces its existing value. This is the same as Set-NodeValue in the underlying Node interface.

It is possible to discover if the attribute value originated from the start-tag of the element, or was supplied as a default by the DTD. If the **getSpecified** method returns a value of 'true', this means that the attribute was defined in the start-tag. A value of 'false' means that the attribute was not present, but the DTD provided the default.

Attribute node children

An Attr node can have children. These nodes represent the value of the attribute in a more complex form than that returned by the getValue method.

In the simplest case, there is a single child node, of type Text (described later). Using getNodeValue on this object returns the same value as does getValue on the parent Attr object. This is of minor benefit, but could be useful if the intention is to extract an attribute value and convert it to element content. The Text node can simply be moved to its new location.

But the real benefits of this approach become apparent when the attribute value includes one or more entity references. In this case, each entity reference is represented by an EntityReference node, and each block of text between entity references is represented by a Text node. EntityReference nodes also have children that contain the replacement value for the reference. Using this scheme, it is possible to see which parts, if any, of an attribute value are entity replacement text.

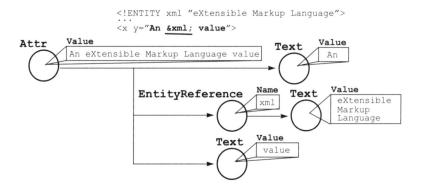

Entity references are discussed in more detail later.

Note that some parsers that claim DOM compliance nevertheless neglect to implement this feature.

Creating attributes

An Attr node can be created using the **createAttribute** method. The name of the attribute to create is passed to this method. In the following example, a new attribute is first created with the name 'status'. It is then given the value 'secret'. Finally, the new attribute is attached to an existing paragraph element:

```
// <para status="secret">
Attr newAttribute = myDoc.createAttribute( "status" );
newAttribute.setValue( "secret" );
myParaElement.setAttributeNode( newAttribute );
```

Character data

Many of the node types still to be discussed have textual content of some kind. The **CharacterData** interface described here is not used directly, but extends the Node interface, adds a number of useful text processing methods, and is further extended by the Text and Comment node types, amongst others. The reason for this arrangement is that all text-based node types have some common requirements. For example, it should be possible to delete a range of characters, insert new text at a given position in the string, and determine the length of the string.

The CharacterData interface contains the following methods:

```
String   getData() throws DOMException;
void     setData( String data ) throws DOMException;
int      getLength();
void     appendData( String arg ) throws DOMException;
String   substringData( int offset, int count )
                                    throws DOMException;
void     insertData( int offset, String arg )
                                    throws DOMException;
void     deleteData( int offset, int count)
                                    throws DOMException;
void     replaceData( int offset, int count, String arg )
                                    throws DOMException;
```

The **getData** method is directly equivalent to the underlying getNodeValue method. The text value can be changed using the **setData** method (which is equivalent to setNodeValue):

```
myText.setData("The DOM is a good thing.");
```

The number of characters in the string can be obtained by calling the **getLength** method:

```
int chars = myText.getLength();
```

New text can be added to the end of the existing string using the **appendData** method:

```
String sub = myText.appendData(" Is it not?");
```

The remaining methods all involve processing just part of the text string, so must be passed a value that represents the position of the first character to be affected, and in most cases also a value that represents the number of characters involved. The offset parameters are integer values, with the value zero representing the first character in the string.

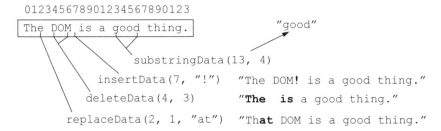

A fragment of the text can be obtained using the **substringData** method. An offset to the start of the text must be provided, as well as a count of the number of characters required. The character at the offset position is included in the extracted string, and is counted as the first character in the range:

```
String sub = myText.substringData(13, 4);
```

Text can be inserted into the string, using the **insertData** method. The first parameter indicates where to insert the new text. The character currently at this position, and all remaining characters, will be moved to the right to make way for the new text:

```
myText.insertData(4, "!");
```

Text can be deleted from the string, using the **deleteData** method. The first parameter indicates the location of the first character to be deleted, and the second parameter indicates how many characters to remove:

```
myText.deleteData(4, 3);
```

Replacing a segment of the text is a common requirement that can be achieved using the delete operation and insert methods. But a more convenient method called **replaceData** is included to achieve this operation in one step. The first two parameters work exactly as described for deleting text, and the third parameter is the replacement string. Note that the replacement string does not have to be the same length as the original. The two examples below are equivalent:

```
// one-step replace
myText.replaceData(2, 1, "at");

// two-step replace
myText.deleteData(2, 1);
myText.insertData(2, "at");
```

Text

Next to Element nodes, **Text** nodes are likely to be the most common in the average DOM tree. They tend to be children of Element nodes, and are always leaf nodes. The Text interface extends the CharacterData interface, so that the content of a Text node can be modified using the methods described above, but also adds the following single method:

```
Text  splitText( int offset ) throws DOMException;
```

The **splitText** method is used to split one Text node into two adjacent Text nodes, at the location in the string given in the parameter. The first part is considered to be the original node. The second part is a new node, and a reference to this new node is returned by the method.

A new Text node can be created using the **createTextNode** method in the Document interface. The following example creates a Text node, appends it to the content of an element, then splits it into two nodes (the element then has two Text child nodes):

```
Text newText = myDoc.createTextNode( "the text" );
anElement.appendNode( newText );
newText.splitText( 3 );
```

Character data sections

Ranges of text, possibly containing markup characters that are not to be inter-preted as markup, can be enclosed in a character data section. A **CDATASec-tion** node represents such a text range. This interface extends the CharacterData interface, and adds no further methods. It is simply used to identify character data nodes. When the value of a CDATASection node is written out to XML, the delimiter markup is added.

A new CDATASection node can be created using the **createCDATASection** method in the Document interface:

```
// <![CDATA[press <ENTER>]]>

CDATASection newCDATA =
        myDoc.createCDATASection( "press <ENTER>" );
```

Comments

Comments are represented by **Comment** nodes. This interface extends Node and CharacterData, and adds no methods. It is simply used to identify nodes that represent comments. When the value of a comment node is written out to XML, the delimiter markup is added.

A new Comment node can be created using the **createComment** method in the Document interface. The following example shows a new comment being cre-ated with the value ' my comment ' (note the surrounding spaces, which are useful to make the comment easier to read within delimiter markup), then the retrieving of a reference to the first child of the document (which may be the root element, a DOCTYPE declaration, a processing instruction, or even an existing comment (though the Sun parser does not preserve comments here)). Finally, the new comment is attached to the document before the existing first node, putting it at the top of the file:

```
// <!-- my comment -->

Comment newComment = myDoc.createComment( " my comment " );
Node firstNode = myDoc.getFirstChild();
myDoc.insertBefore( newComment, firstNode );
```

Processing instructions

Processing Instructions are represented by **ProcessingInstruction** nodes. The name of this type of node is the name of the target application (the first word in the tag). The value of this type of node is the instruction data that occupies the body of the tag.

The white space between the target and the instruction is implied, and most parsers would insert a single space between them when writing out to XML format.

The **CreateProcessingInstruction** method in the Document interface can be used to create new nodes. It takes two parameters, the target name then the instruction:

```
// <?ACME page-break?>

ProcessingInstruction myProc;
myProc =
   myDoc.createProcessingInstruction( "ACME",
                                      "page-break" );
```

Entities and notations

XML documents may include entities, some of them including references to notations, and there will be references to these entities embedded in the text. The DOM includes interfaces for handling notations, entities and references to entities.

Entity references

When parsable entity references appear in an XML document, the parser will either replace the references with the content of the entity before building the DOM tree, or will leave the entity references in place. In the former case, the application simply never knows that they existed. But when the references are left in the text, they should be represented by **EntityReference** nodes (rather than just ignored, and left as embedded character sequences in the text). This interface does not define any additional methods.

The name property reflects the name of the entity, but the value property is not used. Instead, an EntityReference object has children that represent the replacement content of the entity. At a minimum, this would be a single Text node that contains the string as its value:

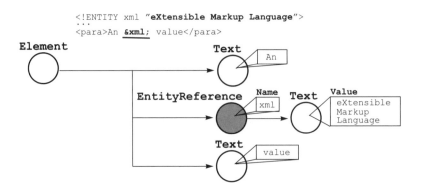

```
<!ENTITY xml "eXtensible Markup Language">
...
<para>An &xml; value</para>
```

Entities

As stated above, the parser may replace entity references, or create EntityReference nodes. Either way, it can be argued that the original entity declaration is now redundant, so can be discarded, and some parsers may do this. However, external binary data cannot be inserted into a DOM tree, so it is important that the original entity definitions for such data be accessible to the application. The application would not otherwise know of the existence of these entities.

The **Entity** interface extends the Node interface, and adds the following methods:

```
String    getPublicId();
String    getSystemId();
String    getNotationName();
```

The **getSystemId** and **getPublicId** methods allow location information to be extracted. An Entity object can represent any kind of entity, but for non-parsable entities it allows the name of the notation to be obtained using the **getNotationName** method:

```
// <!ENTITY MyBoat PUBLIC "BOAT" SYSTEM "boat.gif"
//                                         NDATA GIF>
String pub = ent.getPublicId();       // BOAT
String sys = ent.getSystemId();       // boat.gif
String nota = ent.getNotationName();  // GIF
```

A node representing a parsable entity may have child nodes that represent the replacement value of the entity. If present, these should exactly match the child nodes of each EntityReference node with the same name:

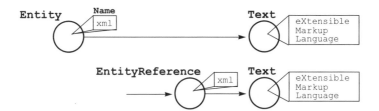

All the entities in a document can be accessed using the getEntities method in the DocumentType object (see below).

It should be noted that the children of an Entity node cannot be edited, and that even if they could be edited the changes would not be dynamically reflected in each reference. Once the DOM has been constructed, there is no connection between references and declarations. To make matters worse, the children of EntityReference nodes cannot be edited either. So, to make a change, it is necessary to actually replace each reference with clones of the children of the Entity node. The inserted nodes can then be edited, at each location. This process is likely to create adjacent Text nodes, so it may be appropriate to call the 'normalize' method after making all edits.

Notations

Having retrieved the name of the notation that a non-parsable entity complies with, it may be necessary to discover more about that notation. Each notation declaration in the document can be represented by an object that implements the **Notation** interface. This interface extends the Node interface, and adds the following methods:

```
String    getPublicId();
String    getSystemId();
```

These methods are the same as for the Entity interface. The **getPublicId** method returns the content of the public identifier (if there is one), and the **get-SystemId** method returns the content of the system identifier.

All the notations in a document can be accessed using the getNotations method in the DocumentType object (see below).

Node lists

Some of the operations described above return lists of nodes that match some criteria. For example, getElementsByTagName returns all element nodes that have a given name, and getChildNodes returns all the children of a given node. For convenience, a single object is returned, of type **NodeList**, and this object acts as a wrapper for the returned nodes.

The nodes contained in this object are organized into a logical, linear sequence. For example, the getChildNodes method returns all the children nodes, in their original order of appearance, so that they can be easily processed in the correct order.

The NodeList interface contains the following two methods:

```
Node   item(int index);
int    getLength( );
```

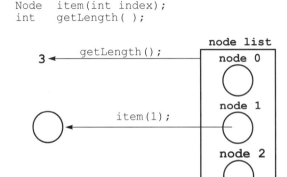

A reference to a node in the list is obtained by calling the **item** method, and providing it with the sequential number of the required node. The first node in the list is assigned the number zero, so to obtain the fourth node it is necessary to request node three:

```
Node myNode = myNodeList.item(3);
```

In order to access all the nodes in a list, or simply to avoid asking for a node that does not exist, it is important to be able to ask the list how many nodes it contains. The **getLength** method returns an integer value that represents the total number of nodes. However, because the first node in the list is numbered zero, the value returned by this method will be one higher than the number of the last node in the list. The following example presents the names of all element children of the root element:

```
Node aChildNode;
NodeList rootsChildren = rootElement.getChildNodes();
for( int i = 0; i < rootsChildren.getLength(); i++ )
{
  aChildNode = rootsChildren.item(i);
  if ( aChildNode.getNodeType() == Node.ELEMENT_NODE )
  {
    System.out.println( aChildNode.getNodeName() );
  }
}
```

Named node maps

In some circumstances, a set of nodes that have no particular ordering significance need to be grouped together. This applies to attributes and to entity and notation declarations. Attributes do, of course, have a location, in that they belong to a specific element instance, but their order of appearance within the start-tag is not significant. Likewise, entity declarations have an order in the data stream, but this order is not significant (beyond the fact that only the first occurrence of duplicate declarations is acted upon). While the location is not significant in these instances, the names of these items certainly *is* significant. Unique names are essential. The **NamedNodeMap** interface is designed to contain nodes, in no particular order, that can be accessed by name. It can be used to hold a set of attributes that belong to a given element, and sets of entity and notation declarations that belong to a document, as the following examples demonstrate:

```
NamedNodeMap rootsAttributes = myElement.getAttributes();
NamedNodeMap docEntities = myDocument.getEntities();
NamedNodeMap docNotations = myDocument.getNotations();
```

The methods defined in the interface are:

```
Node   item(int index);
int    getLength( );
Node   getNamedItem(String nodeName);
Node   setNamedItem(Node theNode) throws DOMException;
Node   removeNamedItem(String nodeName)
                                    throws DOMException;
```

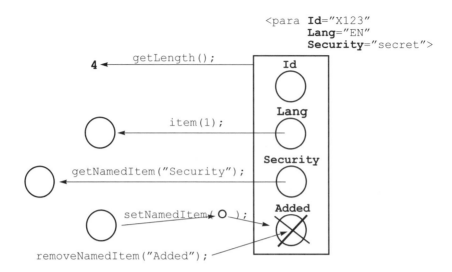

Extracting by name

Because nodes in these lists are distinguished by name, a method called **get-NamedItem** is included. The following example extracts the security status of an element (the node is null if the attribute is not present):

```
NamedNodeMap myMap = myElement.getAttributes();
Attr security = (Attr) myMap.getNamedItem("Security");
```

Removing and adding items

Nodes can be removed and added to the list.

The **removeNamedItem** method removes the node with the given name from the list. However, it does not actually delete the node, but returns a reference to it for reuse elsewhere.

The **setNamedItem** method adds a given node to the list, but despite its name passes a node reference to the list, not the node name (this method is probably so named as a reminder that the operation will not succeed if there is a node with the same name already present in the list).

The following example demonstrates both methods, by first removing the Security attribute, then reinserting it into the list:

```
Node temp = myMap.removeNamedItem("Security");
myMap.setNamedItem(temp);
```

The setNamedItem method also returns a reference to the node just added, which can be useful when the node is added at the same time as it is created:

```
Node newNode =
    myMap.setNamedItem(myDoc.createAttribute("Added"));
```

Extracting without name

Although NamedNodeMap objects have an **item** method that works in the same way as in the NodeList interface, there is no equivalent significance to the item number. The **getLength** and item methods are included so that nodes can be selected even when their names are not known, for example to extract all attributes and display their names:

```
Node aNode;
NamedNodeMap atts = myElement.getAttributes();
for( int i = 0; i < atts.getLength(); i++ )
{
  aNode = atts.item(i);
  System.out.println( aNode.getNodeName() );
}
```

Document fragments

A fragment of the document can be attached temporarily to a 'lightweight' object, formally called a **DocumentFragment** node. This can also be thought of as a 'scratchpad' or 'clipboard'. The most interesting characteristic of this node is that when it is attached to another node as a child, it dissolves. Its children are promoted to be direct children of the node that it was attached to.

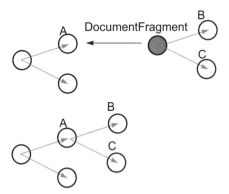

However, if the final location is already known, it is just as easy to move each node directly to its intended location. This node type is probably only useful when the application really does not know the ultimate destination of the nodes at the time they are removed from the document tree. It is therefore very useful when the application is interactive, and provides a 'cut' and 'paste' option.

DOM implementation

The **DOMimplementation** interface defines a single method, called **hasFeature**, which is used to determine the extent of DOM support that the application/ parser has. This method returns a boolean value, with 'true' indicating support for the given feature. This method can be called a number of times, each time testing for support for a particular feature, and the name of the feature is passed as the first parameter. Currently, this method can be called to test for support for 'XML' and for 'HTML'. As DOM support for both these data types is expected to improve over time, it is also necessary to check which version of the DOM is supported in each case, and the version number is therefore passed as the second parameter. Currently, this would be the string '1.0'.

```
if ( theParser.hasFeature( "XML", "1.0" )
{
  // XML is supported
  ...
}
```

16. Character sets

XML markup and document data can only be recognized when the characters they comprise conform to recognized standard encoding schemes. This chapter describes character encoding schemes in general, and the most important standards, including ASCII, ISO 8859, Unicode and ISO 10646. An understanding of the intentions and limitations of these formats is fundamental to appreciation of the purpose and scope of XML, and these standards are very important in their own right.

Characters

XML data is composed of a simple sequence of **characters**, including the **text** of the document and the markup that describes and structures the text. However, computers do not directly understand the concept of characters. Computers are basically calculating machines (once termed 'number crunchers'). In order to store text in a computer, a unique numeric value is used to represent each possible character, including letters, digits and punctuation marks. For example, the value 51 may be used to represent the digit '3', the value 33 may be used to represent the exclamation mark, '!', and the value 84 may be used to represent the letter 'T'. When an operator presses the letter 'T' key on the keyboard, a signal is sent to the computer, which uses a look-up table to determine the value to be stored on disk or in memory.

A group of number-to-character mappings, usually including the characters typically found on a typewriter or computer keyboard, is termed a **character set**. The actual shape of the character will vary depending on which **font** is used to display or print that character. A font table provides a suitable shape for each value in the range encompassed by the character set.

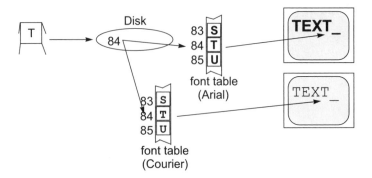

font table
(Arial)

font table
(Courier)

When information is transferred between two computers that use incompatible character sets, the numeric values are preserved but the number-to-character mappings differ, and the text becomes unintelligible when presented to a user of the second system. Assuming the incompatible representation schemes shown below (where every character on System B has a value one lower than on System A), the word 'TEXT' would be corrupted to 'UFYU' on transfer to System B:

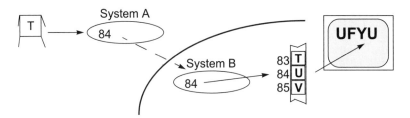

ASCII

Moves to avoid the problem of incompatible character sets resulted in the defining of **ASCII** (the *American Standard Code for Information Interchange*), which assigns an agreed value to commonly used characters. For example, two systems that use the ASCII standard will both assume that the value 84 represents the letter 'T', so they can exchange text data without risk.

A data file that contains only characters conforming to the ASCII format is termed a **text file** (though this term also applies to platform-specific alternatives such as **EBCDIC**). A text file is often used as a simple data format for transfer of information between systems and application software. Many word processors, for instance, have an option such as 'Save as Text' or 'Export ASCII'. Data exchange formats that rest upon the ASCII format include **CSV**, **RTF** and **PostScript**, amongst others.

Text editor applications are designed to work with text files, allowing them to be created, viewed, edited and printed. A simple text editor is therefore a suitable tool for editing XML documents (providing interactive validation is not required).

ASCII defines values for only 128 characters (a **7-bit** representation). Although one character is stored in each **byte** of storage, which can theoretically hold 256 distinct values, the eighth bit is actually reserved for use as a check-bit (used to validate that each byte has been transferred between systems without corruption). This means that ASCII can only represent the characters and symbols that appear on typewriters and computer keyboards, plus a few invisible control characters required to crudely format the text for viewing or printing. There are no spare values to represent foreign accented characters ('Üàó'), Greek letters ('αεϕγ') or scientific symbols ('!∀≤∃').

▨ 1 0 1 0 1 0 0 = 84 = 'T'

The full range of visible ASCII characters are listed by order of ascending value below:

```
!"#$%&'()*+,-./0123456789:;<=>?@ABCDEFGHIJKL
MNOPQRSTUVWXYZ[\]^_`abcdefghijklmnopqrstuvwx
yz{|}~
```

The ASCII format was standardized by the **ISO** (the ***International Organization for Standardization***) under the designation **ISO/IEC 646**. The only modification made was to replace the country-specific currency symbol, such as '$', with the international currency symbol, ' '.

One approach to extending the range of characters that can be represented using the standard ASCII character set is to use several ASCII characters to represent one non-ASCII character. This technique is in common use in SGML and HTML documents, and may be applied to XML equally well. An entity may be defined for each 'extended' character, and given a suitable name such as 'eacute' for the 'é' character. Whenever the character is required in the text, the entity reference 'é' is inserted. Alternatively, the value of a character can be inserted, such as 'é', without needing an entity definition, but relying on an agreed definition of what character the value maps to. These approaches are unwieldy, and should be made redundant when all computer systems adopt the extended character set schemes described below.

Extended ASCII

Modern computers are more reliable than old systems, and do not need a check-bit, so they use an **8-bit** representation (the whole byte) to hold character values, and thus provide for an extra 128 characters. There was originally no agreement on which extra characters to include, and which values to assign to those that were common to some or all systems. For example, the Apple Macintosh uses the value 142 to represent the character 'é', whereas the same character is given a value of 130 in one configuration of an MS-DOS system. A Macintosh text file should not be copied to an MS-DOS system without passing it through a filter that moves the extra characters to their correct positions in the latter's character set.

This problem is addressed by **ISO 8859**, which defines (amongst others) a standard Latin alphabet character set (called **ISO 8859/1**) consisting of 255 characters, currently used by Web browsers, Microsoft Windows and Sun OS UNIX. A chart of this character set is shown in Chapter 20. These sets were designed in the 1980s by **ECMA**.

Backward compatibility with ISO 646 is maintained, so if the high bit of every byte in an 8859 document is zero, it automatically counts as a 646 document as well.

```
0 1 0 1 0 1 0 0   = 84  = 'T'
1 1 0 1 0 1 0 0   = 212 = 'Ô'
```

The '/1' part of the name identifies just one variant of 8859, the standard Latin alphabet, but there are other variants that include different accented characters, to cover the requirements of various languages.

ISO 8859/*x*	Languages Covered
1	ISO Latin-1. ASCII characters plus Danish, Dutch, English, Faroese, Finnish, German, Icelandic, Irish, Italian, Norwegian, Portuguese, Spanish and Swedish characters.
2	ISO Latin-2. ASCII characters plus Croatian, Czech, Hungarian, Polish, Romanian, Slovak and Slovenian characters.
3	ISO Latin-3. ASCII characters plus Esperanto, Maltese, Turkish (though 8859/5 is now preferred for this language) and Galician characters.
4	ISO Latin-4. ASCII characters plus Latvian, Lithuanian, Greenlandic and Lappish.
5	ASCII characters plus Cyrillic characters to cover Byelorussian, Bulgarian, Macedonian, Russian, Serbian and Ukrainian.
6	ASCII characters plus Arabic.

7	ASCII characters plus modern Greek.
8	ASCII characters plus Hebrew.
9	ISO Latin-5. As Latin-1 except six Turkish characters replace six Icelandic letters.
10	ISO Latin-6. ASCII characters plus Lappish, Nordic and Inuit.

Despite the existence of the more powerful standards described later, work still continues on yet more variants of 8859, including the following:

ISO 8859/*x*	Languages Covered
11	Thai.
12	*RESERVED*
13	ISO Latin-7. ASCII characters plus characters for Baltic Rim languages.
14	ISO Latin-8. ASCII characters plus Gaelic and Welsh (all Celtic languages).
15	ISO Latin-9. ASCII characters plus French and Finnish letters and the Euro symbol.

Unicode and ISO/IEC 10646

As there are far more than 256 symbols in use in the world, even ISO 8859 cannot represent them all. One obvious solution is to use more than one byte to encode each character, and two standards have emerged that use this technique. These are the **Unicode** and **ISO/IEC 10646** standards.

Unicode, now at version 2.1 (as of January 1998), was the first initiative, and basically uses two bytes for each character, immediately raising the scope to 65,536 characters. Online charts of the characters covered can be found at http://charts.unicode.org.

As even this scale is insufficient for some needs, such as representing the vast range of Chinese characters, the ISO devised the capacious 10646 scheme, which employs up to four bytes, giving over two billion characters. In response, Unicode 2.0 contains some additional variable-size representation schemes to access some of these additional characters, and exactly 38,887 characters are defined in version 2.1.

XML has adopted ISO 10646 as its character encoding format, as this is seen as the ultimate encoding scheme. It is expected that all operating systems and applications will eventually move to this universal standard.

UCS

ISO 10646 consists of a number of encoding schemes. The simplest schemes utilize a fixed number of bytes to store each character, and are known as **UCS** (***Universal Character Set***) schemes. **UCS-4** is a four-byte scheme. **UCS-2** is a two-byte scheme:

```
             00000000 01010100 = 84 = 'T' (UCS-2)
00000000 00000000 00000000 01010100 = 84 = 'T' (UCS-4)
```

Values below 128 represent the same characters as the equivalent value in ISO 646 (and therefore also ASCII, with just one exception). Values between 128 and 256 are the same as ISO 8859/1, so the character 'é' has the value 233 in both.

As identification of a character by its 16-bit value is hardly intuitive, names have been assigned to groups of values on different scales. For example, a character can be identified as being in group 13, plane 253, row 4, cell 129:

```
┌─────────────────────────────────────────────┐
│ -0000000  00000000  00000000  00000000 │
└─────────────────────────────────────────────┘
   group (128)  plane (256)  row (256)    cell (256)
```

Note that UCS-2 therefore represents all the characters in plane 0.

BMP

As shown above, there are 32,768 planes of 65,536 characters each. The first plane (plane 0) is known as the **BMP** (the ***Basic Multilingual Plane***). All XML names must comprise of characters from the BMP (from UCS-2). At the time of writing, only the BMP has been assigned characters; the vast landscape beyond this set is reserved for future use, which will certainly include the huge Chinese character set.

Note that the standard two-byte Unicode format is now directly equivalent to the BMP set. A valid Unicode character is automatically the same character in the UCS-2 representation, and with two zero-value bytes added is also valid UCS-4. However, discrepancies have temporarily occurred in the past, whenever one standard has been updated before the other, and this may happen again.

UTF

The UCS scheme is certainly simple and efficient. Memory is now relatively cheap, so using two, or even four bytes for each character is not usually of concern, and processing data when all characters occupy the same number of bytes is inherently very efficient. For example, the location in memory of the 39th character is easy to determine (simply multiply 39 by four, then deduct three). Yet this technique is not suitable in all cases. It can appear wasteful when storing data, and dramatically hinder the flow of information over networks.

In many scenarios, the great majority of characters in a file will be the standard alpha-numerics found on the keyboard, in which case only 25 per cent of the bytes stored or transmitted contain useful information (the first three bytes of each character contain zero values). To reduce the size of such files, a scheme that allows common characters to be represented by smaller values would be ideal. Less common characters could still be represented by large values, stored in four, or even more bytes. Schemes that work in this way are termed **UTF** (*UCS Transformation Format*) schemes.

Using UTF, when an ASCII character is encoded, only one byte is needed to represent it, but more exotic characters are encoded using several bytes. In the worst case scenario, where exotic characters comprise the majority of characters in the file, a UTF format produces a slightly larger file than its UCS equivalent, but in the best case is just one-quarter of the size.

UTF-8

UTF-8 uses a single byte to represent 7-bit ASCII characters, and between two and six bytes to represent extended characters. For example, to represent the character with a binary value of '011 11000000 11110000 00111100', it actually employs five bytes. The first byte first states that it is the first of five ('11111'), then represents the first three digits ('011'). Subsequent bytes start with '10' to indicate that they are part of a larger value, then store six bits of the value each.

```
00000000 00000000 00000000 01010100 = 84 = 'T' (UCS-4)
                            01010100 = 84 = 'T' (UTF-8)


00000011 11000000 11110000 00111100                    (UCS-4)

11111011 10110000 10001111 10000000 10111100  (UTF-8)

  = 5 bytes    continuation bytes
```

Although the second example above demonstrates that UTF-8 representation of a character can actually take more bytes than UCS-4, in the vast majority of cases it will take considerably fewer, and most frequently just one byte per character (as in the first example).

All XML processors must be able to process UTF-8 format data.

UTF-16

Some operating systems (such as Windows NT) and programming languages (notably Java) have adopted Unicode as their standard encoding format.

Unicode is based on UCS-2 (its 65,536 characters are the same as those defined in UCS-2, and by implication the same as the low-order 65,536 UCS-4 characters). However, it includes some tricks to represent the additional characters from the full 10646 UCS-4 set. As the limitations of Unicode became apparent (compared with ISO 10646), a technique to access more than just the BMP set of characters from ISO 10646 was developed, first called UCS-2E ('E' for extended), but now known as **UTF-16** (*UCS Transformation Format for Planes of Group 00*). This scheme provides access to a further 16 planes. This is achieved in a similar manner to the UTF scheme described above. Some values are reserved to 'switch in' other planes.

All XML processors must be able to process UTF-16 format data.

Summary

All XML processors must accept UTF-8 and UTF-16 formats as standard. The main point to recall is that most of these standards overlap each other.

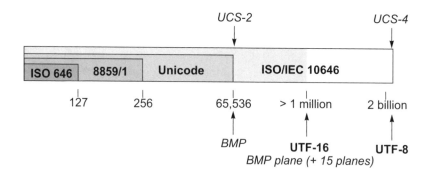

It should be noted, however, that ISO 8859/1 does not fit comfortably into this picture. It is not possible to 'pretend' that an ISO 8859/1 format file is in fact one of these other standards (even Unicode, as it uses two bytes for each character).

Unfortunately, the encoding scheme that is the most popular in the early days of XML is *not* a default XML format.

Unicode support is slowly emerging. The most popular word processors and Web browsers, and some operating systems (such as NextStep, BeOS and Windows NT 4.0) do provide some level of support, but the big problem is finding fonts that include glyphs for all the characters in this huge set.

Character set declarations

The XML processor is informed of the character set used in an XML document via the encoding parameter of the XML declaration:

```
<?xml ... encoding="UTF-8" ... ?>
```

An XML document is assumed to be encoded in UTF-8 if the first four bytes of the file have the values '3C 3F 78 6D ' (in **hexadecimal** notation), which represent the characters '<?xm'. If these characters are not present, but the document does not conform to any of the other options, then UTF-8 is assumed anyway. The encoding parameter is not required because this is the default character set.

If UTF-16 is in use, the characters expected at the start of an XML document could be represented by the values '00 3C 00 3F 00 78 00 6D', as might be expected, or equally by the byte-reversed values '3C 00 3F 00 78 00 6D 00'. In order to resolve this **lo-byte/hi-byte** ordering problem, which is caused by microprocessor design constraints, the first two bytes of any UTF-16 file *must* be reserved for use as a byte order mark. The byte order mark should be 'FF FF' for the first ordering shown above, and 'FF FE' for the latter.

The declaration is required for formats other than UTF-8 and UTF-16. A document that conforms to ISO 646 can 'pretend' to be a UTF-8 file, as it is a valid subset, but an ISO 8859 document must be explicitly identified:

```
<?xml ... encoding="ISO-8859-1" ... ?>
```

Note that a variant of this tag, the **Encoding Processing Instruction (Encoding-Decl[80])**, should appear at the top of each external entity, where it is used to identify entities with a different character encoding to the main file:

```
<?xml encoding="EUC-JP" ?>
```

If an XML document is delivered over the Internet, the character set in use may be determined from the MIME header. When the MIME type is 'text/xml', the character encoding is provided in the 'charset' parameter of the MIME header.

Entities for characters

Until the more advanced character set schemes described above become widely used in operating systems and transfer media, many may prefer to stick with 7-bit ASCII, and rely upon entities to describe additional characters. Most SGML DTDs, for example, contain references to ISO entity sets:

```
<!ENTITY % ISOpub PUBLIC "ISO 8879:1986//
            ENTITIES Publishing//EN"
            SYSTEM "../ISOpub.ent">
<!ENTITY % ISOlat1 PUBLIC "ISO 8879:1986//
            ENTITIES Added Latin 1//EN"
            SYSTEM "../ISOlat.ent">
<!ENTITY % ISOgrk1 PUBLIC "ISO 8879:1986//
            ENTITIES Greek Letters//EN"
            SYSTEM "../ISOgrk.ent">
%ISOpub; %ISOlat1; %ISOgrk1;
```

However, it is perhaps too easy just to add entity declarations that refer to the ISO sets. An ISO set may be added because it contains a few, or even just one, required character definition, but once added a document author can use all the characters in the set. Difficulties arise if a character is used that is not supported by an available font on the printer or in the browser used to publish or present the material. Although more work is required, it is better to create an application-specific entity set that contains exactly the characters required, though it is also advisable to use the official ISO-defined names for these characters.

17. Cascading style sheets (CSS)

This chapter describes CSS, a style sheet format already in widespread use. Initially, this chapter covers the well-supported CSS1 format, then the latest CSS2 extensions, and should be of particular interest to those wishing to use Web browsers to format XML or HTML documents, and those wishing to use the CSS-compatible parts of XSL.

Background

The **CSS** standard was initially developed for use with HTML (by the W^3C in 1996), specifically for implementation within Web browsers, and was born out of growing pressure for more author control over the presentation of Web pages. At the time of writing, version 1 is supported by the most popular HTML Web browsers, but version 2 has not yet been widely adopted. Version 1 can be obtained from http://www.w3.org/pub/WWW/TR/REC-CSS1 and version 2 from http://www.w3.org/TR/REC-CSS2.

An earlier chapter explores the XSL format, and demonstrates how powerful and flexible this language is. It is reasonable to ask why two style sheet standards should exist, and why XSL users should even consider CSS. The answer is partly a simple issue of timing. At the time of writing, CSS exists and is supported by the popular Web browsers, whereas XSL is still just a draft standard. In addition, CSS may be used when XSL is considered too complex for the task, as it is easier to learn. Although CSS is relatively simple in comparison with many style sheet languages, its concentration on screen formatting gives it some unique advantages in this area. In addition, version 2 of the standard addresses some page-related issues missing from the original standard.

It should be noted that the latest drafts of XSL include formatting properties that are copied from CSS equivalents, and that even the names of these properties are the same. This means that once CSS is understood, it should be easier to learn XSL as well.

Format overview

The CSS format utilizes the ASCII text format, so style definitions can be easily created and edited in any text editor or word processor. However, unlike XSL, it does not use XML constructs but defines its own syntax.

A CSS style sheet is composed of at least one style rule. A rule is simply a style specification for an element, pseudo-element or group of similar elements. A typical style sheet will contain many such rules. A rule begins with a selector, which must start a new line in the text file. In the simplest case, the selector is the name of an XML or HTML element. In the following example, the selector is 'title', so the style definition will apply to the content of the Title element, wherever it is used in a document. Curly brackets enclose the style definition, which may span any number of lines:

```
title { ... }
```

Note that when used with HTML, the name is not case-sensitive, so 'body', 'BODY' and 'Body' all identify the HTML Body element. In XML, however, element names are case-sensitive, so the style sheet names must also be case-sensitive, and care must be taken to match exactly the name used in the DTD declaration (or in the document, if there is no DTD).

In some cases, styles can be applied to just part of the text of an element, such as the first line or word, and in other cases user activity can affect the style. Keywords representing these conditions are separated from the element name using a colon:

```
title:first-line { ... }
```

A style definition consists of at least one declaration. Each declaration defines a specific style, such as the name of a font, or size of an indent. A declaration is composed of a property, such as 'font-size', and a value for that property, such as '32pt'. The property is separated from its value by a colon:

```
font-size:32pt
```

For improved readability, spaces may also be included. Although it is possible to place spaces before the colon, perhaps the most readable combination is a colon followed by a space:

```
font-size: 32pt
```

Multiple declarations are separated by semi-colons. In this case, legibility may be improved by including spaces both before and after the separator:

```
font-size: 32pt ; color: blue
```

To summarize these rules, a complete style definition that specifies 23pt blue text for a H1 element appears as follows:

```
h1    { font-size: 32pt ; color: blue }
```

The definition may span multiple lines. This example could be also be formatted as follows:

```
h1    { font-size: 32pt;
        color: blue }
```

Comments can be added to a style sheet, and take the same form as in the C programming language, beginning with the character sequence '/*', and ending with the sequence '*/':

```
H1    {  }   /* HTML Header One Style */
```

Wherever colours are allowed, the choice is from 'aqua', 'black', 'blue', 'fuchsia', 'gray', 'green', 'lime', 'maroon', 'navy', 'olive', 'purple', 'red', 'silver', 'teal', 'white' and 'yellow'. An RGB value can be given, with the keyword 'rgb(r, g, b)' ('r' represents red, 'g' represents green and 'b' represents blue), or with a hexadecimal number in the form '#rgb' or '#rrggbb'. The examples below are equivalent:

```
emph   { ... ; color: rgb(128, 0, 255)  }

emph   { ... ; color: #8000FF  }
```

Wherever sizes are allowed, the choice is from absolute sizes given in points ('pt'), inches ('in'), centimetres ('cm'), millimetres ('mm') or picas ('pc'), and from relative sizes 'em' (height of the element's font), 'ex' (the height of a letter) and 'px' (pixels relative to the canvas). Values can have a '+' (the initial setting) or '-' prefix.

Often, sizes can be given as a percentage of an inherited size, so that '50%' means half the current size. Note that percentage values can be greater than 100, and a size value of '200%' indicates that the object should be twice the inherited size.

Sometimes, an external resource can be called in using a URL. The function 'url(...)' is used for this purpose. Relative URLs have the style sheet document location as their context. Quotes may enclose the actual URL. Significant characters need to be escaped, including '(', ')', ' ' ', ' " ' and ',', by placing a '\' character before them, such as '\('.

Styling properties

CSS has many styling properties, including text properties (dealing with fonts and character styles), colours and backgrounds, margins, and white space around elements, and general object type classifications.

Font styles

Characters are presented in a specified font, at a given size, and possibly rendered with style characteristics such as bold, italic and small caps.

The 'font-family' property specifies the font to display the text in, such as Helvetica. When the font name includes spaces, the name must be quoted, as in the following example:

```
para    { font-family: "Times New Roman" }
```

Because not all systems have the same fonts available, alternatives can be expressed, and are separated by commas. An application should pick the first one that matches an installed font, reading from left to right through the list. To cover situations where no font names match, there are some generic names available, and one of these should be added to the end of the list. They are: 'serif' (a font like Times, or the font used for this paragraph, with lines on the end of each major stroke), 'sans-serif' (a font without serifs, such as Arial or Helvetica, and the titles and headings in this book), 'cursive' (Zapf-Chancery), 'fantasy' (Western) and 'monospace' (a font where all characters are the same width, such as Courier, the font used for the examples in this chapter).

```
title    {font-family: Arial, sans-serif }
```

The 'font-style' property affects the text in other ways, either slanting the letters, properly italicizing them, or using small caps for lower-case letters. The values 'normal', 'italic', and 'oblique' (slanted) are used. Note that oblique is not quite the same as italic, and is often achieved by simply slanting the text electronically:

```
title { ... ; font-style: italic }
```

The 'font-weight' property darkens or lightens the text using the values 'bold' (or '700'), 'normal' (or '400') (the default), '100', '200', '300', '500', '600' and '800', with 'bolder' and 'lighter' adjusting an inherited value up or down by 100.

```
title    { ... ; font-weight: bold }
```

The text can also be displayed in small-caps style, using the 'font-variant' property, which takes a value of 'normal' (the default) or 'small-caps':

```
title { ... ; font-variant: small-caps }
```

The 'font-size' property determines the size to display the text, and is usually given in point sizes, though more vague measures such as 'xx-large', 'x-large', 'large', 'medium', 'small' , 'x-small' and 'xx-small' are also available. It is also possible to increase or decrease the size from an inherited value using 'smaller' and 'larger':

```
title    { ... ; font-size: 24pt   }
para     { ... ; font-size: medium   }
comment { ... ; font-size: smaller   }
```

The 'line-height' property specifies a gap between lines. A value of 'normal' means that no gap is added. A percentage of the inherited value can be given, and a number can be used as a calculation of the inherited height:

```
title    { ... ; line-height: 32pt   }
para     { ... ; line-height: normal   }
comment { ... ; line-height: 0.9   }
```

The 'font' property conveniently combines the properties described above into a single statement, with parameters that specify the font style, the variant, the weight, the size and line height (separated by a '/' character), and the font family. The Title element example below combines all the statements for this element shown above:

```
title    { font: italic small-caps bold
                  24pt/32pt Arial, sans-serif }
```

Colours and backgrounds

Colours, used carefully, greatly enhance the appearance of a document. CSS is able to specify a colour for the text itself, and for the area behind the text. For example, the content of a Warning element could be displayed in red text on a yellow background.

The 'color' property specifies the colour of the text:

```
warning   { ... ; color: red }
```

The 'background-color' property specifies the colour of the background, both behind the text and in the padding area (see below). Apart from the name of a colour, the value can be 'transparent', meaning that the existing background colour shows through, and this is the default setting:

```
warning   { ... ; background-color: yellow }
```

In addition to the colour, a background can also incorporate an image, referenced by URL. The 'background-image' property has a default value of 'none', but can take a url parameter:

```
warning   { ... ; background-image: url(skull-Xbones.gif) }
```

A background image may be smaller than the area it needs to cover. It can therefore be repeated, both across and down, until the whole area is filled. The 'background-repeat' property takes the values 'repeat' (across and down), which is the default value, as well as 'repeat-x' (across only), 'repeat-y' (down only) and 'no-repeat':

```
warning    { ... ; background-repeat: repeat-x }
```

A browser may be able to scroll a background image, along with the text, as the user adjusts the display to read more. Alternatively, it may be able to keep the image in place as the text scrolls over it. Some browsers may be able to do both. The intended behaviour can be set using the 'background-attachment' property, which takes a value of 'scroll' (the default) or 'fixed':

```
warning    { ... ; background-attachment: fixed }
```

The top-left corner of a background image normally lies over the top-left corner of the first character in the text block, so does not cover the padding area (but see below for exceptions). Large, non-repeating images in particular may need to be moved to another location. The 'background-position' property allows the image to be moved to the 'top', 'center' or 'bottom', as well as to the 'left' or 'right' edge. Percentage values or simple length values can also be used, where the first parameter specifies the horizontal, followed by an optional vertical position:

```
warning    { ... ; background-position: center }
```

For the sake of brevity, all the background settings can be combined within the 'background' property:

```
warning    { ... ; background: red url(boat.gif)
                          no-repeat scroll 10% 10% }
```

Text styles

Indentation of first lines, the spacing between words and letters, automated transformation to upper-case or lower-case letters, underlines and overlines, the horizontal and vertical alignment of lines and words, can all be achieved using the following properties.

Additional space can be inserted between words using the 'word-spacing' property. It takes a length parameter, or 'normal' (the default):

```
important   { ... ; word-spacing: 3pt }
```

Additional space can also be inserted between letters in a word, using the 'letter-spacing' property. It takes a length parameter, or 'normal' (the default):

```
important   { ... ; letter-spacing: 1pt }
```

Lines can be added to the text using the 'text-decoration' property, which takes the values 'none' (the default), 'underline', 'overline', 'line-through' (for displaying invalid or replaced text) and 'blink' (strictly for browser rendering):

```
important    { ... ; text-decoration: underline }
```

The 'vertical-align' property aligns the text vertically, taking values of 'baseline' (the default), 'sub', 'super', 'top', 'text-top', 'middle' (useful for centring in-line images), 'bottom' or 'text-bottom', or a percentage value of the current line height:

```
subscript    { vertical-align: sub }
superscript { vertical-align: 50% }
```

Whatever use of upper-case and lower-case letters actually occur in an element, a standard may apply to which they must conform when presented. For example, title text may need to be presented in capitals, even when capitals have not been used in the title text. The 'text-transform' property transforms characters, when necessary, to the desired case. It takes a value of 'capitalize' (the first character of each word is upper-case, the remainder are lower-case), 'uppercase', 'lowercase' or 'none' (no transformations, and overriding inherited value) (the default):

```
title    { ... ; text-transform: uppercase }
```

Text can be aligned in different ways within the space reserved for it. The text can be justified (as the text in this paragraph is), left justified, right justified or centred, with the 'text-align' property taking the value 'left', 'right', 'center' or 'justify' (align on both sides):

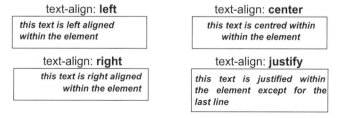

Often, the first line of each paragraph is indented. The 'text-indent' property takes a length or percentage value, with the percentage value representing a fraction of the parent element's width.

```
para    { ... ; text-indent: 3em }
```

Boxes

Text is formatted within a box, called the 'content box'. But text boxes rarely lie directly adjacent to each other. Margins separate these containers, and border lines may also be added, with padding between the text and the border lines, and between the lines and adjacent text blocks. There are properties for each of these areas, including variants that allow the top, right, bottom or left sides to be given individual styles. In the diagram below, a paragraph block is shown, enclosed between two other vertically stacked blocks:

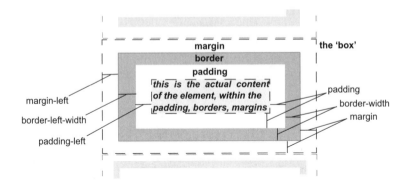

Note that background colours cover the padding area as well as the content area, and that background images should not cover this area, but do so in current versions of the two most popular Web browsers.

The border can be given a specific thickness, colour and style. The 'border-width', 'border-color' and 'border-style' ('none', 'dotted', 'dashed', 'solid', 'double', 'groove', 'ridge', 'inset' or 'outset') properties set these characteristics individually, but the 'border' property combines these features into a single statement. The two examples below are equivalent:

```
p  {  ... ; border-width: 2pt ; border-color: red ;
          border-style: solid }

p  {  ... ; border: 2pt solid red  }
```

When separate styles are required for different borders, the more specific 'border-left', 'border-right', 'border-top' and 'border-bottom' properties can used instead of the 'border' property:

```
p  {  ... ; border-left:    2pt solid red ;
          border-right:   2pt solid red ;
          border-top:     4pt dotted black ;
          border-bottom: 4pt dotted black  }
```

Widths can also be set for individual borders, using the 'border-left-width', 'border-right-width', 'border-top-width' and 'border-bottom-width' properties:

```
p  {  ... ; border-left-width:    2pt ;
          border-right-width:   2pt ;
          border-top-width:     4pt ;
          border-bottom-width: 4pt }
```

The 'padding' property defines the size of the gap between the content and the border. If the padding is different on each side, the 'padding-left', 'padding-right', 'padding-top' and 'padding-bottom' properties are available, although individual top, right, bottom and left values can be defined in the 'padding' property by adding parameters. The examples below are equivalent:

```
p  { ... ; padding-top:    2pt ;
           padding-right:   3pt ;
           padding-bottom: 4pt ;
           padding-left:    5pt }

p  { ... ; padding: 2pt 3pt 4pt 5pt }
```

The 'margin' property (and the more specific 'margin-left', 'margin-right', 'margin-top' and 'margin-bottom' properties) defines the size of the gap between this entire box and any adjacent boxes. Multiple values in the 'margin' property also identify separate top, right, bottom and left margins respectively. The following examples are equivalent:

```
p  { ... ; margin-top:    2pt ;
           margin-right:   3pt ;
           margin-bottom: 4pt ;
           margin-left:    5pt }

p  { ... ; margin: 2pt 3pt 4pt 5pt }
```

Some elements (especially images) may need to be resized (or scaled). The 'height' and 'width' properties can be used to reduce or enlarge the area reserved for the content of the element, and in the case of images actually reduce or increase the size of the image by scaling. Both properties can take a length value, or a value of 'auto' (the default). When 'auto' is used for just one of these properties, the scaling replicates the given scaling for the other property (for images, the ratio is maintained). If both properties use the 'auto' value, an image will appear at its original size. The 'width' property also allows a percentage value:

```
image    { ... ; width: 50% ; height: auto }
```

The 'float' property is used to move boxes to the 'left' or 'right' of the display area, though the default value is 'none'. Other text may wrap around the element. This property is very useful for placing images amongst text.

The 'clear' property ensures that floating elements do not appear next to the current element; it clears the area to the 'left', 'right' or 'both' sides of the element, though the default value is 'none'. When a floating element would have appeared to the left or right of this element, then this element is moved down until it is clear of the floating element. For example, if there is a danger that there will be a floating image immediately preceding a title, it would not be appropriate for the image to occupy the same horizontal space as the title:

```
title    { ... ; clear: both }
```

Display properties

There are a number of additional properties that are used to distinguish between block and in-line elements, identify lists and list items, and elements in which multiple spaces must be preserved. These properties are not essential for working in HTML, where the names of relevant elements in each category are hard-wired into HTML-aware Web browsers. But they are vital for working with XML. The 'display', 'white-space', 'list-style-type', 'list-style-image', 'list-style-position' and 'list-style' properties are therefore discussed later, when exploring important XML-specific features of CSS.

Simple element mapping

As previously described, defining a style rule for a given element requires specification of the element name, the selector, followed by a set of declarations:

```
head1    { font-size: 32pt ; color: blue }
```

More than one rule may be defined for each element. Providing that the declarations do not conflict, they simply accumulate as if they had been defined in a single rule. The example below is functionally identical to the less verbose version above:

```
head1    { font-size: 32pt }
head1    { color: blue }
```

When separate rules *do* conflict, the last rule in the style sheet applies. In the following example, the Head1 element is displayed in green:

```
head1    { font-size: 32pt ; color: blue }
head1    { color: green }
```

However, this behaviour can be reversed by adding an **important** clause to a declaration:

```
head1    { font-size: 32pt ; color: blue ! important}
head1    { color: green }
```

Of course, the original order of importance can be restored by also adding an important clause to the second declaration.

If a number of elements share the same styles, their style specifications can be combined into a single rule. The selector simply consists of all relevant element names, separated by commas:

```
head1, head2, head3    { color: blue }
```

Good style sheet design practice combines the techniques described above to avoid unnecessary repetition. In the following example, the three main header elements should appear in blue, italic style, but have differing point sizes:

```
head1, head2, head3  { color: blue ; font-style: italic }
head1                { font-size: 18pt }
head2, head3         { font-size: 14pt }
```

Contextual rules

There may be occasions where the style of an element should depend on where it appears within the document. For example, an XML DTD may define an element called Title, which is used to hold the title text of a book, a chapter, a section and a table. Typically, the style of the title text should vary, depending on where it is applied. A book title would, for example, be larger than a section title. Reflecting this requirement in a style sheet is known as contextual style mapping:

```
<book>
  <title>The Book Title</title>
  <chapter>
    <title>The First Chapter</title>
    <section>
      <title>The First Section</title>
      <table>
        <title>A Table</title>
        ...
      </table>
      ...
    </section>
    ...
  </chapter>
  ...
</book>
```

The simplest kind of context rule defines a style for an element that applies only when that element is enclosed by another specified element. In the example below, a style is specified for a Title element when it appears within a Book element:

```
book title   { color: blue ; font-size: 36pt }
```

This construction can be misleading. The rule above applies to any descendant Title element, even if it is the title of a chapter or table. CSS1 has no ability to specify a particular parent element, but can override a rule with a more specific rule. In the example below, a Title element inside a Table element is associated with both rules, but the second rule is more specific, and has the final say (so the title text appears in 12pt):

```
book title   { color: blue ; font-size: 36pt }
table title  { font-size: 12pt }
```

It is possible to combine simple selectors and contextual selectors within the same rule. In the example below, the declarations apply to both the Header element, wherever it might appear, and to the Title element, but only when it appears inside a Table element:

```
header, table title  { color: blue ; font-size: 36pt }
```

When a single element has a number of styles, depending on its context, one approach would be to define a rule for each context:

```
book title      { color: blue ; font-size: 36pt }
chapter title   { color: blue ; font-size: 18pt }
section title   { color: green ; font-size: 16pt }
table title     { color: blue ; font-size: 12pt }
```

However, when some or all of these contexts have properties in common, it is more efficient to first define a more generalized description of the element, in a simple, non-contextual rule. In the example above, it is obvious that most of the contexts require the title text to appear in blue, so this rule should be placed in the general Title description, and inherited by the others (unless overridden):

```
title           { color: blue }
book title      { font-size: 36pt }
chapter title   { font-size: 18pt }
section title   { color: green ; font-size: 16pt }
table title     { font-size: 12pt }
```

This approach avoids repetition, and so reduces the size of the style sheet, improves legibility, highlights important rules and makes it easier to modify the style sheet.

When some rules are more specific than others, the simple precedence rule for resolving conflicts does not operate. The most specific rule takes precedence, even if it appears before the less specific rule in the style sheet. However, it is good design practice to define the general case first, as shown above, as this allows the reader to absorb the information in a more natural way. Taking the example above, when a title appears in a book, the first and second rules apply, and the title text appears in 36pt blue style. But when there are conflicting rules, such as the font size property in the chapter title, the more specific rule overrides the less specific rule, so the title text appears in 18pt. In this case, the second rule is effectively ignored, because its single declaration is overridden by the third rule. Care must be taken, however, because unforeseen and undesirable effects may result. It may not be immediately obvious from the example above that the title of a table will in fact appear in green, when it is embedded within a section. This is because the fourth rule also applies, which specifies the colour green, and is more specific than the first rule, and the final rule does *not* override this setting. A good percentage of the time taken to design and debug a style sheet revolves around locating and resolving such clashes.

Traditional formatting techniques include distinct styling of the first character, or the first line of text, particularly within the first paragraph of a chapter
or book. It is not possible to add markup to a single text line, as the actual
number of characters involved is determined only when the browser or pagination engine renders the text to screen or page. The ':first-letter' keyword
tells the application to style the first character in a given way, and the ':first-
line' keyword similarly applies a given style to all the characters on the first
line. These definitions can be combined, as shown below:

```
book title:first-line   { ... ; font-weight: bolder }
book title:first-letter { ... ; font-size: 14pt }
```

Accessing and overriding styles

When using CSS with HTML, the standard can be applied in various ways. XML
is more restrictive in this regard. Where possibly conflicting styles are defined in different places, decisions need to be made regarding which styles to use.

Importing

To assist with the management of style sheets, an importing mechanism is
included. This allows one style sheet to call in another. The '@import' keyword has a URL parameter that locates the other style sheet document. These
commands must appear at the top of the style sheet, before any of the rules:

```
@import url(file:///library/tables.css)
```

One of the ways in which CSS exploits its 'cascading' nature is that imported
rules are considered less important than the rules defined in the main style
sheet, when conflicts arise.

HTML

There are three ways that CSS styles can be applied to HTML documents.
These are the in-line method, the embedded method and the linked method.

The **linked style sheet** approach places the style sheet in a separate data file
that is simply referred to by each document. The remote style sheet is referenced either by a Link element, or by an 'import' command:

```
<!-- HTML -->
<head>
<link rel="STYLESHEET" href="red-colors.css"
                                        type="text/css">
</head>
```

In the **embedded style sheet** approach, the style sheet appears at the top of the document, within the HTML Style element. The styles apply only to the document containing them:

```
<!-- HTML -->
<head>
<style type="text/css">
p { color: green }
</style>
</head>
```

Finally, an **in-line style** is a rule that is applied directly to a specific instance of an element. This approach uses the HTML Style attribute (described later), and does not involve the concept of a style 'sheet' at all:

```
<!-- HTML -->
<p style="color: blue">A blue paragraph</p>
```

Although not part of the specification itself, the 'cascading' nature of CSS may include distinguishing between the three levels of implementation described above. A style specified in a linked style sheet can be replaced by one defined in an embedded style sheet, which can in turn be overridden by an in-line style. The popular browsers work in this way:

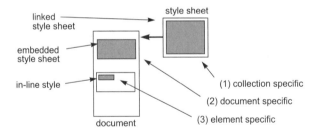

This principle is illustrated below, with the external style sheet defining all elements to be red in colour, the embedded one redefining paragraphs to be green, and an in-line style on one of the paragraphs overriding this to make the paragraph blue:

```
<!-- HTML -->
<head>
<link rel="STYLESHEET" href="red-colors.css"
                                    type="text/css">
<style type="text/css">
p { color: green }
</style>
</head>
<body>
<h1>A Red Header</h1>
<p style="color: blue">A blue paragraph</p>
<p>A green paragraph</p>
```

XML

As shown above, the mechanisms for attaching styles to an HTML document are to a large extent built in via extensions to the HTML specification. Implementors of XML systems need a different approach. There is no equivalent to the Head element in XML, and while in-line styles may be used, the attribute name 'style' would need to be added to every element in the DTD, or some other mechanism must be found for identifying an equivalent attribute. It is clear that the linked style sheet approach is the most suitable.

It is possible for an XML document to refer to the style sheet that should be applied to it using a processing instruction. There is an agreed W^3C standard for such instructions that work for both CSS and XSL. The target name is 'xml-stylesheet', and parameters that look like XML attributes (called 'href' and 'type') are used to locate the style sheet, using a URL, and to identify the type of style sheet in use. In this case, the type is 'text/css' (see Chapter 13 for more details):

```
<?xml-stylesheet href="MyBook.css" type="text/css" ?>
```

XML specifics

Because HTML tags are hard-wired into HTML-aware Web browsers, some information does not need to be supplied in the style sheet. For example, it is known that the Emphasis element is an in-line element, so no line breaks are to be generated around it. It is also known that the Ordered List element contains numbered list items, and that the Preformatted element dictates no formatting of the embedded text. An XML-aware formatter, however, requires explicit information to identify elements that perform these and other roles.

Block and in-line elements

When presenting information the formatting program must distinguish between two types of element content. Some elements contain text that forms just part of a larger block of text. Emphasized text, superscript numbers and hypertext links are typical examples. None of these items, when enclosed by an element, should create a break in the text. They are known as **in-line elements**. In other cases, an element contains text that must be separated from preceding and following information. A title, paragraph, list item or footnote would fall into this category. Such items are described as **block elements**.

```
<p>A block containing an <em>in-line</em> element.</p>
```

At first sight, it is tempting to equate in-line elements with mixed content DTD models, and block features with element content models. But there is no direct correlation. For example, a Paragraph element will usually have mixed content (text and further elements), but an embedded Emphasis element may also have mixed content, yet the first is a block element, and the latter is an in-line element (it *is* possible to detect which elements are block elements from a DTD, though it can only be done by analyzing all content models, starting with the smallest element in each hierarchy, to find the outermost element with mixed content).

The **display property** is used to identify block and in-line elements. The 'display' property can hold values of 'block', 'inline', 'list-item' and 'none' (CSS2 adds some more options). The default value, if the display property is not present, is 'block'. Therefore, the following two examples are equivalent:

```
title    { color: blue }

title    { color: blue ; display: block }
```

A 'block' display value indicates that line breaks will be generated above and below the element content. An 'inline' display value indicates that no line breaks will be generated. A display value of 'none' indicates that the content of the element should not be presented at all:

```
p        { display: block }
secret { display: none }
em       { display: inline }

<p>This is a paragraph.</p>
<secret>THIS IS A SECRET!</secret>
<p>This is another block, with an
<em>in-line</em> embedded element.</p>
```

This is a paragraph.

This is another block, with an **in-line** embedded element.

Lists

It is possible for list item numbers to be generated automatically. The 'list-item' display value indicates that a list item marker is to appear against the content of this element.

```
item { display: list-item }

...
<item>This is an item.</item>
<item>This is another item.</item>
...

...
3. This is an item.
4. This is another item.
...
```

It may also be necessary to identify the element that encloses the entire list, if only to reset item counting, though an application may just assume that numbering starts from the first sibling in a list of items. Whether necessary or not, the parent of the items is a good place to specify the form the numbering will take. The 'list-style-type' property specifies the marker type that will appear against each item. There are many options: 'disc', 'circle', 'square', 'decimal' (1. 2. 3. 4.), 'lower-roman' (i. ii. iii. iv.), 'upper-roman' (I. II. III.), 'lower-alpha' (a. b. c. d.), 'upper-alpha' (A. B. C. D.) and 'none' (blank). The default value is 'disc', which is just a non-sequenced list (sometimes described as a 'bulleted' or 'random' list):

```
list { ... ; list-style-type: disc }
item { display: list-item }
```

• item one

• item two

• item three

The 'list-style-position' property specifies whether the marker appears within the left boundary of the text block, 'inside', or to the left of this block, 'outside' (the default):

1. This is the first list item, with
   the item number appearing inside or outside.

2. This example shows the same effect

When set to 'inside' the marker is 'brought in' to the text block:

```
list { ... ; list-style-position: inside }
```

1. This is the first list item, with
   the item number appearing inside or outside.

2. This example shows the same effect

As an alternative to the list type marker, an image can be displayed before each list item. The image is identified by a URL in the 'list-style-image' property. Apart from its obvious use as a mechanism to include an infinite number of new item markers, this feature is particularly useful for generating appropriate icons against items of different types. For example, the brochure for a hotel could list its features in this way. To achieve this effect, however, the image property must be included in the definition of the item element(s) themselves:

```
food  { list-style-image: url(/images/knife-fork.tif) }
beds  { list-style-image: url(/images/bed.tif) }
pool  { list-style-image: url(/images/pool.tif) }
```

```
<features>
<beds>64 bedrooms</beds>
<pool>full sized swimming pool</pool>
<food>first class restaurant</food>
</features>
```

These disparate properties make list definitions quite cumbersome. Fortunately, all this information can be specified using just the 'list-style' property, which takes a number of parameters; first the type, then an optional image URL, and finally the position:

```
r-list    { list-style: lower-roman inside }
n-list    { list-style: decimal outside }
```

White space

Under normal conditions, any surplus spaces and line-break codes are removed from a block of text. For example, if a text editor is used to create an HTML or XML document, it is normal practice to insert line-break codes into a paragraph at convenient points, so that the text will be legible:

```
<p>This paragraph is quite long so it has[CR]
been broken into separate lines in the text[CR]
editor used to create it. Yet these[CR]
line-breaks are artificial, and should[CR]
not be retained in formatted output.</p>[CR]
```

This paragraph is quite long so it has been broken into separate lines on the text editor used to create it. Yet these line-breaks are artificial, and should not be retained in formatted output.

Most line-break codes are converted into spaces, as shown above, but there are exceptions that apply when the line breaks or original spaces appear between markup tags and text. In the example below, the leading space and carriage return are removed:

```
<p> [CR]
This paragraph is quite short.[CR]
</p>
```

This paragraph is quite short.

This behaviour is described as 'collapsing' the content of the element, effectively into a single text line (though it is re-split by the application at convenient column or window boundaries).

The 'white-space' property must take a value of 'normal' (collapsed), 'pre' (pre-formatted) or 'nowrap' (an HTML-specific feature used in conjunction with the Break element), and has a default value of 'normal'. All spaces and line-break codes can be preserved by setting the 'white-space' property to 'pre':

```
program    { white-space: pre }
```

```
<program>
10 REM This is a BASIC program[CR]
20 PRINT "Hello world"[CR]
30 GOTO 20[CR]
</program>
```

10 REM This is a BASIC program
20 PRINT "Hello world"
30 GOTO 20

See Chapter 7 for more details on this complex but important issue.

Batch composition to HTML

When using an XML-aware browser to display an XML document, it is only necessary to create a suitable CSS style sheet, and reference it from the document. But when using an HTML-aware browser to display an XML document, a software 'filter' is used to transform the document into HTML format.

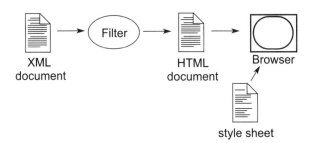

When using a filter program, HTML in-line styles become a practical, and sometimes preferred option. A filter program does not object to repeatedly generating the same style rule, it simply adds the Style attribute directly to each element:

```
<p style="font-size: 9pt ; color: blue">...</p>
<p style="font-size: 9pt ; color: blue">....</p>
<p style="font-size: 9pt ; color: blue">.....</p>
```

This technique can be exploited by XSL conversion filters, as demonstrated in Chapter 7.

Although in-line styles were originally intended for 'tweaking' the appearance of specific objects on design-centred Web pages, the advantage of this approach is the total flexibility it provides. The filter software is able to take complex element and attribute value-based context rules into consideration when determining the style of each HTML element. For example, the content of a Person element may need to be presented in different colours, according to some age grouping category, such as baby, toddler, child, teenager, adult and pensioner, for which appropriate age ranges are assigned, but working from an Age attribute that contains a simple value such as '36'. The software would supply the appropriate colour value using a look-up table of age ranges.

The disadvantages of this approach are the need for an intelligent filter program, and the larger size of the resulting HTML document.

HTML features

HTML contains elements and attributes that have been included specifically to facilitate styling by the CSS mechanism. Conversely, the CSS standard itself contains features aimed at its use with HTML documents. This section has been included for those readers who also work with HTML (either directly, or as an output format derived from XML source documents), and would like to apply CSS to HTML documents.

New attributes (Style and Class)

A new attribute, called Style, has been added to elements in the new HTML 4.0 standard. This attribute contains a style rule that applies only to the specific instance of the element containing it. This in-line rule overrides all other rules:

```
<!-- HTML -->
h3    { color: blue }
...
<h3>Blue Header</h3>
...
<h3 style="color: green">Green Header</h3>
```

This feature is primarily aimed at design-led documents, where there are no predictable patterns to the layout of the text. As such, it is of little relevance to XML (though it was earlier shown how this feature can be used in unexpected ways).

A new HTML 4.0 attribute, called Class, effectively provides a mechanism for extending the HTML DTD. For example, if the document author requires three different kinds of paragraph, the Class attribute can be used to define variants of the single Paragraph element:

```
<!-- HTML -->
<p class="first">The first paragraph.</p>
<p>A normal paragraph.</p>
<p class="note">NOTE: a note paragraph.</p>
```

The style sheet can refer to the content of the Class attribute, creating different rules for each variant. The classification name is placed after the element name, separated by a full-point. For the example above, three rules would be needed:

```
P            { color: blue ; font-size: 12pt }
P.first    { txt-indent: .5in }
P.note     { font-size: 9pt ; margin-left: 1in }
```

When a Class attribute does not appear in a specific paragraph instance, the first of these rules applies. When the Class attribute contains 'first', the second rule *also* applies. When the Class attribute contains 'note', the paragraph is indented, and the point size of the text is reduced.

It is not necessary to match the case of the text. 'FIRST' will match 'first' or 'First', though consistency is encouraged if only for the sake of legibility.

New elements (Div and Span)

Two additional elements have been defined to extend the capabilities of HTML. These are the **Span** and **Division** (**Div**) elements. Unlike other HTML elements, such as Emphasis, they have no implied meaning, and no default styles. Simply adding a Span element or Division element to an HTML document has no effect on embedded text, and in any case they are ignored by older browsers. These elements are only intended to be used to help build style sheet rules (though Div was first introduced to isolate areas of the document that had different alignments, and has an Align attribute to affect embedded structures – but this usage should now be discontinued).

The Span element is an in-line element, which can be used to produce any ad hoc styles the author requires. Whenever the author requires an in-line element that does not exist in HTML, the Span element can be used. For example, if the name of a country is significant, and is to be presented in a unique style, the country name could be embedded within a Span element:

```
<!-- HTML -->
<p>I hear that <span>Belgium</span> is a nice
place to visit.</p>
```

If more than one additional element type is required, the Class attribute can be used. For example, if animal names are to be styled differently, the Class attribute can distinguish these domains:

```
SPAN.country { color: blue }
SPAN.animal  { color: green }
...
<!-- HTML -->
<P>I hear that <span class="country">Belgium</span>
is a nice place to visit. But there are no
<span class="animal">Giraffes</span> there.</p>
```

Link styling

Hypertext links can be styled in different ways, depending on whether or not the link has recently been traversed, and whether or not it is currently selected. The ':link' keyword identifies a hypertext link that has not been activated and is not currently selected. The ':visited' keyword identifies one that has been traversed (assuming that the browser has remembered this fact). The ':active' keyword identifies one that is currently being selected:

```
A:link        { color: green }
A:visited     { color: blue }
A:active      { color: red }
```

CSS 2

CSS2 adds a number of features to the standard that increase its power generally, and improves its utility with XML. It includes more contextual rules and features to support output to paper. Of most importance to XML users, though, are its new display types, which allow arbitrarily named elements to be described as table-building constructs.

The language has more than doubled in size with this release, as it includes 77 new property types. However, CSS2 remains backward compatible with CSS1.

New selection options

Some obvious holes in the element selection capabilities of CSS have been filled in the new version. It is now possible to select an element that is the direct child of another specified element, that is immediately preceded by another specified element, or that is the first child of its parent. In addition, attribute values can be taken into consideration.

The '*' symbol is used as a wildcard, substituting for every element in the document, and also for any number of embedded element levels. However, unlike the XML use of this character in DTDs, it represents one or more descendants (not zero or more). Therefore, the rule below applies to all titles in the book, except for the book title itself (because there must be another element between the two elements), whereas the second rule applies to all titles in the book:

```
book * title { ... }
```

The '>' symbol indicates that the target element must be a child of another specified element. In the following example, the style only applies to Paragraph elements that are directly embedded within Intro elements:

```
intro > para { ... }
```

Child and ancestor selection criteria may be combined. In the following example, the Intro element must also be a descendant of the Book element:

```
book intro > para { ... }
```

The '+' symbol is used to indicate that the target element must immediately follow another specified element. In the following example, the style only applies to a Paragraph element that immediately follows a Title element:

```
title + para { ... }
```

Again, this rule may be mixed with others. The following rule applies to paragraphs that immediately follow a title, but only when they are children of a Chapter element:

```
chapter > title + para { ... }
```

The ':first-child' keyword is used to identify an element that has no prior siblings. For example, the first Paragraph element in a child sequence may be formatted differently to others (perhaps it does not have the usual indent on the first line):

```
para:first-child { ... }
```

The '#' symbol, followed by an ID value, targets an instance of the given element when it has a matching unique identifier. Note that *no* mechanism is included for identifying the name of the attribute concerned when that information is unavailable due to the absence of a DTD. In the following example, the style only applies to the Paragraph element that has a Name value of 'para33':

```
para#para33 { ... }
```

Attribute restrictions are enclosed in square brackets, '[' and ']', following the element name:

```
para[ ... ] { ... }
```

Multiple attributes may be considered, in which case the square brackets are repeated for each one:

```
para[ ... ][ ... ] { ... }
```

The mere presence of a particular attribute may be considered sufficient to select a category of elements. For example, every Paragraph element containing a Security attribute may be indented and displayed in a different colour, regardless of its value:

```
para[security] { ... }
```

However, it is also possible to specify the value the attribute must contain for the match to be successful:

```
para[security="secret"] { ... }
```

A further refinement of this is the ability to match one word in an attribute that contains several space-separated values, by employing the '~' symbol before the equals sign. For example, a Keywords attribute may contain the value 'xml xsl css', but the rule may apply if the text 'css' is present within the value:

```
para[keywords~="css"] { ... }
```

A more constrained variant uses the vertical bar, '|', to match only the first part of an entry, leading up to a hyphen. This feature is mainly intended to be used with language codes, such as 'en-GB'. The following rule would match an English paragraph, no matter what the location:

```
para[keywords|="en"] { ... }
```

When a rule should apply to any element containing a specified attribute, or particular attribute value, the element name is simply omitted. However, it is considered good practice to include the wildcard symbol, '*'. The following two examples are equivalent:

```
[security="secret"] { ... }
*[security="secret"] { ... }
```

Miscellaneous improvements

All properties now have an 'inherit' value option. When this value is used, the element inherits its setting for this property from the current setting, as specified in an enclosing element. In some cases, the 'inherit' option is the default value, which means that the element inherits the characteristic from the parent element, unless an override value is explicitly set.

The 'vertical-align' property can now take a length value, such as '2pt'.

The 'text-align' property can now take a string value that represents the character or characters to centre the text on. This is of most use in tables, where columns of figures may need to be centred on a decimal point.

```
salary      { ... ; text-align: "." }
```

Some languages are written right to left. The 'direction' property takes a value of 'ltr' (left to right) or 'rtl' (right to left). This property specifies the base writing direction of blocks, the direction of table column layouts, the direction of horizontal overflow, and the position of the last line in a block with a 'text-align' property value of 'justify'. The 'unicode-bidi' property works in conjunction with 'direction' to control processing of in-line elements. Refer to the standard for details.

```
hebrew-text    { direction: rtl; unicode-bidi: embed }
```

Fonts and styles

Characters can be stretched or squeezed using the 'font-stretch' property. They can be 'ultra-condensed', 'extra-condensed', 'semi-condensed', 'condensed', 'normal' (the default), 'expanded', 'semi-expanded', 'extra-expanded' or 'ultra-expanded'. The values 'wider' and 'narrower' specify a move to the next setting in either direction:

```
warning-para { ... ; font-stretch: extra-expanded }
```

Shadows can appear around characters using the 'text-shadow' property. Each shadow effect is separated from others using a comma. Each effect involves up to four parameters, including the horizontal offset (which may be negative for backward shadows), the vertical offset (which may also be negative, for shadows above the text), then an optional blurring radius factor, and finally an optional colour:

```
shade-it { text-shadow: 2pt 2pt red }
shade-it-vivid { text-shadow: 2pt 2pt red,
                              -3px -3px 1px green }
```

Font substitution can be risky when a preferred font is not available, and a small point size is specified. The reason is that some fonts are more legible than others at small point sizes, and this is usually due to something called the 'aspect ratio'. This is the height of small, lower-case letters, such as 'x', in relation to the line height. This difference is expressed as a value, such as '0.45'. Substitute fonts with a smaller aspect ratio than the preferred font should be presented at a larger point size to compensate. The 'font-size-adjust' property takes as a parameter the aspect ratio of the preferred font. The application must perform a calculation from the known aspect ratio of the substitution font in order to adjust its size accordingly.

```
para { font: bold italic large Palatino, serif ;
       font-size-adjust: 0.58 }
```

Boxes

The 'border-color' property can now take the value 'transparent'. It is then invisible, but still has its given width.

The new properties 'border-left-color', 'border-right-color', 'border-top-color' and 'border-bottom-color' allow each side to be coloured differently (though 'border-color' with four parameters has the same effect). Similarly, the new properties 'border-left-style', 'border-right-style', 'border-top-style' and 'border-bottom-style' allow each side to be styled differently (though 'border-style' with four parameters has the same effect). The two examples below are equivalent:

```
para { border-color: red green yellow blue ;
       border-style: dotted dashed }

para { border-top-color:    red ;
       border-right-color:  green ;
       border-bottom-color: yellow ;
       border-left-color:   blue ;
       border-top-style:    dotted ;
       border-right-style:  dashed ;
       border-bottom-style: dotted ;
       border-left-style:   dashed}
```

When the content of an element is too much to fit in its containing box, some of the content will overflow. This will only happen when the box cannot expand to encompass the data, because it has been given a set width or height. The content is normally still 'visible', but using the 'overflow' property it is possible to make this content 'hidden', though possibly still make it accessible by giving this property the value 'scroll' (a scroll bar is added to the field). The value 'auto' is also available, but will often be interpreted as being the same as 'scroll':

```
colours-list { ... ; width: 30mm ; height: 80mm ;
                      overflow: scroll }
```

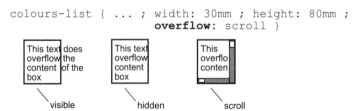

In addition, the normally visible region within the box can be clipped, using the 'clip' property, which by default takes the value 'auto' (the clip region is the same size as the content box, so has no effect). In future, it should be able to take parameters that represent a number of shapes, such as triangles and ovals, but for now it can only take a rectangular-shaped clipping region, 'rect(...)'. This function takes four parameters, each representing the distance from the top, right, bottom and left side of the content box:

```
clip-it { ... ; clip: rect(0px, 10px, 0px 10px) }
```

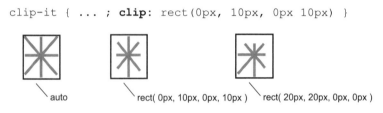

The content box is normally 'visible', but using the 'visibility' property it is possible to make the content 'hidden', while still taking the equivalent space in the flow, or even to 'collapse' the content entirely. The default value is 'inherit'.

```
top-secret { ... ; visibility: collapse }
```

Lists

Additional options have been added to the 'list-style-type' property, including 'decimal-leading-zero', 'lower-greek', 'upper-greek', 'lower-latin' (the same as 'lower-alpha'), 'upper-latin' (the same as 'upper-alpha'), 'hebrew', 'armenian', 'georgian', 'cjk-ideographic', 'katakana', 'hiragana-iroha' and 'katakana-iroha'.

The leading zeros in the first option refer to padding to the same length as the longest number in the list. If the largest number is '87', then values below 10 are padded to two digits, as in '06'. If the largest number is '264', then all values below 100 are padded to three digits, as in '006' and '098'.

```
098  ninety-eighth item
099  ninety-ninth item
100  last item
```

Prefix and suffix generation

In XML documents, the ability to generate prefix and suffix text automatically is very important. For example, a Note element should not actually contain the prefix 'note:', or anything similar, but should only contain the note text itself:

```
<note>This is a note</note>
```

To indicate that this text is in fact a note when it is presented, a suitable prefix may be added. CSS is now able to do this using the 'before' pseudo-element, in conjunction with the new 'content' property:

```
note:before { content: "NOTE: " }
```

As the default value of the display property is 'inline', the prefix 'NOTE: ' is added to the text content of the Note element:

NOTE: This is a note

However, explicitly changing this value to 'block' puts the prefix above the text:

```
note:before { content: "NOTE: " ; display: block }
```

NOTE:
This is a note

All other style properties are available. For example, to make the heading bold, the font-weight property may be used:

```
note:before { content: "NOTE: " ; font-weight: bold }
```

NOTE: This is a note

For suffixes, there is an 'after' pseudo-element that works in exactly the same manner.

```
reference:before { content: "[" }
reference:after { content: "]" }
```

The 'content' property value can be more complex than a simple string of text. Quotes can be generated, with different symbols appearing depending on the language involved, and the placement of quotes within other quotes. Also, the value of an attribute can be extracted and presented.

To enclose the content of an element in quotes, it is advisable to use the 'open-quote' and 'close-quote' keywords:

```
quote:before { content: open-quote }
quote:after { content: close-quote }
```

What actually appears depends on a setting elsewhere, made using the 'quotes' property. For example, an English book may contain the following declaration, which states that left and right double-quote characters will be used, but then goes on to state, using additional parameters, that embedded quotes will be represented by single quote characters:

```
book[xml:lang="en"] { quotes: '"' '"' "\" "'"   }
```

The 'attr(...)' function is replaced by the value of the named attribute. For example, to supply the name of the speaker for each speech in a play:

```
speech:before { content: attr(speaker)   }
```

```
<speech speaker="Macbeth">...</speech>
```

More complex options are made possible due to the fact that the 'content' property can take a number of parameters:

```
speech:before { content: "SPEAKER " attr(speaker) ":"}
```

SPEAKER Macbeth: ......

Finally, it is possible to generate sequential item numbering, in a more powerful way than could be achieved using the 'list-item' property. The 'counter-reset' property defines, and optionally also specifies, the starting value (default '0'). Then the 'counter-increment' property is used to increase the named value. Each increase can be more (or less) than the default of '1', by adding the increment (or decrement) value after the counter name. To display the counter, the 'counter()' function in the 'display' property is used (note that the value shown is one that is current after any reset or increment property is processed, regardless of the ordering of properties in the rule). The following example adds numbers to each item in a list:

```
list          { counter-reset: item 0 }
item          { display: block }
item:before { counter-increment: item ;
               content: counter(item) ". " }
```

1. first item
2. second item

Display options

The 'display' property has some additional options, including 'run-in', 'compact' and 'marker'.

The 'run-in' option is useful for creating specific styles for a range of text at the beginning of a block. An element given this style is assumed to be an in-line element that begins the block content of the next element. The style information only applies to the 'run-in' part of the resulting block. A single space character should appear between the content of the two elements. For example:

```
name { display: run-in ; font-weight: bold }
summary { display: block ; font-weight: medium }

<name>J Smith</name>
<summary>Software Developer, working in Java,
C++ and Perl.</summary>
```

J Smith Software Developer, working in Java, C++ and Perl.

The 'compact' option is used to position text in the margin of the following block element. This feature is especially useful for creating glossaries and definition lists. The example above can be modified slightly as follows:

```
name { display: compact ; font-weight: bold }
summary { display: block ; font-weight: medium }
```

The content is treated as an in-line block if it is followed by a block element, and the content is short enough to fit in the margin. Otherwise, it is treated as a preceding block element.

```
...
<name>M Pumpernickel</name>
<summary>Manager.</summary>
```

The 'marker' option is used within ':before' and ':after' pseudo-elements to separate prefix and suffix items from the main block, and can be used to create flexible list options. Also, the distance between the marker text and the main block can be controlled using the 'marker-offset' property. For example, it could dictate a gap of '3em':

```
note:before { display: marker ;
              marker-offset: 3em ; content: NOTE> }
note:after { display: marker ;
              marker-offset: 3em ; content: <<< }

<note>This is a long note that spans over lines.</note>
```

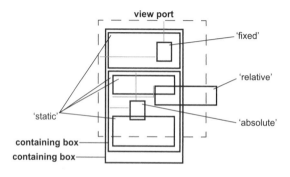

There may be a need to constrain the width or height of an object to a specific minimum and/or maximum size. The 'min-width' and 'min-height' properties take a length or percentage value (with the latter defaulting to '0' and the former being application dependent). The 'max-width' and 'max-height' properties are similar, but both have a default value of 'none'.

```
sidebox    { min-width:  3cm ; max-width: 4cm ;
             min-height: 9cm ; max-height: none }
```

Boxes can even be moved out of the normal flow, using the 'position' property. A value of 'static' (the default) produces a box in the normal flow, but a value of 'relative' allows the box to be moved to a new location relative to its normal position, without affecting subsequent boxes, and a value of 'absolute' allows the box to be moved to a location relative to the position of the containing box (the box generated by the parent of the current element, such as a list box surrounding its item boxes, or the root element box that surrounds all others). A 'fixed' value is similar to 'absolute', but specifies a fixed location in respect to the page or browser view port. A fixed item does not move when the document is scrolled:

```
logo    { ... ; position: fixed }
```

Boxes that are *not* positioned in a 'static' (normal flow) manner can be sized. The default value for the 'top', 'bottom', 'left' and 'right' properties is 'auto', meaning that the box is sized to fit the content, but a length or percentage value can be used to size the box relative to the containing block, or, in the case of relative positioning, to the originally calculated position of this box in the flow. The 'left' property specifies the distance from the left edge of the containing block (or view port) to the left edge of the fixed or absolutely positioned box, and the 'right', 'top' and 'bottom' properties work in the same way for their respective sides. It may be more convenient, however, just to set the left and top edges in this manner, then use the 'width' and 'height' properties to size the box:

```
logo    { ... ; top:    20mm ; left: 150mm ;
                width: 40mm ; height: 40mm }
```

Relatively placed boxes are positioned relative to the box itself. To move the box outside its own boundaries (as in the illustration above), negative values are used.

Positioned boxes can also be placed over or beneath other boxes, creating a stack. The root element automatically creates a default stack, and this element has the position '0' within this stack. By default, all embedded elements share the same position value, so there is no stacking. But positioned elements given a higher stack number, using the 'z-index' property, lie above the the other elements, fully or partially masking them. When 'z-index' is given a value, instead of the default 'auto', the element is positioned in the stack, and also creates a new stacking context for embedded elements.

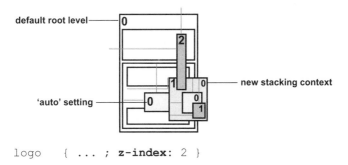

```
logo    { ... ; z-index: 2 }
```

Tables

The table extensions in CSS2 should be of particular interest to XML users wishing to render the content of arbitrary XML elements in a tabular grid. Chapter 6 includes a brief discussion on the use of CSS to apply table styles to arbitrary XML elements, but the model is more powerful than the simple mapping to the table, the row and the cell elements shown there. As the properties described here have been developed to match the capabilities of the

HTML 4.0 table model, readers unfamiliar with this model are advised to read the relevant descriptions in Chapter 18 before continuing.

The display value 'table' corresponds to the HTML Table element. The display values 'table-row' and 'table-cell' correspond to the HTML elements Tr and Td (as well as Th). These three display values are sufficient to map a simple XML structure onto a row-oriented table grid (column-oriented tables cannot be mapped, despite the first impression given by the inclusion of the display types 'table-column' and 'table-column-group', which serve a very different purpose):

```
<prices>
  <prod><code>XYZ-15</code><price>987</price></prod>
  <prod><code>XYZ-22</code><price>765</price></prod>
</prices>

prices { display: table }
prod   { display: table-row }
code   { display: table-cell }
price  { display: table-cell }
```

XYZ-15	987
XYZ-22	765

In HTML 4.0, table row groups specified using the Thead, Tbody and Tfoot elements are defined. Header rows may repeat at the top of each page, and footer rows may repeat at the base of each page containing a reference to them. The equivalent display values are 'table-header-group', 'table-row-group' and 'table-footer-group'.

```
<prices>
  <headers><head>Code</head><head>Price</head></headers>
  ...
</prices>

headers { display: table-header-group }
head    { display: table-cell }
...
```

In the previous example, there is no single row-separating element in the header section. The Head element defines a cell and the Headers element defines a table header group of rows. The missing level need not be explicitly stated, and is assumed to exist around all consecutive cell-level elements. Similarly, a group of row-level elements need not be explicitly encased in a table-level or row-group level element. In the previous example, the two Prod rows are deemed to be table body rows. It would even be possible to create a single-row table using nothing but cell-level elements:

```
<para>Normal text.</para>
<cell>danger</cell><cell>red</cell><cell>1</cell>
<para>More normal text.</para>
```

The means by which the width and height of various parts of a table are determined includes automated calculations based on the content of the elements, or the use of attributes to make these measurements explicit. The 'table-layout' property takes a value 'auto' to specify that this task will be left to the rendering engine, or 'fixed' to ensure that fixed values are used. This property type may be used in the table-level element:

```
prices { display: table ; table-layout: auto}
```

Text can be aligned within a cell using the 'text-align' and 'vertical-align' properties (though only the 'top', 'bottom', 'middle' and 'baseline' values apply for vertical alignment):

```
<prices>
  <prod>
    <code>XYZ-15</code>
    <price>987</price></prod>
  <prod>
    <code>XYZ-22</code>
    <price>312</price></prod>
  </prod>
</prices>
code    { display: table-cell ; text-align: center }
price   { display: table-cell ; text-align: right }
```

XYZ-15	987
XYZ-22	312

Note that it is not possible to extract attribute values in order to determine alignment, or to specify cell spanning. The 'attr()' function mentioned earlier can only be used in the 'content' property, and only to present the content of an attribute. Perhaps the next version of CSS will address this problem. However, there is a crude technique available for providing some of this functionality:

```
code { display:table-cell ; text-align: center }
code[align="L"]       { ... ; text-align: left }
code[align="R"]       { ... ; text-align: right }
```

It is possible to assign XML elements to the roles played by the HTML Col and Colgroup elements, using the 'table-column' and 'table-column-group' display types:

```
left-block    { display:    table-column-group ;
                text-align: left }
```

There are property types to present borders around the table, or individual rows, columns and cells, including 'border' and 'border-collapse', but there are too many options and complications to cover here. See the specification.

A caption can be added to a table, using the 'table-caption' display type, and its location relative to the table can be specified using the 'table-side' property ('top' (the default), 'bottom', 'left' or 'right'):

```
table title { display: table-caption ;
                  caption-side: bottom }
```

Using the 'border-collapse' property, borders around cells can be 'separate' (each cell has four border lines around it, not touching the borders around other cells) or can 'collapse' (the cells share the border lines, so they span the entire table). Collapsed borders are the default setting, but when separate borders are specified, the amount of space between the borders of each cell can be given using the 'border-spacing' property, which takes at least one length value, and up to four values representing the top, right, bottom and left edges respectively. Also, in this model it is possible to omit borders around empty cells, using the 'empty-cells' property, and giving it the value 'hide' ('show' is the default):

```
table   { ... ; border-collapse: separate ;
                  border-spacing: 2pt, 1pt, 2pt, 1pt }
```

When the table is presented by speech, the content of a relevant table header is spoken before each cell, but by default is not repeated if the current cell shares the same header as the previous one. To repeat the header for every cell, the 'speak-header' property can be assigned the value 'always' (the default is 'once').

Printed output

CSS1 concentrates on the task of formatting text for presentation on-screen, within a Web browser. The different needs of printed output are not addressed, though it is possible simply to print out a document using the formatting already applied for screen presentation (the document is simply divided into page-sized chunks and printed in the same format). CSS2 extensions give the style sheet designer the ability to specify the size and orientation of the page output, the elements that should start a new page, how multi-line element content is broken over pages, and styles that only apply to screen or to page, and to define active areas on the page to be printed on.

Before investigating these features in detail, the issue of separating instructions for print from instructions to display must be addressed. An **at-rule**, '@', with a keyword of 'media' and a parameter of 'screen' or 'print', is used to separate screen formatting rules from paper formatting rules. In the example below, the Emphasis element is given differing definitions. For screen, bold style is an appropriate highlighting technique. For paper, italic style is feasible and often preferred.

```
@media screen { em { font-weight: bold } }
@media print  { em { font-style: italic } }
```

An important word.

An **important** word.

An *important* word.

More options are available, including 'aural', 'braille', 'embossed', 'handheld', 'projection', 'tty' (teletype) and 'tv'. The term 'all' is used to encompass all these media types. Combinations are separated by commas:

```
@media screen, tv, handheld { ... }
```

The features of a page, such as its width and height, do not correspond to any element, so another at-rule, the 'page' rule, is used to contain the properties that may be used to specify page-oriented information:

```
@media print {
   @page  { ... }
   ...
}
```

Finally, the first page of a document is often treated differently to the others, particularly when it takes the role of a cover sheet, having narrower margins or a smaller page depth. The 'first' pseudo-class identifies the first page of a document. In the following example, the first page has a larger bottom margin:

```
@page :first { ... }
```

The declarations allowed in the 'page' rule (and all its variants) include those available to block elements ('margin', 'margin-top', 'margin-right', 'margin-bottom' and 'margin-left') plus 'size' and 'marks'.

The 'size' property defines the page area within a sheet of paper. The default setting, 'auto', is to the same size and orientation as the sheet. However, it should be noted that printers cannot usually print to the edges of a sheet, so borders should be used to clear some space around the edges (see below). The value 'landscape' specifies printing across the wider page dimension. A single explicit value provides both the width and height of the page box (defining a square). When two values are provided, the first value defines the width and the second defines the height. The target sheet must be at least this size for the page to be printed successfully:

```
@page  { size: 8.5in 11in }
```

It may also be necessary to consider the space that the binding takes from the reading area. It is common practice to make the inner margin wider than the outer margin, which in practice means defining different margin widths for left-hand and right-hand pages:

```
@page :left  { margin-left: 2cm ; margin-right: 4cm }
@page :right { margin-left: 4cm ; margin-right: 2cm }
```

Printed sheets may need to be trimmed to create a bound document, but the page box area defined above is not usually apparent on the sheet. The 'marks' property ensures that marks are added to reveal the print box area. Crop marks are used to show where the page should be trimmed. Cross marks are used to align pages.

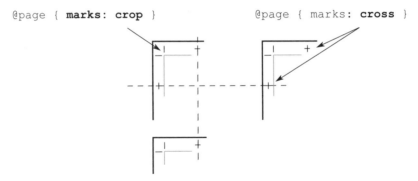

As on-screen browsing involves simply scrolling down through a single, possibly very long page, there is usually no clue as to how this material should be split when it is printed on multiple pages. The most obvious approach is simply to fill each page, regardless of the objects that appear before or after the page-break. If there are any chapter or section titles, for example, they can appear anywhere on the page, even though this does little to highlight their importance:

normal text flow

The 'page-break-before' property can be used to override this simple behaviour, which is represented by the value 'auto' (the default). Alternative values are 'always', 'avoid', 'left' or 'right'. This property may be used with any block element (except those in tables). The default setting specifies that a page-break is not necessary, unless the element happens to fall naturally at the start of a new page. A value of 'always' indicates a forced page-break before this element, even when this means generating a large amount of white space at the bottom of the original page. The value 'avoid' is used to ensure that the element is never the first on a page (the content of the previous element may have to be dragged down to the top of the current page, leaving an even larger space on the previous page). A value of 'left' or 'right' indicates that the element should be placed at the top of the next left-hand or right-hand page respectively. For example, if the text flow had reached the middle of a right-hand page when an element with a 'right' page-break setting was encountered, the rest of that page would be left blank, and the following left-hand page would also be left blank. This technique is typically found in books (like this one) where each chapter begins a new right-hand page:

```
chapter title    { page-break-before: right }
section title    { page-break-before: always }
```

The 'page-break-after' property works in exactly the same manner, except that the page-break appears after the content of the element.

When a paragraph is broken over pages, the split could normally occur at any point within the paragraph, including just after the first line, or just before the last line. This is considered bad practice, and most typesetters avoid such splits by adjusting inter-line and inter-word spacing. A single line at the bottom of a page is called an orphan. A single line left at the top of the page is called a widow. It is possible to specify a minimum number of lines that must appear at the bottom or top of a page using the 'widows' and 'orphans' properties. For example, setting both properties to a value of '2' in the Paragraph element would ensure the following kinds of paragraph break:

Page-breaks can be prevented from occurring within a text block, by moving the entire block down onto the following page. The 'page-break-inside' property can be set to 'avoid' (the default value is 'auto'). Note that this action may create white space at the bottom of the page that would have contained the first part of the block.

User interface

The design of the cursor may be changed as the user places it over a particular element. The 'cursor' property takes a value of 'auto' (the default), 'crosshair', 'default' (*not* the default), 'pointer', 'move', resize in a given compass direction ('e-resize', 'ne-resize', 'nw-resize', 'n-resize', 'se-resize', 'sw-resize', 's-resize' and 'w-resize'), 'text',' 'wait' or 'help', or may take a URL that identifies an image to show instead. Some of the more common representations are shown below:

Lines around objects may be added to highlight a default or currently selected item, particularly within forms. Outlines are similar to borders, except that they do not occupy additional space, and are the same shape as the object (not necessarily rectangular). An outline can have a style, with the same options as the border styles (default 'none'), a colour (with 'invert' added to the normal colour list, and made the default setting) and a width (default 'medium'). The 'outline-style', 'outline-color' and 'outline-width' properties apply these characteristics. Pseudo-classes called ':focus' and ':active' are used to identify an element that has the current focus, or is currently active:

```
name:focus { outline-style: dashed }

:active    { outline-style: dotted ;
             outline-color: red ;
             outline-width: 2pt }
```

These three properties can be combined within the 'outline' property, which specifies first the colour, then the style, and finally the width:

```
name:focus { outline: dashed }

:active    { outline: red dotted 2pt }
```

Aural styles

CSS2 includes a large number of properties to assist the audible presentation of material. Speech presentation is important, not just to those who are visually disabled, but also to anyone who is not able to switch their visual attention from some other task, such as driving.

The 'speak' property is used to render text audibly when given the value 'normal' (the default), or 'spell-out'. The 'spell-out' option is used to pronounce text such as CSS, by spelling out each letter; 'C', 'S', 'S'. A value of 'none' indicates no audible presentation of the content.

One of the most important properties of speech is volume. The 'volume' property can take a number of different types of value. A simple numeric value in the range 1–100 denotes a volume from barely audible to barely comfortable. A percentage value is used for volumes that are relative to inherited values.

```
para      { volume:  60 }
whisper { volume: 50% }
shout     { volume: 150% }

<para>you should <shout>shout</shout> this and
<whisper>whisper</whisper> this.</para>
```

The value 'silent' switches off sound (it should be recalled that a volume of '0' does not indicate silence, just very quiet speech), and there are several named volume values that represent common requirements, including 'x-soft' (the same as a volume of 0), 'soft' (the same as 25), 'medium' (50), 'loud' (75) and 'x-loud' (100). This is simply a recommended or default value that the listener should be able to adjust.

The rate of speech can be defined with the 'speech-rate' property. This property takes a numeric value that represents words per minute, though some convenient named values are also available, including 'x-slow' (80 words per minute), 'slow' (120), 'medium' (180–200), 'fast' (300) and 'x-fast' (500). The values 'slower' and 'faster' adjust an inherited speech rate by 40 words per minute. As before, the listener should be able to override the initial setting.

Voices are also distinguished by type. The most obvious categories are male, female and child, but it is also possible to specify more specific categories (though the standard does not contain such a list of options), or even name an individual. Voice characteristics use an override system that is similar to the font specification, so that generic types can be chosen when specific types are not available on the local system. The 'voice-family' property is used:

```
john       { voice-family: male-cockney, male }
mary       { voice-family: female-irish, female }
ageto12    { voice-family: child }
churchill { voice-family: churchill, male }
```

When generic voice types are used, it is possible to add some variety by specifying the 'pitch'. This property takes a value of 'x-low', 'low', 'medium', 'high' or 'x-high', or a numeric value giving the pitch in Hertz. The named values do not have a pre-defined Hertz equivalent, as it depends on the main voice characteristic chosen, such as 'male' or 'female' (the average pitch for a male voice is around 120Hz, but for a female voice it is around 210Hz):

```
churchill { voice-family: male ; pitch: 90Hz }
```

Some people speak with a steady pitch, and others vary the pitch, even in normal conversation. The 'pitch-range' property specifies the degree to which the pitch can change during the speech, from '0' (no change, a monotonous voice) to '100' (a wildly animated voice), with '50' representing a normal variance.

```
churchill { voice-family: male ; pitch:90Hz
                                  pitch-range: 20 }
```

The voice can be further refined using 'stress' and 'richness' properties that affect the inflection and the prominence or brightness of the voice.

Pauses between words are very important in speech. The ends of sentences, paragraphs, and larger divisions of the text are marked by pauses of different lengths. The 'pause-before' property creates a pause before the content of the element is presented. A set duration can be given, such as '20ms' (20 milliseconds), or a time span that is relative to the speed of the speech can be specified instead, such as '50%' ('100%' represents the time it takes to speak one word, on average, at the current speech rate). The 'pause-after' property works in the same way, but creates a gap after the content. When specifying a pause both before and after, a more convenient 'pause' property is available that takes two parameters, with the first parameter providing the before value, and the second parameter providing the after value. The 'pause' property can take a single parameter, to represent both locations. The following two examples are therefore equivalent:

```
item { pause: 30ms 20ms }
```

```
item { pause-before: 30ms ; pause-after: 20ms }
```

In some cases, the pauses they produce may not be sufficient to identify punctuation, and it may be necessary to be ensure that punctuation is clearly identified. The 'speak-punctuation' property takes a value of 'code' to specify that punctuation is to be read out. For example, 'this, and that' would be read out as 'this comma ...(pause)... and that'. The value 'none' (the default) disables punctuation speech.

Similarly, while numerals are normally spoken as 'continuous' digits, so that '237' is pronounced 'two hundred and thirty seven', it is possible using the 'speak-numeral' property to dictate that the digits are to be read out separately. The value 'digits' ensures that this example is pronounced 'two three seven'.

```
code { speak-numeral: digits }
<p>The alarm code is <code>1254</code>.</p>
```

Sound effects can be played before or after the spoken content. The 'cue-before' property specifies a sound to be played before the speech, and 'cue-after' plays a sound afterward. The 'cue' property is more convenient if surrounding sounds are required, as it takes two values, one for before and one after. Note that a single value to the 'cue' property specifies that the given sound should be played both before and after the speech. Sounds can be inherited from parent elements, but existing sounds can be overridden using the value 'none' (to avoid playing a sound). A sound is identified by URL, using the 'url' function:

```
emergency { cue: url("BELL.WAV") }
```

The 'play-during' property allows a sound to be played throughout the speech. A value of 'auto' means that an existing sound, activated by an ancestor element, should continue to play throughout this fragment of the speech. If there is a possibility (or even a certainty) that the sound will end before the speech ends, it is possible to repeat the sound using the 'sound' parameter. It is also possible to mix a new sound with one that is already playing, by adding the 'mix' parameter. These two parameters must follow the 'url' value, and when both are present they must appear in the order described above.

```
humm { play-during: url("HUMM1.WAV") repeat }
humm-harmony { play-during: url("HUMM2.WAV") mix repeat }
```

Advanced sound systems are able to provide stereo sound, and maybe also surround-sound effects. When there are several people speaking, it can be useful to give each one a separate spatial location. Horizontal locations are specified using the 'azimuth' property, which accepts a value between '0deg' (zero degrees) and '360deg' (the same position). Values increase clockwise from the front-centre. For convenience, some named values are available to correspond to different degree settings, including 'center' (zero degrees), 'center-right' (20 degrees), 'right' (40), 'far-right' (60), 'right-side' (90), 'left-side' (270), 'far-left' (300), 'left' (320) and 'center-left' (340). The values 'leftwards' and 'right-wards' take an inherited value and move the sound left (by deducting 20 degrees) or right (by adding 20 degrees), though both appear to move sound in the wrong direction when it is behind the listener. The parameter 'behind' can be added to a value, moving the sound to the back:

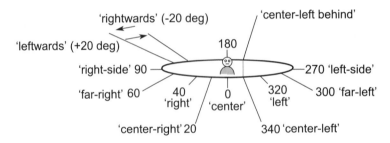

The following example places the Judge at the centre-front, with prosecution and defence at each side:

```
judge          {  azimuth: center }
prosecution  {  azimuth: left-side }
defence        {  azimuth: right-side }
```

Sound sources may also be located at different vertical locations. For example, a Judge should perhaps be elevated above the other speakers. The 'elevation' property specifies a vertical location, from '0deg' (zero degrees) to '90deg' (overhead) or '-90deg' (beneath), with 'level', 'above' and 'below' also representing these extreme positions. The values 'higher' and 'lower' add and subtract 10 degrees respectively:

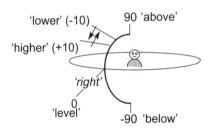

```
judge          {  azimuth: center ;  elevation: 75deg }
```

18. The Internet and HTML

The Internet and HTML have had a major impact on the development of XML. This chapter should be of particular interest to those who are interested in the Internet in general, who need to work with HTML as well as XML, or who need to convert XML documents into HTML format for Web publishing. Browsers that allow XML to be embedded within an HTML page, or HTML within an XML document, are now emerging. Publishing with HTML is a large topic in its own right, and there are many books dedicated to the standard. This chapter introduces the subject and briefly describes the use of each HTML tag, including those recently introduced with HTML 4.0. This chapter ends with a quick look at the next version of HTML, which is likely to be an application of XML (rather than SGML).

The Internet

The **Internet** is a worldwide network of computer systems. Every computer attached to the Internet is called a **host**. Some hosts are **Internet servers**, which hold information on each other to establish the framework of the network. There is no central system or single route between two systems. A message passed between systems could take one of many different routes, passing through several **router** systems. Parts of a message may even take different routes, yet rejoin in the correct order at the receiving end. This is one of the great strengths of the Internet, as it means a failure of one server, or of one connecting line, does not prevent messages from reaching their destination.

The Internet provides a platform for a number of disparate services, including **FTP** (the *File Transfer Protocol*), which allows users to copy files between their own system and a remote server, electronic mail (smtp), and software (rlogin and telnet) that allows a user to run commands on a remote system. Technical reference material on these protocols is available over the Internet itself, and is described as **RFC** (*Request For Comment*) and **FYI** (*For Your Information*) documents. They have file names such as 'RFC1630.txt', but there is also an index ('fyi-index.txt') that matches these numbers to more meaningful names. These documents can be found at ftp://ds.internic.net/rfc/.

A single computer may simultaneously run several programs that connect to the Internet. When a system receives a message or request from another system, there has to be some mechanism for deciding which program is to receive it. Each program therefore connects to a different **port**, which is identified by a unique **port number**, and is only passed incoming messages that quote the same number. Most servers are able to handle simultaneous processes, as a number of clients may wish to connect to them at the same time. A process is created to handle each client connection, and is dedicated to listening, processing and responding to that client. But with all information arriving through the same port, confusion would seem to be inevitable. To avoid crossed wires, both computers create a **socket** (again identified by a unique number) for the duration of an exchange of information. All messages include the socket number, so that they will arrive at the correct process.

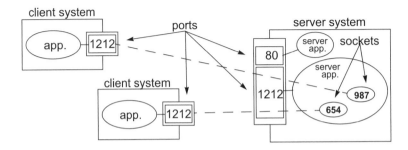

The transfer of information between systems requires a network protocol. The Internet is actually based on a combination of two protocols, with the compound name **TCP/IP**. Amongst the benefits of TCP/IP are its independence of hardware and vendor, its built-in failure recovery, its ability to handle high error rates and its lean size. The individual protocols TCP and IP have very different tasks. **TCP** (*Transmission Control Protocol*) is responsible for ensuring that received data is in the correct order (recall that packets of data may take different routes) and that it has not been corrupted. TCP may request that some packets be re-sent. For one computer on the Internet to send information to another, it must know the 'address' of the remote system. **IP** (the *Internet Protocol*) is responsible for ensuring that data packets are transferred to the correct system, identified by a unique **IP number**. An IP number is often represented in the so-called **dotted decimal** notation, for example '194.193.96.10'. Note that this scheme is (at the time of writing) close to breaking-point, due to the success of the Internet. This problem is being resolved by the introduction of a new, more capacious version of IP called **IPng** (*IP Next Generation*).

IP numbers are far from intuitive. Typing such numbers into a Web browser in order to connect to Web pages, though possible, would simply be unacceptable to most people because they are too difficult to remember. To make things simpler, some special hosts hold a look-up list that matches IP numbers to more natural **domain names**. When the user of an application enters a domain name, such as www.bradley.co.uk, this name is transmitted to a **DNS** (a *Domain Name Server*), which returns the IP number equivalent (194.193.96.10). This is termed **name resolution** because it resolves a name back to its associated number. The application can then refer to the remote system by its true identifier.

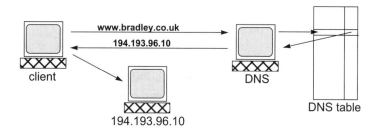

HTTP and HTML

The concept of electronic links between text stored on computer systems is an old one, and many **hypertext** systems have been developed, though most have been confined to linking texts stored on the same system, and have used proprietory technologies.

It was only a matter of time before the Internet became an obvious candidate to support a hypertext system that spans systems and countries. With the infrastructure in place, it was only necessary to define two additional protocols. First, a new access protocol that would allow hypertext documents to be requested from a server, and second, a document markup language that would be used to both style the received document, and locate and enable any embedded Hypertext links. The **HTTP** and **HTML** protocols were devised in 1990 for these purposes.

HTTP (the *HyperText Transfer Protocol*) forms the bridge between a browser and server, so that they can exchange instructions and information over the Internet. An HTTP exchange begins with the browser, which sends a request to the server. By default, an HTTP server application listens for requests on port 80. On receiving a request, the application responds, either with a status message, or by sending the required information. The exchange always works in this way; the server never initiates the two-way communication (this is 'pull' technology).

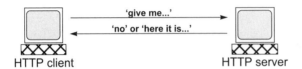

HTTP client   HTTP server

HTML (*HyperText Markup Language*) documents are transferred to the client. HTML documents are also known as '**pages**'.

The page first made available to users is known as the '**home page**', which usually has the default filename of 'index.html' (or 'index.htm').

The browser on the client system interprets the HTML document, removing the tags and presenting the content in an appropriate format. There are implied styles or behaviours associated with each tag. The HTML markup language takes a position half-way between format and structure. It includes style tags, such as the Italic element, where the output format is explicitly stated, but also includes generalized objects, such as the Emphasis element, where output format is left to the browser.

The core feature of HTML – the very reason for its existence – is its ability to let readers follow links to other HTML documents, anywhere on the Internet. When a **URL** reference to another file is selected by the user, the browser extracts the reference and sends a further request to the server (or to another server) for another HTML document, usually to replace the original, but possibly to be presented in a new browser window.

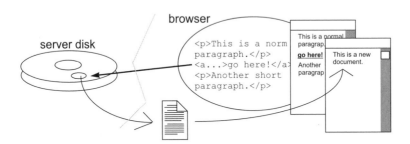

Similarly, an HTML document may contain references to resources that conform to other data formats. In this way, image files and Java applets, amongst other objects, are downloaded to the browser and inserted into the presented version of the document.

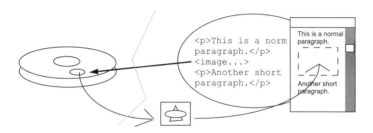

Note that **HTTP 1.0** requires a separate connection for each exchange. Users of HTML browsers accessing complex pages that contain several images will be familiar with the phenomenon of multiple accesses. The status bar shows repeated accesses to the server until the page is complete. The major improvement in the recently defined **HTTP 1.1** standard is that the connection may be kept open during a number of exchanges, so avoiding the time penalty incurred by repeated connections.

HTML is an application of SGML, and is therefore defined by an SGML DTD. It is not currently possible for HTML to be considered an application of XML, as it cannot be accurately described by an XML DTD. It uses advanced features of SGML such as element and attribute minimization, and adopts SGML conventions for representation of empty elements (but see the final section for details on how HTML is about to be moved to XML compliance).

There have been five versions of HTML, known as **HTML Level One**, **HTML Level Two**, **HTML+**, **HTML Level Three** and now **HTML Level Four**, of which HTML+ was an interim to Level Three that included tables. The respective DTDs are named **HTML 2.0**, **HTML 3.2** and **HTML 4.0** accordingly (level one pre-dates full compatibility with SGML). Level Two added an interactive 'forms' feature to the original standard. Level Three added support for tabular output and text alignment options, and is currently supported by all popular browsers. To be precise, version 3.0 never proceeded beyond draft status, but version 3.2 was released in May 1996, by the **W^{3}C** (the *World Wide Web Consortium*), and version 4.0 was released on 18 December 1997. A comparison table of the elements and attributes found in each of these versions is provided in Chapter 20. For further information regarding these and future versions, contact http://www.w3.org.

HTML 2.0

HTML 2.0 is now so widely adopted that there is little point in describing the previous incarnation of HTML. In fact, the next version of HTML is also very well supported, but as version 2.0 still forms the core of following versions, the elements defined are mostly still relevant.

Nevertheless, some of the features of this (and the next) version of HTML are now (as of version 4.0) deprecated, or even obsolete. Discouraged features are indicated below, but are still described because they are appropriate for use with older browsers, and need to be understood when upgrading existing HTML documents to a later version, or to XML. For convenience, a table in Chapter 20 lists all HTML elements and attributes, from all versions of the standard, and indicates which versions support them.

This is the first version of HTML that conforms to SGML syntax. The public identifier for HTML 2.0 is '-//IETF//DTD HTML 2.0//EN', though use of the following SGML document type declaration is only encouraged, not enforced:

```
<!-- HTML -->

<!DOCTYPE HTML PUBLIC "-//IETF//DTD HTML 2.0//EN">
```

As indicated in the declaration above, an HTML-conforming document has a document element called **Html**. Unlike XML, element names are not case-sensitive, so the element may actually be named 'html', 'HTML' or 'Html', and does not need to match either the document type declaration or the end-tag.

The Html element encloses a **Head** section and a main **Body** section. The header contains a **Title**, which is presented in the title bar of the browser. The Body element may contain any of a number of other elements, but will usually begin with the title repeated in a header-one element, **H1**. An **Address** element encloses details of the author of the document, and is usually inserted at the end of the document, where it is displayed in italic, possibly indented or centred:

```
<!-- HTML -->
<html>
   <head>
      <title>What is HTML?</title>
   </head>
   <body>
      <h1>What is HTML?</h1>
      ......
      <address>Neil Bradley
      (http://neil@bradley.co.uk)</address>
   </body>
</html>
```

- all PHRASE definitions
- all FONT definitions

All of the elements defined by the FONT and PHRASE entities may enclose the elements defined in the TEXT definition, which may in turn contain further FONT and PHRASE elements. For example, Sample text (Samp) may contain an Anchor (A), which may contain Keyboard (Kbd) Elements. The HEADING elements may also contain any TEXT elements.

Heading elements

Headers can be used to create crude section and sub-section divisions in the document, or to define outliner levels. The heading elements, **H1** to **H6**, hold title text with varying degrees of highlighting. H1 is the most important, and is typically used only for the title of the document (perhaps in conjunction with the Center element, described later). At the other extreme, H6 is the least important header, and should only be used when six levels of heading are necessary. Each header element is a block, separated from preceding and following objects, including paragraphs and other headers. Although no specific formatting style is indicated, typically the header elements are all displayed in bold typeface, and the point size of the text varies, increasing with the level of importance.

```
<!-- HTML -->
<h1>The Document Title</h1>
<h2>A Section Title</h2>
<h3>A sub-section title</h3>
```

List elements

The most basic type of list is the **Unordered List** type (**Ul**). An unordered list is used when the items do not form a logical sequence or series of steps. It contains a number of **List Item** elements (**Li**). Each of these contains text and is automatically preceded by a bullet, dash or other symbol:

```
<!-- HTML -->
<ul>
<li>First Item
<li>Second Item
<li>Third Item
</ul>
```

- First Item
- Second Item
- Third Item

The **Directory List** element (**Dir**) is intended to hold directory listings, which are very short items that may be formatted in columns (as in UNIX file listings). This tag is now deprecated:

```
<!-- HTML -->
<dir>
<li>MYBOOK.DTD
<li>MYBOOK.XML
<li>PARSER.EXE
<li>REPORT.DAT
</dir>
MYBOOK.DTD    PARSER.EXE
MYBOOK.XML    REPORT.DAT
```

The **Menu** list is intended to be used to represent software menu selections. The content of each item is assumed to be short, and the browser is likely to indent them and omit the bullet. It is now deprecated:

```
<!-- HTML -->
<menu>
<li>Activate
<li>Options
<li>Help
<li>Exit
</menu>
        Activate
        Options
        Help
        Exit
```

The **Ordered List** element (**Ol**), is similar to the unordered list, but each item is preceded by a sequential, automatically generated number. It is used in preference to the Ul element when the items describe a series of steps, or are referred to individually elsewhere:

```
<!-- HTML -->
<ol>
<li>Step 1
<li>Step 2
<li>Step 3 - Go To Step 1
</ol>
```

1. Step 1
2. Step 2
3. Step 3 - Go To Step 1

Some lists consist of a keyword or term, followed by an explanation of that keyword or term. The **Definition List** element (**Dl**), contains a number of items (but *not* Item elements), each one consisting of two parts, a **Definition Term** element (**Dt**) and a **Definition Entry** element (**Dd** – not 'De'!):

```
<!-- HTML -->
<dl>
<dt>SGML<dd>Standard Generalized Markup Language
<dt>DTD<dd>Document Type Definition
<dt>XML<dd>Extensible Markup Language
</dl>
```

SGML Standard Generalized Markup Language
DTD   Document Type Definition
XML   Extensible Markup Language

All of the list types described above may be condensed by closing the gap between items, using the **Compact** attribute (now deprecated in all but the Dl element). This implied attribute has a single value option of 'compact', and the attribute name does not appear:

```
<!-- HTML -->
<ul compact>
```

Again, HTML has inherited this minimization feature from SGML, and it is not available in XML.

Font elements

The font elements are all in-line elements (they do not form a new paragraph block) that specify a change of character style. The **Teletype** element (**Tt**) specifies a mono-spaced font such as Courier. The **Bold** element (**B**) specifies a bold typeface. The **Italic** element (**I**) specifies an italic typeface:

```
<!-- HTML -->
<p>This paragraph contains <b>bold</b>, <i>italic</i>
and <b><i>bold/italic</i></b> text.</p>
```

This paragraph contains **bold**, *italic* and ***bold/italic*** text.

Phrase elements

The phrase elements are all in-line elements that do not specify an output format. However, many have obvious style mappings. **Strong** normally maps to bold typeface and **Emphasis** (**Em**) to italic typeface. The computer sample elements **Code** and **Var**, as well as the **Keyboard** element (**Kbd**), normally map to a mono-spaced font. The **Sample** element (**Samp**) and **Citation** element (**Cite**) may both map to italic typeface:

```
<!-- HTML -->
<p><em>Emphasized text</em>.
<strong>Strong text</strong>.
<code>Computer text</code>.
<kbd>Keyboard text</kbd>.
<var>Variable text</var>.
<samp>Sample text</samp>.
<cite>Citation text</cite>.</p>
```

Emphasized text. **Strong text**. `Computer text.` `Keyboard text.` `Variable text.` *Sample text. Sample text. Citation text.*

Text elements

Text elements are all in-line elements. All the elements described as font elements and as phrase elements are included in this category. Other elements in this group are described below.

The **Image** element (**Img**) identifies an image file, the content of which is to appear within the current line of text. This is an empty element; there is no end-tag. A **Source** attribute (**Src**) specifies the name and location of the image file (often stored in **GIF** format):

```
<!-- HTML -->
...there is a GIF file<img src="myimage.gif">
here.
```

Note that in HTML (as well as in SGML) empty elements are always represented by a normal start-tag, with no end-tag present. This combination is not possible in XML, which either requires the end-tag to be present, or uses the special empty element tag.

The image name alone, as shown above, is sufficient when the image resides in the same directory as the HTML document. The rules for specifying an image file stored in another location are the same as for hypertext links (described later), so need not be covered here. By default the base of the image is likely to be aligned with the baseline of the text. Image alignment can be made specific using the **Align** attribute (now deprecated), which takes a value of 'top', 'middle' or 'bottom'. As some browsers are not able to display images, an **Alternative** attribute (**Alt**) may be used to display alternative text. The second example below demonstrates its use:

```
<!-- HTML -->
...there is a GIF file
<img src="myimage.gif" align="top" alt="No Piccy"> here.
...there is a GIF file   --------   here.
                            |        |
                            --------
...there is a GIF file [no piccy] here.
```

An increasing number of image formats are supported by some browsers, including **XBM**, **JPEG** and the original **GIF**.

The **Anchor** element is also included in this group of elements. This element is the subject of *Internal and External Links* below.

Other elements

The **Isindex** element, which appears in the Head element, simply indicates that the Web server will accept a search request from the browser. The browser displays a text entry box for entry of the term to be searched for. It is now deprecated, and a more wide-ranging facility, called 'forms,' is discussed later.

The **Line Break** element (**Br**) forces a new line to be created. This is very useful for semi-formatting text, such as lines of poetry. It is an empty element:

```
<!-- HTML -->
<p>Break this line here <br>so this is line 2
```

The **Blockquote** element contains a block of text quoted from another source, which is typically indented by the browser.

A more powerful, though visually less pleasing approach to formatting uses the **Preformatted** element (**Pre**), which composes the content in a monospaced font. All spaces and line feed characters are retained, making it possible to use these characters to create simple character-based diagrams, or columns of text. The **Width** attribute (now deprecated) can be used to give the browser a hint as to the maximum length of the lines of text, so that it can choose an appropriate font size to render it.

```
<!-- HTML -->
<pre width="30">
Here is a face:   ---
                 /   \
                [ o o ]
                 \ - /
                  ---
</pre>
```

The **Plaintext** and **Example** (**Xmp**) elements identify text that should be presented exactly as it is stored in the file, including preservation of line breaks. They are therefore indistinguishable from the Pre element (and in future versions of HTML are deprecated or made obsolete).

The **Horizontal Rule** element (**Hr**) draws a line across the screen. It is an empty element.

```
<!-- HTML -->
<p>The next para is in another section</p>
<hr>
<p>New section of the document</p>
```

Internal and external links

The **Anchor** element (**A**) is used to locate both the source and target ends of a link.

When used as a target element, the Anchor element usually contains the title of the referenced text (in order that it may be highlighted on completion of a link to that item) within the **Name** attribute:

```
<!-- HTML -->
<h3><a name="details">The Details</a></h3>
```

When used as a source element, the Anchor contains a **Hypertext Reference** attribute (**Href**) which contains a **URL**, as described in Chapter 4.

```
<!-- HTML -->
<a href="#details">See details</a>
```

A single Anchor may be both the source of a link and the target of a link:

```
<!-- HTML -->
<a name="summary" href="#details">See details</a>
```

The target document does not require an Anchor element, because the entire file is the target. However, it is possible to link to an anchored item in the other file by appending the hash symbol and item name:

```
<!-- HTML -->
<a href="../myfiles/detail.html#part3">See
details, part 3</a>
```

Note: MS-DOS systems should name HTML files with an extension of '.HTM', due to the three-letter limit on file name extensions.

If the path ends with a forward slash, '/', the target Web server supplies the name of the default home page:

```
<!-- HTML -->
<a href="http://www.myserver.com/myfiles/">
See My Server</a>
```

To target a browser at a home page held on the reader's own system, or another system visible over a local area network, the protocol becomes 'file:' (this is not officially a protocol name, and so should not be followed by the double slash):

```
<!-- HTML -->
<a href="file:/myserver/myfiles/me.html">
See My Server Home Page</a>
```

A **Title** attribute may be used to hold a brief description of the target resource, to be displayed by the browser when the mouse is over the link. A **Urn** (Universal Resource Name) attribute (now obsolete) is used to provide a unique name for the resource that will not change if the resource is moved (the intention being to use this in conjunction with a catalogue file, as with XML public identifiers) and a **Methods** attribute (also now obsolete) is used to describe the methods that may be performed on the target.

When relative paths are included in the URL, the starting-point is normally the address of the page containing the link. The **Base** element can be used to provide a new fixed point in the directory structure from which relative links should be calculated. It uses an **Href** attribute to specify the replacement path.

To facilitate automation of unique name identifiers for A elements, The **NextID** element contains an **N** attribute, which holds the next available identifier value. This element has been dropped in later versions of HTML.

The **Link** element identifies other resources that are connected to this Web page, such as a style sheet. To identify the resource, it has an **Href** attribute, and the **Title** attribute holds a brief description of the resource. The Methods and Urn attributes are used as described for the A element.

```
<!-- HTML -->
<link title="big print" href="bigprint.css"
      type="text/css">
```

The A and Link elements may contain a **Rel** (relationship) attribute, which identifies the relationship between the target object and the current page. The **Rev** attribute identifies the previous (reverse) relationship when the links form a chain. A browser could (in theory) style these links differently to others to indicate to the user that there is a preferred path to follow. These attributes are not widely used, but may be useful to Web search engines.

```
<!-- HTML -->
<link rel="alternate stylesheet" title="big print"
href="bigprint.css" type="text/css">
```

Image maps

Following on the theme of hypertext links, a popular feature of HTML is its ability to attach links to parts of an image. This is called an **image map**. For example, a map of the world could be linked to other HTML documents that describe characteristics of each country. The source of the link is therefore an area of the image. In the well-supported concept of a 'server-sided' image map, the browser simply passes the coordinates of the mouse-click to the Web server, which calls a script that decides, depending on the coordinate values, which HTML document to return to the browser. The **Image** element (**Img**) takes an additional attribute, **Ismap**, to indicate that the coordinates of the mouse-click should be sent to the Web server. This implied attribute has a single legal value of 'ISMAP' (the attribute name never appears):

```
<!-- HTML -->
<img src="myimage.gif" ISMAP>
```

However, the Web server must also be told which script to activate when the mouse is clicked on this image. To do this, the Img element is enclosed in an **Anchor** element (**A**) which uses a **URL** to locate the appropriate script:

```
<!-- HTML -->
<a href="/cgi-bin/imagemap/my.map">
<img src="myimage.gif" ISMAP>
</a>
```

This scheme relies upon the use of the **HTTP** protocol, a Web server and **CGI** scripts, so is not particularly suitable for simple intranet solutions, or for publishing HTML files on a CD-ROM. The concept of 'client-side' image maps overcomes this problem, and is introduced later.

Meta-data

The **Meta** element is not used for document markup, and is of most interest to those involved in browser/server communications. The Meta element is placed within the **Head** element to add meta-information not covered by attributes of other elements. The content of the Meta element is not to be displayed in the document, but may be read by the browser or server. It has three attributes, HTTP-Equiv, Name and Content. The **Name** attribute provides the name of the meta-information (almost an attribute name in itself). The **Content** attribute provides the current value for the named item. For example:

```
<!-- HTML -->
<meta name="Index" content="cycle">
```

If more than one Meta element is present, with the same Name attribute value, the various content values are accumulated into a comma separated list; for example 'cycle, bus, car'. The third attribute, **HTTP-Equiv**, allows the content to be inserted into an **HTTP** header field (a topic not explored further in this book).

Forms

The **Form** concept gives the user the ability to send information back to the Web server. The document may contain a questionnaire, for example, which the user fills in and returns. A **Form** element encloses the entire form. It has an attribute called **Action**, which identifies a script that can process the form when it is submitted, and an **Enctype** attribute specifies the **MIME** type used to submit data to the server, such as 'text/xml'.

The Form element may contain a number of **Input** elements, but one of them must have an attribute **Type** value of 'submit', which the browser detects and takes as an instruction to send the content of the form to the Web server (another Input element may be used to define a button that resets the default settings of the form, using a Type attribute value of 'reset'). The example below sends the data entered into the form to the 'myscript.cgi' script running on the Web server when the 'Send' button is selected by the user of the browser:

```
<!-- HTML -->
<form method="POST" action="../mydir/myscript.cgi">
   <input type="submit" value="Send">
   ...
</form>
```

Web server

Note: The Form element has another attribute called **Method**, which in the example has a value of 'POST'. It may also take a value of 'GET'. These values define the exact scheme by which the form sends information back to the server, a subject which is not covered further here.

An Input **Type** value of 'radio' indicates that radio buttons will appear in the form. The browser ensures that only the last radio button selected is highlighted at any one time within a group of buttons. The Name attribute is used to define these groups. All Input elements sharing the same **Name** value are part of a single group. In the example below, two groups are defined, 'vehicle' and 'colour'. From the vehicle group the user may select the radio button labelled 'car', 'truck' or 'van', and from the colour group the user may select 'Red' or 'Blue'. The user may therefore select, for example, a blue car or a red van:

```
<!-- HTML -->
<input type="radio" name="vehicle" value="car">
<input type="radio" name="vehicle" value="truck">
<input type="radio" name="vehicle" value="van">
<input type="radio" name="colour" value="Red">
<input type="radio" name="colour" value="Blue">
```

However, the user will not be able to see which buttons to select unless descriptive names also appear near the Input element, perhaps within List Item elements:

```
<!-- HTML -->
<li>
<input type="radio" name="colour" value="red">
Red option.
<li>
<input type="radio" name="colour" value="blue">
Blue option.
```

Red option
Blue option

The browser is likely to pre-select the first item in each group when the form is displayed, because one option must always be selected, but it is the value selected when the 'submit' button is selected that ultimately matters.

The **Input** element can also be used to provide 'check-boxes,' which differ from radio buttons in that more than one can be selected at any one time. The **Type** attribute contains 'checkbox' and the **Name** attribute contains the name of the item that may be selected. An item can be pre-selected by including the **Checked** attribute, holding the single legal value of 'checked' (the attribute name not appearing). In the example below, the user is presented with two options, 'leather' (seats) and 'CD' (player), and the CD item is already selected. The user can de-select CD player, select leather seats, select both or neither:

```
<!-- HTML -->
<li>
<input type="checkbox" name="car" value="leather">
Leather
<li>
<input type="checkbox" name="car" value="CD" checked>
CD-player
```

☐ Leather
☒ CD-player

The **Input** element can also be used to provide text entry areas. The **Type** attribute either holds a value of 'text', or may be absent (as this is its default value). The **Name** attribute holds the label for the text field. The **Size** attribute may be used to determine the length in characters of the text field, and if not present defaults to 20 characters. Also, the attribute **Maxlength** can be used to strictly limit the number of characters that can be entered, and may be smaller or larger than the text field size:

```
<!-- HTML -->
<input type="text" size="25" maxlength="15">
```

Fifteen chars !

Other Input element options available using the Type attribute include 'file' (attach a file to send with the form), 'hidden' (do not show to the user, and used for passing state information between the server and browser) and 'image' (present a graphic, though the **Src** attribute can also be used to locate an image file that will fill the background of the input field).

To allow for multiple lines of text, the **Textarea** element is used. Each text area is identified using the **Name** attribute. The attributes **Rows** and **Cols** set the height and width of the visible text area in character-sized units. Scroll bars or other devices may allow extra characters or lines of text to be displayed within this area. All line feed characters in the data are retained, including one between the start-tag and the first word, if present (the example below would begin with a blank line if there were a line feed before 'Here').

```
<!-- HTML -->
<textarea name="mybox" rows="3" cols="10">Here
is some
content</textarea>
```

```
Here is
some
content
```

Selection menus are available using the Select and Option elements. The **Select** element encloses the menu. It uses the **Name** attribute to identify the menu. The number of rows visible is determined by the **Size** attribute. By default, it is possible to select only one item from the list, but the **Multiple** attribute can take a value of 'multiple' to allow multiple selections.

Each option in the menu is defined using the **Option** element. The **Value** attribute may be used to replace the content of the element as the value returned to the server if that item is selected, and the **Selected** attribute may be used to pre-select one of the items, by including its only possible value of 'selected':

```
<!-- HTML -->
<select name="mymenu">
<option>Car<option selected>Truck<option>Van
</select>
```

```
Car
Truck
Van
```

The forms mechanism has been extended in HTML 4.0, as described later.

HTML 3.2

HTML 3.2 is well supported by the popular Web browsers and HTML editors. The public identifier for this version of HTML is '-//W3C//DTD HTML 3.2//EN', though use of the following document type declaration is only encouraged, not enforced:

```
<!-- HTML -->
<!DOCTYPE HTML PUBLIC "-//W3C//DTD HTML 3.2 Final//EN">
```

This version of HTML deprecates the **Plaintext** element and makes obsolete the **NextID** element and the **Methods** and **Urn** attributes on the A and Link elements. There are numerous new elements for presenting tables (Table, Caption, Td, Th and Tr), for including Java applets (Applet and Param), for styling text (Center, Font, Basefont, U, Sub and Sup, Strike, Big and Small), for client-side image-based linking (Map and Area) and for structuring the document (Div and Dfn). Also Script and Style elements are introduced for future use.

General

The **Center** element has been added to centre any other structure or group of structures, including possibly the entire document (though it is now deprecated). The **Division** element (**Div**) extends this idea, surrounding segments of the document that share an alignment option. It takes an **Align** attribute, with a value of 'left', 'center' or 'right'. The Center element is, therefore, no different to a Division element with an Align value of 'center'.

Several existing elements have been given an **Align** attribute, with a possible value of 'left', 'center' or 'right', including **P, H1, H2, H3, H4, H5** and **H6**.

The **Horizontal Rule** element (**Hr**) has additional attributes (all now deprecated) that specify the thickness of the line (the **Size** attribute); the width of the line in pixels or as a percentage of the screen width (the **Width** attribute); the alignment of a line narrower than the screen width (the **Align** attribute); and that dictate that the line must be solid (the **Noshade** attribute). The Noshade attribute has a single legal value of 'noshade', and the attribute name does not appear. In the example below, the line must be solid, occupy half the width of the window and be centred:

```
<!-- HTML -->
<hr noshade size="4" width="50%" align="center">
```

A **Type** attribute has been added to the **Ordered List** element, the **Unordered List** element and the **List Item** element (but is now deprecated in the first two cases). An ordered list can take values of 'A' (capital letters), 'a' (small letters), 'I' (large Roman letters), 'i' (small Roman letters) or '1' (digits), which is the default. An unordered list can take values of 'DISC' (bullet), 'CIRCLE' (hollow bullet) or 'SQUARE' (a square hollow bullet). The list item can take the same values, depending which list type it is within, and overrides the current setting for the list within all remaining items. In addition, the ordered list has a **Start** attribute, which indicates a start value for the first item when it is not '1' (or equivalent), and the list item has a **Value** attribute that can only be used within ordered lists to reset the current calculated value:

```
<!-- HTML -->
<ol Type="A" Start="4">
    <li>First Item
    <li Value="G">Second Item
    <li>Third Item
</ol>
```

> D   First Item
> G   Second Item
> H   Third Item

The **Defining Instance** element (**Dfn**) encloses the first occurrence or most significant occurrence of a term used in the text. Potentially, this element may be used by search engines to determine the keywords, and by style sheets to highlight new terms as they are introduced:

```
<!-- HTML -->
... Although <dfn>XML</dfn> is related
to <dfn>SGML</dfn>, XML is also related
to <dfn>HTML</dfn>, as HTML is an application
of SGML.
```

Text and page style

The document background colour and foreground text colour can be specified in the **Body** element (though the following techniques are now deprecated), using the new **Background Color** attribute (**Bgcolor**) and the new **Text** attribute. In both cases, the format of the attribute value comprises either the name of a colour, or a coded RGB (red, green, blue) mix. Available colour names are 'aqua', 'black', 'fuchsia', 'gray', 'green', 'lime', 'maroon', 'navy', 'olive', 'purple', 'red', 'silver', 'teal', 'white' and 'yellow'. The RGB scheme uses three hexadecimal (two-digit) values, preceded by a hash symbol, for example '#FF2250'. The first two digits indicate the amount of Red, the next two digits indicate the amount of Green, and the final two digits indicate the amount of Blue to be mixed to create the desired colour. The example below produces a document with light-gray text on a black background:

```
<!-- HTML -->
<body bgcolor="#000000" text="#F0F0F0">
```

As an alternative, the background can be composed from a picture, often in GIF format. The new **Background** attribute provides a **URL** to the desired picture. When the picture is smaller than the display area, it is repeated across and down until it fills the display area:

```
<!-- HTML -->
<body background="/piccies/mybackgr.gif">
```

A change to the document background or text colour may affect the visibility of **hypertext** links, so three additional attributes are used to set the colour of linking text (all now deprecated). The **Link** attribute sets the colour of a link that is not active and has not been visited. The **Visited Link** attribute (**Vlink**) sets the colour of all links that have been activated in the (recent) past. The **Active Link** attribute (**Alink**) sets the colour of the currently selected link. The format of the values is as described above for document foreground and background colors.

The font size may be varied using the new **Font** element (now deprecated). The **Size** attribute dictates the new font size, either absolutely, as a value between '1' and '7' (the default being '3'), or relatively as a size change from the current value. A relative size is given by inserting a '+' or '-' character:

```
<!-- HTML -->
This text is <font size="+1">bigger</font> than
normal.
```

An additional **Color** attribute uses the scheme described above for changing the document colour in the Body element. Font elements can also be embedded within each other.

The **Basefont** element (now deprecated) is used to specify a new default font size for the whole document, and should therefore be placed at the top of the Body segment. It also uses a **Size** attribute to set the font size:

```
<!-- HTML -->
<basefont size="2">Text size is smaller than normal but
<font size="+1">is now as expected</font>.
```

The **Big** and **Small** elements are complementary, and specify larger and smaller text respectively, but the actual size is determined by the browser. The **Underline** element (**U**) specifies a line under the enclosed text, and the **Strike** element specifies a line through the text (both elements are now deprecated).

The **Subscript** element (**Sub**) and the **Superscript** element (**Sup**) are complementary. The first encloses small text that appears below the baseline and the second encloses small text that appears above the baseline:

```
<!-- HTML -->
The W<sup>3</sup>C is responsible for...
Water is H<sub>2</sub>O.
```

Image handling

The **Image** element (**Img**) takes additional alignment options using the **Align** attribute. In addition to the standard 'middle', 'top' and 'bottom' options, the new 'left' and 'right' options create **floating images** in the left or right margin. New attributes include **Border**, which specifies the thickness of the image   border line, the **Vertical Space** attribute (**Vspace**) and the **Horizontal Space** attribute (**Hspace**) which create extra space around the image, and **Width** and **Height**, which tell the browser the dimensions of the image to speed up downloading:

```
<!-- HTML -->
<img border="3" vspace="2" hspace="2" align="left">
```

Due to the new floating images described above, the **Line Break** element (**Br**) has been extended to allow the break to force the next line to appear below large, horizontally adjacent floating images. Account can be taken of images that appear in just one of the margins. The **Clear** attribute (now deprecated) takes a value of 'all' (an image in either or both margins), 'left' (an image in the left margin only) or 'right' (an image in the right margin only):

```
<!-- HTML -->
<br clear="left">
```

The concept of a 'client-side image map' was introduced earlier. The browser uses HTML tags to identify image areas and associated URLs to other documents or other parts of the same document. This approach provides the benefits of less interaction with the server (making the process more efficient) and independence from the HTTP protocol (making it suitable for simple intranet use, when a Web server may not be needed, as well as for more efficient Internet use), as well as giving prior warning of the effect of clicking on any part of the image (the target URL is displayed as the pointer is moved over the image). The **Usemap** attribute is added to the Img element, and holds the name of a **Map** element that defines areas of the image:

```
<!-- HTML -->
<IMG SRC="/images/myimage.gif" usemap="#mymap">

<map name="mymap"> ..... </map>
```

Within the Map element, each area and associated URL is defined using an **Area** element. This element contains attributes to define the shape of the area, the coordinates of the area and the URL associated with the area. The **Coords** attribute defines the coordinates of the area and the **Href** attribute provides the URL. The **Alt** attribute contains a textual equivalent to the area, to be used by applications that cannot support this feature. The **Nohref** attribute indicates that this area is not active, and has a single possible value of 'nohref'. Consider an example of an image showing a new model of motor car. Each area of interest, such as the wheels, or the engine, could be located and attached to an appropriate HTML document:

```
<!-- HTML -->
<map name="mymap">
   <area shape="circle"
         coords="50, 150, 150, 250"
         href="wheels/back.html"
         alt="Back Wheels">
   <area shape="circle"
         coords="350 200 50"
         href="wheels/front.html"
         alt="Front Wheels">
</map>
```

The default shape is assumed to be a rectangle, with four coordinates representing in pixels the left edge, top edge, right edge and bottom edge of the area. The first example above defines an area for the back wheel – '50' pixels in, '150' pixels down for the left and top edges, and as the diameter of the wheel is 100 pixels, '150' in and '250' down for the right and bottom edges. The optional **Shape** attribute may be used to make this area type explicit, 'shape="rect"'. Another shape option is 'circle', which requires three values, the horizontal and vertical coordinate for the centre of the circle, followed by a radius value. The second example defines the area of the front wheel as a circle with a radius of '50' pixels, '350' pixels across and '200' down.

Backward compatibility can be provided for the benefit of browsers not able to use this facility. Both schemes for creating image maps (client-side and server-side) can co-exist by including both the Ismap attribute and the Usemap attribute in the same Img element. In the example below, a browser that does not support a client-side map scheme uses the Anchor to pass coordinates to 'myscript.cgi':

```
<!-- HTML -->

<a href="myscript.cgi">
    <IMG SRC="/images/myimage.gif"
         usemap="#mymap" ISMAP>
</a>

<map name="mymap">
<!-- image mapping commands -->
</map>
```

Tables

The most significant new feature of HTML 3.2 is its support for tabular material. The **Table** element encloses a table grid. The cells may be separated by border lines, using the **Border** attribute. A number of pixels value may be applied, such as '3' pixels, and a value of '0' indicates no border and no space for a border (which is different from the effect of not including the attribute). Alternatively, the tag may simply include the word 'border', which can be considered the same as a border value of '1':

```
<!-- HTML -->

<table>              no borders, space for them remains

<table border="0">  no borders, no space for them

<table border>      same as 'border=1' using 'dummy'

<table border="10"> very thick border lines
```

This confusing arrangement only makes sense in XML terms if the word 'border' is seen to be a single option value of another attribute, perhaps named 'dummy', and the name is never actually present. This is just another SGML tag minimization technique.

The space between cells can be adjusted. The **Cellspacing** attribute takes a numeric value that states how much space there is between cells (including their borders). It has a default value of '2':

```
<!-- HTML -->
<table border>                <table border cellspacing=8>
```

If a value of zero is used, the border lines overlap each other.

The space between the cell contents and the borders of the cell can also be adjusted using the **Cellpadding** attribute, which takes a numeric value. The default value is '1':

```
<!-- HTML -->
<table border>                <table border cellpadding=8>
```

The width and height of the table are often left under the control of the browser, which composes the table within the restrictions of the available window area. The **Width** attribute may be used to 'encourage' the browser to take into account the wishes of the document author. This attribute takes a numeric value that dictates how many pixels wide the table should be, or what percentage of the available screen width it should occupy. A pure number is interpreted as a pixel value. A percentage symbol indicates a proportion of the screen dimensions.

```
<!-- HTML -->
<table border width=800>
```

The table may have a title, which is contained within a **Caption** element. This element is placed within the Table element, but before the elements described later. The content is by default displayed above the main table grid, but may be explicitly displayed below the table using the **Align** attribute, with a value of 'bottom':

```
<!-- HTML -->
<table>
    <caption align="bottom">Title Below</caption> ...
</table>
```

The table structure is row-oriented, which means that the grid is built by first defining each row, then separating each cell within a row. Each row of data is enclosed in a **Table Row** element (**Tr**), and each cell is enclosed in either a **Table Header** element (**Th**) or a **Table Data** element (**Td**), the only difference being one of emphasis – the Th element content is usually displayed in bold (and centred). Th and Td elements may be mixed within the same row, possibly to create side headings:

```
<!-- HTML -->
<tr><th>Colour<th>Status<th>Level</tr>
<tr><th>Red<td>Danger<td>1</tr>
<tr><th>Green<td>Normal<td>3</tr>
```

Colour	Status	Level
Red	Danger	1
Green	Normal	3

As shown above, a cell may directly contain text. But it may also contain any document body elements, including a complete embedded table. The Line Break element is particularly useful for formatting text within the cell. If a cell is empty, no border lines are drawn.

The width and height of a cell can be 'suggested' in the Td and Th elements, using the **Width** and **Height** attributes. The browser is not required to obey these instructions.

The content of individual cells, or all the cells in a row, may be aligned horizontally and vertically in various ways. The default horizontal alignment is 'left' in Td elements, and 'center' in Th elements, as shown in the example above. The default vertical alignment is 'middle' for both types of cell. The **Align** attribute allows horizontal alignment to be set to 'left', 'right' or 'center'. The **Valign** attribute allows vertical alignment to be set to 'top', 'middle', 'bottom' or 'baseline' (where all cells in the row are horizontally aligned by last line, after the cell with the most lines is aligned to 'top'). An alignment set in the Tr element provides a default for all cells in the row, but individual cells may override this setting.

By default each cell occupies an area dissected by one column and one row, forming a simple position within the table grid, but may be expanded across or down using the **Colspan** and **Rowspan** attributes. These attributes take numeric values, and have implied values of '1' (zero is not a legal option). Higher values than '1' stretch the cell over adjoining areas:

```
<!-- HTML -->
<tr><th>Colour<th>Status<th>Level</tr>
<tr><th>Red<td>Danger<td>1</tr>
<tr><th>Blue<td colspan=2>No Priority<td>2</tr>
<tr><th>Brown</th><!-- NO CELL --><td>3</td></tr>
```

Colour	Status	Level
Red	Danger	1
Blue	No Priority	2
Brown	Status	3

Note that the final row in the example above has only two cell elements, containing 'Brown' and '3', because the middle cell has effectively been replaced by the cell above it.

The content of a cell is normally formatted by the browser as it is composed to fit the available screen width. The **Nowrap** attribute may be used in the Th and Td elements to prevent lines being split. This is another example of a minimized attribute with a single possible value, in this case 'nowrap':

```
<!-- HTML -->
<td nowrap>This line must not be broken</td>
```

Java

Some HTML browsers are able to access and execute **Java** programs (or **applets**). The HTML document contains an element called **Applet** (now deprecated in favour of the new Object element), which identifies the file containing the Java program. An attribute called **Code** holds the **URL** of the program, but as it cannot be an absolute URL, the optional **Codebase** attribute provides the base for relative paths (and if not present, the URL of the HTML document is assumed). The **Name** attribute identifies the applet for inter-communication between active applets. An area of the screen is set aside to display any output from the program when it is activated, using the **Width** and **Height** attributes, which indicate the number of pixels to reserve:

```
<!-- HTML -->
<applet code="MyJava.class" height="150" width="300">
...
</applet>
```

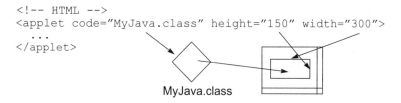

MyJava.class

The remaining attributes, **Align**, **Alt**, **Hspace** and **Vspace** have the same functions as described for the Img element.

The **Parameter** element (**Param**) is used to send parameter values to the program. The **Name** attribute identifies a particular parameter, and the **Value** attribute assigns a value to the named parameter:

```
<!-- HTML -->
<applet code="Clock.class" height="150" width="300">
   <param name="ZONE" value="GMT">
   <param name="REPRESENTATION" value="DIGITAL">
</applet>
```

Browsers that are not Java-aware should simply ignore the Applet element.

Scripts and styles

This version foresees the need for scripts and style sheets to be built into Web pages. Though not defining an exact mechanism to do either of these things, this version of the standard helped prepare the way by including the **Script** and **Style** elements. For now, browsers need to be aware of these elements, if only to avoid displaying their contents.

HTML 4.0

The next version of HTML, version 4.0, was released by the **W³C** in December 1997 (and is the current version, at the time of writing). Some of its features have long been available in at least one of the popular browsers. In particular, the **frame** concept has been in widespread use for some time. There is an SGML DTD for this standard (http://www.w3.org/TR/REC-html40/). As with earlier ones this DTD is not XML compatible (though the next version probably will be).

The new elements in this version allow the window to be split into frames (using the Frameset, Frame, Noframes and Iframe elements), extend the table model (the Tbody, Tfoot, Thead, Col and Colgroup elements), extend the forms model (the Fieldset, Label, Legend, Optgroup and Button elements, as well as the 'button' value added to the Type attribute), adds changed content highlighting (Ins (inserted text) and Del (deleted text)), and a generalized non-HTML object identifier (Object), and introduce some general text descriptions (Abbr (abbreviation), Q (quote) and Acronym). This version also adds a Noscript, Bdo (BiDi override) and S element (strike) (but immediately deprecates it!). The Script and Style elements are put to use, and given various attributes.

It is widely expected that the HTML table model will become the *de facto* standard model for XML documents (just as CALS tables did for SGML).

This version finally makes obsolete the **Listing** element, as well as the **Plaintext** and **Xmp** (example) elements (Pre should be used instead). In addition, it deprecates the **Applet** element (replaced with Object), the **Center** element (replace with Div, aligned 'center'), the **Dir** and **Menu** elements (use Ul) and the Isindex element. To encourage the use of style sheets, a number of text styling elements are also deprecated, including the **Strike**-through and **U** (underline) element, and the **Font** and **Basefont** elements. A number of styling attributes have also been deprecated, for the same reason.

Common attributes

Some useful attributes have now been added to almost every HTML element. The most ubiquitous are four core attributes, **Id**, **Title**, **Class** and **Style**. There are few elements that do not have them, the exceptions being structural tags (Html, Head, Title), background scripts (Script, Style and Area), applet tags (Applet and Param) and meta-data (Base, Basefont and Meta). In addition, many elements have new language attributes, Lang and Dir, and many others have attributes that allow scripts to be activated when the user interacts with the element in some way (Onclick, Ondblclick, Onmousedown, Onmouseup, Onmouseover, Onmouseout, Onkeypress, Onkeydown and Onkeyup).

The **Identifier** attribute (**Id**) gives the element a unique name that may be used for various purposes, such as to provide a target for a hypertext link, to allow a style defined in a separate style sheet to be applied specifically to this element, or to be manipulated in a specific way by an ECMAScript procedure. The following paragraph is given a red colour by the style sheet, and is also the target of a link.

```
para:#Scarborough { color: red }
...
<!-- HTML -->
<para id="Scarborough">This is a paragraph about
Scarborough. A seaside resort in the north of
England.</p>
...
... See <a href="#Scarborough">Scarborough</a>...
```

This technique is familiar to XML and SGML users, and is certainly a less clumsy way to identify the target of a link than wrapping the paragraph text within an A element (using the Name attribute to identify it).

The **Title** attribute allows a brief description of the content of the element to be included. Normally not visible, this text would only be revealed on user request, used to build a simple table of contents, or may be presented in the status bar.

```
<!-- HTML -->
<p title="Scarborough">This is a paragraph about
Scarborough.</P>
```

The **Style** attribute allows **CSS** in-line styles to be applied. See Chapter 17 for details.

```
<!-- HTML -->
<p style="color: red">This is a paragraph about
Scarborough.</p>
```

The **Class** attribute introduces a measure of the generalized markup concept to HTML by allowing category names to be added to element instances. For example, some Anchor elements may need to be presented differently, to indicate whether they take the user to a different document (colour in red), or to another part of the same document (colour in blue):

```
A:{ ... }
A:internal{ color: blue }
A:external{ color: red }
<!-- HTML -->
<p id="Scarborough">This is a paragraph about
Scarborough. A seaside resort in the north of
England</p>
...
... See <a href="#Scarborough" class="internal">Scarbor-
ough</a>, or go to the <a href="http://www.scarborough.org/
" class="external">Scarborough</a> site.
```

The **Lang** attribute describes the human language used for the textual content of the element:

```
<!-- HTML -->
<p lang="EN">This is an English paragraph.</p>
```

The **Direction** attribute (**Dir**) describes the direction of writing that is conventional for the human language concerned. It takes a value of 'ltr' (left to right) or 'rtl' (right to left):

```
<!-- HTML -->
<p lang="EN" DIR="ltr">This is an English
paragraph.</p>
```

The 'On...' attributes all specify an ECMAscript function that is to be activated when the user interacts with the element in some given way.

The **Onclick** attribute activates the named function when the user clicks the mouse button over the element.

```
<!-- HTML -->
<p onclick="MyParaClickFunction()">Click here!</p>
```

Similarly, the **Ondblclick** attribute activates the named function when the user double-clicks the mouse button over the element and **Onkeypress** activates when a key is pressed (and released). The **Onmousedown** and **Onmouseup** attributes detect the pressing and release of the mouse button while it is over the element. The **Onkeydown** and **Onkeyup** attributes work in the same way, but for key presses. Movement of the mouse pointer over the element is detected by the **Onmouseover** and **Onmouseout** attributes.

Descriptive blocks

As stylistic elements are removed or deprecated, they are replaced by new descriptive elements. The following elements help style sheet designers develop more suitable formatting, and Web crawler search engines perform more useful analysis of the document.

The **Abbreviation** element (**Abbr**) is used to identify an abbreviation in the text. It has a **Title** attribute which is used to hold the full term:

```
<!-- HTML -->
...talk to
<abbr title="mister">Mr.</abbr>
Smith ...
```

Similarly, the **Acronym** element holds a form of abbreviation that substitutes each word in a name with one letter. The **Title** attribute is used in the same way:

```
<!-- HTML -->
...the
<acronym title="World Wide Web">WWW</acronym>
is ...
```

The **Quote** element (**Q**) holds an in-line quotation:

```
<!-- HTML -->
...Shakespeare wrote <q>To be or not to be...</q>.
```

The **Deletion** element (**Del**) identifies text that is to be considered as deleted, and is only present to bring attention to the fact that it no longer applies. Such text is typically presented with a line through it. Complementing this is the **Insertion** element (**Ins**), which identifies new text. Typically, new text is highlighted with a change bar in the margin. By convention, they should be used consistently as block-level elements, or as in-line elements, but not both, as it may be difficult to apply a suitable style for both types. They both contain optional **Datetime** and **Citation** attributes (**Cite**), indicating the time the document was changed, and pointing to another document that contains comments on why the change was made, though the Title attribute may also be used to contain a short note on the reason:

```
<!-- HTML -->
... there are <del>fifteen</del><ins>nine</ins> days left
to Christmas ...
```

Table model improvements

The HTML table model has been extended in various ways. The most significant improvements concern identification of logically distinct parts of the table for more intelligent rendering, and more efficient means to define format settings for ranges of cells.

When presenting tables on paper, it is useful to be able to identify header rows, so that the pagination engine can repeat the headings at the top of each page. Similarly, footer rows can be repeated at the base of each page containing a reference to a footnote. When presenting to a scrollable window, a large table body may be collapsed to just a few scrollable rows, sandwiched between fixed, permanently visible headers and footers. The new elements, **Table Head** (**Thead**), **Table Body** (**Tbody**) and **Table Footer** (**Tfoot**) encloses rows of each kind.

Only the Tbody element is required, and for backward compatibility both its start-tag and end-tag may be absent (its presence is then implied). The Thead and Tfoot elements are optional because not all tables have rows that fall into these categories. When present, the Thead element must occur first, as would be expected, but the Tfoot element must *also* precede the body. The reason for this unusual arrangement is that it allows the rendering package to collect the content of a footer, then place it at the base of each page, without needing to process the table twice.

```
<!-- HTML -->
<table>
   <thead>...</thead>
   <tfoot>...</tfoot>
   <tbody>...</tbody>
</table>
```

In addition to the usual array of core, event and language attributes, these three elements also contain the **Align** and **Valign** attribute, so introducing another level of cell content alignment overriding, above the row level. In a table containing mostly currency values, it may be suitable to state that all header cells are centred, that all body cells are aligned on full-point, and that all footer cells are left-aligned.

It is not uncommon to find tables where all the cells in a particular column are aligned in the same way. For example, a price table in a catalogue may have two columns, the first being a description of each product, with the text left-aligned, and the second being the price of that item, aligned on a decimal point. Using the table model described in the previous section, each Entry element would need to contain an Align attribute:

```
<!-- HTML -->
<tr>
<entry align="left">Red coat</entry>
<entry align="char" char=".">12.4</entry>
</tr>
<tr>
<entry align="left">Green coat</entry>
<entry align="char" char=".">12.6</entry>
</tr>
```

Clearly, when many rows are involved, this is very time-consuming to produce, and also wasteful of memory and bandwidth. It is now possible to define a style for all cells in a column, using the **Column** element (**Col**). In the example below, the first Col element specifies an alignment of 'left' for the first column, and the second Col element specifies an alignment on decimal point for the second column, so removing the need to specify these alignments in individual entries:

```
<!-- HTML -->
<col align="left">
<col align="char" char=".">
<tr>
<entry>Red coat</entry>
<entry>12.4</entry>
</tr>
<tr>
<entry>Green coat</entry>
<entry>12.6</entry>
</tr>
...
```

For horizontal alignments, the Col element overrides the Tr element, though individual Entry element styles are still the most significant.

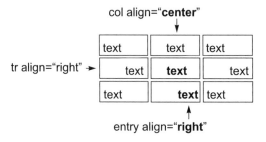

As indicated above, the first Col element is deemed to apply to the first column, the second applies to the next column, and so on. When several columns in a group have the same settings, only one Col element is required, and the **Span** attribute is used to specify how many columns are affected. The total number of columns in a table can be calculated by adding together the span values (when not present, a value of '1' is assumed). In the following example, the table has six columns (it is assumed that if a Col element is used at all, then all table columns must be covered by these elements):

```
<!-- HTML -->
<col align="left">
<col span="3" align="right">
<col span="2" align="center">
```

This element can also be used to pre-define the width of each column, using the **Width** attribute, so that Web browsers and pagination engines can start building the table presentation before reading the entire table. In the following example, the column widths are '30', '40', '40', '40', '50' and '50':

```
<!-- HTML -->
<col width="30" align="left">
<col width="40" span="3" align="right">
<col width="50" span="2" align="center">
```

The width values may also be proportional, so the table width can expand to the area available, and each column is assigned a 'fair' proportion of that width, based on the values in the Width attribute.

A value followed by an asterisk character denotes a proportional value. To make the column widths defined above keep their relative sizes, but allow additional space to be exploited, it is only necessary to append the asterisk to the existing values, though the smaller values '3*', '4*', '4*', '4*', '5*' and '5*' would produce identical results.

SGML Note: Users of CALS tables for SGML tables will be familiar with this concept.

When a large number of consecutive Col elements share some attribute values, but not others, a more efficient technique may be employed using the **Column Group** element (**Colgroup**). This element may enclose a number of Col elements, and has exactly the same attributes, which when used are deemed to apply to each embedded Col element that does not itself contain an explicit definition. In this example, both columns in the group are given a width of 55 pixels:

```
<!-- HTML -->
<colgroup width="55">
   <col align="left">
   <col span="3" align="right">
</colgroup>
<colgroup width="50" span="2" align="center">
</colgroup>
```

The other major benefit of column groups is that they define an identifiable vertical component of a table, consisting of several columns, and regardless of any degree of commonality in style between these columns. This defined object may be the target of a hypertext link, or the trigger for an event, such as Onclick. A Colgroup element does not even have to contain Col elements, if their presence is not appropriate. In this case, it has its own **Span** attribute:

```
<!-- HTML -->
<colgroup span="3" width="35"></colgroup>
<colgroup span="2" width="20"></colgroup>
```

It is not possible to mix Colgroup and Col elements. If just one Colgroup is needed, then all definition must be applied using it. Another way to look at this restriction is to imagine that Col elements must always be contained within a Colgroup element, but, when there are only Col elements present, they are enclosed within an implied column group.

Form improvements

Text that describes the purpose of an object on the form can be made 'active'. Using the **Label** element, the user can click on the text instead of the actual button. For check-boxes and option buttons, clicking on a label changes the value just as clicking on the object itself does. The Label element may surround the object concerned, or, when it is to be displayed at a distance from the objects, it is associated with the identifier of the object using the **For** attribute:

```
<!-- HTML -->
<label><input type="checkbox" ...>Leather</label>

<label for="covertype">Leather</label>
...
<input type="checkbox" id="covertype" ...>
```

It is now possible to use the tab key to select form objects in a pre-defined order using the **Tabindex** attribute. The form control with a Tabindex value of '1' is the first field selected.

Alternatively, the **Accesskey** attribute allows a specific field to be selected instantly when the user depresses a specified key (in combination with the ALT key on a PC):

```
<!-- HTML -->
<input type="checkbox" accesskey="L" ...>Leather</label>
```

Styles and scripts

The **Style** element encloses style sheet instructions. The **Type** attribute is required, and identifies the style sheet language, such as 'text/css' or 'text/xsl'. The **Media** attribute identifies the type of media the style sheet is aimed at, such as 'screen' (the default) or 'paper'. A **Title** attribute is also allowed to identify the style sheet.

```
<!-- HTML -->
<style type="text/css" media="screen">
  p { color: green }
</style>
```

A number of attributes have been added to the **Script** element, which is used to enclose script programs. The **Type** attribute describes the scripting language used, such as 'text/javascript'. The **Src** attribute identifies a remote file containing the scripts, using a URL. When Src is used, the **Charset** attribute may also be used to identify the character set used in the file that contains the scripts. The **Defer** attribute takes a boolean value of 'true' or 'false' to indicate whether or not the browser should defer executing the script. When set to 'true', this is a hint that the script does not alter the document in any way, so the browser can go ahead and render the document.

To prevent older browsers from simply displaying the scripts, it is necessary to surround them with a comment.

The **NoScript** element has been included to hold alternative information in the case that the browser is configured to prevent scripts from running, or is not familiar with the scripting language used.

Frames

Using frames, the screen is divided into areas, with each area possibly displaying a different document, each one scrolled independently. Among other uses, frames facilitate the use of table of contents and button bars that do not vanish as the user scrolls down the main document.

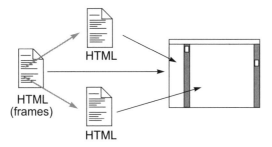

A frame-based document replaces the Body element with a **Frameset** element:

```
<!-- HTML -->
<html>
<head>...</head>
<frameset>...</frameset>
</html>
```

The Frameset element defines an area which generally fills the end user's screen. This area is divided into frames using the **Cols** or **Rows** attribute. These attributes take a value that specifies the width or height of the sub-areas. This value specifies the height or width using one of three methods, the number of pixels (not advised), a percentage of the available space or a proportion of the available space. Values are separated by commas, which also therefore specify the number of columns or rows in the set:

```
<!-- HTML -->

<frameset rows="1500, 1000, 500">

<frameset rows="3*, 2*, *">

<frameset rows="50%, 33%, 16%">
```

The first example above specifies a height of 1,500 pixels for the first row, the second example reserves three proportional units for the first row (the asterisk character alone is equivalent to '1*'), and the third example specifies that the first row should occupy half the available height ('50%'). If the available height were 3,000 pixels, then all three examples above would be equivalent. These value types may be mixed:

```
<!-- HTML -->
<frameset cols="50%, 100, 2*, *">
```

When value types are mixed, fixed values have precedence, followed by percentage values, then proportional values. In the example above, the second column is assigned exactly 100 pixels of horizontal space, the first column is then assigned half of the remaining space, and the remainder is divided among the proportional columns (the third column taking twice the space of the last column):

2nd (percentage)	1st	3rd (proportional)	
50% of remaining area	100 pixels	2*	1*

A Frame Set can contain further embedded Frame Sets. Each embedded Frame Set occupies the space reserved for it by the enclosing Frame Set. Taking the example above, a Frame Set embedded in the first column is restricted to the left half of the screen, and will define subdivisions of this area:

```
<!-- HTML -->
<frameset cols="50%, 100, 2*, *">
   <frameset cols="60%, 40%">
   ...
   </frameset>
   ...
</frameset>
```

|-------- 60 % -------|--- 40 % ---|	100 pixels	2*	1*

A Frame Set may contain a **Noframes** element. This element is intended to hold information to be displayed by a browser that cannot interpret the frames. Its function is therefore similar to the Alt attribute in the Image element. Its content, which may include normal blocks such as paragraphs and lists, is not displayed in frames-aware browsers:

```
<!-- HTML -->
<noframes><p>If you see this, you can't see
FRAMES!</noframes>
```

A frames-aware browser ignores this tag and all its contents. A browser that does not understand frames will not be aware of the Noframes element, but is most likely to remove the tags, while leaving the enclosed text intact for presentation to the user.

Finally, a Frameset element may contain a **Frame** element. This is an empty element, so has no end-tag. It is used to identify the document to be displayed within the frame, to identify the frame itself (so that it can be made the target of links from other frames or documents), to determine whether the width and height of the frame can be altered by the end user, to determine whether scroll bars are used, and to specify the margin widths.

The Frame element has a **Source** attribute (**Src**) which contains the **URL** of the HTML document to be displayed in the frame. If no URL is provided, the area is left blank. The Frame element also has a **Name** attribute, which contains the name of the frame, so that it can be the target of a link from another frame, or from another document:

```
<!-- HTML -->
<frame name="main" src="../areas/myarea.html">
```

By referring to the Name value of another frame, a new document can be requested, and displayed in that other area. This feature is ideal for changing the content of the main window as items are selected in a table of contents frame. The **A** (Anchor) element has a new **Target** attribute to refer to the actual frame in which the content should be displayed:

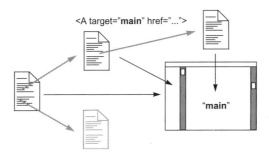

The Frame element also has a **Scrolling** attribute, which indicates whether horizontal and vertical scroll bars are always present, present as required (when the height or width of the page exceeds the space provided on the screen), or never present. A value of 'yes' forces scroll bars to appear even if not needed. A value of 'auto' displays scroll bars when necessary, and is the default value. A value of 'no' disables scroll bars entirely.

The Frame element also has a **Noresize** attribute, which, if present, prevents the end user from changing the height or width of the frame. By default it is absent, and resizing is allowed. In SGML terms, this must be seen as an attribute called Noresize that has an optional, single value of 'NORESIZE', and that minimization is in use to avoid stating the attribute name:

```
<!-- HTML -->
<frame src="../areas/myarea.html" NORESIZE>
```

Finally, the Frame element has **Marginwidth** and **Marginheight** attributes, which specify the space to reserve between the borders of the frame and the enclosed text. Width settings affect the space between the left and right edges. Height settings affect the space above and below the content. Values are in pixels, and if present must be at least '1', and not so large that content cannot be displayed. If absent, the browser provides default settings.

XHTML 1.0 (draft)

As already stated, HTML is currently an application of SGML. However, the popularity of XML since its release has led to the desire to embed XML fragments in HTML documents, and vice versa, and some incompatibilities arise when this is attempted. SGML includes a number of markup techniques that have been adopted by HTML (both before and after HTML became legal SGML), but were omitted from the XML standard. Tag minimization, the lack of well-formed compliance constraints, the format of empty elements, and other issues all need to be addressed.

Many have speculated that the next version of HTML will become an application of XML instead of SGML, largely to solve the problem outlined above, and this view now seems to be taking shape in the form of XHTML, a draft proposal for a reformalization on HTML 4.0 as an XML application. No new functionality or tags have been added, so this cannot be viewed as the 'next' version of HTML in the normal sense. The draft proposal referred to here can be found at http://www.w3.org/TR/1999/WD-html-in-xml-19990304.

Fortunately, because XML is a subset of SGML, an XML variant of HTML 4.0 should still work with SGML tools, and, perhaps more importantly, with Web browsers.

Identifying XHTML documents

This version of HTML must include a DOCTYPE declaration, with a public identifier that matches one of the following strings.

```
-//W3C//DTD XHTML 1.0 Strict//EN
-//W3C//DTD XHTML 1.0 Transitional//EN
-//W3C//DTD XHTML 1.0 Frameset//EN
```

These URLs identify existing variants of HTML 4.0, as represented by three DTDs. A 'strict' document is one that conforms to the strict constraints of

HTML 4.0, and omits all deprecated elements and attributes (the 'strict' variant is recommended in the HTML 4.0 specification). A 'transitional' document is one that may include deprecated features. A 'frameset' document is one that may also contain the Frameset element.

A system identifier is still needed to reference the DTD. By default, these DTDs have names that reflect the types discussed above:

```
xhtml1-strict.dtd
xhtml1-transitional.dtd
xhtml1-frameset.dtd
```

For example:

```
<!DOCTYPE PUBLIC "-//W3C//DTD XHTML 1.0 Strict//EN"
                 "xhtml1-strict.dtd" >
```

The root element must be named 'html', as expected, but this element must also declare a namespace, which is one of the following:

```
http://www.w3.org/Profiles/xhtml1-strict
http://www.w3.org/Profiles/xhtml1-transitional
http://www.w3.org/Profiles/xhtml1-frameset
```

The following is a complete, valid XHTML document that happens to conform to the strict variant:

```
<!DOCTYPE PUBLIC "-//W3C//DTD XHTML 1.0 Strict//EN"
                 "xhtml1-strict.dtd" >
<html
 xmlns="http://www.w3.org/Profiles/xhtml1-strict">
   <head><title>STRICT DOCUMENT</title></head>
   <body><p>STRICT</p></body>
</html>
```

Constraints

Because XML is case-sensitive, all elements and attributes must conform to a strict standard. The DTD is defined using lower-case names. As shown in the example above, lower-case letters must therefore be used for all names.

Empty elements, such as Img, must end with '/>'. Some browsers will only work with such elements when there is a space before the end delimiters in the tag. The start-tag/end-tag combination must not be used for elements of type EMTPY. On the other hand, non-empty elements that happen to contain no child elements or text must use the start-tag/end-tag combination, never the empty element tag. The following example demonstrates correct usage of the Img and Paragraph elements:

```
<p>Image with extra spaces above and below</p>
<p></p>
<img href="...." />
<p></p>
```

XML DTDs cannot override element models to prevent an element from occurring somewhere within itself. For example, in HTML the anchor element (a) should not occur within another anchor element, yet an XML DTC cannot enforce this rule. The following list therefore defines a constraint beyond those in the DTD:

The A, Form and Label elements cannot contain further instances of themselves.

The Pre element cannot contain Img, Object, Big, Small, Sub or Sup elements.

The Button element cannot contain Input, Select, Textarea, Label, Button, Form, Fieldset or Iframe elements.

Script and style coding

To avoid interpretation of '<' and '&' characters, and interpretation of '<' and '&' strings as entity references within the Script and Style elements, a CDATA section must be embedded to enclose the content.

```
<style>
  <![CDATA[
  .............
  ]]>
</style>
```

Like any XML document, an XHTML document must be well-formed, and no tag minimization techniques can be used. It must also conform to the constraints of the chosen DTD.

Mixing HTML with XML

Sometimes it is useful to combine XML and HTML, and there are different approaches to doing this. For some purposes, it is useful to embed XML fragments within HTML documents, and for others it is useful to be able to embed HTML fragments in XML documents.

XML in HTML

Although not officially part of even the latest HTML standard, at least one of the popular browser vendors has added a tag that allows XML fragments to be embedded within an HTML document. There is no guarantee that other parties will agree on the exact mechanism described here, but the need for this capability is undoubted. The Xml tag is used to enclose an embedded XML fragment:

```
<!-- HTML -->
<html>
...
   <p>Normal HTML paragraph.</p>
   <xml id="myXmlFragment">
     <?xml version="1.0">
     <animals>
       <animal>Giraffe</animal>
       <animal>Elephant</animal>
     </animals>
   </xml>
   <p>Another normal HTML paragraph.</p>
</html>
```

Alternatively, it should be possible to link to an existing but separate XML document, in this case using the Src attribute in the Xml tag:

```
<!-- HTML -->
<html>
...
   <p>Normal HTML paragraph.</p>
   <xml id="myXmlFragment" src="animals.xml"></xml>
   <p>Another normal HTML paragraph.</p>
</html>
```

It should be possible to render the XML island directly using CSS or XSL, or make it available for processing and presenting using the DOM.

HTML in XML

Although style sheets are capable of rendering XML elements into general formatting objects such as in-line styles and block structures, support for advanced features such as tables and interactive forms is in its infancy. One way around this problem is to use HTML tags within XML documents. However, a browser needs to be able to distinguish between genuine HTML elements, and XML elements that happen to have the same names as elements in the HTML standard. This can be done using namespaces.

For example, it is currently not possible (using CSS) to render an XML table if it contains cells that span rows or columns. Inserting an HTML table avoids this issue:

```
<para>A normal XML paragraph.</para>
<table xmlns="http://www.w3.org/TR/REC-html40">
   <tr>......</tr>
   <tr>...<td colspan="2">...</td>...</tr>
   <tr>......</tr>
</table>
<para>Another XML paragraph.</para>
```

19. SGML

There are several books dedicated to describing SGML in detail (see the author's own book, *The Concise SGML Companion* (Addison-Wesley – ISBN 0-201-41999-8)). This chapter focuses on the differences between SGML and XML, and should be of particular interest to readers who are still considering which language to adopt, those who need to convert existing SGML documents or DTDs into XML format, and those who wish to use SGML tools to process XML documents.

Concepts

SGML (the ***Standard Generalized Markup Language***) has, at the time of writing, been in existence for over 13 years. The developers of the XML language used their experience of SGML to determine the shape and scope of the new language, and there are therefore many similarities. However, SGML is also a larger (some would say more unwieldy) language.

Due to the complexity of SGML, and the consequential expense of implementing a system based around this format, relatively few organizations have adopted it for document storage, publishing and interchange. Initially, it was almost totally confined to use in government organizations, and focused particularly on technical documentation controlled by the US Department of Defense. As supporting tools became more affordable and more mature, SGML branched out into new domains, and has become a popular solution to some demanding publishing needs.

SGML incorporates the use of a **DTD** (a ***Document Type Definition***), which is very similar to, but slightly more complex than, the XML DTD. However, a DTD *must* exist for each class of document, and that DTD must be used by all SGML-compliant applications. An SGML DTD and its associated documents can be converted into XML equivalent files, should there be any reason to replace SGML tools with XML tools, or to process, deliver or publish SGML data using XML tools. But it may not be possible to achieve this without human intervention, due to the fact that SGML is more complex than XML.

All SGML documents begin with an **SGML Declaration**, which can be seen as a kind of configuration file. Instructions in this section provide values for the characteristics and limitations described below. The SGML declaration logically precedes the DTD. It may be present in the same physical data file as the DTD and document instance, but more typically it applies to many documents, and even to many document types, so is located in a separate data file.

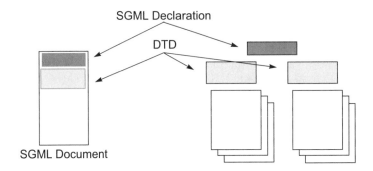

There are default settings for all the features affected by the SGML Declaration. When the default settings are satisfactory, there is no need for an actual SGML Declaration to be present.

At the time SGML was defined, memory and disk space were vastly more expensive than today. The size of documents was therefore a major concern, and keeping markup to a minimum was seen as essential. In addition, there was no expectation that WYSIWYG editing tools would be produced, so techniques designed to minimize the task of keying markup constructs was of prime importance. For these reasons, the SGML specification includes a number of **markup minimization** techniques. For example, it is sometimes possible to omit an end-tag, an attribute name, or even an element name.

HTML Note: Some of these minimization techniques found their way into HTML. In particular, some end-tags may be omitted, and some attribute names are not required (or indeed expected) as in '`<ul compact>`'.

It was foreseen that some implementors would work in environments where the default markup delimiters would be inconvenient, perhaps because the characters used as delimiters are in common use in the document text. For example, the element start-tag open delimiter, by default a '<' character, could easily be changed to '!':

```
!code> <a<b<c !/code>
```

The limited memory available to computers in the early 1980s was a concern. A document could be too large, or too complex for the parser to deal with. For example, a limit of 8,000 could be imposed on the number of elements that can appear in a document, and an element name could be restricted to a maximum length of eight characters.

The SGML Declaration

The **SGML Declaration** segment of an SGML document prepares the parser for the remaining data by specifying character sets in use (usually based on ASCII or ISO 646), setting system variable space limits and selecting optional parts of the SGML standard. These considerations are not relevant to XML, which can take advantage of recent technological developments and has a different target audience. However, it is necessary to know about the SGML declaration if SGML tools are to be used with XML documents, because the default SGML settings need to be modified to make the tools accept documents conforming to the XML syntax.

The start of an SGML declaration is defined by the characters '<!SGML', followed by the version of the standard. It is completed by the close chevron, '>':

```
<!-- SGML -->

<!SGML ISO 8879:1986 ..........>
```

The SGML standard defines the rules that apply to an SGML document, but does not specify exactly how to apply them. Implied rules are defined by an **abstract syntax**, and include, for example, a rule stating that a special character will be used to begin an element start-tag, but without specifying which character this is. A mechanism is provided for defining a **concrete syntax** from the abstract syntax. The concrete syntax specifies the actual keywords and special characters that separate markup from data. For example, it includes a physical value for the character to be used to begin an element start-tag, such as '<'. There is a default concrete syntax, which is known as the **reference concrete syntax**. The defaults include specifying the use of the '<' character to begin a start-tag, and '>' to end one. For example, a start-tag for an element called Name would by default be expected to appear as '<name>'. As the values and settings of the reference concrete syntax are 'hard-wired' into the parser, they need not be physically included in the declarations. But a change to any part of the concrete syntax must be declared, and creates a **variant concrete syntax**. For example, a variant may redefine the start-tag open character to '!', giving '!code>' (though such changes have been rare in practice).

There is also a **reference quantity set** that sets limits on the number or size of various objects, which works in a similar manner. For example, it states that an element name consists of at most eight characters. This too can be changed.

Every SGML application could have its own unique SGML declaration (including a variant concrete syntax and/or a variant quantity set), but due to the desirability of maintaining standards only one variant is in common use. Devised by the US Department of Defense, it is sometimes referred to as the **CALS declaration**.

The **CALS** (*Continuous Acquisition and Life Cycle Support*) variant differs from the reference quantity set mainly in respect of the legal scope of some constraints. For example, the reference quantity set restricts tag names to a maximum length of eight characters, but the CALS variant permits up to 32 characters. The default declaration would enforce a brief element name to identify a 'procedure summary', such as '`<procsum>`', whereas the CALS variant would allow the code to be '`<procedure-summary>`' (if so desired).

The issue of SGML declarations is only relevant to XML when using SGML tools to maintain XML documents. Generally, it is possible to modify an existing declaration, and if the size or number of certain objects is present, they should be reset to '9999999'. It is also necessary to change the definitions for empty elements and processing instructions. This allows document instances to be formatted as required by XML:

```
<!-- SGML -->
CAPACITY
        SGMLREF
        ELEMCAP 999999


DELIM    GENERAL    SGMLREF
         NET    "/>"
         PIC    "?>"


<!-- SGML -->
<p>This is an <empty/> element</p>
<?PROCESS instruction ?>
```

Extra DTD features

An SGML DTD may include features that have been omitted from the simpler XML standard. In some, but not all cases, these features can be emulated using other techniques.

'and' groups

Beyond the sequential and optional model group types that XML permits, SGML also has an option that requires all elements in a group to be present, but allows them to occur in any order. The 'and' connector, '&', is used to signify this rule. For example, an entry in a catalogue may require the presence of Description, Price and Code elements, but not dictate what order they must appear in:

```
<!-- SGML -->
<!ELEMENT entry - - (desc & pr & cd)>
```

The three examples below all conform to this rule:

```
<!-- SGML -->
<entry><desc>...</desc><pr>...</pr><cd>...</cd></entry>

<!-- SGML -->
<entry><cd>...</cd><desc>...</desc><pr>...</pr></entry>

<!-- SGML -->
<entry><cd>...</cd><pr>...</pr><desc>...</desc></entry>
```

Inclusions and exclusions

It is possible to specify the inclusion of a given element in the content models of all elements below a certain point in the DTD hierarchy. For example, instead of explicitly stating that the Indexterm and Emphasis elements are allowed in the content model of each mixed content element, such as the Paragraph, Item, Title and Note elements, they could be defined as 'global' elements at the root of the document. After the model group, a list of included elements appears, separated by one of the token separator characters, '|', '&' or ',' (though it is irrelevant which is chosen) and bounded by brackets that are preceded by a plus symbol, '+'. In this example, a paragraph before the first chapter cannot contain index terms or emphasis, but any paragraph within a chapter can.

```
<!-- SGML -->
<!ELEMENT book      - - (para*, chapter+)>
<!ELEMENT chapter   - - (para|list|note)*
                             +(indexterm|emph)>

<!ELEMENT para      - - (#PCDATA)>
<!ELEMENT list      - - (item+)>
<!ELEMENT note      - - (#PCDATA)>

<!ELEMENT indexterm - - (#PCDATA)>
<!ELEMENT emph      - - (#PCDATA)>

<!-- SGML -->
<para>This is an <emph>important</emph> paragraph.</para>
```

Note that the Chapter element can also directly contain the included elements, so revealing this technique to be a rather blunt instrument, often causing possibly unintended side effects.

It is also possible to specifically exclude an element from the content of all sub-elements, whether they are explicitly (but optionally) defined as part of the model group of some of these sub-elements, or are just included (using the mechanism just described) at a higher level in the document hierarchy. The approach is the same, except that a minus symbol, '-', is used in place of the plus symbol. For example, it may be considered unwise to allow an Indexterm element to contain another Indexterm element, and for an Emphasis element to contain another Emphasis element:

```
<!-- SGML -->
<!ELEMENT indexterm (#PCDATA) -(indexterm)>
<!ELEMENT emph      (#PCDATA) -(emph)>
```

Ignoring markup

When it is inconvenient for significant characters in a particular element to be interpreted as markup, the element content can be defined to consist of normal character data, 'CDATA', or normal character data that may also contain entity references, 'RCDATA' (*Replaceable Character Data*).

```
<!-- SGML -->
<!ELEMENT statement CDATA>
...
<statement>The characters '&<>' are used in
the Standard Generalized Markup Language</statement>

<!-- SGML -->
<!ELEMENT statement RCDATA>
...
<statement>The characters '&amp;<>' are used in
the &SGML;</statement>
```

When this requirement applies only to a range of text, instead of the whole content of an element, marked sections may be used to enclose and identify the text range. XML has adopted the CDATA marked section, but not the **RCDATA** variant:

```
<!-- SGML -->
<statement>The characters <![RCDATA[ '&amp;<>' ]]>
are used in the &SGML;</statement>
```

Similarly, the content of an entity (both internal and external) may be defined as CDATA or as **SDATA** (*System Data*). SDATA is the same thing as CDATA, except that it indicates system-dependent content, which would need to be edited if transmitted to another system.

Markup minimization techniques

Element minimization

The DTD may contain switches within element declarations that specify whether or not the start-tag or the end-tag may be omitted from the document (providing that their presence can be implied by context). When this feature is enabled (by the SGML declaration) two single character tokens appear immediately after the element name. Each token must be either '-' (required) or 'o' (omit), and the first applies to the start-tag, the second to the end-tag. In the following example, the Paragraph element end-tag may be omitted:

```
<!-- SGML -->
<!ELEMENT para - o (.....)>

<!-- SGML -->
<chapter>
<para>This is a paragraph.
<para>This is another paragraph.
</chapter>
```

Markup tags may be shortened or omitted without disrupting the document structure, but only where the context permits, where the DTD rules allow, and when some optional SGML features are enabled on the local system. This is termed **minimization**, and is intended to aid the process of manually keying tags (a process now rarely necessary).

Providing that the following techniques are applied legally, it is possible to convert the document into a non-minimized form at any time. This process is called **normalization** (and by this definition, XML is always normalized). The fragment shown below is a fully normalized structure identifying a company employee:

```
<!-- SGML -->
<employee>
    <name>J. Smith</name>
    <number>9876</number>
    <title>XML Developer</title>
</employee>
```

Though it may seem a confusing contradiction, an element that is officially required to be present may in fact be *omitted* from the document, simply because its presence can be implied. For the sake of following examples, it will be assumed that all the elements shown above are required by the DTD, in the strict order given.

In some cases, the start-tag may be omitted. This is an option where it is obvious by context that the element must have started. In this case, the Employee start-tag is enough to signify the start of its first required child element, Name, and the Name end-tag similarly signifies the start of its next sibling element, Number:

```
<!-- SGML -->
<employee>
    J. Smith</name>
    9876</number>
    XML Developer</title>
</employee>
```

In some cases, as shown below, the end-tag may be omitted. This is an option where it is obvious by context that the element has ended. In this case, the Number start-tag is enough to signify the end of the Name element, and the Employee end-tag similarly signifies the end of the embedded Title element:

```
<!-- SGML -->
<employee>
    <name>J. Smith
    <number>9876
    <title>XML Developer
</employee>
```

Alternatively, the end-tags may be present, but may omit the element names. These are known as **empty end-tag** elements:

```
<!-- SGML -->
<employee>
    <name>J. Smith</>
    <number>9876</>
    <title>XML Developer</>
</employee>
```

Another technique abbreviates both the start-tag and end-tag. The end-tag is a **null end-tag**, '/', and the start-tag is a **net-enabling start-tag** (net = null end-tag), which ends with the same character, '/':

```
<!-- SGML -->
<employee>
    <name/J. Smith/
    <number/9876/
    <title/XML Developer/
</employee>
```

This feature can be convenient when the element content is restricted to text and is likely to be brief:

```
Water is H<sub/2/O
```

Water is H_2O

The start-tag may be empty if it is the same as the previous start-tag. This is known as an **empty start-tag**:

```
<!-- SGML -->
<title>XML Developer</title><>Java Developer</title>
```

Here, the '<>' tag has an implied meaning of '<title>', as this was the previous element in the data stream.

Short references

Markup can be implied from the contextual use of normal text characters using **short reference** mappings. This can be considered the ultimate minimization technique, as it may involve the insertion of *no* extra characters. For example, the use of the quotation mark character to surround quoted text could be interpreted as markup, in which case the following fragments would be considered equivalent:

```
<!-- SGML -->
<p>Alice in Wonderland thought "What is the
use of a book without pictures or convers-
ations?".</p>

<!-- SGML -->
<p>Alice in Wonderland thought <quote>What
is the use of a book without pictures or
conversations?</quote>.</p>
```

The mapping of strings or individual characters to element tags can be made context-sensitive. Taking the example above, a quotation mark found within a Paragraph element is mapped to the start-tag '<quote>', whereas a quotation mark found within a (now opened) Quote element is mapped to the end-tag '</quote>'.

This technique is especially suitable for tabular material, where the line-ending codes are mapped to Row elements and tab or comma characters are mapped to Entry elements:

```
<!-- SGML -->
Red [TAB] 1 [TAB] Danger [CR][LF]
Yellow [TAB] 2 [TAB] Alert [CR][LF]
Green [TAB] 3 [TAB] Normal [CR][LF]
```

Attribute minimization

When an attribute value is restricted to a single word or number the quotes are not necessary. This is because the next space or chevron unambiguously ends the value (though this feature may be disabled in some systems):

```
<!-- SGML -->
<list offset=yes indent=15>
```

An attribute value may be further restricted to one word from a group of words, termed a **name group** (as in XML). In the following example, the Offset attribute value is restricted to a value of either 'yes' or 'no'. Any other value would be illegal (though this is not obvious from the example – the limitation is defined in and controlled by the DTD). In this situation, the attribute name and the **value indicator** ('=') may also be absent:

```
<!-- SGML -->
<list yes>
```

An attribute value may be inherited from the value of the previous occurrence of that attribute. This is a useful technique when its value is likely to switch occasionally. The declaration includes the **#CURRENT** keyword to indicate this behaviour. In the following example, the second and third paragraphs are 'English', whereas the fifth is 'French':

```
<!-- SGML -->
<!-- English paragraphs -->
<para lang="English">...</para>
<para>...</para>
<para>...</para>
<!-- French paragraphs -->
<para lang="French">...</para>
<para>...</para>
```

Converting to XML

The wide range of software supporting XML will prompt some to consider converting SGML documents to XML format. Unfortunately, this is not as simple a task as converting the other way. This is due to the fact that SGML has a far wider range of capabilities.

The SGML Declaration

XML uses the same characters for markup delimiters as specified by the default SGML declarations. For example, the characters '</' indicate the start of an end-tag in XML, just as they do in the SGML reference concrete syntax. If the SGML declaration in use redefines any delimiter, both the SGML declaration must be changed to the default case, and all affected DTDs and document instances must be processed accordingly.

```
<!-- SGML -->
GENERAL
        SGMLREF
        STAGO "**"              (start-tag open)
        ETAGO "@@"              (end-tag open)
        TAGC  "!!"              (tag close)
```

**p!!This is a simple paragraph@@p!!

The example declaration and document shown above must be changed as follows:

```
<!-- SGML -->
GENERAL
        SGMLREF
        STAGO "<"               (start-tag open)
        ETAGO "</"              (end-tag open)
        TAGC  ">"               (tag close)

<!-- SGML -->
<p>This is a simple paragraph</p>
```

In fact, the instructions can be removed entirely when their value is the same as the reference concrete syntax. There are a number of SGML books on the market which provide a full list of the keywords used to modify capacity limits and markup delimiters, along with their default, reference concrete syntax values.

Converting the DTD

Element and attribute names, as well as attribute values, are not usually case-sensitive in SGML. It is possible for the DTD to contain a definition of an element using lower-case letters, yet for a conforming document instance to contain upper-case letters. Care must be taken to ensure that all names defined in the DTD are consistent with each other, and with element names in the document, unlike the following example:

```
<!-- SGML -->
<!ELEMENT Chapter .....>
<!ELEMENT para .....>

<chapter>
<PARA>This is a paragraph</PARA>
...
</CHAPTER>
```

As element minimization techniques are not part of the XML format, the minimization tokens must, if present, be removed from SGML element declarations. Alternatively, they can be replaced by a parameter entity reference. This will be accepted by an XML processor, though the entities concerned must contain no text when processed as XML, and is useful if the DTD is still to be applied to SGML documents as well as XML documents:

```
<!-- XML -->
<!ENTITY % YesYes ''>   <!-- for SGML make 'o o' -->
<!ENTITY % NoNo   ''>   <!-- for SGML make '- -' -->
<!ENTITY % NoYes  ''>   <!-- for SGML make '- o' -->
<!ENTITY % YesNo  ''>   <!-- for SGML make 'o -' -->

<!ELEMENT para %NoYes (#PCDATA)>
```

SGML allows comments to be embedded in declarations of various types, including element declarations. An embedded comment must be moved out of the declaration, and, if it is still required, must be placed within dedicated comment declarations.

```
<!-- SGML -->
<!ELEMENT IMG EMPTY -- Image Reference -->

<!-- XML -->
<!-- Image Reference -->
<!ELEMENT IMG EMPTY>
```

SGML allows PCDATA to be mixed with elements (in a mixed content model), with the tokens appearing in any order. XML insists on the PCDATA token appearing first:

```
<!-- XML -->
<!ELEMENT para %NoYes (#PCDATA | sub | super)*>
```

Although strongly discouraged, connectors other than the choice connector may be used in a mixed content model, and the content may not have to be repeatable. But XML insists on the choice connector, and repeatability in mixed content models, so as to avoid ambiguities.

```
<!-- SGML -->
<!ELEMENT title - - (prefix, #PCDATA)>

<!-- XML -->
<!ELEMENT title %NoNo (#PCDATA | prefix)*>
```

When several elements share the same content model, a single element declaration may be used to define them all. The element names are grouped. It is necessary to create individual element declarations for the XML DTD.

```
<!-- SGML -->
<!ELEMENT (para|note|item) - - (#PCDATA|emph)*>

<!-- XML -->
<!ELEMENT para     %NoNo   (#PCDATA|emph)*>
<!ELEMENT note     %NoNo   (#PCDATA|emph)*>
<!ELEMENT item     %NoNo   (#PCDATA|emph)*>
```

SGML allows a content model to include tokens that represent elements which must appear, but in any order, using the 'and' connector, '&'. This connector type may *not* be used in XML. In practice, it is rarely used in SGML too, but where it *is* used it can often be changed to a sequence connector without many complaints from document authors. However, doing this may invalidate old documents which include these elements in a different order to that chosen in the new DTD. Alternative approaches to this problem include resequencing invalid combinations (see *Converting the Document instance* below) or explicitly allowing all combinations. The latter approach involves less work, but can result in complex chains of rules, particularly because it is necessary to avoid ambiguity in DTD models.

```
<!-- SGML -->
<!ELEMENT entry - - (desc & pr & cd)>

<!-- XML -->
<!ELEMENT entry   ( (desc, pr, cd) | (desc, cd, pr) |
                    (pr, desc, cd) | (pr, cd, desc) |
                    (cd, desc, pr) | (cd, pr, desc) )>
```

The XML equivalent shown above is actually illegal, because it is ambiguous. On encountering the element Desc, for example, the parser would not know which of the first two model groups apply. The solution is to modify the example as follows:

```
<!-- XML -->
<!ELEMENT entry   (
                  (desc, ((pr, cd) | (cd, pr)) ) |
                  (pr, ((desc, cd) | (pr, (cd, desc)) ) |
                  (cd, (desc, pr)) | (cd, (pr, desc)) )
                  )>
```

A number of SGML attribute types are not available in XML. The table below shows all SGML attribute types, and gives recommended substitutions for those types not supported by XML:

SGML	XML
CDATA	CDATA
ENTITY	ENTITY
ENTITIES	ENTITIES
ID	ID
IDREF	IDREF
IDREFS	IDREFS
NAME	**NMTOKEN**
NAMES	**NMTOKENS**
NMTOKEN	NMTOKEN
NMTOKENS	NMTOKENS
NUMBER	**NMTOKEN**
NUMBERS	**NMTOKENS**
NUTOKEN	**NMTOKEN**
NUTOKENS	**NMTOKENS**
NOTATION	NOTATION

In all cases, the more specific token types are simply reassigned to name tokens, which in their XML incarnation are less rigidly defined (for example, they may start with a digit).

In SGML, marked section keywords may be surrounded by spaces, and the TEMP keyword is available. In XML, marked section keywords must not have spaces around them, and 'TEMP' is not allowed, so 'TEMP' should be converted to 'INCLUDE' (or 'IGNORE' if not currently wanted) (the same is true for keywords specified via an entity reference).

Inclusions and exclusions

Where an inclusion has been used purely as a convenience, to avoid specifying the element in many content models, conversion is a simple matter of entering the element name in these content models. For example, a DTD that includes an Indexterm element at the root element must be modified to specify the Indexterm element explicitly in each element where it may be used. The DTD becomes more verbose, but this is unavoidable. There is, in fact, one virtue to doing this, as more control is provided over the placement of the included element. For example, an Indexterm element could contain a Chapter element (assuming it has a content of ANY):

```
<!-- SGML -->
<!ELEMENT book    - - (chapter)* +(indexterm)>
<!ELEMENT title   - - (#PCDATA)*>
<!ELEMENT para    - - (#PCDATA|emph)*>

<!-- XML -->
<!ELEMENT book    (chapter)*>
<!ELEMENT title   (#PCDATA|indexterm)*>
<!ELEMENT para    (#PCDATA|emph|indexterm)*>
```

Where an inclusion is used to enable certain structures within parts of a document, it is necessary to invent new elements. For example, where an Indexterm may be used in paragraphs contained in chapters, but not paragraphs contained within preliminary matter, the solution is to replace the single Paragraph element with two elements, one containing the Indexterm element:

```
<!-- SGML -->
<!ELEMENT book     - - (para*, chapter+)>
<!ELEMENT chapter  - - (para|list|note)* +(indexterm|emph)>
<!ELEMENT para     - - (#PCDATA)>

<!-- XML -->
<!ELEMENT book     (intro_para*, chapter+)>
<!ELEMENT chapter  (para|list|note)* >
<!ELEMENT intro-para (#PCDATA)*>
<!ELEMENT para     (#PCDATA|indexterm)>
```

Where an exclusion has been used for the same purpose, an identical approach should be used, but where an exclusion has been used to avoid recursion, either the rule must be removed (and replaced with written instructions), or more drastic remodelling introduced. For example, a Table element may include an exclusion on embedded tables, because each cell of the table may contain any block-level element, including the Table element, yet some software applications may not be able to handle embedded tables:

```
<!-- SGML -->
<!ENTITY % block "para|list|table">
...
<!ELEMENT table - - (row)* -(table)>
<!ELEMENT row  - - (cell)*>
<!ELEMENT cell - - (%block)*>
<!-- XML -->
<!ENTITY % block "para|list|table">
...
<!ELEMENT table  (row)*>
<!ELEMENT row    (cell)*>
<!ELEMENT cell   (para|list)*>
```

Converting the document instance

The default SGML Declaration states that element and attribute names are not case-sensitive. Although it can be changed, most SGML documents conform to this setting. When the DTD and document authors work with case-insensitive material it is typically the case that inconsistent use will be made of upper- and lower-case letters in names. These inconsistencies must be removed during the conversion to XML. Entities are usually case-sensitive in SGML, so no further thought needs to be given to these.

SGML documents containing minimized and/or omitted tags must be **normalized**. All start-tags and all end-tags must be present and complete to be valid XML element tags. Thankfully, most modern SGML-aware applications produce fully normalized data. In other cases, there are a number of SGML tools that can perform the normalization process quickly and efficiently.

SGML allows external entities to be identified by only a public identifier. Resolution to an actual file name is assumed to be the task of an entity manager:

```
<!-- SGML -->
<!DOCTYPE mybook PUBLIC "-//MyCorp//DTD My Book//EN">
```

XML does not allow for public identifiers without accompanying system identifiers. A public identifier in a document type declaration must be converted to a system identifier, which unambiguously locates a named file on the system:

```
<!-- SGML or XML -->
<!DOCTYPE mybook SYSTEM "/DTDS/MYBOOK.DTD">
```

Primarily, conversion of the document instance requires the reformatting of empty elements:

```
<!-- SGML -->
This is an <empty> element.
```

```
<!-- XML -->
This is an <empty/> element.
```

All processing instructions must start with a keyword, and end in '?>', but it is unlikely that existing processing instructions will be relevant in a new XML-based environment. It is more likely that old processing instructions would simply be removed by eliminating all text beginning '<?' and ending '>'.

Marked section content defined as RCDATA must be converted to CDATA, and any embedded entities must be replaced by their content:

```
<!-- SGML -->
<statement>The characters <![RCDATA[ '&amp;<>' ]]>
are used in the &SGML;</statement>

<!-- XML -->
<statement>The characters <![CDATA[ '&<>' ]]>
are used in the &SGML;</statement>
```

In addition, markup characters in elements defined to be of type CDATA or RCDATA must be replaced by entity references (as well as changing the DTD to #PCDATA).

```
<!-- SGML -->
<!ELEMENT statement CDATA>
...
<statement>The characters '&<>' are used in
the Standard Generalized Markup Language</statement>

<!-- XML -->
<!ELEMENT statement (#PCDATA)>
...
<statement>The characters '&amp;&lt;&gt;' are used in
the Standard Generalized Markup Language</statement>
```

20. Charts and tables

The charts and tables included in this chapter are:

Acronyms list

ASCII	American Standard Code for Information Interchange
CSS	Cascading Style Sheets
DIS	Draft International Standard
DOM	Document Object Model
DSSSL	Document Style Semantics and Specification Language
DTD	Document Type Definition
EBCDIC	Extended Binary Coded Decimal Interchange Code
EDI	Electronic Data Interchange
IEC	International Electrotechnical Commission
IP	Internet Protocol
IS	International Standard
ISO	International Organization for Standardization
HTML	HyperText Markup Language
HTTP	HyperText Transport Protocol
MIME	Multi-purpose Independent Mail Extensions
RFC	Request For Comments
SAX	Simple API (Application Programmers Interface) for XML
SGML	Standard Generalized Markup Language
TCP	Transmission Control Protocol
UCS	Universal Multi-Byte Octet Character Set (ISO10646)
URI	Uniform Resource Identifier
URL	Uniform Resource Locator
UTF	**UCS** Transform Format
W³C	World Wide Web Consortium
WWW	World Wide Web
XLL	XML Linking Language (now **XLink** and **XPointer**)
XLink	XML Linking Language (not including **XPointer**)
XML	eXtensible Markup Language
XPointer	XML Pointer linking (not including **XLink**)
XSL	XML Stylesheet Language (now excludes **XSLT**)
XSLT	XML Stylesheet Language – Transformation

Useful Web pages

Useful resources	
`http://www.w3.org/pub/WWW/xml/`	Main XML site
`http://www.lists.ic.ac.uk/` `hypermail/xml-dev/`	Archive of newsgroup discussions on the specification and usage of XML
`http://www.ucc.ie/xml/`	XML frequently asked questions (FAQ)
`http://www.ietf.cnri.` `reston.va.us/lid-abstracts`	Current Internet-Drafts
XML standards	
`http://www.w3.org/pub/WWW/TR/WD-` `xml-lang`	The XML standard
`http://www.textuality.com/` `sgml-erb/WD-xml-link`	XML linking standard (XLL)
`http://www.w3.org/TR/NOTE-XSL`	XML style sheet proposal (XSL)
`http://www.w3.org/TR/1998/` `NOTE-xml-names`	Namespaces proposal
XML influences	*(standards that influenced the XML design and standards that XML relies upon)*
`http://www.w3.org/Addressing/` `Addressing#term`	Web Naming and Addressing Overview (URIs, URLs, ...)
`http://www.unicode.org/unicode/` `standard/wg2n1036.html`	UCS Transformation Format 8 (UTF-8)
`http://www.unicode.org/unicode/` `standard/utf16.html`	UCS-2 Encoding Format (UTF-16)
`ftp://info.cern.ch/pub/www/doc/` `http-spec.txt.Z`	HTTP standard
`http://http://www.w3.org/pub/` `WWW/TR/REC-HTML32.dtd`	HTML 3.2
`http://http://www.w3.org/TR/` `REC-html40`	HTML 4.0
`http://www.sgmlopen.org/`	SGML (SGML Open)
`http://www.w3.org/markup/dom/` `drafts/requirements.html`	The Document Object Model (DOM)

`http://sunsite.unc.edu/pub/`
`sun-info/standards/dsssl/`
`dssslo.htm`
	The DSSSL-O specification

XML-based standards	*(standards and proposed standards that rely upon XML as a base syntax)*
`http://www.w3.org/TR/Math/`	Mathematics specification
`http://www.w3.org/TR/` `NOTE-rdfarch`	RDF specification
`http://www.venus.co.uk/omf/cml/` `doc/index.html`	Chemical markup language (CML)
`http://207.201.154.232/murray/` `specs/xml-sd.html`	Structuring XML data
`http://www.otp.org`	XML for OTP (Open Trade Protocol)

http://www.geocities.com/ WallStreet/Floor/5815/	XML for EDI home page
http://www.otp.org	Open Trading Protocol
Other useful resources	
http://www.cis.ohio-state.edu/ text/faq/usenet/graphics/ fileformats-faq/part3/faq.html	Graphics File Formats FAQ (Part 3 of 4): Where to Get File Format Specifications

XML design goals

At the start of the process that led to the development of XML, the W³C group responsible decided to define some guiding principles, or goals, which would be used to ensure that the final specification addressed the concerns that first prompted the drive for a new language. The ten goals they defined are listed below, together with some personal and rather subjective assessments of their realization or otherwise in the final specification.

Goal 1. *XML shall be straightforwardly usable over the Internet*. XML has purposely adopted HTML conventions to make the progression to XML as simple as possible.

Goal 2. *XML shall support a wide variety of applications*. XML provides a convenient mechanism for describing a very wide variety of information, from highly structured database fields to semi-structured publishing material, from push technology and client-sided processing, to document management and multiple media publishing.

Goal 3. *XML shall be compatible with SGML*. XML is defined as a subset of SGML, so can be processed using SGML tools, occasionally at the expense of clarity in the XML specification. (Whenever it is perceived that some detail of the XML language is superfluous, redundant or irrelevant, it is almost invariably there to provide backward compatibility with the more complex SGML format.)

Goal 4. *It shall be easy to write programs which process XML documents*. The major differences between XML and SGML are the removal of minimization and other options and the stricter rules on the format of remaining markup. For example, in XML the literal string '`<![CDATA[`' is significant, whereas in SGML the same instruction may be formatted in various ways, such as '`<![   CDATA   [`' or '`${CharData{`'. An XML processor is therefore much easier to develop than a similar SGML tool, because there are fewer options and variants to consider in the data syntax.

Goal 5. *The number of optional features in XML is to be kept to the absolute minimum, ideally zero*. In one sense, almost all the features of XML are optional, so it is difficult to assess the success of this goal. However, in the sense that there are rarely two or more ways to achieve one effect, XML has met this aim. This goal is really just part of Goal 4.

Goal 6. *XML documents should be human legible and reasonably clear*. As XML is based on SGML, a human-readable markup language resting on the ASCII text format, and also has no minimization features (see Goal 10), it is a given that XML is legible and clear (but see Goal 3 for exceptions).

Goal 7. *The XML design should be prepared quickly.* This goal is difficult to assess. Development began in the summer of 1996 and the final specification was released in February 1998. It is left to the reader to decide whether this goal was met.

Goal 8. *The design of XML shall be formal and concise.* XML is specified by a set of rules that conform to a formal grammar. See Chapter 21, which illustrates the design of XML in chart form.

Goal 9. *XML documents shall be easy to create.* Software can create an XML document using simple text line output commands, and humans can create XML documents using any tool that can export ASCII text.

Goal 10. *Terseness in XML markup is of minimum importance.* The SGML language includes many optional features that allow a document author to omit keying tags or parts of tags, when context alone allows software to infer the presence of this markup. Even in HTML, it is possible to omit end-tags, such as the '`</p>`' tag, without introducing ambiguity. XML has no such minimization features. All tags must be present, and complete, which helps with Goal 4, and reflects the fact that modern XML-aware word processors make issues of keying individual markup characters irrelevant.

XML fragments

Each major feature of XML is labelled in the diagram below to facilitate quick look-up of any unknown concepts:

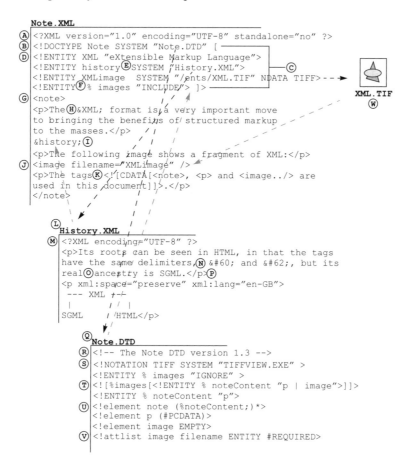

```
Note.XML
Ⓐ <?XML version="1.0" encoding="UTF-8" standalone="no" ?>
Ⓑ <!DOCTYPE Note SYSTEM "Note.DTD" [ ──────────────
Ⓓ <!ENTITY XML "eXtensible Markup Language">
   <!ENTITY history Ⓔ SYSTEM "History.XML">──── Ⓒ
   <!ENTITY XMLimage  SYSTEM "/ents/XML.TIF" NDATA TIFF>───►
   <!ENTITY Ⓕ% images "INCLUDE"> ]> ─────────────
Ⓖ <note>
   <p>The Ⓗ &XML; format is a very important move
   to bringing the benefits of structured markup
   to the masses.</p>
   &history; Ⓘ
   <p>The following image shows a fragment of XML:</p>
Ⓙ <image filename="XMLimage" />
   <p>The tags Ⓚ <![CDATA[<note>, <p> and <image../> are
   used in this document]]>.</p>
   </note>

                                          XML.TIF
                                            Ⓦ

Ⓛ History.XML
Ⓜ <?XML encoding="UTF-8" ?>
   <p>Its roots can be seen in HTML, in that the tags
   have the same delimiters, Ⓝ &#60; and &#62;, but its
   real Ⓞ ancestry is SGML.</p> Ⓟ
   <p xml:space="preserve" xml:lang="en-GB">
   --- XML
   |
   SGML    /  /HTML</p>

Ⓠ Note.DTD
Ⓡ <!-- The Note DTD version 1.3 -->
Ⓢ <!NOTATION TIFF SYSTEM "TIFFVIEW.EXE" >
   <!ENTITY % images "IGNORE" >
Ⓣ <![%images[<!ENTITY % noteContent "p | image">]]>
   <!ENTITY % noteContent "p">
Ⓤ <!element note (%noteContent;)*>
   <!element p (#PCDATA)>
   <!element image EMPTY>
Ⓥ <!attlist image filename ENTITY #REQUIRED>
```

Key:

- (A) the XML Declaration – Chapter 3, *Declarations* (29)
- (B) the document type declaration – Chapter 5, *DTD structure* (51)
- (C) the internal subset – Chapter 5, *DTD structure* (51) and *DTD processing issues* (67)
- (D) an entity declaration – Chapter 4, *Defining an entity* (39)
- (E) an external entity declaration – Chapter 4, *Defining an entity* (39)
- (F) a parameter entity declaration – Chapter 4, *Defining an entity* (39)
- (G) the document element – Chapter 3, *Elements* (23)

- (H) an entity reference to an internal text entity – Chapter 4, *Defining an entity* (39)
- (I) an entity reference to an external text entity – Chapter 4, *Concepts* (35)
- (J) an empty element – Chapter 3, *Elements* (23)
- (K) a character data section – Chapter 3, *Declarations* (29)
- (L) an external XML entity file – Chapter 4, *Concepts* (35) and Chapter 11, *Locating Documents (URLs)* (139)
- (M) an encoding declaration – Chapter 13, *Character set declarations* (295)
- (N) a character reference – Chapter 4, *Defining an entity* (39)
- (O) preserved space – Chapter 3, *Reserved attributes* (27) and Chapter 8, *Preserved space* (100)
- (P) text language – Chapter 3, *Reserved attributes* (27) and this chapter, *ISO 639 language codes* (438)
- (Q) the external subset file (the DTD) – Chapter 5, *DTD structure* (51)
- (R) a comment – Chapter 3, *Declarations* (29)
- (S) a notation declaration – Chapter 5, *Notation declarations* (65)
- (T) an ignored or included section declaration – Chapter 5, *Conditional sections* (64)
- (U) an element declaration – Chapter 5, *Element declarations* (52)
- (V) an attribute list declaration – Chapter 5, *Attribute declarations* (58)
- (W) a binary entity file – Chapter 4, *Defining an entity* (39)

SAX methods

The following table shows all the methods in the SAX API, in alphabetic order, the interfaces they are defined in, the parameters they take and their return values:

Method	Interfaces	Parameters	Returns
characters	DocumentHandler	char ch[], int start, int length	void
endDocument	DocumentHandler		void
endElement	DocumentHandler		void
error	ErrorHandler	SAXParseException err	void
fatalError	ErrorHandler	SAXParseException err	void
getByteStream	InputSource	InputStream byteStream	InputStream
getCharacterStream	InputSource	Reader charStream	Reader
getColumnNumber	Locator		int
getEncoding	InputSource		String
getLength	AttributeList		int
getLineNumber	Locator		int
getName	AttributeList	int i	String
getPublicId	Locator, InputSource		String
getSystemId	Locator, InputSource		String
getType	AttributeList	int i *or* String name	String
getValue	AttributeList	int i *or* String name	String
ignorableWhitespace	DocumentHandler	char ch[], int start, int length	void
InputSource	InputSource	*NONE or* String SysId *or* InputStream byteStream *or* Reader charStream	
notationDecl	DTDHandler	String name, String pubId, String sysId	void
parse	Parser	InputSource src, *or* String url	void
processingInstruction	DocumentHandler	String target, String data	void
resolveEntity	Entityresolver	String pubId, String sysId	InputSource

getByteStream	InputSource	InputStream byteStream	InputStream
setByteStream	InputSource	InputStream byteStream	void
setCharacterStream	InputSource	Reader charStream	void
setDocumentHandler	Parser	DocumentHandler dh	void
setDocumentLocator	DocumentHandler	Locator myLoc	void
setDTDHandler	Parser	DTDHandler dtdh	void
setEncoding	InputSource	String encoding	void
setEntityResolver	Parser	EntityResolver er	void
setErrorHandler	Parser	ErrorHandler eh	void
setLocale	Parser	Locale loc	void
setPublicId	InputSource	String pubId	void
setSystemId	InputSource	String sysId	void
startDocument	DocumentHandler		void
startElement	DocumentHandler		void
unparsedEntityDecl	DTDHandler	String name, String pubId, String sysId, String notaName	void
warning	ErrorHandler	SAXParseException err	void

DOM methods

The following table shows all the methods in the DOM API in alphabetic order, the interfaces they are defined in, the parameters they take and their return values:

Method	Interfaces	Parameters	Returns
appendChild	Node	Node newChild	Node
appendData	CharacterData	String arg	void
cloneNode	Node	boolean deep	Node
createAttribute	Document	String name	Attr
createCDATASection	Document	String data	CDATASection
createComment	Document	String text	Comment
createDocumentFragment	Document		DocumentFragment
createElement	Document	String tagname	Element
createEntityReference	Document	String name	EntityReference
createProcessingInstruction	Document	String target, String data	ProcessingInstruction
createTextNode	Document		Text
deleteData	CharacterData	int offset, int count	void
getAttribute	Element	String name	String
getAttributeNode	Element	String name	Attr
getAttributes	Node		NamedNodeMap
getChildNodes	Node		NodeList
getData	CharacterData		String
getDoctype	Document		DocumentType
getDocumentElement	Document		Element
getElementsByTagName	Document, Element		NodeList
getEntities	DocumentType		NamedNodeMap
getFirstChild	Node		Node
getImplementation	Document		DOMImplementation
getLastChild	Node		Node

getLength	CharacterData, NodeList, Named NodeMap		int
getName	DocumentType, Attr		String
getNamedItem	NamedNodeMap	String nodeName	Node
getNextSibling	Node		Node
getNodeName	Node		String
getNodeType	Node		short
getNodeValue	Node		String
getNotationName	Entity		String
getNotations	DocumentType		NamedNodeMap
getOwnerDocument	Node		Document
getParentNode	Node		Node
getPreviousSibling	Node		Node
getPublicId	Entity, Notation		String
getSpecified	Attr		boolean
getSystemId	Entity, Notation		String
getTagName	Element		String
getValue	Attr		String
hasChildNodes	Node	String value	boolean
insertBefore	Node	Node newChild, Node oldChild	Node
insertData	CharacterData	int offset, String arg	void
item	NodeList, Named NodeMap	int index	Node
normalize	Element		void
removeAttribute	Element	String name	void
removeAttributeNode	Element	Attr oldAttr	void
removeChild	Node	Node oldChild	Node
removeNamedItem	NamedNodeMap	String nodeName	Node
replaceChild	Node	Node newChild, Node oldChild	Node
replaceData	CharacterData	int offset, int count, String arg	void

setAttribute	Element	String name, String value	void
setAttributeNode	Element	Attr newAttr	void
setData	CharacterData	String data	void
setNamedItem	NamedNodeMap	Node theNode	Node
setNodeValue	Node	String value	void
setValue	Attr	String value	void
splitText	Text	int offset	Text
substringData	CharacterData	int offset, int count	String

XSL formatting objects and properties

Formatting objects

The following table lists all the XSL formatting objects and the properties they can take (the values these properties can take are shown in the next table).

Some groups of properties are repeated in a number of objects, so are defined first for convenience:

AbsolutePositions – bottom, left, position, right, top.

Aurals – azimuth, cue, cue-before, cue-after, cursor, elevation, pause, pause-after, pause-before, pitch, pitch-range, play-during, richness, speak, speak-header, speak-numeral, speak-punctuation, speech-rate, stress, voice-family, volume (*see CSS properties*).

Fonts – font, font-family, font-size, font-size-adjust, font-stretch, font-style, font-variant, font-weight (*see CSS properties*).

Hyphenations – country, hyphenate, hyphenation-char, hyphenation-push-char-count, hypenation-remain-char-count, language, script.

Margins – margin-top, margin-bottom, margin-left, margin-right, margin, end-indent, space-after, space-before, space-end, space-start.

Borders+Paddings+Backgrounds – background, background-attachment, background-color, background-image, background-position, background-repeat, border, border-after-color, border-after-style, border-after-width, border-before-color, border-before-style, border-before-width, border-bottom, border-bottom-color, border-bottom-style, border-bottom-width, border-color, border-end-color, border-end-style, border-end-width, border-left, border-left-color, border-left-style, border-left-width, border-right, border-right-color, border-right-style, border-right-width, border-start-color, border-start-style, border-start-width, border-style, border-top, border-top-color, border-top-style, border-top-width, padding, padding-after, padding-before, padding-bottom, padding-end, padding-left, padding-right, padding-start, padding-top.

Formatting object	Properties
Pagination and layout	
root	id
page-sequence	format, letter-value, digit-group-sep, n-digits-per-group, sequence-src, id, initial-page-number
sequence-specification	id
sequence-specifier-single	id, page-master-name

sequence-specifier-alternating	id, page-master-first, page-master-even, page-master-odd, page-master-blank-even, page-master-last-even, page-master-last-odd
sequence-specified-repeating	id, page-master-first, page-master-repeating
layout-master-set	id
simple-page-master	id, page-master-name, page-height, page-width, reference-orientation, size, writing-mode, *Margins*
region-body	clip, column-count, column-gap, id, overflow, vertical-align, reference-orientation, writing-mode, *Margins, Borders+Paddings+Backgrounds*
region-before	clip, extent, id, overflow, precedence, vertical-align, reference-orientation, writing-mode, *Borders+Paddings+Backgrounds*
region-start	clip, extent, id, overflow, precedence, vertical-align, reference-orientation, writing-mode, *Borders+Paddings+Backgrounds*
region-end	clip, extent, id, overflow, precedence, vertical-align, reference-orientation, writing-mode, *Borders+Paddings+Backgrounds*
flow	flow-name, id
static-content	flow-name, id
Blocks	
block	color, hyphenation-keep, hyphenation-ladder-count, last-line-end-indent, line-height, line-height-shift-adjustment, line-stacking-strategy, orphans, page-break-inside, span, text-align, text-align-last, text-indent, visibility, white-space-treatment, widows, wrap-option, writing-mode, z-index, *AbsolutePositions, Aurals, Borders+Paddings+ Backgrounds, Fonts, Hyphenations, Margins*
display-graphic	height, href, id, max-height, max-width, min-height, min-width, scale, span, width, *AbsolutePositions, Aurals, Borders+Paddings+Backgrounds, Keeps+Breaks, Margins*
display-included-container	clip, height, id, overflow, reference-orientation, span, width, writing-mode, *AbsolutePositions, Borders+Paddings+Backgrounds, Keeps+Breaks, Margins*
display-rule	color, id, length, rule-orientation, rule-style, rule-thickness, span, text-align, *AbsolutePositions, Aurals, Borders+Paddings+Backgrounds, Keeps+Breaks, Margins*
display-sequence	id
Inline	
bidi-override	color, direction, id, letter-spacing, line-height, line-height-shift-adjustment, score-spaces, text-decoration, text-shadow, text-transform, word-spacing, *AbsolutePositions, Aurals, Borders+Paddings+Backgrounds, Fonts*

character	character, color, font-height-override-after, font-height-override-before, id, inhibit-line-breaks, letter-spacing, line-height, line-height-shift-adjustment, score-spaces, text-decoration, text-shadow, text-transform, vertical-align, word-spacing, *AbsolutePositions, Aurals, Borders+Paddings+ Backgrounds, Fonts, Margins*
first-line-marker	id, letter-spacing, line-height, line-height-shift-adjustment, score-spaces, text-decoration, text-shadow, text-transform, word-spacing, *Aurals, Borders+Paddings+ Backgrounds, Fonts*
inline-graphic	height, href, id, inhibit-line-breaks, line-height, line-height-shift-adjustment, max-height, max-width, min-width, max-width, scale, vertical-align, width, *AbsolutePositions, Aurals, Borders+Paddings+ Backgrounds, Margins*
inline-included-container	clip, id, inhibit-line-breaks, line-height, line-height-shift-adjustment, overflow, reference-orientation, vertical-align, width, writing-mode, *AbsolutePositions, Borders+Paddings+Backgrounds, Margins*
inline-rule	color, id, inhibit-line-breaks, length, line-height, line-height-shift-adjustment, rule-orientation, rule-style, rule-thickness, vertical-align, *AbsolutePositions, Borders+Paddings+Backgrounds, Margins*
inline-sequence	id. (all inheritable properties apply to embedded objects, including characters)
page-number	id, inhibit-line-breaks, letter-spacing, line-height, line-height-shift-adjustment, score-spaces, text-decoration, text-shadow, text-transform, word-spacing, vertical-align, *AbsolutePositions, Aurals, Borders+Paddings+Backgrounds, Fonts, Margins*
page-number-citation	id, inhibit-line-breaks, letter-spacing, line-height, line-height-shift-adjustment, ref-id, score-spaces, text-decoration, text-shadow, text-transform, word-spacing, vertical-align, *AbsolutePositions, Aurals, Borders+Paddings+Backgrounds, Fonts, Margins*
Tables (and captions)	
table-and-caption	caption-side, id, *AbsolutePositions, Aurals, Borders+Paddings+Backgrounds, Margins*
table	border-collapse, border-spacing, id, table-height, table-layout, table-omit-middle-footer, table-omit-middle-header, table-width, *AbsolutePositions, Aurals, Borders+Paddings+ Backgrounds, Keeps+Breaks, Margins*
table-column	column-number, column-width, id, n-columns-repeated, n-columns-spanned, visibility, *Borders+Paddings+Backgrounds*
table-caption	caption-width, id, *AbsolutePositions, Aurals, Borders+Paddings+Backgrounds*
table-header	id, *AbsolutePositions, Aurals, Borders+Paddings+Backgrounds*

table-footer	id, *AbsolutePositions, Aurals, Borders+Paddings+Backgrounds*
table-body	id, *AbsolutePositions, Aurals, Borders+Paddings+Backgrounds*
table-row	id, may-break-after-row, may-break-before-row, row-height, *AbsolutePositions, Aurals, Borders+Paddings+Backgrounds*
table-cell	cell-height, column-number, empty-cells, ends-row, id, n-columns-spanned, n-rows-spanned, starts-row, *AbsolutePositions, Aurals, Borders+Paddings+ Backgrounds*
Lists	
list-block	id, provisional-distance-between-parts, provisional-label-separation, space-between-list-rows, *AbsolutePositions, Aurals, Borders+Paddings+ Backgrounds, Keeps+Breaks, Margins*
list-item	id, *AbsolutePositions, Aurals Borders+Paddings+Backgrounds,Keeps+Breaks, Margins*
list-item-body	id
list-item-label	id
Links	
simple-link	id, indicate-destination, inhibit-line-breaks, internal-destination, line-height, line-height-shift-adjustment, show-destination, space-above-destination-start, space-above-destination-block, vertical-align, *AbsolutePositions, Aurals, Borders+Paddings+Backgrounds, Margins*
multi-switch	auto-restore, id
multi-case	id, initial, name, title
multi-toggle	id, switch-to
multi-properties	id
multi-property-set	id, state
Out-of-line Formatting	
float	id, clip, overflow, max-height, span, visibility, z-index, *Borders+Paddings+Backgrounds, Margins*
footnote	id, clip, overflow, max-height, overflow, span, visibility, z-index, *Borders+Paddings+Backgrounds, Margins*
footnote-citation	id, inhibit-line-breaks, letter-spacing, line-height, line-height-shift-adjustment, score-spaces, text-decoration, text-shadow, text-transform, word-spacing, vertical-align, *AbsolutePositions, Aurals Borders+ Paddings+Backgrounds, Fonts, Margins*

Properties

The following table lists all the values each property described above can take. They are sorted into alphabetic order for ease of look-up from entries in the table above.

Entries marked with a '*' have the same name and purpose as a property in CSS, and where the text '*same as CSS*' appears, the values it can take are also exactly the same (as described in the next section). Note that all aural styles, font and character style details, most basic table building constructs, and many border, padding and margin settings are copied directly from CSS.

Length values with no suffix are deemed to be calculated in metres, so would normally be very small, such as '0.002', but other measures are allowed, including 'cm' (0.01 of a metre), 'mm' (0.001), 'in' (inch) (0.0254), 'pt' (point) (0.000352) and 'pica' (0.004233).

Color – '#rrggbb' for RGB values in hexadecimal.

Boolean – 'true' or 'false'.

ID – a string of characters, conforming to NMTOKEN, and unique.

IDREF – a string of characters, conforming to NMTOKEN, and referring to a unique *ID*.

Char – a Unicode character.

String – a sequence of characters, such as 'abcdefgh'.

Name – a string of characters, conforming to NMTOKEN.

Percent – a percentage as a signed real value, such that '33.9' is 339/1000.

SL (Signed Length) – a real number plus a unit qualifier, such as '-1.3pt'.

UL (Unsigned Length) – a real number plus a unit qualifier, such as '1.3pt' or '0pt'.

PL (Positive Length) – a real number, greater than zero, plus a unit qualifier, such as '1.3pt'.

SI (Signed Integer) – an integer with '+' or '-' prefix, such as '+33' or '-2'.

UI (Unsigned Integer) – an integer, such as '33' and '0'.

PI (Positive Integer) – an integer greater than zero, such as '1'.

SR (Signed Real) – signed real number, with optional '+' or '-' preceding, such as '-33.4'.

UR (Unsigned Real) – unsigned real number, such as '33.4' and '0'.

PR (Positive Real) – positive real number, such as '1.1'.

Property	Example values	Values
auto-restore	false	*Boolean* (default true)
azimuth*	center-left	*same as CSS*
background*	red url(boat.gif) no-repeat scroll top	*same as CSS*
background-attachment*	fixed	*same as CSS*
background-color*	red	*same as CSS*
background-image*	url(boat.gif)	*same as CSS*
background-repeat*	no-repeat	*same as CSS*
background-position*	top	*same as CSS*
border*	thin solid #FF00FF 3pt transparent	combination of width, style and color, for all sides
border-after-color	#FF0000	transparent, *Color*
border-after-style	thin	*same as CSS* (eg border-top-style)
border-after-width	thin 2.5pt	medium (the default), thin, thick, *UL*
border-before-color	#FF00FF	transparent, *Color*
border-before-style	solid	*same as CSS* (eg border-style-top)
border-before-width	thin 2.5pt	medium (the default), thin, thick, *UL*
border-bottom*	thin solid #FF00FF 3pt transparent	combination of width, style and color, for one side only
border-bottom-color*	#800000	transparent, *Color*
border-bottom-style*	double	*same as CSS*
border-bottom-width*	thin 2.5pt	medium (the default), thin, thick, *UL*
border-collapse*	separate	*same as CSS*
border-color*	#FF00FF	*Color*
border-end-color	#808080	transparent, *Color*
border-end-style	solid	*same as CSS* (eg border-top-style)
border-end-width	thin 2.5pt	*same as CSS*
border-left*	thin solid #FF00FF 3pt transparent	combination of width, style and color, for one side only
border-left-color*	#FFFFFF	transparent, *Color*
border-left-style*	dashed	*same as CSS*
border-left-width*	thin 2.5pt	medium (the default), thin, thick, *UL*
border-right*	thin solid #FF00FF 3pt transparent	combination of width, style and color, for one side only
border-right-color*	#008080	transparent, *Color*
border-right-style*	dotted	*same as CSS*
border-right-width*	thin 2.5pt	medium (the default), thin, thick, *UL*

border-spacing*	2pt	*same as CSS*
border-start-color	#FF7F00	transparent, *Color*
border-start-style	hidden	*same as CSS* (eg border-top-style)
border-start-width	thin 2.5pt	medium (the default), thin, thick, *UL*
border-style*	solid dotted solid dotted solid	*same as CSS*
border-top*	thin solid #FF00FF 3pt transparent	combination of width, style and color, for one side only
border-top-color*	#12FF34	transparent, *Color*
border-top-style*	solid	*same as CSS*
border-top-width*	thin 2.5pt	medium (the default), thin, thick, *UL*
border-width*	2pt thick 2pt thin 5pt	medium (the default), thin, thick, *UL*, (repeatable as in CSS)
bottom*	3cm	*same as CSS*
break-after	even-page	auto (the default), column, page, even-page, odd-page
break-before	column	auto (the default), column, page, even-page, odd-page
caption-side*	bottom	*same as CSS* + (before (default in place of 'top'), after, start, end)
caption-width	50%	auto, *Length, Percent*
cell-height	7mm	auto, *Length, Percent*
clear*	right	*same as CSS*
clip*	rect(5pt 5pt 10pt 10pt)	*same as CSS*
color*	#FF7F08	*same as CSS*
column-count	2	*PI* (default 1)
column-gap	9pt	*SL* (default 12pt)
column-number	3	*PI* (default 1 + last column)
column-width	10mm	*UL*
country	use-document	none (the default), use-document
cue*	url(squeek.gif) url(go.gif) url(stop.gif)	*same as CSS*
cue-after*	url(stop.gif)	*same as CSS*
cue-before*	url(go.gif)	*same as CSS*
digit-group-sep	,	*Char* (',' = '1,000,000' or '.' = '1.000.000')
direction*	ttb	*same as CSS* + btt (bottom-to-top), ttb (top-to-bottom)
elevation*	far-right behind 240deg	*same as CSS*
empty-cells*	hide	*same as CSS*
end-indent	-2pt	*SL*
ends-row	yes	no (the default), yes
extent	9pt	*UL* (default 0.0pt)
external-destination	file://dest.xml	URL

float	left	*same as CSS*
flow-name	xsl-body	*Name*
font*	italic small-caps bold 18pt/22pt Helvetica, sans-serif	*same as CSS*
font-family*	Helvetica, sans-serif	*same as CSS*
font-height-override-after		*SL*, font metric
font-height-override-before		*SL*, font metric
font-size*	12pt narrower	*same as CSS*
font-stretch*	condensed narrower	*same as CSS*
font-size-adjust*	5.45 none	*same as CSS* (but no negative numbers allowed)
font-style*	italic	*same as CSS*
font-variant*	small-caps	*same as CSS*
font-weight*	bold	*same as CSS*
format	01	'1' = '1 2 3 4', '001' = '001 002 003 004', 'a' = 'a b c d', 'A' = 'A B C D', 'i' = 'i ii iii iv', 'I' = 'I II III IV'
height*	7cm	*same as CSS* (default auto)
href	file://destfile.xml	none (the default), URL
hyphenation-char	-	*Char*
hyphenation-keep	column	column, none, page, spread
hyphenation-ladder-count	2	none (the default), URL
hyphenation-push-char-count	3	*PI*
hyphenation-remain-char-count	2	*PI*
hyphenate	true	*Boolean*
id	MyID	*ID*
indicate-destination	true	*Boolean* (default false)
inhibit-line-breaks	true	*Boolean* (default false)
initial	false	*Boolean* (default true)
initial-page-number	1	*UI* (default to 1, probably)
internal-destination	ThisObjectId	HREF
keep-with-next	true	*Boolean*
keep-with-previous	true	*Boolean*
language	use-document	none (the default), use-document
last-line-end-indent	-1cm	*SL*
left*	3cm	*same as CSS*
length	12cm	auto (the default), *UL*
letter-spacing*	normal 1pt	*same as CSS*
letter-value	other	other, alphabetic
line-height	80%	normal, *Length*, *Number*, *Percent*
line-height-shift-adjustment	disregard-shifts	consider-shifts, disregard-shifts
line-stacking-strategy	line-height	line-height (the default), font-height, max-height

margin*	2pt	*same as CSS*
	2pt 4pt	
margin-bottom*	2pt	*same as CSS*
margin-left*	2pt	*same as CSS*
margin-right*	2pt	*same as CSS*
margin-top*	2pt	*same as CSS*
max-height*	10cm	*same as CSS*
max-width*	8cm	*same as CSS*
may-break-after-row	yes	no (the default), yes
may-break-before-row	yes	no (the default), yes
min-height*	2cm	*same as CSS*
min-width*	3cm	*same as CSS*
n-columns-repeated	2	*PI* (default 1)
n-columns-spanned	3	*PI* (default 1 (no span))
n-digits-group-sep	3	*PI* ('3' = '1,000,000' or '2' = '1.00.00.00')
n-rows-spanned	3	*PI* (default 1 (no span))
name	MyName	*Name*
orphans*	2	*same as CSS*
overflow*	scroll	*same as CSS*
padding*	2pt	*UL* repeating as in CSS
	2pt 3pt 2pt 3pt	
padding-after	2pt	*UL* (default 0.0pt)
padding-before	2pt	*UL* (default 0.0pt)
padding-bottom*	2pt	*UL* (default 0.0pt)
padding-end	2pt	*UL* (default 0.0pt)
padding-left*	2pt	*UL* (default 0.0pt)
padding-right*	2pt	*UL* (default 0.0pt)
padding-start	2pt	*UL* (default 0.0pt)
padding-top*	2pt	*UL* (default 0.0pt)
page-break-inside*	avoid	*same as CSS*
page-height	indefinite	auto (the deafult), indefinite, *UL*
	12cm	
page-master-blank-even	MyEvenBlankMaster	*Name*
page-master-even	MyEvenMaster	*Name*
page-master-first	MyFirstPageMaster	*Name*
page-master-last-even	MyEvenLastMaster	*Name*
page-master-last-odd	MyOddLastMaster	*Name*
page-master-name	MyMasterName	*Name*
page-master-odd	MyOddMaster	*Name*
page-master-repeating	MyRepeatMaster	*Name*
page-width	indefinite	auto (the deafult), indefinite, *UL*
	12cm	
pause*	12ms 9ms	*same as CSS*
pause-after*	9ms	*same as CSS*
pause-before*	12ms	*same as CSS*
pitch*	low	*same as CSS*
	200Hz	
pitch-range*	44	*same as CSS*

play-during*	url(squeek.gif) repeat auto	*same as CSS*
position*	relative	*same as CSS*
precedence	true	*Boolean*
provisional-distance-between-starts	12pt	*UL* (default 24.0pt)
provisional-label-separation	3pt	*UL* (default 6.0pt)
ref-id	TargetObject	*IDREF*
richness*	70	*same as CSS*
right*	3cm	*same as CSS*
row-height	12mm	auto, *Length, Percent*
rule-orientation	horizontal	escapement (the default), horizontal, line-progression, vertical
rule-style	solid	none (the default), solid
rule-thickness	2pt	*UL* (default 1.0pt)l
scale	0.9	*PR*
score-spaces	true	*Boolean* (default false)
script	use-document ISO/IEC 10179:1996/ /Script::Han	none (the default), use-document, *String* (ISO defined script)
sequence-src	file:///numlist.txt	URL (numlist.txt containing whitespace separated numbers – '2 4 6 8 last'
show-destination	new	replace (the default), new
size*	8cm 12cm	*same as CSS*
space-above-destination-block	12pt	*UL*
space-above-destination-start	12pt	*UL*
space-after	2pt 5pt 3pt 0 retain	*minimum + maximum + optimum + precedence + conditionality (retain, discard)*
space-before	2pt 5pt 3pt 0 discard	*minimum + maximum + optimum + precedence + conditionality (retain, discard)*
space-end	1pt 1pt 1pt 0 discard	*minimum + maximum + optimum + precedence + conditionality (retain, discard)*
space-start	1pt 1pt 1pt 0 discard	*minimum + maximum + optimum + precedence + conditionality (retain, discard)*
span	all	none (the default), all
speak*	spell-out	*same as CSS*
speak-header*	always	*same as CSS*
speak-numerals*	digits	*same as CSS*
speak-punctuation*	code	*same as CSS*
speech-rate*	faster 120 *(words per minute)*	*same as CSS*
start-indent	2pt	*SL*
starts-row	yes	no (the default), yes
state		a DOM state or event

stress*	53	*same as CSS*
switch-to	#following Option1 Option2	#preceding, #following, #any (the default) or *Name* (repeating)
table-height	12cm	*Length, Percent*, auto
table-layout*	fixed	*same as CSS*
table-omit-middle-footer	yes	no (the default), yes
table-omit-middle-header	yes	no (the default), yes
table-width	12cm	*Length, Percent*, auto
text-align*	justified	start, centered, end, justified, page-outside, page-inside (also CSS left and right are interpreted as start and end)
text-align-last	start	relative (the default), start, end, justified
text-decoration*	underline	*same as CSS*
text-indent*	1em	*same as CSS*
text-shadow*	#FF00FF 1pt 1pt 1pt	*same as CSS*
text-transform*	uppercase	*same as CSS*
title	OptionalContent3	*String*
top*	3cm	*same as CSS*
vertical-align*	text-top	*same as CSS*
visibility*	hidden	*same as CSS* (but visible is now default)
voice-family*	churchill female	*same as CSS*
volume*	medium	*same as CSS*
white-space-treatment	collapse	preserve (the default), collapse, ignore
widows*	2	*same as CSS*
width*	5cm	*same as CSS*
word-spacing*	normal 1pt	*same as CSS*
wrap-option	no-wrap	wrap (the default), no-wrap
writing-mode	lr-inverting-rl-bt	use-page-writing-mode (the default), lr-tb, rl-tb, tb-rl, tb-lr, bt-lr, bt-rl, lr-bt, rl-bt, lr-alternating-rl-bt, lr-alternating-rl-tb, lr-inverting-rl-bt, lr-inverting-rl-tb, tb-rl-in-rl-pairs
z-index*	12	*same as CSS*

CSS properties

The following table lists all the CSS properties (53 from CSS1 and an additional 77 from CSS2) and the values that they can take, grouped by appropriate function. Common parameter value types are described below.

Length – inches (in), centimetres (cm), millimetres (mm), points (pt), picas (pc), ems (em), x-height (ex), pixels (px). A '+' or '-' prefix is allowed.

Percent – '+' or '-', followed by number, then '%', e.g. 200% = twice size.

Color – black, navy, blue, aqua, purple, maroon, green, red, gray, fuchsia, teal, lime, yellow, white, olive, silver, #rgb (hexadecimal), #rrggbb (hexadecimal), rgb(r,g,b) (each value decimal, or percent).

Number – digits, optionally prefix with '+' or '-', may include decimal point.

Integer – digits, optionally prefix with '+' or '-', not including decimal point.

Time – Number plus 'ms' (milliseconds) or 's' (seconds).

String – Quotes characters, single or double, no embedded quotes of same type, use '\"' or '\'' instead. Newline is '\A' and just '\' to split text over lines in style sheet.

Note that, beyond the values shown below, CSS2 also adds the Inherit value to all properties.

Property	Ver	Example values	Values
Font properties			
font	1	italic small-caps bold 18pt/22pt Helvetica, sans-serif	combination of next six properties – font-style, font-variant, font-weight, font-size, line-height and font-family, with '/' between size and line height
	2	caption	... caption, icon, menu, message, small-caption, status-bar
font-style	1	italic	normal (the default), italic, oblique
font-variant	1	normal	normal (the default), small-caps
font-weight	1	bold	normal (the default), bold, bolder, lighter, 100, 200, 300, 400, 500, 600, 700, 800, 900
font-size	1	18pt larger	*Length*, xx-large, x-large, large, medium (the default), small, x-small, xx-small, smaller, larger

font-family	1	Helvetica, sans-serif 'Times New Roman'	comma separated alternative font names, first has preference, can be generic name (serif, sans-serif, cursive, fantasy, monospace), (quote name with spaces, "Times New Roman" (use single quotes in Style attributes))
font-size-adjust	2	0.58	*Number*, none (the default)
font-stretch	2	narrower	normal (the default), wider, narrower, ultra-condensed, extra-condensed, condensed, semi-condensed, semi-expanded, expanded, extra-expanded, ultra-expanded
Color and background			
color	1	blue #FF0	*Color*
background	1	red url(boat.gif) no-repeat scroll 10% 10%	combination (background-color, background-image, background-repeat, background-attachment, background-position)
background-color	1	green	*Color*, transparent (the default)
background-image	1	url(boat.gif)	URL, none (the default)
background-repeat	1	repeat-x	repeat (default), repeat-x, repeat-y, no-repeat
background-attachment	1	fixed	scroll (default), fixed
background-position	1	top 10mm 15mm	top, center, bottom, left, right, *Percent*, (*Length* – x, y)
Text properties			
text-decoration	1	underline	none (the default), underline, over-line, line-through, blink
vertical-align	1	sub	baseline (the default), sub, super, top, text-top, middle, bottom, text-bottom, *Percent*
	2	2pt	... *Length*
text-align	1	center	left, right, center, justify
	2	"."	... *String*
text-indent	1	1cm	*Length* (default '0') (first line of text block, minus value gives hanging indent), *Percent*
letter-spacing	1	2pt	normal (the default), *Length*
word-spacing	1	normal	normal (the default), *Length*
text-transform	1	uppercase	capitalize, uppercase, lowercase, none (the default)
line-height	1	22pt	none, (default), *Number*, *Length*, *Percent*
text-shadow	2	3px 3px red 2pt 4pt, -2pt -4pt 1pt blue	normal (default), *Length* (across) *Length* (down) *Length*? (blur angle) *Color*? (plus more optional shadows separate by commas)
Box properties			

margin	1	.3cm	*Length*, *Percent*, auto – repeated ('x' = all margins, 'x x' = vertical and horizontal and 'x x x x' = top/right/bottom/left)
margin-left	1	.3cm	*Length* (default 0), *Percent*, auto
margin-right	1	.3in	*Length* (default 0), *Percent*, auto
margin-top	1	9pt	*Length* (default 0), *Percent*, auto
margin-bottom	1	10%	*Length* (default 0), *Percent*, auto
padding	1	1pt	*Length* (default 0), percent*** – repeated ('x' = all edges, 'x x' = vertical and horizontal and 'x x x x' = top/right/bottom/left)
padding-left	1	1pt	*Length* (default 0), *Percent*
padding-right	1	auto	*Length* (default 0), *Percent*
padding-top	1	1em	*Length* (default 0), *Percent*
padding-bottom	1	5pt	*Length* (default 0), *Percent*
border	1	1in	*Length* – repeated ('x' = all borders, 'x x' = vertical and horizontal and 'x x x x' = top/right/bottom/left) or URL (or from V2, also set width, color and style – see below)
border-left	1	.3cm	*Length* or URL (or from V2, also set width, color and style – see below)
border-right	1	.3in	*Length* or URL (or from V2, also set width, color and style – see below)
border-top	1	9pt	*Length* or URL (or from V2, also set width, color and style – see below)
border-bottom	1	10%	*Length* or URL (or from V2, also set width, color and style – see below)
border-width	1	thick, thin 2pt 4pt 2pt 4pt	thin, medium, thick, *Length* – repeated ('x' = all borders, 'x x' = vertical and horizontal and 'x x x x' = top/right/bottom/left)
border-left-width	1	thick	thin, medium (default), thick, *Length*
border-right-width	1	thin	thin, medium (default), thick, *Length*
border-top-width	1	medium	thin, medium (default), thick, *Length*
border-bottom-width	1	3pt	thin, medium (default), thick, *Length*
border-color	1	blue green	*Color* – repeated ('x' = all borders, 'x x' = vertical and horizontal and 'x x x x' = top/right/bottom/left)
	2	transparent	… , transparent
border-left-color	2	red	*Color*
border-right-color	2	black	*Color*
border-top-color	2	white	*Color*
border-bottom-color	2	red	*Color*
border-style	1	solid ridge solid ridge	none, hidden, dotted, dashed, solid, double, groove, ridge, inset, outset – repeated ('x' = all borders, 'x x' = vertical and horizontal and 'x x x x' = top/right/bottom/left)
border-left-style	2	dotted	none, hidden, dotted, dashed, solid, double, groove, ridge, inset, outset

border-right-style	2	ridge	none, hidden, dotted, dashed, solid, double, groove, ridge, inset, outset
border-top-style	2	dashed	none, hidden, dotted, dashed, solid, double, groove, ridge, inset, outset
border-bottom-style	2	dotted	none, hidden, dotted, dashed, solid, double, groove, ridge, inset, outset
width	1	50px	*Length*, *Percent*, auto (default)
min-width	2	50px	*Length*, *Percent*
max-width	2	50px	*Length*, *Percent*, none (default)
height	1	auto	*Length*, auto (default)
	2	15%	*... Percent*
min-height	2	50px	*Length*, *Percent*
max-height	2	50px	*Length*, *Percent*, none (default)
float	1	left	left, right, none (the default)
clear	1	left	left, right, both, none (the default)
overflow	2	hidden	visible (the default), hidden, scroll, auto
clip	2	auto	*Shape*, auto (the default)
visiblity	2	visible	visible, hidden, collapse (default is 'inherit')
z-index	2	12	auto (the default), *Integer*
Generated content			
content	2	open-quote "My prefix" close-quote	*String*, URI, *Counter*, attr(...), open-quote, close-quote, no-open-quote, no-close-quote (and any combination)
quotes	2	none "«" "»" "<" ">"	none, *String String* (repeating)
counter-reset	2	section -1 imagenum 99	none (the default) or *Identifier Integer?* (repeating)
counter-increment	2	section 10 item 1	none (the default) or *Identifier Integer?* (repeating)
list-style	1	decimal outside	combination of list-style-type, list-style-image, list-style-position
list-style-type	1	circle	disc, circle (the default), square, decimal, lower-roman, upper-roman, lower-alpha, upper-alpha, none
	2	circle	... decimal-leading-zero, lower-greek, upper-greek, lower-latin, upper-latin, hebrew, armenian, georgian, cjk-ideographic, hiragana, katakana, hiragana-iroha, katakana-iroha
list-style-position	1	inside	inside, outside (the default)
list-style-image	1	url(boat.gif)	URL, none (the default)
Paged media			
size	2	8cm 12cm	auto (the default), protrait, landscape, *Length* (one or twice)
marks	2	crop cross	none (the default), crop cross
page-break-before	2	left	auto (the default), always, avoid, left, right

page-break-after	2	always	auto (the default), always, avoid, left, right
page-break-inside	2	avoid	auto (the default), avoid
page	2	auto	auto (the default), *Identifier*
orphans	2	3	*Integer* (default '2')
widows	2	3	*Integer* (default '2')
Tables			
caption-side	2	left	top (the default), bottom, left, right
table-layout	2	fixed	auto (the default), fixed
border-collapse	2	separate	collapse (the default), separate
border-spacing	2	3pt 3pt 5pt	*Length* (default '0') *Length*?
empty-cells	2	hide	show (the default), hide
speak-header	2	always	once (the default) always
User interface			
cursor	2	crosshair, default url(eggtimer.gif), wait	auto (the default), crosshair, default, pointer, move, e-resize, ne-resize, nw-resize, n-resize, se-resize, sw-resize, s-resize, w-resize, text, wait, help, or URL() (repeating?)
outline	2	red dashed 2pt	combination of outline-color, out-line-style, outline-width
outline-width	2	2pt	thin, medium (the default), thick, *Length* – repeated ('x' = all borders, 'x x' = vertical and horizontal and 'x x x x' = top/right/bottom/left)
outline-style	2	dashed	none (the default) , hidden, dotted, dashed, solid, double, groove, ridge, inset, outset – repeated ('x' = all borders, 'x x' = vertical and horizontal and 'x x x x' = top/right/bottom/left)
outline-color	2	red	invert (the default), *Color*
Aural styles			
volume	2	medium	*Number*, *Percent*, silent, x-soft, soft, medium (the default), loud, x-loud
speak	2	spell-out	normal (the default), non, spell-out
pause	2	12ms 9ms	combination of pause-before and pause-after
pause-before	2	12ms	*Time*, *Percent*
pause-after	2	9ms	*Time*, *Percent*
cue	2	url(squeek.gif) url(go.gif) url(stop.gif)	combination of cue-before and cue-after
cue-after	2	url(squeek.gif)	url(...), none (the default)
cue-before	2	url(squeek.gif)	url(...), none (the default)
play-during	2	url(squeek.gif) repeat auto	auto (the default), none, url(...) mix? repeat?

azimuth	2	far-right behind 240deg	*nnn* deg, leftwards, rightwards or left-side, far-side, left, center-left, center (the default), center-right, right, far-right, right-side followed by behind
elevation	2	far-right behind 240deg	*nnn* deg, below, level (the default), above, lower, higher
speech-rate	2	faster 120 *(words per minute)*	*nnn*, x-slow, slow, medium (the default), fast, x-fast, faster, slower
voice-family	2	churchill female	male, female, child, (specific voice such as 'comedian')
pitch	2	low 200Hz	x-low, low, medium (the default), high, x-high, *nn* Hz
pitch-range	2	44	0–100 (default 50)
stress	2	53	0–100 (default 50)
richness	2	70	0–100 (default 50)
speak-punctuation	2	code	code, none (the default)
speak-numerals	2	digits	digits, continuous (the default)
Classifications			
display	1	inline	none, block (**default**), inline, list-item
	2	block compact table-row	none, block, inline (**default**), list-item ...*PLUS*... run-in, compact, marker, table, inline-table, table-row-group, table-header-group, table-footer-group, table-row, table-column-group, table-column, table-cell, table-caption
marker-offset	2	section 10 item 1	*Length*, auto (the default)
position	2	relative	static (the default), relative, absolute, fixed
top	2	2pt	*Length*, *Percent*, auto
bottom	2	2pt	*Length*, *Percent*, auto
left	2	2pt	*Length*, *Percent*, auto
right	2	2pt	*Length*, *Percent*, auto
direction	2	rtl	ltr (the default), rtl (right-to-left)
unicode-bidi	2	embed	normal (the default), embed, bidi-override
white-space	1	pre	normal (the default), pre (pre-formatted), nowrap (single line)

This book DTD

The following is an example DTD (based on the SGML DTD that was used to produce this book), included to illustrate the concepts described in Chapters 5 and 10:

```
<!-- XML BOOK DTD
            DTD for The XML Companion
            AUTHOR: N.Bradley (neil@bradley.co.uk)
            VERSION: 1.3 (5/1/98) -->


<!-- ENTITY DECLARATIONS -->

<!-- specify names and locations of external entities -->
<!ENTITY % CALStable SYSTEM "TABLE.DTD">
<!ENTITY % ISOnum
        PUBLIC "ISO 8879:1986//ENTITIES Numeric and Special
                Graphic//EN" SYSTEM "ISOnum.ent">
<!ENTITY % ISOlat1
        PUBLIC "ISO 8879:1986//ENTITIES Added Latin 1//EN"
        SYSTEM "ISOlat1.ent">
<!ENTITY % ISOgrk1
        PUBLIC "ISO 8879:1986//ENTITIES Greek Letters//EN"
        SYSTEM "ISOgrk.ent">
<!ENTITY % ISOpub
        PUBLIC "ISO 8879:1986//ENTITIES Publishing//EN"
        SYSTEM "ISOpub.ent">

<!-- merge-in the external entities -->

%CALStable;
%ISOnum;
%ISOlat1;
%ISOgrk1;
%ISOpub;

<!-- define internal entities -->
<!ENTITY % Blocks     "(para | markup-para | graphic |
                       list | table | road-map)*" >

<!ENTITY % SuperSub   "sup | sub" >
<!ENTITY % Hilite "markup | emph-strong | emph-weak" >


<!-- MAIN STRUCTURE -->

<!-- Book document element -->
<!ELEMENT book          (front, body, back)>
<!ATTLIST book          id      ID      #REQUIRED>

<!-- Title -->
<!ELEMENT title         (#PCDATA | %SuperSub;)*>


<!-- FRONT SECTION -->

<!-- front matter -->
```

```
<!ELEMENT front      (title, edition, author, publisher)>

<!-- edition of book -->
<!ELEMENT edition    (#PCDATA)>

<!-- author of book -->
<!ELEMENT author     (first, second, e-mail?)>
<!ELEMENT first      (#PCDATA)>
<!ELEMENT second     (#PCDATA)>
<!ELEMENT e-mail     (#PCDATA)>

<!-- publisher of book -->
<!ELEMENT publisher (pub-name, address)
<!ELEMENT pub-name   (#PCDATA)>
<!ELEMENT address    (#PCDATA)>


<!-- BODY SECTION -->

<!ELEMENT body      (part+ | chapter+)>

<!-- part (in body) -->
<!ELEMENT part      (title, chapter+)>

<!-- chapter (in body or part) -->
<!ELEMENT chapter     (title, %Blocks;, section*)>
<!ATTLIST chapter     id      ID      #REQUIRED>

<!-- section (in chapter) -->
<!ELEMENT section     (title, %Blocks;, sub-section*)>
<!ATTLIST section     id      ID      #REQUIRED>

<!-- subsection (in section) -->
<!ELEMENT sub-section (title, %Blocks;)
<!ATTLIST sub-section id      ID      #REQUIRED>

<!-- roadmap charts have different pagination and
     font size rules -->
<!ELEMENT road-map    (para | markup-para)*>


<!-- BACK SECTION -->

<!-- back matter -->
<!ELEMENT back        (glossary)>

<!-- glossary (special form of chapter) -->
<!ELEMENT glossary    (para*, section*)>


<!-- BLOCK STRUCTURES -->

<!-- paragraph -->
<!ELEMENT para        (#PCDATA | %Hilite; | %SuperSub; |
                      x-ref)*>

<!-- graphic image - placeholder -->
<!ELEMENT graphic     EMPTY>
<!ATTLIST graphic     id      ID      #IMPLIED
```

```
                               ident   ENTITY    #REQUIRED>

<!-- list -->
<!ELEMENT list            (item+)>

<!-- list item -->
<!ELEMENT item            (#PCDATA | %Hilite; |
                           %SuperSub; | x-ref)*>
<!ATTLIST item            type      (number|random)  "random"

<!-- text block dislayed in mono-space -->
<!ELEMENT markup-para     (markup-line*)>
<!ATTLIST markup-para     splitable (loose | together)
                                                     "loose">

<!-- markup line - one line of text in markup fragment-->
<!ELEMENT markup-line     (#PCDATA | %Hilite; | %SuperSub;
                           | presented)*>


<!-- IN-LINE STRUCTURES -->

<!-- example of rendered output -->
<!ELEMENT presented (#PCDATA | %Hilite; | %SuperSub;)*>

<!-- XML example fragments in text -->
<!ELEMENT markup          (#PCDATA | %SuperSub; |
                           emph-strong | emph-weak)*>

<!-- emphasized text - shown in bold -->
<!ELEMENT emph-strong     (#PCDATA | markup | emph-weak |
                           %SuperSub; | x-ref)*>

<!-- stressed (names) - shown in italic -->
<!ELEMENT emph-weak       (#PCDATA | markup |
                   emph-strong | %SuperSub; | x-ref)*>

<!-- superscript -->
<!ELEMENT sup             (#PCDATA)>

<!-- subscript -->
<!ELEMENT sub             (#PCDATA)>

<!-- cross-references to other text in the book -->
<!ELEMENT x-ref           (#PCDATA)>
<!ATTLIST x-ref           source  IDREF   #REQUIRED>

<!-- END END END -->
```

ISO 8859/1 character set

The character set describing European letters, numbers and symbols. This character set is used by HTML, and forms the basis of Microsoft Windows fonts (although reserved places are filled with extra characters in the Windows version) and UNIX fonts (for example, Open Windows). The first 128 characters are derived from the **ISO/IEC 646** version of **ASCII**. The remaining 128 characters cover European accented characters, and further common symbols. The official ISO name for each character is placed in brackets, for example 'Solidus (slash)'.

The ISO character entity sets, **ISOnum** (numeric and special graphic), **ISOlat1** (latin accents) and **ISOdia** (diacritic marks), provide an alternative means of specifying most of the characters in this set. Each entity reference is identified as belonging to one of these sets as follows:

- N = ISOnum
- L = ISOlat1
- D = ISOdia

For example, '< N' indicates that entity reference '<' belongs to the ISOnum set. Those not covered by any ISO entity set are shown as character entities, '&#...;'. When an entry appears in italic, the character is easily available from the keyboard, and has no significance in any XML context (so the entity reference is not generally needed), or it is unused within an XML context (mainly redundant control codes).

All the entities in the following table may be used in HTML documents presented using Internet *Explorer 3.0* and *Navigator 3.0* onwards, except for ', | (use the normal vertical bar '|') and ½ (use the alternative form: ½).

Decimal and Hex		Character entities	Description
000 00		*&#00;*	*NUL – no effect*
001 01		*&#01;*	*SOH – Start of Heading*
002 02		*&#02;*	*STX – Start of Text*
003 03		*&#03;*	*ETX – End of Text*
004 04		*&#04;*	*EOT – End of Transmission*
005 05		*&#05;*	*ENQ – Enquiry*
006 06		*&#06;*	*ACK – Acknowledge*
007 07		*&#07;*	*BEL – Bell*
008 08		*&#08;*	*BS – Backspace*
009 09		&#09;	HT – Horizontal Tab, **HTML** Tab
010 0A		&#10;	LF – Line Feed, **HTML** new-line (with or without '013'), **record start (RS)**
011 0B		*&#11;*	*VT – Vertical Tabulation*
012 0C		&#12;	FF – Form Feed

013 0D		&#13;	CR – Carriage return, **HTML** new-line (with or without '010'), **record end (RE)**
014 0E		*&#14;*	*SO – Shift Out*
015 0F		*&#15;*	*SI – Shift In*
016 10		*&#16;*	*DLE – Data Link Escape*
017 11		*&#17;*	*DC1 – Device Control (1)*
018 12		*&#18;*	*DC2 – Device Control (2)*
019 13		*&#19;*	*DC3 – Device Control (3)*
020 14		*&#20;*	*DC4 – Device Control (4)*
021 15		*&#21;*	*NAK – No Acknowledge*
022 16		*&#22;*	*SYN – Synchronize*
023 17		*&#23;*	*ETB – End of Transmission Block*
024 18		*&#24;*	*CAN – Cancel*
025 19		*&#25;*	*EM – End of Medium*
026 1A		*&#26;*	*SUB – Substitute Character*
027 1B		*&#27;*	*ESC – Escape*
028 1C		*&#28;*	*FS – File Separator*
029 1D		*&#29;*	*GS – Group Separator*
030 1E		*&#30;*	*RS – Record Separator*
031 1F		*&#31;*	*US – Unit Separator*
032 20		&#32;	Space (space)
033 21	!	*!* N	Exclamation (exclam)
034 22	"	*"* N	Quotation (quotedbl), literal (use " in attributes with literal delimiters)
035 23	#	*#* N	Number sign (numbersign), **reserved name indicator** ('#PCDATA')
036 24	$	*$* N	Dollar sign (dollar)
037 25	%	*%* N	Percent sign (percent), parameter entity reference open delimiter ('%ent;')
038 26	&	& N	Ampersand (ampersand), entity reference open delimiter ('&ent;'), character reference open delimiter ('&#26;')
039 27	'	' N	Apostrophe sign, literal alternative delimiter (use ' in attributes with literal alternative delimiters)
040 28	(	(N	Left parenthesis (parenleft), group open delimiter ('(a, b)')
041 29	)	) N	Right parenthesis (parenright), group close delimiter ('(a, b)')
042 2A	*	*** N	Asterisk (asterisk), optional and repeatable symbol ('a, b*')
043 2B	+	*+* N	Plus sign (plus), required and repeatable symbol ('a, b+')
044 2C	,	*,* N	Comma (comma), **sequence connector** ('a, b, c')
045 2D	-	*‐* N	Hyphen (hyphen), comment delimiter ('-- my comment --')
046 2E	.	*.* N	Full point (period)
047 2F	/	/ N	Solidus (slash), end-tag open delimiter ('</tag>')
048 30	0	&#48;	Zero (zero)
049 31	1	&#49;	One (one)
050 32	2	&#50;	Two (two)
051 33	3	&#51;	Three (three)
052 34	4	&#52;	Four (four)
053 35	5	&#53;	Five (five)
054 36	6	&#54;	Six (six)
055 37	7	&#55;	Seven (seven)
056 38	8	&#56;	Eight (eight)
057 39	9	&#57;	Nine (nine)
058 3A	:	*:* N	Colon (colon)

059 3B	;	; N	Semicolon (semicolon), **reference close** ('&ent;')
060 3C	<	< N	Less than (less), start tag open delimiter, end-tag open delimiter ('</'),
061 3D	=	= N	Equals (equal), **value indicator** ('attrib=" value" ')
062 3E	>	> N	Greater than (greater), **markup declaration close** ('<!.......>'), **processing instruction close** ('<?proc>'), **tag-close** ('<tag>')
063 3F	?	? N	Question mark (question), **optional occurrence indicator** ('a | b'), **processing instruction open** ('<?')
064 40	@	@ N	Commercial at (at)
065 41	A	&#65;	A
066 42	B	&#66;	B
067 43	C	&#67;	C
068 44	D	&#68;	D
069 45	E	&#69;	E
070 46	F	&#70;	F
071 47	G	&#71;	G
072 48	H	&#72;	H
073 49	I	&#73;	I
074 4A	J	&#74;	J
075 4B	K	&#75;	K
076 4C	L	&#76;	L
077 4D	M	&#77;	M
078 4E	N	&#78;	N
079 4F	O	&#79;	O
080 50	P	&#80;	P
081 51	Q	&#81;	Q
082 52	R	&#82;	R
083 53	S	&#83;	S
084 54	T	&#84;	T
085 55	U	&#85;	U
086 56	V	&#86;	V
087 57	W	&#87;	W
088 58	X	&#88;	X
089 59	Y	&#89;	Y
090 5A	Z	&#90;	Z
091 5B	[	[N	Left square bracket (bracketleft), **declaration subset open** ('<!DOCTYPE ... [...]>'), **data tag group open**
092 5C	\	\ N	Reverse solidus (backslash)
093 5D	]	] N	Right square bracket (bracketright), **declaration subset close** ('<!DOCTYPE ... [...]>'), **data tag group close, marked section close** (']]')
094 5E	^	ˆ D	Caret (asciicircum)
095 5F	_	― N	Underscore (underscore)
096 60	`	` D	Grave accent
097 61	a	&#97;	a
098 62	b	&#98;	b
099 63	c	&#99;	c
100 64	d	&#100;	d
101 65	e	&#101;	e
102 66	f	&#102;	f
103 67	g	&#103;	g
104 68	h	&#104;	h
105 69	i	&#105;	i
106 6A	j	&#106;	j
107 6B	k	&#107;	k

108 6C	l	&#108;	l	
109 6D	m	&#109;	m	
110 6E	n	&#110;	n	
111 6F	o	&#111;	o	
112 70	p	&#112;	p	
113 71	q	&#113;	q	
114 72	r	&#114;	r	
115 73	s	&#115;	s	
116 74	t	&#116;	t	
117 75	u	&#117;	u	
118 76	v	&#118;	v	
119 77	w	&#119;	w	
120 78	x	&#120;	x	
121 79	y	&#121;	y	
122 7A	z	&#122;	z	
123 7B	{	{ N	Left curly brace (braceleft)	
124 7C	|	| N	Vertical bar (bar), **or connector**	
125 7D	}	} N	Right curly brace (braceright)	
126 7E	~	˜ D	Tilde (asciitilde)	
127 7F		&#127;	Delete (del), Checkerboard effect	
128 80			WINDOWS CHARS, delete (del)	
....			...	
....			...	
....			...	
159 9F			WINDOWS CHARS	
160 A0		N	NBS – Non-break space	
161 A1	¡	¡ N	Inverted exclamation (exclamdown)	
162 A2	¢	¢ N	Cent sign (cent)	
163 A3	£	£ N	Pound sterling (pound)	
164 A4	¤	¤ N	General currency symbol (currency)	
165 A5	¥	¥ N	Yen sign (yen)	
166 A6	¦	¦ N	Broken vertical bar (pipe)	
167 A7	§	§ N	Section sign (section)	
168 A8	¨	¨ D	Umlaut (dieresis)	
169 A9	©	© N	Copyright (copyrightserif)	
170 AA	ª	ª N	Feminine ordinal (ordfeminine)	
171 AB	«	« N	Left angle quote (guillemotleft)	
172 AC	¬	¬ N	Not sign (logicalnot)	
173 AD	-	&#173;	Soft hyphen (hyphen)	
174 AE	®	® N	Registered trademark (registerserif)	
175 AF	¯	¯ D	Macron accent (macron)	
176 B0	°	° N	Degree sign (ring)	
177 B1	±	± N	Plus or minus (plusminus)	
178 B2	²	² N	Superscript two (Reserved)	
179 B3	³	³ N	Superscript three (Reserved)	
180 B4	´	´ D	Acute accent (acute)	
181 B5	μ	µ N	Micro sign (Reserved)	
182 B6	¶	¶ N	Paragraph sign (paragraph)	
183 B7	·	· N	Middle dot (periodcentered)	
184 B8	¸	¸ D	Cedilla (cedilla)	
185 B9	¹	¹ N	Superscript one (Reserved)	
186 BA	º	º N	Masculine ordinale (ordmasculine)	
187 BB	»	» N	Right angle quote (guillemotright)	
188 BC	¼	¼ N	Fraction one-fourth (Reserved)	
189 BD	½	½ N ½ N	Fraction one-half (Reserved)	
190 BE	¾	¾ N	Fraction three-fourths (Reserved)	
191 BF	¿	¿ N	Inverted question mark (questiondown)	
192 C0	À	À L	Capital A grave (Agrave)	

193 C1	Á	Á L	Capital A acute (Aacute)
194 C2	Â	Â L	Capital A circumflex (Acircumflex)
195 C3	Ã	Ã L	Capital A tilde (Atilde)
196 C4	Ä	Ä L	Capital A umlaut (Adieresis)
197 C5	Å	Å L	Capital A ring (Aring)
198 C6	Æ	Æ L	Capital AE dipthong (AE)
199 C7	Ç	Ç L	Capital C cedilla (Ccedilla)
200 C8	È	È L	Capital E grave (Egrave)
201 C9	É	É L	Capital E acute (Eacute)
202 CA	Ê	Ê L	Capital E circumflex (Ecircumflex)
203 CB	Ë	Ë L	Capital E umlaut (Edieresis)
204 CC	Ì	Ì L	Capital I grave (Igrave)
205 CD	Í	Í L	Capital I acute (Iacute)
206 CE	Î	Î L	Capital I circumflex (Icircumflex)
207 CF	Ï	Ï L	Capital I umlaut (Idieresis)
208 D0	Ð	Ð L	Capital Eth Icelandic (Reserved)
209 D1	Ñ	Ñ L	Capital N tilde (Ntilde)
210 D2	Ò	Ò L	Capital O grave (Ograve)
211 D3	Ó	Ó L	Capital O acute (Oacute)
212 D4	Ô	Ô L	Capital O circumflex (Ocircumflex)
213 D5	Õ	Õ L	Capital O tilde (Otilde)
214 D6	Ö	Ö L	Capital O umlaut (Odieresis)
215 D7	×	× N	Multiply sign (Reserved)
216 D8	Ø	Ø L	Capital O slash (Oslash)
217 D9	Ù	Ù L	Capital U grave (Ugrave)
218 DA	Ú	Ú L	Capital U acute (Uacute)
219 DB	Û	Û L	Capital U circumflex (circumflex)
220 DC	Ü	Ü L	Capital U umlaut (Udieresis)
221 DD	Ý	Ý L	Capital Y acute (Reserved)
222 DE	Þ	Þ L	Capital THORN Icelandic (Reserved)
223 DF	ß	ß L	Small sharp s, sz ligature (germandbls)
224 E0	à	à L	Small a grave (agrave)
225 E1	á	á L	Small a acute (aacute)
226 E2	â	â L	Small a circumflex (acircumflex)
227 E3	ã	ã L	Small a tilde (atilde)
228 E4	ä	ä L	Small a umlaut (adieresis)
229 E5	å	å L	Small a ring (aring)
230 E6	æ	æ L	Small ae dipthong, ligature (ae)
231 E7	ç	ç L	Small c cedilla (ccedilla)
232 E8	è	è L	Small e grave (egrave)
233 E9	é	é L	Small e acute (eacute)
234 EA	ê	ê L	Small e circumflex (ecircumflex)
235 EB	ë	ë L	Small e umlaut (edieresis)
236 EC	ì	ì L	Small i grave (igrave)
237 ED	í	í L	Small i acute (iacute)
238 EE	î	î L	Small i circumflex (icircumflex)
239 EF	ï	ï L	Small i umlaut (idieresis)
240 F0	ð	ð L	Small eth Icelandic (Reserved)
241 F1	ñ	ñ L	Small n tilde (ntilde)
242 F2	ò	ò L	Small o grave (ograve)
243 F3	ó	ó L	Small o acute (oacute)
244 F4	ô	ô L	Small o circumflex (ocircumflex)
245 F5	õ	õ L	Small o tilde (otilde)
246 F6	ö	ö L	Small o umlaut (odieresis)
247 F7	÷	÷ N	Division sign (Reserved)
248 F8	ø	ø N	Small o slash (oslash)
249 F9	ù	ù N	Small u grave (ugrave)
250 FA	ú	ú N	Small u acute (uacute)
251 FB	û	û N	Small u circumflex (ucircumflex)

252 FC	ü	ü N	Small u umlaut (udieresis)
253 FD	ý	ý N	Small y acute (Reserved)
254 FE	þ	þ N	Small thorn Icelandic (Reserved)
255 FF	ÿ	ÿ N	Small y umlaut (ydieresis)

ISO 639 language codes

ISO 639 language codes are used in **xml:lang** attributes and **public identifiers**. The following table shows some of the most common. The full list can be found in **RFC 1766** (see ftp://ds.internic.net/rfc/rfc1766.txt):

Code	Language	Code	Language
aa	Afar	mk	Macedonian
ab	Abkhazian	ml	Malayalam
af	Afrikaans	mn	Mongolian
am	Amharic	mo	Moldavian
ar	Arabic	mr	Marathi
as	Assamese	ms	Malay
ay	Aymara	mt	Maltese
az	Azerbaijani	my	Burmese
ba	Bashkir	na	Nauru
be	Byelorussian	ne	Nepali
bg	Bulgarian	nl	Dutch
bh	Bihari	no	Norwegian
bi	Bislama	oc	Occitan
bn	Bengali	om	Oromo
bo	Tibetan	or	Oriya
br	Breton	pa	Punjabi
ca	Catalan	pl	Polish
co	Corsican	ps	Pashto
cs	Czech	pt	Portuguese
cy	Welsh	qu	Quechua
ch	Chinese	rm	Rhaeto-Romance
da	Danish	rn	Kirundi
de	German	ro	Romanian
dz	Bhutani	ru	Russian
el	Greek	rw	Kinyarwanda
en	English	sa	Sanskrit
eo	Esperanto	sd	Sindhi
es	Spanish	sg	Sangro
et	Estonian	sh	Serbo-Croatioan
eu	Basque	si	Singalese
fa	Persian	sk	Slovak
fi	Finnish	sl	Slovenian
fj	Fiji	sm	Samoan
fo	Faeroese	sn	Shona
fr	French	so	Somali
fy	Frisian	sq	Albanian
ga	Irish	sr	Serbian
gd	Gaelic	ss	Siswati
gl	Galician	st	Sesotho
gn	Guarani	su	Sudanese
gr	Greek	sv	Swedish
ha	Hausa	sw	Swaheli
he	Hebrew	ta	Tamil
hi	Hindi	te	Tegulu

hr	Croatian	tg	Tajik
hu	Hungarian	th	Thai
hy	Armenian	ti	Tigrinya
ia	Interlingua	tk	Turkman
id	Indonesian	tl	Tagalog
ie	Interlingue	tn	Setswana
ik	Inupiak	to	Tonga
in	Indonesian	tr	Turkish
is	Icelandic	ts	Tsonga
it	Italian	tt	Tatar
iu	Inuktitut	tw	Twi
ja	Japanese	ug	Uigur
jw	Javanese	uk	Ukrainian
ka	Georgian	ur	Urdu
kk	Kazakh	uz	Uzbek
kl	Greenlandic	vi	Vietnamese
km	Cambodian	vo	Volapuk
kn	Kannada	wo	Wolof
ko	Korean	xh	Xhosa
ks	Kashmiri	yi	Yiddish
ku	Kurdish	yo	Yoruba
ky	Kirghiz	za	Zuang
la	Latin	zh	Chinese
ln	Lingala	zu	Zulu
lo	Laothian		
lt	Lithuanian		
lv	Latvian		
mg	Magalasy		
mi	Maori		

ISO 3166 country codes

ISO 3166 country codes are used in e-mail addresses, such as '... .co.uk' and in the **xml:lang** attribute to identify variations on the same languages (such as 'en-UK' and 'en-US'):

Code	Country	Code	Country
AD	Andorra	LA	Laos
AE	United Arab Emirates	LB	Lebanon
AF	Afghanistan	LC	Saint Lucia
AG	Antigua and Barbuda	LI	Liechtenstein
AI	Anguilla	LK	Sri Lanka
AL	Albania	LR	Liberia
AM	Armenia	LS	Lesotho
AN	Netherland Antilles	LT	Lithuania
AO	Angola	LU	Luxembourg
AQ	Antarctica	LV	Latvia
AR	Argentina	LY	Libya
AS	American Samoa	MA	Morocco
AT	Austria	MC	Monaco
AU	Australia	MD	Moldova
AW	Aruba	MG	Madagascar
AZ	Azerbaijan	MH	Marshall Islands
BA	Bosnia-Herzegovina	MK	Macedonia
BB	Barbados	ML	Mali
BD	Bangladesh	MM	Myanmar
BE	Belgium	MN	Mongolia
BF	Buerkina Faso	MO	Macau
BG	Bulgaria	MP	Northern Mariana Islands
BH	Bahrain	MQ	Martinique
BI	Burundi	Mr	Mauritania
BJ	Benin	MS	Montserrat
BM	Bermuda	MT	Malta
BN	Brunei Darussalam	MU	Mauritius
BO	Bolivia	MV	Maldives
BR	Brazil	MW	Malawi
BS	Bahamas	MX	Mexico
BT	Bhutan	MY	Malaysia
BV	Bouvet Island	MZ	Mozambique
BW	Botswana	NA	Namibia
BY	Belarus	NC	New Caledonia
BZ	Belize	NE	Niger
CA	Canada	NF	Norfolk Island
CC	Cocos Islands	NG	Nigeria
CF	Central African Republic	NI	Nicaragua
CG	Congo	NL	Netherlands
CH	Switzerland	NO	Norway
CI	Ivory Coast	NP	Nepal
CK	Cook Islands	NR	Nauru
CL	Chile	NU	Niue
CM	Cameroon	NZ	New Zealand

CN	China	OM	Oman
CO	Colombia	PA	Panama
CR	Costa Rica	PE	Peru
CU	Cuba	PF	Polynesia
CV	Cape Verde	PG	Papua New Guinea
CX	Christmas Island	PH	Philippines
CY	Cyprus	PK	Pakistan
CZ	Czech Republic	PL	Poland
DE	Germany	PM	St Pierre and Miquelon
DJ	Djibouti	PN	Pitcairn
DK	Denmark	PR	Puerto Rico
DM	Dominica	PT	Portugal
DO	Dominican Republic	PW	Palau
DZ	Algeria	PY	Paraguay
EC	Ecuador	QA	Qatar
EE	Estonia	RE	Reunion
EG	Egypt	RO	Romania
EH	Western Sahara	RU	Russian Federation
ER	Eritrea	RW	Rwanda
ES	Spain	SA	Saudi Arabia
ET	Ethiopia	SB	Solomon Islands
FI	Finland	SC	Seychelles
FJ	Fiji	SD	Sudan
FK	Falkland Islands	SE	Sweden
FM	Micronesia	SG	Singapore
FO	Faeroe Islands	SH	St Helena
FR	France	SI	Slovenia
FX	France	SJ	Svalbard and Jan Mayen Islands
GA	Gabon	SK	Slovakia
GB	Great Britain (UK)	SL	Sierra Leone
GD	Grenada	SN	Senegal
GE	Georgia	SO	Somalia
GF	Guyana	SR	Surinam
GH	Ghana	ST	St Tome and Principe
GI	Gibraltar	SV	El Salvadore
GL	Greenland	SY	Syria
GM	Gambia	SZ	Swaziland
GN	Guinea	TC	Turks and Caicos Islands
GP	Guadeloupe	TD	Chad
GQ	Equatorial Guinea	TF	French Southern Territory
GR	Greece	TG	Togo
GS	South Georgia and South Sandwich Islands	TH	Thailand
GT	Guatemala	TJ	Tadjikistan
GU	Guam	TK	Tokelau
GW	Guinea Bissau	TM	Turkmenistan
GY	Guyana	TN	Tunisia
HK	Hong Kong	TO	Tonga
HM	Heard and McDonald Islands	TP	East Timor
HN	Honduras	TR	Turkey
HR	Croatia	TT	Trinidad and Tobago
HT	Haiti	TV	Tuvalu

HU	Hungary	TW	Taiwan
IE	Ireland	TZ	Tanzania
IN	India	UA	Ukraine
IQ	Iraq	UG	Uganda
IR	Iran	UK	United Kingdom
IS	Iceland	US	United States
IT	Italy	UY	Uraguay
JM	Jamica	UZ	Uzbekistan
JO	Jordan	VA	Vatican City State
JP	Japan	VC	St Vincent and Grenadines
KE	Kenya	VE	Venezuela
KG	Kyrgyz Republic	VG	Virgin Islands
KH	Cambodia	VN	Vietnam
KI	Kiribati	VU	Vanuatu
KM	Comoros	WF	Wallis and Futuna Islands
KN	St Kitts Nevis Anguilla	WS	Samoa
KP	Korea (North)	YE	Yemen
KR	Korea (South)	YT	Mayotte
KW	Kuwait	YU	Yugoslavia
KY	Cayman Islands	ZA	South Africa
KZ	Kazachstan	ZM	Zambia
		ZR	Zaire
		ZW	Zimbabwe

HTML 2/3/4 elements and attributes

The following table shows the elements and attributes defined in each significant version of HTML. Items marked with an asterisk, '*', are not supported by the latest version of at least one of the most popular Web browsers, so should be used with caution.

There are a very large number of attributes first defined in HTML 4.0. Many of them are defined using entities. To keep this table to a reasonable size, these groups are described here, and given the names 'Core', 'Events' and 'Lang' for reference under appropriate elements.

Core attributes: Id, Type, Class, Style.

Language attributes: Lang, Dir.

Event attributes: Onclick, Ondblclick, Onmousedown, Onmouseup, Onmouseover, Onmouseout, Onkeypress, Onkeydown, Onkeyup.

However, note that when an attribute in one of these groups applies to earlier versions of HTML, it is also included explicitly.

Similarly, HTML 2.0 contains a number of SDA attributes to aid conversion of HTML elements into the ICADD DTD format. These attributes are not covered here.

Elements and Attributes	HTML 2.0	HTML 3. 2	HTML 4.0
A	YES	YES	YES
Core & Events & Lang			YES
accesskey *			YES
coords *			YES
charset *			YES
href	YES	YES	YES
hreflang *			YES
methods	YES	obsolete	
name	YES	YES	YES
onblur *			YES
onfocus *			YES
rel	YES	YES	YES
rev	YES	YES	YES
shape *			YES
tabindex *			YES
target			YES
type *			YES
title	YES	YES	YES
urn	YES	obsolete	
ABBR			**YES**
Core & Events & Lang			YES
ACRONYM			**YES**
Core & Events & Lang			YES

ADDRESS	YES	YES	YES
Core			YES
APPLET		YES	deprecated (use Object)
align		YES	
alt		YES	
archive			
code		YES	
codebase		YES	
height		YES	
hspace		YES	
name		YES	
object *			
title			
vspace		YES	
width		YES	
AREA		YES	YES
accesskey *			
alt		YES	
coords		YES	
href		YES	
nohref		YES	
onblur *			
onfocus *			
shape		YES	
tabindex *			
target			
B	YES	YES	YES
Core & Events & Lang			YES
BASE	YES	YES	YES
href	YES	YES	YES
target			YES
BASEFONT		YES	deprecated
color *			
face *			
id *			
name *			
size		YES	
BDO			YES
Core			
dir *			
lang *			
BIG *		YES	YES
Core & Events & Lang			YES
BLOCKQUOTE	YES	YES	YES
Core & Events & Lang			YES
cite *			YES
BODY	YES	YES	YES
Core & Events & Lang			YES
alink		YES	deprecated
background		YES	deprecated
bgcolor		YES	deprecated
link		YES	deprecated
onload *			YES
onunload *			YES
text		YES	deprecated
vlink		YES	deprecated
BR	YES	YES	YES
Core			YES
clear		YES	deprecated

BUTTON			**YES**
Core & Events & Lang			YES
accesskey *			YES
clear		YES	
disabled *			YES
name *			YES
onblur *			YES
onfocus *			YES
tabindex *			YES
type *			YES
value *			YES
CAPTION		YES	**YES**
Core & Events & Lang			YES
align		YES	deprecated
CENTER		YES	**deprecated**
Core & Events & Lang			
CITE	YES	YES	**YES**
Core & Events & Lang			YES
CODE	YES	YES	**YES**
Core & Events & Lang			YES
COL *			**YES**
Core & Events & Lang			
align			
char *			
charoff *			
span			
valign *			
width			
COLGROUP *			**YES**
Core & Events & Lang			
align *			
char *			
charoff *			
span *			
valign *			
width *			
DD	YES	YES	**YES**
Core & Events & Lang			YES
DEL			**YES**
Core & Events & Lang			
cite *			
datetime *			
DFN *		YES	**YES**
Core & Events & Lang			YES
DIR	YES	YES	**deprecated** (use UL)
Core & Events & Lang			YES
compact *	YES	YES	YES
DIV		YES	**YES**
Core & Events & Lang			YES
align		YES	YES
DL	YES	YES	**YES**
Core & Events & Lang			YES
compact	YES	YES	YES
DT	YES	YES	**YES**
Core & Events & Lang			YES
EM	YES	YES	**YES**
Core & Events & Lang			YES

EMBED			YES
Core & Events & Lang			
FIELDSET			YES
Core & Events & Lang			
language *			
title *			
FONT		YES	deprecated
Core & Lang			
color		YES	
size		YES	
FORM	YES	YES	YES
Core & Events & Lang			
action	YES	YES	
accept-charset *			
enctype *	YES	YES	
method	YES	YES	
onreset			
onsubmit			
target			
FRAME			YES
Core			
frameborder			
langdesc *			
marginheight			
marginwidth			
name			
noresize			
scrolling			
src			
FRAMESET			YES
Core			
cols			
onload *			
onunload *			
rows			
H1	YES	YES	YES
Core & Events & Lang			YES
align		YES	deprecated
H2	YES	YES	YES
Core & Events & Lang			YES
align		YES	deprecated
H3	YES	YES	YES
Core & Events & Lang			YES
align		YES	deprecated
H4	YES	YES	YES
Core & Events & Lang			YES
align		YES	deprecated
H5	YES	YES	YES
Core & Events & Lang			YES
align		YES	deprecated
H6	YES	YES	YES
Core & Events & Lang			YES
align		YES	deprecated
HEAD	YES	YES	YES
Lang			YES
profile *			YES
HR	YES	YES	YES
Core & Events			YES
align		YES	deprecated

noshade		YES	deprecated
size		YES	deprecated
width		YES	deprecated
HTML	**YES**	**YES**	**YES**
Lang			YES
version *			deprecated
I	**YES**	**YES**	**YES**
Core & Events & Lang			YES
IFRAME			**YES**
Core			
align *			
frameborder *			
langdesc *			
marginwidth *			
marginheight *			
marginwidth *			
name *			
scrolling *			
src *			
width *			
IMG	**YES**	**YES**	**YES**
Core & Events & Lang			YES
align	YES	YES	deprecated
alt	YES	YES	YES
border		YES	deprecated
height		YES	YES
hspace		YES	YES
ismap	YES	YES	YES
langdesc *			YES
src	YES	YES	YES
usemap		YES	YES
vspace	YES	YES	YES
width	YES	YES	YES
INPUT	**YES**	**YES**	**YES**
Core & Events & Lang			
accept *			
accesskey *			
align	YES	YES	
alt *			
checked *	YES	YES	
disabled *			
langdesc *			
maxlength *	YES	YES	
name *	YES	YES	
onblur *			
onchange *			
onfocus *			
onselect *			
readonly *			
size	YES	YES	
src	YES	YES	
tabindex *			
type	YES	YES	
usemap *			
value	YES	YES	
INS			**YES**
Core & Events & Lang			
cite *			
datetime *			

ISINDEX	YES	YES	deprecated (use INPUT)
Core & Lang			
prompt		YES	
KBD	YES	YES	YES
Core & Events & Lang			YES
LABEL			YES
Core & Events & Lang			
accesskey *			
for *			
lang *			
language *			
onblur *			
onfocus *			
title *			
LEGEND *			YES
Core & Events & Lang			YES
accesskey *			YES
align *			deprecated
LI	YES	YES	YES
Core & Events & Lang			YES
type		YES	YES
value		YES	deprecated
LINK	YES	YES	YES
Core & Events & Lang			
charset *			
href	YES	YES	
hreflang *			
media *			
rel	YES	YES	
rev	YES	YES	
title	YES	YES	
LISTING	deprecated	deprecated	obsolete (use PRE)
MAP		YES	YES
Core & Events & Lang			YES
name		YES	YES
MENU	YES	YES	deprecated (use UL)
Core & Events & Lang			
compact	YES	YES	
META	YES	YES	YES
Lang			YES
content	YES	YES	YES
http-equiv	YES	YES	YES
name	YES	YES	YES
scheme *			YES
NEXTID	YES	obsolete	
N	YES	obsolete	
NOSCRIPT			YES
Core & Events & Lang			YES
NOFRAMES			YES
Core & Events & Lang			YES
OBJECT *			YES
Core & Events & Lang			YES
align *			YES
archive *			YES
border *			deprecated
classid *			YES
codebase *			YES
codetype *			YES

declare *			YES
height *			YES
hspace *			YES
name *			YES
standby *			YES
tabindex *			YES
type *			YES
usemap *			YES
vspace *			YES
width *			YES
OL	**YES**	**YES**	**YES**
Core & Events & Lang			YES
compact	YES	YES	deprecated
start		YES	deprecated
type		YES	deprecated
OPTGROUP			**YES**
Core & Events & Lang			
disabled *			
label *			
OPTION	**YES**	**YES**	**YES**
Core & Events & Lang			YES
selected	YES	YES	YES
value	YES	YES	YES
P	**YES**	**YES**	**YES**
Core & Events & Lang			YES
align		YES	deprecated
disabled *			YES
label *			YES
PARAM		**YES**	**YES**
id *			YES
name		YES	YES
type *			YES
value		YES	YES
valuetype *			YES
PLAINTEXT	**YES**	**deprecated**	**obsolete** (use PRE)
PRE	**YES**	**YES**	**YES**
Core & Events & Lang			YES
width	YES	YES	deprecated
Q			**YES**
Core & Events & Lang			YES
cite *			YES
SAMP	**YES**	**YES**	**YES**
Core & Events & Lang			YES
SCRIPT		**YES**	**YES**
charset *			YES
defer *			YES
language			deprecated
src *			YES
type *			YES
SELECT	**YES**	**YES**	**YES**
Core & Events & Lang			
disabled *			
multiple	YES	YES	
name	YES	YES	
onchange *			
onblur *			

onfocus *			
size	YES	YES	
tabindex *			
SMALL *		YES	YES
Core & Events & Lang			YES
SPAN			YES
Core & Events & Lang			
align			
STRIKE		YES	deprecated
Core & Events & Lang			YES
STRONG	YES	YES	YES
Core & Events & Lang			YES
STYLE		YES	YES
Lang			
media *			
title *			
type *			
SUB *		YES	YES
Core & Events & Lang			YES
SUP *		YES	YES
Core & Events & Lang			YES
TABLE		YES	YES
Core & Events & Lang			YES
align		YES	deprecated
bgcolor *			deprecated
border		YES	YES
cellpadding		YES	YES
cellspacing		YES	YES
frame *			YES
rules *			YES
summary *			YES
width		YES	YES
TBODY *			YES
Core & Events & Lang			
align *			
valign *			
TD		YES	YES
Core & Events & Lang			YES
abbr *			YES
align		YES	YES
axis *			YES
colspan		YES	YES
headers *			YES
height		YES	deprecated
nowrap		YES	deprecated
rowspan		YES	YES
scope *			YES
valign		YES	YES
width		YES	deprecated

TEXTAREA	**YES**	**YES**	**YES**
Core & Events & Lang			
accesskey *			
cols	YES	YES	
disabled *			
name	YES	YES	
onblur *			
onchange *			
onfocus *			
onselect *			
readonly *			
rows	YES	YES	
tabindex *			
TFOOT *			**YES**
Core & Events & Lang			
align *			
valign *			
TH		**YES**	**YES**
Core & Events & Lang			YES
abbr *			YES
align		YES	YES
axis *			YES
colspan		YES	YES
headers *			YES
height		YES	deprecated
nowrap		YES	deprecated
rowspan		YES	YES
valign		YES	YES
width		YES	YES
THEAD *			**YES**
Core & Events & Lang			
align *			
valign *			
TITLE	**YES**	**YES**	**YES**
Lang			YES
TR		**YES**	**YES**
Core & Events & Lang			
align		YES	
bgcolor *			
valign		YES	
TT	**YES**	**YES**	**YES**
Core & Events & Lang			YES
U		**YES**	**deprecated**
Core & Events & Lang			YES
UL	**YES**	**YES**	**YES**
Core & Events & Lang			YES
compact	YES	YES	deprecated
type		YES	deprecated
VAR	**YES**	**YES**	**YES**
Core & Events & Lang			YES
XMP	**deprecated**	**deprecated**	**obsolete** (use PRE)

21. XML road map

This chapter is intended to be used as an aid to 'steering' through the XML standards, and the enclosed charts are referenced from terms appearing in the main text and Glossary.

Map formats

The 'road map' appearing in this chapter is derived from the rules that comprise the XML 1.0 standard, released in February 1998.

Each rule defines a **symbol**, using an **expression**:

```
symbol ::= expression
```

The expression is composed of at least one **token**. A token may be literal text, such as '<!', or the name of another rule, which may be considered a 'sub-rule' (so building a hierarchy of rules):

```
symbol ::= expression
           /       \
          /      symbol ::= expression
         /
      symbol ::= expression
               /     \
              /      symbol ::= expression
             /
          symbol ::= expression
```

Each rule is numbered (from 1 to 93 in the Syntax specification, and 1 to 21 in the Linking specification), and is represented in this chapter by an appropriately numbered chart. The charts appear in numeric order, just as the rules do in the standard. However, alphabetically ordered listings are included in tables that precede the charts, and the rules are also described in alphabetical order in the Glossary.

Each chart has a two-digit number, enclosed by curly brackets. For example, rule 8 is represented by the chart numbered '{08}'. The symbol name appears next to the number, and the associated expression is drawn beneath the symbol name, using a simple diagrammatic structure. In the example below, symbol one, 'aRule', includes two tokens. In this case, both components of the expression happen to be references to other expressions:

```
{17} aRule

----- anotherRule
         |
      lastRule
```

The connecting lines can only be followed across to the right or down, starting from the top-left corner of the chart. In the example above symbol one, 'anotherRule', leads down to symbol two, 'lastRule'.

The next example shows how optional structures are represented. In this example, the expression describes a structure that consists of either 'aRule' or 'alternate Rule' (followed by 'lastRule'):

```
----- aRule
  |
  --- alternateRule
         |
      lastRule
```

Occurrence rules for each token are shown using the official convention, '?' for optional, '+' for repeatable and '*' for optional and repeatable.

```
----- aRule ?
  |
  --- alternateRule *
         |
      lastRule +
```

Most charts are followed by one or more examples of their use, which appear in italic style. For example:

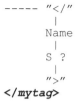

```
----- "</"
         |
      Name
         |
      S ?
         |
      ">"
</mytag>
```

Most examples only show typical usage, and should not be assumed to cover all possibilities. In some cases, however, several examples are employed to show various options. In this case, the examples are numbered:

```
1. </mytag>
2. </mytag    >
```

A space character is represented by the '^' symbol when it is not otherwise obviously present.

```
1. name
2. ^^name^^^
```

Most expressions contain symbols that refer to other rules. The reader can locate a 'sub-rule' by referring to the number appearing in curly brackets after the symbol name:

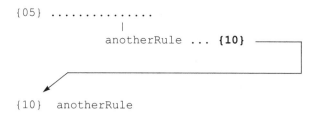

When studying a rule, it is sometimes useful to know how and where that rule is used in other charts. This can be described as 'backward' linking, and allows the reader to analyze a rule, then trace its contextual location in the standard. Every symbol in an expression is numbered, as in '{05.8}' in the example above. This is done to facilitate precise location of the reference in the other chart. Most rules form sub-units of a larger rule. The location of the reference to this rule appears next to the symbol name:

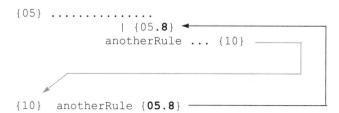

A rule may be referenced from more than one other location, in which case there will be multiple references to it, such as '{05.8} {19.12}'. When a rule is referenced several times from a single expression, an abbreviated format is used, giving '{05.8 .11}' in place of '{05.8} {05.11}'.

When specific characters are referred to, they are identified by a four-digit hexadecimal number that specifies their location in the Unicode/UCS-4 ISO 10646 character set. Note that the first 256 characters in this set are identical to ISO 646, so the ASCII/ISO 646 value for the TAB character, which is given as hexadecimal value '#x09', would be represented as '#x0009'.

Content lists

The structure of an XML document is described by hierarchies of charts. Apart from the obvious hierarchy describing the logical structure of a complete XML document, **document**$^{\{01\}}$, there are other 'top-level' charts that describe a data file that contains an external DTD, **extSubset**$^{\{30\}}$, or fragment thereof, **extPE**$^{\{79\}}$, an external text entity, **extParsedEnt**$^{\{78\}}$, and the value of an attribute when it is a set of names, **Names**$^{\{06\}}$, name tokens, **Nmtokens**$^{\{08\}}$, or a language code, **languageID**$^{\{33\}}$.

The table below lists the charts in the order that they are defined in the standard, and as they are presented in this chapter:

01 document	31 extSubsetDecl	61 conditionalSect
02 Char	32 SDDecl	62 includeSect
03 S	**33 LanguageID**	63 ignoreSect
04 NameChar	34 Langcode	64 ignoreSectContents
05 Name	35 ISO639Code	65 Ignore
06 Names	36 IanaCode	66 CharRef
07 Nmtoken	37 UserCode	67 Reference
08 Nmtokens	38 Subcode	68 EntityRef
09 EntityValue	39 element	69 PEReference
10 AttValue	40 STag	70 EntityDecl
11 SystemLiteral	41 Attribute	71 GEDecl
12 PubidLiteral	42 ETag	72 PEDecl
13 PubidChar	43 content	73 EntityDef
14 CharData	44 EmptyElemTag	74 PEDef
15 Comment	45 elementdecl	75 ExternalID
16 PI	46 contentspec	76 NDataDecl
17 PITarget	47 children	77 TextDecl
18 CDSect	48 cp	**78 extParsedEnt**
19 CDStart	49 choice	**79 extPE**
20 CData	50 seq	80 EncodingDecl
21 CDEnd	51 Mixed	81 EncName
22 Prolog	52 AttlistDecl	82 NotationDecl
23 XMLDecl	53 AttDef	83 PublicID
24 VersionInfo	54 AttType	84 Letter
25 Eq	55 StringType	85 BaseChar
26 VersionNum	56 TokenizedType	86 Ideographic
27 Misc	57 EnumeratedType	87 CombiningChar
28 doctypedecl	58 NotationType	88 Digit
29 markupdecl	59 Enumeration	89 Extender
30 extSubset	60 DefaultDecl	

The table below lists the charts in alphabetic order:

53 AttDef	09 EntityValue	58 NotationType
52 AttlistDecl	57 EnumeratedType	
41 Attribute	59 Enumeration	72 PEDecl
54 AttType	25 Eq	74 PEDef
10 AttValue	42 ETag	69 PEReference
	89 Extender	16 PI
85 BaseChar	75 ExternalID	17 PITarget
	78 extParsedEnt	22 Prolog
20 CData	**79 extPE**	13 PubidChar
21 CDEnd	**30 extSubset**	12 PubidLiteral
18 CDSect	31 extSubsetDecl	83 PublicID
19 CDStart		
02 Char	71 GEDecl	67 Reference
14 CharData		
66 CharRef	36 IanaCode	03 S
47 children	86 Ideographic	32 SDDecl
49 choice	65 Ignore	50 seq
87 CombiningChar	63 ignoreSect	40 STag
15 Comment	64 ignoreSectContents	55 StringType
61 conditionalSect	62 includeSect	38 Subcode
43 content	35 ISO639Code	11 SystemLiteral
46 contentspec		
48 cp	34 Langcode	77 TextDecl
	33 LanguageID	56 TokenizedType
60 DefaultDecl	84 Letter	
88 Digit		37 UserCode
28 doctypedecl	29 markupdecl	
01 document	27 Misc	24 VersionInfo
	51 Mixed	26 VersionNum
39 element		
45 elementdecl	05 Name	23 XMLDecl
44 EmptyElemTag	04 NameChar	
81 EncName	**06 Names**	
80 EncodingDecl	76 NDataDecl	
70 EntityDecl	07 Nmtoken	
73 EntityDef	**08 Nmtokens**	
68 EntityRef	82 NotationDecl	

Maps

{01} document *(no enclosing structures – describes logical document structure)*:

```
         {01.1}
----- Prolog ... {22}
     | {01.2}
     element ... {39}
     | {01.3}
     Misc * ... {27}

<?XML version="1.0"?>
<!-- start document type -->
<!DOCTYPE mybook SYSTEM "mybook.dtd">
<!-- start actual document -->
<mybook> ... </mybook>
<!-- end document -->
<?END my end of file processing instruction ?>
```

{02} Char (Character) {15.1} {16.3} {20.1} {65.1} {S37.1} *(also a general description of the characters allowed in a document)*:

```
----- #x0009 (tab)
  |
  --- #x000a (line feed)
  |
  --- #x000d (carriage return)
  |
  --- #x0020 > #xD7FF
  |
  --- #xE000 > #xFFFD
  |
  --- #x10000 > #x10FFFF
```

{03} S (Space) {06.2} {08.2} {16.2} {23.4} {24.1} {25.1 .2} {27.3} {28.1 .3 .5 .8 .9} {31.4} {32.1} {40.2 .4} {42.2} {44.2 .4} {45.1 .3 .5} {49.1 .3 .4 .6} {50.1 .3 .4 .6} {51.1 .2 .3 .4 .5 .7} {52.1 .3 .5} {53.1 .3 .5} {58.1 .2 .4 .5 .7} {60.1} {62.1 .2} {63.1 .2} {71.1 .3 .5} {72.1 .2 .4 .6} {75.1 .3 .5} {76.1 .2} {77.3} {80.1} {82.1 .3 .6} {83.1}:

```
  -----
    |
(repeatable)
    |
    --- #x0020 (space)
    |
    --- #x000a (line feed)
    |
    --- #x000d (carriage return)
    |
    --- #x0009 (tab)
```

{04} NameChar (Name Character) {05.2 .3 .4} {07.1}:

```
         {04.1}
----- Letter ... {84}
   |     {04.2}
   --- Digit ... {88}
   |     (04.3}
   --- CombiningChar ... {87}
   |     (04.4}
   --- Extender ... {89}
   |
   --- '.'
   |
   --- '-'
   |
   --- '_'
   |
   --- ':'
```

{05} Name {06.1 .3} {17.1} {28.2} {40.1} {41.1} {42.1} {44.1} {45.2} {48.1} {51.6} {52.2} {53.2} {58.3 .6} {59.1 .3 .4 .6} {68.1} {69.1} {71.2} {72.3} {76.3} {82.2}:

```
           {05.1}
----- Letter ... {84}
   |    |  {05.2}
   |   Namechar * ... {04}
   |
   --- " "
   |    ⊤  (05.3)
   |   NameChar * ... {04}
   |
   --- ":"
        |  (05.4)
       NameChar * ... {04}
```

1. *My•Name*
2. *_MyName*
3. *:SPECIAL*

{06} Names *(not part of any other rule – however, **TokenizedType**[56] refers to 'IDREFS' content, which is of type Names)*:

```
         {06.1}
----- Name ... {05}
     |
   (optional)
   (repeatable)
     |  {06.2}
    S (space) ... {03}
     |  {06.3}
    Name ... {05}
```

1. *MyName*
2. *My_Name Another_Name*

{07} Nmtoken (Name Token) {08.1 .3} {59.2 .5}:

```
         {07.1}
----- NameChar + ... {04}
```

66_Token

{08} Nmtokens (Name Tokens) *(not part of any other rule – however, **Token-izedType**{56} refers to 'NMTOKENS' content)*:

```
            {08.1}
----- Nmtoken ... {07}
       |
   (optional)
   (repeatable)
        |   {08.2}
        S (Space) ... {03}
        |   {08.3}
        Nmtoken ... {07}


1. 66_Token
2. 66_Token Another_Token
```

{09} EntityValue {73.1} {74.1}:

```
----- " " "
      |     |
      |    ----
      |     |
      |   (optional)
      |   (repeatable)
      |       |
      |      ---(text except for '%', '&' and '"')
      |       |     {09.1}
      |      --- PEReference ... {69}
      |       |     {09.2}
      |      --- Reference ... {67}
      |       |
      |      ----
      |         |
      |       " " "
   " ' "
      |
     ----
      |
   (optional)
   (repeatable)
       |
      ---(text except for '%', '&' and ' ' ')
       |     {09.3}
      --- PEReference ... {69}
       |     {09.4}
      --- Reference ... {67}
       |
      ----
         |
       " ' "


1. "An entity value"
2. 'an entity value with %paramRef; and &reference; in it'
```

{10} AttValue (Attribute Value) {41.3} {60.2}:

```
_____ " " "
  |     |
  |    ----
  |     |
  |  (optional)
  |  (repeatable)
  |     |
  |     ---(text except for '<', '&' and '"')
  |     |       {10.1}
  |      --- Reference ... {67}
  |     |
  |    ----
  |      |
  |     " " "
" ' "
  |
 ----
  |
 (optional)
 (repeatable)
  |
  ---(text except for '<', '&' and '"')
  |       {10.2}
  --- Reference ... {67}
  |
 ----
    |
   " ' "
```

1. `"An attribute value"`
2. `'the % is not significant'`

{11} SystemLiteral {75.2 .6}:

```
_____ " " "
  |     |
  |  (chars except for " " ")
  |     |
  |    " " "
" ' "
  |
(chars except for " ' ")
  |
 " ' "
```

1. `"C:\DTDS\MyDoc.DTD"`
2. `'C:\DTDS\MyDoc.DTD'`

{12} PubidLiteral (Public Identifier Literal) {75.4} {83.2}:

```
_____ " " "
  |     |  {12.1}
  |  PubidChar * ... {13}
  |     |
  |    " " "
" ' "
  |  {12.2}
 PubidChar * (except for " ' ") ... {13}
  |
 " ' "
```

1. `"The Big DTD"`
2. `'Another DTD Version 1.4'`
3. `'-//MyCorp/ENTITIES My Entities/EN'`

{13} PubidChar (Public Identifier Character) {12.1 .2}:

```
----- #x000a (line feed)
   |
   --- #x000d (carriage return)
   |
   --- #x0020 (space)
   |
   --- "a - z" "A - Z" "0 - 9"
   |
   --- " -'()+,./:=?;!*#@$_% "
```

{14} CharData (Character Data) {43.2}:

```
----- (not '<', '&' or ']]>')
```

```
This is character data
```

{15} Comment {27.1} {29.6} {43.6}:

```
----- "<!--"
   | {15.1}
     Char * (except "--") ... {02}
   |
   "-->"
```

```
<!--A Comment, characters < & % are all ignored-->
```

{16} PI (Processing Instruction) {27.1} {29.5} {43.5}:

```
----- "<?"
   | {16.1}
     PITarget ? ... {17}
   | {16.2}
     S ... {03}
   | {16.3}
     Char * (not including "?>") ... {02}
   |
   "?>"
```

```
<?MyInstruct AVOID ? BEFORE > IN PI ?>
```

{17} PITarget (Processing Instruction Target) {16.1}:

```
        {17.1}
----- Name (not including "xml" or "XML") ... {05}
```

```
MyInstruct
```

{18} CDSect (Character Data Section) {43.4}:

```
         {18.1}
----- CDStart ... {19}
      | {18.2}
        CData ... {20}
      | {18.3}
        CDEnd ... {21}
```

```
<![CDATA[This is <normal> text]]>
```

{19} CDStart (Character Data Start) {18.1}:

```
----- "<![CDATA["
```

```
<![CDATA[
```

{20} CData (Character Data) {18.2}:

```
        {20.1}
----- Char * (excluding "]]>") ... {02}
```

This is <normal> text

{21} CDEnd (Character Data End) {18.3}:

```
----- "]]>"
```

]]>

{22} Prolog {01.1}:

```
          {22.1}
----- XMLDecl ? ... {23}
       | {22.2}
       Misc * ... {27}
       |
  (optional)
       | {22.3}
       doctypedecl ? ... {28}
       | {22.4}
       Misc * ... {27}
```

<?XML version="1.0"?>
<!-- start document type -->
<!DOCTYPE mybook SYSTEM "mybook.dtd">
*^^^<!-- start actual document -->^^<?SHOW Show this message?>^*

{23} XMLDecl (XML Declaration) {22.1}:

```
----- "<?xml"
         | {23.1}
         VersionInfo ... {24}
         | {23.2}
         EncodingDecl ? ... {80}
         | {23.3}
         SDDecl ? ... {32}
         | {23.4}
         S (Space) ? ... {03}
         |
         "?>"
```

1. *<?XML version="1.0"?>*
2. *<?XML version='1.0' encoding="UTF-8" ?>*
3. *<?XML version='1.0' encoding="UTF-8" standalone="yes" ?>*

{24} VersionInfo {23.1}:

```
          {24.1}
----- S (Space) ... {03}
       |
     "version"
       | {24.2}
       Eq (Equals) ... {25}
       |
      ----- " ' "
      |        | {24.3}
      |        VersionNum ... {26}
      |        |
      |        " ' "
      |
     " ' "
       | {24.4}
       VersionNum ... {26}
       |
      " ' "
```

```
1. VERSION="1.0"
2. version = '1.0'
```

{25} Eq (Equals) {24.2} {32.2} {41.2} {80.2}:

```
           {25.1}
----- S (Space) ? ... {03}
      |
      "="
      |   {25.2}
      S (Space) ? ... {03}
```

{26} VersionNum {24.3 .4}:

```
  -----
      |
  (repeatable)
      |
      --- "a - z" "A - Z" "0 - 9"
      |
      --- " - "
```

```
1. 1.0
2. 1.1
3. version X99
```

{27} Misc (Miscellaneous) {01.3} {22.2 .4}:

```
           {27.1}
----- Comment ... {15}
   |    {27.2}
   --- PI (Processing Instruction) ... {16}
   |    {27.3}
   --- S (Space) ... {03}
```

```
1. <!-- end document -->
2. <?MY-PROC my processing instruction ?>
3. ^^^
```

{28} doctypedecl (document type declaration) {22.3}:

```
----- "<!DOCTYPE"
      | {28.1}
      S (Space) ... {03}
      | {28.2}
      Name ... {05}
      |
      |-----
      |     | {28.3}
      |     S (Space) ... {03}
      |     | {28.4}
      |     ExternalID ... {75}
      |     |
      -----|
            | {28.5}
            S ? (Space) ... {03}
            |
            |-----
            |     |
            |    "["
            |     |
            | (repeatable)
            |     |          {28.6}
            |    --- markupdecl ... {29}
            |     |          {28.7}
            |    --- PEreference ... {69}
            |     |          {28.8}
            |    --- S (Space) ... {03}
            |     |
            |     -----
            |         |
            |        "]"
            |         | {28.9}
            |        S ? (Space) ... {03}
            |         |
            ---------------
                     |
                    ">"
```

1. `<!DOCTYPE mybook>`
2. `<!DOCTYPE mybook SYSTEM "mybook.dtd">`
3. `<!DOCTYPE mybook SYSTEM "mybook.dtd" [ ... ] >`
4. `<!DOCTYPE mybook [ ... ] >`
5. `<!DOCTYPE mybook PUBLIC "MyPublicId" "mybook.dtd" [ ... ]>`
6. `<!DOCTYPE mybook PUBLIC "-//MyCorp//DTD My Book//EN" "mybook.dtd">`

{29} markupdecl (Markup Declarations) {28.6} {31.1}:

```
-----
   |
(optional)
(repeatable)
   |      {29.1}
  --- elementdecl ... {45}
   |      {29.2}
  --- AttlistDecl ... {52}
   |      {29.3}
  --- EntityDecl ... {70}
   |      {29.4}
  --- NotationDecl ... {82}
   |      {29.5}
  --- PI ... {16}
   |      {29.6}
  --- Comment ... {15}
```

```
<?SHOW formatted?>
<!NOTATION ......>
^^^<!-- DTD fragment -->
%OtherDecs;
<!ENTITY ...>
<!ELEMENT ...>   <!ATTLIST ...>
```

{30} extSubset (External Subset) *(no enclosing structures – the DTD file)* :

```
            {30.1}
--- TextDecl ? ... {77}
     |   {30.2}
     extSubsetDecl ... {31}

<!xml version="1.0" encoding="ISO-8859-1">
<!NOTATION ......>
<!ELEMENT ...>
%elementSet;
<!ATTLIST ...>
<![IGNORE[
   <!ELEMENT ...>
]]>
```

{31} extSubsetDecl (External Subset Declaration) {30.2} {62.3} {79.2}:

```
------
       |
   (optional)
   (repeatable)
       |        {31.1}
       --- MarkupDecl   ... {29}
       |        {31.2}
       --- conditionalSect ... {61}
       |        {31.3}
       --- PEReference ... {69}
       |        {31.4}
       --- S (Space) ... {03}

<!NOTATION ......>
<!ELEMENT ...>
%elementSet;
<!ATTLIST ...>
<![IGNORE[
   <!ELEMENT ...>
]]>
```

{32} SDDecl (Standalone Document Declaration) {23.3}:

```
            {32.1}
----- S (Space) ... {03}
       |
     "standalone"
       |   {32.2}
       Eq (Equals) ... {25}
       |
       |--------------------
       |                    |
     " " "                " ' "
       |                    |
       --- "yes" -----      --- "yes" -----
       |            |       |            |
       --- "no" -------|    --- "no" -------|
                  " " "              " ' "
```

```
1. standalone="no"
2. ^^^standalone = 'yes'
```

{33} LanguageID (Language Identifier) *(no enclosing structures – the value of the 'xml:lang' attribute, as described in RFC 1766)*:

```
                {33.1}
----- Langcode ... {34}
         |
     (optional)
     (repeatable)
         |
        "_"
         |  {33.2}
        Subcode ... {38}
```

1. *en*
2. *en-GB*
3. *i-Yiddish*
4. *x-MyCode*

{34} Langcode (Language Code) {33.1}:

```
                {34.1}
------ ISO639Code ... {35}
    |          {34.2}
    --- IanaCode ... {36}
    |          {34.3}
    --- UserCode ... {37}
```

1. *en*
2. *i-Yiddish*
3. *x-Cardassian*

{35} ISO639Code {34.1}:

```
-----   "a - z" "A - Z"
            |
        "a - z" "A - Z"
```

1. *en*
2. *fr*

{36} IanaCode {34.2}:

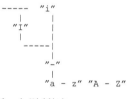

```
-----   "i"
   |         |
  "I"        |
   |         |
   -----|
        |
       "_"
        |
     "a - z" "A - Z"
```

1. *i-Yiddish*
2. *I-Yiddish*

{37} UserCode {34.3}:

```
-----   "x"
   |         |
  "X"        |
   |         |
   -----|
        |
       "_"
        |
     "a - z" "A - Z" +
```

1. *x-Cardassian*
2. *X-Cardassian*

{38} Subcode {33.2}:

```
----- "a - z" "A - Z" +

GB
```

{39} element {01.2} {43.1}:

```
            {39.1}
----- EmptyElemTag ... {44}
   |     {39.2}
  --- STag ... {40}
      | {39.3}
      content ... {43}
      | {39.4}
      ETag ... {42}
```

```
1. <image name="image13"/>
2. <para>Some content</para>
3. <para></para>
4. <para/>
```

{40} STag (Start Tag) {39.2}:

```
----- "<"
      |  {40.1}
     Name ... {05}
      |

      -----
      |    |
      | (repeatable)
      |    |  {40.2}
      |  S (Space) ... {03}
      |    |  {40.3}
      |  Attribute ... {41}
      |    |
      -------
              |  {40.4}
             S (Space) ? ... {03}
              |
             ">"
```

```
1. <emph>
2. <emph type="2">
3. <emph type = "2" style = "bold" >
```

{41} Attribute {40.3} {44.3}:

```
            {41.1}
----- Name ... {05}
      | {41.2}
      Eq (Equals) ... {25}
      | {41.3}
      AttValue ... {10}
```

```
1. type="2"
1. border = '5mm 10mm 2" 3"'
```

{42} ETag (End Tag) {39.4}:

```
----- "</"
      | {42.1}
      Name ... {05}
      | {42.2}
      S ? (Space) ... {03}
      |
     ">"
```

```
1. </emph>
2. </emph >
```

{43} content {39.3} {78.2}:

```
-----
    |
 (optional)
 (repeatable)
    |      {43.1}
    --- element ... {39}
    |    {43.2}
    --- CharData ... {14}
    |    {43.3}
    --- Reference ... {67}
    |    {43.4}
    --- CDSect ... {18}
    |    {43.5}
    --- PI ... {16}
    |    {43.6}
    --- Comment ... {15}
```

```
<!-- Some Content -->
<?ACME-WP  new_page ?>
<para>
An entity reference, such as &ref;, is not recognized in
when <![CDATA[appearing in here]]>.
</para>
```

{44} EmptyElemTag {39.1}:

```
----- "<"
      |  {44.1}
     Name ... {05}
      |
      -----
      |    |
      | (repeatable)
      |    |  {44.2}
      |   S (Space) ... {03}
      |    |  {44.3}
      |   Attribute ... {41}
      |    |
      -------
             |  {44.4}
            S (Space) ? ... {03}
             |
            "/>"
```

```
1. <revisionStart/>
2. <image name="image13" />
```

{45} elementdecl (element declaration) {29.1}:

```
----- "<!ELEMENT"
      |  {45.1}
     S (Space) ... {03}
      |  {45.2}
     Name ... {05}
      |  {45.3}
     S (Space) ... {03}
      |  {45.4}
     contentspec ... {46}
      |  {45.5}
     S ? (Space) ... {03}
      |
     ">"]
```

Note: an entity reference that contains nothing may appear after the name (because it is then just part of the space). It is included to allow the entity to contain SGML tag omission indicators, '- O', in an SGML variant of the same DTD.

```
1. <!ELEMENT image EMPTY>
2. <!ELEMENT para (#PCDATA | sub | super)* >
3. <!ELEMENT %para; (#PCDATA | sub | super)* >
4. <!ELEMENT para %paraContent;>
```

{46} contentspec (content specification) {45.4}:

```
-------- "EMPTY"
      |
     --- "ANY"
      |     {46.1}
     --- Mixed ... {51}
      |     {46.2}
     --- children ... {47}

1. EMPTY
2. ANY
3. (#PCDATA | sub | super)*
4. (title, para*)
```

{47} children {46.2}:

```
            {47.1}
----- choice ... {49}
  |      |
  |     --47-----------------
  |      {47.2}             |
  |-- seq (sequence) ... {50} |
  |      |                   |
       ---------------------|
                            |
                       --- "?"
                            |
                       --- "*"
                            |
                       --- "+"
                            |
                            *

1. (name, address, telphone)
2. (para | list)*
```

{48} cp (content particle) {49.2 .5} {50.2 .5}:

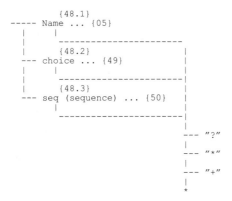

```
            {48.1}
----- Name ... {05}
  |      |
  |     ---------------------
  |      {48.2}             |
  --- choice ... {49}        |
  |      |                   |
  |     ---------------------|
  |      {48.3}             |
  --- seq (sequence) ... {50} |
         |                   |
        ---------------------|
                            |
                       --- "?"
                            |
                       --- "*"
                            |
                       --- "+"
                            |
                            *

1. address
2. address+
1. (..., ..., ...)
2. (... | ...)*
```

{49} choice {47.1} {48.2}:

```
----- "("
      | {49.1}
    S ?(Space) ... {03}
      | {49.2}
    cp ... {48}
      |
    -------
      |       |
      | (repeatable)
      |       | {49.3}
      |     S ? (Space) ... {03}
      |       |
      |     "|"
      |       | {49.4}
      |     S ? (Space) ... {03}
      |       | {49.5}
      |     cp ... {48}
      |       |
    ---------
              | {49.6}
            S ? (Space) ... {03}
              |
            ")"
```

1. *(para|list)*
2. *(para | Nlist | Alist)*
3. *(para | %listTypes;)*
4. *(company | (firstname, secondname))*

{50} seq (sequence) {47.2} {48.3}:

```
----- "("
      | {50.1}
    S ?(Space) ... {03}
      | {50.2}
    cp ... {48}
      |
    -------
      |       |
      | (repeatable)
      |       | {50.3}
      |     S ? (Space) ... {03}
      |       |
      |     ","
      |       | {50.4}
      |     S ? (Space) ... {03}
      |       | {50.5}
      |     cp ... {48}
      |       |
    ---------
              | {50.6}
            S ? (Space) ... {03}
              |
            ")"
```

1. *(para)*
2. *(%paraType;)*
3. *(name, address, tel)*
4. *(name, %addrType;, tel)*
5. *(title, (para | note)*)*

{51} Mixed (mixed content) {46.1}:

```
------ "("
   |    | {51.1}
   |    S ? (Space) ... {03}
   |    |
   |    "#PCDATA"
   |    | {51.2}
   |    S ? (Space) ... {03}
   |    |
   |    ")"
   |
  "("
   | {51.3}
   S ? (Space) ... {03}
   |
  "#PCDATA"
   |
   |-----
   |    |
   | (repeatable)
   |    | {51.4}
   |    S ? (Space) ... {03}
   |    |
   |    "|"
   |    | {51.5}
   |    S ? (Space) ... {03}
   |    | {51.6}
   |    Name ? ... {05}
   |    |
   ----------
             | {51.7}
             S ? (Space) ... {03}
             |
             ")*"
```

1. *(#PCDATA)*
2. *(#PCDATA)*
3. *(%someMixedContent;)**
4. *(#PCDATA|emph)**
5. *(#PCDATA | emph | code | name)**
6. *(#PCDATA | emph | %other; | name)**

{52} AttlistDecl (Attribute list Declaration) {29.2}:

```
----- "<!ATTLIST"
      | {52.1}
      S (Space) ... {03}
      | {52.2}
      Name ... {05}
      | {52.3}
      S ? (Space) ... {03}
      | {52.4}
      AttDef * ... {53}
      | {52.5}
      S ? (Space) ... {03}
      |
      ">"
```

1. *<!ATTLIST report date   NMTOKEN   #REQUIRED*
   author CDATA   #IMPLIED
   status (draft|final) "draft" >
2. *<!ATTLIST %para type   CDATA   "normal"*
   %otherAttrib;   >

{53} AttDef (Attribute Definition) {52.4}:

```
            {53.1}
----- S (Space) ... {03}
      | {53.2}
      Name ... {05}
      | {53.3}
      S (Space) ... {03}
      | {53.4}
      AttType ... {54}
      | {53.5}
      S (Space) ... {03}
      | {53.6}
      DefaultDecl ... {60}

 1. date NMTOKEN #REQUIRED
 2. author CDATA #IMPLIED
 3. status (draft|final) "draft" >
 4. %colourAttName; %colourGroup; %colourDefault; >
```

{54} AttType (Attribute Type) {53.4}:

```
            {54.1}
----- StringType ... {55}
    |     {54.2}
    --- TokenizedType ... {56}
    |     {54.3}
    --- EnumeratedType ... {57}

 1. CDATA
 2. NMTOKEN
 3. (draft|final)
 4. NOTATION (Tex|TROFF)
```

{55} StringType {54.1}:

```
----- "CDATA"
```

{56} TokenizedType {54.2}:

```
----- "ID"
    |
    --- "IDREF"
    |
    --- "IDREFS"
    |
    --- "ENTITY"
    |
    --- "ENTITIES"
    |
    --- "NMTOKEN"
    |
    --- "NMTOKENS"

 NMTOKEN
```

{57} EnumeratedType {54.3}:

```
            {57.1}
----- NotationType ... {58}
    |     {57.2}
    --- Enumeration ... {59}

 1. NOTATION (Tex|TROFF)
 2. (draft|final)
```

{58} NotationType {57.1}:

```
----- "NOTATION"
      | {58.1}
      S (Space) ... {03}
      |
      " ("
      | {58.2}
      S ? (Space) ... {03}
      | {58.3}
      Name  ... {05}
      |
      -----     |
      |         |
      | (repeatable)
      |     | {58.4}
      |     S ? (Space) ... {03}
      |     |
      |   " | "
      |     | {58.5}
      |     S ? (Space) ... {03}
      |     | {58.6}
      |   Name  ... {05}
      |     |
      -------
            | {58.7}
            S ? (Space) ... {03}
            |
          " ) "
```

```
1. NOTATION (Tex|TROFF)
2. NOTATION ( Tex | TROFF )
3. %NOTA; ( %imageFormats; | PostScript | %mathFormats; )
```

{59} Enumeration {57.2}:

```
----- " ("
      | {59.1}
      S ? (Space) ... {03}
      | {59.2}
      Nmtoken ... {07}
      |
      -----
      |     |
      | (repeatable)
      |     | {59.3}
      |     S ? (Space) ... {03}
      |     |
      |   " | "
      |     | {59.4}
      |     S ? (Space) ... {03}
      |     | {59.5}
      |   Nmtoken ... {07}
      |     |
      -------
            | {59.6}
            S ? (Space) ... {03}
            |
          " ) "
```

```
1. (Activate)
2. (yes|no)
3. ( red | amber | green )
4. ( %colours; )
```

{60} DefaultDecl {53.6}:

```
------ "#REQUIRED"
   |
  --- "#IMPLIED"
   |
  --------- "#FIXED"
       |         | {60.1}
       |         S (Space) ... {03}
       |         |
    --------|
             | {60.2}
             AttValue ... {10}
```

1. *#REQUIRED*
2. *#IMPLIED*
3. *"giraffe"*
4. *%defaultAnimal;*
5. *#FIXED "giraffe"*

{61} conditionalSect {31.2}:

```
        {61.1}
------ includeSect ... {62}
   |    {61.2}
  --- ignoreSect ... {63}
```

1. *<![INCLUDE[...]]>*
2. *<![IGNORE [...]]>*

{62} includeSect (included Section) {61.1}:

```
----- "<!["
      | {62.1}
      S ? (Space) ... {03}
      |
      "INCLUDE"
      | {62.2}
      S ? (Space) ... {03}
      |
      "["
      | {62.3}
      extSubsetDecl ... {31}
      |
      "]]>"
```

1. *<![INCLUDE[...%decl1;...%decl2;...]]>*
2. *<![%Switch;[...]]> <!-- when entity value is "INCLUDE" -->*

{63} ignoreSect (ignored Section) {61.2}:

```
----- "<!["
      | {63.1}
      S ? (Space) ... {03}
      |
      "IGNORE"
      | {63.2}
      S ? (Space) ... {03}
      |
      "["
      | {63.3}
      ignoreSectContents * ... {64}
      |
      "]]>"
```

1. *<![IGNORE[...%decl1;...%decl2;...]]>*
2. *<![%Switch; [...]]> <!-- when entity value is "IGNORE" -->*

{64} ignoreSectContents (ignored Section Contents) {63.3} {64.2 (recursive)}:

```
            {64.1}
----- ignore ... {65}
        |
 (repeatable)
        |
      "<!["
      | {64.2}
      ignoreSectContents ... {64}  (RECURSIVE)
        |
      "]]>"
      | {64.3}
      ignore ... {65}
```

Note: this rule calls itself, allowing nesting of ignored sections.

```
1. "ignore contents of this string"
2. ...<!-- a comment-->...
3. ...<?CODE new-page?>...
4. ...<![IGNORE[ ... <![IGNORE[...]]> ... ]]>...
```

{65} Ignore {64.1 .3}:

```
            {65.1}
----- Char * (but not '<![' or ']]>') ... {02}
```

This text must not contain consecutive "< ! [" or "]] >".

{66} CharRef (Character Reference) {67.2}:

```
----- "&#"
  |     |
  |   "0"-"9" +
  |     |
  |   ";"
  |
  --- "&#x"
        |
      "0"-"9" "a"-"f" "A"-"F" +
        |
      ";"
```

```
1. &#123;
2. &#xE2;
3. &#x7FFF;
```

{67} Reference {09.2 .4} {10.1 .2} {43.3}:

```
            {67.1}
----- EntityRef ... {68}
  |         {67.2}
  --- CharRef ... {66}
```

```
1. &myent;
2. &#123;
3. &#x7FFF;
```

{68} EntityRef (Entity Reference) {67.1}:

```
----- "&"
      | {68.1}
      Name ... {05}
        |
      ";"
```

```
&myref;
```

{69} PEReference (Parameter Entity Reference) {09.1 .3} {28.7} {31.3}:

```
----- "%"
      |  {69.1}
      Name ... {05}
      |
      ";"
```

```
%myref;
```

{70} EntityDecl {29.3}:

```
             {70.1}
----- GEDecl ... {71}
      |      {70.2}
      --- PEDecl ... {72}
```

```
1. <!ENTITY myent      "a general entity" >
2. <!ENTITY myent      %someGeneralContent>
3. <!ENTITY %EntName; "a general entity">
4. <!ENTITY % myent     "a parameter entity" >
5. <!ENTITY % %otherEnt; "a parameter entity">
6. <!ENTITY % %otherEnt; %someParameterContent; >
```

{71} GEDecl (General Entity Declaration) {70.1}:

```
----- "<!ENTITY"
      |  {71.1}
      S (Space) ... {03}
      |  {71.2}
      Name ... {05}
      |  {71.3}
      S (Space) ... {03}
      |  {71.4}
      EntityDef ... {73}
      |  {71.5}
      S (Space) ? ... {03}
      |
      ">"
```

```
1. <!ENTITY myent      "a general entity" >
2. <!ENTITY myent      %someGeneralContent;>
3. <!ENTITY %EntName; "a general entity" >
```

{72} PEDecl (Parameter Entity Declaration) {70.2}:

```
----- "<!ENTITY"
      |  {72.1}
      S (Space) ... {03}
      |
      "%"
      |  {72.2}
      S (Space) ... {03}
      |  {72.3}
      Name ... {05}
      |  {72.4}
      S (Space) ... {03}
      |  {72.5}
      PEDef ... {74}
      |  {72.6}
      S (Space) ? ... {03}
      |
      ">"
```

```
1. <!ENTITY % myent      "a parameter entity" >
2. <!ENTITY % %otherEnt; "a parameter entity">
3. <!ENTITY % %otherEnt; %someParameterContent; >
```

{73} EntityDef (Entity Definition) {71.4}:

```
        {73.1}
----- EntityValue... {09}
|       {73.2}
  --- ExternalID ... {75}
      | {73.3}
        NDataDecl ? ... {76}

1. "this is my entity"
2. PUBLIC "-//MyCorp/TEXT My entity/EN" "/ents/myent.ent"
3. SYSTEM "file:///ents/myent.ent" NDATA cgm
```

{74} PEDef (Parameter Entity Definition) {72.5}:

```
        {74.1}
----- EntityValue... {09}
|       {74.2}
  --- ExternalID ... {75}

1. "this is my entity"
2. PUBLIC "-//MyCorp/TEXT My entity/EN" "/ents/myent.ent"
3. SYSTEM "file:///ents/myent.ent"
```

{75} ExternalID {28.4} {73.2} {74.2} {82.4}:

```
----- "SYSTEM"
    |   | {75.1}
    |   S (Space) ... {03}
    |   | {75.2}
    |   SystemLiteral ... {11}
    |
    --- "PUBLIC"
        | {75.3}
        S (Space) ... {03}
        | {75.4}
        PubidLiteral ... {12}
        | {75.5}
        S (Space) ... {03}
        | {75.6}
        SystemLiteral ... {11}

1. SYSTEM "/ents/myent.ent"
2. PUBLIC "-//MyCorp/TEXT My entity/EN" "/ents/myent.ent"
```

{76} NDataDecl (Notational Data Declaration) {73.3}:

```
        {76.1}
----- S (Space) ... {03}
    |
      "NDATA"
      | {76.2}
      S (Space) ... {03}
      | {76.3}
      Name ... {05}

^^^NDATA TeX
```

{77} TextDecl (Text Declaration) {30.1} {78.1} {79.1}:

```
----- "<?xml"
      | {77.1}
      VersionInfo ? ... {24}
      | {77.2}
      EncodingDecl ... {80}
      | {77.3}
      S ? (Space) ... {03}
      |
      "?>"
```

Note: describes optional information appearing at the top of each external XML format entity file.

```
1. <?XML encoding = "UTF-8"?>
2. <?XML VERSION="1.0" encoding = "UTF-8"?>
```

{78} extParsedEnt (external Parsed Entity) *(no enclosing structures – well-formed entity containing a document fragment)*:

```
        {78.1}
----- TextDecl ? ... {77}
      | {78.2}
      content ... {43}
```

```
<?XML encoding = "UTF-8"?>
<chapter>...</chapter>
```

{79} extPE (external Parameter Entity) *(no enclosing structures – the external DTD or fragment of the DTD)*:

```
        {79.1}
----- TextDecl ? ... {77}
      | {79.2}
      extSubsetDecl ... {31}
```

```
<?XML version="1.0" encoding = "UTF-8"?>
<!ELEMENT book ...>
<!ATTLIST book ...>
<!ELEMENT chapter ...>
```

{80} EncodingDecl (Encoding Declaration) {23.2} {77.2}:

```
        {80.1}
----- S (Space) ... {03}
      |
      "encoding"
      | {80.2}
      Eq (Equals) ... {25}
      |
      |--- " " "
      |        | {80.3}
      |        EncName ... {81}
      |        |
      |     " " "
      |        |
       ------|
               |
             " ' "
               | {80.4}
             EncName ... {81}
               |
             " ' "
```

```
1. encoding="UTF-8"
2. ^^^encoding = 'UTF-8'
```

{81} EncName {80.3 .4}:

```
----- "A"-"Z" "a"-"z"
      |
   (optional)
   (repeatable)
      |
      --- "A"-"Z" "a"-"z" "0"-"9"
      |
      --- "-"
      |
      --- "_"
      |
      --- "."
```

```
UTF-8
```

{82} NotationDecl (Notation Declaration) {29.4}:

```
----- "<!NOTATION"
      | {82.1}
      S (Space) ... {03}
      | {82.2}
      Name ... {05}
      | {82.3}
      S (Space) ... {03}
      | {82.4}
      |----- ExternalID ... {75}
      |          |
      | {82.5}   -------------
      PublicID ... {83}        |
      |                        |
      -----------------------|
                             |  {82.6}
                             S ? (Space) ... {03}
                             |
                             ">"
```

1. *<!NOTATION mynota SYSTEM "/nota/mynota.not" >*
2. *<!NOTATION mynota PUBLIC "MY NOTATION" "/nota/mynota.not">*
3. *<!NOTATION mynota SYSTEM "">*
4. *<!NOTATION %aNotatName; SYSTEM "/nota/mynota.not">*
5. *<!NOTATION mynota &aNotatID;>*
6. *<!NOTATION %aNotatName; %aNotatID>*

{83} PublicID (Public Identifier) {82.5}:

```
----- "PUBLIC"
      | {83.1}
      S (Space) ... {03}
      | {83.2}
      PubidLiteral ... {12}
```

Note: describes optional information appearing at the top of each external XML format entity file.

1. *<?XML encoding = "UTF-8"?>*
2. *<?XML VERSION="1.0" encoding = "UTF-8"?>*

{84} Letter {04.1} {05.1}:

```
            {84.1}
----- BaseChar ... {85}
   |        {84.2}
   --- Ideographic ... {86}
```

Note: this rule is too large to illustrate in chart form – refer to the standard.

1. *e*
2. *e´*

{85} BaseChar (Base Character) {84.1}:

```
----- (a large range of letters from many languages)
```

Note: this rule is too large to illustrate in chart form – refer to the standard.

{86} Ideographic {84.2}:

```
----- (various unicode character ranges)
```

Note: this rule is too large to illustrate in chart form – refer to the standard.

{87} CombiningChar (Combining Character) {04.3}:

```
----- (various unicode character accents, such as "´")
```

Note: this rule is too large to illustrate in chart form – refer to the standard.

{88} Digit {04.2}:

```
----- "0"-"9"
  |
  --- (various Unicode non-Arabic digits)
```

Note: this rule is too large to illustrate in chart form – refer to the standard.

{89} Extender {04.4}:

```
----- "•" (middle dot)
  |
  --- (various Unicode characters)
```

Note: this rule is too large to illustrate in chart form – refer to the standard.

Glossary

The glossary contains a list of terms related to XML and to the additional topics covered in this book. It includes:

- XML and Xlink concepts, delimiter characters, keywords and production charts
- XSLT concepts and keywords (but not XSL or CSS formatting properties)
- SGML concepts
- HTML elements and attributes, and Internet-related terminology
- other related ISO and *de facto* standards
- database and publishing-related terminology, including popular image formats

All text before the dash, '—', is used to sort the entries, even when not highlighted. For example, '**Title** attribute — ...' appears before '**Title** element —...'.

When a term has more than one definition, each definition is preceded by a number in square brackets, starting at '*[1]*'. As an exception to this rule, element and attribute names are separated from other entries, and are distinguished by using a capital first letter (as in the text). For example, there are separate entries for 'superscript' (raised character) and 'Superscript' (the element name). But two elements with the name 'Superscript' would be numbered as described above.

Acronyms are pronounced by spelling out the letters ('XML' is pronounced 'ex-em-el') except when the entry contains '[pronounced ...]'. For example, the JPEG entry contains '[pronounced 'jay-peg']'. To make the pronunciation as clear as possible, the term is sometimes expanded to a known word that contains the sound. For example, the entry for SAX contains '[pronounced 'sax'ophone]'.

A reference to another entry is highlighted in bold typeface. In some cases, a term is not referenced from the main text at all, only from other entries in the glossary. Note that in this case the term does not appear in the index, because the index does not cover this glossary.

As in the main text, a highlighted word or phrase followed by a superscript number is actually a syntactic variable, and the number may be used to locate the relevant chart in Chapter 21.

Symbols and digits

" — Literal delimiter, '`attrib="value"`'.

— *[1]* Reserved name indicator delimiter, prefixing **INCLUDE**, **IGNORE**, **FIXED** and **PCDATA**, as in '`#INCLUDE`'. *[2]* Character separating a URL for an Internet-based document from a subdocument location, `http:www.myserver.com/mydoc#chapter2`. *[3]* Also part of character reference delimiter.

% — Parameter entity reference open delimiter, '`%entity;`'.

& — Entity reference open delimiter, '`&entity;`'.

&# — Character reference open delimiter, '`&#123;`'.

' — Literal alternative delimiter, '`attrib='value'`'.

(— Group open delimiter, '`((a & b) | c)`'.

) — Group close delimiter, '`((a & b) | c)`'.

* — *[1]* Optional and repeatable indicator, '`(a*,b,c+)`'. *[2]* In expressions, used as a wildcard to represent any element name.

+ — Required and repeatable indicator, '`(a*,b,c+)`'.

, — Sequence connector, '`(a,b,c)`'.

-- — Comment delimiter (both open comment and close comment), '`-- comment --`'.

. — In **XPath** expressions, used to represent the current node.

.. — In **XPath** expressions, used to represent the parent node.

/ — In **XPath** expressions, used as a location path step separator.

/> — Empty element close indicator, '`The house<image id="x123" />`'.

; — Reference close delimiter, '`&entity;`'.

: — In **Namespaces**, used to separate the namespace prefix from the element name, as in '`html:h3`'.

:: — In **XPath** expressions, used to separate a location direction keyword, such as 'parent' or 'child', from the name of the element, as in '`parent::chapter`'.

< — *[1]* Start-tag open delimiter, '`<element>`'. *[2]* Used in expressions to indicate less-than comparison, returning true or false.

<! — Markup declaration open delimiter, '`<!ELEMENT ..>`'.

</ — End-tag open delimiter, '`</element>`'.

<? — Processing instruction open, '`<?BREAK page?>`'..

= — *[1]* Value indicator, '`attrib=value`'. *[2]* In expressions, used to compare two expressions, returning true or false.

> — *[1]* Markup declaration close delimiter, '`<!ELEMENT ..>`'. *[2]* Tag close delimiter, '`</element>`'. *[3]* Used in expressions to indicate larger-than comparison, returning true or false.

? — Optional occurrence indicator, '`(a?, b, c?)`'.

?> — Processing instruction close delimiter, '`<?BREAK page?>`'.

@ — *[1]* Used in Internet mail addresses to separate the user ID from the domain name, as in '`neil@bradley.co.uk`'. *[2]* Used in **CSS** to identify an **at-rule**. *[3]* Used in expressions to indicate an attribute (the name follows).

[— Declaration subset open delimiter, '`<!DOCTYPE [...]>`'.

] — Declaration subset close delimiter. '`<!DOCTYPE [...]>`'.

]] — Optional section close delimiter. '`<[INCLUDE[...]]>`'.

| — Optional connector. '`(a|b|c)`'.

16-bit — Character set that uses 16 binary digits, which allows 65,536 values for representing characters. **Unicode** is a 16-bit character set.

32-bit — Character set that uses 32 binary digits, which allows 4,294,967,296 values for representing characters. **ISO/IEC 10646** is a 32-bit character set. See **7-bit** and **8-bit**.

7-bit — Character set or image format that uses 7 binary digits (**bit**s) for each character or pixel. The smallest memory unit most computer systems deal with is a **byte**, which is **8 bit**s. But data formats that use 7 bits employ the final bit for validating data transmitted between systems (making all values even or odd by setting the last bit on or off accordingly, then checking that no even (or odd) values are received at the other end). The bit combinations '0000000' to '1111111' are used to represent the decimal values '0' to '127'. **ASCII** and **ISO/IEC 646:1991** are 7-bit character sets. More reliable systems have made 7-bit data formats unnecessary. See **8-bit**.

8-bit — Character set or image format that uses 8 binary digits (**bit**s) for each character or pixel. The binary values '00000000' to '11111111' are used to represent decimal values '0' to '255'. **ISO/IEC 8859/1** is an 8-bit character set.

A

A element — An **HTML** element that locates the source or target of an **anchor**.

AAP *(American Association of Publishers)* — Organization of publishers that have defined various standard **DTDs** for **SGML**, which have been used as the basis for the latest **ISO** DTDs. See **ISO 12083**.

Abbrev element — An **HTML 4.0** element that encloses an abbreviation, using a **Title** attribute to hold the full term. See **Acronym**.

Abbreviation — See **Abbrev** element.

absolute link — A **hypertext link** that identifies a resource by its full address. See **relative link**.

absolute path — An **XPath** navigation method that locates an object by its unique identifier, rather than by its contextual location. See **relative path**.

abstract syntax — An **SGML** concept not applicable to XML that allows SGML markup syntax to be configurable, so that a **start-tag** could, for example, be described by '[para]' instead of '<para>'.

accent — A diacritical mark that modifies a base letter. For example, 'é'. The **ISOlat1** set of **entities** defines references for common European accented characters. For example, '`&eacute;`'.

access server — A computer that provides access to remote users, providing transparent access to remote networks. Sometimes called a **remote access server**.

Accesskey attribute — An **HTML 4.0** attribute to various form-related elements, holding a keyboard character that, when pressed, selects this field. A faster way to access a specific field than to step through the fields using the **Tabindex** attribute.

Acronym element — An **HTML 4.0** element that encloses an acronym, using a **Title** attribute to hold the full term. See **Abbrev**.

Action attribute — An **HTML** element to the **Form** element that identifies the **CGI** script that can process the filled-in form.

Active Link attribute — See **ALink** attribute.

Actuate attribute — The default name for the **Xlink** attribute that specifies whether a link is followed automatically (as soon as it appears on-screen) (a value of 'auto'), or is followed only when the user selects it (a value of 'user'). It is closely associated with the **Show** attribute.

Address element — An **HTML** element used to store the name and location of the author of the **page**.

address resolution protocol — See **ARP**.

Adobe Acrobat — A program that displays page images on-screen, or outputs them to paper, using the **PDF** data format. A suitable electronic publishing method when the screen presentation must exactly match page formatting.

agent — A program that operates on a user's behalf, performing its task in the background and delivering results at the end of its task. A **Web** agent may roam over the **Internet** for information of interest to the user.

Align attribute — Available in several **HTML** elements, where it is used to horizontally justify an object.

ALink attribute — An **HTML** attribute to the **Body** element that specifies the colour of hypertext links (in **A** elements) when the user is selecting that link. See **Link** attribute and **VLink** attribute.

Alt attribute — An **HTML** attribute to the **Img** element (Image) that contains suitable text to be presented if the browser is not able to display the image itself.

Alternative attribute — See **Alt** attribute.

American Standard Code for Information Interchange — See **ASCII**.

amp — The name of a reserved entity that represents the ampersand character, '&', used to avoid confusing a data character with an entity reference delimiter.

ancestor — A concept derived from the family tree describing an **element** that encloses the subject element, either directly as a **parent**, or indirectly as part of a larger **hierarchy** of elements. For example, a Book element would be the ancestor of a Paragraph, and also of the Chapter containing the Paragraph. See **child** and **sibling**.

ancestor:: — An **XPath** expression that selects an ancestor of the current node, with the given name. See **descendant::**.

anchor — A **tag** embedded in the text that serves as the **source** or **destination** of a **hypertext link**. The link is 'anchored' because it stays with the relevant text if it is moved due to insertions or deletions earlier in the document. Sometimes used to describe an element that serves as both the **target** and **source** ends of a link.

Anchor element — See **A** element.

and — Used in an expression in **XPath** to test two sub-expressions, returning true only if both sub-expressions are true. See **or**.

ANY — A keyword used to indicate that an **element** may contain all other elements defined in the **DTD** (including itself). Rarely used in practice, due to the lack of constraint on structure it encourages.

API *(Application Program Interface)* — A specification for the interface of a software package by which other programs can utilize that package. An **XML processor** must have an API through which applications can receive XML data. See **JAX** and **DOM**.

Apply Template element — An **XSLT** element used to specify that the content of the current element is to be processed against other templates. A **Select** attribute can be used to specify selected elements to be processed, and to select elements from elsewhere in the document.

apos — The name of a reserved entity that represents the apostrophe character, ' ' ', used to avoid confusing a data character with an attribute value delimiter.

appendChild method — A **DOM** method in the **Node** interface. Adds a new node to the end of the child list. It is passed the new **Node**. Returns the same Node object.

appendData method — A **DOM** method in the **CharacterData** interface. Adds the given text string to the end of the current value.

applet — A self-contained program that runs in a specific environment, usually a **Web browser**. See **applet (Java)**.

Applet element — An **HTML** element used to reference a Java program, or **applet**, via a **URL**. For example, `<applet code="http://mycorp.com/java/code/myprog.class" ...>`.

applet (Java) — A semi-compiled **Java** program accessed by a **Web browser** for activation on the local system. Source code has an extent of '.java'. Semi-compiled code, or 'bytecode', has an extent of '.class'. Machine-specific compilers are available from http://java.sun.com/download.html. See **Applet** element.

arc — A connection between two **node**s.

architectural form — The use of XML constructs to add a further layer of meaning. A syntax that rests upon XML, just as XML rests upon **Unicode**. Only specialist software applications make use of the additional information. Typically, a processing instruction format, element name, or attribute name and value provides the extra information. See **ICADD** and **XML-Link** for example applications.

area — In **XSL**, a rectangular region into which text is flowed. See **inline area** and **display area**.

Area element — An **HTML** element used in the **Map** element to assign a **URL** to a specified area of an image. Part of the 'client-sided' **image map** scheme.

area container — In **XSL**, a rectangular region containing an **area**. It has a coordinate system, but this is not utilized by **DSSSL-O** or XSL, only by the full **DSSSL** standard, which allows objects to be placed anywhere on a page.

Argument element — See **Arg** element.

ARP *(address resolution protocol)* — A **TCP/IP** protocol for locating the physical address of a node on the network.

ascending — A possible value for the **Order** attribute in **XSLT**, indicating that 'a' appears before 'b' in a sorted list.

ASCII *(American Standard Code for Information Interchange)* — [pronounced 'ass-key'] The most popular scheme for representing common characters (Latin alphabet, Arabic digits and typewriter symbols) in computer memory. Defined by ANSI (*American National Standards Institute*). A unique **7-bit** value is assigned to each character, including '65' for the letter 'A' and '49' for the digit '1' (the value of a character should not be confused with a digit character, such as '1'). The values 0 to 31 are non-printing control characters; 32 to 127 represent letters, numbers and symbols. The only relevant alternative is **EBCDIC**, used on IBM mainframe systems. See **ISO/IEC 646:1991, ISO/IEC 8859/1** and **Unicode**.

at-rule — A **CSS** rule that is used to create definitions for objects that do not map to elements, such as page layout characteristics. So called because it is identified by a 'commercial at' symbol', '@'.

AttDef[53] *(Attribute Definition)* — The part of an **attribute list declaration** (**AttlistDecl**[52] that describes one attribute for the **element**, including its name and any restrictions on the value it can take.

ATTLIST keyword — The keyword that identifies an **attribute declaration**, used to declare and define the content of one or more attributes.

AttlistDecl[52] *(Attribute list Declaration)* — The markup used to define attributes and assign them to a specific element. Although there may be more than one attribute list declaration for an element, for compatibility with SGML only one should be used.

Attr interface — Defined in the **DOM** standard, to represent an XML attribute. A subclass of the **Node** interface, adding the **getName**, **getValue** and **getSpecified** methods. Accessed using the **getAttribute** method in the **Element** interface, or the **getAttributes** method in the **Node** interface.

attribute — An **element** parameter that modifies or refines the meaning of the element, and consists of a name and a value. The attribute is named to distinguish it from other attributes and values in the same element.

Attribute — See **Attribute**[41].

attribute:: — An **XPath** expression that selects a given attribute of the current node.

Attribute[41] — The name and value of a single attribute instance, embedded in the **start-tag** (**STag**[40]), or **EmptyElemTag**[44].

Attribute class — A **DOM** class. Each instance represents one **attribute**, including its name and value.

Attribute definition — A single **attribute** definition, including its name, its requirement status, and possibly its default and allowed values. See **AttDef**[53].

Attribute element — An **XSLT** element used to create an attribute and attach it to the enclosing element (perhaps created using **Element** or **Copy**). The name of the attribute to create is given in the **Name** attribute, and optionally the **Namespace** attribute. See **Attribute Set**.

attribute list declaration — See **AttlistDecl**[52].

attribute name — The name of a defined **attribute**.

Attribute Set element — An **XSLT** element used to create a group of attributes, and give the group a reference name in the **Name** attribute, referred to using the **Use Attribute Sets** attribute in various elements. Contains a number of **Attribute** elements.

attribute type — An attribute is assigned to a category, such as 'CDATA' (character data) or 'ID' (unique identifier). See **AttType**[54].

attribute value — The value of a specific **attribute** instance. See **AttValue**[10].

AttributeList interface — Defined in the **SAX** standard, implemented by the parser. A value passed to the **startElement** method in the object that instantiates the **DocumentHandler** interface so that the application can extract details on attributes in the **start-tag**. Defines the **getLength**, **getName**, **getType** and **getValue** methods.

AttType[54] *(Attribute Type)* — A category of attribute, applied to a specific attribute. Whenever that attribute is used, its value is simply restricted in some way ('**NMTOKEN**', '**NMTOKENS**' and **enumerated** values) or may also be deemed to have some special significance ('**ID**', '**IDREF**', '**IDREFS**', '**ENTITY**', '**ENTITIES**' and '**NOTATION**').

AttValue[10] *(Attribute Value)* — The value of an attribute as its appears in the element start-tag.

auto — One possible value of the **Actuate** attribute in **XLink**, indicating that the **hypertext link** is followed without user intervention. See **user**.

AVI *(Audio Video Interleave)* — Full motion video format developed by Microsoft.

axis — In **XPath**, a direction through the document structure. Ascendents, descendants, parent, children, preceding siblings, following siblings, preceding elements (to the start of the document) following elements (to the end of the document), and attribute lists are all examples. Used in expressions with a keyword and a node filter, separated by double colons, '::', as in 'parent::chapter'.

B

B element — An element containing bold style text in the **HTML** model.

Background attribute — Used in the **Body** element in **HTML** to fill the **page** background pattern from a picture.

Background Color — See **Bgcolor** attribute.

bandwidth — The capacity of a communications channel (the amount of data transferrable in a given unit of time), specified by megabits per second (Mbps). Standard Ethernet has a bandwidth of 10Mbps.

Base element — An **XML Catalog** element for defining a base directory location, from which relative URLs are calculated, using the **PublicId** attribute.

Base Character — See **BaseChar**[85].

base64 — A data encoding scheme that transforms a **binary data** object into plain **ASCII**, so that it can be safely transferred over networks designed to handle only text. There are suggestions around for a special mechanism in XML to be defined to include embedded base64 data, usually representing image data.

BaseChar[85] *(Base Character)* — Part of a compound character, being combined with an accent or other **Ideographic**[86].

Basefont element — An **HTML** element that uses a **Size** attribute to set the default font size.

basic link — In **XLink**, a simple **hypertext link**, with one **source** and one **destination**. See also **simple link** and **extended link**.

Basic Multilingual Plane — See **BMP**.

batch composition — Document format preparation done automatically, usually on many documents in series. A suitable approach only when the source data is self-describing, such as XML documents. See **database publishing**.

batch validation — The comparison of one or more document instances against its (or their) DTD as a single process. The result is a report of errors encountered (if any). See **interactive validation**.

baud rate — the rate at which discrete signal events are transmitted on a communications channel. See **bps**.

Bgcolor attribute — Used in the **Body** element in **HTML** to set the **page** background colour. See **Text** attribute.

Big element — An **HTML** element that specifies a larger font. See **Small** element.

binary date — Data that does not conform to a textual encoding scheme. Most **image format**s use binary data files, where each byte represents a combination of pixels. In a binary format, no pre-determined meaning can be given to any particular value, as any value is possible in an image. There can be no 'end-of-file' or 'end-of-line' code.

binary entity — An **entity** with content that is either not XML format, or is XML but is not to be parsed as part of the document. It must be an **external entity**. Typically used for image data (see http://www.cis.ohio-state.edu/text/faq/usenet/graphics/fileformats-faq/part3/faq.html). See **parsed entity**.

bit — A 'binary digit'. The smallest unit of information on a computer, taking a value of '0' or '1' (or 'on' or 'off'). Collections of bits make larger units, with values that can be calculated using binary arithmetic ('00' = 0, '01' = 1, '10' = 2, '11' = 3). For example, 8 bits combine to form a **byte**, and a **7-bit** character set uses 7 bits to store unique character values, allowing only 128 possibilities.

Bits Per Second — See **BPS**.

block element — An **element** that contains a block of text, such as a title, paragraph or table cell. A block element is separated from previous and following elements by at least a line break. See **in-line element**.

Blockquote element — An **HTML** element that identifies a block of quoted text, possibly to be presented in italic style.

BMP *(Basic Multilingual Plane)* — The first 65,536 characters of **ISO/IEC 10646**, and equivalent to **Unicode** (though the two standards have diverged slightly as one is updated before the other).

BNF *(Backus-Naur Form)* — See **EBNF**.

Body element — An **HTML** element that encloses the actual document, following the **Head** element that contains information *about* the document.

bold — A heavy variation of a normal typeface. Cross-referenced terms in this glossary appear in bold typeface.

Bold — See **B** element.

boolean() — A function in an expression used in **XPath** that returns the boolean value of the enclosed expression. See **not()**.

Border attribute — Used in the **HTML** elements **Img** and **Table** to determine the thickness (or presence) of border lines.

BPS *(Bits Per Second)* — A measurement of the rate of transfer of data. A 100bps transfer rate means 12 **ASCII** characters are transmitted by one system and received by the other each second.

Br element — An **HTML** element that forces a new line.

Browser — An application designed to read and display tagged text, allowing **hypertext links** to be followed. See **HTML Browser**.

BTW — Abbreviation for 'By The Way' used in online conversation. Others include **IMHO** (In My Humble Opinion), **FWIW** (For What It's Worth), **FYI** (For Your Information) and **OTOH** (On The Other Hand).

byte — A unit of memory composed of 8 **bit**s (short for 'by eight'). Using binary arithmetic, a byte can store values between '00000000' and '11111111' (or '0' to '255' in decimal). Currently, most **character set**s use one byte to represent one character, giving 256 combinations for an **8-bit** character set. When one bit is ignored, or used for parity checking, this leaves only 128 character values available in a **7-bit** set, such as **ASCII**. Proposed character sets use two or four bytes for each character, vastly expanding the range of available characters. Some image formats use byte values to represent pixels.

C

Call Template element — An **XSLT** element that is used to call in a pre-defined reusable template, using the **Name** attribute.

CALS *(Continuous Acquisition and Lifecycle Support)* — [pronounced 'kalz'] Set of standards (before 1994 standing for *Computer-aided Acquisition and Logistics Support*), including **DTD**s, **CCITT Group IV**, **CGM** and **IGES**, and an electronic delivery standard for transfer of documentation between defence contractors and the US Department of Defense. Notable for **CALS table**s and the **CALS declaration**. Contact http://www.acq.osd.mil/cals/.

CALS declaration — An **SGML Declaration** defined for use with **CALS** DTD. Notable primarily for extending the number of characters allowed in element and attribute names from 8 to 32.

CALS table — An **SGML** table model defined in the **DTD**s developed in the **CALS** initiative, now used in many other applications due to widespread software support, including **WYSIWYG** editing. Defined in 'MIL SPEC 28001-B Appendix A-50', and refined by the **SGML Open** committee in 1995.

canonical — An idea or object reduced to its simplest possible representation. This concept applies to string comparisons when each string may contain the same information, but originally coded using different options.

CAPS *(Computer Aided Publishing System)* — [pronounced 'caps'] Combined database and pagination system, possibly used for on-demand printing, and feasibly involving the use of XML.

Caption element — An **HTML** element that holds the title of a table, to be placed above or below the table contents.

carriage return — See **CR**.

Cascading Style Sheets — See **CSS**.

case folding — The act of converting **lower-case** characters to **upper-case** equivalents to assist string comparisons where differences of case are not relevant. After case folding, the string 'This Text' will match the string 'THIS TEXT', or 'this text'.

Case Order attribute — An **XSLT** attribute to the **Sort** element, specifying how lower-case and upper-case letters, such as 'a' and 'A', are sorted in relation to each. When set to '**lower-first**', 'a' appears before 'A'. When set to '**upper-first**', 'A' appears before 'a'. See **Order**.

catalog — A file containing mappings between a **public identifier** and its **system identifier** counterparts. For example, 'MyEnt' may be mapped to '/ENTS/MYENT.XML' and '-//MyCorp//DTD My DTD//EN' may be mapped to '/ENTS/MYDTD.DTD'. Used by an **entity manager**. See **SGML Open** for a standard catalog format.

catalogue — UK spelling of **catalog**.

CCITT Group IV — Compression scheme for bi-level (on/off pixels, not suited for representing gray scales or colours) bit-mapped (**raster**) image data, optimized for images containing lines of text. Adopted as an **ODA** format (along with CCITT Group III). Adopted as one of the **CALS** standards. May be stored in a **TIFF** file 'wrapper'.

CDATA *(Character Data)* keyword — The keyword that identifies data consisting of normal text characters; no markup recognition is attempted on encountering significant markup delimiter characters.

CDATASection interface — Defined in the **DOM** standard, to represent an XML character data section. A subclass of the **Node** interface, adding no new methods. A CharacterData object is created using the factory method **createCDATASection** in the **Document** interface.

CData[20] *(Character Data)* — Data consisting of normal text characters; no markup recognition is attempted on encountering significant markup delimiter characters. Part of a Character Data Section (**CDSect**[18]).

CDEnd[21] *(Character Data End)* — The terminating markup delimiters of a Character Data Section (**CDSect**[18]). The characters ']]>' end the special treatment of characters.

CDF *(Channel Definition Format)* — A standard for the use of XML markup to identify a Web site with push capability, including which pages are channel pages, the icon to display, a title and a description of the channel.

CDSect[18] *(Character Data Section)* — A section of the document consisting of normal text characters; no markup recognition is attempted on encountering significant markup delimiter characters. It is bounded by the **CDStart**[19] delimiter, '<![CDATA[', and the **CDEnd**[21] delimiter, ']]>'.

CDStart[19] *(Character Data Start)* — The starting markup delimiters of a Character Data Section (**CDSect**[18]). The characters '<![CDATA[' begin special treatment of characters.

ceiling() — Used in an expression in **XPath** to convert a real number into an integer by rounding up to the nearest whole number. See **round()** and **floor()**.

Cellpadding attribute — Used by the **Table** element in **HTML** to adjust the space between the cell content and its borders. See **Cellspacing** attribute.

Cellspacing attribute — Used by the **Table** element in **HTML** to adjust the space between cells. See **Cellpadding** attribute.

Center element — An **HTML** element used to centre all enclosed structures. See **Div** element.

CERT *(Computer Emergency Response Team)* — Organization formed to increase awareness of Internet security issues. Contact cert@cert.org.

CGI *(Common Gateway Interface)* — A standard method for software to dynamically create customized **HTML** pages, facilitating a two-way exchange of information between the **Web server** and the user of a **Web browser**. A CGI script can be written in any language (though the most popular is Perl), and can therefore access various sources of information, such as an SQL database. One use of a CGI script is to process **form**s that are filled in by the user (using the **Action** attribute), and another is to create and return customized HTML pages based on information gathered from such a form. Contact comp.infosystems.www.authoring.cgi' news group and http://hoohoo.ncsa.uiuc.edu/cgi/interface.html.

CGM *(Computer Graphics Metafile)* — An **ISO** standard (ISO 8632) for representing two-dimensional object based **vector** images. Adopted as part of the **CALS** standard (MIL-D-28003). Contact http://www.agocg.ac.uk:8080/agocg/CGM.html.

Channel Definition Format — See **CDF**.

Char[02] *(Character)* — The character set of XML, from the **ISO 10646** set. Also see **Unicode**.

character — A letter, digit or symbol represented within a computer by a numeric code. Generally grouped into **character set**s.

Character — See **Char**[02].

Character Data — Data that does not contain markup, so markup delimiter characters may be safely used without risk of confusion. See **CData**[20].

Character Data End — The markup construct that identifies the end of a **Character Data Section**. See **CDEnd**[21].

Character Data Section — Part of an XML document that may contain markup delimiter characters which are not to be interpreted as markup. See **CDSect**[18].

Character Data Start — The markup construct that identifies the start of a **Character Data Section**. See **CDStart**[19].

character number — A value that represents a character. For an **8-bit** character set, the number will be in the range 0–255. As the letter 'A' has a value of 65 (decimal) in **ASCII**, its character number would be '65'. **Hexadecimal** notation is often used, especially in **Character Reference**s.

Character Reference — A markup construct that represents a single character (usually a character that is normally interpreted as a markup delimiter or is not possible to generate directly from the keyboard). For example, 'Ӓ' represents the **Unicode** character with the **hexadecimal** value 1234. See **CharRef**[66].

character set — An ordered set of **character** definitions. A value is assigned to each character shape (or 'glyph'). The number of characters held in a set is determined by the number of **bit**s assigned to each character. Currently, most character sets are **8-bit** sets, holding 256 characters. See **ASCII**, **EBCDIC**, **ISO/IEC 646:1991** and **ISO/IEC 10646**.

CharacterData interface — Defined in the **DOM** standard, to represent objects that have text content (the **Text**, **Comment** and **CDATASection** interfaces) that may need additional editing functions. A subclass of the **Node** interface, adding the **getData**, **setData**, **getLength**, **appendData**, **substringData**, **insertData**, **deleteData** and **replaceData** methods.

characters method — A **SAX** method defined in the **DocumentHandler** interface. Called by the parser when a block of text in an element is detected. A character array, start offset and length value are passed to it. See **ignorableWhitespace** method.

CharData[14] *(Character Data)* — The textual content of an XML document, as distinct from the various **markup** constructs.

CharRef[66] *(Character Reference)* — A special form of **entity reference** that has a replacement value of a single **character**. Requires a preceding '#' symbol. For example, '`&#1234;`'. A **hexadecimal** value can be used by inserting the letter 'x' before the digits. For example, '`&#x1F8D;`'.

Charset attribute — An **HTML 4.0** attribute to the **Script** element. Used in conjunction with the **Src** attribute to identify the character set used in the file.

Checked attribute — An **HTML** attribute to the **Input** element. Used to pre-select a check-box option.

Chemical Markup Language — See **CML**.

child — A concept derived from family trees that describes an **element** that is enclosed by another element (as part of a **hierarchy** of elements). One element is the child of another, and an element may have several children. For example, a Chapter element may be the child of a Book element, and itself may contain several Section children. See **parent** and **sibling**.

child:: — An **XPath** expression that selects a node by name that is a child of the current node. Abbreviates to nothing, so 'child::para' is the same as 'para'.

Children[47] — The legal content of an element, including text and/or **child** elements.

Choice — See **Choice**[49].

Choice[49] — The content of an element, when defined in the **DTD** to be a choice of one or more elements. The '|' symbol is used to separate the names of available elements. The alternative model is **Seq**[50] (sequence).

choice connector — The '|' symbol used to separate the names of available elements, to be used in any order.

Choose element — An **XSLT** element used to test options within a template, reducing the number of templates needed. Each option is enclosed in **When** elements. A more specialized form of test than the **If** element provides, as there is a default condition enclosed by the **Otherwise** element.

Citation element — See **Cite** element or **Cite** attribute.

Cite attribute — An **HTML 4.0** attribute to the **Del** and **Ins** elements, specifying the location of a document that contains details on the deletion or insertion made. See **Datetime** attribute.

Cite element — An **HTML** element used to contain a citation (reference or quotation).

Class attribute — An **HTML** attribute added to almost all elements in **HTML 4.0**, allowing any element to be divided into sub-groups which may be distinctly processed or given a specific style from a remote **style sheet**.

Clear attribute — An **HTML 3.2** attribute to the **Br** element that forces following text to clear 'all' floating images (the default), or just the floating images on the 'left' or 'right' sides.

client — An application that requests services from a **server** application, usually over a network. For example, a **Web browser** acts as a client to each **Web server** it connects to. See **peer-to-peer**.

cloneNode method — A **DOM** method in the **Node** interface. Returns a copy of the given **Node** object. If a boolean parameter is set to true, all descendants are also copied to create a duplicate tree fragment.

CML *(Chemical Markup Language)* — A private initiative to determine an XML markup scheme for chemical formulae. See http://www.venus.co.uk/omf/cml/doc/index.html.

Code element — An **HTML** element used to contain examples of computer code, typically displayed in a mono-spaced font.

Codebase attribute — An **HTML** attribute to the **Applet** element, specifying the name and location of the **Java** program to run.

Col element — An **HTML 4.0** element that allows one or more columns to be identified by name and styled (overriding the style given to a row). See **Colgroup** element.

Colgroup element — An **HTML 4.0** element that allows one or more columns to be identified by name and styled (overriding the style given to a row). May enclose **Col** elements that define different styles to single or multiple sub-groups of columns.

collapsed space — The replacement of a consecutive **white space** characters with a single space character, such as ' [TAB] [CR][CR] [LF][TAB] ' with ' '.

Color attribute — An **HTML** attribute to the **Font** element that changes the colour of the text. See **Text** attribute.

Cols attribute — An **HTML** attribute to the **Textarea** and **Frameset** elements.

Colspan attribute — An **HTML 3.2** attribute to the **Td** and **Th** elements, used to span a table cell over subsequent columns. See **Rowspan**.

Column — See **Col** element.

Column Group — See **Colgroup** element.

Combining Character — See **CombiningChar**{87}.

CombiningChar{87} *(Combining Character)* — Various characters built from two **Unicode** character shapes. This technique avoids having to define thousands of extra characters, and forms part of the **NameChar**{04} rule for defining names of markup constructs.

Comment — See **Comment**{15}.

Comment{15} — A **markup** declaration that holds explanatory text not considered part of the document content. Similar to comments in program source code. Comments have no effect on processing and do not appear in published documents. A comment may be inserted by a **DTD** author or by a document author. It is delimited by '<!--' and '-->'.

comment() — A function of a navigation expression used in **XPath** that identifies any **comment** object in the document tree. See **node()**.

Comment element — An **XSLT** element used to create a comment in the output file (using a real comment in the style sheet does not work, as this is a comment for the style sheet, not the output document). See **Processing Instruction** element.

Comment interface — Defined in the **DOM** standard, to represent an XML comment. A subclass of the **CharacterData** interface, adding no new methods. A Comment object is created using the factory method **createComment** in the **Document** interface.

Common Gateway Interface — See **CGI**.

Compact attribute — An **HTML** attribute to various list type elements, indicating that items in the list should be as close together as possible.

compile — The automated conversion of information from a human-readable form into a more efficient, machine-readable format. For example, keywords are converted into numeric tokens, which can be read faster by machine, but are unintelligible to people. A computer program that is compiled (such as C) operates faster than one that is merely **interpreted** (using an **interpreter**) (such as Perl). An XML DTD and even XML documents may be compiled for use with a specific software application in order to improve performance (though often at the expense of usability with other software).

compiler — A software application or module of a larger program that **compile**s information.

component management — The storage of document parts in a document management system that is able to re-create the document or parts of the document at will and allows parts to be shared by many documents.

compose — The process of converting **tag**ged data into formatted output, including hyphenation and justification of the text.

composition — See **compose**.

compound document — A document containing more than just text, for example images and sound.

concat() — In an **XPath** expression, used to concatenate strings into a single string.

concrete syntax — In **SGML**, the instructions that define the system environment and choose optional features of the language in the **SGML Declaration**.

conditional Section — See **conditionalSect**[61].

conditionalSect[61] *(Conditional Section)* — A segment of the document that is marked for explicit inclusion (**includeSect**[62]) or exclusion (**ignoreSect**[63]), using a **markup declaration** that includes the 'INCLUDE' or 'IGNORE' keywords respectively. Only allowed in the **external subset** of a **DTD**.

connector — A symbol that connects tokens and describes the relationship between them. The optional connector, '|', indicates a choice of tokens; 'a | b' provides a choice between A and B. The sequence connector, ',', indicates a sequence; 'a , b' specifies that A precedes B.

container element — An element that contains text and/or other elements, enclosed in a **start-tag** and **end-tag** pair. See **empty element**.

contains() — Used in an expression in **XPath** to test for the presence of one string within another. See **starts-with()** and **normalize()**.

content — See **content**[43].

content[43] — The content of an **element**, delimited by a **start-tag** and **end-tag**. An **empty element** has no content.

Content attribute — An **HTML** attribute to the **Meta** element that provides a value associated with meta data (identified by the **Name** attribute).

Content Role attribute — An attribute used in **XLink** to provide a role or classification for an in-line linking element.

content specification — See **contentspec**[46].

contentspec[46] — The definition of the content of an **element**, including **child** elements, **mixed text**, or **empty** element.

content particle — See **cp**[48].

Content Title attribute — An attribute used in **XLink** to provide a title for the content of an in-line linking element, so that browsers of other documents in the relationship can identify it and decide whether to follow a link to it. See **Title** attribute.

content token — Part of a **model group**, defining the use of text, or an **element** or **group** of elements.

control character — A non-visible character that is used by the system to perform special tasks, such as end a line or page of text.

Copy element — An **XSLT** element used to output a copy of the source element. Attributes can be added to the output element using the **Attribute** element.

Copy Of element — An **XSLT** element used to select (using a **Select** attribute) a fragment of the source document for direct copy through to output, without processing the content of the fragment.

Coords attribute — An **HTML** attribute to the **Area** element, used to define the coordinates of an active area of an image.

count() — Used in an expression in **XPath** to return the number of matches found by the embedded expression.

Count attribute — An **XSLT** attribute to the **Number** element, used to specify which elements are to be included in a multi-part counter. Used in conjunction with the **Format** attribute. For example, 'count="chapter|table"' and 'format="1.A"' would number each table with a numeric count of the containing chapter and an alphabetic count of the table within the chapter.

cp[48] *(content particle)* — One token in a list of elements in an element declaration, including an occurrence indicator for the named element, which can be '?' (optional), '*' (optional and repeatable) or '+' (must occur and is repeatable).

CR *(Carriage Return)* — A control character used to terminate lines, alone or in combination with **LF** *(Line Feed)*, by many operating systems. The RE *(Record End)* is assigned to this character by the **reference concrete syntax**.

createAttribute method — A **DOM** method in the **Document** interface. It is passed the name of the **attribute** to create. Returns a newly created **Attr** object.

createCDATASection method — A **DOM** method in the **Document** interface. It is passed the name of the **character data section** to create. Returns a newly created **CDATASection** object.

createComment method — A **DOM** method in the **Document** interface. It is passed the name of the **comment** to create. Returns a newly created **Comment** object.

createDocumentFragment method — A **DOM** method in the **Document** interface. It returns a newly created **DocumentFragment** object.

createElement method — A **DOM** method in the **Document** interface. It is passed the name of the **element** to create. Returns a newly created **Element** object.

createEntityReference method — A **DOM** method in the **Document** interface. It is passed the name of the **entity reference** to create. Returns a newly created **EntityReference** object.

createProcessingInstruction method — A **DOM** method in the **Document** interface. It is passed the name of the **processing instruction** to create. Returns a **ProcessingInstruction** object.

createTextNode method — A **DOM** method in the **Document** interface. Returns a newly created **Text** object.

CRLF — See **CR**.

crop marks —Marks on a sheet of paper that identify the edge of the page it contains, so that it can be cut (or 'cropped') for binding into a book. See **cross marks**.

cross marks —Marks on a sheet of paper that allow pages to be aligned for folding and binding into a book. See **crop marks**.

CSS *(Cascading Style Sheets)* — A **W³C** standard for applying styles to elements. A 'style sheet' is a set of instructions (at least one **CSS rule**) held remotely from the elements they refer to. It is 'cascading' because an **in-line** definition overrides a definition at the top of a document, which in turn overrides a definition in a separate style sheet. Supported by the most popular **Web browser**s. An extended version, known as 'CSS2', is under development (see http://w3.org/TR/WD-css2/). See **XSL**.

CSS declaration — A **CSS** instruction that defines styles for an element, possibly in a specific context, using at least one **CSS rule**.

CSS rule — A **CSS** instruction that defines a style to an element, all or part of a **CSS declaration**.

CSS selector — Each **CSS rule** must start with a 'selector' which identifies an element, or an element in context, that 'trips' this rule.

CSV *(Comma Separated Values)* — A **text file** that uses commas to separate values and line-end characters to separate rows. Typically used as an interchange format between spreadsheet applications and simple **flat-file database**s.

```
object,animal,vegetable,mineral
cat,yes,no,no
cabbage,no,yes,no
```

current attribute — An **SGML** attribute requirement option of 'CURRENT', indicating that the attribute value, if not stated, is the same as a previously declared value. For example, if the Section element for section one had a Status value of 'secret', and the Section element for section two had no value, its Status attribute would inherit the value of 'secret'.

D

data content — The element can only contain data, not **child** elements. Not described by a formal rule, but an informal name for any content model that includes the #PCDATA keyword.

data entity — Non-parsable, non-XML data. See **parser** and **XML Entity**. Alternative term for **binary entity**.

data stream — Term used to describe the processing of a data file, character by character, with the first character in the file heading the stream of input to the application. Some data formats are designed to assist processing in a single direction, including XML, which is why the **prolog** must precede the **document instance** (at no point should a **parser** need to 'rewind' to an earlier point in the file).

Data Type attribute — An **XSLT** attribute to the **Sort** element, specifying strings that consist of digits should be sorted. When set to '**text**', '12' appears before '7' because the first character '1' has a smaller **ASCII** value than '7'. When set to '**number**', '7' appears before '12' because it is a smaller value. See **Order**.

Datetime attribute — An **HTML 4.0** attribute to the **Del** and **Ins** elements, specifying the date and time the deletion or insertion was made. See **Cite** attribute.

database — A collection of information, organized to be easily accessible. The term is often used in a stricter sense, to describe a **table**, containing **record**s, or several tables that are interlinked via unique record identifiers. See **flat-file database**, **relational database** and **object database**.

DataBase Management System — See **DBMS**.

database publishing — Publishing directly from a database. Suitable for highly structured information. For example, bus timetable. The term may be used in a wider sense, to describe publishing of any highly organized, self-describing information, such as a collection of XML documents, when it would include **batch composition** as a necessary component of the system.

DBMS *(DataBase Management System)* — The software that provides access to a **database**, controlling concurrent access to the data, and interpreting commands framed in a **query language**.

Dd element — An **HTML** element describing a definition entry, following a definition term, **Dt** element, and containing any number of other text structures. Enclosed by a **Dl** element.

DDML *(Data Definition Management Language)* — See **schema**.

Decimal Separator attribute — An **XSLT** attribute to the **Locale** element, specifying the character to use as a separator in deimal numbers (full-point, '.' in English).

declaration — A **tag** that is used to help specify the document structure.

declaration subset — A mechanism by which some **declaration**s can contain other declarations, by enclosing them in square brackets, '[' and ']'. For example, the declarations that form all or part of the **DTD** are enclosed in the **doctypedecl**$^{\{28\}}$.

Default Declaration — See **DefaultDecl**$^{\{60\}}$.

DefaultDecl$^{\{60\}}$ — The final part of an attribute definition (**Attdef**$^{\{53\}}$), which declares whether the attribute is required, optional, fixed, or has a default value should none be provided by the document author.

default entity — An **SGML** concept (not applicable to XML). An entity that provides a replacement value for all references to non-existent entities. Possibly used to prevent error messages, or replace references to unknown entities with a message, such as 'SOMETHING MISSING HERE'. There can be only one default entity in an SGML **DTD**.

default namespace — A **namespace** that does not have to be made explicit in each element or attribute, by adding a prefix.

Default Space attribute — An **XSLT** attribute to the **Stylesheet** element, used to indicate that **white space** can be removed from the source document, when its value is set to 'strip'. Used with the **Preserve Space** or **Strip Space** elements to create a list of specific elements from which to strip white space.

default value — The value of an **attribute** when no value is entered by the document author during insertion of the **element** containing that attribute. Alternatively, the value can be pre-defined (FIXED), be REQUIRED or optional (IMPLIED), or take the same value as the previous occurrence of the attribute (CURRENT).

Defer attribute — An **HTML** attribute to the **Script** element, specifying when set to 'true' that running the script can be left until after rendering the document content, as the script does not modify the content of the document.

Defining Element — See **DFN** element.

Definition Entry — See **Dd** element.

Definition List — See **Dl** element.

Definition Term — See **Dt** element.

Del element — An **HTML 4.0** element used to highlight text officially deleted from the document, but still present to show the history of the document. Typically styled with a line-through. Optional **Datetime** and **Cite** attributes specify the time of the amendment and locate a comment regarding the change. See **Ins** element.

deleteData method — A **DOM** method in the **CharacterData** interface. Removes text from the string value of the **Node**. It is passed start and length values and returns. Returns nothing.

Delegate element — An **XML Catalog** element for delegating entity mappings to subsidiary catalogue files, using common **public identifier** prefixes, using the **PublicId** and **HRef** attributes. For example, '-//ACME' identifies all entities beginning with this string, and queries the catalogue file named in the HRef attribute for a fully matching entry mapping. See **Extend**.

Deletion — See **Del** element.

delimiter role — A character or series of characters that identify **markup** embedded within the text have a delimiter role. The '<' character has a delimiter role, sometimes in conjunction with other characters, such as '<!' and '<?'.

descendant — An element that is enclosed either directly or indirectly by another element. All elements are descendants of some other element, except for the **document element** (the 'root' element).

descendant:: — An **XPath** expression that selects a descendant of the current node, with the given name. See **ancestor::**.

descendant-or-self:: — An **XPath** expression that selects all nodes that conform to the given name and are children, or other descendents of the current node. 'self:node()/descendant-or-self::node()' is the same as './/'

descending — A possible value for the **Order** attribute in **XSLT**, indicating that 'b' appears before 'a' in a sorted list.

descriptive markup — A **markup** scheme that describes the significance of each part of a document, without referring to how the document should appear when published, which is the task of **procedural markup**. Both XML and **SGML** facilitate descriptive markup, but do not enforce it. A descriptive document can easily be translated into procedural markup, but the opposite is not true.

designated resource — An **XLink** term used to describe a **resource** that is designated (pointed to) in some way.

DeskTop Publishing — See **DTP**.

DFN element — An **HTML** element that identifies the first or most significant occurrence of a key term.

digit — A numeric character ('0'–'9'). See **digit**{88}.

digit{88} — The characters '0'–'9'. Optionally appearing as part of a name (**Name**{05}), or name token (**Nmtoken**{07}).

Dir attribute — An **HTML** attribute added to almost all elements in **HTML 4.0**, indicating the writing direction used for the text, which is closely associated with the **Lang** attribute.

Dir element — An **HTML** element that contains a directory listing. Rarely used.

Directed Linked Graph — See **DLG**.

Directory List element — See **Dir**.

DIS *(Draft International Standard)* — An **ISO** standard in progress to becoming an **IS** (*Industry Standard*).

display property — A CSS property type that is rarely used in HTML style sheets but is vital for XML as it defines what kind of object the XML element is. For example, a Paragraph element and a Title would be assigned as 'block' types, whereas Emphasis and Subscript elements would be 'in-line'.

Div element — An **HTML 3.2** element that groups other structures that are aligned in the same way, using an **Align** attribute. See **Center** element and **Span** element.

Division — See **Div** element.

Dl element — An **HTML** element describing a definition list, containing at least one pair of **Dt** and **Dd** elements. Commonly used for glossary lists.

DLG (*Directed Linked Graph*) — A system of representing relationships using **arc**s and **node**s. Inherent in the **XML-Data** and **RDF** schemes.

DNS *(Domain Name Server)* — A server that stores the relationships between **domain name**s and **IP address**es (e.g. 'bradley.co.uk' is the domain name for IP address '194.73.182.107').

DocBook DTD — See **OASIS**.

doctypedecl{28} *(document type declaration)* — A markup declaration that appears at the top of an XML **document**, specifying the document element, enclosing the **internal subset** of a **DTD** and pointing to the **external subset**.

document — In this context, an entire XML formatted document, but not including the external DTD subset or other entity. See **document**{01}.

document{01} — The top-level rule describing the format of an XML document, including the **internal subset** of a **DTD**.

Document class — A **DOM** class. Each instance represents one XML document, and includes methods for setting and retrieving the **document element**.

Document Context class — A **DOM** class. Each instance contains general information about an XML document. At the moment, this only includes retrieving the **Document class**.

Document element — The default name for the **XLink** element that identifies one document in a group of interlinked documents. See **Group** element.

document element — The outermost **element** in the document **hierarchy**. The ultimate **ancestor** of all elements in the document. The 'root' element.

document entity — The **entity** that is not called in from any other entity, contained in the file that is selected by the user or given to the **parser**. It contains the **document type declaration** and *may* contain the bulk of the **document instance** data.

document instance — The 'real' document, following system and document defining rules. Defines the content of the document, including **markup** and text.

Document interface — Defined in the **DOM** standard, to represent an XML document. A subclass of the **Node** interface, adding the **getDoctype, getImplementation, getDocumentElement** and **getElementsByTagName** methods.

document management — The task of storing and controlling documents. A document management system provides receipt, creation, referencing, retrieval, distribution, output and disposal features. A **database** forms the core of the system, so allowing documents to be located quickly and easily. See **editorial system**.

Document Object Model — See **DOM**.

document structure — The allowed combination of elements in a given document type, including hierarchical and sequential constraints.

Document Style Semantics and Specification Language — See **DSSSL**.

Document Style Semantics and Specification Language – Online — See **DSSSL-O**.

document type declaration — See **doctypedecl**[28].

Document Type Definition — See **DTD**.

DocumentHandler interface — Defined in the **SAX** standard, to be implemented by objects that can process document events, such as start-tags, comments and text blocks. Defines the **startDocument, endDocument, startElement, endElement, characters, ignorableWhitespace, processingInstruction** and **setDocumentLocator** methods. Must be registered with the parser using the **setDocumentHandler** method in the object that instantiates the **parse** interface. See the **EntityResolver, AttributeList, DTD Handler** and **ErrorHandler** interfaces.

DocumentType interface — Defined in the **DOM** standard, to represent non-structural information about an XML document, including notations and entities, and the name of the root element. A subclass of the **Node** interface, adding the **getName, getEntities** and **getNotations** methods. It is accessed using the **getDoctype** method in the **Document** interface.

DOM *(Document Object Model)* — [pronounced 'dom'estic] A software interface to the document structure, with methods that allow a program to manipulate the elements in a document or read their contents. See http://www.w3.org/markup/dom/drafts/requirements.html. For event-driven processing see **SAX**.

DOM class — A **DOM** class that, for the moment, is only used to retrieve a **DOM Factory** class.

DOM Factory — The class used to create new document objects for insertion into a document stored in memory and accessed via the **DOM** class.

domain name — The natural language equivalent of an **IP address**. For example, 'bradley.co.uk' is the domain name for IP address '194.193.96.10'. The **IANA** *(Internet Assigned Numbers Authority)* is responsible for coordinating and managing the assignment of domain names, which must be unique (there cannot be two 'bradley.co.uk' names). The database that matches domain names to IP numbers is maintained by Network Solutions Inc. (NSI), and currently contains almost 30 million entries (nearly 50,000 are added each day). Part of the name denotes the type of organization ('.org' = organization, '.com' = commercial, '.co' = commercial, '.edu' = education, '.gov' = governmental). The final part of the name denotes the country (see **ISO 3166**) (omitted for the United States). See www.networksolutions.com or www.nominet.org.uk for UK names.

Domain Name Server — See **DNS**.

Dots Per Inch — See **DPI**.

dotted decimal — The notation used for domain names, which are composed of four numbers, each having 256 possible values. The representation '194.193.96.10' shows these numbers in decimal (0–255), with dots between them.

down-convert — Term used to describe the process of converting data from an information-rich format, such as XML, to a less rich, or display-oriented format, such as **RTF**. Generally categorized as a **low energy** conversion process. See **up-convert**.

DP *(Draft Proposal)* — See **ISO**.

DPI *(Dots Per Inch)* — A measure of the **resolution** of text or image data as presented on screen or page. Better quality results from a 'higher' resolution. A 600 DPI laser page proof is easier to read than a 72 DPI screen presentation.

DSSSL *(Document Style Semantics and Specification Language)* — [pronounced 'dis-sell'] An **ISO** standard (ISO/IEC 10179:1995) language (based on the Scheme programming language) used to specify transformation and format information relating to **SGML** structured documents, replacing the more limited **FOSI** approach. More recently, used as the basis for the XML Style specification. Released in April 1996. Contact http://occam.sjf.novell.com:8080/dsssl/dsssl96. For a brief tutorial see http://itrc.uwaterloo.co:80/~papresco/dsssl/tutorial.html. See **DSSSL-O**. Due to reliance on programming language concepts, considered too complex for many users, an issue addressed by the development of **XSL** and **XSLT**.

DSSSL Lite— Previous name for **DSSSL-O**.

DSSSL Online— See **DSSSL-O**.

DSSSL-O *(Document Style Semantics and Specification Language – Online)* — Previously called 'DSSSL Lite', this is a subset of the full **DSSSL** standard aimed at adding remote formatting instructions to **SGML** documents. The online version is used to **compose** SGML documents on-screen. This approach potentially offers a more powerful alternative to the current use of **HTML** on the **Web**, as no prior conversion is needed to a generic **DTD**, and the information provider controls the appearance of the information when it is rendered on the user's system. Contact   http://occam.sjf.novell.com:8080/docs/dsssl-o/do951212.htm   or   http://sunsite.unc.edu/pub/sun-info/standards/dsssl/dssslo.htm.

Dt element — An **HTML** element describing a definition term, preceding a definition entry, **Dd** element, and containing text that describes the following definition. Enclosed by a **Dl** element.

DTD *(Document Type Definition)* — The instructions that codify rules for a particular type of document. Used by a **parser** to check that a **tag**ged document conforms to the pre-defined document structure rules.

DTDHandler interface — Defined in the **SAX** standard, to be implemented by objects that can deal with notations and binary entities that conform to these notations. Must be registered with the parser using the **setDTDHandler** method in the object that instantiates the **Parser** interface. See the **DocumentHandler**, **AttributeList**, **ErrorHandler** and **Locator** interfaces.

DTP *(DeskTop Publishing)* — An application designed to **compose** and **paginate** documents, and operate on desktop computers, usually employing a **WYSIWYG** interface.

DTR *(Draft Technical Report)* — See **ISO**.

Dynamic HTML — A marketing term used to describe the capabilities of the latest **Web browser**s, but resting on the new capabilities of **HTML 4.0**, in particular the now universal **Id** attribute and the various 'on...' event attributes, as well as **Cascading Style Sheets**.

dynamic information — Information that is constantly updated, usually from a database. A feature of online publishing is the continual update of the information. See **static information**.

E

EBCDIC *(Extended Binary Coded Decimal Interchange Code)* — [pronounced 'ebserdick'] An equivalent to **ASCII** used on IBM mainframe systems. Similar characters are represented, but are assigned different values (in fact there are several variants of EBCDIC). A text file copied from an EBCDIC-based computer to an ASCII-based computer should be translated, or the result will be unintelligible.

EBNF *(Extended Backus-Naur Form)* — A notation for expressing the rules of a language in a formal, precise and terse manner. The **XML** specification uses EBNF to define the syntax of XML documents and **DTD**s. EBNF is very difficult to understand (the charts in this book representing the XML specification are included for this reason).

ECMA *(European Computer Manufacturers Association)* — [pronounced 'eck-ma'] Organization responsible for **ECMAScript** and for the **ISO 8859** character sets. Contact www.ecma.ch.

ECMAScript — [pronounced 'eck-ma-script'] A scripting language employed in **Web browser**s, defining a standard version of the popular 'JavaScript' language, produced by **ECMA**. Formally named ECMA-262.

EDI *(Electronic Data Interchange)* — [pronounced 'ed-dee'] The exchange by electronic means of structured business information, such as inventories and accounts. An abstract concept that requires concrete specifications, such as **EDIFACT**. See http://www.geocities.com/Wall-Street/Floor/5815/ for an XML initiative.

EDIFACT — [pronounced 'ed-dee-fact'] An implementation of **EDI** aimed at administration, commerce and transport, and involving a standard character set, and agreed field separators ('+' is a segment tag and data separator, ' ' ' is a segment terminator, ':' is a component data element separator and '?' is a release character) and identifier codes ('5848' stands for 'amount'). Sections of an EDIFACT message may be mandatory or optional, and may be repeatable (simply changing the specification to XML syntax would bring the advantages of cost-effective, off-the-shelf parsers, format translators and output engines, but the parser cannot check field lengths and restricted field contents).

Editable Node List class — A **DOM** class. Each instance represents a sequence of nodes and allows nodes to be removed or replaced by new nodes, and new nodes to be inserted.

editorial system — A **document management** system that includes **workflow** features and is aimed at supporting document production departments.

Electronic Data Interchange — See **EDI**.

element — See **element**[39].

ELEMENT keyword — The keyword that identifies an **element declaration**, used to declare and define the content of an element.

element[39] — An identifiable object in a text document. When the object contains text and/or other elements it is a **container element**, otherwise it is an **empty element** (**EmptyElemTag**[44]). The legal content of an element may be pre-defined in a **DTD** using an **elementdecl**[45]. The attributes allowed may also be pre-defined using an **AttlistDecl**[52].

Element class — A software module forming part of the **DOM** that represents an instance of an element in a document. It includes methods for setting and retrieving the name of the element and its attribute values (by means of the **Attribute List** class).

element content — The text and/or child elements contained within an element. An **empty element** has no content.

element declaration — See **elementdecl**[45].

Element element — An **XSLT** element used to create an element in the output stream. This is an alternative to simply placing the output element in the style sheet, avoiding namespace issues. The **Namespace** and **Name** attributes provide the name of the output element. See **Attribute** element.

element instance — One instance of an element appearing in a document. For example, a book that contains nine chapters will have nine Chapter element instances. This term is often used to avoid confusion with an **element declaration**.

elementdecl[45] *(element declaration)* — A markup declaration that contains the specification of an element, including the element name and its allowed content, which may include the names of other elements, so building the **document hierarchy**. It may be associated (by name) with an attribute declaration (**AttlistDecl**[52]), which specifies attributes allowed in this element.

element content — An element that may contain **child** elements, but not text. All line-feed characters in element content are ignored (not treated as spaces).

Element interface — Defined in the **DOM** standard, to represent an XML element. A subclass of the **Node** interface, adding the **getTagName**, **normalize** and **getElementsByTagName** methods, and for attribute processing the **getAttribute**, **setAttribute** and **removeAttribute** methods (but see also the **Attr** interface).

Element Structure Information Set — See **ESIS**.

Elements attribute — An **XSLT** attribute to the **Preserve Space** and **Strip Space** elements. Used to list the names of elements to be given particular white space preserving or stripping treatment.

Em element — An **HTML** element that encloses text to be emphasized. No particular style is dictated.

embed — Place one **element** inside another element. When an element can directly or indirectly contain instances of its own type, such elements are termed **nested** elements.

emphasis — Text that is highlighted to bring attention to its importance, often using bold or italic styling.

Emphasis — See **Em** element.

Empty Element — See **EmptyElemTag**[44].

empty end-tag — An **SGML** markup minimization feature, where '</>' signifies the end of the element last opened in the text stream. Not applicable to XML.

empty start-tag — An **SGML** markup minimization feature, where '<>' signifies reoccurrence of the previous element in the text stream. Not applicable to XML.

EmptyElemTag[44] *(Empty Element Tag)* — An empty element is simply an element with no content. The **end-tag** may be omitted, but if present must immediately follow the start-tag. An element represented by a single tag, there being no element content. If the end-tag is omitted, the **start-tag** takes a different form from usual, indicating its empty status to a parser (which should not then look for the end-tag). The end of tag **delimiter** is '/>' in place of '>'. For example, '<x></x>' or '<x/>'.

EncName[81] — A parameter of the **Encoding declaration** that specifies the character set in use in the document.

encoding — a parameter of the **XML Declaration**, stating the character encoding in use in the document.

Encoding Declaration — See **EncodingDecl**[80].

EncodingDecl[80] *(Encoding declaration)* — A parameter of the **XMLDecl**[23] and **TextDecl**[77] codes, specifying the character set in use.

Encoding Name — See **EncName**[81].

Enctype attribute — Used in the **Form** element to specify the **MIME** type.

end-tag — Markup that ends a **container element**, and optionally ends an **empty element**, providing it immediately follows the **start-tag**. See **ETag**[42].

endDocument method — A **SAX** method defined in the **DocumentHandler** interface. Called by the parser when the end of the document is detected. See **startDocument** method.

endElement method — A **SAX** method defined in the **DocumentHandler** interface. Called by the parser when the end of an element is detected (empty elements are reported, even when there is no end-tag present). See **startElement** method.

entity — A named object that can be referred to. In **SGML**, a data fragment usually stored in a separate file or delimited by quotes, referred to by an **EntityDecl**[70].

entity declaration — The **markup declaration** that defines an **entity** name and associated content (either directly or by reference). See **EntityDecl**[70].

Entity Definition — See **EntityDef**[73].

entity end — See **EE**.

Entity interface — Defined in the **DOM** standard, to represent an XML **entity**. A subclass of the **Node** interface, adding the **getPublicId**, **getSystemId** and **getNotationName** methods. These objects are obtained using the method **getEntities** in the **DocumentType** interface, and are wrapped in a **NamedNodeMap** object. See **EntityReference** interface.

ENTITY keyword — The keyword that identifies an **entity declaration**, used to declare and define the content of an **entity**.

entity manager — Software designed to locate and access data held in an **entity**. An essential component of a **parser**. May use a **catalog** file to match entity names to **public identifiers**.

entity reference — Special character sequence identifying an external object (an **entity**) to be inserted at the current point in the data. In the document a **general entity** is used. In the DTD a **parameter entity** is used.

entity set — A group of **entity** declarations within the **document type declaration**. May be held in an **external entity**, where they are typically used to represent extended characters, such as the **ISOlat1** set. See ENTITY.

entity text — The content of an **entity**, either enclosed in quotes within the declaration, or referenced from the declaration.

entity type — The type of an **entity**, identifying its content as a sub-document, character data, system specific data or non-SGML data with associated notation name.

entity value — See **EntityValue**[09].

EntityDecl[70] *(Entity Declaration)* — The declaration of an entity name, and the content of the entity, which may be held in the declaration itself, or may be stored elsewhere (in which case the declaration contains a pointer to it).

EntityDef[73] *(Entity Definition)* — The value of a **general entity**, or a reference to the value if it is stored remotely. For parameter entities see **PEDef**[74].

EntityReference interface — Defined in the **DOM** standard, to represent an XML **entity reference**. A subclass of the **Node** interface, adding no new methods. This object is created using the factory method **createEntityReference** in the **Document** interface. See **Entity** interface.

EntityRef[68] *(Entity Reference)* — A reference to a **general entity**. For example, '`&myentity;`'. Declared using a **GEDecl**[71]. For parameter entity references see **PEReference**[69].

EntityResolver interface — Defined in the **SAX** standard, to be implemented by objects that can intercept calls to external entities. Must be registered with the parser using the **setEntityResolver** method in the object that instantiates the **Parser** interface. Defines the **resolveEntity** method. See the **DocumentHandler**, **AttributeList**, **DTD Handler**, **ErrorHandler** and **Locator** interfaces.

EntityValue[09] — A literal value for the entity that appears within the entity declaration.

enumerate — Create a list of possible values, which, for ease of computer processing are assigned unique numeric values. See **Enumeration**[59].

enumerated type — See **EnumeratedType**[57].

EnumeratedType[57] *(Enumerated Type)* — An Attribute Type (**AttType**[54]) that constrains its value to one of a list of options, being either a list of notation types or of other tokens. For example, '(draft|final)' or 'NOTATION (TEX|TIFF)'.

enumeration — See **Enumeration**[59].

Enumeration[59] — An Attribute Type (**AttType**[54]) that constrains its value to one of a list of tokens. For example, '(red|amber|green)'.

EPS *(Encapsulated PostScript)* — A **PostScript** fragment that is not part of a specific page, so may be included in any number of pages, and considered a separate object that can be stored and transmitted. A file format.

Eq[25] *(Equals)* — The equals symbol, '=', optionally surrounded by spaces, as used to separate attribute names from their values.

equals — See **Eq**[25].

error method — A **SAX** method defined in the **Errorhandler** interface. Triggered by the parser whenever a serious, but recoverable error occurs. See **fatalError** and **warning**.

ErrorHandler interface — Defined in the **SAX** standard, to be implemented by objects that can intercept or report errors. Defines the **warning**, **error** and **fatalError** methods. Must be registered with the parser using the **setErrorHandler** method in the object that instantiates the **Parser** interface. See the **DocumentHandler**, **AttributeList**, **DTD Handler** and **Locator** interfaces.

escape code — a character sequence in a **data stream** that generates a special character, or performs some other function.

ESIS *(Element Structure Information Set)* — [pronounced 'ee-sys'] The **ISO** standard (**ISO/IEC 13673:1995**) that describes the content and structure of a document. Used for conformance testing.

ETag[42] *(End Tag)* — A **tag** that indicates the end of the named **element**. For example, '</book>'. See **STag**[40].

Evaluate element — See **Eval** element.

event-driven — Software that reacts to markup as it is encountered while reading the **data stream**. Such software is unable to 'look ahead' for context, copy or move material to earlier points in the stream. See **tree-manipulation**.

Example — See **Xmp** element.

expression — *[1]* A rule that defines part of the XML or **XLink** language. The expression comprises at least one **token** and is given a name (the **symbol**). *[2]* A means of locating elements by their context in a document, used to create a **pattern** for matching **XSLT** templates to source document elements, possibly including a **location path** to the element, and to target objects for reuse or extraction (in **XQL**) or linking (in **XPointer**). All three use an expression language defined by the **XPath** standard.

Extend element — *[1]* The name of the **XLink** element that identifies the source of a **hypertext link** that may have multiple **target** resources. See **Simple** element. *[2]* An **XML Catalog** element for linking catalogue files, using the **HRef** attribute. See **Delegate**.

extended — See **extended link**.

extended document — In **XLink**, a pointer to a document that participates in a network of linked documents. All the extended document pointers are contained in an **extended group**.

extended group — The container in **XLink** for a number of **extended document** pointers.

extended link — A **hypertext link** concept in **XLink** that allows a number of **resources** to be linked together, so each target points to multiple sources, and all links are two-directional. See **simple link**. See **Extend** element.

extended link group — The **XLink** concept that allows a set of documents that contains links to each other to be easily identified, so that a browser can parse them all for links and display all the resources involved in the current document. See **extended group**.

Extended Pointer — A hypertext link that refers to an object by its contextual location.

Extender[89] — Used in **NameChar**[04] only to include special characters.

extender — See **Extender**[89].

Extensible Markup Language — See **XML**.

Extensible Stylesheet Language — See **XSL** (and also **XSLT**).

external entity — An **entity** stored outside the main XML document, usually in a separate file, and located by a **public identifier** or **system identifier**. A **binary entity** *must* be an external entity.

External Identifier — See **ExternalID**[75].

external link — A **hypertext link** to another document, or to part of another document, which is not supported by the ID and IDREF linking scheme, but is supported by the **HyTime** standard and by **Web browsers** working with **HTML** documents. See **internal link**.

external Parameter Entity — See **extPE**[79].

external Parsed Entity — See **extParsedEnt**[78].

external subset — See **extSubset**[30]

external text entity — An **entity** held in a separate file (an **external entity**) that contains XML data to be parsed and merged into the document.

ExternalID — See **ExternalID**[75].

ExternalID[75] *(External Identifier)* — A **system identifier** and possibly also a **public identifier** that identifies an **external entity**.

extParsedEnt[78] *(External Parsed Entity)* — An **external entity** that contains a fragment of the XML document, so will be parsed as part of the document structure.

extPE[79] *(External Parameter Entity)* — An **external entity** that contains a fragment of the **DTD**.

expression — In **XPath**, a text string that represents a query regarding objects in an XML document. This includes **patterns** ('`position() = 3`') and **location paths** ('`book/chapter/title`').

extranet — An **intranet** that has been opened up to selected clients, partners or suppliers, but is still closed to the wider **Internet** community.

extSubset[30] — Part of the **DTD** that is held in a separate file so that it can easily be applied to many documents. Consisting of **extSubsetDecl**[31] declarations. See **internal subset**.

extSubsetDecl[31] — DTD building declarations that are embedded in a remote file or inside an **included section**.

F

false() — An **XPath** expression function that returns the value 'false' in a boolean test.

family — A group of related **font**s. Perhaps a **roman** typeface, **italic** typeface and **bold** typeface, all based on the same character shape designs.

FAQ *(Frequently Asked Questions)* — Abbreviation for a document, usually made available on the **Intnernet**, that includes answers to the most common questions asked of a particular technology or protocol.

fatalError method — A **SAX** method defined in the **Errorhandler** interface. Triggered by the parser whenever a very serious, non-recoverable error occurs. See **error** and **warning**.

field — A single unit of information in a **record**. Every record in a **table** has the same fields, which can be thought of as the columns of the table. Each column has a name, such as 'name', 'employee number' and 'department', but each record may have a different field value, such as 'J. Smith', '6435' and 'Accounts'. In some ways similar to an **attribute** in XML, and information transferred between an XML document and a database is typically copied from attributes to fields, or vice versa. See **key-field**.

firewall — Software or hardware that protects an internal network from unauthorized external access. A firewall may be needed to separate private **Intranet** pages from public **Internet** pages.

FIXED keyword — An attribute type that contains a pre-defined value which cannot be altered by the document author. Used mainly in **architectural form**s.

fixed-pitch — See **mono-spaced**.

fixed attribute — See **FIXED**.

flat-file — A simple type of **database**, which contains a single **table**. The problem with flat-file databases is that they may contain duplicate information in some of the columns. The **relational database** or **object database** approach avoids this problem. Information is typically transferred between flat-file database systems using the **CSV** format.

flat-file database — See **flat-file**.

floating image — An **HTML** concept introduced in **HTML 3.2** that allows images to be placed in the left or right margin of the document. They are 'floating' because text within the document is not broken by the presence of the images. However, the **Br** element may optionally place following text below the images. See **Img** element.

floor() — Used in an expression in **XPath** to convert a real number into an integer by rounding down to the nearest whole number. See **round()** and **ceiling()**.

following:: — An **XPath** expression that selects a node that follows the current node in document order. Similar to **following-sibling::**, except that the search goes forward to the end of the document, at all levels in the following structures. See **preceding::**.

following-sibling:: — An **XPath** expression that selects a sibling of the current node, that follows the node in document order. See **preceding-sibling::**.

font — A set of **character**s, including at least the standard alphabet, conforming to a consistent design, traditionally of a fixed size and style, and tailored for a particular output device (though this is no longer typical). Also called 'fount'. Several related fonts may form a **family**.

Font element — An **HTML 3.2** element that uses a **Size** attribute to set the **font** size.

for attribute — An **HTML 4.0** attribute to the **Label** element that identifies the element being described when the Label element does not actually surround the control. Used when the text is not very close to the control it describes.

For Each element — An **XSLT** element used to apply the embedded template to each occurance of the element given in the **Select** attribute. A technique that can reduce the number of templates needed, and improves clarity of the process, when dealing with highly regular structures like tables.

Form element — An **HTML** element that identifies a section of the document that can be filled in by the user for transmission back to the **Web server**. Includes elements that specify buttons, radio buttons, check-boxes, text fields and menus. See **Input** and **Select** elements.

Format attribute — An **XSLT** attribute to the **Number** element, used to specify how a multi-part number is formatted with intermediate punctuation, and using which scheme, such as alphabetic and roman numerals. For example 'A.i.' dictates such sequences as 'M.ii', 'M.iii', 'M.iv', 'N.i' and '001)' generates such sequences as '009)', '010)', '011)'.

Formatting Objects DTD — A **DTD** defined as part of the **XSL** standard that is used to describe documents that contain XSL formatting instructions as well as the raw text data. Also called the **FO DTD**. This DTD defines such elements as 'block' to hold text blocks and 'inline-sequence' to hold in-line text.

formal public identifier — An organized and strictly formatted version of a **public identifier**. Each required part of the name is separated from other parts by two solidus characters '//'.

Formatting Output Specification Instance — See **FOSI**.

FOSI *(Formatting Output Specification Instance)* — [pronounced 'fozi'] A **CALS** defined (MIL-STD-28001 Appendix B) vendor-independent format for specifying publishing formats and styles for each tagged object in an **SGML** document. Currently supported by several applications that are designed to work with technical manuals. A precursor to the **DSSSL** and **XSL** standards that is rapidly losing favour. A FOSI is in fact an SGML document that conforms to the FOSI 'outspec' **DTD**. The elements and attributes defined in this DTD are used to describe the formats and styles to be applied to elements defined in the user's own DTD. Contact http://www.neuro.sfc.keio.ac.jp/~ayako/CALS/CALS2/MIL-M-28001.app-b10-. In the example below, the 'e-i-c' element (element-in-context) specifies settings for an element called 'Sub', when it appears within an element called 'Para'. The Charlist element (characteristics list) specifies that the 'Sub' element inherits all style information from the current settings, but then the Font element overrides the point size and baseline positioning to create the effect of subscript text:

```
<e-i-c gi="sub" context="para">
 <charlist inherit="1">
 <font size="6pt" offset="-1pt">
</e-i-c>
```

fragment identifier — The '#' symbol following a URL that indicates the presence of information that identifies a specific fragment of the document.

frame — An **HTML 4.0** feature already supported by the popular **Web browsers**. A single window is split into frames, each frame holding a different document which can be scrolled independently. Particularly useful for holding a table of contents or banner. See **Frame** element.

Frame element — An **HTML** element that specifies and encloses a **frame**.

Frameset element — An **HTML** element used in **frame**s that specifies an area divided into columns and rows using the **Cols** and **Rows** attributes.

From attribute — An **XSLT** attribute to the **Number** element, used to specify which element resets a counter when it is not reset by the parent of the source element (the **Level** attribute has a value of 'any').

FTP *(File Transfer Protocol)* — A standard method for computers to access files on other, remote computers. Used by **Anchor** elements in **HTML** to locate and access documents on servers that supports FTP anywhere on the **Web**. Specified in a **URL** using 'ftp://.....'. See alternative **HTTP** connection method.

FWIW — Abbreviation for 'For What Its Worth' used in online conversation. Others include **BTW** (By The Way), **IMHO** (In My Humble Opinion), **FYI** (For Your Information) and **OTOH** (On The Other Hand).

FYI *(For Your Information)* — *[1]* A document explaining an Internet protocol defined by one or more **RFC**s. To reach the index file, contact ftp://ds.internic.net/rfc/fyi-index.txt. *[2]* Abbreviation used in online conversation. Others include **BTW** (By The Way), **IMHO** (In My Humble Opinion), **FWIW** (For What Its Worth) and **OTOH** (On The Other Hand).

G

G4MIL-R-28002 — The **CALS** standard for a bit-mapped image format and compression scheme (actually **CCITT group IV**).

GCA *(Graphic Communications Association)* — A non-profit association formed in 1986 to apply computer technology to printing and publishing. A promoter of XML and other standards through training and development committees and the organization of conferences, including 'SGML/XML 9*x* Europe' and 'SGML/XML 9*x* (USA)' (at which **SGML Open** holds its committee meetings). Contact http://gca.sgml.com.

GEDecl$^{\{71\}}$ *(General Entity Declaration)* — A declaration for a **general entity**, which can be referred to in document text using an **EntityRef**$^{\{68\}}$. For parameter entities see **PEDecl**$^{\{72\}}$.

general entity — An **entity** that may be referenced from the general text, as opposed to a **parameter entity**, which can only be used within **markup**. A reference to a general entity is preceded by an ampersand character ('`&myent;`'). See **general entity reference**.

General Entity Declaration — See **GEDecl**$^{\{71\}}$.

general entity name — The name of the **general entity**.

generalized — See **generic**.

generalized markup — Document markup that uses **generic coding** techniques, and also defines the document structure to aid automated processing. A generalized markup language is sometimes also called a DMA (Declarative Markup Language). See **SGML** and, of course, XML.

generic — Not designed for a specific purpose. A generic **tag** would describe an important word as an emphasized word instead of an italic word, so allowing a different choice of style to be applied depending on the needs of particular media (for example, italic for paper output, red for screen output). See **generic coding**.

generic coding — Document markup that does not specify format and style explicitly, but refers to general names, such as 'title'. The name identifies a **macro** or style sheet name which contains the explicit format or style information. This is a significant step toward **generalized markup**.

geometric graphics — See **vector**.

getByteStream method — A **SAX** method defined in the **InputSource** interface. Used by the parser to get a reference to a supplied byte stream.

getCharacterStream method — A **SAX** method defined in the **InputSource** interface. Used by the parser to get a reference to a supplied character stream.

getColumnNumber method — A **SAX** method defined in the **Locator** interface. Returns the number of the character (within the line given by **getLineNumber**) where the error occurred. See **getSystemId** and **getPublicId**.

getEncoding method — A **SAX** method defined in the **InputSource** interface. Used by the parser to get a reference to a supplied character set encoding scheme.

getLength method — A **SAX** method defined in the **AttributeList** interface. Used to discover how many attributes are present in the element (as well as any defaulted from the DTD). See **getName**, **getValue** and **getType**.

getLineNumber method — A **SAX** method defined in the **Locator** interface. Returns the number of the line the error occurred on. See **getColumnNumber**, **getSystemId** and **getPublicId**.

getName method — A **SAX** method defined in the **AttributeList** interface. Used to discover the name of the attribute at the given (random) position index. See **getLength**, **getValue** and **getType**.

getPublicId method — *[1]* A **SAX** method defined in the **Locator** interface. Returns the **public identifier** of the entity that contained the error. See **getLineNumber**, **getSystemId** and

getColumnNumber. *[2]* A **SAX** method defined in the **InputSource** interface. Used by the parser to get a supplied public identifier.

getAttribute method — A **DOM** method in the **Element** interface. Returns the value of the named attribute as a string. See **getAttributeNode**.

getAttributeNode method — A **DOM** method in the **Element** interface. Returns the value of the named attribute as an **Attr** object. See **getAttribute**.

getAttributes method — A **DOM** method in the **Node** interface. Returns a list of attributes wrapped in a **NamedNodeMap** object.

getChildNodes method — A **DOM** method in the **Node** interface. Returns a list of nodes wrapped in a **NodeList** object. See **getElementsByName**.

getData method — A **DOM** method in the **CharacterData** interface. Returns the text value of the **Node**. See **getValue**.

getDoctype method — A **DOM** method in the **Document** interface. Returns information on the document in general (entity and notation declarations, and the root element name) wrapped in a **DocumentType** object.

getDocumentElement method — A **DOM** method in the **Document** interface. Returns an **Element** object representing the root element.

getElementsByTagName method — A **DOM** method in the **Document** and **Element** interfaces. Returns a **NodeList** object containing all **Element** objects within the given document or element within the document, that match the given name.

getEntities method — A **DOM** method in the **DocumentType** interface. Returns a **NamedNodeMap** object containing all **Entity** objects within the document.

getFirstChild method — A **DOM** method in the **Node** interface. Returns a **Node** object representing the first child object of the current node, if it has any children. See **getNextChild** and **getLastChild**.

getImplementation method — A **DOM** method in the **Document** interface. Returns a **DOMImplementation** object representing the DOM features supported by the application.

getLastChild method — A **DOM** method in the **Node** interface. Returns a **Node** object representing the last child object of the current node, if it has any children. See **getPreviousChild** and **getFirstChild**.

getLength method — A **DOM** method in the **CharacterData**, **NodeList** and **NamedNodeMap** interfaces. Returns an integer value representing the length of the text string, or the list of nodes. Often used with **item** to iterate through a list of nodes.

getNextSibling method — A **DOM** method in the **Node** interface. Returns a **Node** object representing the next (the following) sibling of the current node, if it has any more siblings. See **getPreviousSibling** and **getLastChild**.

getName method — A **DOM** method in the **DocumentType** and **Attr** interfaces. Returns the name of the document (the root element) or the attribute. See **getValue**.

getNamedItem method — A **DOM** method in the **NamedNodeMap** interface. Returns a **Node** that has the given name, if one exists in the list.

getNodeName method — A **DOM** method in the **Node** interface. Returns the name of the **Node** as a string. See **getNodeValue** and **getNodeType**.

getNodeType method — A **DOM** method in the **Node** interface. Returns the type of the **Node** as a short. See **getNodeValue** and **getNodeName**.

getNodeValue method — A **DOM** method in the **Node** interface. Returns the value of the **Node** as a string. See **getNodeName** and **getNodeType**.

getNotationName method — A **DOM** method in the **Entity** interface. Returns the name of the **notation** as a string.

getNotations method — A **DOM** method in the **DocumentType** interface. Returns all notation declarations, wrapped in a **NamedNodeList** object. See **getEntities**.

getOwnerDocument method — A **DOM** method in the **Node** interface. Returns the **Document** object that represents the document containing the current node.

getParentNode method — A **DOM** method in the **Node** interface. Returns a **Node** object representing the parent **element** of the current node, if it has a parent. See **getChildNodes**.

getPreviousSibling method — A **DOM** method in the **Node** interface. Returns a **Node** object representing the previous (the preceding) sibling of the current node, if it has any previous siblings. See **getNextSibling** and **getFirstChild**.

getPublicId method — A **DOM** method in the **Entity** and **Notation** interfaces. Returns a string representing the **public identifier** of the entity of notation declaration. See **getSystemId**.

getSystemId method — *[1]* A **SAX** method defined in the **Locator** interface. Returns the **system identifier** of the entity that contained the error. See **getLineNumber**, **getPublicId** and **getColumnNumber**. *[2]* A **SAX** method defined in the **InputSource** interface. Used by the parser to get a supplied system identifier. *[3]* A **DOM** method in the **Entity** and **Notation** interfaces. Returns a string representing the **system identifier** of the entity of notation declaration. See **getPublicId**.

getTagName method — A **DOM** method in the **Element** interface. Returns a string representing the name of the **element**.

getType method — A **SAX** method defined in the **AttributeList** interface. Used to discover the type of the attribute at the given (random) position index, or of the attribute with the given name. When no DTD is in use, this will always default to 'CDATA'. See **getLength**, **getValue** and **getName**.

getValue method — *[1]* A **SAX** method defined in the **AttributeList** interface. Used to discover the value of the attribute at the given (random) position index, or of the attribute with the given name. This is returned as a string. See **getLength**, **getType** and **getName**. *[2]* A **DOM** method in the **Attr** interface. Returns a string value representing the value of the **attribute**.

GIF *(Graphic Interchange Format)* — [pronounced 'gif't] The *de facto* **raster** 8-bit image format used with **HTML** on the **Web**. Although the data is compressed (using **LZW**), no information is ever lost. Originally GIF 87, transparent backgrounds were added with **GIF 89**. Up to 256 colours are available, and are chosen from the image content, so a picture of a sunset could contain 256 shades of red. Used in preference to **JPEG** on the Web for graphical logos, button images and rules, but not for natural colour images (particularly photographs). See **X-Bitmap**, **X-Pixelmap** and **PNG**.

GIF 87 — See **GIF**.

GIF 89 — Latest version of **GIF** that adds transparent backgrounds. Also provides multiple pass decompression, slowly improving image quality while allowing the download to be cancelled at any time.

glyph — A graphic symbol, as it appears on paper or screen. Every **character** is realized as a glyph from a specified **font**.

GML *(Generalized Markup Language)* — Precursor to **SGML**, developed in 1969 by IBM. A pioneer of the **generic markup** approach.

granularity — The degree to which an element is divided into **child** elements. A complex **hierarchy** denotes a 'fine' granularity. Simple structures with few levels indicate a 'coarse' granularity. For example, a Name element may simply contain a person's name in full, or may contain child elements that separate the first name from the second name. It should be noted that the cost of **up-converting** legacy data to XML format is affected by the degree of granularity chosen. A fine granularity is likely to involve more manual intervention. A difficult and costly process of this kind may be termed a **high energy** process. The reward for this effort, however, is **low energy**, totally automated **down-conversion** to various output formats. The choice of granularity is therefore dictated by balancing the extra cost of a finer granularity, against the likely future benefits of having a richer database. For example, creation of a list of names, sorted by second name, is much simpler to achieve using a finer granularity, as the required information is unambiguously identified for software extraction

Graph Representation Of property ValuEs — See **grove**.

Graphic Communications Association — See **GCA**.

Group element — The default name for the **XLink** element that encloses Document elements to identify all the documents in a web of links.

group — A collection of names, typically **element** names, possibly organized in a strict fashion using the connector symbols, '&', '|' and ',', and possibly quantified using the symbols '*', '+' and '?'. A group is bounded by brackets, '(' and ')'.

Grouping Separator attribute — An **XSLT** attribute to the **Number** and **Locale** elements, used to specify the character to be used to split large numbers into smaller pieces. In English, the comma is used, as in numbers such as '3,000,012'. The number of digits in each group is dictated by the **Grouping Size** attribute.

Grouping Size attribute — An **XSLT** attribute to the **Number** element, used to specify the number of digits to be inluded in each part of a large number, split into smaller pieces and separated by a character dictated by the **Grouping Separator** attribute. In English, the a value of '3' is used, as in numbers such as '3,000,012'.

grove *(Graph Representation Of property ValuEs)* — An abstract description of a means to represent SGML constructs, which may be given concrete form in terms of a **grove plan**.

grove plan — A strategy for deciding what types of information are to be held in a grove for a specific purpose. For example, one plan may omit **comment** and **processing instruction** tags if they are not needed for the processing that will be performed on the grove.

gt — The name of a reserved entity that represents the greater-than character, '>', used to avoid confusing a data character with a tag delimiter. See also **lt**.

H

H1 element — An **HTML** element that encloses a major heading, usually the title of the document. The most important of six levels of heading, with the smallest having the name **H6**.

H2 element — An **HTML** element that encloses an important heading. Less important than **H1**, but more important than **H3**.

H3 element — An **HTML** element that encloses a heading. Less important than **H2**, but more important than **H4**.

H4 element — An **HTML** element that encloses a heading. Less important than **H3**, but more important than **H5**.

H5 element — An **HTML** element that encloses a heading. Less important than **H4**, but more important than **H6**.

H6 element — An **HTML** element that encloses a minor heading. Less important than all other headers, and should only be used when a sixth level of heading is required.

HandlerBase class — A **SAX** class that implements various interfaces on behalf of the application, so that it only needs to override the methods it needs.

hasChildNodes method — A **DOM** method in the **Node** interface. Returns a boolean value stating, if true, that the node nas children. If false, it has no child nodes.

head — Start-point of a **hypertext link**. Equivalent to the **source** of a link. Points to the **tail**. In **HTML** the head is an **Anchor** element (**A**) containing an **Href** attribute.

Head element — An **HTML** element that encloses information about the document, including the document **Title** element, as opposed to the **Body** element which encloses the document content.

Height attribute — An **HTML 3.2** attribute to the **Img** and **Applet** elements, used to specify the height of the image or **applet** working area, and to the **Tr** and **Th** elements to provide a suggested height for the cell. See **Width**.

hexadecimal — The base 16 notation for representing numeric values. In this notation there are 16 value symbols in place of the normal 10. The first 10 are the same, '0' to '9', and the letters 'A' to 'F' represent the additional six values. A = 10, B = 11, C = 12, D = 13, E = 14 and F = 15. Hexadecimal is popular in computing because base 16 is a multiple of two, so is a simple multiple of binary, or base 2. Four bits can represent values between zero ('0000' in binary) and 15 ('1111' in binary), which can be represented by a single hexadecimal digit. Two digits are required to represent the value of a single byte, with 'FF' standing for 255, or '11111111' (binary).

hi-byte — When a single value requires more than one byte to store it, because it may be larger than 255, a sequence of bytes are assigned. Depending on the microprocessor used, a two-byte value may be stored in an unexpected order, **lo-byte** followed hi-byte. To determine the full value stored, the value in the hi-byte is multiplied by 256, then the value in the lo-byte is added to the result.

hierarchy — A concept derived from family trees that describes **element** relationships. The elements Book/Chapter/Section/Paragraph would form a hierarchy, with each layer viewed as one branch of a **tree**, from which smaller branches diverge to create the next level.

high energy — A complex task involving human intervention, which is therefore costly. A term typically used to describe the process of **up-convert**ing data to XML format. See **low energy**.

home page — The initial 'welcome' **Web page** that contains links to other pages on an **Internet** site. Usually named 'index.html' (which is assumed by the **Web browser** if no file name appears in the **URL**).

Horizontal rule — See **Hr** element.

Horizontal space — See **Hspace** attribute.

host — A computer that is connected to the **Internet**. A host may be a server or a client in any particular transaction.

hot spot — An area of a graphical image that acts as a link to associated information when selected.

Hr element — An **HTML** element that generated a horizontal rule.

Href attribute — *[1]* In XML, the default name for the attribute that contains a reference to a **resource** in a simple link. In the **HTML** standard an attribute of the **Anchor**, **Area** and **Link** elements that contains the **URI** location of a document, or a specific location within the remote or current document. The '#' symbol separates a **URL** for a document from the sub-document named location. *[2]* An **XSLT** attribute to the **Import** and **Include** elements, containing a **URL** that identifies the file containing additional templates.

HRef attribute — An **XML Catalog** attribute used in the **Map**, **Remap**, **Delegate**, **Extend** and **Base** elements to identify entity resources and other catalogue files.

Hspace attribute — An **HTML 3.2** attribute to the **Img** element, used to determine the horizontal space to make available for the image.

HTML *(HyperText Markup Language)* — A non-application-specific **DTD** developed for delivery and presentation of documents over the **Web**, to be **composed** using an **HTML browser**. Contact alt.html and comp.infosystems.www.html newsgroups. See **HTML Level One**, **HTML Level Two** and **HTML Level Three**.

HTML 1.0 — See **HTML Level One**.

HTML 2.0 — See **HTML Level Two**.

HTML 3.0 — A proposed version of HTML that was never accepted due to its complexity. This version was abandoned, but some of its ideas were later incorporated into **HTML 3.2**.

HTML 3.2 — See **HTML Level Three**.

HTML 4.0 — See **HTML Level Four**.

HTML browser — A **browser** application that understands and **composes** from HTML markup. Recognizes and activates **Anchor** element links.

Html element — An **HTML** element that encloses the entire document (or **page**), including the **Head** element and **Body** element.

HTML Level Four — Latest version of **HTML** (4.0), released by the W^3C on 18 December 1997. It can be downloaded from http://www.w3.org/TR/REC-html40. An **SGML** application, including a **DTD**. Includes support for **frame**s, more complex tables, and attributes to support processing via a **DOM**.

HTML Level One — First and universally supported version of **HTML**. Loosely related to **SGML** (a **DTD** was later retro-fitted). No support for **form**s, tables or **frame**s. Superseded by **HTML Level Two**.

HTML Level Three — Most widely adopted version of **HTML**. Released June 1996. It can be downloaded from http://www.w3.org/pub/WWW/TR/REC-HTML32.dtd. An **SGML** application, including a **DTD**. Includes support for tables and **frame**s. Now superseded by **HTML Level Four**.

HTML Level Two — Second and well-supported version of **HTML**. Closely related to **SGML**, including a **DTD**. Includes support for **form**s. Superseded by **HTML Level Three**.

HTML-aware — An application that is able to produce or understand **HTML** markup, such as a Web browser or authoring package.

HTML+ — See **HTML**.

HTTP *(HyperText Transfer Protocol)* — The commonest means of communication between a **Web server** and **Web browser**, using a **URL**. Used by **Anchor** elements in **HTML** to locate and access documents on servers that support HTTP anywhere on the Web, 'http://www. ...'. Contact ftp:// info.cern.ch/pub/www/doc/http-spec.txt.Z. See **HTTP 1.1** and **HTTPS**. Also see **FTP**.

HTTPS *(HTTP Security)* — A variation of HTTP that provides security for online transactions, using the SSL scheme. Also called **S-HTTP**.

HTTP 1.0 — See **HTTP**.

HTTP 1.1 — A new version of **HTTP** that allows multiple transactions without having to reconnect to the server each time, so saving time.

Http-equiv attribute — An **HTML** attribute to the **Meta** element, used to place information in a **HTTP** header field.

hyperlink — See **hypertext link**.

hypermedia — The same concept as **hypertext**, with the addition of allowing a mix of information types, including audio and visual media. See **HyTime** and **multimedia**.

Hypermedia/Time-based Document Representation Language — See **HyTime**.

hypertext — Text that does not follow a single narrative flow. A **hypertext link** allows the reader to follow an alternative path through a document. In electronic versions of traditional documents, this may mean simply activating references to other parts of the text. Sometimes, the 'text' part of the name is taken to mean any part of a document, including images, and the term is then used interchangeably with **hypermedia**.

hypertext link — A link between a **source** reference and a **target** object. Sometimes called a 'hyperlink'. Such links enable the creation of **hypertext** documents. See **ID** and **IDREF**, **XLink** and **Hytime**. See **absolute link** and **relative link**.

HyperText Markup Language — See **HTML**.

Hypertext Reference — See **Href** attribute.

HyperText Transfer Protocol — See **HTTP**.

HyTime *(Hypermedia/Time-based Document Representation Language)* — Standard mechanism for use of **SGML** to represent time-based data such as music, animation or film. Released in 1992, and defined as **ISO/IEC 10744**. See **HyTime application**. Several techniques allow **hypertext** linking between SGML documents and between SGML and other format documents, including methods that identify target objects by their location in the file. Contact http://www.sgmlopen.org/sgml/docs/ library/archform.html and http://www.techno.com/TechnoTeacher/HyTime.html.

HyTime application — A **HyTime**-compliant **DTD**, including **HyTime elements** that conform to a **HyTime architectural form**.

HyTime architectural form — An **architectural form** defined in the **HyTime** standard. Specific attribute names and value are recognized by a HyTime-aware application.

HyTime element — An **SGML** defined **element** that includes **attributes** and attribute values recognizable to a **HyTime** application. An attribute called 'HyTime' takes a value that identifies the **HyTime architectural form** – for example 'hytime NAME #FIXED 'clink''.

I

I element — An **HTML** element that contains text to be displayed in **italic** typeface.

IANA *(Internet Assigned Number Authority)* — Authority responsible for assigning default **port numbers** to common applications on the **Internet**. Also responsible for character set identifiers, and the current list can be accessed from ftp://ftp.isi.edu/in-notes/iana/assignments/languages (the procedure for proposing a new variant is described in **RFC 1766**. See **IanaCode[36]**).

IanaCode[36] — A language identifier defined by the **IANA** (the *Internet Assigned Number Authority*), used for variants not covered by **ISO 639**. Part of the **Langcode[34]** rule, which is used in the **xml:lang** attribute.

ICADD *(International Committee for Accessible Document Design)* — A committee formed in 1992 to promote access to documents by print-impaired readers. An ICADD-compliant **DTD** uses **fixed attributes** to map complex structures to a simpler pre-defined document structure. The DTD effectively carries information on how to convert a **document instance** to another document conforming to the ICADD DTD. Once converted, existing software can represent the contained information in various forms suitable for those who are print-impaired, including Grade 2 Braille, large print and voice synthesis. Included in **ISO 12083** (the SGML DTD for general book and periodical publishing). See **SDA**. Contact icadd@asuvm.inre.asu.edu and http://www.sil.org/sgml/ICADDiso.html.

ICR *(Intelligent Character Recognition)* — An improved form of **OCR**, which does not use pre-defined templates to locate characters on an image. The ICR software understands the general shape of each character, and analyzes lines and curves to deduce the character, so is not restricted to specific **fonts**.

id() — A function in an expression used in **XPath** that selects the node with the given unique identifier. It can only be used at the start of an **absolute path**. See **key()**.

Id attribute — *[1]* An **HTML** attribute added to almost all elements in **HTML 4.0**, allowing any element instance to be identified for linking, styling or dynamic updating. *[2]* An **XSLT** attribute to the **Stylesheet** (or **Transform**) element, used for reference to a built-in style sheet from the **xml-stylesheet** processing instruction.

ID keyword — The keyword that defines an **attribute** to be the **target** of an **internal link**. The 'identifier' keyword. See **IDREF**.

Identifier — See **Id** attribute.

identifier type — The type of **public identifier**, '-//', (unregistered), '+//' (registered) or 'ISO ...//' (ISO defined).

Ideographic — See **Ideographic**{86}.

Ideographic{86} — A category of character in **ISO/IEC 10646**.

IDREF keyword — The keyword that identifies an attribute as one that references another element. The value of this attribute must match the value of another attribute of type **ID** in another element.

IDREFS keyword — The keyword that identifies an attribute as one that contains several values of type **IDREF**.

IEC *(International Electrotechnical Commission)* — Organization working on standards, sometimes in partnership with the **ISO**. The next version of **SGML** will be labelled 'ISO/IEC 8879'. Contact http://www.hike.te.chiba-u.ac.jp/ikeda/IEC/.

IETF *(Internet Engineering Task Force)* — The international community (comprising network designers, operators, researchers and vendors) concerned with the smooth operation and future of the **Internet** architecture. An IETF working group defined **HTML**, but this group dissolved in 1995 after defining version 2.0 (the role was taken over by the **W³C**). Contact http://www.ietf.org/.

If element — An **XSLT** element used to test options within a template, reducing the number of templates needed. The **Test** attribute contains an expression that, when it returns true, indicates that the content of this element should be processed. See **Choose**.

IGES *(Initial Graphics Exchange Specification)* — A three-dimensional **vector** CAD drawing data format. Used as part of the **CALS** standard (MIL-D-28000).

ignorable white space — Spaces and line-end codes that occur directly within elements that are defined in a DTD to contain only other elements (not #PCDATA). This white space is deemed not to be part of the content of the actual document, but only appears to format the tags.

ignorableWhitespace method — A **SAX** method defined in the **DocumentHandler** interface. Called by the parser when a block of white space characters in an element is detected, providing that the DTD states that this element can only contain other elements (not #**PCDATA**). A character array, start offset and length value are passed to it. See **characters** method.

Ignore{65} — A sub-rule of **ignoreSectContents**{64} that helps distinguish characters in an ignored section from embedded ignored section contents.

IGNORE keyword — The keyword that identifies a segment of the document (the **ignoreSect**{63}) which is not to be processed. Replacing this keyword with 'INCLUDE' enables processing.

ignore Section — See **ignoreSect**{63}.

ignore Section Contents — See **ignoreSectContents**{64}.

ignoreSect{63} *(ignore Section)* — A section of the document marked for non-inclusion. Enclosed declarations are to be ignored by parsers building the document model. See **includeSect**{62}.

ignoreSectContents{64} *(ignore Section Contents)* — The content of an excluded portion of the document (an **ignoreSect**{63}), which is not processed, but may include further, embedded ignored sections. All the content is ignored, even if an embedded include section is present.

Image element — See **Img** element.

image format — A data format that is used to store graphic data, as opposed to text data. Two main categories are **raster** and **vector** types. On the **Internet**, **GIF** and **JPEG** are commonly used, but **PNG** should also be popular. **CGM** (vector) is used for technical drawings and publishers tend to use **TIFF** (raster). Compression techniques such as **LZW**, **JPEG** and **CCITT Group IV** are used to reduce the file size (a monochrome A4 sized image at 300 dpi would be over one megabyte if uncompressed, but Group IV would typically reduce it to about 30 kilobytes, assuming it comprised mainly of lines of text (this format is used by FAX machines)). Unlike **text format**s, even uncompressed image formats are rarely readable due to the need to keep the file size down. See www.cis.ohio-state.edu/text/faq/usenet/graphics/fileformats-faq/part3/faq.html.

image map — An **Internet** concept. Areas within an image, such as a circle or rectangle, can be identified and made active. When the mouse is clicked on an image associated with a map, the coordinates of the cursor are transmitted to the **Web server**, which uses the map coordinates to determine whether an active area has been selected, and an appropriate script is activated. This is termed a 'server-sided' image map. Some **Web browser**s can link areas directly to **URL**s specified in the **HTML** page. This, more direct method, is called 'client-sided'. Typically, an image map is used to provide an attractive menu screen that accesses other **page**s. See the **Ismap** attribute.

Img element — An **HTML** element that references an image data file using the **Src** attribute. An **Ismap** attribute is used to help create an **image map**.

IMHO — Abbreviation for 'In My Humble Opinion' used in online conversation. Others include **BTW** (By The Way), **FWIW** (For What It's Worth), **FYI** (For Your Information) and **OTOH** (On The Other Hand).

IMPLIED keyword — The keyword that identifies an attribute which does not have to be explicitly given a value by a user. There may be a default value assigned in the DTD. If not, the application must decide on a default action (if any) to take. See **REQUIRED**.

implied attribute — See **IMPLIED**.

Import element — An **XSLT** element used to import another style sheet. Imported templates are considered to be less important than other templates. The rules are located by **URL**, using the **Href** attribute. See **Include** element.

in-line — *[1]* An object that is embedded in a sequence of other objects, such as a Paragraph element that follows and precedes similar text structures. See **out-of-line**. *[2]* Element content that does not force a **line break** in the flow of text. See **in-line element**. *[3]* An element that identifies a **hypertext link** which is embedded with (or surrounds) the referencing text, so moves with that text when earlier text is added or deleted. See **in-line link**.

in-line element — An element that does not imply a line break in the flow of text. Typical examples are Emphasis, Name, Superscript and Xref elements. See **block element**.

in-line link — A **hypertext link** that is specified by an element embedded in (or around) the text that forms the **source** of the link. The benefit of this approach is that the source part of the link is maintained if preceding text is edited, because the linking element is 'anchored' to the reference text. See **out-of-line** link.

in-line style — A style definition that is applied to a particular instance of an element in one document, giving document authors the ability to 'design' a page, but a wasteful technique when every instance should be styled the same. See **style sheet**.

Include element — An **XSLT** element used to import another style sheet. Imported templates are considered to be just as important as other templates. The rules are locates by **URL**, using the **Href** attribute. See **Import** element.

INCLUDE keyword — The keyword that identifies an included section (**includeSect**[62]). The content must be included in **XML processor** output (in other words, it has no effect but may be easily changed to **IGNORE** and back as required).

include section — See **includeSect**[62].

includeSect[62] *(include Section)* — A section of the document explicitly marked for inclusion in **XML processor** output. It has no effect on the document in itself, but it may be changed to an **ignore Section** at any time by changing the keyword from 'INCLUDE' to 'IGNORE'.

Indent Result attribute — An **XSLT** attribute to the **Stylesheet** element. Used to specify (when set to 'yes') that the output document should contain leading spaces to highlight the document structure by creating different levels of indent for each embedded structure.

inferior — See **subscript**.

infobahn — An alternative term used for the 'information superhighway' (the **Internet**).

information superhighway — An alternative term used for the 'infobahn' (the **Internet**).

Inline attribute — An XLink attribute that, when set to 'false', removes the linking element from the web of interlinked resources it identifies (so a user cannot link to this element). Doing this creates an **out-of-line link**.

Input element — An **HTML** element used in the **Form** element to provide user input objects. One must have a **Type** attribute value of 'submit', creating a button that, when selected, sends all current values back to the **Web server**.

InputSource method — A **SAX** constructor method defined in the **InputSource** interface. It may take a single parameter that identifies the source, either as a URL, a byte stream or a character stream, though the **setSystemId**, **setByteStream** and **setCharacterStream** methods can be used afterwards instead. See also **setPublicId**.

Ins element — An **HTML 4.0** element used to highlight text newly added to an existing document for simple tracking of changes. Optional **Datetime** and **Cite** attributes specify the time of the amendment and locate a comment regarding the change. See **Del** element.

insertBefore method — A **DOM** method in the **Node** interface. Used to add a new node to the child list, at a position immediately above the referenced node. Returns a reference to the new node. See **appendChild**.

insertData method — A **DOM** method in the **CharacterData** interface. Used to insert text into an existing string. The first paramter is the positional identifier, and the second is the string to insert. See **replaceData** and **appendData**.

Insertion — See **Ins** element.

insignificant white space — Spaces, tabs, and **line break** codes which are not considered to be part of the document text, but are only used to make markup easier to read, so should not appear when the document is presented. See **significant white space**.

interactive validation — Comparison of an XML DTD with a document instance that should conform to it, while that document is being created or edited. A technique used by XML-aware text editors to prevent document structure rules from being broken. See **batch validation**.

internal entity — An **entity** that exists within the main XML document, and is named and stored within an **entity declaration**. The content is delimited by quote characters. See **external entity**.

internal link — A **hypertext link** that has a **source** point and a **target** point in the same document. See **external link**.

internal reference — See **internal link**.

internal subset — Part of a **DTD** that is stored at the top of a document instance, allowing a document author to add document-specific characteristics. See **external subset**.

internal text entity — A **text entity** that includes the replacement text inside the **entity declaration**. See **external text entity**.

International Committee on Accessible Document Design — See **ICADD**.

International Electrotechnical Commission — See **IEC**.

International Organization for Standardization — See **ISO**.

International Standards Organization — See **ISO** (which, despite appearances, is not actually an abbreviation of this name, and in any case is properly called the 'International Organization for Standardization').

Internet — Scheme for connecting computer systems using the **TCP/IP** network protocols, originating in US defence, gaining popularity within universities, then business, and latterly as a general platform for the **Web** and electronic mail. Overseen by the **IETF**. For details on standards see http://www.ietf.cnri.reston.va.us/1id-abstracts.

Internet Assigned Number Authority — See **IANA**.

Internet Engineering Task Force — See **IETF** .

Internet protocol — The Internet supports a number of communication protocols, including **HTTP** (the *HyperText Transfer Protocol*) and **FTP** (the *File Transfer Protocol*), file (local file access), gopher, mailto, news, telnet, rlogin, tn3270 and wais (*Wide Area Information Servers*).

Internet server — An application that accepts requests from other systems connected to the Internet, returning the data requested. A form of Internet server that accepts **HTTP** requests for **HTML** documents is termed a **Web server**.

InterNIC — The organization responsible for assigning unique **IP addresses** (or blocks of numbers) to individuals, organizations and companies, or to intermediaries (the access providers). Contact User Assistant Services on 1-703-742-4777.

interpret — The step-by-step process of a software application that reads a data file containing instructions that are mainly designed to be human legible. This is known to be a slow process, and must be repeated each time the file is read. To improve speed, such information is often processed by a **compiler** (though the resulting compiled file may not be readable by other software not familiar with the compacted format).

interpreter — A module of a larger program that needs to read data designed to be also human-readable. See **interpret**.

intranet — A local 'closed' version of the **Internet**, for access by a local community (typically by company employees) using tools developed for the Internet, including **Web browser**s. See **extranet**.

IP *(Internet Protocol)* — The method by which computers connected to the **Internet** communicate with each other. See **TCP** and **IP address**.

IP address — Unique **Internet** host identifier number, for example '145.123.252.231'. For ease of use they are associated with easier to remember **domain name**s, such as 'bradley.co.uk', on a **DNS**.

IP number — See **IP address**.

IPng — See **IPv6**.

IPv6 — The 'next generation' of **IP address**, which allows for many more unique machine identifiers, data security, support for mobile computing and many other initiatives. Developed by the **IETF**.

IRV *(International Reference Version)* — Standard version of **ISO/IEC 646:1991**, using the currency symbol, ' ', in place of the dollar character, '$', found in **ASCII**.

IS *(International Standard)* — A standard released by the **ISO**.

Isindex element — An **HTML** element that accepts a user input value that is passed back to the **Web server** for processing. See **form** for a better, more flexible approach.

Ismap attribute — An **HTML** attribute to the **Img** element that indicates an **image map** is associated with the image.

ISO *(International Organization for Standardization)* — [pronounced 'eye-so'] The organization responsible for release of the **SGML** standard under the designation 'ISO 8879' and various other standards. Most of the related standards discussed in this book are released by the working group **WG8**. An 'IS' is an International Standard. A DTR is a 'Draft Technical Report'. Located at 'ISO Central Secretariat/1, rue de Varembe/CH-1211 Geneva 20/Switzerland'. The name 'ISO' is not an abbreviation, but is intended to describe equality, just as it is used in a name such as '*iso*sceles' (a triangle with two *equal* sides).

ISO 10179 — See **DSSSL**.

ISO 10180 — See **SPDL**.

ISO 10744 — See **HyTime**.

ISO 12083 — Ratified versions of the **AAP DTDs**. Devised for general publishing needs.

ISO 2022 — A standard for extending the range of a character set by the use of the **ESC** 'escape sequence' codes, which switch in and switch out alternative blocks of characters.

ISO 3166 — A list of two-letter country codes, such as 'UK' (United Kingdom), as used in e-mail addresses such as 'neil@bradley.co.uk' and in **xml:lang** attributes to specify a dialect, such as 'en.UK' and 'en.US'.

ISO 639 — Definition of codes specifying the language of an **entity**. For example, 'EN' identifies the English language. Used in the **xml:lang** attribute. See **IANA**.

ISO 646 — See **ISO/IEC 646:1991**.

ISO 8632 — See **CGM**.

ISO 8859 — A group of character sets now controlled by the **ISO**, but originally defined by **ECMA**. See **ISO/IEC 8859/1** for one common character set in this group.

ISO 8859/1 — See **ISO/IEC 8859/1**.

ISO 8879 — See **SGML**.

ISO 8879:1986 — See **SGML**. '1986' is the year of issue.

ISO 9069 — See **SDIF**.

ISO 9070 — Official scheme for determining an **owner identifier** in a **formal entity declaration**.

ISO owner identifier — An **external entity** that has been defined by the **ISO**, and has owner details consisting of the ISO publication number. For example 'ISO 8879:1986'. The first part of a **formal public identifier** referring to an ISO-owned entity.

ISO text description — The formal text description of an **ISO**-defined **entity** within a **formal public identifier**. For example, the text description for one of the character entity sets is 'Added Latin 1'.

ISO/IEC 10179 — See **DSSSL**.

ISO/IEC 10180 — See **SPDL**.

ISO/IEC 10646 — An **ISO**-defined **32-bit** coded **character** set for information interchange. See **ASCII** and **ISO/IEC 646:1991**. It defines a unique computer value for 4,294,967,296 characters. The lower seven bits correspond to the **ASCII** (US) **7-bit** character set, the lower eight bits correspond to **ISO/IEC 8859/1** (Latin-1), and the lower 16 bits correspond to the **Unicode** character set.

ISO/IEC 10744:1991 — See **HyTime**.

ISO/IEC 13673:1995 — See **RAST**.

ISO/IEC 646:1991 — The **ISO** defined **7-bit** coded **character set** for information interchange. Almost identical to **ASCII**, from which it is derived. See the first 128 entries of the **ISO/IEC 8859/1** character set. Also see **ISO/IEC 10646**.

ISO/IEC 8859/1 — A **character set** based on **ASCII**, but adding symbols and European accented characters (see **ISOlat1**) by employing an **8-bit** character set. Used in **HTML**, Microsoft Windows and some UNIX systems. See also **ISO/IEC 646:1991**, of which it is a superset, and both **Unicode** and **ISO/IEC 10646**, of which it is a subset.

ISO/IEC 8859/2 — A **character set** based on **ASCII**, but adding characters for Croatian, Czech, Hungarian, Polish, Romanian, Slovak and Slovenian languages.

ISO/IEC 8859/3 — A **character set** based on **ASCII**, but adding characters for Esperanto, Maltese, Turkish (though 8859/5 is now preferred for this language) and Galician languages.

ISO/IEC 8859/4 — A **character set** based on **ASCII**, but adding characters for Latvian, Lithuanian, Greenlandic and Lappish languages.

ISO/IEC 8859/5 — A **character set** based on **ASCII**, but adding characters for Cyrillic characters to cover Byelorussian, Bulgarian, Macedonian, Russian, Serbian and Ukrainian languages.

ISO/IEC 8859/6 — A **character set** based on **ASCII**, but adding characters for the Arabic language.

ISO/IEC 8859/7 — A **character set** based on **ASCII**, but adding characters for modern Greek.

ISO/IEC 8859/8 — A **character set** based on **ASCII**, but adding characters for Hebrew.

ISO/IEC 8859/9 — A **character set** based on **ASCII**, similar to 8859/1, but replacing Icelandic characters with Turkish characters.

ISO/IEC 8859/10 — An **character set** based on **ASCII**, but adding Lappish, Nordic and Inuit characters.

ISO/IEC 8879 — Official designation of forthcoming update to the **SGML** standard.

ISO/IEC TR 9573 — Technical report complementing **ISO 8879**, which includes techniques for encoding general text, tables, mathematical formula and Japanese text. The mathematical structures are widely supported by software, but tables are commonly coded using the **CALS table** model.

ISO639Code[35] — A language identifier that conforms to the **ISO** standard **ISO 639**.

ISOdia *(ISO Diacritics)* — A **character set**, grouped under **formal public identifier** 'ISO 8879:1986//ENTITIES Diacritical Marks//EN', consisting of marks that are added to letters such as '¨' (German umlaut) and '´' (French acute).

ISOgrk1 *(ISO Greek Letters)* — A **character set**, grouped under **formal public identifier** 'ISO 8879:1986//ENTITIES Greek Letters//EN', consisting of Greek letters such as '&Agr;' (Alpha Greek).

ISOlat1 *(ISO Added Latin 1)* — A **character set**, grouped under **formal public identifier** 'ISO 8879:1986//ENTITIES Added Latin 1//EN', consisting mostly of European accented letters such as 'é'.

ISOnum *(ISO Numeric and Special Characters)* — A **character set**, grouped under **formal public identifier** 'ISO 8879:1986//ENTITIES Numeric and Special Graphic//EN', consisting mostly of fractions such as '⅜', mathematical symbols such as '÷' and currency symbols such as '¥'.

ISOpub *(ISO Publishing)* — A **character set**, grouped under **formal public identifier** 'ISO 8879:1986//ENTITIES Publishing//EN', consisting of characters used in publishing, such as ' ' (em space) and 'ﬁ' (fi ligature (the 'f' and the 'i' character are merged into a single symbol)).

ISOtech *(ISO General Technical)* — A **character set**, grouped under **formal public identifier** 'ISO 8879:1986//ENTITIES General Technical//EN', consisting mostly of mathematical symbols such as '∞' (infinity).

italic — Characters that are slanted and cursive (script-like), as in '*italic*'. See **roman**.

Italic — See **I** element.

item method — A **DOM** method in the **NamedNodeMap** and **NodeList** interfaces. Used to gain a reference to a node in the list. The parameter is the number of the node to access, with the first node numbered zero. See **getLength**.

J

Java — A multi-platform object-oriented programming language developed by Sun. Originally developed in 1992, it was intended to be embedded in consumer devices. In 1995 it was enhanced, and aimed at **Internet** applications. Semi-compiled Java code modules, or **applets**, are accessed by a **Web browser**, interpreted or compiled (just-in-time compilation), then executed on the local machine. Platform independence includes machine and operating system neutral interfaces, including a graphical user interface. Contact http://Java.sun.com and comp.lang.java newsgroup.

Java API XML — See **JAX**.

JAX *(Java API XML)* — [pronounced 'jacks'] An effort to define an open, standard method for interfacing with **event-driven** XML processors, so that an application can choose at run-time which one to use to process a document. Contact http://www.microstar.com/xml/jax. For tree-driven processing see **DOM**.

JPEG — [pronounced 'jay-peg'] Popular 24-bit **raster** image format devised by the Joint Photographic Experts Group. An efficient compression scheme, but at the cost of accuracy as it does not faithfully reproduce the original image, and is therefore described as a 'lossy' format. May be stored within a **TIFF** file 'wrapper'. Used on the **Web** and **Internet** in general, in preference to **GIF** for natural colour images, particularly photographs, but not for button images, rules or logos. See **PNG**.

K

Kbd element — An **HTML** element that encloses text representing keyboard input, usually displayed in a mono-spaced font.

Key element — An **XSLT** element that defines a set of keys, which are special element identifiers that are more flexible than provided by the **ID** attribute type. The **Name** attribute gives the key set a name for later reference. The **Match** attribute selects the elements that are to be included in the range ('*' means all elements). The **Use** attribute specifies what values are to be deemed to be key values (it does not have to be an attribute of the given element, or an attribute at all). Keys are accessed using the **key()** function in an expression.

key() — A function in an expression used in **XSLT** that selects the node with the given unique key identifier. The first parameter names a key set, as defined using the **Key** element.

key-field — A **field** with the special property that it must contain a different (unique) value in every **record** in the **table**. It is especially useful in a **relation** database, because it allows information stored across a number of tables to be unambiguously linked.

Keyboard — See **Kbd** element.

keyword — A word appearing in **markup** that identifies the purpose of the tag, or some part of it. For example, 'IGNORE' is a keyword that identifies a portion of the document to be ignored.

L

Label attribute — An **HTML 4.0** attribute to various form-related elements, allowing text describing the form control to become 'clickable'. Uses the **For** attribute when the text is separate from the control so as to match the Label element to the **Id** value of the control.

Lang attribute — An **HTML** attribute added to almost all elements in **HTML 4.0**, indicating the human language used for the enclosed text. See **Dir** attribute. For the XML equivalent see **xml:lang**.

Langcode{34} — A human language identifying code, possibly user defined, but preferably an **ISO** or **IANA** defined code.

language — *[1]* Defined **markup** scheme. See **meta-language**. *[2]* Part of a **public identifier** that indicates the human language used in the data contained in the **entity**. English text contains the identifier 'EN'.

Language Code — See **Langcode{34}**.

Language Identifier — See **LanguageID{33}**.

LanguageID{33} — A human language identifying code, possibly user defined, but preferably an **ISO** or **IANA** defined code, and possibly including a subcode that identifies a regional dialect.

last() — A function in an expression used in **XPath** that returns the location of the last node in its list of siblings, as returned by the expression. Usually used for comparisons, such as '[not(position() = last())]'. See **position()**.

L^AT_EX — [pronounced 'lay-teck'] Popular **macro**-based extension to the T_EX typesetting language, facilitating **descriptive markup**.

leaf — A node that has no sub-nodes. In **DTD** markup, an **empty element** or element that contains only text. In document markup, an element that contains no child elements or text (pseudo element).

Letter — See **Letter{84}**.

Letter{84} — A subset of the **Unicode** character set containing characters that are deemed to be described as 'letters'.

Letter Value attribute — An **XSLT** attribute to the **Number** element, used to specify whether the primary numbering scheme for the language concerned is used (in English, 'A', 'B', 'C'), indicated with a value of 'alphabetic', or an alternate scheme is used (in English, the Roman system, 'i', 'ii', 'iii', 'iv'), indicated by a value of 'other'.

Level attribute — An **XSLT** attribute to the **Number** element, used to specify whether the counter is reset at the parent element ('single') or not ('any'), or whether the number is made of several parts ('multiple').

LF *(Line Feed)* — Special character used to end a line in **ASCII** and **ISO/IEC 646:1991**. Theoretically, the action of moving down one line, with the carriage return (**CR**) used to move back to the left edge of the page, though operating systems vary in their usage of one or both of these characters to start a new line.

Li element — An **HTML** element that is used within the **Ol** and **Ul** elements to identify a single item in a list.

line break — a break in a line of text due to the presence of the right edge of the page or border of the screen, or because a line break control character (or combination) is present. See **CR** and **LF**.

Line Break element — See **Br** element.

line feed — See **LF**.

Link attribute — An **HTML 3.2** attribute to the **Body** element that specifies a new colour for **hypertext** reference text contained in the **A** element. The colour for a link not yet visited. See **Alink** and **Vlink**.

Link element — An **HTML** element that identifies resources connected with this page.

link role — In XLink, an attribute of each link that assigns it to a user-defined category, for such purposes as styling each class differently or having different actions taken on selection.

link step — The number of steps an XLink process should take when collecting together documents that are interlinked. By setting a limit, this avoids possibly every document in the world being processed before all the possible links to a particular document can be shown.

linked style sheet — The term used to describe a **style sheet** conforming to the **CSS** standard which is held separately from the document or documents to which it applies.

linking element — An **element** that contains an **attribute** that identifies another **resource** (of possible interest to the reader).

List Item — See **Li** element.

lo-byte — When a value is too large (greater than 255) to be stored in a single byte, two bytes must be used. This gives 256 multiplied by 256 possible values (65,536), and is known as a **16-bit** value. But one byte must be identified as the one that increments by one each time the other reaches 255. This is the **hi-byte**. The other byte is the lo-byte.

local-part() — Used in an **XPath** expression to extract the local name part of an element name that includes a **Namespace** prefix, as in 'h3' from 'html:h3'. See **namespace()**.

Locale element — An **XSLT** element that specifies a local language number format, using the **Decimal Separator** and **Grouping Separator** attributes (amongst many others).

location source — In **XLink**, the fixed-point from which to navigate to a required **resource**. Typically, the **document element**.

location term — One of the directions in an **extended pointer**. For example, 'go to the top of the document', 'go down to the third chapter' and 'go in to the fifth paragraph' are all equivalent to location terms, though keywords are actually used.

locator — In **XLink**, something that points to a resource. A 'locator' is actually an attribute value in a **linking element**.

Locator interface — Defined in the **SAX** standard, to be implemented by objects that can accept details on the location of errors. Must be registered with the parser using the **setLocale** method in the object that instantiates the **Parser** interface. See the **DocumentHandler**, **AttributeList**, **DTD Handler** and **ErrorHandler** interfaces.

low energy — A process that is fully or highly automated, relatively effortless to perform (once the necessary software filters are written), and therefore cost efficient. Often used to describe conversions from XML format to other formats (known as a **down-convert**ing process). See **high energy**.

lower-case — Small letters. The lower-case equivalent of the **upper-case** letter 'A' is 'a'. The name is derived from the fact that these **character**s were found in the lower part of the printer's type case.

lower-first — A possible value for the **Case Order** attribute in **XSLT**, indicating that 'a' appears before 'A' in a sorted list.

lt — The name of a reserved entity that represents the less-than character, '<', used to avoid confusing a data character with a tag delimiter. See also **gt**.

LZW — An compression scheme for **image format** data, owned by CompuServe and used in **GIF**.

M

macro — A group of typesetting instructions that may be activated by reference to a name. One instruction replaces many, and may take a meaningful name. A feature of **generic coding** schemes. For example, a **macro call** named 'Title' will activate a **macro definition** of the same name (it may contain instructions to centre the following text, and compose it in 18pt Helvetica typeface). An equivalent feature, termed 'style-sheets', is found in some modern word processors and DTP systems.

macro call — A named reference to a **macro definition**. See **macro**.

macro definition — A collection of one or more **markup** tags given a name for use by a **macro call** in the **data stream**. See **macro**.

many-to-many — A term used to describe relationships between items in separate domains. Most frequently found describing records in separate tables of a **relational database**, where a many-to-many relationship, such as 'an author (possibly) writes many documents and a document is (possibly) written by many authors' would be normalized into a more manageable form by adding an intermediate table, with **one-to-many** relationships to the original two tables. Also see **one-to-one**.

Map element — *[1]* An **HTML** element that defines active areas for an associated image, using **Area** elements. The **Name** attribute value links the map to a specific **Img** element. *[2]* An **XML Catalog** element for mapping public identifiers to system identifiers, using the **PublicId** and **HRef** attributes. See **Remap** and **Base**.

Marginheight attribute — An **HTML** attribute to the **Frame** element, specifying the space between the top and bottom margins of a frame and its enclosed text.

Marginwidth attribute — An **HTML** attribute to the **Frame** element, specifying the space between the left and right margins of a frame and its enclosed text.

markup — A **tag** added to electronic data to specify style (**descriptive markup**) or add structure (**procedural markup** or **generalized** markup) to the data. In XML, a document component is identified by an **element**[39].

markup declaration — A special tag in XML that is *not* used to mark up a document, but is used for many other purposes, such as to build the document structure rules (the **DTD**), identify and locate each **entity** or define alternative document segments. Delimited by '<!' and '>' characters. See **markupdecl**[29].

markup delimiter — A character or characters that signify the start or end of **markup** embedded in the text. In XML, some markup delimiters are '<', '</', '>', '/>', '<?', '?>', '<!', '&', '%' and ';'. If these characters are required as data, they are represented by an **entity reference** such as '<' (less than, '<'). In **SGML**, they may be changed in a **variant concrete syntax**.

markup minimization — A feature of **SGML** (and to some extent **HTML**) whereby some parts of a tag (or even the whole tag) can be safely omitted as its presence can be implied. XML does not have any minimization features.

markupdecl[29] — The various markup declaration tags that define **entities** and construct a **DTD**.

Match attribute — An **XSLT** attribute to the **Template** element. Used to specify the **pattern** that identifies when the template is to be activated

MathML — A proposal from the W^3C for encoding of mathematical formulae using XML markup, described using an XML **DTD**. As with earlier schemes, such as part of the **ISO 12083** standard, some of the tags describe the formatting of a formula, but to this model is added another which describes the content of the formula logically, making it possible to compare formula when searching data. MathML is designed to be compatible with both ISO 12083 and **TeX**, to the extent that data can be automatically converted into MathML. Work began in 1994 and is nearing completion. See http://www.w3.org/TR/WD-math.

Maxlength attribute — An **HTML** attribute to the **Input** element, specifying the maximum number of characters that may be entered in a text field.

MCF *(Meta-Content Framework)* — A proposal for an XML-based standard to describe information about information (meta-data). See **XML-Data** and **RDF**.

Media attribute — An **HTML 4.0** attribute to the **Style** element that identifies the media at which the style rules are aimed, such as 'paper' or 'screen'.

Menu element — An **HTML** element containing a list of short items, ideally a list of menu options from a program.

Message element — An **XSLT** element that holds a message to be output by the system performing the transformation. In a command-line system, this would be a message to the command-line. In a GUI system, this may be a pop-up window. Used primarily as a debugging aide.

Meta element — An **HTML** element containing information intended to be read and interpreted by the browser.

meta-data — Data about data, existing only to identify or describe some 'genuine' information. In a book, the table of contents and index are types of meta-data. In a relational database, the primary key may only exist to link records in different tables. Online databases often have a 'keywords' field for finding appropriate records.

meta-language — A language for defining another **language**. XML is an example, using a **DTD** to define a bespoke **markup** language.

Methods attribute — An **HTML 2.0** only attribute to the **A** and **Link** elements that describes the methods allowed in these links. See also **Urn**.

MIME *(Multi-purpose Independent Mail Extensions)* — [pronounced 'mime'] A standard for identifying the formats in a mixed media mail or **HTTP** message, including pictures and text. **HTML** is a MIME format, as specified by the header line 'Content-Type: text/html'. **JPEG** is another, identified by 'content-Type: image/jpeg'. MIME is used by the **Web** to send information on the file content type. Contact 'comp.mail.mime' newsgroup. See **RFC 1590**.

minimization — In **SGML** and **HTML**, one or more techniques for omitting markup that can be implied from context. Not applicable to XML.

Miscellaneous — See **Misc**[27].

Misc[27] *(Miscellaneous)* — Non-hierarchically sensitive markup that may occur after the **document element**, and around the document type declaration (**doctypedecl**[28]). Any mixture of spaces (**S**[03]), **Comment**[15] and processing instructions (**PI**[16]).

Mixed — See **Mixed**[51].

Mixed[51] — The definition of the content of an **element**, when both sub-elements and document text are allowed, in any combination. The keyword '**#PCDATA**' identifies the allowed presence of text, and must appear first in the content model ('(#PCDATA | emph | quote)').

mixed content — A combination of text and elements. For example, a paragraph may contain text and Emphasis and Quote elements. See **Mixed**{51}.

mod — Used in an expression in **XPath** to get the remainder after dividing one number by another.

mode — In **XSLT**, different style rules may apply to the content of an element, depending on the context in which that content is presented. For example, the content of a Title element typically appears differently for its presentation at the top of a new chapter, compared to its appearance in a table of contents. See **Mode** attribute.

Mode attribute — An **XSLT** attribute to the **Template** element, which identifies a **mode** by name.

model group — a sequence or option group in an element declarations, possibly enclosing other model groups. Brackets enclose the group.

mono-spaced — A font that contains characters that are all the same width, which can be useful for illustrating typewriter or old computer output, or for lining up vertically aligned textual structures (see **Pre** element in **HTML**). Also termed 'fixed pitch'.

Multi-purpose Independent Mail Extensions — See **MIME**.

multimedia — The same as **hypermedia**, except that differing information types may be synchronized – for example, music accompanying a video clip, described by a scrolling caption. See **HyTime**.

Multiple attribute — An **HTML** attribute to the **Select** element, with a single possible value of 'multiple', which allows several items to be selected in the menu.

N

Name — See **Name**{05}.

Name{05} — A group of characters that can be considered the name of an element, attribute etc. By definition, starting with a letter, '-' or ':', and thereafter consisting of optional further letters, digits, '.', '-', '_', ':' and other **Unicode** characters.

Name attribute — *[1]* An **XSLT** attribute to the **Processing Instruction** (PI) element, specifying the name of the target application (the content of the pi element is the processing instruction itself), and to the **Variable** element to identify the variable name. Also to the **Template** element, to make it a re-usable template, to be referenced from **Call Template** elements. Also to the **Param** and **With Param** elements to name and reference parameter variables. Also to the **Element** element, providing the name of the output element. *[2]* An **HTML** attribute to the **A** element, where it is used to identify the **target** object of the link; in the **Meta** element, where it is used to name a unit of information; in the **Input** element, where it is used to group buttons for selection purposes; in the **Applet** element, where it is used to identify an **applet** for communication with other active applets; in the **Param** element, where it is used to identify a parameter value; and in the **Frame** element, where it is used to identify the frame for use as a target.

Name Character — See **NameChar**{04}.

name group — A set of tokens that define an attribute's possible values.

name resolution — The replacement of a **domain name** by its associated **IP number**, as the first step to finding a resource on the **Internet**.

name server — A computer attached to the **Internet** that converts **domain name**s into **IP address**es.

name token — See **Nmtoken**{07}.

name tokens — See **Nmtokens**{08}.

NameChar[04] *(Name Character)* — A subset of the Unicode character set that defines characters allowed in a **Nmtoken**[07] and, except for the first character, allowed in a **Name**[05], consisting of letters, digits and miscellaneous characters ('.', '-', '_' and ':').

NamedNodeMaps interface — Defined in the **DOM** standard, to represent a set of nodes that have no sequential context, but do have unique names. It contains the **item**, **getLength**, **getNamedItem**, **setNamedItem** and **removeNamedItem** methods. This object is returned by the methods **getAttributes** and **getChildNodes**. See **NamedNodeMap** interface.

Names — See **Names**[06].

Names[06] — One or more names (**Name**[05]) words separated by **white space**. A top-level rule, but referred to as value constraints in attribute values.

Namespace — An 'environment' within which element names and attribute names are guaranteed to be unique. A DTD defines a single namespace. The namespace 'problem' emerges when documents include elements from different DTDs or schema. See http://www.w3.org/TR/1998/NOTE-xml-names.

namespace() — Used in an **XPath** expression to extract the global part of an element name that includes a **Namespace** prefix, as in 'html' from 'html:h3'. See **local-part()**.

Namespace attribute — An optional **XSLT** attribute to the **Element** and **Attribute** elements, used to declare the **Namespace** prefix (the rest of the element name is provided by the **Name** attribute).

NDataDecl[76] *(Notational Data Declaration)* — The information that an external entity conforms to a **notation** type other than XML, such as 'NDATA TeX'.

NDATA keyword — The **reserved name** for the keyword that indicates the content of an **external entity** is composed of non-XML data (for example, an image format). The 'non-XML data' keyword. A name follows the keyword, identifying the format to match declarations to references. Such entities must be referenced using an attribute value, not an entity reference.

nested element — An **element** that may contain itself, directly, or indirectly via another element, thus allowing potentially endless recursion.

net-enabling start-tag — Single character delimiter option for brief elements in **SGML**. Set to solidus, '/', in the **reference concrete syntax**. For example, 'Water is H<sub/2/O' is shorthand for 'Water is ₂O'.

Network Information Center — See **NIC**.

new — An **XLink** value in the **Show** attribute, indicating that the resource pointed to should be displayed in a new window, leaving the source text on-screen.

NIC *(Network Information Center)* — A system that holds information on **Internet** standards, including **RFC** documents and FYI (For Your Information) documents, made available using **FTP**.

NMTOKEN — A keyword that restricts the value of an attribute to a single word. See **Nmtoken**[07].

Nmtoken[07] *(Name token)* — An attribute type that consists of a single word. Similar to a **Name**[05], except that there is no special restriction on the first character value.

NMTOKENS — A keyword that restricts the value of an attribute to one or more **NMTOKEN**s. See **Nmtokens**[08].

Nmtokens[08] *(Name tokens)* — More than one name token, separated by spaces, such as 'green red white blue'.

No Break — See **Nobr** element.

Nobr element — An **HTML 3.2** element used to contain text which should not be wrapped over multiple lines. The 'no break' element. The **Wbr** element can override this rule at specific points in the text.

node — An object in a **grove**, consisting of at least one **property**. An element definition in a DTD can be represented by a node, with properties for its attribute definitions and its content model. An element instance in a document can also be represented by a node, with properties for its attribute values and its actual content. See **leaf** and **node()**.

node() — A function of a navigation expression used in **XPath** that identifies any object in the document tree, including elements, attributes, comments, processing instructions and text. See **text()**, **processing-instruction()** and **comment()**.

Node interface — Defined in the **DOM** standard, to represent any component of an XML document, including an element, an attribute, a comment and a block of text. Contains the **getNodeType**, **getNodeName**, **getNodeValue**, **hasChildNodes**, **getAttributes** and **getOwnerDocument** characteristics methods, the **getFirstChild**, **getLastChild**, **getNextSibling**, **getPreviousSibling**, **getParentNode** and **getChildNodes** navigation methods; and the **removeChild**, **insertBefore**, **appendChild**, **replaceChild** and **cloneNode** manipulation methods. Subclassed by **DocumentFragment**, **Document**, **CharacterData**, **Attr**, **Element**, **DocumentType**, **Notation**, **Entity**, **EntityReference** and **ProcessingInstruction** interfaces for more specific handling of these objects.

Node Enumerator class — A **DOM** class that represents a sequence of **sibling** elements. Each instance of this class has methods that make it easy to traverse through a list of nodes, including methods to get the first node in the list and to get the next node in the list.

Node List class — A **DOM** class. Each instance represents a list of sibling nodes and has methods to select one and discover how many there are. This class is usually extended by a **Node Enumerator** class.

NodeList interface — Defined in the **DOM** standard, to represent a set of nodes that have sequential context. It contains the **item** and **getLength** methods. This object is returned by the methods **getElementsByTagName** and **getChildNodes**. See **NamedNodeMap** interface.

Noframes element — An **HTML** element used in a **frame** to contain text which should be displayed if the browser has no frame capability. See **Frame** element.

non-validating — An **XML processor** that does *not* compare usage of elements and attributes against the rules defined in a **DTD**. However, correct use of syntax and requirement for the document to be **well-formed** is checked. See **validating parser**.

Noresize attribute — An **HTML** attribute to the **Frame** element to specify that the frame cannot be re-sized by the user.

normalization — When **minimization** has been used in a document, normalization is the process of inserting the missing markup. For example, in **SGML** and **HTML** it is possible to omit end-tags. A document is normalized if these tags are inserted. A significant part of converting SGML documents into valid XML documents involves normalizing it.

normalize method — A **DOM** method in the **Element** interface. Used to merge adjacent **Text** nodes in all descendants of the element.

normalize() — Used in an expression in **XPath** to remove leading and trailing spaces, and reduce multiple spaces to a single space.

normalized space — To separate terms in various contexts it is sufficient to insert a single space character between them, yet **DTD** and document authors may use other **white space** characters, or multiple spaces. To facilitate parsing and text comparison, an **XML processor** detects a sequence of white space characters and reduces it to a single space.

Noshade attribute — An **HTML 3.2** attribute to the **Hr** element, used to specify no shading of the horizontal rule.

not() — A function in an expression used in **XPath** that returns the opposite booleanvalue to the result of the embedded expression. This example returns true if the current node is not the last in the list: '`[not(position() = last())]`'.

notation — Representation of natural phenomena by signs. Speech is represented by a written notation (involving letters, punctuation and left-to-right or right-to-left ordering), and also by a braille notation. In computing this term is used interchangeably with 'data format', such as **ASCII**, **CGM** and **SGML**.

NOTATION — The keyword that asserts the value of an attribute will be a valid **notation** name, as defined in a **Notation Declaration**.

notation declaration — A **declaration** that assigns a unique name to a non-XML format, and may identify a document describing the format, and/or a program capable of processing the format. See **NotationDecl**[82].

Notation interface — Defined in the **DOM** standard, to represent an XML **notation declaration**. A subclass of the **Node** interface, adding the **getPublicId** and **getSystemId** methods. These objects are obtained using the **getEntities** method in the **DocumentType** interface, and are wrapped in a **NamedNodeMap** object. See **Entity** interface.

notation type — An attribute type, indicating that the attribute contains the name of a notation for a data format other than XML. See **NotationType**[58].

Notational Data Declaration — See **NDataDecl**[76].

notationDecl method — A **SAX** method defined in the **DTDHandler** interface. Used by the parser to pass information extracted from **notation declaration**s to the application. See **unparsed EntityDecl**.

NotationDecl[82] *(Notation Declaration)* — A declaration that names a notation and identifies the location of a program that can process the data.

NotationType[58] — Part of an attribute definition (**AttDef**[53]) that is used to identify the notation used for the data in the element, when it is not XML format.

NSGMLS — The 'New SGML Structured' parser that replaces **SGMLS**. A freely available command-line-based SGML parser, but with the correct **SGML declaration** may also be used to validate XML documents. Contact jjc@jclark.com.

null end-tag — An SGML **end-tag** that consists of a single special character, which is used again at the end of the **start-tag**. For example, 'H<sub/2/0' is the same as 'H₂0'.

number — A possible value for the **Data Type** attribute in **XSLT**, indicating that '12' appears after '7' in a sorted list, ignoring the normal **ASCII** code of each character. See **text**.

number() — Used in an expression in **XPath** to convert the result of an embedded expression into a number. See **string()** and **boolean()**.

Number element — An **XSLT** element used to generate number sequences in such things as numeric lists. Counting is affected by the **Level**, **Format**, **Count** and **From** attributes. The format of the number is affected by the **Grouping Separator** and **Grouping Size** attributes.

numeric character reference — A **character reference** containing a numeric value representing a character. Identified by leading '&#', consisting of the decimal value of a character, and concluding with a semi-colon, ';'. For example, 'A' represents 'A' in **ASCII**.

O

o — The reserved name for the **SGML** keyword that indicates that a **start-tag** or **end-tag** may be omitted from the document. The 'omit' keyword. May be changed to another name in a **variant concrete syntax**.

OASIS — The new name for **SGML Open**.

object — An identifiable unit of information, possibly containing both discrete data units and also functions that operate on that data.

object database — A database technology that can represent complex data structures easily, unlike the **relational database** approach, which organizes data into simple tables. The **ODMG** (*Object Database Management Group*) devised the ODMG object database standard (currently ODMG 2.0), which includes OQL (the *Object Query Language*). Suitable for permanent storage of objects created using object-oriented programming languages, such as **Java**. Also utilized by SGML-aware and XML-aware **document management** systems for storage of document components. Contact http://www.odmg.org.

OCR *(Optical Character Recognition)* — The automated recognition of character shapes on an image of a page containing text, from which **ASCII** text is output to allow manipulation or searching of this text. More explicitly the earliest technology for achieving this, which relied on pre-defined template matching to specific shapes on the image. The weakness of this approach is that unknown **font**s are not recognized. See **ICR**.

ODA *(Open Document Architecture)* — Until 1990 known as 'Office Document Architecture'. A standard (ISO 8613) for defining document components for interchange between differing word processors and desktop publishing systems. An attempt to classify the features of such systems. It combines a structure view of the document (in similar fashion to **SGML**), with a layout view that specifies where on the page, and possibly on *which* page, an object appears. Contact http://sil.org/sgml/odanov10.html. In 1986 this format was discontinued as an ISO standard.

Office Document Architecture — Old name for 'Open Document Architecture'. See **ODA**.

Ol element — An **HTML** element containing an ordered list, consisting of **Li** elements.

omitted tag minimization — Determines whether the SGML **start tag** or **end tag** of a declared **element** may be absent in the document.

Onclick attribute — An **HTML** attribute added to almost all elements in **HTML 4.0**, allowing any element instance to activate an **ECMAScript** function when the mouse is clicked in that element. The **Onmousedown** and **Onmouseup** events also occur. Also see **Ondblclick**.

Ondblclick attribute — An **HTML** attribute added to almost all elements in **HTML 4.0**, allowing any element instance to activate an **ECMAScript** function when the mouse is double-clicked in that element. See **Onclick**.

one-to-many — A term used to describe relationships between items in different domains. For example, 'an author (possibly) writes many documents'. An ideal form of relationship in a **relational database**, but see also **one-to-one** and **many-to-many**.

one-to-one — A term used to describe relationships between items in different domains. For example, 'a document has one title'. See **one-to-many** and **many-to-many**.

Onkeydown attribute — An **HTML** attribute added to almost all elements in **HTML 4.0**, allowing any element instance to activate an **ECMAscript** function when key is depressed (but not yet released) while the mouse pointer is over that element. See **Onkeyup**.

Onkeypress attribute — An **HTML** attribute added to almost all elements in **HTML 4.0**, allowing any element instance to activate an **ECMAscript** function when a key is pressed while the mouse pointer is over that element. The **Onkeydown** and **Onkeyup** events also occur.

Onkeyup attribute — An **HTML** attribute added to almost all elements in **HTML 4.0**, allowing any element instance to activate an **ECMAscript** function when key is depressed (but not yet released) while the mouse pointer is over that element. See **Onkeyup**.

Onmousedown attribute — An **HTML** attribute added to almost all elements in **HTML 4.0**, allowing any element instance to activate an **ECMAscript** function when the mouse button is depressed while the pointer is in that element. See **Onmouseup**.

Onmouseout attribute — An **HTML** attribute added to almost all elements in **HTML 4.0**, allowing any element instance to activate an **ECMAscript** function when the mouse pointer is moved away from that element. See **Onmouseover**.

Onmouseover attribute — An **HTML** attribute added to almost all elements in **HTML 4.0**, allowing any element instance to activate an **ECMAscript** function when the mouse pointer is moved over that element. See **Onmouseout**.

Onmouseup attribute — An **HTML** attribute added to almost all elements in **HTML 4.0**, allowing any element instance to activate an **ECMAscript** function when the mouse button is released while the pointer is in that element. See **Onmousedown**.

Open Document Architecture — See **ODA**.

Open Trading Protocol — See **OTP**.

Option element — An **HTML** element used within the **Select** element to identify a single item in a menu list. The **Selected** attribute to this element pre-selects one item in the list.

optional feature — A feature of the **SGML** language that is optional, switched on or off within the **SGML declaration** using **reserved name**s ('SHORTREF', 'CONCUR', 'DATATAG', 'OMITTAG', 'RANK', 'SHORTTAG', 'SUBDOC', 'FORMAL', 'IMPLICIT' and 'EXPLICIT'). Not applicable to XML.

or — Used in an expression in **XPath** to test two sub-expressions, returning true if either sub-expression is true. See **and**.

Order attribute — An **XSLT** attribute to the **Sort** element, specifying how to order the sorted result, either 'ascending' (ABC) or 'descending' (CBA). See **Select**.

Ordered List — See **Ol** element.

OTOH — Abbreviation for 'On The Other Hand' used in online conversation. Others include **BTW** (By The Way), **IMHO** (In My Humble Opinion), **FYI** (For Your Information) and **FWIW** (For What Its Worth).

OTP *(Open Trading Protocol)* — A proposed, independent standard for an interoperable message protocol for payments, invoices and receipts. Contact http://www.otp.org.

out-of-line — An object that is not part of a sequence of objects, such as paragraphs on a page. Used to describe a type of **hypertext** link where the element that describes the link is not embedded in the text, and also used to describe document objects, such as images, which do not need to appear at the point in the text where they are referenced. See **in-line**.

out-of-line link — A type of **hypertext** link where the element that describes the link is not embedded in the text. The benefit of this is that links can be added to read-only documents, and are more easily maintained if grouped together.

owner identifier — The part of a **formal public identifier** that identifies the owner of the specified **external entity**.

P

P element — An **HTML** element used to contain a paragraph.

page — Common term for an **HTML** document. See **Web page**.

Page Description Language — See **PDL**.

Page Wide — See **Pgwide** attribute.

paginate — The process of placing **compose**d text and other parts of a document, such as images, onto at least one page, or as an intermediate step into a **PDL** (*Page Description Language*) such as **PostScript**.

Paragraph element — See **P** element.

Param element — *[1]* An **HTML** element used within an **Applet** element to deliver parameter values to the **Java** applet. *[2]* An **XSLT** element used to define a parameter variable, using the **Name** attribute to provide the name of the attribute, and the content of the element provides the default value, which may be overriden using the **With Param** element.

parameter — Feature of a **tag** that can contain modifying variables. A parameter value may have a meaning associated with its location in the tag (for example, name followed by size, '`*FONT times 18:`') or indicated by a parameter name (for example, 'name' and 'size', '`<font size="18" name="times">`'). An **attribute** is an XML element parameter, and each attribute has a name and value (so the order of parameter appearance is not significant).

Parameter element — See **Param** element.

parameter entity — An **entity** that may be referred to only within **markup**. Used mostly to aid construction of a **DTD**, but may also be used by document authors in the **internal subset** to override or select DTD options. A parameter entity may share the same name as a **general entity** without confusion, as it is distinguished by the '%' character in both the declaration and reference.

Parameter Entity Declaration — See **PEDecl**[72].

Parameter Entity Definition — See **PEDef**[74].

parameter entity reference — An **entity reference** that can be entered only within **markup**, so is mostly the province of the **DTD** author rather than the document author. See **general entity reference**.

Parameter Entity Reference — See **PEReference**[69].

parent — A concept derived from family trees that describes an **element** that encloses another element as part of a **hierarchy** of elements. For example, a Book element may be the parent of several Chapter elements. See **child** and **sibling**.

parent:: — An **XPath** expression that selects the parent of the current node, if it conforms the given name, which may be '**node()**' to avoid exclusion in all cases. Abbreviates to '..', so '`parent::node()`' is the same as '..'.

parse — Decoding and understanding, using the rules of a grammar. In XML, the process of checking the legal use of **markup**, as performed by the **validating parser** module of an **XML processor**.

parse method — A **SAX** method defined in the **Parser** interface. Used to activate parsing. Accepts a String (**URL**) or **InputSource** object for streamed parsing.

parsed entity — An entity whose content is valid XML data, forming part of the document structure, so is required to be parsed by any validating **parser**. See **binary entity**.

parser — Software designed to **parse** the content of a document for syntactical and possibly also logical errors, forming part of an **XML processor** software module. May aid and control the authoring or editing process. A term that is casually used to describe the entire XML processor. See **validating parser**.

Parser interface — Defined in the **SAX** standard, to be implemented by objects that perform the task of parsing and making the data and error messages available to a calling application. Defines the **parse**, **setDocumentHandler** (see **DocumentHandler** interface), **setErrorHandler** (see **ErrorHandler**), **setDTDHandler** (see **DTD Handler**), **setEntityResolver** (see **EntityResolver**) and **setLocale** ((see **Locator**)) methods.

pattern — An **expression** that is used to match a given node in the document tree against a pre-defined template. The pattern 'chapter/title' matches any title that is the direct child of a Chapter element.

PCDATA — The **keyword** that represents normal character data. The 'parsable character data' keyword. Preceded by the hash-symbol, '#', to avoid confusion with an identical **element** name, when used within a **model group** (for example, '(#PCDATA | PCDATA)*'). See **Mixed**[51].

PDF *(Portable Document Format)* — The **PDL** used by **Adobe Acrobat**, derived from **PostScript** for on-screen page display. Contact comp.text.pdf newsgroup.

PDL *(Page Description Language)* — Data format for describing the content of a page of information. Includes commands for positioning each line of text on the page, drawing lines and painting graphics. **PostScript** is a popular PDL.

PEDecl[72] *(Parameter Entity Declaration)* — A declaration that defines a **parameter entity**, referred to in the **DTD** using a **PEReference**[69]. For general entities see **GEDecl**[71].

PEDef[74] *(Parameter Entity Definition)* — The part of a **PEDecl**[72] that holds the actual entity value or the identifier of an external value.

peer-to-peer — Two computers connected on a network where neither system has the set role of **server** or **client**, and at least some applications running on both systems can assume either of these roles.

PEReference[69] *(Parameter Entity Reference)* — A reference to a **parameter entity**, which must occur within markup, so as not to be confused with document entity references. For general entities see **EntityRef**[68].

PI[16] *(Processing Instruction)* — A special instruction that is to be interpreted by the receiving application, only to be used for information that cannot be expressed by the XML language.

PI class — A Java or C++ class in the **DOM** that is used to hold each instance of a **processing instruction**.

PICT — [pronounced 'pict'ure] A Macintosh-based **vector** (but also **raster**) **image format**. See **WMF** for PC variant and **CGM** for widely used standard.

PITarget[17] *(Processing Instruction Target)* — The part of a **PI**[16] that identifies the application which the instruction is aimed at. The target name 'xml' is a special case.

Plaintext element — An **HTML 2.0** element that identifies data that is to be presented exactly as stored in the file (now deprecated (along with **Xmp**), use the **Pre** element instead).

PNG *(Portable Network Graphics)* — An **Internet**-based **image format** devised in 1995 over the Internet by a number of independent developers. Likely to be a successor to **GIF** due to its vendor independence and increased capabilities. Strengths include consistent appearance on different computer platforms and a faster interlacing technique.

port — A communication channel through which an Internet application sends or receives data. See **port number**.

port number — To distinguish one application from another when a computer receives data or requests from other systems, each application is assigned a number. The client must know the port number of the server application in order to communicate with it. A port number must be in the range '0' to '65535' (a 16-bit number). Some applications are so common that they are assigned 'well known' port numbers by the **IANA**, including 7 for the echo utility, 25 for smtp (simple mail transport protocol), 70 for gopher and 80 for **HTTP**. Other registered port numbers fall into the range 1024 through 49151. A port number may appear in a **URL** when a server application is 'listening' on a different port to the default. A secondary HTTP server may be assigned to port '8080' (although this number is registered, a browser looks on '80' unless told otherwise), such as http://occam.sjf.novell.com:**8080**/dsssl/dsssl96. Remaining values are left unassigned for user-specific applications.

Portable Document Format — See **PDF**.

Portable Network Graphics — See **PNF**.

position() — A function in an expression used in **XPath** that returns the location of the current node in its list of siblings, as returned by the expression. See **last()**.

PostScript — The widely used **PDL** developed by Adobe. See **PDF**.

Pre element — An **HTML** element that encloses text which is not to be reformatted for presentation. Specifically, **line break**s are retained.

preceding:: — An **XPath** expression that selects a node that precedes the current node in document order. Similar to **preceding-sibling::**, except that the search goes back to the beginning of the document, at all levels in the document structure. See **following::**.

preceding-sibling:: — An **XPath** expression that selects a sibling of the current node, that precedes the node in document order. See **following-sibling::**.

Preformatted element — See **Pre** element.

Preserve Space element — An **XSLT** element, used to list in the **Elements** attribute all source document elements for which white space is to be preserved.

preserved space — A sequence of **white space** characters that are not normalized to a single space for presentation, parsing or comparison.

Priority attribute — An **XSLT** attribute used in the **Template** element to rank templates that match the same target element. There should always be one template that can be selected by its ranking value.

procedural markup — A **markup** scheme that describes how a document should look, possibly including **font** descriptions, and character styles such as **roman** and **italic**. See **RTF** and **descriptive markup**.

processing instruction — Application-specific text (to be processed by an application). To be used only when absolutely necessary.

Processing Instruction — See **PI**[16].

Processing Instruction element — An **XSLT** element used to create a processing instruction in the output file (using a real processing instruction in the style sheet does not work, as this is processed while reading the style sheet, not the output document). A **Name** attribute is used to provide the target application. See **Comment** element.

processing-instruction() — A function of a navigation expression used in **XPath** that identifies any **processing instruction** object in the document tree. See **node()**.

Processing Instruction Target — See **PITarget**[17].

ProcessingInstruction interface — Defined in the **DOM** standard, to represent an XML **processing instruction**. A subclass of the **Node** interface, adding no new methods. This object is created using the factory method **createProcessingInstruction** in the **Document** interface.

processingInstruction method — A **SAX** method defined in the **DocumentHandler** interface. Called by the parser when a **processing instruction** is detected. Two strings, representing the target application name and the data, are passed to it.

Prolog — See **Prolog**[22].

Prolog[22] — The first part of a **document**[01], specifying the version of XML in use, the document character set and requirements for DTD processing, and possibly either containing or referring to a **DTD**.

property — One piece of information in an **object**. For example, an object that describes a person may have a property for the age of that person and another to describe their height. See **property type**.

property type — The 'template' for a **property** within an object. Each instance of that property may have a different value. For example, three objects that each describe a person may all have an 'age' property, but each age property may hold a different value.

pseudo-element — A unit in the document hierarchy that is not a markup construct. Specifically, a string of text appearing before, after or between **in-line** elements, so that it can be considered a sibling to these elements when the document is viewed as a **tree**. The term has relevance to the advanced hypertext linking schemes in **XLink**, the **DOM** and **grove**s in general. For example, '`<p>this is a pseudo-element <em>but not this</em>.</p>`'.

PubidChar[13] *(Public identifier Character)* — One character in the quoted text of a **public identifier**, which identifies an object by a non-location-specific name. The text must not contain the same quote character used to enclose it.

PubidLiteral[12] *(Public identifier Literal)* — The literal text that identifies an object by a neutral name, including quotes to define the boundaries of the text, which may contain spaces.

public identifier — An **external entity** identifier that is not system specific (in terms of identifying either format or **entity** location). This identifier is expected to be compared with an entry in a **catalog** file, which provides the location and name of the system file. The public identifier may be a **formal public identifier**, in which case it has a rigid format that describes the owner, registered status and language of the entity.

Public Identifier — See **PublicID**[83].

Public identifier Character — See **PubidChar**[13].

Public identifier Literal — See **PubidLiteral**[12].

public text class — The part of a **formal public identifier** that describes the content of an **external entity**. Various class options include 'DTD' and 'ENTITIES'. In the latter case, the entity may only contain more entities.

public text description — The part of a **formal public identifier** that describes the information contained in the **external entity**. Enlarges on information provided by the **public text class**.

public text display version — The part of a **formal public identifier** that distinguishes between versions of public text stored in an entity.

public text language — The part of a **formal public identifier** that identifies the language used in the **external entity**. A two-character **ISO 639** defined code, such as 'EN' for English.

PublicID[83] *(Public Identifier)* — Strictly as used, a public identifier for a notation declaration. Perhaps this rule should also form part of **ExternalID**[75], which includes an identical fragment for identifiers in various other constructs.

PublicId attribute — An **XML Catalog** attribute used in the **Map** and **Delegate** elements to identify the **public identifier** of an **entity**, so that it can be mapped to a **system identifier** for the resource, or to a catalogue file.

publishing database — A **database** that exists purely to provide a platform from which information can be published. Often a half-way house for information derived from a number of different databases that are used for other purposes.

push technology — A term used to describe selected information that is delivered to a **Web browser** based on prior user selection of categories of interesting material. In reality, with current technology the browser still 'pulls' the **Web page** from the server.

Q

Q element — An **HTML 4.0** element that encloses an in-line quotation.

qualified name — an element or attribute name that includes a **namespace** prefix, to ensure that it is unique when mixed among markup from other namespaces.

quantity indicator — The number of times an **element** may appear at a given point in the document structure is governed by a special symbol, '?' (optional), '+' (repeatable) or '*' (optional and repeatable). When no symbol is present, the element is required and may not repeat. For example, '(title,para+)' indicates a required Title element, followed by at least one Paragraph element.

query — A question asked of a **DBMS** to retrieve specific information. The **SQL** query 'SELECT NAME FROM EMPLOYEES WHERE DEPARTMENT = 'Accounts'' returns the names of all employees (held in the 'name' **field** of the 'employees' **table**) in the accounts department.

query language — A computer language designed for the purpose of requesting information from a database. A request formed in such a language is termed a **query**.

quot — The name of a reserved entity that represents the double quote character, ' " ', used to avoid confusing a data character with an atribute value delimiter. See also **apos**.

Quotation — See **Q** element.

R

raster — Method of representing images electronically using computer memory to create a grid, with one or more bits representing a pixel (one bit allows black and white pictures, four bits allow 16 colours, or shades of grey, and 16 bits allow over 65,000 colors). The resolution (pixels per inch) is determined at the time of creation, and the resulting picture is not usually amenable to scaling or rendering at a different resolution. Compression schemes include **JPEG** and **CCITT Group IV**. The alternative representation scheme, designed to overcome some of the limitations of the raster technique, is the **vector** scheme.

RCDATA — An **SGML** concept that identifies text which may contain entity references, but no other markup is expected, so other **markup delimiter**s, such as '<', are safely considered to be data characters. Not applicable to XML.

RDF *(Resource Description Framework)* — A W^{3}C working draft for a foundation for processing metadata on the Web. Applications cited in the specification include providing better search engine capabilities and cataloguing the content of a Web site. See http://www.w3.org/TR/WD-rdf-syntax; it provides interoperability.

RE *(Record End)* — An **SGML** concept that surrounds each 'record' of data with **RS** *(Record Start)* and RE characters.

record — One row of a **table** in a **database**. A table containing details on employees would have one record for each employee. The record is split into a number of **field**s (which are the columns of the table).

record end — See **RE**.

record start — See **RS**.

recursive — Something that may contain itself. From programming circles, the term is used to describe a function that is able to call itself in order to break down a problem into smaller chunks. In XML, an element that may directly or indirectly contain another instance of itself (an **embedded** element).

Reference — See **Reference**[67].

Reference[67] — A reference to a **general entity**, such as '&myEnt;' or the value of a character, such as '{'.

reference concrete syntax — A number of default concrete settings in **SGML** that define quantity limits and the SGML language syntax. For example, the length of a tag has the implied maximum value of '960' and a start tag open delimiter is '<' by default. Values may be overridden within the **SGML declaration**.

reference capacity set — A number of default concrete settings in **SGML** that define the maximum number of various object types allowed. For example, the maximum number of elements that may appear in a document. Not applicable to XML, where no limits are defined.

registered — A **public identifier** for an **external entity** that is registered to ensure that it is unique, so that it can be referred to without ambiguity. See **registered owner identifier**.

registered owner identifier — A **public identifier** registered with the **ISO**, and therefore guaranteed unique. The public identifier begins with '+//', followed by the name of the owner. When an entity is owned by the ISO it has a different format, consisting of the publication number. See **ISO owner identifier**.

Rel attribute — An **HTML** attribute to the **A** and **Link** elements that indicates the contained **URL** is a pointer to the next logical part of a multi-page document. Other, contradictory, uses have been described. Try to avoid. See **Rev**.

relational database — A **database** technology that allows a number of **table**s to be interlinked by **key-field**s. This approach allows all duplication to be removed, by creating new tables where necessary, thus helping to ensure better consistency of the content than a **flat-file** database can provide. See **object database**.

relative link — A **hypertext link** that identifies the location of a resource in relation to some other resource, typically the location of the source document or element. See **absolute link**.

relative location — A hypertext link target that is not identified by a unique code, but by its location relative to other elements. For example, a link could be made to the fifth paragraph in the third chapter in a document. **XLink** has this capability. The weakness of this approach is that insertions and deletions to the text before the target make the link invalid. See **relative path**.

relative path — A navigation method in **XPath** that locates an object by its contextual location, rather than by a unique identifier. See **absolute path**.

Remap element — An **XML Catalog** element for mapping system identifiers to locally valid system identifiers, using the **SystemId** and **HRef** attributes. See **Map** and **Base**.

removeAttribute method — A **DOM** method in the **Element** interface. Used to remove an attribute from the element. The string attribute names the attribute. See **getAttribute** and **setAttribute**.

removeAttributeNode method — A **DOM** method in the **Element** interface. Takes the **Attr** object that represents the attribute as its parameter. Used to remove an attribute from the element. See **getAttributeNode** and **setAttributeNode**.

removeChild method — A **DOM** method in the **Node** interface. Used to remove a child node. A reference to the node to be removed is passed to the method, and this node is returned. See **replaceChild**.

removeNamedItem method — A **DOM** method in the **NamedNodeMap** interface. Used to remove a node in the list . A reference to the node to be removed is passed to the method.

replace — A possible value for the **Show** attribute in **XLink**. The target resource 'replaces' the reference text in the browser window. See **new** and **embed**.

replaceable character data — Text that may contain an **entity reference**, but not element tags. Any references will be replaced by the entity content. See **RCDATA**.

replaceChild method — A **DOM** method in the **Node** interface. Used to replace one child node with another, given as a parameter. A node representing the new node is returned. See **removeChild**.

replaceData method — A **DOM** method in the **CharacterData** interface. Used to replace one character string with another, given as a parameter, following the offset position and a value giving the number of original characters to delete first.

replacement text — The text defined in an **entity** that replaces all references to that entity.

required attribute — An **attribute** that must have a value entered by the document author as the **element** is created. In the **element declaration** this is indicated with the '**REQUIRED**' keyword. Typically, an XML-aware word processor automatically presents a dialogue box for entry of a required attribute value when such an element is inserted into the document. See **implied attribute**.

REQUIRED keyword — A keyword that identifies an **attribute** that must be given a value each time the element containing it is used.

reserved attribute — An **attribute** name that cannot be defined for ad hoc use by DTD authors, because it has special significance in all XML applications. All reserved attributes begin with 'xml'. For example 'xml:lang' is always used to identify the language of the content of an element.

reserved name — In **SGML**, the default name for a keyword, used to help create a **concrete syntax** from the **abstract syntax**. For example, the reserved name for the keyword that allows characters to be assigned to the role of indicating the beginning of a **start-tag** is 'STAGO', and a definition of 'STAGO !' assigns '!' to this role (replacing the default value of '<'). Not applicable to XML.

reserved name indicator — The symbol that precedes a keyword when it is used where element names or other special tokens are also allowed, to avoid confusing one with the other. The '#' symbol is used. For example, if the **DTD** author creates an element called PCDATA, it must not be confused with the PCDATA keyword: '(#PCDATA | PCDATA)*'.

Resize attribute — An **HTML** attribute to the **Frame** element. Its single value, 'resize', specifies that the panes of the frame can be resized (probably by dragging a boundary line).

resolution — The size of pixels (on screen) or dots (on paper). The smaller the dots, the 'higher' the resolution, and the better the quality of the text or image. Quantified in 'dots-per-inch', or **DPI**.

resolveEntity method — A **SAX** method defined in the **EntityResolver** interface. Called by the parser each time a reference to a binary entity is detected, allowing the application the opportunity to intercept and redirect to another resource.

resource — An object that is the target of a **hypertext link**.

Resource Description Framework — See **RDF**.

resource title — The title of a **resource**, used to provide a user with information prior to selecting a link to that resource.

Result Encoding attribute — An **XSLT** attribute to the **Stylesheet** and **Transform** elements that specifies which character set encoding scheme to use in the output file.

Result Namespace attribute — An **XSLT** attribute to the **Stylesheet** and **Transform** elements that is used to indicate the namespace prefix used for output elements, and if mapping to significant namespaces, such as the **FO DTD** namespace, then the **XSL** processor should take additional actions, such as directly formatting the text rather than outputting an XML file.

Result Version attribute — An **XSLT** attribute to the **Stylesheet** and **Transform** elements that specifies which version of XML is to be used in the output file.

Rev attribute — An **HTML** attribute to the **A** and **Link** elements that indicates the contained **URL** is a pointer to the previous logical part of a multi-page document. Other, contradictory, uses have been described in other sources. Try to avoid. See **Rel**.

RFC *(Request For Comments)* — An Internet-related standard proposal. There are usually a number of RFCs for each Internet protocol. Every RFC has a number, and most are accessible over the Internet. RFCs are maintained by the **IETF**. To reach the index file, contact ftp://ds.internic.net/rfc/rfc-index.txt. See **FYI**.

RFC 1590 — An **RFC** that describes the codes which may be used to identify a data type for multi-media-capable e-mail and **HTTP** browsers. The formal description of **MIME**.

RFC 1766 — An **RFC** that describes the codes which may be used to identify a human language.

Rich Text Format — See **RTF**.

RIP *(Raster Image Processor)* — [pronounced 'rip'] A program or computer chip that converts **vector** format data into **raster** output at a specified **resolution**. A **PostScript** RIP converts PostScript data into a page 'image', ready for output to screen or paper.

role — A feature of **XLink** that uses an attribute (default name **Role**) to create categories of link which may affect the style of the linking text or the behaviour of a specialist browser.

roman — A character style. The characters are printed upright, as these words are. See **italic**.

root element — Another term for **document element**. The element that encloses the entire document (the only element that has no **parent**).

round() — Used in an expression in **XPath** to convert a real number into an integer by rounding down or rounding up to the nearest whole number. See **ceiling()** and **floor()**.

router — A intermediate computer that passes **Internet** data between other systems.

Rows attribute — An **HTML** attribute to the **Textarea** element and **Frameset** element (a Netscape extension). Used to specify how many rows of text can appear.

Rowspan attribute — An **HTML** attribute to the **Th** element and **Td** element. Used to specify how many table rows the cell spans over. See **Colspan** attribute.

RS *(Record Start)* — An **SGML** concept that surrounds each 'record' of data with **RE** *(Record End)* and RS characters.

RTF *(Rich Text Format)* — A proprietary format developed by Microsoft that describes the format and style of a text-based document using **tag**s. Particularly suited to exchange of documents between computer platforms. For the specification, contact ftp://ftp.primate.wisc.edu/pub/RTF.

S

S-HTTP *(Secure HTTP)* — A variant of **HTTP** that offers security for commercial transactions using authentication (the client is who they say they are) and encryption (the data cannot be read by other parties). Also called 'HTTPS'.

S{03} *(Space)* — An character with no visible appearance, used to separate words and markup parameters, and to break the document into convenient lines of text. Apart from the space character itself, ' ', this includes the horizontal tab character and the two characters commonly used to start a new text line (**CR** and **LF**).

Samp element — An **HTML** element that contains text identified as sample data. To be displayed in a distinctive fashion.

Sample — See **Samp** element.

SAX *(Simple API for XML)* — [pronounced 'sax'ophone] A standard interface for applications to receive data from XML parsers. Includes a number of interfaces, including the **Parser** interface (implemented by the parser vendor) as well as the **DocumentHandler**, **EntityResolver**, **AttributeList**, **DTD Handler**, **ErrorHandler** and **Locator** interfaces. For tree-driven processing see **DOM**.

schema — The definition of a document structure, including value constraints and relationships between objects. Similar to a **DTD**, but potentially more powerful. See **DDML**.

Scrolling attribute — An **HTML** attribute to the **Frame** element that controls the presence of scroll bars to view content larger than the **frame** area.

Script element — An **HTML 4.0** element that contains scripts to make the Web page dynamic. The **Type** attribute identifies the scripting language. The **Src** identifies by a URL a remote style script file.

SDA *(SGML Document Access)* — A specification for an **architectural form**, specifically using **fixed attribute**s to support the **ICADD** initiative. Attribute names are significant; they specify how the following fixed value should be used in the SDA **DTD**. This DTD defines the following elements: Anchor (mark spot on page); Au (author); B (bold); Book (document element); Box (sidebar info); Fig (figure title); Fn (footnote); H1–H6 (headers); Ipp (ink print page); It (italic); Lang (language); Lhead (list heading); List; Litem (list item); Note; Other (emphasis); Para (paragraph); Pp (print page number); Term (or keyword); Ti (book title) and Xref (cross-reference). Allowable attribute names are **Sdaform**, **Sdarule**, **Sdabdy**, **Sdapref** and **Sdasuff**. See **ISO 12083** (Annex A.8) for more details. An example, mapping the Title element of a user-defined DTD to the ICADD element H1:

```
<!ATTLIST title SDAFORM  CDATA  #FIXED "h1"
```

Sdabdy attribute — Used to place an element in a wider context. Element mapping can be different for an element occurring in a body location as opposed to it occurring in a part location. See **Sdapart**.

Sdaform attribute — The name of an attribute that maps fixed attribute values to an element in the **SDA**-defined **DTD** created by **ICADD**. The example below maps a Title element in the source DTD to the Ti element in the SDA DTD:

```
<!ATTLIST title SDAFORM   CDATA  #FIXED  "ti"
```

Sdapart attribute — Used to place an element in a wider context. Element mapping can be different for an element occurring in a part location as opposed to it occurring in a body location. See **Sdabdy**.

Sdapref attribute — The name of an attribute that maps fixed attribute values to prefix text that replaces an element during transformation to the **SDA**-defined **DTD** created by **ICADD**. The example below maps an Abstract element in the source DTD to an obvious header in the SDA DTD. This may be usefully combined with the **Sdaform** attribute. See **Sdasuff** attribute.

```
<!ATTLIST abstract SDAPREF
                CDATA  #FIXED  '<h1>Abstract</h1>'
```

Sdarule attribute — The name of an attribute that maps fixed attribute values to an element in the **SDA**-defined **DTD** created by **ICADD**. Much like **Sdaform**, but with contextual rules. The example below maps a Title element appearing in a Chapter element in the source DTD to a H2 element in the SDA DTD. The Title of a Section is converted into H3.

```
<!ATTLIST chap SDARULE  CDATA #FIXED  "title h2"
<!ATTLIST sect SDARULE  CDATA #FIXED  "title h3"
```

Sdasuff attribute — The name of an attribute that maps fixed attribute values to suffix text that replaces an element during transformation to the **SDA**-defined **DTD** created by **ICADD**. The example below maps a Quote element in the source DTD to the quote character in the SDA DTD (as well as using **Sdapref** to prefix the content with another quote). This may be usefully combined with the **Sdaform** attribute.

```
<!ATTLIST quote SDASUFF   CDATA  #FIXED  '"'
                SDAPREF   CDATA  #FIXED  '"'>
```

SDATA — A keyword used in **SGML** to identify element and attribute content that is system dependent, so will need editing when the document is transferred to another system.

SDDecl[32] *(Standalone Document Declaration)* — The part of the **XMLDecl**[23] that states whether or not an external DTD needs to be read in order to accurately interpret the content of the document. A value of 'no' indicates the **DTD** is required, perhaps because it contains fixed attribute values, default attribute values of defines entities that are used in the document. A value of 'yes' indicates that the document can stand alone.

SDIF *(SGML Document Interchange Format)* — [pronounced 's-dif'ference] An **SGML**-related **ISO** standard (ISO 9069) for combining related **entity** objects into a single file object, generally for transfer to another system. Not widely used.

Select attribute — An **XSLT** attribute holding an **expression**, used in a number of elements. In the **Apply Templates** element, it is used to select the specific children or elements elsewhere in the document for immediate processing. In the **Sort** element, it specifies the element or attribute content that is to be used as the sort field. In the **Variable** element it generates the value of the variable. In the **Copy Of** element, it is used to find the elements to copy and output. In the **Value Of** element, it is used to locate the element or text fragment to convert into a value. In the **For Each** element, it selects each occurance of the named element to which the template must be applied.

Select element — An **HTML** element that encloses a menu from which a single item can be selected. Each option is defined using an **Option** element.

Selected attribute — An **HTML** attribute to the **Option** element that pre-selects that item in the **Select** list. The only possible value is 'selected', and the attribute name is typically omitted.

self:: — An **XPath** expression that selects the current node, if it conforms the given name, which may be '**node()**' to avoid exclusion in all cases. Abbreviates to '.', so 'self::node()' is the same as '.'.

self-describing — The main feature of a **generalized markup** language is that the names of elements make the information they contain self-describing. For example, text enclosed in an element called Quote is obviously a quote. The benefit is that software can process the data meaningfully, and document style decisions can be made later, using a **style sheet**.

separator — One or more characters used within a defined context to separate objects, such as one markup **parameter** from another.

seq[50] *(sequence)* — The definition of the content of an **element** when the content must be a strict series of other (child) elements and/or groups ('(title,author,(chap|sect),index)').

Sequence — See seq[50].

sequence connector — The character that takes the role of specifying a choice of token, '|'. For example, '(#PCDATA | emph | subscript | superscript)'.

serialization — The process of converting multi-dimensional object relationships and **one-to-many** relationships into a simple data stream, to facilitate transfer of information between systems. XML is a suitable carrier for serialized data.

server — An application that provides services to a **client** application, usually over a network. For example, a **Web server** provides HTML pages to **Web servers**. See **peer-to-peer**.

setAttribute method — A **DOM** method in the **Element** interface. Used to add an attribute to the element, giving first the name, then the value, both as strings. See **setAttributeNode** and **getAttribute**.

setAttributeNode method — A **DOM** method in the **Element** interface. Used to add an attribute to the element, giving a reference to the **Attr** object representing the attribute. See **setAttribute**.

setByteStream method — A **SAX** method defined in the **InputSource** interface. Used to specify a byte stream that contains XML data to be parsed. See also **setCharacterStream**.

setCharacterStream method — A **SAX** method defined in the **InputSource** interface. Used to specify a character stream that contains XML data to be parsed. See also **setByteStream**.

setData method — A **DOM** method in the **CharacterData** interface. Used to specify the text (actually the value property, so **setValue** in the **Node** interface is equivalent).

setDocumentHandler method — A **SAX** method defined in the **Parser** interface. Used to register an object that implements the **DocumentHandler** interface (that deals with document events such as start-tags and text blocks).

setDocumentLocator method — A **SAX** method defined in the **DocumentHandler** interface. Called by the parser to pass an object that implements the **Locator** interface to the application, so that the application can access information on the location of errors and warnings after the **Warning**, **Error** or **fatalError** method has been called.

setEncoding method — A **SAX** method defined in the **InputSource** interface. Used to specify a character set encoding scheme for the XML data to be parsed.

setEntityResolver method — A **SAX** method defined in the **Parser** interface. Used to register an object that implements the **EntityResolver** interface (that intercepts calls to external entities).

setErrorHandler method — A **SAX** method defined in the **Parser** interface. Used to register an object that implements the **ErrorHandler** interface (that handles or reports error messages).

setLocale method — A **SAX** method defined in the **Parser** interface. Used to register an object that tells the parser which language to use for errors and warnings.

setNamedItem method — A **DOM** method in the **NamedNodeMap** interface. Used to add a node to the list, passing a reference to the node to add. The method returns a reference to the same node.

setNodeValue method — A **DOM** method in the **Node** interface. Used to add a node to the list, passing a reference to the node to add. See **getNodeValue**.

setPublicId method — A **SAX** method defined in the **InputSource** interface. Used to specify a **public identifier** for the XML data to be parsed. See also **setSystemId**.

setSystemId method — A **SAX** method defined in the **InputSource** interface. Used to specify a **system identifier** for the XML data to be parsed. See also **setPublicId**.

setDTDHandler method — A **SAX** method defined in the **Parser** interface. Used to register an object that implements the **DTDHandler** interface (that handles notations and binary entities).

setValue method — A **DOM** method in the **Attr** interface. Used to change the value of an attribute (essentially the same as **setNodeValue**). A string value is passed to the method. See **getValue**.

SGML *(Standard Generalized Markup Language)* — The ISO 8879 standard developed in 1986 to assist electronic delivery and publication of text-based documents. Classified under 'Information processing – Text and office systems'. Developed and maintained by the ISO/IEC JTC1 SC18/**WG8** committee. A language is defined for creation of document structure rules in a **DTD**. Contact comp.text.sgml newsgroup. See **SGML Users' Group** and **SGML Open**.

SGML Declaration — The first part of an **SGML** document, providing defaults such as the **concrete syntax** and the **reference capacity set**.

SGML Document Access — See **SDA**.

SGML Open — A non-profit international consortium of suppliers supporting and promoting **SGML** and **XML** (now renamed **OASIS**). Responsible for setting or rationalizing standards that rest upon SGML. As examples, a standard **catalog** format has been agreed (but see **XML Catalog**), and the **CALS table** model refined and harmonized. Contact http://www.sgmlopen.org/. See **GCA** and **SGML Users' Group**. For **HTML** equivalents see **IETF** and **W³C**.

SGML Users' Group — A non-profit organization formed in 1984 to promote the use of **SGML** and the sharing of information. It has many regional and national chapters. Contact http://sil.org/sgml/sgmlug.html. See **GCA** and **SGML Open**.

SGMLS — A popular and freely available **parser** developed for use with **SGML**, but with the correct **SGML declaration**, may also be used to validate XML documents. See **NSGMLS**.

Shape attribute — An **HTML** attribute to the **Area** element, that specifies the shape of an active area on the image. For example, a circle or a rectangle.

short reference — An **SGML** feature that allows data characters to stand in for markup. This is an ultimate **minimization** feature. For example, the quote character can be recognized as both a Quote element start-tag and end-tag (depending on the context). In a table, the tab character could be equivalent to a Cell element and the line-end character to a Row element. This feature is not applicable to XML.

Show element — The default name for an **XLink** attribute that specifies how to present the target of a hypertext link. The possible values are 'new', 'replace' and 'embed'.

sibling — A concept derived from the family tree that describes an **element** that is adjacent to other elements within a **hierarchy** of elements (much like brothers and sisters). It is at the same level, following and/or preceding other elements. For example, a Chapter element is likely to be a sibling to other Chapter elements. See also **parent** and **child**.

significant white space — Spaces, tabs, and **line break** codes which are considered to be part of the document text, so should be preserved and appear when the document is presented. See **insignificant white space**.

Simple API for XML — See **SAX**.

Simple element — The name of the **XLink** element that identifies the source of a **hypertext link** that has a single **target** resource. See **Extend** element.

simple link — An **XLink** link that is in-line and one-directional. See **Simple** element.

Size attribute — An **HTML** attribute to the **Hr** element, defining the thickness of the line, the **Font** and **Basefont** elements, defining the size of the text, and to the **Select** element, defining the number of rows visible in the menu.

Small element — An **HTML 3.2** element that encloses text to be displayed in a smaller point size. See **Big**.

SMDL *(Standard Music Description Language)* — Standard use of **SGML** to describe real-time music samples, related to (and precursor of) the **HyTime** concept. Contact http://www.techno.com/SMDL.html.

SMIL *(Synchronized Multimedia Integration Language)* — An application of XML designed to provide a platform for multimedia presentations over the Web, composed from disparate multimedia objects. For example, a SMIL file may refer to a number of image files and to an oral narrative (audio file), specifying what order to display the images and when to start the audio track.

socket — A single **Internet** server program may be communicating simultaneously with several client applications. Each message received includes a socket number (assigned by the server when the connection is first initiated) that allows the data to be processed by the correct thread.

soft line-break — A break in the flow of text produced by the presentation software due to reaching a page, column or screen edge. Typically, 'hard' line-end codes are replaced by spaces before this happens.

Sort element — An **XSLT** element, used to sort the selected nodes from the source document into order, before writing them out to the output document. The **select** attribute can be used to customize the sort on specific elements and/or attributes in the content. The **Order** attribute can be set to 'descending' instead of 'ascending'. Numeric sorting is possible by setting the **Data Type** attribute to 'number' instead of 'text'. The **Case Order** attribute determines whether 'A' becomes before or after 'a'.

Source — See **Src** attribute.

Space — See **S**$^{\{03\}}$.

Span attribute — An **HTML** attribute to the **Col** and **Colgroup** elements that specifies a multicolumn span (default value '1').

Span element — An **HTML 4.0** element that has no explicit stylistic effect, but may be used to apply document-specific styles (with the **Class** attribute) to ranges of text. An **in-line** equivalent to the **Div** element.

SPDL *(Standard Page Description Language)* — An **ISO** standard (ISO/IEC 10180) that defines a language for representing text and graphics on a page. Released in December 1995. Equivalent and similar to the *de facto* **PostScript** language, except that PostScript commands are embedded within **SGML** elements (in the 'clear-encoding', non-compressed form).

```
<picture>
 <tkseqn>
    200 200 moveto
    100 200 rlineto
 </tkseqn>
</picture>
```

splitText method — A **DOM** method in the **Text** interface. Used to split a single Text node into two nodes, returning a reference to the second node (the new one). The split point is given as an integer value.

SQL *(Structured Query Language)* — [pronounced 'S.Q.L.' or 'sequel'] A very popular, vendor-neutral **query language** for extracting information from a **relational database**. For example, the SQL query 'SELECT name, telephone FROM employees WHERE name = "John"' returns the telephone number of a person from an employee database table.

Src attribute — An **HTML** attribute to the **Img** element, locating and identifying the image file, and to the **Frame** element, containing a **URL** locating an HTML file to display in the frame. Also to the **Script** element to identify a remote script file (see also **Charset**).

SSADM *(Structured Systems Analysis and Design Method)* — A scheme developed by the UK government in 1982 for development of information systems by government departments, but now more widely used.

STag[40] — First part of an **element**, coupled with the end-tag (**ETag**[42]) to hold the content of the element, when not empty. Also the container of **attribute** values.

standalone — The name of a parameter in an **XML declaration** that is used to specify when a separate **DTD** file is (or is not) required to correctly interpret the content of the document. This means that the DTD does not define any default attribute values, or any entities that are referred to in the document. See **SDDecl**[32].

Standalone Document Declaration — See **SDDecl**[32].

Standard Generalized Markup Language — See **SGML**.

Standard Page Description Language — See **SPDL**.

Start attribute — An **HTML 3.2** attribute to the **Ol** element, specifying a start value for the first item in the list. The default value is '1'.

Start Tag — See **STag**[40].

start-tag — The first part of a **container element**, '<...>'. The *only* part of an **empty element** defined using the alternative syntax, '<.../>'. See **end-tag**.

startDocument method — A **SAX** method defined in the **DocumentHandler** interface. Called by the parser when the start of the document is detected. See **endDocument** method.

startElement method — A **SAX** method defined in the **DocumentHandler** interface. Called by the parser when the start of an element is detected. A reference to an object that implements the **AttributeList** interface is passed so that attribute details can be obtained. See **endElement** method.

starts-with() — Used in an expression in **XPath** to test for the presence of one string within another, but only if the contained string is at the start of the larger string. See **contains()** and **normalize()**.

static information — Information that is not easily updated, typically because it takes the form of a published document or book. See **vector information**.

Strike element — An **HTML 3.2** element that encloses text to be displayed with a line through it, indicating that the text has been 'removed'.

Strikethrough — See **Strike** element.

string() — Used in an expression in **XPath** to convert the result of an embedded expression into a string value. See **boolean()** and **number()**.

string-length() — In an **XPath** expression, used to return the length in characters of the string identified by the parameter. '`string-length("abc")`' reutrns three.

StringType[55] — An attribute type, indicating normal characters may be used in the attribute, including spaces, using the '**CDATA**' keyword in the **DTD**.

Strip Space element — An **XSLT** element, used to list in the **Elements** attribute all source document elements for which white space is to be removed.

Strong element — An **HTML** element that encloses text to be highlighted, usually in a **bold** typeface.

Structured Query Language — See **SQL**.

style — The appearance of text when it is printed or presented on-screen, including the font used and the point size.

Style attribute — An **HTML** attribute added to almost all elements in **HTML 4.0**, allowing any element instance to be styled using an embedded **CSS** style property.

Style element — An **HTML** attribute in **HTML 4.0**, used to hold a style sheet. The **Type** attribute identifies the scripting language. The **Media** attribute identifies the output media the styles are intended to be used with. An optional **Title** attribute identifies the style sheet.

style sheet — A set of style rules held together, perhaps in a separate data file, to be applied to all element instances which match, in name and context, one or more of these rules. See **in-line style**.

Stylesheet element — An **XSLT** element that encloses a complete style sheet. An alternative element called **Transform** may be used.

Sub element — An **HTML 3.2** element containing **subscript** text. For example, '`a<sub>b</sub>c`' is 'a_bc'.

subcode[38] — Additional information about a language in the **LanguageID**[33], such as the country, 'en-GB' (Great Britain).

subelement — An **element** that is directly contained within another element. Formal name for the **child** of another element.

subscript — Text positioned below the baseline, as in 'H_2O'. Also known as 'inferior' text. See **superscript**. See **Sub** element.

Subscript element — See **Sub** element.

substring() — Used in an expression in **XPath** to extract part of a string, from a given character, for a specific number of characters. See **substring-before()** and **substring-after()**.

substring-after() — Used in an expression in **XPath** to extract the last part of a string, from a given character in that string. See **substring-before()** and **substring()**.

substring-before() — Used in an expression in **XPath** to extract the first part of a string, up to a given character in that string. See **substring-after()** and **substring()**.

substringData method — A **DOM** method in the **CharacterData** interface. Used to extract a fragment of the string value, taking offset and count parameters.

superior — See **superscript**.

Sup element — An **HTML 3.2** element containing **superscript** text. For example, 'a^bc' is 'a^{b}c'.

superior — See **superscript**.

superscript — Text positioned above the base line, as in 'W^{3}C'. Also known as 'superior' text. See **subscript** and **Sup** element.

Superscript element — See **Sup** element.

symbol — A rule that defines part of the XML or **XLink** language. The symbol is a name given to an **expression**, which is composed of at least one **token**.

Synchronized Multimedia Integration Language — See **SMIL**.

syntax — All languages, including English, have defined rules of grammar. The XML syntax defines how **tags** and **markup declarations** are stored and identified.

System Data — An **SGML** concept that describes data which is system dependent, and must be modified when transmitted to an incompatible system. Not applicable to XML. See **SDATA**.

system identifier — System-specific **external entity** identifier. Typically a file name and location. For example, '../ENTS/MYBOOK.DTD'.

System Literal — See **SystemLiteral**$^{\{11\}}$.

SystemLiteral$^{\{11\}}$ *(System Literal)* — A quoted string containing a file name, and possibly a file path, used to locate entities and notational data handlers.

T

Tabindex attribute — An **HTML 4.0** attribute to various form-related elements, a field to be selected by repeated pressing of the TAB key. Each control has a different Tabindex value to specify the sequence by which fields become active. The first field has a value of '1'.

table — A collection of data arranged into rows and columns, from which a **flat-file** or **relational** database package can locate required information.

Table Body — See **Tbody** element.

Table Data — See **Td** element.

Table element — Table enclosing **element** in HTML 3.2.

Table Foot — See **Tfoot** element.

Table Head — See **Thead** element.

Table Header — See **Th** element.

Table Row — See **Tr** element.

tag — A code embedded in the text, signifying the structure, format or style of the data. A tag is recognized from surrounding text by the use of **delimiter** characters. A common delimiter character for an XML tag is the chevron, '<'.

tag close — The character(s) indicating the end of a tag.

tail — The end-point of a **hypertext link**. Equivalent to the **target** of a link. A reference is traversed from the **head** to the tail. For example, a chapter Title element may be the tail of many references.

target — The object of a **hypertext link**. It must be identified by a unique name or code, which can be used within a **source** object to form the link. See **Target attribute** and **ID**.

Target attribute — An **attribute** that holds a unique value suitable for reference by **source** elements. See **ID**.

Tbody element — An **HTML 4.0** element that isolates the rows of a table that contain body text. Implied if not made explicit, this section follows the optional **Thead** and **Tfoot** sections.

TCP *(Transmission Control Protocol)* — See **TCP/IP**.

TCP/IP *(Transmission Control Protocol/Internet Protocol)* — Data transport protocol for the **Internet**. Used by **HTTP** and **FTP** file transfer protocols. Contact comp.protocols.tcp-ip/ newsgroup.

Td element — An **HTML 3.2** element used in the **Table** element to hold the content of one normal cell. See **Th** element.

TEI *(Text Encoding Initiative)* — A group of representatives from learned societies in the humanities and social sciences, defining common **DTD**s for the coding and interchange of relevant documents. Contact http://mes01.di.uminho.pt/Manuals/HTML/html-howto/tei.html or http://www.uic.edu:80/orgs/tei/.

Teletype — See **Tt** element.

template — In **XSLT**, a template is used to describe how a specific element in the source document is to be transformed in an output document. This may involve formatting the content of the element by replacing source elements with elements from the **FO DTD**, defined in the **XSL** specification.

Template element — An **XSLT** element. Used to create a template for conversion of a specific element in the source document, perhaps in a given contextual circumstance. See **Match** attribute.

Test attribute — An **XSLT** attribute to the **If** and **When** elements, used to contain an expression that, when it returns true, will indicate that the content of this element should be processed.

T$_E$X — [pronounced 'teck'] Popular typesetting language. Particularly strong on mathematical formulae. It is sometimes found embedded in **SGML** documents due to the absence of a widely accepted SGML-based tagging convention for formulae (but see **Math-ML** for XML). Contact 'http://www.fi.muni.cz/TeXhelp/TeX-homepage.html' and 'comp.text.tex' newsgroup. See **L^{A}T$_E$X**.

text — A possible value for the **Data Type** attribute in **XSLT**, indicating that '7' appears after '12' in a sorted list, because the **ASCII** code for '7' is greater than the code for '1'. See **number**.

text() — A function of a navigation expression used in **XPath** that identifies any text object in the document tree. See **node()**.

text — A series of **characters**.

Text attribute — An **HTML 3.2** attribute to the **Body** element that specifies the colour of the document text.

Text element — An **XSLT** element. Used to enclose white space that is not to be stripped from the style sheet template.

Text Encoding Initiative — See **TEI**.

text entity — In a **public identifier**, an **entity** that contains simple text.

text file — A data file containing textual characters, possibly conforming to the **ASCII** standard, or to **Unicode**. Each character is represented by a unique value. There is no provision for styling the text, and little provision for formatting the text. A **markup** language assigns significance to sequences of ASCII characters, forming **tags**. A text editor works directly with ASCII data, and most word processors can export and import text files.

text format — A data format that contains text characters, usually to represent textual information. Simple text formats comprise of nothing more than **character sets** like **ASCII**, **Unicode** and **EBCDIC**. More complex data structures are described by assigning significance to some characters, such as the comma in **CSV**. Using **markup**, even more complex structures are described in **HTML**, XML, **SGML** and TeX. See **image format**.

Text identifier — The major part of a **formal public identifier**, describing the type, description and language of an **entity**.

Text interface — Defined in the **DOM** standard, to represent a block of characters within an element. A subclass of the **CharacterData** interface, adding the **splitText** method. A Text object is created using the factory method **createTextNode** in the **Document** interface.

Textarea element — An **HTML** element that uses **Cols** and **Rows** attributes to define a text box for entry of multi-line text input.

TextDecl[77] *(Encoding Processing Instruction)* — A processing instruction that appears at the top of a **DTD** file, a fragment thereof, or an external **parsed entity**, when its content conforms to a different character set or version of XML to the main document.

Tfoot element — An **HTML 4.0** element that isolates the rows of a table that contain footer text, possibly for repeating at the bottom of each presented page that contains a reference to it. It is placed before the **Tbody** element to avoid the need for multiple parsing. See **Thead**.

Th element — An **HTML 3.2** element containing a table header cell.

Thead element — An **HTML 4.0** element that isolates the rows of a table that contain header text, possibly for repeating at the top of each presented page. See **Tfoot** and **Tbody**.

TIFF *(Tagged Image File Format)* — [pronounced 'tiff'] An **image format** devised by Microsoft and Aldus, now maintained by Adobe. The actual image data is held in one of several **raster** formats, depending on the compression requirements. Options include **CCITT Group IV** and **JPEG** compression, or no compression at all. The current version is 6.0. Contact http://www.adobe.com/Support/TechNotes.html.

Title attribute — An **HTML** attribute, added to almost all elements in **HTML 4.0**, allowing any element instance to be identified with a label.

Title element — An **HTML** element that provides the title of the document, for display in the title bar of a document window. Part of the **Head** element content. Also used in the **Abbrev** and **Acronym** elements to hold the content of the full term of an abbreviation or acronym. Added to almost all **HTML 4.0** elements as a simple 'help system' for users.

token — *[1]* A unit of information in a **group**. Either a single object, such as the name of an **element**, or an entire embedded group which also contains tokens. *[2]* A building block of the rules that comprise the definition of the XML and XLink standards. A number of tokens build an **expression**, which is named with a **symbol** (which may be used as a token in another expression).

Tokenized Type — See **TokenizedType**[56].

TokenizedType[56] *(Tokenized Type)* — An **attribute type** declared in the **DTD**. A single word, or **token**, or a list of tokens.

Tr element — An **HTML 3.2** element containing a table row. Each row consists of **Th** and/or **Td** elements.

transclusion — A **hypertext** concept that involves replacing the **source** reference with the **target** resource. The link is not so much followed, as brought to the reference. An ideal mechanism for ensuring that a reference to a title is always accurate, even when the target title is edited, or for calling in an image without needing to use an **entity declaration**.

Transform element — An **XSLT** element that encloses a complete style sheet. An alternative element called **Stylesheet** may be used. It may be better to use the Transform element when the embedded templates are used to create a new, descriptive XML output file (rather than to simply style the content using **HTML** or **XSL** elements) as it is more descriptive for this purpose.

translate() — Used in an expression in **XPath** to replace specific characters with other characters.

Transmission Control Protocol — See **TCP/IP**.

transversal — A term used for following a **hypertext link** to a references **resource**.

tree — A hierarchical structure which resembles a tree in that the structure can be viewed as branches. **SGML** elements form hierarchies, and are sometimes described using the family tree concept, including the use of names such as **ancestor**, **parent**, **child** and **sibling**.

tree-manipulation — Editing a tree, such as changing the order or location of an element, inserting or deleting an element, or copying and duplicating an element.

tree walking — The process of stepping from one document **node** to another, processing the document in the same order as treating the content as a linear **data stream**. A common technique when processing using the **DOM**.

true() — An **XPath** expression function that returns the value 'false' in a boolean test. See **false()** and **boolean()**.

Tt element — An **HTML** element containing text representing teletype output, usually displayed in a mono-spaced font.

Type attribute — An **HTML** attribute to the **Input** element, specifying the type of input control, such as check-box, radio button and push button. Also in **HTML 3.2** to the **Ol**, **Ul** and **Li** elements, where it specifies the type of list item identifier, such as '1' or 'A'. Also in HTML 4.0 to the **Style** element to identify the style sheet language, and to the Script element to identify the scripting language.

typesetting — The process of converting tagged data, possibly in XML format, into completed pages. A combination of the **compose** and **paginate** operations.

typesetting language — A computer language that comprises a list of codes to be embedded in a **text file**, specifying a style or location for text that follows the code.

U

U element — An **HTML** element that contains text to be underlined.

UCS (*Universal Multiple-Octet Coded Character Set*) — The core **ISO10646** multi-byte data format. Transformation formats reduce the size by using single bytes for common characters. These formats are called **UTF**, with 'U' standing for UCS.

UCS Transformation Format — See **UTF**.

UCS Transformation Format 16 Bit Form — See **UTF-16**.

UCS-2 — An **ISO/IEC 10646** and **Unicode** character encoding scheme that uses two bytes to store each character. See **UCS-4**. May be converted to a **UTF** format for transfer.

UCS-4 — An **ISO/IEC 10646** and **Unicode** character encoding scheme that uses four bytes to store each character. See **UCS-2**. May be converted to a **UTF** format for transfer.

Ul element — An **HTML** element that contains an unordered list, using **Li** elements. See also **OL** (*Ordered List*).

unavailable text indicator — An entity that is not available to the general public, perhaps only for use within an organization. Part of a **formal public identifier**, following the **public text class** and consisting of the trailing characters '-//'. For example, '+//MyCorp//DTD MyDTD -// ...... '.

Underline — See **U** element.

Unicode — A **16-bit** character set devised by the Unicode Consortium (a group of largely American hardware and software suppliers). Several coding schemes are allowed, but in the canonical scheme every bit combination represents a distinct character. Using this scheme, Unicode can be viewed as a superset of **ASCII** (US) with '0000' to '00FF' (hexadecimal) being equivalent to ASCII '00' to 'FF'. Unicode has been adopted as a subset of **ISO/IEC 10646**, with '00000000' to '0000FFFF' being equivalent to the Unicode characters '0000' to 'FFFF'. Contact http://www.stonehand.com/unicode.html.

Universal Multiple-Octet Coded Character Set — See **UCS**.

Uniform Resource Locator — See **URL**.

Universal Resource Identifier — See **URI**.

unparsed entity — An entity that is given a notation, so is not deemed by the XML processor to be XML data that can be parsed (even if it does happen to be XML, or simple text data). It must be an external entity.

unparsedEntityDecl method — A **SAX** method defined in the **DTDHandler** interface. Used by the parser to pass information extracted from **entity declaration**s to the application, when the entity is external and conforms to a notation other than XML. The method is passed the name of the entity, the **public identifier** and **system identifier**, then the name of the notation. See **notationDecl**.

Unordered List — See **Ul** element.

unregistered owner identifier — A **public identifier** that has not been officially registered, so cannot be guaranteed to be unique. See **registered owner identifier**.

up-convert — Conversion of typeset data to XML format. Usually a semi-manual, **high energy** task. The expense of up-converting to XML is often cited as the main reason for not adopting XML, though in some cases this cost is more than offset by the reduced cost of **down-convert**ing to various output formats.

upper-case — Capital letters, such as 'THIS'. The upper-case equivalent of the **lower-case** letter 'a' is 'A'. The name is derived from the fact that these **character**s were found in the upper part of the printer's type case.

upper-first — A possible value for the **Case Order** attribute in **XSLT**, indicating that 'A' appears before 'a' in a sorted list.

URI *(Uniform Resource Identifier)* — The **Internet** addressing scheme. Includes the **URL** standard. Contact http://www.w3.org/pub/WWW/Addressing/Addressing.html.

URN *(Uniform Resource Name)* — Subset of the **URI** protocol for schemes that do not require direct reference to a filename and location. See **URL**.

Urn attribute — An **HTML 2.0** only attribute to the **A** and **Link** elements that describes the resource in a neutral, permanent manner. See also **Methods**.

Use Attribute Sets attributes — An **XSLT** attribute to the **Attribute Set**, **Element** and **Copy** elements, used to call-in a set of attributes, defined in an Attribute Set element, by referencing its **Name** attribute.

Usemap attribute — An **HTML 3.2** attribute to the **Img** element that indicates the image is associated with an **image map** of active areas.

user — A legal value of the **Actuate** attribute in **XLink**, indicating that the **hypertext link** is only followed when selected by a user. See **auto**.

UserCode[37] — A user-defined language code used in the **xml:lang** attribute. Must begin with 'x-' or 'X-'. See **IanaCode**[36] and **ISO639Code**[35].

UTF *(UCS Transformation Format)* — A mechanism for compressing **UCS-2** and **UCS-4** encoded data for transfer between systems. The two-byte or four-byte UCS character representation schemes are often wasteful when relatively common characters are in use. A text file can easily be compressed by as much as 75 per cent. Two variants, UTF-8 (8-bit) and UTF-16 (16-bit), offer different levels of character range support.

UTF-16 — See **UTF**.

UTF-8 — See **UTF**.

V

V.32bis — A modulation protocol for modems that transmit or receive data at a maximum of 14,400 bits per second (bps).

V.34 — A modulation protocol for modems that transmit or receive data at a maximum of 28,800 bits per second (bps). More recently allowing up to 33,600 bps.

V.42 — A modulation protocol for modems that allows errors to be corrected by retransmitting packets of data.

V.42bis — A modulation protocol for modems that includes data compression to achieve greater throughput.

validate — The process of comparing a **document instance** against its **DTD**. See **validating parser**.

validating parser — A **parser** that compares the usage of **element**s and **attribute**s in a document against the rules of a **DTD**. For example, if the DTD states that a Chapter element can only contain a Title element followed by Section elements, then an error will result should a document contain a Paragraph element directly within a Chapter element.

Valign attribute — An **HTML 3.2** attribute to various table-related elements that vertically aligns text within table cells.

Value attribute — *[1]* An **HTML 3.2** attribute to the **Li** element that provides an overriding list item value (out of the normal sequence), to the **Param** element, where it assigns a value to a parameter identified using a **Name** attribute, and to the **Option** element, where it replaces the element content as the return value. *[2]* An **XSLT** attribute to the **Number** element, used to hold an expression for generating the automatic number to insert, which is particularly useful when the numbered elements have already been sorted or other wise transformed, as it sequentially numbers after such processed (normal technique do not).

value indicator — In **SGML**, the equals sign that separates an attribute name from its value may be redefined to another character, but is always called a 'value indicator'. In some SGML **minimization** techniques, the character may be omitted.

Value Of element — An **XSLT** element used to convert the object specified by its **Select** attribute into a string.

Var element — An **HTML** element that contains text identified as a computer program variable, usually displayed in a mono-spaced font.

Variable element — An **XSLT** element that is used to define a variable. The **Name** attribute holds the variable name and the value is either generated from an expression in the **Select** attribute, or is provided by the content of the element.

variant concrete syntax — An **SGML** concept whereby the default characters used as **markup delimiter**s are changed to suit the requirements of a particular computer platform or document type. A concept that does not apply in XML.

vector — Method of representing images electronically using resolution and scale independent drawing commands, producing lines, points, arcs, filled areas and text. For example, '`DRAWTO 60 35; MOVETO 75 90; CIRCLE 50; ...`'. Also known as 'geometric graphics'. Some formats use text-based commands as in the example, others use more compact machine-readable schemes. **CGM** allows for both representations. The alternative representation is called a **raster** format (though a vector-based image must be converted into a raster-based image when rendered using an appropriate resolution). See also **IGES**, **PICT** and **WMF**.

Version Information — See **VersionInfo**[24].

Version Number — See **VersionNum**[26].

VersionInfo[24] *(Version information)* — A statement of the version of XML in use by the document. Part of the XML declaration (**XMLDecl**[23]). At the time of writing, the only version of XML that exists is '1.0'.

VersionNum[26] *(Version Number)* — The actual value of the version of XML in use, such as '1.0'.

Vertical Space attribute — See **Vspace** attribute.

Virtual Reality Modelling Language — See **VRML**.

Visited Link attribute — See **Vlink** attribute.

Vlink attribute — An **HTML 3.2** attribute to the **Body** element that specifies the colour of the **source** of a **hypertext link** that has already been traversed.

VRML *(Virtual Reality Modelling Language)* — A language that describes three-dimensional objects. Used on the **Internet** to create 'virtual worlds'. Developed by Silicon Graphics, who also shaped VRML 2.0 (1996), which adds behaviours, sensors, sound and animation (from its 'Moving Worlds' specification). Contact http://vrml.sgi.com/moving-worlds.

Vspace attribute — An **HTML 3.2** attribute to the **Img** element that specifies additional space above and below the image.

W

W³C *(World Wide Web Consortium)* — An industry consortium founded in 1994 that comprises over 120 organizations. Involved in the establishment of standards for the **Web**, including XML and **DTD**s for versions of **HTML**. In agreement with major vendors, responsible for the latest versions of HTML, starting with **HTML 3.2** in June 1996 and **HTML 4.0** on 18 December 1997. This organization has a close relationship with the **IETF** (see **SGML Open** for equivalent **SGML** monitoring organization). Contact http://www.w3.org/.

warning method — A **SAX** method defined in the **Errorhandler** interface. Triggered by the parser whenever a low-level error occurs. See **error** and **fatalError**.

Wbr element — An **HTML 3.2** element contained within a **Nobr** element to specify points in the text where a line break can be made (if necessary). The 'word break' element.

Web — Common abbreviation for the World Wide Web. An **Internet** service that uses the **HTTP** protocol and **HTML** format data files to provide an attractive document delivery service over standard telephone lines. Information is passed between a **Web server** and a **Web browser**. Various graphic formats are also supported, including **GIF** and **JPEG**. Created by researchers at CERN in Switzerland (http://www.w3.org). Not owned by any company, the Web is overseen by the **W³C** (and the Internet is overseen by the **IETF**).

Web browser — A computer application that receives **Web page**s from a **Web server** via the **Internet**, and **render**s them on-screen. See **Web**.

Web page — A data file containing **HTML** or XML tagged text ready to be displayed by a **Web browser**. Although called a 'page', the file may be much longer than a physical page, and a closer analogy would be a scroll. However, Web page designers are encouraged to split long documents into smaller units, so as to keep network traffic to a minimum, and the name 'page' is a reminder of this philosophy.

Web server — A computer attached to the **Internet** that stores **Web page**s and delivers them to a **Web browser**. See **Web**.

well-formed — An XML or SGML document that contains properly embedded tags, with all objects explicitly bounded by start-tags and end-tags. An **SGML** document *may* be well-formed, but an XML document *must* be well-formed in order to be valid. In addition, the document must be complete (an **entity** defined outside the document must not be referenced).

WG8 *(ISO/IEC JTC1 SC18/WG8)* — The **ISO** working group responsible for a number of standards, starting with **SGML** in 1986, but recently including **HyTime** (1992), **SPDL** (1995) and **DSSSL** (1996). Contact http://www.ornl.gov/sgml/wg8/wg8home.htm.

When element — An **XSLT** element used within the **Choose** element to test an option within a template. The **Test** attribute contains an expression that, when returning true, indicates that the content of this element is to be processed. See **Otherwise** element.

white space — A character used to separate words in text, and parameters in markup, including the space character, ' ', the horizontal tab character and the end-of-line codes **CR** and **LF**. See **ignorable white space**.

whitespace —See **white space**.

Width attribute — An **HTML** attribute to the **Hr** element that specifies the width of the line in comparison with the width of the window, to the **Table** and **Applet** elements to define the width of the table or **applet** working area, to the **Pre** element to give the browser an opportunity to choose a suitable font size to handle the lines of text, and to the **Tr** and **Th**, **Col** and **Colgroup** elements that allows the widths of columns in a table to be 'suggested'.

Windows MetaFile — See **WMF**.

With Param element — An **XSLT** element used to pass a parameter variable value to a named template. The **Name** attribute refers to a parameter variable, defined using the **Param** element.

With Parameter element — See **With Param** element.

WMF *(Windows MetaFile)* — A Microsoft Windows-based **vector** image format. See **PICT** and **CGM**.

Word Break element — See **Wbr** element.

workflow — The movement of documents through a number of separate preparation stages, such as 'create', 'proof', 'edit', 'approve' and 'publish'. A necessary component of an **editorial system**, which may automatically deliver documents to operators assigned given tasks as they become ready. A workflow system may also automatically re-route documents as necessary, alert users to scheduling problems and provide statistics on throughput.

World Wide Web — See **Web**.

World Wide Web Consortium — See **W^{3}C** .

WWW *(World Wide Web)* — See **Web**.

WYSIWYG *(What You See Is What You Get)* — [pronounced 'wizz-e-wig'] Acronym describing one approach to viewing data on-screen, where an attempt is made to replicate published output (What You See *on the screen* Is What You Get *on the page*). Text markup is hidden, and the text is composed using representative fonts and styles.

X

X-Bitmap — Simple 1-**bit** per pixel **raster** image format used on UNIX systems and also used by the **Web**. Pixels are set to black or transparent. Typical file extent is '.xbm'. Actually C language source code (an array) to be read by a compiler rather than a graphic viewer. See **JPEG**, **GIF** and **X-Pixelmap**.

X-Pixelmap — Simple **8-bit**s per pixel **raster** image format used on UNIX systems (and X-Windows icons) and used by the **Web**. Pixels are set to one of 256 colours. Actually C language source code (an array) to be read by a compiler rather than a graphic viewer. Less memory efficient than **GIF**. Typical file extent is '.xpm'. See **JPEG** and **X-Bitmap**.

XBM — See **X-Bitmap**.

XLink *(XML Linking Language)* — An adjunct standard to XML that defines a specification for hypertext linking. See http://www.w3.org/TR/WD-xml-link. See **XPointer**.

XML — A **generalized markup language** based on **SGML**, with some influence from **HTML**, aimed primarily at the **Web**. Subscribe to xml-dev@ic.ac.uk.

XMLCatalog element — An optional **XML Catalog** element that describes an entire document, containing entity mappings, and containing the elements **Map**, **Remap**, **Base**, **Extend** and **Delegate**.

XML Catalog — A private initiative, well supported, for defining a standard format for entity management catalogues. Based on **SGML Open** format, but simplified and with an optional XML-based syntax. See **XMLCatalog**.

XML Declaration — See **XMLDecl**[25].

XML processor — A software module that allows XML documents to be read by an application. It includes an **entity manager**, and optionally a **parser**. The XML document is made available to the application as a **data stream**, or as a **grove**. Commonly, the term 'parser' is used to describe what is formally an XML processor. See **SAX** and **DOM**.

xml:lang — A reserved XML attribute name, used to identify a value that represents the human language used for the content of the current element. Its value is a code, defined in **LanguageID**[33]. See **IANA** and **ISO 639**.

XML:Link attribute — The default name for the **XLink** attribute that identifies a linking element.

xml:space — A reserved XML attribute name, used to identify elements that contain **white space** which must be preserved.

XML-aware — A software application that recognizes the XML data format and understands XML concepts, such as document structure, entities, and possibly also the hypertext linking or stylesheet supplementary standards, so is able to perform meaningful operations on that data. An XML-aware editor, for example, would use the **DTD** to control and guide the authoring process. Other terms used include 'XML-capable' and 'XML-sensitive'. An XML-aware application must include at least an **XML processor**.

XML-capable — See **XML-aware**.

XML-Data — A proposed XML schema for defining and documenting object classes. Contact http://www.microsoft.com/standards/xml/xmldata.htm. See **RDF**.

XML-sensitive — See **XML-aware**.

xml-stylesheet — The target name for a processing instruction that is used to link a style sheet to the XML document to format that document.

XML Stylesheet Language — See **XSL**.

XMLDecl[25] *(XML Declaration)* — The first part of an XML document, specifying the version of XML in use (**VersionInfo**[24]), the character set in use (**EncodingDecl**[80]) and the requirements, or otherwise, of DTD processing to correctly interpret the content of the document (**SDDecl**{32}).

Xmp element — An **HTML 2.0** element that identifies example data, to be presented exactly as stored in the file (now deprecated (along with **Plaintext**), use the **Pre** element instead).

XPath — a standard for an **expression** language that can be used for searching an XML document (see **XQL**), creating links into documents (see **XPointer**) and applying specific formats to each element type within contextual constraints (see **XSLT**). Contact www.w3.org/TR/xpath.

XPM — See **X-Pixelmap**.

XPointer — a standard that complements **XLink** to allow links to objects that do not have a unique identifier, but do have a significant contextual location in the document.

XQL *(XML Query Language)* — A proposal for a query language to extract information from XML documents.

XSL *(XML Stylesheet Language)* — A proposal for a **style sheet** language for XML, including **CSS** equivalent features. See http://www.w3.org/TR/WD-xsl or http://www.mulberrytech.com/xsl/xsl-list. An **XSLT** style sheet may be used to create an XML document that contains elements and attributes as a concrete format for XSL features, confroming to the **FO DTD**.

XSL Transformations — See **XSLT**.

XSLT *(XSL Transformations)* — A proposal for a transformation language that has the primary use of creating **XSL** documents from arbitrary XML documents, but can also be used to translate one XML document into another XML document of a different structure. Contact 'http://www.w3.org/TR/WD-xslt'.

Index

NOTES : This index identifies terms introduced in the main text (where they are displayed in bold). The glossary is not indexed, so a term in the glossary that is only referenced from other terms in the glossary will not appear in this index. All entries are shown in the present tense, singular form (except where the term is a syntactic token name or keyword, or is always used in another form). For example the 'hierarchy' entry also identifies usage of the word 'hierarchical.' Entries in capitals, such as 'ENTITY,' are XML keywords. Entries with an initial capital letter, such as 'Table,' are DTD-specific element or attribute names, and as they may be used in more than one DTD they are identified using bracketed qualifiers; for example, there is an entry for 'Title (XLink)' and another entry for 'Title (HTML)' (but note that these names are case-sensitive, and usually differ from this convention).